Mastering SQL

Mastering™ SQL

Martin Gruber

SYBEX®

San Francisco • Paris • Düsseldorf • Soest • London

Associate Publisher: Richard Mills
Contracts and Licensing Manager: Kristine O'Callaghan
Acquisitions & Developmental Editor: Denise Santoro-Lincoln
Editor: Linda Recktenwald
Project Editor: Julie Sakaue
Coauthor of Chapter 26: Keith Hare
Technical Editors: Keith Hare and John Zukowski
Technical Reviewer: David Thompson
Book Designer: Kris Warrenburg
Graphic Illustrators: Tony Jonick and Jerry Williams
Electronic Publishing Specialist: Kris Warrenburg
Project Team Leaders: Lisa Reardon and Teresa Trego
Proofreaders: Patrick Peterson, Dave Nash, Nancy Riddiough,
and Emily Hsuan
Indexer: Ted Laux
CD Coordinator: Kara Schwartz
CD Technicians: Ginger Warner and Keith McNeil
Cover Designer: Design Site
Cover Illustrator/Photographer: Sergie Loobkoof, Design Site

Library of Congress Card Number: 99-64121
ISBN: 0-7821-2538-7

Manufactured in the United States of America

10 9 8 7 6 5 4 3 2 1

CONTENTS AT A GLANCE

TABLE OF CONTENTS

INTRODUCTION

SQL (usually pronounced "sequel") stands for Structured Query Language; because of the pronunciation, this book will refer to "*a* SQL (sequel) statement" rather than "*an* SQL (S-Q-L) statement". SQL is a language that enables you to create and operate on *relational databases*, which are sets of related information stored in tables. Relational databases are managed by programs called database management systems (DBMSs), of which a variety are on the market: IBM's DB2 Universal Database, Oracle, Microsoft SQL Server and Access, Sybase Adaptive Server Enterprise and SQL Anywhere Studio, Informix Information Server, Ingres, MySQL, mSQL, and others. These products use SQL for all of their database operations. Although they all extend standard SQL to support proprietary features, they all conform to standard SQL, as defined by the standards organizations ANSI and ISO. This book covers standard SQL.

Mastering SQL provides an introduction to database concepts, an in-depth tutorial in the SQL language, and a complete reference on the currently dominant ANSI/ISO standard. It assumes no background for the reader but is designed to be a book you won't outgrow quickly. The idea is to work through the first five parts, which teach you how to use the language. These chapters contain numerous examples, including ideas on how to deal with variations on the standard situations as well as exercises at chapter's end, so you can strengthen your mastery. If you already have some SQL background, you can skim through these chapters to fill in the blanks.

Part VI covers SQL99, a new SQL standard that, as of this writing, has just been published and is therefore not yet implemented. It also contains a sizable chapter on combining SQL with Java, in accordance with the SQLJ and JDBC standards. This is the forward-looking part of the book.

Part VII is the reference, which is divided into three chapters. The first chapter of the reference is a separate introduction just for the reference, so you should look there for details. As you gain mastery of the language, the reference will come in increasingly handy. It is more concise than the earlier material, which means it does not walk you through as many examples, but it does provide more thorough coverage. Read the earlier chapters to understand how things work and then check the reference to explore all the possibilities. This arrangement enables the main body of the book to move quickly and explain things clearly without getting bogged down in a mass of detail. The reference provides the detail. Most SQL books take one or the other of these approaches (ease of understanding or thoroughness), so we believe we offer the best of both worlds.

The database world is becoming more and more integrated, which has boosted the importance of a standard language that can be used to operate in many different kinds of computer environments and on many different DBMSs. A standard language allows you to learn one set of commands and use it to create, retrieve, alter, and transfer information regardless of whether you are working on a personal computer, a workstation, or a mainframe. It also enables you to write applications that access multiple databases, as we frequently see with applications that use the ODBC API. In our increasingly interconnected computer world, a user equipped with such a language has tremendous power to utilize and integrate information from a variety of sources in a great number of ways.

Because of its elegance and independence from machine specifics, as well as its support by the industry leaders in relational-database technology, SQL has become, and will for the foreseeable future remain, that standard language. For this reason, anyone who expects to work with databases in the early 21st century needs to know SQL.

The SQL standard is defined jointly by ANSI (American National Standards Institute) and the ISO (International Organization for Standardization). These organizations have jointly published a series of SQL standards since 1986. Each such standard is a superset of its predecessors. These standards tend to be ahead of the industry by several years, believe it or not. As of this publication (2000), most commercial products conform to SQL92, so this book focuses on that standard. Elements of SQL92 have not yet been widely implemented even now, but the book focuses on those that have. Part of the book covers SQL99, which is a more recent standard. However, as we mentioned, most commercial database programs extend SQL beyond the ISO definition, adding other useful features. In this book, we basically will be following the ISO standard, but with an eye toward the most common variations. You should consult the documentation on the software package(s) you will be using to see where they vary from the standard.

Who Can Use This Book?

Mastering SQL requires no more than a minimal knowledge of computers and none of databases. SQL is in a number of ways considerably easier to use than many languages that are less compact because it doesn't require you to define the procedures used to achieve the desired results. This book will lead you through the language step by step, providing examples along the way and exercises in each chapter to sharpen your comprehension and skills. You will be able to perform useful tasks almost immediately; then you will build more complex skills layer by layer.

Because SQL is part of so many programs that run on so many different computers, we make no assumptions about the specific context in which you are using it. SQL can be used interactively, coded in applications, or dynamically generated by applications. We designed this book to be as general purpose as possible. You will be able to apply what you learn here directly to any context in which SQL is used.

Although *Mastering SQL* is designed to be accessible to database beginners, it presents SQL in considerable depth. We created the examples to reflect a variety of situations, many of which commonly occur in business environments. Certain examples are fairly complex in the interest of showing all the implications of a particular feature. The discussion of SQL is not restricted to what is technically correct; it also explores the implications of various features and approaches. We believe you will not find another book on SQL that has the accessibility and the depth of this one.

How Is This Book Organized?

Mastering SQL is divided into seven parts, each of which covers a logical category of SQL statements. These parts are subdivided further into chapters. Parts I through VI have a narrative flow; each chapter builds on what came before and concludes with practice questions to sharpen and solidify your understanding. (Appendix A contains the answers to all practice questions.) Part VII is the reference, which is divided into three chapters. Following the reference is Appendix A, which, as just mentioned, contains the answers to all practice questions. To find even more reference information, please go to the companion CD. There, you will find Appendices B through I, in addition to an electronic version of Appendix A.

Depending on how you will be using SQL, you may find that some of the later information exceeds your needs. Not all users design databases or write applications for them. As a tutorial, this book is written so that one chapter will flow into the next, but feel free to skim sections that you may not require.

We use a single set of tables to derive the bulk of the book's examples. You will become quite familiar with these tables—and thus be able to understand clearly the points being made with them.

Here is a complete summary of the contents of *Mastering SQL*:

- Part I introduces the basic concepts that underlie databases and SQL.

  - Chapter 1 defines a relational database, including the important concept of primary and foreign keys, and gives examples similar to real-life situations. It also contains the three tables from which we will derive the bulk of our examples and explains their contents.

  - Chapter 2 orients you to the world of SQL. It covers such general issues as the structure of the language, the different types of data recognized by SQL, and some common SQL conventions and terminology. It also provides a few simple examples of SQL statements to give you a flavor of the language.

- Part II shows you how to set up a database, including creating the basic structures and filling them with data.

  - Chapter 3 explains how to create tables. After reading this chapter, you will be able to do useful work with SQL.

  - Chapter 4 shows you how to constrain the data that can be entered into tables, so as to enforce both structural features of the database and the business rules.

  - Chapter 5 elaborates on constraints to show you how to build and enforce parent and foreign key relationships.

  - Chapter 6 demonstrates how to enter data into the tables you have created, how to change it, and how to delete it.

- Part III shows you how to retrieve and work with information from your database.

- Chapter 7 introduces queries, which are requests for information from the database. Queries are the most elaborate aspect of SQL, and the next several chapters expand on them.

- Chapter 8 introduces some operators that are specific to the SQL language. It also discusses aggregate (or summary) functions, a set of operators that derive data from tables rather than simply extracting it. Aggregate functions provide single values dynamically derived from groups of values in the database.

- Chapter 9 explains some things you can do with value expressions, such as those that constitute the output of a query. These things include performing mathematical operations on the value expression, inserting text in it, ordering it in various ways, converting it between datatypes, and enabling its value to be conditional.

- Chapter 10 shows one way a single query can draw information from more than one table at a time. The approach shown in this chapter is called a *join*. A join combines information from multiple tables, typically in terms of a relationship expressed in the join.

- Chapter 11 discusses subqueries. These are queries nested within other SQL statements, whose output becomes part of the statements that contain them.

- Chapter 12 introduces SQL operators that work with subqueries. These include EXISTS, ANY, ALL, SOME, and, in some cases, IN. By using subqueries, these operators act on entire queries rather than on simple values.

- Chapter 13 shows you how to combine the output of multiple queries directly, rather than placing one inside another, as with subqueries, or defining a relationship between the tables, as with joins.

- Part IV explains some features of how databases work beyond the simple data, including such things as access and concurrency control.

  - Chapter 14 talks about the view, a "window" that shows the partial contents of some other table or group of tables. Even if you do not expect to create tables as such, you may want to look over this discussion of views, because they are quite useful and are commonly created by many users who don't create tables.

- Chapter 15 concentrates on the complex issue of changing the values in a view. When you change the values in a view, you actually change them in the underlying table. Some related issues are also discussed in this chapter.

- Chapter 16 talks about privileges—who has the ability to query tables, who has the ability to change their contents, how these abilities can be given to and taken from users, and so on.

- Chapter 17 deals with how changes to the data can be made permanent or reversed and how the DBMS deals with simultaneous access to the same data by different users or applications.

- Chapter 18 describes how SQL database systems keep your data structured and shows you how to access and use this information.

- Part V covers database design, optimization, internationalization, and application development.

  - Chapter 19 shows you how to analyze a real-life situation and derive a logical design for a database schema.

  - Chapter 20 details internationalization issues—specifically, how standard SQL deals with multiple character sets.

  - Chapter 21 focuses on the special problems and procedures associated with putting SQL statements inside other languages to create applications. This is commonly referred to as Embedded SQL. The chapter includes SQL features relevant only to the embedded form, such as cursors and the FETCH command.

  - Chapter 22 is about Dynamic SQL. This term refers to applications that generate SQL statements dynamically at runtime.

  - Chapter 23 addresses optimization techniques, which are ways of making your SQL code more efficient.

- Part VI covers SQL99 and SQLJ.

  - Chapter 24 provides an overview of SQL99, showing how the whole standard fits together.

  - Chapter 25 covers Core SQL99. This is the basic functionality of SQL99 that provides a foundation for all of the optional enhancements.

- Chapter 26 is about combining SQL with Java. The two relevant standards here are SQLJ and JDBC. We discuss both, though we cover SQLJ in more detail since it has received less attention and promises to be more important in the long run.

- Part VII is a complete reference to SQL92, which is the standard commercially implemented as of this writing (2000).

  - Chapter 27 explains how the reference fits together and provides a glimpse at some of the more obscure features of the standard.

  - Chapter 28 is an alphabetical listing of all SQL statements recognized by the standard. Each entry has a syntax diagram, an explanation, some examples, and a summary of the levels of standard conformance relevant to that statement.

  - Chapter 29 is an alphabetical listing of the basic elements other than data objects with which SQL deals. These include datatypes, Authorization IDs, special value functions, and such things.

- Appendices

  - Appendix A provides answers to the exercises that close Chapters 1 through 26 of the text.

  - Appendix B describes the changes needed to transition between one version of standard SQL and another.

  - Appendix C describes the standard error and status message that SQL statements return.

  - Appendix D discusses the standard INFORMATION_SCHEMA, a set of tables that describes the content of the database itself.

  - Appendix E describes how datatypes and other elements map between SQL and other languages. You employ this information when you develop applications in other languages and use SQL to access the database, as you do in Embedded and Dynamic SQL.

  - Appendix F describes the standard approach to creating standalone modules of SQL code that can be called by applications.

  - Appendix G provides a formal definition of the linguistic elements of SQL, the conventions for identifiers, the rules regarding separators, and so on.

- Appendix H provides a formal description of how applications can generate and execute SQL dynamically.

- Appendix I is the Glossary.

NOTE You will find Appendices B through I along with an electronic version of Appendix A on the companion CD.

Conventions of This Book

The main text of *Mastering SQL* refers frequently to the more detailed information in the reference. These references conform to the following conventions:

- Term references written in ALL CAPS are to Chapter 28, which covers complete SQL statements. Example: see "SELECT" in the reference.

- Term references written in Initial Caps are to Chapter 29, which covers elements common to multiple SQL statements. Example: see "Datatypes" in the reference.

Words in *italics* are terminology. In the text, terms are italicized when they are first explained. Example: a *primary key* is a value that uniquely distinguishes each row of a table. In the syntax diagram explaining SQL statements, terms are italicized to indicate that they stand for something other than themselves. Example: ALTER TABLE *table name*. The italics on *table name* indicate that this represents the name of some table, rather than the words "table name".

In our examples, we will show you the text you should enter into your database program and then show you the output as it appears in one database product (we used DB2 Universal Database, the flagship database product from IBM, for taking our screenshots). Not all statements produce output as such, though all should produce some acknowledgment of execution when they are used interactively. Output from other products may look different, but the content will be the same.

Occasionally in the text and consistently in the reference, we will describe the syntax of a statement formally using the industry-standard BNF (Backus Naur Form, aka Backus Normal Form) conventions with a few extensions. The conventions are as follows.

- The symbol ::= means "is defined as". It is used to further clarify parts of a statement's syntax diagram.

- Keywords appear in all uppercase letters. These reserved words are literals that are actually written as part of the statement.

- Placeholders for specific values, such as *domain name* in the CREATE DOMAIN statement, appear in italic type. These placeholders identify the type of value that should be used in a real statement; they are not literals to be written as part of the statement. This use of italics takes the place of items in angle brackets in conventional BNF diagrams.

- Optional portions of a statement appear in square brackets ([and]).

- A vertical bar (|) indicates that whatever precedes it may optionally be replaced by whatever follows it.

- Braces ({ and }) indicate that everything within them is to be regarded as a unit for the purpose of evaluating other symbols (e.g., vertical bars or ellipses).

- Ellipses (…) indicate that the preceding portion of the statement may be repeated any number of times.

- Ellipses with an interposed comma (.,..) indicate that the preceding portion may be repeated any number of times, with the individual occurrences separated by commas. The final occurrence should not be followed by a comma.

NOTE The above is not a standard BNF convention; we use it for clarity in representing the many SQL statements that use this construct. If we did not adopt this convention, the syntax diagrams would be considerably more awkward and difficult to read.

- Parentheses (()) used in syntax diagrams are literals. They indicate that parentheses are to be used in forming the statement. They do not specify a way of reading the diagram as braces or square brackets do.

- Carriage returns or line feeds in SQL are treated the same as blanks—they simply delimit the elements of statements. We used carriage returns and spacing in our syntax diagrams simply for readability; you need not duplicate them in your SQL code. For more detail on SQL's lexical conventions, see Appendix G.

PART I

Introducing SQL

CHAPTER
ONE

1

Introducing Relational Databases

- What Is a Relational Database?

- How a Relational Database Fits Together

- A Sample Database Schema

Before you can use SQL, you must understand what relational databases are. In this chapter, we will explain this concept and show you how relational databases are useful. We won't discuss SQL specifically here, so if you already understand these concepts fairly well, you may wish to merely skim this chapter. In any case, you should look at the three tables that are introduced and explained at the chapter's end; these will be the basis of most of our examples in this book. A second copy of them is available on the inside cover.

What Is a Relational Database?

A *database* is a structured set of persistent information stored by a computer program. The term *persistent* means the data survives the termination of the program or user session that created it. A *relational database* is a body of such information stored in two-dimensional tables. There are other structures that could be used—at one time, most databases were structured as hierarchies or as networks—but the relational approach has proved superior for most purposes and is currently the industry standard. Ted Codd, then a researcher for IBM, developed the relational model in the 1970s.

A simple way to picture a relational database is to think of an address book. The book contains many entries, each of which corresponds to a given individual. For each individual, there may be several independent pieces of data, such as name, telephone number, and address. Suppose you were to format this address book as a table with rows and columns. Each row would correspond to a certain individual; each column would contain a value for each type of data—name, telephone number, and address—represented in each row. Assuming it is an address book of clients, the address book might look like Table 1.1.

TABLE 1.1: The Clients Table

Name	Address	City	State	Country
Gerry Farish	127 Caesar Chavez St.	San Francisco	CA	USA
Celia Brock	246 3rd St.	Sonoma	CA	USA
Julio Abregon	778 Avenida Tarragon	Patzcauro	MICH	MEX

NOTE

> You may find the terms "record" for row and "field" for column used in the database literature.

There is only one problem with an address book like this—what if there were two Celia Brocks? Among your personal circle of friends, this situation may be unlikely, but databases often grow to have thousands or even millions of entries, so it is a real problem.

You might think that the solution would be to reference the rows by their order in the table. But which order should this be? The order in which they are entered? This order is arbitrary. The order in which they are stored in the computer's file system? Also arbitrary. It is much better to be independent of order, and such independence is one of the strengths of the relational approach. To maintain maximum flexibility, the rows of the table are, by definition, in no particular order. A database differs from a conventional address book in this respect. The entries in an address book are usually ordered alphabetically. In relational database systems, users have the powerful capability of ordering their information in whatever manner they like as they retrieve it.

To make this process work, you assign each person a unique identifier—a value, almost always a number, that is different for each person. The number can be either one already associated with the person— such as social security number—or one you assign them yourself. This number, which must be unique for each person in the database, is called the *primary key*. Every table you create in a database must have a primary key so that the individual rows can be logically identified.

Here's the Clients table with a primary key column added. As you can see, the primary key in Table 1.2 is an identification number that gives a unique number to each client.

TABLE 1.2: The Clients Table with Primary Key Added

Id_Num	Name	Address	City	State	Country
1007	Gerry Farish	127 Caesar Chavez St.	San Francisco	CA	USA
1008	Celia Brock	246 3rd St.	Sonoma	CA	USA
1010	Julio Abregon	778 Avenida Tarragon	Patzcauro	MICH	MEX

What we have here is the foundation of a relational database as defined at the beginning of this discussion—a two-dimensional (row and column) table of information. Relational databases seldom consist of a single table, however. Such a table is little more than a filing system. By creating several tables of interrelated information, you can perform more complex and powerful operations on your data. The power of the database lies in the relationships that you can construct between the pieces of information, rather than in the pieces of information themselves.

The Need for a Second Table

What happens when a column can logically have multiple values for the same row? Let's suppose we need to add a telephone number column to the Clients table. Well, most people have at least two phone numbers—home and work; and they may have more—fax, cell phone, beeper, vacation home, voice mail, and so on. One of the basic premises of the relational model is that column values are atomic—one value per column in each row, period. Put in more than one value and the DBMS (Database Management System) will treat them as one value anyway.

The solution is to build another table (called, say, Client_Phone), with one column for the phone number and a second for a description of the type of number—home, fax, e-mail, and so on (we use the underscore in Client_Phone because SQL does not permit spaces within the names of objects). Of course, we also have to relate the phone number to the person we will find on the other end—the person represented in our first table—so we must find a way to relate the two tables to one another.

We do this by also putting the primary key—our unique identifying column from the Clients table—in the Client_Phone table. Since this number is unique for every client, we always know which client a given number matches. (For clarity's sake, we could also include the name in Client_Phone, but this would be redundant and take up more disk space. Since the number links the two tables, we can always determine the correct name to match a given number.) The id_num column in Client_Phone is called a *foreign key*, and we say that it references the primary key of Clients. (In this book, keys referenced by foreign keys are called *parent keys*.) Table 1.3 illustrates this relationship. If all the foreign key values in Client_Phone reference values that actually are present in Clients, the system has *referential integrity*. If they do not, we're in trouble, because it would mean that there are phone numbers in the database for clients who are nonexistent or who cannot be identified.

TABLE 1.3: The Client_Phone Table

Id_Num	Phone	Type
1007	4156479772	home
1008	7074568232	work
1008	7079402092	home

We also need a primary key for the Client_Phone table—every table should have a primary key. We can't use id_num because it is not unique (it will be repeated for each phone number of the same client, as for the two numbers for 1008, Celia Brock, above). What about using the phone number itself? This solution is better, but it is possible that we will get two clients in the same household or office. If this were to happen, we still would want to track their phone numbers separately. If we were to use the phone number as the primary key, we could use it in only one row of the Client_Phone table and therefore could associate it with only one id_num. But it is the phone number of two clients. What if one of the clients moved and the other did not? This situation would require a lot of special handling that it probably wouldn't get.

A primary or a foreign key need not be a single column. We can combine the id_num and phone columns. Such a combination should always be unique because, if we list the same number for the same person twice, we've really made the same entry twice and should delete one anyway. So the combination of id_num and phone is the logical primary key of the Client_Phone table. A key of more than one column is variously referred to by different products as a *multicolumn, composite, or concatenated key.*

To summarize, each table has a group of one or more columns that must, as a group, have different values for each row. This value, or group of values together, makes up the primary key and serves to identify the row. A table may also have a group of one or more columns that indicate a relationship to another table. This group is called a *foreign key*, and the group of columns in the other table to which it relates is called its *parent key*. A parent key must be a unique identifier, so that you can tell which row of the parent key table a foreign key is referring to. The foreign key will have the same number and type of columns as the parent key, although it may use different names. The foreign key values do not have to be, and generally are not, unique in their own table, only in the table of the parent key. A system has referential integrity if all foreign key values are present in the referenced parent key.

NOTE

As we said, a parent key must be a unique identifier, which means it must be either a primary key or a *unique key*. A unique key is a group of one or more columns that must be distinct for logical reasons, although not for the sake of database structure. For example, if your database stores insurance ID numbers for employees, but uses social security numbers as the primary key in a table, the insurance ID numbers might be a unique key. Generally, parent keys are primary keys. Since every table should have a primary key, there should always be one that you can use. Since primary keys, like foreign keys, are a fundamental part of the database structure, they are also a more logical choice than unique keys, which are distinct for reasons external to the database structure.

Joining Tables

Now, how do we relate the second table to the first so we can relate the client telephone numbers to the other information from the first table? The two tables remain separate entities in the database, but when we extract the information contained in them, we can link each foreign key value to its parent key and to whatever other columns we might want to see from either table. We don't need to specify any other kind of linkage between the two tables. The fact that one has foreign key values that match values in the primary key of the other is sufficient to determine which rows of the two tables are related (in this case, refer to the same client). Therefore, you perform operations by specifying them logically.

An operation that extracts information from the database is called a *query*. Queries are implemented in SQL with the SELECT statement, which we will briefly introduce in the next chapter. A query that extracts data from more than one table at the same time by relating columns in one table to columns in the other(s) is called a *join*. A join of a foreign key to its parent key is usually (although not in the official SQL92 standard) called a *natural join*, because it is built into the structure of the database. It reunites what we put asunder in separate tables for the sake of the relational structure. With a join, you could produce all of your information for each client—name, address, phone number, and so on—and it will all be correctly correlated. We will explain joins more thoroughly in Part III of this book.

Columns Are Named, Numbered, and Typed

Unlike the rows, the columns of a table are ordered and named. Thus, in our Clients table, Table 1.2, the third column from the left is the address column. Naturally, this means that each column of a given table must have a different name to avoid ambiguity. These names should indicate the content of the column. In the sample tables in this book, we will use some abbreviations as column names, such as *cname* for customer name and *odate* for order date. We have also given each table a single numeric column as a primary key. Like many nerdly conventions, these help to save you typing. The next section will explain these tables and their keys in detail.

Columns also have *datatypes*. All data in a given column will be of the same type: text, numeric, date, and so on. This is because each entry in a column is logically supposed to contain the same type of information about each row.

How a Relational Database Fits Together

Now that you understand the pieces that make up a relational database, let's look at how those pieces fit together. There are two basic matters with which we should be concerned.

First of all, there is the question of how tables are to be grouped. Must all tables in a database be interrelated? No. A group of interrelated tables is called a *schema*. A database can contain any number of *schemata* (sometimes the informal plural *schemas* is used instead of *schemata* in the database literature). Originally (in SQL89), all tables under control of a single user were automatically in the same schema. The SQL92 standard changed this situation, but you may still encounter the old practice. We further discuss the implications of this below. The various SQL standards, including SQL99, are further explained in Chapter 2.

Second, there is the question of users. An operating system intended for use only on a standalone personal computer or an embedded system may or may not recognize individual users, but one intended for most any other use will recognize distinct users. Likewise, any DBMS capable of being used anywhere but on a standalone PC (and even some of those) will recognize individual users. A database user does not necessarily correspond to an OS user, however. Many OS users may appear the same to the database, and a particular OS user may connect as different database users. Database users do, however, have the following features in common with OS users:

- They are identified with a logon procedure, generally involving a username and password.

- Once they log on, they initiate a *session* (also called a *connection*) with the DBMS. This session continues until terminated. Within the session, a sequence of statements (or commands) is issued. Statements from simultaneous sessions of the same or different users form independent sequences.

- They have a set of privileges that indicate what they may and may not do.

- Just as an OS user typically has ownership of some set of files and directories and may have access to others as well, a database user typically has ownership of one schema and may have access to others as well. Depending on the particular database system used, a database user can own one or several schemata. Often an application that must access a schema does so as the same user regardless of which OS user is executing the application. This simplifies matters considerably.

A Sample Database Schema

Tables 1.4, 1.5, and 1.6 constitute a simple relational database that is small enough to follow easily, but complex enough to illustrate the major concepts and practices involved in using SQL. These tables are printed in this chapter and also on the inside cover as we will refer to them throughout this book.

You will notice that the first column of each table contains numbers whose values are different for every row. As you may have guessed, these are the primary keys of the tables. Some of these numbers also appear in columns of other tables. These are foreign keys referencing the primary keys. Although it is not necessary that foreign keys have the same names as the primary keys they reference, we have adopted this convention for clarity's sake.

TABLE 1.4: Salespeople

Snum	Sname	City	Comm
1001	Peel	London	.12
1002	Serres	San Jose	.13
1004	Motika	London	.11
1007	Rifkin	Barcelona	.15
1003	Axelrod	New York	.10

TABLE 1.5: Customers

Cnum	Cname	City	Rating	Snum
2001	Hoffman	London	100	1001
2002	Giovanni	Rome	200	1003
2003	Liu	San Jose	200	1002
2004	Grass	Berlin	300	1002
2006	Clemens	London	NULL	1001
2008	Cisneros	San Jose	300	1007
2007	Pereira	Rome	100	1004

TABLE 1.6: Orders

Onum	Amt	Odate	Cnum	Snum
3001	18.69	10/03/2000	2008	1007
3003	767.19	10/03/2000	2001	1001
3002	1900.10	10/03/2000	2007	1004
3005	5160.45	10/03/2000	2003	1002
3006	1098.16	10/03/2000	2008	1007

TABLE 1.6 (CONTINUED): Orders

Onum	Amt	Odate	Cnum	Snum
3009	1713.23	10/04/2000	2002	1003
3007	75.75	10/04/2000	2004	1002
3008	4723.00	10/05/2000	2006	1001
3010	1309.95	10/06/2000	2004	1002
3011	9891.88	10/06/2000	2006	1001

The snum field of the Customers table indicates to which salesperson a customer is assigned. The snum number relates to the Salespeople table, which gives information about these salespeople. Obviously, the salespeople to whom the customers are assigned should exist—that is to say, the snum values in the Customers table should also be present in the Salespeople table. If such is the case, we say that the system is in a state of *referential integrity*.

The tables themselves are intended to resemble a real-life business situation, where you would use SQL to keep track of the salespeople, their customers, and the customers' orders. They are, of course, much simplified over all the material that would need to be tracked in a realistic example. Let's take a moment to look at these three tables and the meaning of their various columns.

The columns of the Salespeople table

COLUMN	CONTENT
snum	A unique number assigned to each salesperson (an employee number). This is the primary key of the table.
sname	The last name of the salesperson.
city	The location of the salesperson. This indicates one of a set of company offices.
comm	The salesperson's commission on orders in decimal form.

The columns of the Customers table

COLUMN	CONTENT
cnum	A unique number assigned to each customer. This is the primary key of the table.
cname	The last name of the customer.
city	The location of the customer. This actually indicates a company office, rather than the city where the customer resides.
rating	A numeric code indicating the level of preference assigned to this customer. Higher numbers indicate greater preference. NULL indicates a customer who has not yet been assigned a rating.
snum	The number of the salesperson assigned to this customer. This is a foreign key referencing Salespeople (snum). Since we don't want a customer to languish if his assigned salesperson is not available, we have enabled a mechanism for other salespeople to handle this customer when the one normally assigned is not available. We explain this mechanism below.

The columns of the Orders table

COLUMN	CONTENT
onum	A unique number given to each purchase.
amt	The amount of the purchase.
odate	The date of the purchase.
cnum	The number of the customer making the purchase. This is foreign key referencing Customers (cnum).
snum	The number of the salesperson credited with the sale. This is a foreign key referencing Salespeople (snum). It normally would be the salesperson assigned to the customer in the Customers table, but may not be, as explained below.

There are a number of things to note about the above design. First, detailed information about salespeople and customers, such as full names and contact information, is not included. A realistic database would obviously include such information and may well put some of it in these tables (we discuss when and how to do so under "Designing a Database" in Part V of this book). We have omitted it here to keep the tables as simple as possible, so that the complexity of the tables would not get in the way of understanding examples.

Second, customers are assigned to salespeople, and then each order is associated with both a salesperson and a customer. Does each match of salesperson and customer in the Orders table have to be the same as the matches in the Customers table? In other words, does the salesperson assigned to a customer invariably get credit for each order of that customer? We have assumed not. If we had assumed so, the snum column in the Orders table would be superfluous, since we could use the Customers table to determine which salesperson would get credit for the sale. Doing it this way is more flexible. If the salesperson assigned to a customer is unavailable, another could handle the sale, and the two could split the commission. Such complexity may be introduced into a database by the business rules, and we thought it best to deal with it straight on. For the sake of simplicity, however, we have not introduced any such anomalies into the sample data.

Finally, the commission in the Salespeople table need not be static. It may be something that is periodically calculated on, for example, year-to-date sales. Certain issues arise from storing derived information directly in the database this way, and we will discuss those issues under database design in Part V of this book. Suppose that calculating the commission is complex or involves accessing several databases. In such cases, it makes sense to occasionally (say, monthly) derive the commission and store it here. Otherwise, another approach may be better.

Status of Relational and Other Systems

Relational database systems are the most widely used database systems in the world today. These systems have solved many of the problems that plagued the earlier nonrelational products. Those products required programmers and database administrators to become engaged with the details of how the data was stored and structured in the database, which made applications complex to develop and nightmarish to modify. It also made the problem of having several applications use the same data more complex. Relational systems allow you to work with the data at a higher level. All operations on the data are handled by a program called a DBMS, which responds only to statements expressed in a high-level language.

Another kind of database that is becoming popular is the object-oriented database model derived from the object-oriented programming methodology. In object-oriented (OO) programming languages such as Java and C++, program modules are independent entities called *objects* that encapsulate both data and the operations that can be performed on it. If you have a need for a persistent store of such objects—that is to say, if you wish these objects to keep track of some data between one execution of the program and another—you would create an object-oriented database (OODB). Object-oriented programming has a number of advantages, all of which are beyond the scope of this book. Suffice it to say that the importance of OO programming, coupled with the established position and usefulness of relational systems, has led to a clamor for a graceful combination of the two approaches. This is one of the problems the SQL99 standard, explained in Part VI of this book, addresses.

Summary

Now you know what is meant by a relational database, a concept that sounds more complicated than it really is. You also have learned some fundamental principles about how tables are structured—how rows and columns work, how primary keys distinguish rows from one another, and how columns can refer to values in other columns.

You are now familiar with the sample tables. Brief and simple as they are, they are adequate to demonstrate most of the features of the language, as you shall see. On occasion, we will introduce another table or postulate some different data in one of these tables to show you some other possibilities.

Now you are ready to dive into SQL itself. The next chapter gives you a bird's-eye view of the language, orienting you to the terrain and putting a lot of the material you may need to refer to in one familiar place.

Putting SQL to Work

1.   What is the primary key of the Orders table?

2.   What is another word for row? For column?

3.   Why can you not ask to see the first five rows of a table?

CHAPTER

TWO

2

SQL: An Overview

- How Does SQL Work?

- The Various Types of Data

- Some Basic SQL Statements

This chapter will acquaint you with the structure of the SQL language as well as with certain general issues, such as the types of data that columns can contain and the status of the various official SQL standards and local variations. This is intended to provide a context for the more specific information in subsequent chapters. You will also get a quick tour of the language, including sample statements, so you can see how the language works. You do not need to remember every detail mentioned in this chapter. The overview presented here consolidates, in one easily located area, many of the details that you may need to refer to as you proceed to master the language. We have put all this information at the beginning of the book to orient you to the world of SQL without oversimplifying it and to give you a familiar place to go back to when you have questions. This material will become much clearer when we move into the specifics of SQL statements, starting in Chapter 3.

How Does SQL Work?

SQL is a language oriented specifically around relational databases. It eliminates a lot of the work you would have to do if you were using a general-purpose programming language, such as C. To build a relational database in C, you would have to start from scratch. You would have to define an object called a *table* that could grow to have any number of rows, and then create step-by-step procedures for putting values in it and retrieving them. If you wanted to find some particular rows, you would have to enumerate each step of the process like this:

1. Look at a row of the table.

2. Perform a test to see if it is one of the rows you want.

3. If so, store it somewhere until the whole table is examined.

4. See if there are any more rows in the table.

5. If there are more rows, go back to step 1.

6. If there are no more rows, output all values stored in step 3.

(Of course, this is not an actual set of C instructions, just an English-language rendition of the logical steps that would be involved.)

SQL, however, spares you all this. Commands in SQL (traditionally called *statements*) can operate on entire tables as single objects and can treat any quantity of information extracted or derived from them as a single unit as well.

How Do the Standards Fit In?

As we mentioned in the Introduction, the SQL standard is defined jointly by the *ISO* (International Organization for Standardization) and *ANSI* (the American National Standards Institute). Since ANSI is part of the ISO, we will refer to both organizations jointly as the ISO. SQL was not invented by these bodies; it is essentially a product of IBM research. But other companies picked up on SQL right away. In fact, at least one company beat IBM to the punch with a marketable SQL product.

After a number of competing SQL products were on the market, the ISO defined the standard to which they would all conform (defining such standards is the ISO's function). Doing this after the fact, however, presented some problems. The early ISO standards were somewhat limited: The ISO simply left a lot of material out of the standard, so that existing products would not have too much trouble conforming without sacrificing the upward compatibility of their previous versions. Later standards were more complete. Here is the list of the major ANSI/ISO SQL standards:

SQL86　This provided a minimum functionality that all existing products had in common. Hence, it basically standardized syntax that was somewhat at variance.

SQL89　This made only one major change to SQL86, which was to add support for mechanisms to enforce foreign key relationships (referential integrity).

SQL92　This was a major update of the standard. Instead of simply certifying and standardizing the overlap among existing products, the ISO specified future growth for the language, including much functionality that had not yet been implemented by anyone, at least not in the way specified. Since conforming to this standard is rather ambitious, the ISO specified three distinct levels of conformance: Entry, Intermediate, and Full. As of this publication (2000), most database vendors are still at Entry level, with some features from the higher levels thrown in.

SQL99   This is the new standard being finalized as this book is written. It further extends SQL92 to include integration with object-oriented approaches, programmatic extensions, and other features.

This book provides a tutorial in SQL92. The reference section in Part VII covers SQL92 completely. Part VI covers SQL99.

Note that database vendors still have local variations on the standard. Many vendors provide both a standard and a non-standard mode so that you can choose whether to code to the standard or to use the local variations.

Forms of SQL

In a sense, there are three SQLs: Interactive, Static, and Dynamic. For the most part, the forms operate the same way, but they are used differently.

- Interactive SQL is used to operate directly on a database to produce output for human utilization. In this form of SQL, you enter a statement now, it is executed now, and you can see the output (if any) immediately.

- Static SQL consists of SQL statements hard-coded as part of an application or code module. The most common form of this is *Embedded SQL*, where SQL code is interspersed in the source code of a program written primarily in another language, such as C or Pascal. Enabling these other languages to deal with SQL's structure and its style of data management does require some extensions to Interactive SQL. The output of SQL statements in Embedded SQL is "passed off" to variables or parameters usable by the program in which it is embedded.

- Dynamic SQL is also part of an application or code module, but the specific SQL code to be executed is generated at runtime rather than coded in advance. Some extensions to Static SQL are required to make this possible.

In this book, we will present SQL first in its interactive form. This will enable us to discuss statements and their effects without worrying about how they interface with other languages. Interactive SQL is also the common ground, as almost everything about Interactive SQL applies to the other forms as well, and it constitutes the bulk of the language. We'll deal with the changes needed to use the static and dynamic forms in the latter parts of this book.

The Subdivisions of SQL

In all of its forms, SQL has multiple sections, or subdivisions. Since you are likely to encounter this terminology when reading about SQL, we will provide some explanation. Unfortunately, these terms are not used consistently in all implementations. They are emphasized by the ISO and are useful on a conceptual level, but many SQL products do not treat them separately in practice, so they essentially become functional categories of SQL statements. The most commonly referenced areas are:

- Data Definition Language (DDL, also called Schema Definition Language by the ISO) consists of those commands that create the objects (tables, indexes, views, and so on) in the database.

- Data Manipulation Language (DML) is a set of commands that determine which values are present in the tables at any given time.

- Data Control Language (DCL) consists of features that determine whether a user is permitted to perform a particular action. The ISO considers this part of DDL.

Don't let these names put you off. These are not different languages per se, but divisions of SQL statements into groups according to their functions.

The Various Types of Data

Although all of the data in a given column is of the same logical type, not all the types of values that can occupy the columns of a table are the same. The most obvious distinction is between numbers and text. You can't put numbers in alphabetical order or subtract one name from another. Since relational database systems enable you to construct ad-hoc relationships between pieces of information, the various types of data must be clearly distinguished from one another so that the appropriate processes and comparisons can be applied.

In SQL, you do this by assigning each column a *datatype* that indicates the kind of value the column will contain. All of the values in a given column must be of the same type. In the Customers table, for example, cname and city are strings of text, whereas rating, snum, and cnum are numbers. For this reason, you could not enter Highest or None into the rating column, which has a numeric datatype. This limitation is fortunate because it imposes some structure on your data. You frequently will be comparing some or all of the values in a given column so that you can perform an action on some rows and not on others. You could not do this if the column's values had mixed datatypes.

The standard datatypes can be divided into the following categories:

NOTE   This is a list of logical categories, not of types. There are several distinct datatypes in most of these categories.

- Text, such as single characters, fixed-length text strings, and varying-length text strings. These are enclosed in single quotes (apostrophes) when referenced, as follows: 'I am a text string'.

- Some products also support double-quotes or single left and right quotes, but these are non-standard. Pairs of apostrophes should always work.

- Exact numeric, such as integers and decimal numbers. An integer would be 2, and a decimal number would be 2.5.

- Approximate numeric, which is to say floating point numbers with a base of 10, as are used in scientific notation.

- Datetime. These can be date only, time only, or a combination. For example, 1/1/2000.

- Intervals, which is to say intervals of time between datetime values, such as ten seconds or three months. To see how these are represented and used, see "Datatypes" in the reference.

- Binary, which is to say binary data that, in a computer, could represent anything.

For details on these datatypes, see "Datatypes" in the reference section. Some vendors supplement the above categories with special-purpose types like money.

The ISO defines several different types of number values, the distinctions between which are frequently subtle and sometimes confusing. The complexity of these types can, at least in part, be explained by the effort to make SQL compatible with a variety of other languages.

Table 2.1 shows the ISO types we shall rely on for most of the discussion in this book.

TABLE 2.1: Datatypes Most Commonly Referenced

Datatype	Description
CHAR(*num*)	A fixed-length text string of *num* characters. If *num* is omitted, the default is 1.
VARCHAR(*num*)	A varying-length text string of no more than *num* characters. If *num* is omitted, the default is defined by the implementation. The chief difference between a fixed and varying length string is that the former allocates enough disk space for the maximum for each entry, which wastes space but can make searches more efficient.
INTEGER	An exact numeric type with no decimal point. Also written INT.
DECIMAL	An exact numeric type with a written or implied decimal point. Also written DEC.
DATE	A datetime type with the fields year, month, and day.

The character types consist of all the printable characters, including the numbers. However, the number 1 is not the same as the character '1'. The character '1' is just another printable piece of text, not recognized by the system as having the numeric value 1. While $1 + 1 = 2$, '1' + '1' does not equal '2'.

CHARACTER values are stored in the computer as binary values, but appear to the user as printable text. The conversion follows a format defined by the system you are using. For English and some other languages, this conversion format will almost always be ASCII (possibly with extensions), though it may also be EBCDIC (used in some larger computers). Certain operations, such as alphabetical ordering of column values, may vary with the format. Generally speaking, the default sorting for alphabetical ordering will be determined by the format, but, in SQL92, you can override this with the use of explicit collating sequences, as explained in Chapter 20.

Terminology

Following are some key SQL terms that you should be familiar with:

- Keywords are words that have a special meaning in SQL. They are understood to be instructions or parts of instructions, not text or names of objects. We will indicate keywords by printing them in all CAPS. You should take care not to confuse keywords with terminology. SQL has certain special terms that are used to describe it. Among these are such words as "query", "clause", and "predicate", which are important in describing and understanding the language, but do not mean anything to SQL itself.

- Statements, or commands, are instructions you give to a SQL database. Statements consist of one or more logically distinct parts called *clauses*. Clauses generally begin with a keyword for which they are named and consist of keywords and arguments. Examples of clauses you will encounter are FROM Salespeople and WHERE city = 'London'. *Arguments* complete or modify the meaning of a clause. In the examples above, Salespeople is the argument, and FROM is the keyword of the FROM clause. Likewise, city = 'London' is the argument of the WHERE clause.

- Objects are structures in the database that are given names and stored persistently. They include base tables, views (the two kinds of tables), and indexes. Notice that this differs from the meaning of "object" used in object-oriented programming.

Conventions

When we show you how statements are formed, we will generally do so by example. There is, however, a more formal method of describing statements using a set of standardized conventions called the Backus-Naur Form (BNF). We use this extensively in the reference and occasionally elsewhere. We have extended this slightly (with the .,.. convention) to cover a common SQL construct that otherwise would complexify the diagrams considerably. We also use italics rather than angle brackets for placeholders, as explained below. The conventions we use are as follows:

- The symbol ::= means "is defined as". It is used to further clarify parts of a statement's syntax diagram.

- Keywords appear in all uppercase letters. These reserved words are literals that are actually written as part of the statement.

- Placeholders for specific values, such as *domain name* in the CREATE DOMAIN statement, appear in italic type. These placeholders identify the type of value that should be used in a real statement; they are not literals to be written as part of the statement. These take the place of items in angle brackets in conventional BNF diagrams. White space within italicized terms is for readability, not separation. *Table name* is one term, not two. Outside of italicized terms, blanks and other white space separate distinct statement elements.

- Optional portions of a statement appear in square brackets ([and]).

- A vertical bar (|) indicates that whatever precedes it may optionally be replaced by whatever follows it.

- Braces ({ and }) indicate that everything within them is to be regarded as a whole for the purpose of evaluating other symbols (e.g., vertical bars or ellipses).

- Ellipses (…) indicate that the preceding portion of the statement may be repeated any number of times.

- Ellipses with an interposed comma (.,..) indicate that the preceding portion may be repeated any number of times, with the individual occurrences separated by commas. The final occurrence should not be followed by a comma. Note: This is not a standard BNF convention; we use it for clarity in representing the many SQL statements that use the construct. If we did not adopt this convention, the syntax diagrams would be considerably more awkward and difficult to read.

- Parentheses () used in syntax diagrams are literals. They indicate that parentheses are to be used in forming the statement. They do not specify a way of reading the diagram as braces or square brackets do.

- Carriage returns or line feeds in SQL are treated the same as blanks—they simply delimit the elements of statements. We use carriage returns and spacing in our syntax diagrams simply for readability; you need not duplicate them in your SQL code.

Some Basic SQL Statements

In order for you to get a flavor of SQL, we're going to show you some sample SQL statements. Don't worry if you do not fully understand them right now. The object here is to let you see how the pieces we will be examining in detail fit into the larger picture.

Assuming you are not working on a standalone PC system, you must begin by connecting to the DBMS, so that your identity and privileges can be established. This will create a session between you as a database user and the DBMS (for the time being, we will set aside the preliminaries like creating the database in the first place and defining the various users). The most common way to initiate a session with a DBMS is with a statement like the following:

```
CONNECT TO MyDatabse USER Darvin/Sasquatch;
```

This statement is an example based on Full SQL92 conformance. Since most products are not at this level of conformance, they may not support this precise syntax. Check your system documentation for details.

- CONNECT is the keyword that indicates which SQL statement this is. SQL statements begin with keywords.

- TO MyDatabase is the database to which you are connecting.

- Darvin is your database username. It need not correspond to your operating system username.

- Sasquatch is your database password. If you had not wanted to type this in the clear, you could have omitted it, and you would then have been prompted to enter it hidden (in most implementations). If your database is so configured, you could also possibly connect without a password. In this case, the database authorizes you based on your OS user identity, though this still does not imply a one-to-one correspondence between OS and database users.

- The semi-colon (;) is the SQL statement terminator. Although a semi-colon is the official SQL statement terminator, some implementations support alternative ones as well. If you use Embedded SQL, the statement terminator is simply whichever terminator is normally used in the host language (the language within which you are embedding SQL, for example, C, Pascal, or Java).

When you enter this statement, you should get some acknowledgment of success or failure, such as:

```
user Darvin connected.
```

Now suppose you wanted to create the Salespeople table we introduced in the preceding chapter. You would use the CREATE TABLE statement, as follows:

```
CREATE TABLE Salespeople
    (snum      INTEGER       NOT NULL PRIMARY KEY,
     sname     CHAR(15)      NOT NULL,
     city      CHAR(15)      NOT NULL,
     comm      DECIMAL);
```

The components of this statement are as follows:

- CREATE TABLE are the keywords indicating what this statement does.

- Salespeople is the name given the table.

- The items in parenthesis are a list of the columns in the table. Each column has a name and a datatype. It may also have one or more constraints (NOT NULL, PRIMARY KEY), which we will explain later.

Again, the spacing is for readability. We could have put all this code on one line with no change in effect. This statement too will produce a response, such as:

```
Table Salespeople created.
```

Though you have created the table, as yet it contains no data. To put a row in the table, you would enter the following:

```
INSERT INTO Salespeople VALUES (1001, 'Peel', 'London', .12);
```

This inserts the list of values in parentheses into the Salespeople table. Note that the values are given in the same order as the columns into which they are being inserted and that the text data values are enclosed in right-single quotes (apostrophes).

Finally, let's assume that you want to retrieve the row you just placed in the Salespeople table. The operation that retrieves data from the database is called a *query* and is implemented with the SELECT statement, which is the most sophisticated in SQL. With SELECT, you choose criteria that determine which rows of a table to output. This set of criteria is called a *predicate*. The use of predicates is consistent with the general relational approach of defining operations by logic rather than by details of implementation. Here is a SELECT statement to retrieve Peel's row:

```
SELECT snum, sname, city, comm
     FROM Salespeople
     WHERE sname = 'Peel';
```

This statement would select all columns for **every** salesperson named Peel. There happens to be only one, of course, but if there were more, all would be selected. To get around this, and choose exactly the row you want, you should use a predicate that tests for the PRIMARY KEY, which is snum, thusly:

```
SELECT snum, sname, city, comm
     FROM Salespeople
     WHERE snum = 1001;
```

Finally, if you wanted to take out the row you had entered, you would do it with a predicate, just like you did for the query, as follows:

```
DELETE FROM Salespeople
     WHERE snum = 1001;
```

It is not necessary to name any columns because a DELETE statement always takes out the entire row. To take out individual column values, you would use a different statement, UPDATE, which we will discuss later.

That concludes the brief tour. We have only superficially touched on each of these statements to give you an idea how it all fits together. In the following chapters, we will look at these and other statements in detail.

Summary

Whew! You have quickly covered a lot of ground in this chapter. But our intention has simply been to fly high over the SQL territory so you could have an idea of its overall shape. When we return to the ground in the next chapter, things will become much more concrete. Now you know a fair amount about SQL—how it is structured, how it is used, how it conceives of data, how and by whom it is defined (and some inconsistencies emerging from that), and some of the conventions and terminology used to describe it. You have also seen simple examples of some of its most important statements. In that discussion, we defined two concepts that will become very important:

- The *predicate*, which is a set of criteria used to decide whether a statement will or will not be executed against a particular row of a table. This concept will become more concrete as we discuss it further.

- The *query*, which is a request for information from the database. In other words, a SELECT statement.

We've given you a lot of information for a single chapter; you don't have to remember all of the details, but you can refer to them as you need to. The important thing is the big picture.

In Chapter 3, we will go hands-on, showing the CREATE TABLE statement in greater detail.

Putting SQL to Work

1. Which SQL statement is used to place data in tables?

2. Which subdivision of SQL is used to create tables?

3. What is a predicate?

4. What is a query?

PART II

Creating a Database

CHAPTER

THREE

Creating, Changing, and Dropping Tables

- Defining the Environment

- Using the CREATE TABLE Command

- Altering a Table Once It Has Been Created

- Dropping a Table

3

In this chapter, we will show you how to create a database schema and populate it. We will discuss the creating, altering, and dropping of tables. This refers to the definitions of the tables themselves, not to the data stored in them. You may or may not need to perform these operations yourself, but a conceptual understanding of them will increase your comprehension of SQL and of the nature of the tables that you use. This puts us in the area of SQL called DDL (Data Definition Language), where SQL data objects are created.

Defining the Environment

Since users must perform all actions in a database, including the creation of objects, one of the first logical steps in setting up a database is to create some users. Unfortunately, the whole business of creating users and databases is an area where the standard is weak or silent, and companies need to take their own approaches. Also, if you are in a large multi-user environment, you probably will not have to create users and databases anyway. You will be using a set of user accounts and schemata that have already been established. Nonetheless, we will give you some flavor of how this process works. Keep in mind that what we show here is a typical syntax and procedure, but your mileage may vary depending on the specific DBMS platform you are using. Once we get into areas where the standard is more developed (which are most areas), you will be better able to use our code samples without modification.

The DBMS automatically defines one or more users so that this process has a place to begin. It will also define at least one default schema for you to CONNECT to. For the most part, these are database superusers such as SYS (for System), which will naturally have a default password. Therefore, you would first CONNECT as SYS:

```
CONNECT TO DEFAULT USER SYS/SomePassword;
```

Once you have so connected, you can create users:

```
CREATE USER Chris IDENTIFIED BY pumpkin;
```

This statement creates a new user with a database login name of Chris and a password of pumpkin. Note that although Chris and pumpkin are, in a sense, text strings, they are not enclosed in single quotes. This is because they are not

SQL data values, but are rather *identifiers*. An identifier is simply a name for something that is or will become meaningful to the DBMS.

In some systems, you will also have to give Chris the right to connect to the DBMS. We will explain rights such as these later in the book. For now, just realize that you may also have to enter a statement like the following:

```
GRANT CONNECT TO Chris;
```

Now that you have created Chris, you can CONNECT as her, to wit:

```
CONNECT TO DEFAULT USER Chris/pumpkin;
```

This initiates a new database session where you are the user Chris. Your previous session is terminated.

When you created the user called Chris, you also created a default schema called Chris where objects created by this person can be stored. This schema is initially empty, and Chris does not necessarily have the right to place objects in it. Giving Chris this power is something we will cover in Chapter 16, "Determining Who Can Do What". In some systems (specifically those that are at least Intermediate-level SQL92-compliant, and possibly others that have decided to implement this feature), multiple schemata could be created for Chris either by her or by others. For more information on this feature, look up CREATE SCHEMA in the statement reference. For the most part, we will assume that there is one (possibly empty) schema per user and that the schema and user share the same name. Such is the usual situation and was required in earlier versions of SQL.

For now, let's assume that the user Chris now exists and has the privileges necessary to begin constructing a database schema. How does she go about doing so? This question actually contains two logical parts: How does she go about determining which tables to create? And how does she construct the SQL statements needed to construct the tables? The first question brings up the whole topic of database design, which would be a major digression at this point. We will cover that topic in Part V of this book. By all means, skip ahead to Part V if you need to design a practical database right away.

For the time being, suffice it to say the following:

- A schema should map some set of real-world entities and the relationships between them. For example, the schema we introduced previously tracks the activities of three inter-related entities: Salespeople, Customers, and

Orders. Each of these has a definable existence in the world quite apart from the needs of our database.

- Relationships between entities are generally expressed with foreign key/parent key mechanisms. For example, in the company we are modeling, customers are assigned to salespeople. We express this by having a foreign key called snum in the Customers table that references the primary key, also called snum, of the Salespeople table.

Those things being said, let's move on to the specific SQL statement used to create SQL tables.

Using the CREATE TABLE Command

We define tables with the CREATE TABLE command. This command creates an initially empty table—a table with no rows. We enter values with the INSERT statement, which we will explain later in this book. The CREATE TABLE command basically defines a table name as describing a set of named columns in a specified order. It also defines the data types and sizes of the columns. Each table must have at least one column. Here is the syntax of the CREATE TABLE command:

```
CREATE TABLE tablename
    ({columnname datatype[(size)]}.,...);
```

> **NOTE**   This and other syntax diagrams follow the extended BNF notation that we described in Chapter 2 of this book.

Note that the above is a simplified syntax description. It doesn't include constraints, which we will discuss in the next chapter, nor does it include temporary tables or indexes, which we will discuss later in this book. For a complete syntax of CREATE TABLE, see the reference under "CREATE TABLE".

As mentioned in Chapter 2, datatypes vary somewhat between products. For the sake of compatibility with the standard, however, they should all at least support the standard ISO types. These are enumerated in the reference under "Datatypes".

Since blank spaces are used to separate parts of statements in SQL, they may not be part of a table's name (or that of any other object, such as an index). An underscore (_) is most commonly used to separate words in table names.

The meaning of the size argument varies with the datatype. If you omit it, your system will assign a value automatically. For numeric values, this is usually the best course, because it will make all your fields of a given type the same size and release you from concern about union compatibility (see Chapter 13 or the reference under "SELECT"). Besides, the use of the size argument with some of the numeric types is not a simple matter. If you need to store large numbers, however, you will naturally want to ensure that the columns are long enough and of the appropriate scale to contain them.

The one datatype for which you should generally assign a size is CHAR. Here the size argument is an integer that specifies the maximum number of characters that the column can hold. The column's actual number of characters can range from zero to this number. The default is 1, which means the column can contain only a single letter. This is not what you usually want.

The user who creates the tables owns them, and the names of all tables in a given schema must be different from one another, as must the names of all the columns within a given table. Separate tables may use the same column names, even if they are in the same schema. An example of this is the city column in both the Salespeople and Customers tables. Users other than the owner of a table will refer to that table by preceding its name with that of its schema followed by a dot; for example, Chris' table Employees would become Chris.Employees when referred to by another user. The following command would create the Salespeople table:

```
CREATE TABLE Salespeople
     (snum INTEGER,
     sname CHAR(10),
     city  CHAR(10),
     comm  DECIMAL);
```

The order of the columns in the table is determined by the order in which they are specified. In other words, since snum comes first, snum will be the first column of the table. Each column definition consists of a column name, the datatype, and optionally the size. The column definitions do not have to be on separate lines as above—that is done only for readability—but they do have to be separated by commas.

Altering a Table Once It Has Been Created

The ALTER TABLE statement is used to change the definitions of extant tables. Because this is so often necessary in practical terms, most vendors have implemented ALTER TABLE since the early days of SQL. However, it was not part of the SQL standard until SQL92 and was only required for Intermediate conformance then. Therefore, there is still some inconsistency in how this statement works, but there is also increasing convergence between the versions. In SQL92, ALTER TABLE can do the following:

- Add a column to a table.

- Drop a column from a table.

- Add a table constraint to a table.

- Drop a constraint from a table.

- Add a default value to a column.

- Drop a default value from a column.

The syntax to achieve this is as follows:

```
ALTER TABLE tablename
{ ADD [COLUMN] column definition }
| {ALTER [COLUMN] column name
     {SET DEFAULT default option } | {DROP DEFAULT }}
| { DROP [COLUMN] column name }
| {ADD table constraint definition }
| { DROP CONSTRAINT constraint name  };
```

Note that the above is slightly simplified. For a complete explanation, see ALTER TABLE in the reference. Let's look at some examples of ALTER TABLE usage.

The following statement adds a column called fname (for first name) to the Salespeople table:

```
ALTER TABLE Salespeople ADD fname char(10);
```

Note the following:

- The syntax of the column definition is the same as used in the CREATE TABLE statement.

- We didn't include the keyword COLUMN after ADD, although we could have. The syntax diagram indicates it is optional, and it doesn't change the meaning at all. This makes the standard compatible with different existing products.

- If any rows currently exist in the table (i.e., if the table is not empty), the column is added with NULLs in place for those rows.

- The new column will be the last column of the table.

If we wanted London to be the default city, we could achieve it as follows:

```
ALTER TABLE Salespeople ALTER COLUMN city ADD DEFAULT 'London';
```

ALTER TABLE is invaluable when you need to redefine a table, but you should design your database as much as possible to avoid relying on it. Changing the structure of a table already in use is full of hazards. Views of the table, which are secondary tables extracting data from other tables (see Part IV), may no longer function properly, and applications may run incorrectly or not at all. In addition, you must make the implications of the change clear to all users accessing the table. For these reasons, you should try to design your tables to meet your anticipated, as well as current, needs and use ALTER TABLE only as a last resort.

If your system doesn't support ALTER TABLE, or if you want to avoid using it, you can simply create a new table with the desired change in its definition, and transfer the old data to it. You will need to independently grant users with access to the old table access to the new table.

Dropping a Table

Dropping a table is actually a two-step process, as follows:

- First you must empty the table of any data by using the DELETE statement.

- Then you can destroy the definition of the table by using the DROP TABLE statement.

You must own (have created) the schema in which a table resides in order to drop it. The syntax to remove the definition of your table from the system once it is empty is

```
DROP TABLE tablename [RESTRICT | CASCADE];
```

The RESTRICT or CASCADE clause refers to what happens when other objects (such as views, see Part IV) exist that depend on this table. If RESTRICT is specified, the DROP is disallowed; if CASCADE is specified, dependent objects are automatically dropped as well. DROP TABLE is required only for intermediate-level SQL92 conformance. Implementations that don't claim such conformance do, in fact, support DROP TABLE, but usually without the RESTRICT or CASCADE business. In the standard, the RESTRICT or CASCADE business can also apply to ALTER TABLE DROP COLUMN.

Once this statement is issued, the table name is no longer recognized and no more statements can be given on that object.

Summary

You are now fluent in the basics of data definition. You can create, modify, and drop tables. In creating tables, you specify the columns they will contain and the datatypes of each. You also know how to add columns or constraints to a table or to drop them. DROP TABLE allows you to get rid of tables that have outlived their usefulness. It drops only empty tables, and therefore does not destroy data.

In the next chapter, we will cover a more sophisticated aspect of table creation: constraints. These enable you to control which values may or may not be entered into tables.

Putting SQL to Work

1. Write a CREATE TABLE statement that would produce our Customers table.

2. Write an ALTER TABLE statement that would drop the rating column from the Customers table. Assume the table is currently empty.

3. Write a statement that would drop the Customers table and the Order table that references it.

CHAPTER

FOUR

4

Constraining the Values of Your Data

- Declaring Constraints

- Using Constraints to Exclude NULLs

- Specifying the Primary Key

- Making Sure Values Are Unique

- Checking Column Values

- Naming and Dropping Constraints

- Deferring Constraints

- Assigning Default Values

In the previous chapter, you learned how tables are created. Now we will elaborate on that point to show you how you can place constraints on tables. *Constraints* are parts of a table definition that limit the values you can enter into its columns. We will also show you how to define default values in this chapter. A *default* is a value that is inserted automatically into any column of a table when a value for that column is omitted from an INSERT statement on that table. NULL is the most widely used default, but we will show you how to define others. Technically, defaults are not constraints, but the procedures involved in defining the two are quite similar.

Declaring Constraints

When you create a table (or, sometimes, when you alter one), you can place constraints on the values that can be entered into its columns. If you do this, SQL generally will reject any values that violate the criteria you define. (The exception is if the constraint is deferred. See "Constraints" in the reference.) The two basic types of constraints are column constraints and table constraints. The difference between the two is that *column constraints* apply only to individual columns, whereas *table constraints* apply to groups of one or more columns.

In CREATE TABLE statements, you append column constraints to the end of column definitions after the datatype and before the comma. You place table constraints at the end of the table definition, after the last column definition but before the closing parenthesis. The following is the syntax for the CREATE TABLE statement, expanded to include constraints:

```
CREATE TABLE tablename
     ({columnname datatype column constraint}...,
     [table constraint (columnname .,..) .,..];
```

(For the sake of brevity, we have omitted the size argument, which is sometimes used with datatype.) The columns given in parentheses after the table constraint(s) are those to which the given table constraint applies. The column constraints, naturally, apply to the columns whose definitions they follow. The rest of this chapter will describe the various types of constraints and their use.

Unless otherwise noted, table constraints described in this chapter can also be added to tables after the fact by using the ALTER TABLE statement explained in the previous chapter.

Using Constraints to Exclude NULLs

You can use the CREATE TABLE statement to prevent a column from permitting NULLs by using the NOT NULL constraint. This constraint can be only of the column variety.

NULLs are special designations that mark a column as having no value for the row at hand. As useful as NULLs can be, there are cases where you will want to ensure against them. Obviously, primary keys should never be NULL, as this would severely undermine the functionality of primary keys, which is identifying each row of a table. There would be no way to distinguish the NULL rows from one another. In addition, columns such as names should, in many cases, be required to have definite values. For example, you would probably want a name for every customer in the Customers table.

If you place the keywords NOT NULL immediately after the datatype (including size) of a column, any attempts to put NULL values in that column will be rejected. Otherwise, SQL will assume that NULLs are permitted.

For example, let us improve our definition of the Salespeople table by not allowing NULLs in the snum or sname columns:

```
CREATE TABLE Salespeople
    (snum INTEGER NOT NULL,
    sname CHAR(10) NOT NULL,
    city CHAR(10),
    comm DECIMAL);
```

It is important to remember that any column with a NOT NULL constraint must be assigned values in every INSERT clause that affects the table. In the absence of NULLs, SQL will have no values to put in these columns unless a default value, described later in this chapter, is assigned.

Specifying the Primary Key

Until now, we have been discussing primary keys solely as logical concepts. Although we should know, for any table, what the primary key is and how it is to be used, we have not assumed that SQL "knows". There is, however, a constraint you can use to define a group of one or more columns as a primary key. Unsurprisingly, this is called the PRIMARY KEY constraint. The PRIMARY KEY constraint can be of the table or column variety. Only one primary key (of any number of columns) can be defined for a given table. Primary keys cannot allow NULL values. In the older (pre-SQL92) standards, this meant they had to be explicitly declared NOT NULL. More recently, PRIMARY KEY automatically implies NOT NULL. Check your system documentation to see what it requires. Most systems do not reject the inclusion of NOT NULL even if it is not required. Therefore, that is the convention we will follow in the examples in this book.

Here is an improved version of our definition of the Salespeople table:

```
CREATE TABLE Salespeople
    (snum INTEGER NOT NULL PRIMARY KEY,
    sname CHAR(10) NOT NULL,
    city CHAR(10),
    comm DECIMAL);
```

Primary Keys of More Than One Column

The PRIMARY KEY constraint can also apply to multiple columns, forcing a unique combination of values. Suppose your primary key is a name (this is not recommended and is only mentioned for the purpose of illustration), and you have first and last names stored in two different columns (so you could organize the data by either one). Obviously, neither the first nor last names can be forced to be unique by themselves, but we may well wish every combination of the two to be unique. We can apply the PRIMARY KEY table constraint to the pair:

```
CREATE TABLE Namefield
    (firstname CHAR(10) NOT NULL,
    lastname CHAR(10) NOT NULL,
    city CHAR(10),
    PRIMARY KEY (firstname, lastname));
```

One problem with this approach is that we may have to force the uniqueness—by entering Mary Smith and M. Smith, for example—which can easily be confusing, because your employees may not know which is which. This is one reason it is better to define some numeric column that can distinguish one row from another and have it be the primary key. You can then apply the UNIQUE constraint (described below) to the two name columns, if desired.

Making Sure Values Are Unique

At times, you will want to make sure that all of the values entered into a column are different from one another. Primary keys clearly call for this, but there are also other situations where it may be appropriate. If you place the UNIQUE column constraint on a column when you create a table, the database will reject any attempt to introduce into that column a value in one row that is already present in another. The UNIQUE constraint differs from the PRIMARY KEY constraint in the following ways:

- A table may use the PRIMARY KEY constraint only on one column or group of columns. It may use the UNIQUE constraint any number of times.

- Columns with the PRIMARY KEY constraint may not contain NULLs. Those with the UNIQUE constraint may.

- These constraints interact differently with the FOREIGN KEY constraint. We'll introduce this difference in the next chapter.

Here is a further refinement of our definition of the Salespeople table:

```
CREATE TABLE Salespeople
    (snum INTEGER NOT NULL PRIMARY KEY,
    sname CHAR(10) NOT NULL UNIQUE,
    city CHAR(10),
    comm DECIMAL);
```

As you can see, UNIQUE columns can also be declared in the same table as PRIMARY KEY columns. What you accomplish by declaring the sname column to be unique is to ensure that two Mary Smiths will be entered in different ways—Mary Smith and M. Smith, for example. While doing so is not necessary from a functional standpoint—the snum column as the primary key provides a distinction between the two rows—it may be easier for people using the data in the tables to keep the two Smiths separate in their minds if the names are not identical.

More to the point, the UNIQUE constraint should be used wherever data values are required to be distinct for logical reasons unrelated to database structure. For example, we are using a locally generated number called snum to identify our salespeople. We may also track their social security numbers for tax or other purposes. In this case, we may add an SSN column to the Salespeople table. From the viewpoint of the database structure, there is no reason why the SSN column could not permit duplicate values. We don't rely on it as a primary key. Since we know, however, that every employee should have a different SSN, and that data entry errors are common with long numbers, it may make sense to force SSNs to be unique. Non-unique SSNs almost certainly indicate a data error, even though they are no problem for our database as such. Columns (other than primary keys) whose values are required to be unique are often called *unique keys*.

Note that NULLs are considered distinct for the purposes of the UNIQUE constraint. That is to say, a column with a UNIQUE constraint can have any number of NULL values, and these will not be considered duplicates.

Should we then allow our prospective SSN column to contain NULLs? Probably. What would happen if we got an employee who was not a US citizen? Perhaps this person would have a similar identification number from his own country, but there is no authority, as far as I know, that ensures that foreign identification numbers will not clash with US social security numbers. If you wanted to do this, you should create a second column indicating nationality and create a UNIQUE constraint on the two in combination with a UNIQUE table constraint.

Declaring a group of columns unique differs from declaring the individual columns unique in that it is the combination of values, not each individual value, that must be unique. Group uniqueness is respective of order, so that a pair of rows with the column values 'a', 'b' and 'b', 'a' are considered to be different from one another. Our database is structured so that each customer is assigned one and only one salesperson. This means that each combination of customer number and salesperson number in the Customers table should be unique. You can ensure this by defining the Customers table in the following manner:

```
CREATE TABLE Customers
    (cnum INTEGER NOT NULL,
    cname CHAR(10) NOT NULL,
    city CHAR(10),
    rating INTEGER,
    snum INTEGER NOT NULL,
    UNIQUE (cnum, snum));
```

Notice that this table constraint is not necessary if we use the PRIMARY KEY (or, for that matter, UNIQUE) constraint on cnum, as we should. If the cnum column is different for each row, there cannot be two rows with identical combinations of cnum and snum. The same would apply if we had declared the snum column unique, although this would not be appropriate in this instance because salespeople can be assigned multiple customers. Therefore, the UNIQUE table constraint is most useful when we do not want to force the individual columns to be unique.

Suppose, for example, that we designed a table to keep track of the total orders per day per salesperson. Each row of this table would represent a total of any number of orders, rather than an individual order. In this case, we could eliminate some possible errors by ensuring that each day has no more than one row for a given salesperson, that is, that each combination of snum and odate is unique. Here's how we could create such a table called Salestotal:

```
CREATE TABLE Salestotal
     (snum,   INTEGER NOT NULL,
      odate,  DATE NOT NULL,
      totamt, DECIMAL,
      UNIQUE  (snum, odate));
```

What about cases where NULLs are permitted in groups of columns that have the UNIQUE table constraint? We can summarize the rules for evaluating these cases as follows:

- If two rows are identical in all their non-NULL columns, and neither has a NULL in a column where the other does not have one, the two rows are not UNIQUE and violate the constraint.

- If the two rows are entirely NULL, the constraint is not violated.

- In any other case, the constraint is not violated.

Checking Column Values

Of course, you might want to place any number of restrictions on the data that can be entered into your tables—to see if the data is in the proper range or the correct format, for example—that SQL cannot possibly account for beforehand. For this reason, SQL provides the CHECK constraint, which allows you to define a condition that a value entered into the table must satisfy before it can be accepted. The CHECK constraint consists of the keyword CHECK followed by a parenthesized predicate, which employs the column(s) in question. Any attempt to update to or insert column values that will make this predicate FALSE will be rejected. Note that the predicate must actually be FALSE, not merely UNKNOWN. For more information, see "Predicates" in the reference.

Let's look once more at the Salespeople table. The comm column is expressed as a decimal, so that it can be multiplied directly with a purchase amount to produce the right dollar figure. Someone used to thinking of it in terms of percentages, however, might be inclined to forget this. If that person were to enter 14 instead of .14 for a commission, it would be equivalent to 14.0, a legitimate decimal value, and would be accepted. To guard against this possibility, we can impose a CHECK column constraint to make sure that the value entered is less than 1.

```
CREATE TABLE Salespeople
     (snum INTEGER NOT NULL PRIMARY KEY,
     sname CHAR(10) NOT NULL,
     city CHAR(10),
     comm DECIMAL CHECK (comm < 1) );
```

Using CHECK to Predetermine Valid Input Values

We can even use a CHECK constraint to restrict a column to specific values and thereby reject mistakes. For example, suppose the only cities in which we had sales offices were London, New York, San Jose, and Barcelona. As long as we know that all of our salespeople will be operating from one of these offices, we need not allow other values to be entered. If nothing else, using a restriction such as this will prevent typographical and similar errors from being accepted. Here is how we would restrict a column to specific values:

```
CREATE TABLE Salespeople
     (snum INTEGER  NOT NULL PRIMARY KEY,
     sname CHAR(10) NOT NULL,
     city CHAR(10) CHECK
     (city IN ('London', 'New York','San Jose', 'Barcelona')),
     comm DECIMAL CHECK (comm < 1) );
```

Of course, if you are going to use such a restriction, you should realize that you may have to use the ALTER TABLE statement to change the constraints whenever your company opens a new office (hopefully this is frequently). To do this, you would have to name the constraint so that you could later drop it and add a new one that would include the new office among the valid values. If you were using a system that could not use ALTER TABLE to remove constraints, you would have to CREATE a new table and transfer the information from the old table to it whenever you need to change a constraint. This is not something you will want to do often, and at times it may not be practical at all. A better way to do this is with a second table listing valid values and a FOREIGN KEY constraint. We will show how in the next chapter.

CHECK Conditions Based on Multiple Columns

You can also use CHECK as a table constraint, which is useful for those cases where you want to involve more than one column of a row in a condition. Suppose that commissions of .15 and above were permitted only for salespeople in Barcelona. We could enforce this with the following CHECK table constraint:

```
CREATE TABLE Salespeople
    (snum INTEGER PRIMARY KEY,
    sname CHAR(10) NOT NULL UNIQUE,
    city CHAR(10),
    comm DECIMAL,
    CHECK (comm < .15 OR city = 'Barcelona') );
```

As you can see, two different columns have to be examined to determine if the predicate is true. Keep in mind, however, that they are two different columns of the *same* row. Many SQL implementations are not capable of referencing multiple rows of a table in a CHECK constraint. In this case, you could not use a CHECK constraint to make sure all the commissions in a given city were the same, for example. One way to get around this would be to define a view using WITH CHECK OPTION as discussed in Part IV and under "CREATE VIEW" in the reference.

Naming and Dropping Constraints

Starting with Intermediate-level SQL92, constraints can be named. Although not many vendors claim this level of conformance as of this publication (2000), some do support constraint naming. The point of naming constraints is so that you can drop them. Note that a constraint name must be different from every other constraint or assertion name (see "CREATE ASSERTION" in the reference) in the same schema.

Here's how to create a version of Salespeople that provides a named version of a CHECK table constraint we used previously:

```
CREATE TABLE Salespeople
    (snum INTEGER NOT NULL PRIMARY KEY,
    sname CHAR(10) NOT NULL UNIQUE,
    city CHAR(10),
    comm DECIMAL,
    CONSTRAINT LuckyBarcelona CHECK
    (comm < .15 OR city = 'Barcelona') );
```

The name of the constraint is LuckyBarcelona (strictly speaking, it is LUCKYBARCELONA, since SQL92-compliant systems convert the names of objects to entirely uppercase). To drop this constraint from the Customers table, you use the ALTER TABLE statement introduced in the previous chapter, as follows:

```
ALTER TABLE Customers DROP CONSTRAINT LuckyBarcelona;
```

You could also have omitted the optional word CONSTRAINT.

Deferring Constraints

As of SQL92, it is possible to defer the checking of constraints. This means that the constraint is not tested immediately when a statement that may violate it is issued, but is instead checked later. There are two main reasons for doing so:

- Some legitimate sequences of operations require constraints to be temporarily violated.

- Sometimes it is better for performance to check batches of constraints all at once.

We can't discuss this situation meaningfully until we talk about transactions in Part IV of this book. This feature is not universally supported anyway. You can find out about it in the reference under "Constraints".

Assigning Default Values

When you insert a row into a table without having a value in it for every column, SQL must have a default value to put in the excluded column(s) or the statement will be rejected. The most common default value is NULL. This is the default by default. That is to say, it is the default for any column that has not been given a NOT NULL constraint or had another default assigned with the clause we explain here.

DEFAULT value assignments are defined in the CREATE TABLE statement in the same way as column constraints, although, technically speaking, DEFAULT values are not constraints—they do not limit the values you can enter, but merely specify what happens if you do not enter any. Suppose you are running the New York office of your company, and the vast majority of your salespeople are based in New York. You might decide to define New York as the default city value for your Salespeople table, saving the trouble of entering it each time:

```
CREATE TABLE Salespeople
     (snum INTEGER PRIMARY KEY,
     sname CHAR(10) NOT NULL,
     city CHAR(10) DEFAULT = 'New York',
     comm DECIMAL CHECK (comm < 1) );
```

Of course, entering New York into a table each time a new salesperson is assigned is not such a great deal of trouble, and habitually omitting a column may lead to its being neglected even when it should have some other value. A default value of this type might be more advisable if, for example, you had a long office number, indicating your own office, in the Orders table. Long numeric values are error prone, so, if the vast majority (or all) of your orders will have your own office number on them, it may be advisable for that number to become the default. If the updating of the data in your database is achieved through an application rather than interactively, it may also make sense to enforce defaults there, though usually it does not. Putting the default right in the database ensures that it is not neglected by some future application that updates the data. It also makes changing the default much easier, since it has to be changed in only one place.

Default Values and NULLs

First, let's briefly summarize the rules regarding default values and NULLs:

- If a column has neither a NOT NULL constraint nor a DEFAULT clause, any INSERT into that table that fails to provide a value for that column will insert a NULL into that column.

- If a column has a DEFAULT clause, regardless of whether it has a NOT NULL constraint, any INSERT into that table that fails to provide a value for that column will insert the indicated default value into that column.

- If the column has a NOT NULL constraint and no specified default value, every INSERT into the table must provide a value for that column or the INSERT will be rejected as an error.

In the second option above, we can use a default value as an alternative to a NULL. Why would we want to do this? Since NULLs utilize three-valued logic, they tend to have the following disadvantages:

- They tend to be excluded from a lot of predicates. For example, you might think that a predicate such as $(x < 5)$ OR $(x >= 5)$ would have no choice but to always be TRUE. If, however, x is NULL, the predicate is UNKNOWN. Operations such as SELECT and UPDATE statements that use such predicates to determine which rows to affect will never affect the rows with the NULLs unless you account for these sorts of effects.

- They create counterintuitive logic problems in advanced query situations such as subqueries and joins. We will cover these situations in Chapter 7 of this book. See also "Three-Valued Logic" under the Predicates entry in the reference.

For these reasons, you may decide that NULLs are more trouble than they are worth. You can define a special default value, such as zero or blank, that actually functions less as a value than as an indication that there is no value present—in other words, a custom-made NULL. The difference between this and a regular NULL is that SQL will treat this the same as any other value. In fact, the problems created by NULLs are so great that one prominent writer in the field, Chris Date, recommends that you do exactly this. Others, however, disagree, since conventional defaults have their own problems.

Suppose that customers are not assigned ratings initially. Every six months, you raise the rating of all your lower-rated customers, including those who previously had no rating assigned, provided that all has gone well with them. If you want to select all these customers as a group, a query such as the following would exclude all customers with NULL ratings:

```
SELECT *
     FROM Customers
     WHERE rating <= 100;
```

However, if you had defined a DEFAULT of 000 for the rating column, customers without ratings would have been selected along with the others. Which method is better depends on the situation. If you were using the column in question to determine which rows to select with a query, would you usually want to include the rows without values or exclude them?

Another characteristic of defaults of this type is that they make it a good idea for you to declare the column in question NOT NULL. If you are using a default in order to avoid NULLs, this is probably good protection against mistakes. Of course, you could just reserve NULLs for cases where there really is no value that applies, not even the default, but mixing NULLs and defaults is error-prone, so you are usually better off picking one approach or the other.

You could also, in principle, use a UNIQUE or PRIMARY KEY constraint with this column. If you do, however, keep in mind that only one row at a time may have the default value. Any row that contains the default value will have to be updated before another row with the default could be inserted. This is not how you usually want to use defaults, so default values are not usually given to rows with UNIQUE and PRIMARY KEY constraints (especially the latter).

Summary

You have now mastered several ways of controlling the values that can be entered into your tables. You can use the NOT NULL constraint to exclude NULLs, the UNIQUE constraint to force all the values in a group of one or more columns to be different, the PRIMARY KEY constraint to do basically the same thing as UNIQUE but to a different end, and the CHECK constraint to define your own custom-made criteria that values must meet before they can be entered. In addition, you can use a DEFAULT clause, which will automatically insert a default value into any column not named in an INSERT, just as NULLs are inserted when the DEFAULT clause is not present and there is no NOT NULL constraint.

The FOREIGN KEY or REFERENCES constraint that you will learn about in Chapter 5 is similar to these, except that it relates a group of one or more columns to another and thereby affects the values that can be entered into either of these groups at once.

Putting SQL to Work

1.   Create the Orders table so that all onum values as well as all combinations of cnum and snum are different from one another and so that NULL values are excluded from the date column.

2.   Create the Salespeople table so that the default commission is 10 percent with no NULLs permitted, and snum is the primary key.

3.   Create the Orders table, making sure that the onum is greater than the cnum and the cnum is greater than the snum (these restrictions, of course, will probably be of little practical use, but they provide exercise in the use of the constraints). Allow no NULLs in any of these three columns.

Maintaining Referential Integrity

- Foreign and Parent Keys

- The FOREIGN KEY Constraint

When we introduced the sample tables in this book, we pointed out certain foreign and parent key relationships that existed among some of their columns. The snum column of the Salespeople table, for example, matches the snum column of both the Customers and Orders tables. The cnum column of the Customers table matches the cnum column of the Orders table, as well. We called this type of relationship *referential integrity*.

In this chapter, you will be investigating referential integrity more closely and finding out about the constraint that you can use to maintain it. You will also see how this constraint is enforced when you update the data. Because referential integrity involves relating columns or groups of columns to one another, its enforcement can be somewhat more complex than that of the other constraints. For this reason, it is good to have a basic familiarity with it, even if you do not plan to create tables. Your update statements can be affected by referential-integrity constraints (as by other constraints, but referential-integrity constraints can affect other tables besides those in which they are located). Certain query functions, such as joins, are frequently structured in terms of referential-integrity relationships (as we will show in Chapter 10).

Foreign and Parent Keys

As shown in Chapter 1, when all of the values in one column of a table must be present in a column of another table, we say that the first column refers to, or *references*, the second. It indicates a direct relationship between the meaning of the two columns. For example, the customers in the Customers table each have an snum column that indicates the salesperson to whom he or she is assigned in the Salespeople table. For each order in the Orders table, there is one and only one salesperson and one and only one customer, as indicated by the snum and cnum columns in the Orders table. Therefore, the snum column of the Customers table is a foreign key, and the snum column it references in the Salespeople table is its parent key. Likewise, the cnum and snum columns of the Orders table are foreign keys referring to their parent keys of the same names in the Customers and Salespeople tables.

A foreign key indicates that any given row of a given table references one and only one row of the table containing the parent key, although multiple foreign key values may reference the same parent-key value. For this reason, the parent key must have a constraint that enforces uniqueness: either the PRIMARY KEY or the UNIQUE constraint. Generally speaking, it should be the former. Also, it is worth pointing out that the foreign key must match the entire primary or unique parent key; if the primary key has three columns, all three must be in the foreign key that references it.

When a column is a foreign key, it is specially linked to the table it references. You are, in effect, saying "every value in this column (the foreign key) is directly related to a value in another column (the parent key)". Each value (each row) of the foreign key should unambiguously refer to one and only one value (row) of the parent key. If this is, in fact, the case, your system is said to be in a state of referential integrity.

You can see why this is so. The foreign key snum in the Customers table has the value 1001 for the rows of Hoffman and Clemens. Suppose we had two rows in the Salespeople table with the snum = 1001. How would we know to which of the two salespeople Hoffman and Clemens were assigned? Likewise, if there were no such rows in the Salespeople table, we would have Hoffman and Clemens assigned to a salesperson who did not exist! The implication is clear: every value in the foreign key must be present once, and only once, in the parent key.

The fact that a given foreign-key value can refer to only one parent-key value does not imply the reverse: any number of foreign keys can refer to the same parent-key value. You can see this in the sample tables. Both Hoffman and Clemens are assigned to Peel, so both of their foreign-key values match the same parent key, which is fine. A foreign-key value must refer to only a single parent-key value, but that parent-key value can be referred to by any number of foreign-key values.

The FOREIGN KEY Constraint

SQL supports referential integrity with the FOREIGN KEY constraint. This constraint restricts the values you can enter into your database to force a foreign key and its parent key to conform to the principles of referential integrity. One effect of an enforced FOREIGN KEY constraint is to reject values for the column(s) constrained as a foreign key that are not already present in the parent key. This constraint also affects your ability to change or remove the values of the parent key (we will discuss this later in the chapter).

Declaring Columns As Foreign Keys

You use the FOREIGN KEY constraint in the CREATE TABLE (or possibly ALTER TABLE) statement as you would any other constraint (see the previous chapter). You name the parent key you are referencing within the FOREIGN KEY constraint. Like most constraints, it can be of the table or column variety, with the table form allowing multiple columns to be used as a single foreign key.

FOREIGN KEY As a Table Constraint

Here is the syntax of the FOREIGN KEY table constraint:

```
FOREIGN KEY column list REFERENCES pktable [column list]
```

You can use this syntax in either a CREATE TABLE or an ALTER TABLE statement. The first column list is a parenthesized list of one or more columns of the table being created or altered in this command, separated by commas. The *pktable* is the table containing the parent key. This may be the same table that is being created or altered by the current command (more on this point later). The second column list is a parenthesized list of those columns that will constitute the parent key. The two column lists—that of the foreign key and that of its parent key—must be compatible. Compatibility is defined by the following criteria:

- The lists must have the same number of columns.

- In the sequence given, the first, second, third, and so on, column of the foreign-key column list must have the same datatypes and sizes as the first, second, third, and so on, of the parent-key column list. The columns in the two column lists need not have the same names, although we have done it this way in our examples to make the relationship clearer.

Here is the definition of the Customers table with snum defined as a foreign key referencing the Salespeople table:

```
CREATE TABLE Customers
(cnum INTEGER NOT NULL PRIMARY KEY,
cname CHAR(10),
city CHAR(10),
snum INTEGER,
FOREIGN KEY (snum) REFERENCES Salespeople(snum));
```

FOREIGN KEY As a Column Constraint

The column-constraint version of the FOREIGN KEY constraint is also called the REFERENCES constraint, because it does not actually contain the words FOREIGN KEY. It simply uses the word REFERENCES and then names the parent key, like this:

```
CREATE TABLE Customers
(cnum INTEGER NOT NULL PRIMARY KEY,
cname CHAR(10),
city CHAR(10),
snum INTEGER REFERENCES Salespeople(snum));
```

The above defines Customers snum as a foreign key whose parent key is Salespeople.snum. It is equivalent to this table constraint:

```
FOREIGN KEY (snum) REFERENCES Salespeople(snum)
```

Omitting Primary-Key Column Lists

With either table or column FOREIGN KEY constraints, you may omit the column list of the parent key if the parent key has the PRIMARY KEY constraint. In case of multiple-column keys, naturally, the order of the columns in the foreign and primary keys must match, and, in any case, the principles of compatibility between the two keys still apply. For example, if we had placed the PRIMARY KEY constraint on the snum column in the Salespeople table, we could use it as a foreign key in the Customers table (similar to the previous example) with this command:

```
CREATE TABLE Customers
(cnum INTEGER NOT NULL PRIMARY KEY,
cname CHAR(10),
city CHAR(10),
snum INTEGER REFERENCES Salespeople);
```

This feature has been built into the language to encourage you to use primary keys as parent keys.

Using FOREIGN KEY to Predetermine Valid Input Values

In the previous chapter, we showed you how to use a CHECK constraint to restrict the possible cities for your salespeople to the small number of cities you know to be valid. As we mentioned there, a drawback of this approach is the necessity to change the constraint each time your company adds or closes an office. An alternative would be to store the valid values in another table and make the city column in Salespeople a foreign key referencing it. The sequence of operations to do this would be as follows:

```
CREATE TABLE Officecities
    (office CHAR(10) NOT NULL PRIMARY KEY);

CREATE TABLE Salespeople
    (snum INTEGER  NOT NULL PRIMARY KEY,
    sname CHAR(10) NOT NULL,
    city CHAR(10)  REFERENCES Officecities,
    comm DECIMAL CHECK (comm < 1) );
```

The advantage of this is that changing the set of valid city values is simply a matter of updating the Officecities table, which is much less of a hassle than dropping and adding a constraint. This example also illustrates the use of a parent key with a different name than the foreign key referencing it.

Primary vs. Unique Parent Keys

Having your foreign keys reference only primary keys, as we have done in the sample tables, is a good policy. When you use foreign keys, you are not linking them simply to the parent keys that they reference; you are linking them to the specific row of the table where that parent key is found. The parent key by itself provides no information that is not already present in the foreign key.

The significance, for example, of the snum column as a foreign key in the Customers table is the link it provides, not to the snum value that it references, but to the other information in the Salespeople table, such as the salespeople's names, their locations, and so on. A foreign key is not simply a link between two identical values; it is a link, through those two values, between two entire rows of the tables in question. You can use that snum column to relate any information in a row from the Customers table to the referenced row of the Salespeople table, such as whether they live in the same city, who has a longer name, or whether the salesperson of a given customer has any other customers.

Since the purpose of a primary key is to identify rows uniquely, it is the most logical and least ambiguous choice for a foreign key. For any foreign key that takes a unique key as a parent key, you should be able to create a foreign key that takes the primary key of that same table to the same effect. Having a foreign key that has no other purpose but to link rows, like having a primary key with no other purpose but to identify them, is a good way to keep the structure of your database clear and simple and is therefore less likely to create difficulties.

Foreign Key Restrictions

In general, a foreign key may contain only values that are actually present in the parent key or NULLs. Any other values you attempt to enter into that key will be rejected. We have noted one exception in the reference under "Constraints" in the discussion of the MATCH clause. You may declare foreign keys to be NOT NULL, but it is not necessary and, in many cases, not desirable. For example, suppose you enter a customer without knowing at first to which salesperson he will be assigned. The best way to deal with this situation would be with a NULL that could later be updated to a valid value.

Multicolumn Foreign Keys

In actuality, a foreign key need not consist of only a single column. Like a primary key, a foreign key can be of any number of columns, all of which are treated as a unit. A foreign key and the parent key it references must, of course, have the same number and types of columns, in the same order. We have used single-column foreign keys exclusively in our sample tables; they are perhaps the most common. For the sake of keeping our discussion simple, we will often speak of a foreign key as a single column, but this is not necessarily the case. Unless otherwise noted, whatever we say about a column that is a foreign key will also hold true for a group of columns that is a foreign key.

In general—that is, unless you specifically disallow it with NOT NULL constraints—a foreign key can contain NULLs. For a single-column foreign key, this is fairly straightforward; a NULL in the foreign key is valid but means that there is no parent key that the foreign key matches. A NULL parent key would not be a match, because a NULL is not considered a proper value, but rather a marker for the fact that there is no value present and the appropriate value is unknown or inapplicable.

For a multicolumn foreign key, though, this becomes a bit trickier, since such a key can be partially NULL and partially filled with valid values. If the parent key is a UNIQUE rather than a PRIMARY KEY, then it too can be partially NULL. How should matches of these be evaluated? Strictly speaking, we cannot say whether NULLs match known data items or even each other because they represent unknown content. There is considerable debate in this area, which we won't go into here. Suffice it to say that NULLs don't match anything—not even other NULLs.

To deal with this, SQL92 lets you specify a MATCH clause that controls the desired behavior. The MATCH clause is rather complicated, so rather than go into it here, we refer you to "Constraints" in the reference, where it is explained.

Understanding the Foreign Keys in the Sample Tables

Let's assume that all of the foreign keys built into our sample tables are declared and enforced with FOREIGN KEY constraints. The code to create our three sample tables is shown in Listing 5.1.

LISTING 5.1   **Code to Create Sample Tables with Foreign Keys**

```
CREATE TABLE Salespeople
(snum INTEGER NOT NULL PRIMARY KEY,
sname CHAR(10) NOT NULL,
city CHAR(10),
comm DECIMAL);
CREATE TABLE Customers
(cnum INTEGER NOT NULL PRIMARY KEY,
cname CHAR(10) NOT NULL,
city CHAR(10),
rating INTEGER,
snum INTEGER,
FOREIGN KEY (snum) Custtosales REFERENCES Salespeople);
CREATE TABLE Orders
(onum INTEGER NOT NULL PRIMARY KEY,
amt DECIMAL,
odate DATE NOT NULL,
cnum INTEGER NOT NULL,
```

```
snum INTEGER NOT NULL,
FOREIGN KEY (snum) Ordtosales REFERENCES Salespeople,
FOREIGN KEY (cnum) Ordtocust REFERENCES Customers);
```

Several attributes of these definitions merit discussion. As we stated when we first introduced these tables, we chose not to make the cnum and snum columns of the Orders table a single foreign key referencing Customers because we want flexibility in crediting a salesperson for a sale even if he is not the salesperson normally assigned to the customer. Suppose the business rules had changed, and we had to modify the tables to assume that the salesperson assigned to the customer got credit for every sale. Here is one possibility:

```
ALTER TABLE Orders DROP CONSTRAINT Ordtosales;
ALTER TABLE Orders DROP COLUMN snum;
```

Now the only way to determine which salesperson gets credited with a sale is to look in the Customers table to see which salesperson is assigned to the Customer. This ensures that for every customer credited with an order, the salesperson credited with that order is the same as indicated in the Customers table.

On the other hand, perhaps you will be so frequently accessing the Orders table that you do not want to reference the Customers table each time to determine the correct salesperson. Making this linkage requires an operation called a *join* that is not without performance cost. Therefore, it might be better for practical reasons to include both the snum and cnum in the Orders table, as we do, but to make sure the match of the two is the same as it is in the Customers table. You could achieve this with the following:

```
ALTER TABLE Orders DROP CONSTRAINT Ordtosales;
ALTER TABLE Orders DROP CONSTRAINT Ordtocust;
ALTER TABLE Orders ADD CONSTRAINT Bothmatch
     FOREIGN KEY (cnum, snum) REFERENCES Customers (cnum, snum);
```

Defining the foreign key in this manner maintains the integrity of the database, even though it does prevent you from making exceptions and crediting any salesperson other than the one assigned to a customer with sales for that customer. Excluding mistakes often means also excluding the ability to make exceptions, and, of course, whether to allow exceptions is a business, not a database, decision.

The Effects of the Constraints

How do these constraints affect what you can and cannot do with update statements? For the columns defined as foreign keys, the answer is fairly straightforward: Any values you put into these columns with an INSERT or UPDATE statement (explained in Chapter 6) must already be present in their parent keys. You may put NULLs in these columns, even if NULLs are not allowed in the parent keys, unless the foreign-key columns have NOT NULL constraints. You may DELETE any rows with foreign keys without affecting the parent keys at all.

As far as changes to the parent-key values are concerned, the answer is a little trickier. As defined previously to SQL92, any parent-key value currently referenced by a foreign-key value cannot be deleted or changed. This means, for example, that you could not remove a customer from the Customers table while he or she still has orders in the Orders table. Depending on exactly how you are using these tables, this rule can be either desirable or troublesome. It is certainly better, however, than a system that would allow you to remove a customer with current orders and leave the Orders table referencing nonexistent customers.

Referential Triggered Actions

In SQL92, the question of how parent-key changes affect foreign keys became considerably more complicated through the introduction of *referential triggered actions*. These are not yet universally supported, so we will just briefly touch on them here. Referential triggered actions enable you to specify when creating a FOREIGN KEY constraint what you would like to have happen to the foreign-key values when the referenced parent-key values are deleted or changed. There are two kinds of operations that can change the present content of a parent key, as follows:

- UPDATE statements change existing values in the database. The relevant issue here is what happens to a foreign-key value when the parent-key value it references is changed.

- DELETE statements remove existing rows from the database. The relevant issue here is what happens to a foreign-key value when the parent-key row it references is deleted.

A third kind of operation that changes the existing content of a database table is INSERT, which adds a new row. Since a new row cannot previously have been referenced by a foreign key, referential triggered actions do not apply to INSERT.

You determine the proper behavior for UPDATE statements and DELETE statements independently by specifying UPDATE effects and DELETE effects, respectively. Either of these offers the same four possibilities:

- CASCADE means that the foreign-key value will be changed to match the parent-key value. For UPDATE effects, this means the foreign-key value will be changed to the new parent-key value. For DELETE effects, this means that all rows containing foreign keys that match a parent key being deleted are deleted as well. Note that, since foreign-key relationships are really relationships between rows, it is the entire row, rather than simply the foreign-key values themselves, that is deleted.

- SET NULL means that the foreign-key value will be set to NULL. Naturally, this is not an option if the foreign key has the NOT NULL constraint.

- SET DEFAULT means that the foreign-key value will be set to the specified DEFAULT value or, if there is none such, to NULL. This is not an option if the foreign key has the NOT NULL constraint *and* has no DEFAULT specified.

- NO ACTION is the default and is the behavior expected from systems that do not support referential triggered actions as such. In this scenario, the foreign key remains unchanged. If, however, this would leave the foreign key with an invalid reference, the statement attempting to change the parent key is rejected.

The syntax you use to specify referential triggered actions is as follows:

```
[ ON UPDATE { CASCADE
    | SET NULL
    | SET DEFAULT
    | NO ACTION } ]
[ ON DELETE { CASCADE
    | SET NULL
    | SET DEFAULT
    | NO ACTION } ]
```

You can specify one and only one effect of each type, or you can omit one or both entirely. Let's look at some examples.

For the sake of argument, let's suppose you have reason to change the snum column of the Salespeople table on occasion. Perhaps these numbers are actually assigned by divisions and change when your salespeople are transferred. (Routinely changing primary keys is actually *not* something we recommend in practice. This is one argument for having primary keys that have no other use or meaning than to act as primary keys: they should not need to be changed.) When you change a salesperson's number, you want him to keep all of his customers. If he is leaving the company, however, you do not want to remove his customers when you remove him from the database. Instead, you want to make sure you assign them to someone else. To achieve this, you could specify an UPDATE effect of CASCADE and a DELETE effect of NO ACTION, as shown here:

```
CREATE TABLE Customers
(cnum INTEGER NOT NULL PRIMARY KEY,
cname CHAR(10) NOT NULL,
city CHAR(10),
rating INTEGER,
snum INTEGER REFERENCES Salespeople
     ON UPDATE CASCADE ON DELETE NO ACTION);
```

If you now tried to remove Peel from the Salespeople table, the statement would be rejected unless you changed the snum values of customers Hoffman and Clemens to that of another salesperson. On the other hand, you could change Peel's snum value to 1009, and those of Hoffman and Clemens would automatically change as well.

Another possibility is SET NULL. Perhaps when salespeople leave the company, their current orders are not credited to anyone. On the other hand, you want to cancel all orders automatically for customers whose accounts you remove. Changes of salesperson or customer number can simply be passed along. This is how you would create the Orders table to have these effects:

```
CREATE TABLE Orders
(onum INTEGER NOT NULL PRIMARY KEY,
amt DECIMAL,
odate DATE NOT NULL,
cnum INTEGER NOT NULL REFERENCES Customers
     ON UPDATE CASCADE ON DELETE CASCADE,
snum INTEGER REFERENCES Salespeople
     ON UPDATE CASCADE ON DELETE SET NULL);
```

There is also some variation in how referential triggered actions behave according to the MATCH clause you specify. See "Constraints" in the reference.

Note that many commercial products already supported some or all of this functionality before it became part of the standard, so you may encounter non-standard variations of it. Here are the preceding two examples as implemented using one common non-standard variation:

```
CREATE TABLE Customers
(cnum INTEGER NOT NULL PRIMARY KEY,
cname CHAR(10) NOT NULL,
city CHAR(10),
rating INTEGER,
snum INTEGER REFERENCES Salespeople,
UPDATE OF Salespeople CASCADES,
DELETE OF Salespeople RESTRICTED);
```

and

```
CREATE TABLE Orders
(onum INTEGER NOT NULL PRIMARY KEY,
amt DECIMAL,
odate DATE NOT NULL,
cnum INTEGER NOT NULL REFERENCES Customers,
snum INTEGER REFERENCES Salespeople,
UPDATE OF Customers CASCADES,
DELETE OF Customers CASCADES,
UPDATE OF Salespeople CASCADES,
DELETE OF Salespeople NULLS);
```

Foreign Keys That Refer Back to Their Own Tables

As we mentioned, the FOREIGN KEY constraint can name its own table as its parent-key table. Far from being a simple anomaly, this feature can come in handy. Suppose we had an Employees table with a column called manager. This column contains the employee number of each employee's manager. However, since each manager is also an employee, he or she will be present in this table as well. Let's create the table, declaring empno (employee number) as the primary key and manager as a foreign key referencing it:

```
CREATE TABLE Employees
(empno INTEGER NOT NULL PRIMARY KEY,
name CHAR(10) NOT NULL,
manager INTEGER REFERENCES Employees);
```

(Since the foreign key is referencing the primary key of the table, naturally we can omit the column list.) Here are some possible contents of Table 5.1.

TABLE 5.1:   A Sample Employees Table

Empno	Name	Manager
1003	Terrence	2007
2007	Atali	NULL
1688	McKenna	1003
2002	Collier	2007

As you can see, everyone but Atali references another employee in the table as his or her manager. Atali, being the highest in the table, must have his value set to NULL. This brings up another principle of referential integrity. A foreign key that refers back to its own table must allow NULLs. If it does not, how could you insert the first row? Even if this first row referred to itself, the parent-key value is supposed to be already present when the foreign-key value is entered.

This principle holds true even if a foreign key refers to its own table indirectly—that is, by referring to another table that then refers to the foreign key's table. For example, suppose our Salespeople table had an additional column that referenced the Customers table, so that each table referred to the other, as shown in the following CREATE TABLE statement:

```
CREATE TABLE Salespeople
(snum INTEGER NOT NULL PRIMARY KEY,
sname CHAR(10) NOT NULL,
city CHAR(10),
comm DECIMAL,
cnum INTEGER REFERENCES Customers);
CREATE TABLE Customers
(cnum INTEGER NOT NULL PRIMARY KEY,
cname CHAR(10) NOT NULL,
city CHAR(10),
rating INTEGER,
snum INTEGER REFERENCES Salespeople);
```

This functionality is variously called *circular relationships*, *recursive relationships*, *reflexive relationships*, or *cross-referencing*. SQL supports it theoretically, but this functionality can present problems in practice. Whichever table of the two is created first will reference a table that does not yet exist, for one thing. In the interest of supporting circularity, SQL will actually allow this, but neither table is usable until both are created. On the other hand, if these two tables are created by different users, the problems become more difficult. Circularity can be a useful tool, but it is not without its ambiguities and hazards. The preceding example, for instance, is not very usable: it restricts salespeople to a single customer, and it needn't be circular, even to achieve that. We recommend that you be very careful how you use it and study closely exactly how your system handles update and delete effects as well as privileges and transaction processing before you create a circular system of referential integrity. (We'll discuss privileges and transaction processing in Chapters 22 and 23, respectively. See also the discussion of database design in Part V.)

Summary

Now you have a pretty good handle on referential integrity. The basic idea is that all foreign-key values refer to a specific row of the parent key. This means that each foreign key value must be present once and only once in the parent key. Whenever a value is placed in a foreign key, the parent key is checked to make sure that value is present; otherwise, the statement is rejected. The parent key must have a PRIMARY KEY or UNIQUE constraint to ensure that a value will not be present more than once. Attempts to change a parent-key value that is currently present in the foreign key will have the effect you specify in a referential triggered action; by default, they are rejected. In the next chapter, you will learn how to place data into the tables we have created using the INSERT, UPDATE, and DELETE statements.

Putting SQL to Work

1. Create a table called Cityorders. This will contain the same onum, amt, and snum columns as the Orders table and the same cnum and city columns as the Customers table, so that each customer's order will be entered into this table along with his or her city. Onum will be the primary key of Cityorders. All of the columns in Cityorders will be constrained to match the Customers

and Orders tables. Assume the parent keys in these tables already have the proper constraints.

2.   Here is an advanced problem. Redefine the Orders table as follows: add a new column called prev, which will identify, for each order, the onum of the previous order for that current customer. Implement this with a foreign key referring to the Orders table itself. The foreign key should refer as well to the cnum of the customer, providing a definite enforced link between the current order and the one referenced.

3.   Let's assume each order can contain any number of items, which must be individually tracked for inventory purposes. The relationship of items to orders, then, is a classic many-to-one relationship requiring the use of another table. This table will be called Items and will include, for each item, the item number, name, price, and the associated order number, from which all the order information can be derived. Create the Items table.

4.   Redefine the Customers table so that a deletion of a salesperson sets the salesperson assignment of all his customers to NULL, while an update of a salesperson's snum value is automatically reflected in the Customers table, so that all the salesperson's customers remain properly assigned.

CHAPTER

SIX

Entering, Deleting, and Changing Data

- ■ Entering Values into Tables—The INSERT Statement

- ■ Removing Rows from Tables—The DELETE Statement

- ■ Changing Field Values—The UPDATE Statement

This chapter introduces the statements that control which values are present in a table at any given time. When you have finished this chapter, you will be able to place rows into a table, remove them, and change the individual values present in each row. We'll explore the use of queries to generate entire groups of rows for insertion, as well as the use of predicates to control the changing of values and the deletion of rows. The material in this chapter constitutes the bulk of the knowledge you need to create and manipulate the information in a database.

NOTE   Values are placed in and removed from fields with three Data Manipulation Language (DML) statements: INSERT, UPDATE, and DELETE. Confusingly enough, these are all referred to in SQL as *update* statements in a generic sense. We shall simply use the lowercase "update" to indicate these statements generically and the uppercase for the keyword UPDATE, as for all keywords.

Entering Values into Tables—The INSERT Statement

You enter all rows in SQL using the update command INSERT. In its simplest form, INSERT uses the following syntax:

```
INSERT INTO table name
    VALUES( value .,..);
```

So, for example, to enter a row into the Salespeople table, you could use the following statement:

```
INSERT INTO Salespeople
    VALUES (1001, 'Peel', 'London', .12);
```

Update statements produce no output as such, but your program should give you some acknowledgment that data has been affected. The table name (in this case, Salespeople) must have been defined previously in a CREATE TABLE statement, and each value enumerated in the VALUES clause must match the datatype of the column into which it is being inserted. The values, of course, are entered into the table in the order named, so that the first value named goes into column 1 automatically, the second into column 2, on so on.

Inserting NULLs

If you have to enter a NULL, you do it just as you would a value. Suppose you did not yet have a city field for Peel. You could insert her row with a NULL in that field as follows:

```
INSERT INTO Salespeople
    VALUES(1001, 'Peel', NULL, .12);
```

Since NULL is a special marker, not a character value, it is not enclosed in single quotes.

Naming Columns for Insert

You can also specify the columns into which you wish to insert a value by name. This allows you to insert into them in any order. Suppose you are taking values for the Customers table from a printed report, which puts them in the following order: city, cname, and cnum. For simplicity's sake, you want to enter the values in that same order:

```
INSERT INTO Customers(city, cname, cnum)
    VALUES('London', 'Hoffman', 2001);
```

You will notice that we have omitted the rating and snum columns. This means that they will be set automatically to default values for this row. The default will be either NULL or an explicitly defined default, as explained in Chapter 4. If a constraint prevents a NULL from being accepted in a given column, and that column has no explicit default, you must provide that column with a value for any INSERT command against the table.

Listing the column names is often a good idea even when it is not strictly necessary. It makes your code more understandable and maintainable.

Inserting the Results of a Query

You can also use the INSERT command to take or derive values from one table and place them in another by using it with a query. As we mentioned in Chapter 2, a query is a SELECT statement. It retrieves data from the database. When used within an INSERT statement, it takes data from one place in the database and puts it into another in a single step. To do this, you simply replace the VALUES clause with an appropriate SELECT statement, as in this example:

```
INSERT INTO Londonstaff
     SELECT *
     FROM Salespeople
     WHERE city = 'London';
```

This statement takes all values produced by the query—that is, all rows from the Salespeople table with the city value = 'London'—and places them in the table called Londonstaff. In order for this to work, the Londonstaff table must fulfill the following conditions:

- It must have already been created with a CREATE TABLE command.

- It must have four columns that match those of the Salespeople table in terms of datatype; that is, the first, second, and so on columns of each table must be of a comparable type (they need not have the same name; comparable datatypes are outlined in the reference under "Datatypes").

The general rule is that the columns of the table being inserted into must match the columns output by the query, in this case, the entire Salespeople table.

Londonstaff is now an independent table that happens to have some of the same values as Salespeople. If the values in Salespeople change, the change will not be reflected in Londonstaff (although you could create this effect by defining a view, as discussed in Part IV). Because either the query or the INSERT statement can specify columns by name, you can, if you wish, move only selected columns as well as reorder the columns that you select. You could also use the values in expressions. For example, you could give everyone in London a raise thusly:

```
INSERT INTO Londonstaff
     SELECT snum, sname, city, comm * 1.1
     FROM Salespeople
     WHERE city = 'London';
```

Of course, the old commission values would still be intact in the Salespeople table itself. If you actually wanted to use this approach, you would probably have to DELETE the London people from Salespeople, as shown later in this chapter.

Suppose you decide to build a new table called Daytotals, which would simply keep track of the total dollar amount ordered each day. You have to fill Daytotals with the information already present in Orders. Assuming that the Orders table covers the past fiscal year, rather than the few days in our example, you can see the advantages of using the following INSERT statement to calculate and enter the values:

```
INSERT INTO Daytotals(date, total)
    SELECT odate, SUM(amt)
    FROM Orders
    GROUP BY odate;
```

This would be a useful query in an application that you would run periodically as a batch job. If so, you might want to modify it with a where clause that only selected the recent dates, rather than reinserting what had already been placed in the table.

Note that, as we suggested earlier, the column names of the Orders and Daytotals tables do not have to match. Also, if date and total are the only columns in the table, and they are in the given order, their names could be omitted.

Removing Rows from Tables—The DELETE Statement

You can remove rows from a table with the update command DELETE. This command can remove only entire rows, not individual column values, so no column argument is needed or accepted. To remove all the contents of Salespeople, you would enter the following statement:

```
DELETE FROM Salespeople;
```

The table would now be empty and could be destroyed with a DROP TABLE command, as we explained in Chapter 3.

Usually, you want to delete just some specific rows from a table. To determine which rows are deleted, you use a predicate. As you may recall, a predicate is an expression that can be TRUE, FALSE, or (in the presence of NULLs) UNKNOWN. For instance, to remove salesperson Axelrod from the table, you would enter

```
DELETE FROM Salespeople
    WHERE snum = 1003;
```

We used snum instead of sname because it is the best policy to use primary keys when you want an action to affect one and only one row. That is what primary keys are for.

Of course, you can also use DELETE with a predicate that selects a group of rows, as in this example:

```
DELETE FROM Salespeople
    WHERE city = 'London';
```

Changing Field Values—The UPDATE Statement

Now that you can enter and delete rows from a table, you need to learn how to change some or all of the values in an existing row. You do so with the UPDATE statement. This statement has an UPDATE clause that names the table affected and a SET clause that indicates the change(s) to be made to certain column(s). For example, to change all customers' ratings to 200, you would enter

```
UPDATE Customers
    SET rating = 200;
```

Updating Only Certain Rows

Of course, you do not always want to set all rows of a table to a single value, so UPDATE, like DELETE, can take a predicate. Here's how to perform the same change on all customers of salesperson Peel (snum 1001):

```
UPDATE Customers
    SET rating = 200
    WHERE snum = 1001;
```

Updating Multiple Columns at Once

You need not, however, restrict yourself to updating a single column per UPDATE statement. The SET clause can accept any number of column assignments, separated by commas. All of these assignments will still be made to the table a single row at a time. Suppose Motika had resigned, and we wanted to reassign her number to a new salesperson named Gibson:

```
UPDATE Salespeople
    SET sname = 'Gibson', city = 'Boston', comm = .10
    WHERE snum = 1004;
```

This would give Gibson all of Motika's current customers and orders, because these are linked to Motika by snum. In practice, however, reassigning primary keys is usually not a good idea. For one thing, it would become difficult to disentangle Gibson from Motika in the archived historical data.

You cannot, however, update multiple *tables* in a single statement, partly because you cannot use table prefixes with the columns being changed by the SET clause. In other words, you cannot say SET Salespeople.sname = 'Gibson' in an UPDATE statement; you can say only SET sname = 'Gibson'.

Using Value Expressions in UPDATE

It is possible to use value expressions in the SET clause of the UPDATE statement, however, including expressions that employ the column being modified. Suppose you decide to double the commission of all your salespeople. You could use the following expression:

```
UPDATE Salespeople
    SET comm = comm * 2;
```

Whenever you refer to an existing column value in the SET clause, the value produced will be that of the current row before UPDATE makes any changes. Naturally, you can combine features to, say, double the commission of all salespeople in London with this statement:

```
UPDATE Salespeople
    SET comm = comm * 2
    WHERE city = 'London';
```

Updating to NULL Values

The SET clause can update to NULLs much as the INSERT statement inserts them. So, if you wanted to set all ratings for customers in London to NULL, you would enter the following statement:

```
UPDATE customers
```

```
SET rating = NULL
WHERE city = 'London';
```

This will null all the ratings of customers in London.

Summary

You have now mastered the essentials of manipulating the contents of your database with three simple statements: INSERT is used to place rows in the database; DELETE, to remove them; and UPDATE, to change the values in rows previously inserted. You have learned to use predicates with UPDATE and DELETE to determine which rows will be affected by the statement. Of course, predicates as such are not meaningful for INSERT, because the row in question does not exist in the table until after the INSERT statement is executed. You can, however, use queries with INSERT to put entire sets of rows into a table at once. And you can do this with the columns in any order. You have learned that you can place default values in columns if you do not explicitly state a value. You have also seen the use of the standard default value, which is NULL. You can also use subqueries in these statements, which we will discuss after we have more thoroughly explained queries in the next part of the book.

Putting SQL to Work

1. Write a command that puts the following values, in their given order, into the Salespeople table: city—San Jose, name—Blanco, comm—NULL, snum—1100.

2. Write a command that removes all orders from customer Clemens from the Orders table.

3. Write a command that increases the rating of all customers in Rome by 100.

4. Salesperson Serres has left the company. Assign her customers to Motika.

PART III

Queries

CHAPTER
SEVEN

7

Using SQL to Retrieve Information from Tables

- Making a Query

- Using the SELECT Statement

- Qualified Selection—The WHERE Clause

In this chapter we will show you how to retrieve information from tables. We will teach you how to omit or reorder columns and how to automatically eliminate redundant data from your output. To do this, we will elaborate on the SELECT statement that was briefly introduced in Chapter 2 and will be discussed for the next several chapters.

Making a Query

SQL stands for Structured Query Language, though these days the acronym is much more commonly used than the name. The name is derived from the fact that queries are the most frequently used aspect of SQL. What is a query? A query is a statement you give your DBMS that tells it to produce certain specified information. Queries in SQL are all constructed from a single statement. The structure of this statement is deceptively simple, because you can extend it enough to allow some highly sophisticated evaluating and processing of data. This statement is called SELECT.

Using the SELECT Statement

In its simplest form, SELECT instructs the database to retrieve the contents of a table. For example, you could produce the Salespeople table by typing the following:

```
SELECT snum, sname, city, comm
    FROM Salespeople;
```

The output for this query is shown in Figure 7.1.

In other words, this statement simply outputs all of the data in the table. Here is an explanation of each part of the statement:

SELECT   A keyword that tells the database this statement is a query. All queries begin with this word followed by white space.

snum, sname ...   A list of the columns from the table that are being selected by the query. Any columns not listed here would not be included in the output of the statement.

FROM Salespeople   A keyword, like SELECT, that must be present in every query. It is followed by a space and then the name of the table being used as the source of the information. In this case, that table is Salespeople.

FIGURE 7.1:

The SELECT statement

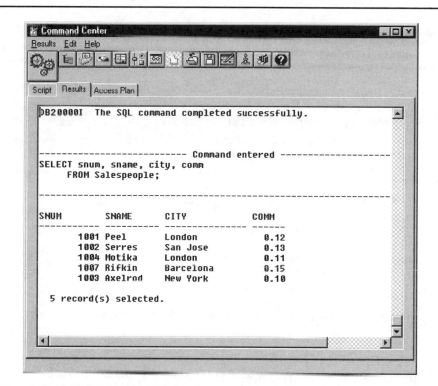

It is worth noting here that a query of this nature will not necessarily order its output in any particular way. The same statement executed on the same data at different times may not even produce the same ordering. You can order output from SQL statements directly through the use of a special clause. Later, we will explain how to do this. For now, simply recognize that, in the absence of explicit ordering, your output will not necessarily come in a definite order.

Selecting All Columns the Easy Way

If you want to see every column of a table, there is an optional abbreviation you can use. You can substitute an asterisk (*) for a complete list of the columns as follows:

```
SELECT *
    FROM Salespeople;
```

Doing so will produce the same result as our previous statement.

To sum up, the SELECT statement begins with the keyword SELECT. After this comes a list of the names of the columns you wish to see, separated by commas. If you wish to see all of the columns of a table, you can replace this list with an asterisk (*). The keyword FROM is next, followed by a space and the name of the table that is being queried.

Selecting Only Certain Columns

To look only at specific columns of a table, simply omit the columns you do not wish to see from the SELECT clause. For example, this query

```
SELECT sname, comm
    FROM Salespeople;
```

will produce the output shown in Figure 7.2.

You will often see tables that have a large number of columns containing data, not all of which is relevant to the purpose at hand. Therefore, you will find the ability to pick and choose your columns quite useful.

By the way, even though the columns of a table do have a specific order (unlike the rows), this does not mean that you have to retrieve them in that order. An asterisk (*) will produce all the columns in their proper order, but if you indicate the columns separately, you can put them in any order you want. Although these are very simple examples, they say something important about queries, which is that queries enable you to extract and rearrange, rather than simply output, your data. As we go further into the SELECT statement in the next few chapters, it will become clear that a single SELECT statement can access, correlate, and derive information across the entire database.

FIGURE 7.2:

Selecting certain columns

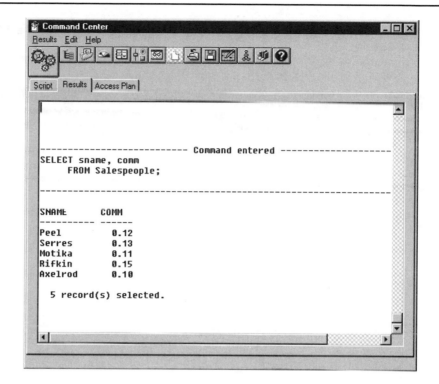

Eliminating Redundant Data

DISTINCT is an argument that provides a way for you to eliminate duplicate values from your output. You put DISTINCT in the SELECT clause. Suppose you want to know which salespeople currently have orders in the Orders table. You don't need to know how many orders each one has; you need only a list of salesperson numbers (snums). You could enter

```
SELECT snum
    FROM Orders;
```

to get the output shown in Figure 7.3.

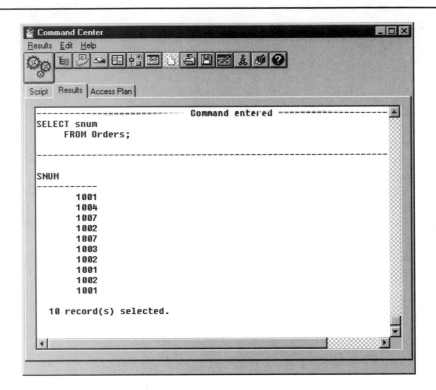

To produce a list without duplications, which would be easier to read, you could enter the following:

```
SELECT DISTINCT snum
     FROM Orders;
```

The output for this query is shown in Figure 7.4.

In other words, DISTINCT keeps track of which values have come up before, so they will not be duplicated on the list. This is a useful way to avoid redundant data, but it is important that you be aware of what you are doing. *If you should not have redundant data, then you should not use DISTINCT*, because it can hide a problem. For example, you might assume that all your customers' names are different. If someone put a second Clemens in the Customers table, however, and you used SELECT DISTINCT cname, you would not even see evidence of the duplication. Both would appear to be a single customer. Since you don't expect redundancy in this case, you shouldn't use DISTINCT. Also, if DISTINCT is really not needed, it can cause your system to do extra work, which will make your queries run more slowly.

FIGURE 7.4:

SELECT without duplicates

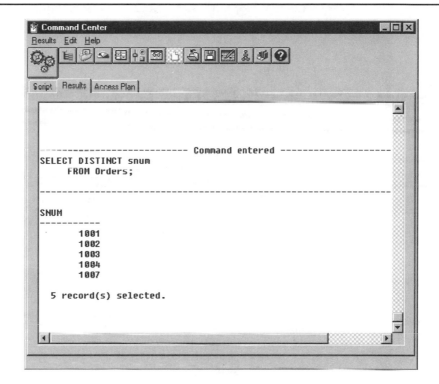

The Parameters of DISTINCT

DISTINCT applies to all of the columns in the SELECT clause. When the combination of all output columns is a duplicate of a previously selected combination, the duplicate is eliminated. Therefore, it can be specified only once in a SELECT statement (except when used within aggregate functions, as explained in Chapter 8). If the clause shown in Figure 7.4 had selected multiple columns, DISTINCT would have eliminated the rows where all of the column values were identical. Rows in which some values were the same and some different would have been retained. Since DISTINCT applies to the entire output row, not a specific column, it makes no sense to repeat it.

DISTINCT vs. ALL

As an alternative to DISTINCT, you may specify ALL. This has the opposite effect: duplicate output rows are retained. Since this effect is also what happens if you specify neither DISTINCT nor ALL, ALL is essentially a clarifier, rather than a functional argument.

Qualified Selection—The WHERE Clause

Tables tend to get very large as time goes on and more and more rows are added. Because usually only certain rows interest you at a given time, SQL enables you to define criteria to determine which rows are selected for output. The WHERE clause of the SELECT statement enables you to define a *predicate*, a condition that can be TRUE, FALSE, or UNKNOWN for any given row of a table. The statement extracts only those rows from the table for which the predicate is TRUE. We have seen predicates before, of course—in Chapters 4 and 6, for example—but SELECT tends to make more sophisticated use of them than other statements (we will discuss predicates more thoroughly later in this chapter).

By the way, a common term for the rows of a table that are being evaluated by a predicate is *candidate rows*. Those rows that make the predicate TRUE are the *selected rows*.

Suppose you want to see the names and commissions of all salespeople in London. You could enter this statement:

```
SELECT sname, city
    FROM Salespeople
    WHERE city = 'London';
```

When a WHERE clause is present, the database program goes through the entire table one row at a time and examines each row to determine if the predicate is TRUE. Therefore, for the Peel record, the program will look at the current value of the city column, determine that it is equal to 'London' and include this row in the output. The Serres record will not be included, and so on. The output for the above query is shown in Figure 7.5.

Notice that the city column is not included in the output, even though its value is used to determine which rows are selected. This is perfectly acceptable. It is not necessary for the columns used in the WHERE clause to be present among those selected for output.

FIGURE 7.5:

SELECT with a
WHERE clause

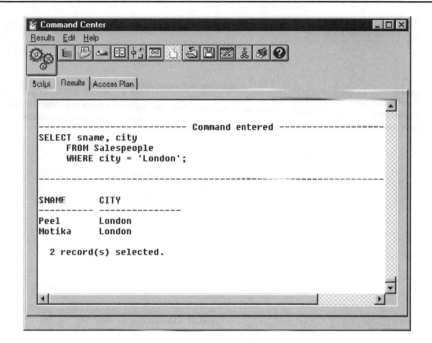

Let's try an example with a numeric field in the WHERE clause. The rating field of the Customers table is intended to separate the customers into groups based on some criteria that can be summarized by a number, such as a credit rating or a rating based on the volume of previous purchases. Such numeric codes can be useful in relational databases as a way of summarizing complex information. We can select all customers with a rating of 100 as follows:

```
SELECT *
     FROM Customers
     WHERE rating = 100;
```

We didn't use the single quotes here because rating is a numeric field. The results of the query are shown in Figure 7.6.

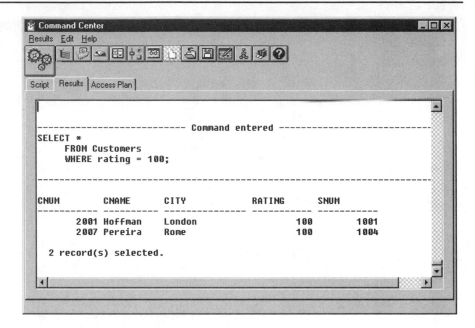

```
-------------------------- Command entered --------------------------
SELECT *
     FROM Customers
     WHERE rating = 100;


CNUM         CNAME        CITY             RATING      SNUM
-----------  -----------  ---------------  ----------- -----------
        2001 Hoffman      London                   100        1001
        2007 Pereira      Rome                     100        1004

 2 record(s) selected.
```

Using Inequalities in Predicates

A *relational operator* is a mathematical symbol that indicates a certain type of comparison between two values. You have already seen how equalities, such as 2 + 3 = 5 or city = 'London', are used. There are other relational operators as well. Suppose you want to see all salespeople with commissions above a certain amount. You would use a greater-than type of comparison. These are the relational operators that SQL recognizes:

=   Equal to

>   Greater than

<   Less than

>=   Greater than or equal to

<=   Less than or equal to

<>   Not equal to

As with equalities, all of these operators are UNKNOWN when NULLs are used in a comparison.

These operators have the standard meanings for numeric values. For example, suppose you wanted to see all customers with a rating above 200. Since 200 is a scalar value, as are the values in the rating column, you could use a relational operator to compare them:

```
SELECT *
     FROM Customers
     WHERE rating > 200;
```

The output for this query is shown in Figure 7.7.

FIGURE 7.7:

A query using an inequality

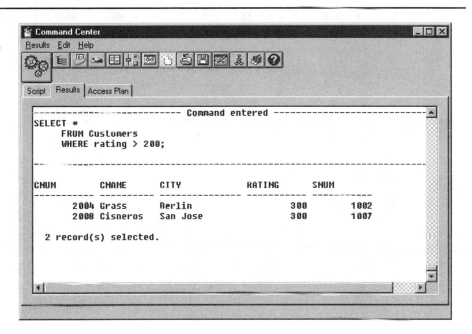

Of course, if you also wanted to see the customers with a rating equal to 200, you would use the predicate:

```
rating >= 200
```

For character values, the meaning of relational operators depends on the sorting order, with the following possibilities:

- If the DBMS is fully SQL92-compliant, it will support *collations* (also known as *collating sequences*). A collation is a database object that specifies how a set of characters is to be sorted. You have considerable flexibility in creating and assigning collations. A DBMS that supports collations will almost inevitably have a sensible default sorting order for any character sets whose support is built into the program. Much of the point of treating characters sets and collations as objects, rather than simply as part of database functionality, is that doing so makes it possible to expand a DBMS to support more character sets than it was originally intended to do.

- If the DBMS is not fully SQL92-compliant, it may simply default to sorting the characters according to the binary numbers that represent them internally. For the English language, this sorting will almost always follow the ASCII standard mappings, possibly with extensions. ASCII mappings sort in alphabetical order provided that the case is consistent; however, all uppercase letters precede all lowercase. Therefore, 'a' < 'b', but 'a' > 'B'. Conceivably, you could be using an EBCDIC-based system. In this scheme, sortings are alphabetical, but all lowercase letters precede all uppercase.

- The DBMS may provide a sensible, case-insensitive sort that cannot be altered and is therefore part of the product's functionality rather than a database object like a collation.

In any of the above schemes, the question arises of how to sort non-alphabetic (i.e., numbers and punctuation) characters within the character set. There will be some defined order, and it should be specified in your system documentation, but there are no general rules, since these sorts are not commonly meaningful (what would '*' < 'a' mean?).

Another standard datatype you can use with inequalities is DATETIME. This, of course, can refer to dates, times, or combinations of both and is therefore not always sortable: '11/24/99' > '11:52:43' is, of course, meaningless.

By the way, values that can be sorted are called *scalar values*. SQL predicates typically compare scalar values using either relational operators or special SQL operators to see if the comparison is TRUE. We explain some special SQL operators in the next chapter.

For at least two SQL datatypes, inequality comparisons may make no sense:

- Straight binary data, often referred to as BLOBs (Binary Large Objects). Suppose you stored jpeg images of your employees in a database. Sorting these by their binary representations would simply order them based on the color of their first pixels—a rather meaningless sort.

- SQL99 permits users to create abstract structured datatypes (UDTs). Sort orders may not be meaningful for these.

That being said, application developers do sometimes use these types in ways such that sorting is useful, and the semantics of SQL permits such sorts.

NOTE   For more on SQL99, see Part VI.

Working with NULL Values

Frequently, a table will contain rows that do not contain values for every column, either because the information is incomplete or because the column simply does not apply to every case. SQL provides for these instances by allowing you to enter a NULL into the column in place of a value. When a column value is NULL, it means that the database program has specially marked that column as not having any value for that row. Since NULL is technically not a value, it does not have a datatype. It can be placed in any type of column. Nonetheless, a NULL in SQL is frequently referred to as a NULL value.

Suppose you have a new customer who has not yet been assigned a salesperson. Rather than wait for the salesperson to be assigned, you want to enter the customer into the database now, so that he or she does not get lost in the shuffle. You can enter a row for the customer with a NULL for snum and fill in that column with a value later, when a salesperson is assigned. NULLs, however, significantly change the way that the logic of SQL works, as we show in the next section.

Using Boolean Operators in Predicates

The basic Boolean operators used in most programming languages are recognized in SQL but operate a little differently than usual because of NULLs. In most computer languages, Boolean expressions are expressions that can be either TRUE or

FALSE. In SQL, they can also be UNKNOWN. Hence, SQL uses three-valued logic (3VL), rather than the traditional two-valued kind. Boolean operators relate one or more Boolean values and produce a single Boolean value: TRUE, FALSE, or UNKNOWN. The Boolean operators recognized in SQL are the standard AND, OR, and NOT. Other, more complex, Boolean operators exist (such as "exclusive or", often written XOR), but you can build them from our three simple pieces. In traditional (two-valued) Boolean logic, the operators work as follows:

- NOT takes a single Boolean expression (in the form NOT A) as an argument and changes its value from FALSE to TRUE or from TRUE to FALSE.

- AND takes two Boolean expressions (in the form A AND B) as arguments and evaluates to TRUE if they are both TRUE. Otherwise, it is FALSE.

- OR takes two Boolean expressions (in the form A OR B) as arguments and evaluates to TRUE if either is TRUE. Otherwise, it is FALSE.

Of course, SQL's three-valued logic makes this considerably more complex. Tables 7.1, 7.2, and 7.3 illustrate how NOT, OR, and AND work in 3VL.

TABLE 7.1:   Truth Values Using NOT in Three-Valued Logic

Expression	Truth Value
NOT TRUE	FALSE
NOT FALSE	TRUE
NOT UNKNOWN	UNKNOWN

As you can see, the difference here is that NOT does not change the value of UNKNOWN. It is still UNKNOWN. This is an important difference for SQL predicates, since UNKNOWN in most respects behaves the same as FALSE, and this difference can mislead you if you have not accounted for it. The following two tables are formatted somewhat like the multiplication tables of which you were so fond in elementary school. The truth values are given across the top row and along the left column. To find the result of an OR (in Table 7.2) or an AND (in Table 7.3) applied to two truth values, look at the intersection of the row for one truth value with the column of the other.

TABLE 7.2:   Truth Values Using OR in Three-Valued Logic

OR	TRUE	FALSE	UNKNOWN
TRUE	TRUE	TRUE	TRUE
FALSE	TRUE	FALSE	UNKNOWN
UNKNOWN	TRUE	UNKNOWN	UNKNOWN

You can remember this logic as follows:

- TRUE OR (*any truth value*) is TRUE.
- UNKNOWN OR (*any truth value other than TRUE*) is UNKNOWN.
- FALSE OR FALSE is FALSE.

TABLE 7.3:   Truth Values Using AND in Three-Valued Logic

AND	TRUE	FALSE	UNKNOWN
TRUE	TRUE	FALSE	UNKNOWN
FALSE	FALSE	FALSE	FALSE
UNKNOWN	UNKNOWN	FALSE	UNKNOWN

You can remember this logic as follows:

- FALSE AND (*any truth value*) is FALSE.
- UNKNOWN AND (*any truth value other than FALSE*) is UNKNOWN.
- TRUE AND TRUE is TRUE.

By relating Boolean expressions with Boolean operators, you can greatly increase the sophistication of predicates. Suppose you want to see all customers in London who have a rating below 200:

```
SELECT *
    FROM Customers
    WHERE city = 'London'
    AND rating < 200;
```

The output for this query is shown in Figure 7.8. There is only one customer who fills the bill.

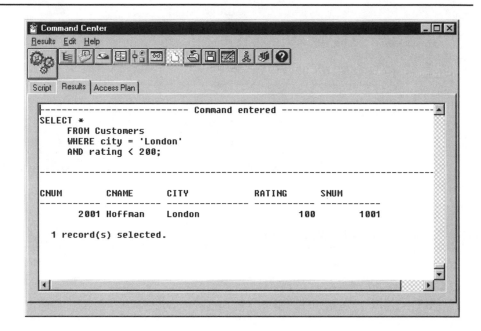

What, you may ask, about Clemens, Customer #2006? He is in London but has a NULL rating. Let's examine the logic. For Clemens, `city = 'London'` is TRUE, and `rating < 200` is UNKNOWN (it translates to NULL < 200). Therefore, the predicate is TRUE AND UNKNOWN, which is UNKNOWN. Since a predicate selects only rows that make it TRUE, Clemens is not selected. Notice that if we had said `rating > 200`, he still would not have been selected. SQL provides a special operator for dealing with NULLs, which we will introduce in the next chapter.

If you had used OR, you would have gotten all customers who fulfilled either condition. The following query select all who were either located in San Jose or had a rating above 200:

```
SELECT *
    FROM Customers
    WHERE city = 'San Jose'
    OR rating > 200;
```

The output for this query is shown in Figure 7.9.

FIGURE 7.9:

SELECT using OR

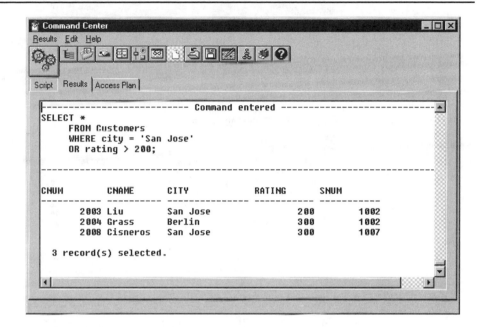

You can use NOT to reverse the value of a Boolean. Here is an example of a NOT query:

```
SELECT *
     FROM Customers
     WHERE city = 'San Jose'
     OR NOT rating > 200;
```

This query's output is shown in Figure 7.10.

FIGURE 7.10:

SELECT using NOT

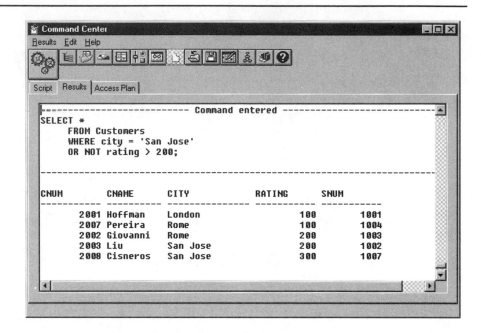

The query selected all of the records except Grass and Clemens. Grass was not in San Jose, and his rating was greater than 200, so he failed both tests. Clemens failed the city test, and his rating was UNKNOWN. Each of the other rows met one *or* the other (or both) of these criteria. Notice that the NOT operator must precede a Boolean whose value it is to change, not be located before the relational operator as you might do in English. It is *incorrect* to enter

```
rating NOT > 200
```

as a predicate, even though that is how we would say it in English.

This brings up another point. How would SQL evaluate the following?

```
SELECT *
    FROM Customers
    WHERE NOT city = 'San Jose'
    OR rating > 200;
```

Does the NOT apply only to the `city = 'San Jose'` expression or to both that and the `rating > 200` expression? As written, the correct answer would be the former. SQL will apply NOT only to the Boolean expression immediately following it. The output for this query is shown in Figure 7.11.

FIGURE 7.11:

SELECT using a
compound NOT

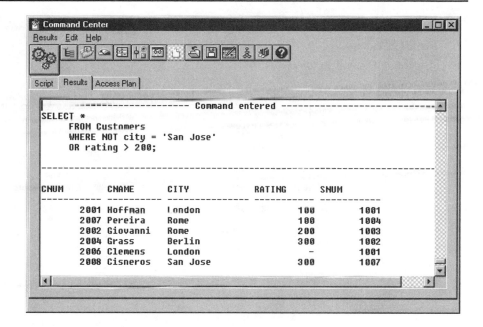

You could obtain another result with this statement:

```
SELECT *
    FROM Customers
    WHERE NOT (city = 'San Jose'
    OR rating > 200);
```

SQL understands parentheses to mean that everything inside them will be evaluated first and treated as a single expression by everything outside them (which is the standard interpretation in Boolean logic, much other mathematics, and many programming languages). In other words, SQL takes each row and determines if the city = 'San Jose' or the rating > 200. If either condition is TRUE, the Boolean expression inside the parentheses is TRUE. However, if the Boolean expression inside the parentheses is TRUE, the predicate as a whole is FALSE, because NOT turns the TRUEs into FALSEs and vice versa. The output for this query is shown in Figure 7.12.

FIGURE 7.12:

SELECT with NOT and
parentheses

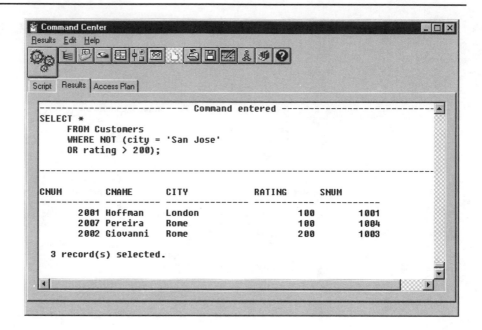

Here is a deliberately complex example. See if you can follow its logic (the output is shown in Figure 7.13):

```
SELECT *
     FROM Orders
     WHERE NOT ((odate = '10/03/2000' AND snum > 1002)
     OR amt > 2000.00);
```

Although Boolean operators are simple individually, they are not so simple when combined into complex expressions. The way to evaluate a complex Boolean is to evaluate the Boolean expression(s) most deeply nested in parentheses, combine these into a single Boolean value, and then combine this value with the higher nested values.

Here is a detailed explanation of how we evaluated the example in Figure 7.13.

- First of all, none of the columns tested (odate, snum, and amt) happen to contain NULLs. Therefore, there will be no UNKNOWN predicates, and we can limit ourselves to conventional (two-valued) Boolean logic, which for this example will be complex enough. In a realistic situation, you could only be justified in this assumption if all the columns being tested had the NOT NULL constraint.

FIGURE 7.13:

A complex query

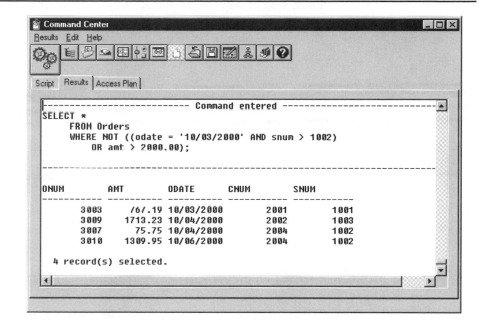

```
Command Center                                          _ □ ×
Results  Edit  Help

Script   Results  Access Plan

|--------------------- Command entered ---------------------|▲
|SELECT *                                                   |
|    FROM Orders                                            |
|    WHERE NOT ((odate = '10/03/2000' AND snum > 1002)      |
|        OR amt > 2000.00);                                 |
|                                                           |
|-----------------------------------------------------------|
|                                                           |
|ONUM        AMT       ODATE      CNUM        SNUM          |
|----------- --------- ---------- ----------- ----------    |
|       3003     767.19 10/03/2000        2001        1001  |
|       3009    1713.23 10/04/2000        2002        1003  |
|       3007      75.75 10/04/2000        2004        1002  |
|       3010    1309.95 10/06/2000        2004        1002  |
|                                                           |
| 4 record(s) selected.                                     |▼
|◄                                                        ►|
```

- The most deeply nested Boolean expressions in the predicate—odate = '10/03/2000' and snum > 1002—are joined by an AND, forming one Boolean expression that will evaluate to TRUE for all rows that meet both of these conditions. Call this compound Boolean expression B1.

- B1 is joined with the amt > 2000.00 expression (B2) by an OR, forming a third expression, B3.

- B3 is TRUE for a given row if either B1 or B2 is TRUE for that row.

- B3 is wholly contained in parentheses preceded by a NOT, forming the final Boolean expression, B4, which is the condition of the predicate. Thus B4, the predicate of the query, is TRUE whenever B3 is FALSE and vice versa.

- B3 is FALSE whenever B1 and B2 are both FALSE.

- B1 is FALSE for a row if the order date of the row is not 10/03/2000 or if its snum value is not greater than 1002.

- B2 is FALSE for all rows with an amount that is not above 2000.00. Any row with an amount above 2000.00 would make B2 TRUE; as a result, B3 would be TRUE and B4 FALSE. Therefore, all such rows are eliminated from the output.

- Of the remaining rows, those on October 3 with snum greater than 1002 (such as the row for onum 3001 on October 3 with snum of 1007), make B1 TRUE, thereby making B3 TRUE and the predicate of the query FALSE. These are also eliminated. The output shows the rows that are left.

Here is an alternative, slightly simpler, formulation of the above query:

```
SELECT *
    FROM Orders
    WHERE (odate <> 10/03/2000 OR snum <= 1002)
    AND amt <= 2000.00;
```

Summary

Now you know several ways to make a table give you the information that you want, rather than simply spilling out its contents. You can reorder the columns of the table or eliminate any of them. You can decide whether you want to see duplicate values.

Most important, you can define a condition called a predicate that determines whether a particular row of a table, possibly from among thousands, will be selected for output. Predicates can become very sophisticated, giving you great precision in controlling which rows are selected by a query. It is this ability to decide exactly what you want to see that makes SQL queries so powerful. The next several chapters will consist, for the most part, of features that expand the power of predicates.

You can find values that relate to a given value in any one of a number of ways—all definable with the various relational operators. You can also use the Boolean operators AND and OR to combine multiple conditions, each of which could stand alone in predicates, into a single predicate. The Boolean operator NOT, as you have seen, can reverse the meaning of a condition or group of conditions. You can control the effect of all of the Boolean and relational operators by the use of parentheses, which determine the order in which the operations are performed. You can take these operations to any level of complexity; you have had some taste of how conditions that are quite involved can be built up out of these simple parts.

Now that we have shown how standard mathematical operators are used, we can move on to operators that are exclusive to SQL. We will do this in the next chapter.

Putting SQL to Work

1. Write a SELECT statement that produces the order number, amount, and date for all rows in the Orders table.

2. Write a query that produces all rows from the Customers table for which the salesperson's number is 1001.

3. Write a query that produces the Salespeople table with the columns in the following order: city, sname, snum, comm.

4. Write a query that will produce the snum values of all salespeople with orders currently in the Orders table without any repeats.

5. Write a query that will give you the names and cities of all salespeople in London with a commission above .10.

6. Write a query on the Customers table whose output will exclude all customers with a rating < = 100, unless they are located in Rome.

7. What will be the output from the following query?

```
SELECT *
     FROM Orders
     WHERE (amt < 1000
OR
          NOT (odate = '10/03/2000'
          AND cnum > 2003));
```

8. What will be the output of the following query?

```
SELECT *
     FROM Orders
     WHERE NOT ((odate = '10/03/2000' OR snum > 1006)
          AND amt > = 1500);
```

9. What is a simpler way to write this query? Assume that the comm column cannot contain NULLs.

```
SELECT snum, sname, city, comm
     FROM Salespeople
     WHERE (comm >= .12
OR
          comm < .14);
```

CHAPTER

EIGHT

8

Using IN, BETWEEN, LIKE, IS NULL, and Aggregate Functions

- ■ The IN Operator

- ■ The BETWEEN Operator

- ■ The LIKE Operator

- ■ The IS NULL Operator

- ■ Summarizing Data with Aggregate Functions

In addition to the relational and Boolean operators we discussed in the last chapter, SQL uses a group of special operators that includes IN, BETWEEN, LIKE, and IS NULL. In this chapter, you will learn how to use these, as you would the relational operators, to produce more sophisticated and powerful predicates.

You will also move beyond simply using queries to extract values from the database and discover how you can use them to derive information from those values. You will do so with aggregate or summary functions that take groups of values and reduce them to a single value. You will learn how to use these functions, how to define the groups of values to which they will be applied, and how to determine which of the resulting grouped values are selected for output. You will also see under what conditions you can combine column values with this derived information in a single query.

The IN Operator

IN explicitly defines a set in which a given value may or may not be included. Based on what you have learned up to now, if you wanted to find all salespeople who were located in either Barcelona or London, you would have to use the following query (its output is shown in Figure 8.1):

```
SELECT *
    FROM Salespeople
    WHERE city = 'Barcelona'
    OR city = 'London';
```

Here is an easier way to get the same information:

```
SELECT *
    FROM Salespeople
    WHERE city IN ('Barcelona', 'London');
```

The output for this query is shown in Figure 8.2.

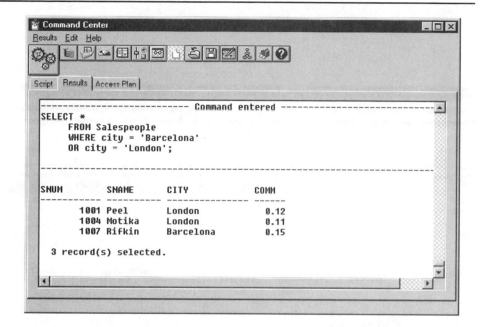

FIGURE 8.1:

Finding salespeople in
Barcelona or London

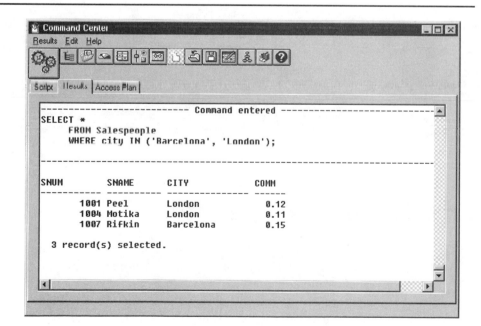

FIGURE 8.2:

SELECT using IN

As you can see, IN defines a set by explicitly naming the members of the set in parentheses, separated by commas. It then checks the various values of the named column to try to find a match. If it finds one, the predicate is TRUE. When the set contains numeric rather than character values, of course, the single quotes are omitted. Let's find all customers matched with salespeople 1001, 1007, and 1004. The output for the following query is shown in Figure 8.3:

```
SELECT *
     FROM Customers
     WHERE snum IN (1001, 1007, 1004);
```

FIGURE 8.3:
SELECT using IN with numbers

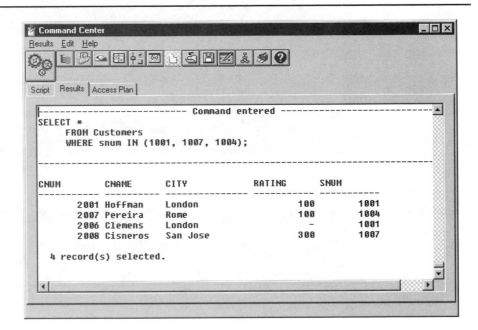

The BETWEEN Operator

The BETWEEN operator is similar to IN. Rather than enumerating a set as IN does, BETWEEN defines a range that values must fall into to make the predicate TRUE. You use the keyword BETWEEN followed by the beginning value, the keyword AND, and the ending value. Unlike IN, BETWEEN is sensitive to order, and the first value in the clause must be first in alphabetic or numeric order (notice that, unlike English, SQL does not say *value* "is BETWEEN" *value* and *value*, but simply *value* "BETWEEN" *value* and *value*). This format applies as well to the LIKE operator. (The keyword IS is reserved for use in the IS NULL operator). The following query will extract from the Salespeople table all salespeople with commissions between .10 and .12 (the output is shown in Figure 8.4):

```
SELECT *
    FROM Salespeople
    WHERE comm BETWEEN .10 AND .12;
```

FIGURE 8.4:
SELECT using BETWEEN

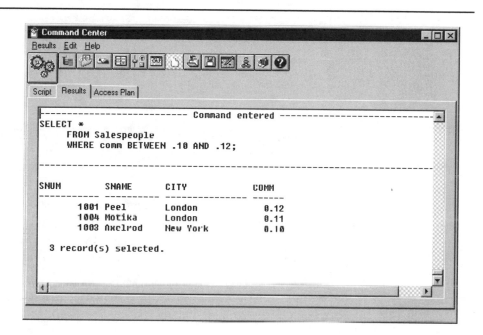

Notice that the BETWEEN operator is inclusive; that is, values matching either of the two boundary values (in this case, .10 and .12) cause the predicate to be TRUE. SQL does not directly support a noninclusive BETWEEN. You must either define your boundary values so that an inclusive interpretation is acceptable or do something like this:

```
SELECT *
    FROM Salespeople
    WHERE (comm BETWEEN .10, AND .12)
    AND NOT comm IN (.10, .12);
```

The output for this query is shown in Figure 8.5.

FIGURE 8.5:
Making BETWEEN
noninclusive

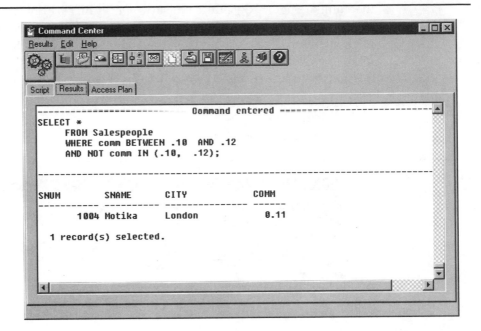

Admittedly, this statement is a bit clumsy, but it does show how you can combine these new operators with Boolean operators to produce more complex predicates. Basically, you use IN and BETWEEN just as you do relational operators to compare values, one of which happens to be a set (for IN) or a range (for BETWEEN).

In BETWEEN, it is important to emphasize the importance of the order in which the boundary values are given. Take, for example, the following query:

```
SELECT *
     FROM Salespeople
     WHERE comm BETWEEN .12 AND .10;
```

This is not equivalent to the previous example. In fact, this version will never be TRUE, because .12 > .10. BETWEEN is interpreted as meaning that the first value precedes or equals the target, and the second follows or equals the target, never the reverse. Literally, the preceding BETWEEN example is translated as follows:

```
SELECT *
     FROM Salespeople
     WHERE comm >= .12 AND comm <= .10;
```

This, of course, is not true for any real number. Although this may seem obvious enough as it stands, it can cause confusion in applications where the numbers used in the SQL statement may be variables instead of constants. The principle to remember is that the first comparison value in the BETWEEN clause should always be less than the second.

Also like relational operators, BETWEEN operates on character columns in terms of the collation. This means you can use it to select ranges from alphabetical ordering. It is important when you do so to be consistent in your use of capitalization.

This query selects all customers whose names fall in a certain alphabetical range:

```
SELECT *
    FROM Customers
    WHERE cname BETWEEN 'A' AND 'G';
```

The output for this query is shown in Figure 8.6.

FIGURE 8.6:
Using BETWEEN
alphabetically

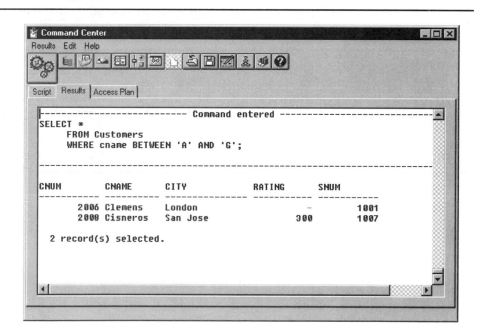

Notice that Giovanni and Grass are omitted, even though BETWEEN is inclusive. This is because of the way BETWEEN compares strings of unequal length. The string 'G' is shorter than the string 'Giovanni', so BETWEEN pads the 'G' with blanks. The blanks precede the letters in alphabetical order (in most common collations), so Giovanni is not selected. The same applies to Grass. It is important to remember this if you are using BETWEEN to extract alphabetical ranges. You will usually go one letter beyond the last letter you want to include or add a *z* (several if necessary) after your second boundary value. If the system you use is fully SQL92-compliant, a particular collation will have a PAD ATTRIBUTE that determines whether the padding with blanks described above actually occurs. For more information, see "Collations" in the reference.

The LIKE Operator

LIKE is used with text string datatypes, against which it is used to find substrings. In other words, it searches a text column to see if part of it matches a string. To do this, it uses *wildcards*, special characters that will match anything. There are two types of wildcards used with LIKE:

- The underscore character (_) stands for any single character. For example, 'b_t' will match 'bat' or 'bit', but it will not match 'brat'.

- The percent sign (%) stands for a sequence of any number of characters (including zero characters). '%p%t' will match 'put', 'posit', or 'opt', but not 'spite'.

Let's find all the customers whose names begin with *G* (the output is shown in Figure 8.7):

```
SELECT *
    FROM Customers
    WHERE cname LIKE 'G%';
```

LIKE can be handy if you are searching for a name or other value and you cannot remember all of it. Suppose you were unsure whether to spell the name of one of your salespeople Peal or Peel. You can simply use the part you know and the wildcards will find all possible matches (the output of this query is shown in Figure 8.8):

```
SELECT *
    FROM Salespeople
    WHERE sname LIKE 'P_ _l';
```

FIGURE 8.7:
SELECT using LIKE with %

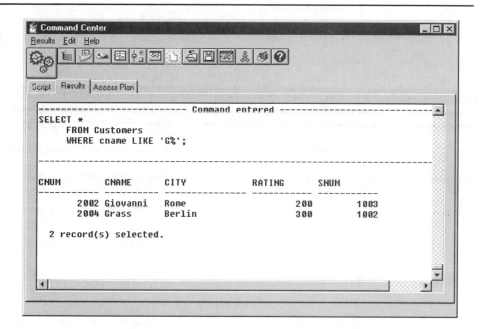

FIGURE 8.8:
SELECT using LIKE with _
(underscore)

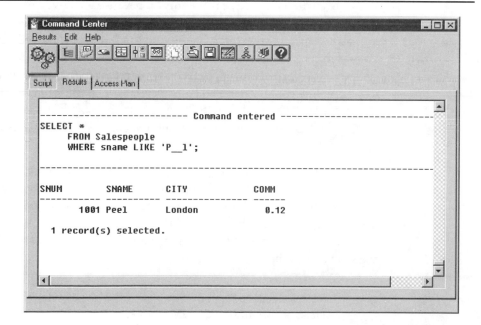

The underscore wildcards each represent a single character, so a name like Prettel would not show up. A % wildcard at the end of the string is necessary in many implementations if the length of the sname column is greater than the number of characters in the name Peel and the sname column is a fixed-length (CHAR) rather than varying-length (VARCHAR) text datatype. In such a case, the sname column value is actually stored as the name Peel, followed by a series of spaces to bring the total number of characters up to the fixed length specified for the column. Therefore, the character 'l' is not considered the end of the string. The % wildcard simply matches all the empty padding. This would not be necessary if the sname column were of type VARCHAR.

So what do you do if you need to search for a percent sign or an underscore in a string? In a LIKE predicate, you can define any single character as an *escape character*. An escape character is used immediately before a percent sign or underscore in the predicate and means that the percent sign or underscore will be interpreted literally as a character rather than as a wildcard. For example, we could search our sname column for the presence of underscores, as follows:

```
SELECT *
    FROM Salespeople
    WHERE sname LIKE '%/_%' ESCAPE '/';
```

With the current data there is no output, because we have not included any underscores in our salespeople's names. The ESCAPE clause defines / as an escape character. The escape character is used in the LIKE string, followed by a percent sign, an underscore, or itself (to be explained shortly). Whenever such a character is so prefixed, it will be searched for as a literal, rather than with its usual wildcard meaning. The escape character must be a single character and applies only to the single character immediately following it. In the example above, both the beginning and ending percent signs are still treated as wildcards—only the underscore represents itself.

As we mentioned, the escape character can also be used on itself. In other words, if you want to search the column for your escape character, you will simply enter it twice. The first one acts as an escape character meaning "take the following character literally as a character", and the second one is that character—the escape character itself. Here is the preceding example revised to search for occurrences of the string _/ in the sname column:

```
SELECT *
    FROM Salespeople
    WHERE sname LIKE '%/_//%' ESCAPE '/';
```

Again, there is no output with the current data. The string being matched consists of any sequence of characters (%), followed by the underscore character (/_), the escape character (//), and any sequence of trailing characters (%).

The IS NULL Operator

As we discussed in the previous chapter, when a NULL is compared to any value, even another NULL, the result is neither TRUE nor FALSE, but *UNKNOWN*. Often you will need to distinguish between FALSE and UNKNOWN—between rows containing column values that fail a predicate condition and those containing NULLs in those columns. For this reason, SQL provides the special operator IS, which is used with the keyword NULL to locate and treat NULL values.

To find all records in our Customers table with NULL values in the city column, we could enter:

```
SELECT *
     FROM Customers
     WHERE city IS NULL;
```

This query currently produces no output because we have no NULL values in the city column. NULL values are very important, and we will return to them later.

Using NOT with Special Operators

The special operators we have covered in this chapter can be immediately preceded by the Boolean NOT. This is in contrast to relational operators, which must have the NOT before the entire expression. For example, if we want to eliminate NULLs from our output rather than finding them, we would use NOT to reverse the meaning of the operator:

```
SELECT *
     FROM Customers
     WHERE city IS NOT NULL;
```

In the absence of NULLs (which is currently the case), this query would produce the entire Customers table. It is the equivalent of entering

```
SELECT *
     FROM Customers
     WHERE NOT city IS NULL;
```

which is also acceptable.

In Intermediate-level SQL92, IS NULL can test sets of values, rather than simply testing single values. Some products that do not claim Intermediate conformance may nonetheless support this functionality. In this case, NOT *value, value* IS NULL is not necessarily the same as *value, value* IS NOT NULL. For details, look in the reference under "Predicates."

We can also use NOT with IN:

```
SELECT *
    FROM Salespeople
    WHERE city NOT IN ('London', 'San Jose');
```

This is another way of saying

```
SELECT *
    FROM Salespeople
    WHERE NOT city IN ('London', 'San Jose');
```

The output for this query is shown in Figure 8.9. You can use NOT BETWEEN and NOT LIKE the same way. By the way, these queries will not produce any rows that have NULL city values. For those rows, the predicate NULL IN ('London', 'San Jose') is unknown. Hence the predicate NOT (NULL IN ('London,' 'San Jose')) is also unknown, as implied by the 3VL truth table from the previous chapter. Again, if you have to deal with NULLs, use the IS NULL operator. That's what it's for. If you wanted to include NULL city values among those not in San Jose or London, you could rephrase the query like this:

```
SELECT *
    FROM Salespeople
    WHERE NOT city IN ('London', 'San Jose')
    OR city IS NULL;
```

FIGURE 8.9:
Using NOT with IN

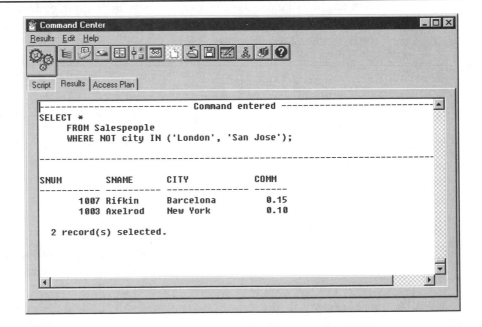

Summarizing Data with Aggregate Functions

A query can produce generalizations about groups of values as well as individual column values. It does this through the use of *aggregate functions*. Aggregate functions produce a single value for an entire group of columns. Here is a list of these functions:

- COUNT produces the number of rows or non-NULL column values that the query selected.

- SUM produces the arithmetic sum of all selected values of a given column.

- AVG produces the average (mean) of all selected values of a given column.

- MAX produces the largest of all selected values of a given column.

- MIN produces the smallest of all selected values of a given column.

How Do You Use Aggregate Functions?

Aggregate functions are used like column names in the SELECT clause of queries and, with one exception, take column names as arguments. Only numeric columns can be used for SUM and AVG. For COUNT, MAX, and MIN, any datatype can be used. When used with character columns, MAX and MIN will be interpreted in terms of the collation, which is to say that, generally speaking, MIN will mean first and MAX last, in alphabetical order (for more information, see "Collations" in the reference). NULL values are ignored in all calculations.

To find the SUM of all of our purchases from the Orders table, we could enter the following query, whose output is shown in Figure 8.10:

```
SELECT SUM(amt)
    FROM Orders;
```

This query, of course, differs substantially from selecting a column in that it returns a single value, regardless of how many rows are in the table. Because of this restriction, you cannot select aggregate functions and columns at the same time, unless you use the GROUP BY clause (described shortly).

Finding the average amount would be a similar operation (the output of the following query is shown in Figure 8.11):

```
SELECT AVG(amt)
    FROM Orders;
```

FIGURE 8.10:
Selecting a sum

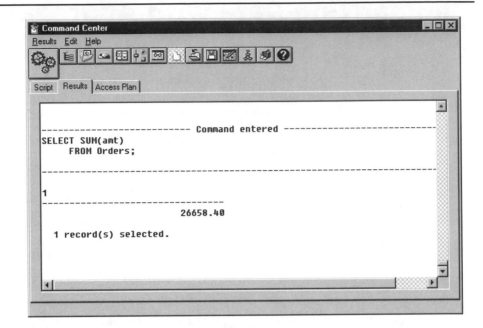

FIGURE 8.11:
Selecting an average

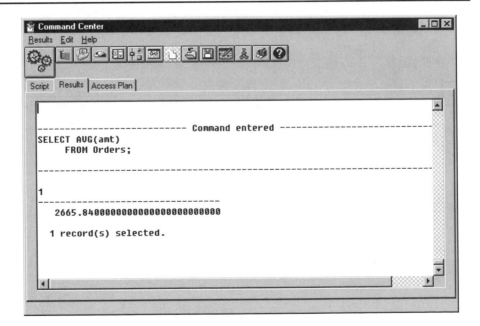

Special Attributes of COUNT

The COUNT function is slightly different. It counts the number of values in a given column or the number of rows in a table. When it is counting column values, you can combine it with DISTINCT to produce a count of the different values in a given column.

Counting Values   We could use COUNT, for example, to count the salespeople currently listing orders in the Orders table (the output is shown in Figure 8.12):

```
SELECT COUNT(DISTINCT snum)
    FROM Orders;
```

If we had not specified DISTINCT, we would have gotten a count of all rows that had non-NULL snum values. This would be a count of the number of orders for which any salesperson was credited, which is a different question from the number of salespeople.

FIGURE 8.12:
Counting column values

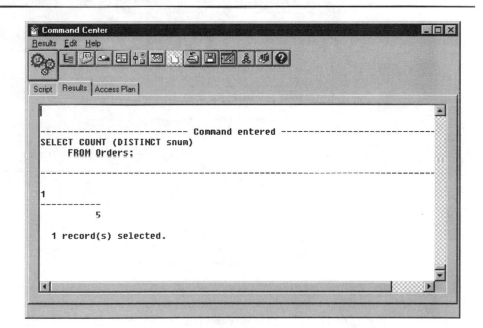

Notice in the above example that we placed DISTINCT, followed by the name of the column it is being applied to, in parentheses, not immediately after SELECT as we have seen DISTINCT used before. You can select multiple COUNTs of DISTINCT columns in a single query, and you can mix DISTINCT and non-DISTINCT aggregates.

You can use DISTINCT in this way with any aggregate function, but you most often use it with COUNT. With MAX and MIN, it simply has no effect, and with SUM and AVG, you usually want to include repeated values, because these legitimately affect the total and the average of all column values.

Counting Rows   To count the total rows in a table, use the COUNT function with an asterisk in place of a column name, as in the following example, the output of which is shown in Figure 8.13:

```
SELECT COUNT(*)
    FROM Customers;
```

FIGURE 8.13:
Counting rows instead
of values

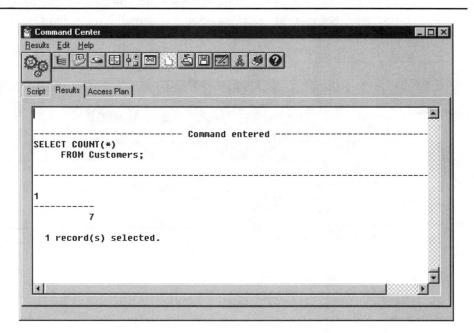

COUNT with the asterisk includes both NULLs and duplicates, so you cannot use DISTINCT. For this reason, it can produce a higher number than the COUNT of a particular column, which eliminates all rows that have NULL data in that column and may also eliminate duplicates.

Including Duplicates in Aggregate Functions   Aggregate functions can also take the argument ALL, which is placed before the column name, like

DISTINCT, but means the opposite: to include duplicates. The differences between ALL and * when used with COUNT are as follows:

- ALL still takes a column name as an argument.

- ALL will not count NULL values.

Since * is the only argument that includes NULLs and it is used only with COUNT, functions other than COUNT disregard NULLs in any case. The following statement will COUNT the non-NULL rating columns in the Customers table (including repeats):

```
SELECT COUNT(ALL rating)
     FROM Customers;
```

Aggregates Built on Expressions

Until now, you have used aggregate functions with single columns as arguments. You can now also use aggregate functions with arguments that consist of scalar expressions involving one or more columns. (If you do this, DISTINCT is not allowed.) We will cover expressions more thoroughly in the next chapter. Just to give you a taste of using expressions, however, suppose you wanted to represent the commission values as percentages rather than decimals. You would simply multiply them by 100, of course. If you wanted to find the average commission and express it as a percentage, you could use the following query, the output of which is shown in Figure 8.14:

```
SELECT AVG(comm * 100)
     FROM Salespeople;
```

The preceding query was phrased to illustrate the use of expressions within aggregate functions. As it happens, however, that is not always the best place to put them. It would probably be more efficient to write

```
AVG(comm) * 100
```

than to write

```
AVG(comm * 100)
```

because the latter only has to do the mathematical calculation once. Although it is conceivable that your DBMS will be clever enough to figure this out and execute the second version as though it were written like the first, don't count on it.

FIGURE 8.14:
An aggregate built on a value expression

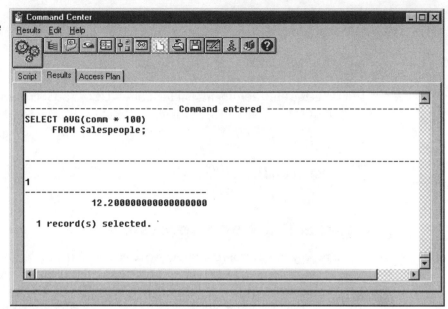

The GROUP BY Clause

The GROUP BY clause allows you to define a subset of the values in a particular column and apply an aggregate function to the subset. The subset is a group defined as having the values in some column other than the one being aggregated in common. For example, suppose you wanted to find the largest order taken by each salesperson. You could do a separate query for each salesperson, selecting the MAX amt from the Orders table for each snum value. GROUP BY, however, lets you put it all in one statement. You group the query by the snum values and then calculate the MAX separately for each such group. Here is the code to achieve this:

```
SELECT snum, MAX(amt)
      FROM Orders
      GROUP BY snum;
```

The output for this query is shown in Figure 8.15.

FIGURE 8.15:
Finding maximum amounts
for each salesperson

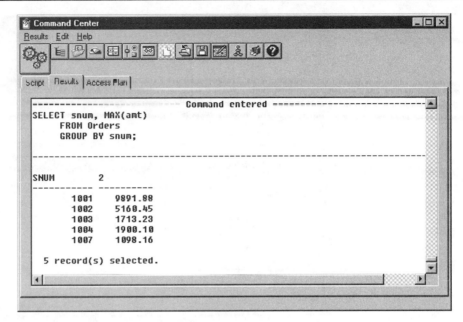

```
SELECT snum, MAX(amt)
    FROM Orders
    GROUP BY snum;
```

As you can see, GROUP BY applies the aggregate functions independently to a series of groups that are defined as having a column value in common. In this case, each group consists of all the rows with the same snum value, and the MAX function is applied separately to each such group. This means the column to which GROUP BY applies has, by definition, only one value per output group, as do the aggregate functions. The result is a compatibility that allows aggregates and columns to be combined in this way.

You can also use GROUP BY with multiple columns. To refine the above example further, suppose you wanted to see the largest order taken by each salesperson on each date. To do this, you would group the Orders table by the combination of date and salesperson, and apply the MAX function to each group, like this:

```
SELECT snum, odate, MAX(amt)
    FROM Orders
    GROUP BY snum, odate;
```

The output for this query is shown in Figure 8.16. Of course, empty groups—that is, dates when the current salesperson had no orders—are not shown.

FIGURE 8.16:

Finding each salesperson's
largest orders for each day

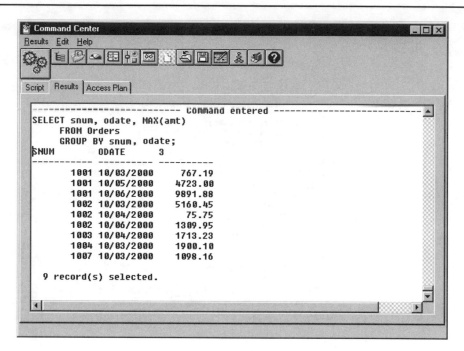

The HAVING Clause

Suppose, in the previous example, you had wanted to see just the maximum
purchases over $3,000.00. You cannot use aggregate functions in a WHERE
clause (unless you use a subquery, as explained later), because predicates are
evaluated in terms of a single row, whereas aggregate functions are evaluated
in terms of groups of rows. This means you could *not* do something like the
following:

```
SELECT snum, odate, MAX(amt)
    FROM Orders
    WHERE MAX(amt) > 3000.00
    GROUP BY snum, odate;
```

In a strict ISO interpretation of SQL, this query would be rejected. It is awkward
and illogical anyway: the WHERE clause is for filtering rows *before* they are formed
into groups by GROUP BY. To filter the groups—for example, to see the maximum
purchases over $3,000.00—you would use the HAVING clause. The HAVING clause
defines criteria used to eliminate certain groups from the output, just as the WHERE
clause does for individual rows. The correct statement would be the following.

```
SELECT snum, odate, MAX(amt)
    FROM Orders
    GROUP BY snum, odate
    HAVING MAX (amt) > 3000.00;
```

The output for this query is shown in Figure 8.17.

FIGURE 8.17:
Eliminating groups of aggregate values

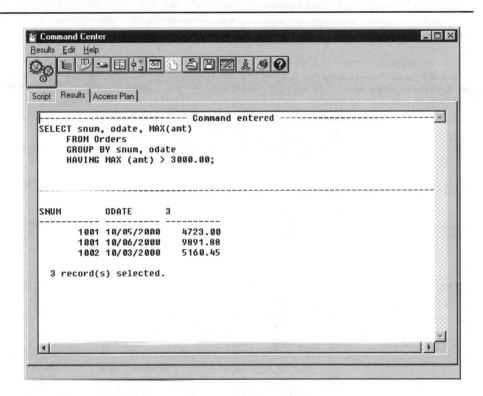

Arguments to the HAVING clause follow the same rules as those to the SELECT clause of a command using GROUP BY. They must have a single value per output group. The following statement would be illegal:

```
SELECT snum, MAX(amt)
    FROM Orders
    GROUP BY snum
    HAVING odate = '10/03/2000';
```

The HAVING clause cannot reference the odate column because it can have (and indeed does have) more than one value per output group. Hence, for a given group, the odate can be both equal and unequal to '10/03/2000', depending on the group member with which you are concerned. To avoid this situation, the HAVING clause must reference only aggregates themselves and columns chosen by GROUP BY. Here is the correct way to state the above query (the output is shown in Figure 8.18):

```
SELECT snum, MAX(amt)
    FROM Orders
    WHERE odate = '10/03/2000'
    GROUP BY snum;
```

FIGURE 8.18:
Each salesperson's maximum for October 3

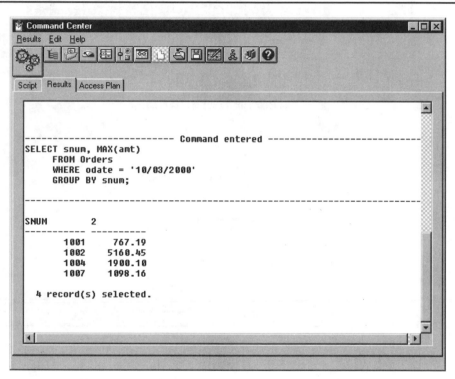

As we mentioned, HAVING can take only arguments that have a single value per output group. In practice, references to aggregate functions are the most common, but columns chosen by GROUP BY are also permissible. For instance, we could look at the largest orders for Serres and Rifkin:

```
SELECT snum, MAX(amt)
    FROM Orders
    GROUP BY snum
    HAVING snum IN (1002, 1007);
```

The output for this query is shown in Figure 8.19.

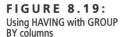

FIGURE 8.19:
Using HAVING with GROUP
BY columns

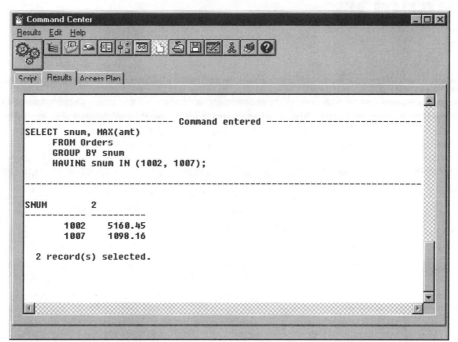

Don't Nest Aggregates

In a strict interpretation of ISO SQL, you cannot take an aggregate of an aggregate. Suppose you wanted to find out which day had the higher total amount ordered. If you tried to do this

```
SELECT odate, MAX( SUM(amt))
    FROM Orders
    GROUP BY odate;
```

your statement would probably be rejected. (Some implementations don't enforce this restriction, which is advantageous because nested aggregates can be useful, even if they are somewhat problematic.) In the above command, for example, SUM is to be applied to each odate group and MAX to all of the groups, producing a single value for all of the groups. Yet, the GROUP BY clause implies that there should be one row of output for each odate group.

Summary

Now you can construct predicates in terms of relationships specially defined by SQL. You can search for values in a certain range (BETWEEN) or in an enumerated set (IN), or you can search for character values that match text within parameters that you define (LIKE). You have also learned some things about special functionality that SQL needs to deal with missing data—a reality of the database world—and the NULL values used to represent it. You can extract or exclude NULLs from your output by using the IS NULL (or IS NOT NULL) operator.

You are also able to use queries a little differently by deriving, rather than simply locating, data. This very powerful tool goes beyond the aggregate functions introduced in this chapter. It means that you may not necessarily have to keep track of certain information if you can formulate a query to derive it. A query will give you up-to-the-minute results, whereas a table of totals or averages will be only as good as the last time it was updated. This is not to suggest that aggregate functions can completely supplant the need to track such information independently, but they frequently can, and it is better when they do.

You can apply these aggregates to groups of values defined by a GROUP BY clause. These groups have a column value in common, and they can reside within other groups that have a column value in common. Meanwhile, predicates are still used to determine to which rows the aggregate function is applied. Combined, these features make it possible for you to produce aggregates based on tightly defined subsets of the values in the column. Then you can define another condition to exclude certain of the resulting groups with the HAVING clause.

Now that you have become adept with many facets of how a query produces values, we will show you, in the next chapter, some things that you can do with the values it produces.

Putting SQL to Work

1. Write two queries that will produce all orders taken on October 3 or 4, 2000.

2. Write a query that will produce all of the customers whose names begin with a letter from A to G.

3. Write a query that selects all customers whose names begin with C, either upper- or lowercase.

4. Write a query that selects all orders save those with zeros or NULLs in the amt (amount) column.

5. Write a query that counts all orders for October 3.

6. Write a query that counts the number of different non-NULL city values in the Customers table.

7. Write a query that selects each customer's smallest order.

8. Write a query that selects the first customer, in alphabetical order, whose name begins with G.

9. Write a query that selects the highest rating in each city.

10. Write a query that counts the number of salespeople registering orders for each day. (If a salesperson has more than one order on a given day, he or she should be counted only once.)

CHAPTER

NINE

9

Working with Expressions

- Using Value Expressions in the SELECT Clause

- More Advanced Uses of Value Expressions

- Ordering Output by Column Values

This chapter will extend your ability to work with the output produced by queries. You will learn how to insert text and constants among the selected columns, how to use the selected columns in mathematical expressions, whose results will then become the output, how to convert datatypes, how to select conditionally among a set of candidate values, how to work with entire rows and tables as single values, and how to make the values you output emerge in a specified order. This last feature includes the ability to order your output by any column or any values derived from a column.

Most of these expressions are not limited to queries but can be used wherever value expressions are used in statements like UPDATE and INSERT as well.

Using Value Expressions in the SELECT Clause

Many SQL-based databases provide special features that allow you to refine the output from your queries. Naturally, these vary greatly from product to product, and discussion of them is beyond our scope here. However, there are some standard features that allow you to do more than simply output column values and aggregate data.

Expressions among Selected Columns

Let's suppose you want to perform simple numeric computations on the data to put it in a form more appropriate to your needs. SQL allows you to place scalar expressions and constants among the selected columns. These expressions can supplement or replace columns in the SELECT clauses, and they can involve one or more selected columns themselves. For example, you might consider it desirable to present your salespeople's commissions as percentages rather than decimal numbers. Simple enough:

```
SELECT snum, sname, city, comm * 100
    FROM Salespeople;
```

The output from this query is shown in Figure 9.1.

FIGURE 9.1:

Putting an expression in
your query

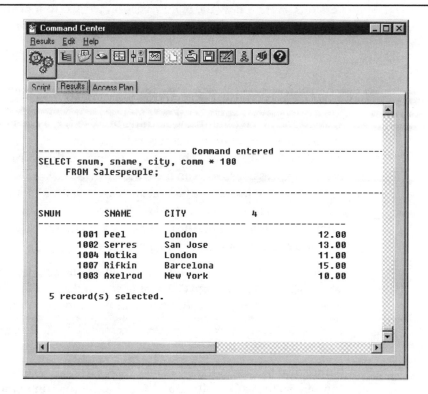

Naming Expression Columns in Output

The last column output by the preceding example has no name as such. Its name
is not properly *comm*, because its content is not the same as the comm column
from which its content is derived. The columns output by the SELECT clause are
called *output columns*. As this example shows, output columns are not necessarily
table columns. We will refer to columns that are not directly taken from tables as
expression columns. Expression columns do not automatically have names. It is up
to the implementation to label such columns. There are two commonly used possibilities: either the column is unlabeled, or it is labeled with the expression that
produced it, in this case comm * 100.

SQL92 includes a way for you to provide names for columns in output by including an AS clause. Some implementations had previously supported this feature
with alternative syntax and may therefore still use their previous version or both

versions. Here is how the SQL92 version works. To repeat the above example, labeling the new column "percentage", you would enter the following query:

```
SELECT snum, sname, city, comm * 100 AS percentage
    FROM Salespeople;
```

Putting Text in Your Query Output

The letter *A*, when signifying nothing but itself, is a constant, just as the number *1* is. You have the ability to insert constants in the SELECT clause of a query, including text. However, character constants, unlike numeric constants, cannot be used in expressions. You can have the expression 1 + 2 in your SELECT clause, but you cannot use an expression such as 'A' + 'B'. This restriction is reasonable if you keep in mind that *A* and *B* here are simply letters, not variables or symbols for anything besides themselves. Nonetheless, the ability to insert text in the output from your queries is quite handy.

You could refine the previous example by marking the commissions as percentages with the percent sign (%). Doing so enables you to put such items as symbols and comments in the output, as in the following example:

```
SELECT snum, sname, city, '%', comm * 100 AS percentage
    FROM Salespeople;
```

Notice also the use of the AS clause. This provides a column name for the derived column, so that there will be a header for the column in the output. If you neglect to provide such a header, your system will typically default either to a blank header or to the expression, in this case, comm * 100.

You can use this same feature to label output with inserted comments. You must remember, however, that the same comment will be printed with every row of the output, not simply once for the table. Therefore, this feature is seldom useful for more than display niceties. Suppose you are generating output for a report that indicates the number of orders for each day. You could label your output (see Figure 9.2) by forming the query as follows:

```
SELECT 'For', odate, ', there are',
    COUNT(DISTINCT onum), 'orders.'
    FROM Orders
    GROUP BY odate;
```

FIGURE 9.2:

Combining text, column values, and aggregates

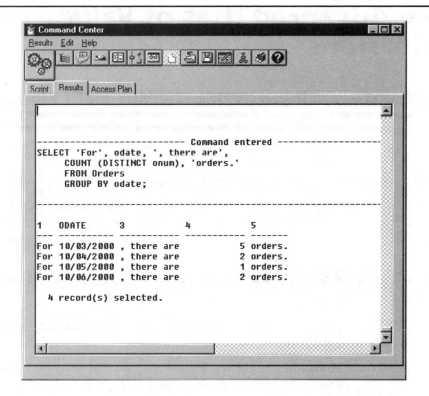

```
-------------------------------- Command entered --------------------
SELECT 'For', odate, ', there are',
       COUNT (DISTINCT onum), 'orders.'
       FROM Orders
       GROUP BY odate;


1   ODATE      3          4          5
--- ---------- ---------- ---------- -------
For 10/03/2000 , there are          5 orders.
For 10/04/2000 , there are          2 orders.
For 10/05/2000 , there are          1 orders.
For 10/06/2000 , there are          2 orders.

  4 record(s) selected.
```

We cannot correct the grammar of the output for October 5 without making this query much more complicated than it is. As you can see, a single unvarying comment for each row of a table can be helpful but has limitations. It is sometimes more elegant and useful to produce a single comment for the output as a whole or different comments for different rows.

The various programs using SQL often provide tools, such as report generators or form interfaces, that are designed to format and refine output. Embedded SQL can also exploit the formatting capabilities of the language in which it is embedded. SQL itself is primarily concerned with operating on data. Its output is essentially information, and a program using SQL can often take that information and put it in a more attractive form. Doing so, however, is beyond the scope of SQL itself.

More Advanced Uses of Value Expressions

SQL92 provides a number of more sophisticated forms and uses of value expressions. Basically, value expressions in SQL92 fall into the following categories:

- Numeric expressions are mathematical expressions involving EXACT or APPROXIMATE NUMERIC datatypes. We have already seen some examples of these.

- String expressions are specific to the manipulation of text or binary string datatypes. We have seen examples of these as well. SQL92 provides for a rather rich set of string expressions, not all of which are widely implemented as yet. For more information on these, see Chapter 29 under "String Value Functions".

- Datetime expressions are specific to the manipulation of DATETIME datatypes.

- Interval expressions are specific to the manipulation of INTERVAL datatypes.

- Value functions are special expressions that have values set by the DBMS. They fall into the following categories:

  - User value functions, which represent database users

  - Datetime value functions, which give system-defined values such as the current date

- CAST expressions are expressions that convert one datatype to another.

- CASE expressions are expressions that can have one of several values depending on the values of some predicates. This is similar to the CASE logic, or multiple uses of the IF…THEN logic, found in many programming languages. Note, however, that conditional expressions are still value expressions. That is to say, they are used in place of values within SQL statements, rather than controlling a flow of execution from one statement to another.

- Row and table value constructors are expressions that enable you to directly specify a set of values that will function as a row or a table within a SQL statement. These effectively function as subqueries, and we defer discussion of them until we cover subqueries.

These expressions come into play at varying levels of SQL92 conformance, although some of them, such as user value functions, have been supported by many implementations regardless of the standard for some time. We will cover them here, so that you will have all the possibilities (save row and table constructors) outlined in one place.

You have seen value expressions used in the SELECT clause of queries. In the older versions of SQL, this was pretty much the only option. In SQL92, however, you can use a value expression most anywhere that you could use a simple value of the same datatype and structure (for row and table value constructors).

Datetime and Interval Expressions

Since datetime expressions involve the use of INTERVALs, we will discuss the two together. There are a number of expressions you can use that are specific to the DATETIME datatypes. Those datatypes are as follows:

- DATE represents a date, such as 12/16/99.

- TIME represents a time, such as 4:26:55.

- TIMESTAMP represents a combination of date and time, such as 12/16/99 4:26:55.

NOTE　Some implementations use the term "timestamp" differently, to mean an indication of the precise time when an event occurred, or even as a term for optimistic locking (see Chapter 17), since the latter inevitably involves timestamps.

Note that the datatype simply determines the type of content the column contains. It does not determine how that content is represented. Most DBMSs give you a choice of several kinds of display, such as 12/28/02, December 28, 2002, or Dec-28-2002. A corollary of this is that you cannot tell whether the date is represented internally with two or four digits simply by seeing how it is displayed.

INTERVALs represent periods of time between DATETIME values, for example, one week, one hour, or three days, ten minutes, and four seconds. Using INTERVALs, you can add and subtract DATETIME values intelligently. You can also apply NUMERIC operations to INTERVALs (such as multiplying a number of weeks by two). INTERVALs must deal with the somewhat mutable character of dates. A month can have any number of days from 28 to 31, and the INTERVAL value of a month must change dynamically when used to reflect this reality. Because of such complexities, there are a number of restrictions to how INTERVALs can be used, which are outlined in Chapter 29 under "Datatypes". What we offer here is a brief overview of INTERVALs.

INTERVALs look much like DATETIME values. Both DATETIME and INTERVAL types, when used as literals, are delimited with single quotes and preceded by the name of the datatype. For example, here is the INTERVAL 4 years, 11 months:

```
INTERVAL YEAR TO MONTH '4/11'
```

(We do not end the preceding expression with a semicolon because it is not a SQL statement. It is merely a value expression you would use within a SQL statement.) So, if you wanted to specify a date 4 years and 11 months past a specified date, you could do it as follows:

```
DATE '2/4/98' + INTERVAL YEAR TO MONTH '4/11'
```

You can also derive INTERVALs by adding and subtracting DATETIME values. Here is an example:

```
DATE '2/4/98' - DATE '2/2/98'
```

This expression would produce an INTERVAL value of days that would be written as follows:

```
INTERVAL DAY '2'
```

Value Functions

Value functions are functions built into SQL that produce values based on the context in which the issuing statement is executed. They fall into the following categories:

- User value functions identify a user whose identity is relevant to the question at hand.

- Datetime value functions provide context information such as the current date and time.

The purpose of the user value functions is to identify the *user* issuing a statement. For example, suppose you have an HTML form that is dynamically generated and used to update the database. You may want to fill this form with default values, depending on who the user is. This gets a little more complicated than it would seem at first glance, however. Let's look at these three variations:

- SESSION_USER is the database user identified in the CONNECT statement that created the current session.

- CURRENT_USER is the user whose privileges actually determine what can or cannot be done. By default and usually, this is the same as the SESSION_ USER, but there are exceptions that are a bit complicated to go into now. See Chapter 29 under "Authorization IDs".

- SYSTEM_USER is the OS user.

You can refer to any of these users in a SQL statement and get a text string containing the current value for that parameter.

Datatype Conversion (CAST) Expressions

It's possible to convert one datatype to another within a SQL statement. Doing so, of course, does not affect the datatype of the data in the database; it just changes the datatype for the purposes of the current SQL statement. SQL can, in fact, perform some kinds of conversion automatically. The primary reasons to change datatypes are:

- To make comparisons that would otherwise be invalid.

- To control how a conversion that could be done automatically is actually performed.

- To produce a datatype that can be properly handled in another language, for example in Embedded SQL, or in an interface.

You convert datatypes using the CAST expression. Here is an example:

```
CAST ('12/03/2001' AS DATE)
```

This expression coverts the given text string into a date. Why didn't we just declare it a date in the first place? Usually, you would use this expression with variables or values retrieved from the database, rather than with literals. Suppose we were developing an Intranet application that would use material from our database. Everything in an HTML page is text. Therefore, depending on how we went about creating our application (there are innumerable possibilities), we might need to convert text to other datatypes that SQL recognizes or vice versa. Here is a SQL statement that converts two numeric columns from the Orders table into text:

```
SELECT CAST(onum AS CHAR), CAST(amt AS CHAR)
    FROM Orders;
```

For more information, including a table of valid datatype conversions, see "CAST Expressions" in Chapter 29.

Conditional (CASE) Expressions

A conditional expression can have any one of several values, depending on which of several predicates is satisfied or on which of several values is matched. Here is the syntax:

```
{ CASE value expression
{ WHEN value expression
THEN   { value expression | NULL } }...
| { WHEN predicate
THEN   { value expression | NULL } }...
[ ELSE { value expression | NULL } ]
END }
| { NULLIF (value expression, value expression) }
| { COALESCE (value expression.,...) }
```

Stated less formally, the CASE expression has three forms, each of which begins with a keyword: CASE, NULLIF, and COALESCE. Actually, there are four forms, because there are two variations on the CASE form, one using value expressions and one using predicates. The value expression form of CASE works like this: suppose we had made a mistake and realized that Peal's name was not spelled the way we had thought. We should, of course, fix this in the database, but if we are not privileged enough users to update the contents of the Salespeople table but only to display it, we cannot do this ourselves. To keep Peal from spotting the goof, we could use a line like this in a query:

```
SELECT CASE sname WHEN 'Peel' THEN 'Peal' END
    FROM Salespeople
    WHERE snum = 1001;
```

This expression goes through the Salespeople table and finds Peel's row. The CASE statement then checks the sname value of each selected row (in this case, there is only one, but this need not be so). If it finds the sname is `'Peel'`, the value of the expression is `'Peal'`, so our substitution is effected in the output, though the data in the table is still incorrect. What would happen if it found a row with a different sname? Although in this case we would probably want it to leave the sname alone, the truth is that it would set it to NULL (in the output; again the value in the database would not be affected). To get around this problem, you could do the following:

```
SELECT CASE sname WHEN 'Peel' THEN 'Peal' ELSE sname END
    FROM Salespeople
    WHERE snum = 1001;
```

Here is a predicate form version that does the same thing:

```
SELECT CASE WHEN sname = 'Peel' THEN 'Peal' ELSE sname END
    FROM Salespeople
    WHERE snum = 1001;
```

Notice that with the predicate form, you need not and do not put a value directly after the keyword CASE. The predicate version is also more complex in that it is based on three-valued logic (see Chapter 7), which you must keep in mind. On the other hand, you can perform much more complex operations with a string of predicates that you can by simply attempting to match an expression.

Regardless of which form of CASE you use, the following rules apply:

- You cannot mix the two forms. A given CASE expression is either all value expression form or all predicate form.

- Either form can take any number of WHEN...THEN clauses. These are traversed in order, and the first one that satisfies the test determines the value. If you have more than one WHEN condition that fulfill the criteria, this is not a problem, but be aware that only the first one in the sequence counts.

- An optional ELSE clause may follow all the WHEN...THEN clauses. If the ELSE clause is not included, ELSE NULL is implied.

- Finally, the entire CASE form is terminated with the keyword END.

NULLIF is a simple variation on CASE. It takes two values as arguments. If the two are the same, it produces a NULL; otherwise, it produces the first value of the two. Here is an example:

```
SELECT NULLIF(snum, 1001), sname
    FROM Salespeople;
```

For Peel's row, `snum = 1001`, this query would produce a NULL and the name `'Peel'`. For other rows, it would produce the snum and matching sname.

COALESCE is somewhat similar. It traverses a list of values and produces the first one that is not NULL. If all are NULL, it produces NULL. Note that all the values used in a COALESCE expression must be comparable, though they need not be the exact same datatype. Rules determining which datatypes are comparable are given in Chapter 29 under "Datatypes". Here is an example:

```
SELECT COALESCE(snum, cnum)
    FROM Orders;
```

If snum is not NULL, COALESCE equals the value of snum. Else, if cnum is not NULL, COALESCE equals the value of cnum. Otherwise, it is NULL.

A good use of COALESCE is to generate values where NULLs are found. Suppose you were writing some code to insert orders into the Orders table. You derive values for the various columns from user input, except for onum. The value for onum is the previous highest value plus one. How would you insert the first row? When there is no previous highest value—i.e., when there are no rows in the table—the MAX value is NULL. However, NULL + 1 is NULL, not 1, whereas 1 is the starting value you want. Many DBMSs provide mechanisms called *sequences* to deal with this (common) situation, but if you had to do it by hand, you could do the following:

```
INSERT INTO Orders (onum, odate, amt, cnum, snum)
    VALUES (1 + COALESCE(SELECT MAX(onum) FROM Orders, 0),
            '10/14/2000', 42.66, 2002, 1001);
```

COALESCE here will equal the highest current onum value in the Orders table, unless there is none such, in which case it will coalesce to its second value, which is 0. Add 1 to COALESCE and you have the next logical onum.

Ordering Output by Column Values

As we have pointed out, tables are unordered sets, and the data that comes out of them does not necessarily emerge in any particular sequence. SQL uses the ORDER BY statement to allow you to impose an order on your output. This statement orders the query output according to the values in one or more selected columns. Multiple columns are ordered one within another, just as with GROUP BY, and you can specify ascending (ASC) or descending (DESC) for each column. Ascending is the default.

Let's look at our Orders table arranged by customer number (notice the values in the cnum column):

```
SELECT *
    FROM Orders
    ORDER BY cnum DESC;
```

The output is shown in Figure 9.3.

FIGURE 9.3:

Ordering output by a
descending column

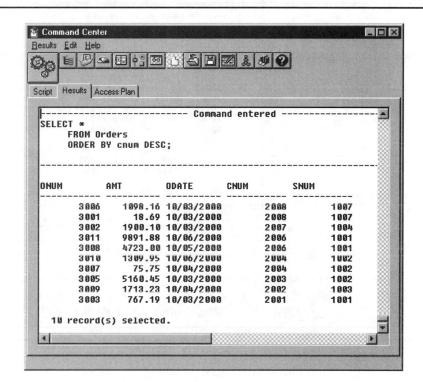

Ordering by Multiple Columns

We could also order the table by another column, amt for example, within the cnum ordering (the output is shown in Figure 9.4):

```
SELECT *
    FROM Orders
    ORDER BY cnum DESC, amt DESC;
```

FIGURE 9.4:

Ordering output by
multiple columns

You can use ORDER BY in this manner with any number of columns at once. Notice that, in all cases, the columns being ordered are among the columns selected. This is an ISO requirement that most, but not all, systems enforce. The following statement, for instance, would be illegal:

```
SELECT cname, city
    FROM Customers
    ORDER BY cnum;
```

Since cnum was not a selected column, ORDER BY cannot find it to use for ordering the output. Even if your system does allow this, the significance of the ordering would not be evident from the output, so including all columns used in the ORDER BY clause is usually advisable.

Ordering Aggregate Groups

You can also use ORDER BY with GROUP BY to order groups. If so, ORDER BY always follows the GROUP BY and HAVING clauses. Here's an example from the last chapter with an added ORDER BY clause. In that example, the output was grouped, but the order of the groups was arbitrary; now we force the groups to be placed in sequence:

```
SELECT snum, odate, MAX(amt)
    FROM Orders
    GROUP BY snum, odate
    ORDER BY snum;
```

The output is shown in Figure 9.5. Since we did not specify ascending or descending order, ascending is used by default.

FIGURE 9.5:

Ordering by a group

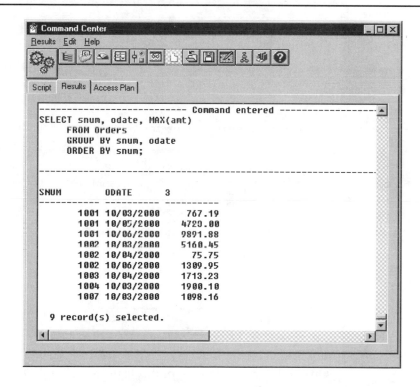

Ordering Output by Column Number

In place of column names, you can use numbers to indicate the columns being used to order the output. These numbers will refer not to the order of the columns in the table, but to their order in the output. In other words, the first column mentioned in the SELECT clause is, for the purposes of ORDER BY, column number 1, regardless of where it is found in the table. For example, you can use the following statement to see certain columns of the Salespeople table, ordered in descending order of commission (the output is shown in Figure 9.6):

```
SELECT sname, comm
     FROM Salespeople
     ORDER BY 2 DESC;
```

FIGURE 9.6:

Ordering using numbers

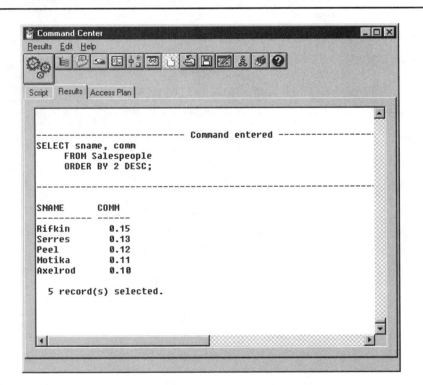

One of the main purposes of this feature of the ORDER BY clause is to enable you to use ORDER BY with unlabeled output columns as well as table columns. Columns resulting from aggregate functions, constants, or expressions in the SELECT clause of a query are perfectly usable with ORDER BY, provided that you refer to them by number. For example, let's count the orders of each of our salespeople and output the results in descending order:

```
SELECT snum, COUNT(onum)
    FROM Orders
    GROUP BY snum
    ORDER BY 2 DESC;
```

In this case, you should use the column number, because an output column has no name; you should not use the aggregate function itself. In strict ISO SQL, the following query would not work, although some systems relax this requirement:

```
SELECT snum, COUNT(DISTINCT onum)
    FROM Orders
    GROUP BY snum
    ORDER BY COUNT(DISTINCT onum) DESC;
```

Using ORDER BY with NULLs

If the column that you are using to order your output contains NULL values, they will either follow or precede every other value in the column. ISO has left this option up to the individual program. A given program uses one or the other form.

Summary

In this chapter, you have learned how to make your queries do more than produce column values or aggregate function data from a table. You can use columns in expressions. For example, you can multiply a numeric column by 10 or even multiply it by another numeric column. In addition, your ability to put constants, including characters, in your output allows you to put text directly in a query and have it output with the table data. This enables you to label or explain your output in various ways. You can use special functions to reference the current user, date, or time and perform arithmetic using dates. You have learned how to use conditional value expressions and how to convert datatypes one to another.

You have also learned how to impose an order on your output. Even though the table itself remains unordered, the ORDER BY clause enables you to control the order of the rows of a given query's output. Query output can be in ascending or descending order, and columns can be nested one within another.

Now that you have seen what you can do with the output from a query based on a single table, it is time to move on to the advanced query features. In Chapter 10, you will learn how to query any number of tables in a single statement, forging relationships between them as you do so.

Putting SQL to Work

1. Assume each salesperson has a 12 percent commission. Write a query on the Orders table that will produce the order number, the salesperson number, and the amount of the salesperson's commission for that order.

2. Write a query on the Customers table that will find the highest rating in each city. Put the output in this form:

   ```
   For the city (city), the highest rating is: (rating).
   ```

3. Write a query that lists customers in descending order of rating. Output the rating column first, followed by the customer's name and number.

4. Write a query that totals the orders for each day and places the results in descending order.

5. Write a query that shows the city of all Paris customers as Brussels but leaves all the other customers listed with their correct cities.

6. Write an UPDATE statement that increases the ratings of all customers by 100. Assume that customers can have NULL ratings, in which case their ratings should be set to 100.

CHAPTER

TEN

10

Querying Multiple Tables at Once

- Joining Tables

- Joining a Table to Itself

- More Complex Uses of Joins

Up until now, each query we have examined has been based on a single table. In this chapter, you will learn how to query any number of tables with a single statement. This is an extremely powerful feature because it not only combines output from multiple tables, but also expresses the relationships between them and can be used to construct relationships that were not originally built into the database design. You will learn about the various forms these relationships can take, as well as how to define and use them to answer specific needs.

Joining Tables

One of the most important features of SQL queries is their ability to define relationships between multiple tables and draw information from the tables in terms of these relationships, all within a single statement. This kind of operation is called a *join*, and it is one of the powerhouse operations of SQL. As we showed in Chapter 1, you break related information down into separate tables when you represent it in a relational database structure. This is part of what is called *normalization*. Joins are the technique you use to reconstruct those relationships on the fly. Joins, however, are logical operations, like other SQL statements. They do not rely on FOREIGN KEY constraints or the other mechanisms by which the integrity of normalized data is maintained. Therefore, you can also use joins to find kinds of patterns in your data other than those you deliberately built in the structure of the schema. With joins, you can directly relate the information in any number of tables and thus are able to make connections between disparate pieces of data.

In a join, the tables are listed in the FROM clause of the query, separated by commas. The predicate of the query can refer to any column of any table joined and, therefore, can be used to make connections between them. Usually, the predicate will compare the values in columns of different tables to determine whether a WHERE condition is met.

Table and Column Names

The name of a column of a table actually consists of the table name followed by a dot and then the column name. Here are some examples:

```
Salespeople.snum
Customers.city
Orders.odate
```

Previously, you have been able to omit the table names because you were querying only a single table at a time, and SQL is intelligent enough to assume the proper table-name prefix by default in this case. Even when you query multiple tables, you will still be able to omit the table names, provided that all of the columns in the various tables have different names. But such is not always the case. For example, we have two sample tables with columns called "city." If we were to join them (as we will momentarily), we would have to say Salespeople.city or Customers.city, so that the DBMS could know which one we meant.

Making a Natural Join

The most common kind of join is called a *natural join*. Natural joins are so named because they express relationships that already exist in the structure of the database. You may recall from Chapter 1 that when we design a database schema, we often put related information about an entity in separate tables. For example, we put the telephone numbers of our clients in a different table than the rest of the information we had about them. Later we showed you how to use the CREATE TABLE statement to define foreign and parent keys that embody the relationships between the various tables. Now we will show you the SQL operation used to rejoin what was put asunder for the sake of normalizing the database structure.

For example, to show the names of all customers matched with the salespeople serving them, we would use this query:

```
SELECT Customers.cname, Salespeople.sname
    FROM Customers, Salespeople
    WHERE Salespeople.snum = Customers.snum;
```

The output of this query is shown in Figure 10.1.

What SQL basically does in a join is take the tables joined and examine every combination of rows possible, taking one row from each of the two (or more) joined tables (this operation is known as a Cartesian product, after Rene Descartes). These combinations are then tested against the predicate, just as individual rows are tested in a single table query. In the preceding example, the DBMS first took the row of salesperson Peel from the Salespeople table and combined it with each row of the Customers table, one at a time. If a combination produced values that made the predicate TRUE—in this case, if the snum field of a Customer table row were 1001, the same as Peel's—the DBMS selected the requested values from that combination for output. It then did the same thing for every other salesperson in the Salespeople table. Formally speaking, the join creates a Cartesian product of the two tables and then selects from the result based on the predicate. (If you don't understand Cartesian products, don't worry about it, but such an understanding may clarify the logic of the operation.) Even though you need to include the table name only when the column name by itself is ambiguous, it is often a good idea to include all table names in joins for the sake of clarity and consistency. Despite this suggestion, we will, in our examples, generally use table names only when necessary, so that it will be clear when they are needed and when they are not.

FIGURE 10.1:

Joining salespeople to their customers

Our preceding example also illustrates a join in which the columns used to determine the predicate of the query—in this case, the snum columns of both tables—have been omitted from the output, which is perfectly all right. The output shows which customers are serviced by which salespeople; the snum values that constitute the link are not, in themselves, relevant here. If you do omit such columns, however, you should make sure the output is self-explanatory.

Making an Unnatural Join

Since the whole idea of relational databases was conceived with them in mind, natural joins are far the most common kind. However, *unnatural joining* is also an option (there is no standard term for "other than natural" joins, but the obvious one may seem a bit amusing). This means that you can find relationships based on the data content rather than the database design. Suppose you had not yet assigned your customers to salespeople and you wanted to match your salespeople to your customers according to the city in which they lived so that you could make the assignment. To see all the combinations of salespeople and customers who shared a city, you would need to take each salesperson and search the Customers table for all customers in the same city as that salesperson (or you could do the reverse and search for salespeople who matched customers). You could do this by entering the following statement (the output is shown in Figure 10.2):

```
SELECT Customers.cname, Salespeople.sname,
      Salespeople.city
   FROM Salespeople, Customers
   WHERE Salespeople.city = Customers.city;
```

FIGURE 10.2:

An unnatural join

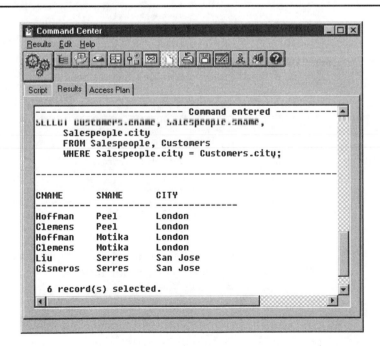

Compound and Join Predicates

Suppose in the preceding example that we were interested only in customers and salespeople in the cities of Barcelona or London. In this case, we would modify the query as follows:

```
SELECT Customers.cname, Salespeople.sname,
       Salespeople.city
       FROM Salespeople, Customers
       WHERE Salespeople.city IN ('London', 'Barcelona')
       AND Salespeople.city = Customers.city;
```

The output of this query is shown in Figure 10.3.

FIGURE 10.3:

A join with a compound predicate

The compound predicate consists of a join predicate, `Salespeople.city = Customers.city`, and a conventional predicate, `Salespeople.city IN ('London', 'Barcelona')`. Notice that we put the conventional predicate first for the sake of efficiency. Because joins involve combining many rows, they can be slow to execute. By eliminating irrelevant data before the join is performed, we lessen the size of the resulting join. In practice, this may or may not make a difference. Since performance is so important for many database uses, DBMSs include an *optimizer* that attempts to find the most efficient way to execute a query regardless of how it is phrased. Optimizers are not perfect, however, so it still makes sense to try to phrase your queries with performance in mind. This is particularly the case with unnatural joins, because the DBMS expects to perform joins over foreign keys and therefore prepares for them. Ad hoc joins like this are unexpected and may take longer, so it is more likely to be useful to optimize them by hand. We will cover this subject in more detail in Chapter 23 of this book.

Equijoins and Non-equijoins

Joins that use predicates based on equalities are called *equijoins*. Our examples in this chapter up to now have all fallen into this category because the conditions in the WHERE clauses have all been based on equality expressions—for example, City = 'London' or Salespeople.snum = Orders.snum. Equijoins are the most common sort of join, but there are others. You can, in fact, use any of the SQL operators in a join. Here is an example of another kind of join (its output is shown in Figure 10.4):

```
SELECT sname, cname
    FROM Salespeople, Customers
    WHERE sname < cname
    AND rating < 200;
```

This statement is seldom useful. It produces all combinations of salesperson and customer names such that the former precedes the latter alphabetically and the latter has a rating of less than 200. Usually, you will not need to construct such complex relationships, and, for this reason, you will probably find equijoins to be the most useful, but it is good to be acquainted with the other possibilities. One area where obscure sorts of joins can come into play is what is called *data mining*. If you have a lot of information in your database, you can use ad hoc joins like this to find patterns, such as those used for demographic analysis.

FIGURE 10.4:

A join based on an inequality

OUTER Joins

An important issue concerns the possible incompleteness of joins. For example, suppose we added the following row to the Salespeople table:

Snum	Sname	City	Comm
1020	Wang	Bangkok	.11

Now suppose we wanted to see a list of our salespeople with each one's current orders listed. We could do this with a natural join of the Salespeople and Orders tables, as follows:

```
SELECT Salespeople.snum, onum, odate
FROM Salespeople, Orders
    WHERE Salespeople.snum = Orders.snum;
```

The results of this query are shown in Figure 10.5.

FIGURE 10.5:

A join excluding Wang

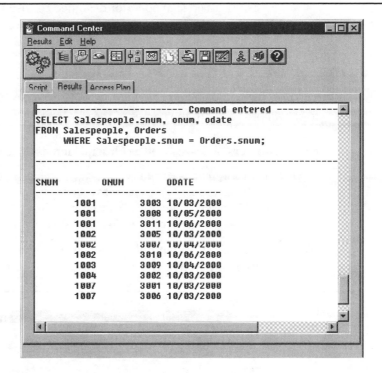

Our new salesperson, Wang, does not show up in the results because, being new, he has no orders yet. There is no row in the Orders table that uses his snum. In this a problem? It depends on which information we wanted. If we were interested in seeing only the current orders, along with their associated salespeople, then it is not. But if we had wanted a complete list of salespeople, including the orders for each, perhaps for use in a monthly report, this result would definitely be problematic. In the latter case, we want a result that lists all salespeople, along with their orders, if any. Such a query is called an *OUTER join*. A join like the above that does not include unmatched rows is called an *INNER join*. You have seen how INNER joins are done. How do you perform OUTER joins? Three approaches are in common usage:

- You can use a subquery with the EXISTS operator. We'll cover this in Chapter 12.

- You can combine two queries using the UNION operator. We'll cover this in Chapter 13.

- You can use a special operator designed for use with OUTER joins. We cover this in this chapter in the section "Special Join Operators."

Joins of More Than Two Tables

You can also construct queries joining more than two tables. Suppose we wanted to see all orders, with the names of the salesperson and customer for each. Since we want the names and not just the numbers, we have to look in the Salespeople and Customers tables, as well as Orders. Here is the code to do it:

```
SELECT sname, cname, onum
    FROM Salespeople, Customers, Orders
    WHERE Orders.snum = Salespeople.snum
        AND Orders.cnum = Customers.cnum;
```

Notice that this is still a natural join, since both of the join predicates connect foreign keys to their parents. The output from this query is shown in Figure 10.6.

FIGURE 10.6:

Joining three tables for complete order information

Here's a less common, double-join example. Suppose we wanted to find all orders by customers not located in the same cities as the salespeople who took their orders. This would involve relating all three of our sample tables (the output is shown in Figure 10.7):

```
SELECT onum, cname, Orders.cnum, Orders.snum
     FROM Salespeople, Customers, Orders
     WHERE Orders.snum = Salespeople.snum
     AND Orders.cnum = Customers.cnum
     AND Customers.city <> Salespeople.city;
```

FIGURE 10.7:

Joining three tables to find anomalies

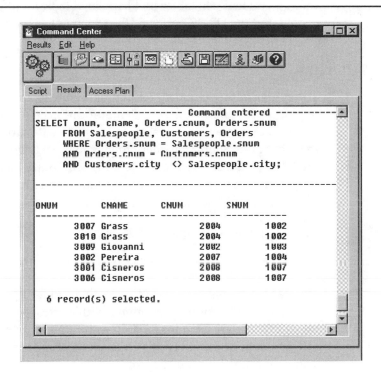

Although this statement looks rather complex, you can see its logic in the following steps:

- First, perform the two natural joins. These are the first two predicates; they match each order to the correct salesperson and customer. This part is the same as the earlier example.

- For each such order, eliminate the row if the salesperson's and customer's cities are the same. This is the third predicate.

- The rows that remain are output.

Joining a Table to Itself

Joining a table to itself is, in principle, just like joining it to another table. It is as though you had two tables that happened to be identical. The table is not actually copied, but the DBMS performs the statement as though it were.

Aliases

The syntax of the statement for joining a table to itself is the same as that for joining multiple tables, with a single modification. When you join a table to itself, all of the column names are repeated, complete with table-name prefixes. To refer to these columns within the query then, you must have two different names for the same table. You can do this by defining temporary names for the table. There are three common names for these temporary names in the database literature:

- Range variables

- Correlation variables

- Aliases

Note that *synonym* is a term frequently used for a permanent alternative names for a table. Don't confuse synonyms with aliases. Aliases are defined in a SQL statement and are meaningful only within that statement. You define them in the FROM clause of the query. It's quite simple: type the name of the table, leave a space, and then type the alias for it.

Here is an example of a self join that finds all pairs of customers having the same rating (the output is shown in Figure 10.8):

```
SELECT first.cname, second.cname, first.rating
    FROM Customers first, Customers second
    WHERE first.rating = second.rating;
```

FIGURE 10.8:

Joining a table to itself

In the above statement, SQL behaves as though it were joining two tables called "first" and "second". Both of these are actually the Customers table, but the aliases allow them to be treated independently. The aliases first and second are defined in the FROM clause of the query, immediately following the names of the tables being copied. Notice that the aliases are also used in the SELECT clause, even though they are not defined until the FROM clause. This is fine. SQL will initially accept any such aliases on faith, but will reject the statement if they are not defined immediately in the FROM clause of the query. The life of an alias is only as long as the statement takes to execute. Once the query is finished, the aliases used in it are no longer meaningful.

Now that it has two copies of the Customers table to work with, SQL can treat this operation just as it would any other join, taking each row from one alias and matching it with each row of the other.

Notice that our output shows every combination of values twice, the second time in reverse order. This is because each value shows up once in each alias, and the predicate is symmetrical. Therefore, value A in alias first is selected in combination with value B in alias second, *and* value A in alias second is selected in combination with value B in alias first. In our example, Cisneros was selected with Grass, and then Grass was selected with Cisneros. The same thing happened with Liu and Giovanni. Also, each row was matched with itself to output rows such as Liu and Liu.

A simple way to avoid this duplication is to impose an order on the two values so that one will have to be less than the other or precede it in alphabetical order. Doing so makes the predicate asymmetrical in order that the same values in reverse order will not be selected again. For example:

```
SELECT first.cname, second.cname, first.rating
    FROM Customers first, Customers second
    WHERE first.rating = second.rating
    AND first.cname < second.cname;
```

The output of this query is shown in Figure 10.9.

FIGURE 10.9:

Eliminating redundant output from a self join

Hoffman precedes Periera in alphabetical order, so that combination satisfies both conditions of the predicate and appears in the output. When the same combination comes up in reverse order—when Periera in alias first is matched with Hoffman in alias second—the second condition is not met. Likewise, Hoffman is not selected for having the same rating as himself because his name doesn't precede itself in alphabetical order.

More on Aliases

Although joins of a table with itself are the first situation you have encountered in which aliases are necessary, you are not limited to using them to differentiate between copies of a single table. You can use them anytime you want to create alternate names for your tables in a statement. For example, if your tables have long and complex names, you can define simple one-letter aliases, such as a and b, and use these instead of the table names in the SELECT clause and predicate. Aliases will also be used with correlated subqueries.

Using Self Joins with Circular Relationships

Probably the most common way to use self joins is to deal with circular relationships. Recall the discussion "Foreign Keys That Refer Back to Their Own Tables" in Chapter 5. There we pointed out that tables sometimes contain circular foreign keys and offered in the following example:

Empno	Name	Manager
1003	Terrence	2007
2007	Atali	NULL
1688	McKeen	1003
2002	Collier	2007

In this table, manager is a foreign key referencing empno. The idea is that each employee has a manager, who is also an employee and therefore is represented in the Employees table. Suppose we wanted to see each employee coupled with his or her manager. We could do this with a self join of the Employees table, as follows:

```
SELECT under.empno, under.name, over.name
    FROM Employees under, Employees over
    WHERE under.manager = over.empno;
```

The output of this query is shown in Figure 10.10. Note that "over" and "under", though used here for clarity, may be keywords in some implementations, requiring you to select other aliases. The logic is as follows:

- In effect, two copies of the Employees table are created. These are called by the aliases under and over.

- For each row in under, the row in over with the empno matching under's manager value is found.

- The empno and name from under are produced along with the name from over, which contains the row for under's manager.

FIGURE 10.10:

A self join using a circular relationship

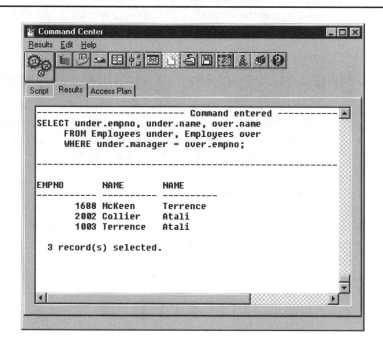

```
------------------------- Command entered -----------
SELECT under.empno, under.name, over.name
     FROM Employees under, Employees over
     WHERE under.manager = over.empno;


EMPNO      NAME        NAME
---------- ----------  ----------
      1688 McKeen      Terrence
      2002 Collier     Atali
      1003 Terrence    Atali

 3 record(s) selected.
```

Notice that Atali's row is not produced. Why? Because he has no manager—he is the boss. One of the exercises at the end of this chapter will be revising this query to include Atali.

More Complex Uses of Joins

Another way we can use joins and some other advanced features of SQL is to check for certain kinds of data anomalies. We designed our sample database with certain business rules in mind. For example, we assume that salespeople can take orders for customers to whom they are not assigned, though this is not the case with the actual sample data. What should we do when this happens? Perhaps the assigned and actual salespeople split the commission in this case. If so, we may need a query that will find cases where the salesperson who made a sale is not the one assigned. Here is such a query:

```
SELECT a.snum, b.snum, a.cnum., a.onum
    FROM Orders a, Customers b
    WHERE a.cnum = b.cnum
        AND a.snum <> b.snum;
```

The first snum output is that of the salesperson who actually took the order; the second is that of the salesperson regularly assigned. This query will produce only cases where the two are different.

Finding Patterns in the Data

Databases are increasingly used for data analysis. Joins are a very powerful tool you can use to find patterns and relationships in your data. We'll give you a couple of simple examples here, but you can take this technique to any level of complexity.

You can use any number of aliases for a single table in a query, although you would seldom use more than two in a given SELECT clause. Suppose you had not yet assigned your customers to your salespeople. Company policy is to assign each salesperson three customers initially, one at each of the three rating values. You, personally, are to decide which customers to assign to each salesperson, but you use the following query to see all of the possible combinations of customers you can assign (the output is shown in Figure 10.11):

```
SELECT a.cnum, b.cnum, c.cnum
    FROM Customers a, Customers b, Customers c
WHERE a.rating = 100
    AND b.rating = 200
    AND c.rating = 300;
```

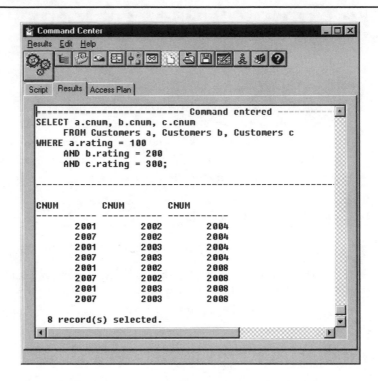

As you can see, this query finds all combinations of customers with the three rating values, so that the first column consists of customers with a 100 rating, the second of those with a 200 rating, and the last of those with a rating of 300. These are repeated in all possible combinations. You cannot create this sort of grouping with GROUP BY or ORDER BY, as these clauses compare values only in a single output column.

Joining Tables That Are Not Used in the Output

You should also realize that it is not always necessary to use every alias or table mentioned in the FROM clause of a query in the SELECT clause. Sometimes an alias or table is queried solely so that it can be referenced in the predicate of the query. For example, the following query finds all customers located in cities where salesperson Serres (snum 1002) has customers (the output is shown in Figure 10.12):

```
SELECT b.cnum, b.cname
    FROM Customers a, Customers b
WHERE a.snum = 1002
    AND b.city = a.city;
```

FIGURE 10.12:

Finding customers in the same cities as those of Serres

Here is the logic of this query broken down into steps:

- The first predicate is FALSE, except when the snum column value of alias a is 1002. So alias a eliminates all but Serres' customers.

- The second predicate uses alias b and will be TRUE for all rows with the same city value as the current city value of a. Over the course of the query, a will have values equal to the various cities of customers with an snum of 1002, that is, the customers of Serres.

- A row of alias b will be TRUE once for every time its city value is present in a. Finding these rows of alias b is the only purpose of alias a, so we did not select any columns from it. As you can see, Serres' own customers are selected for being in the same city as themselves, so selecting them from alias a is unnecessary.

- In short, alias a contains the rows of Serres' customers, Liu and Grass. Alias b finds all customers located in either of their cities (San Jose and Berlin, respectively) including, of course, Liu and Grass themselves.

You can also construct joins that involve both different tables *and* aliases of a single table. The following query joins the Customers table to itself to find all pairs of customers served by a single salesperson. At the same time, it joins the customer to the Salespeople table to name that salesperson (the output is shown in Figure 10.13):

```
SELECT sname, Salespeople.snum, a.cname, b.cname
     FROM Customers a, Customers b, Salespeople
     WHERE a.snum = b.snum
     AND Salespeople.snum = a.snum
     AND a.cnum < b.cnum;
```

Why is that last predicate included? This will be one of the questions in your chapter end exercises.

FIGURE 10.13:

Joining a table to itself and to another table

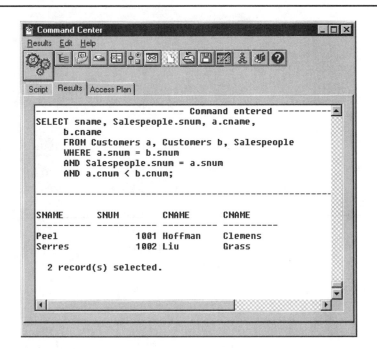

Special Join Operators

SQL92 provides a special syntax to make it easier to perform certain kinds of common join operations. Though this is not required for Entry-level SQL92 conformance, many vendors support this functionality with proprietary syntax that achieves similar effects, and some have implemented the standard syntax even though they may not be generally up to Intermediate conformance. Much of this functionality is also required for Core SQL99 conformance (see Appendix B). For a more complete explanation of these operators, look in the reference under "SELECT".

The built-in join operators in SQL92 divide joins into a three-part hierarchy. At the highest level, there are four kinds: CROSS JOINs, NATURAL JOINs, specified joins, and UNION JOINs. These are defined as follows. (Don't worry if some of these brief explanations are not perfectly transparent. We will elaborate and provide examples shortly.)

- CROSS JOIN. This is equivalent to a join without a join predicate. In other words, it is a straight Cartesian product. Support for this feature is not required until Full SQL92 conformance, and it is frankly not that commonly useful for business applications, though perhaps so for scientific ones.

- NATURAL JOIN. As we stated, "natural joins" ordinarily refers to joins based on matching foreign-key values to parent-key values. In the SQL92 standard, however, this term is used slightly differently: in a natural join, any two columns with the same name are matched as though they were parent and foreign key. The idea is that the NATURAL JOIN operator should be used when a convention of the database design ensures that matching column names do, in fact, imply parent and foreign keys. This is purely a convention, but it is a useful and common one. We will return to this point.

- Specified join. This is a join based on a condition directly specified in the query. All of the joins we have seen until now have been specified joins, but these new join operators provide new mechanisms for you to do this in the FROM, rather than the WHERE, clause of the query. The new specified joins are of the following types:

  - ON joins. These use a predicate to define the join. They are, therefore, just like the joins we have seen, save that the predicate is part of the FROM, rather than the WHERE, clause of the query.

  - USING joins. These operate on a list of like-named columns, one from each table joined, and perform an equijoin over those columns.

- UNION JOIN. This is different from the UNION operator used to combine multiple queries. A UNION JOIN is similar to a CROSS JOIN in that it uses no stated or implied predicate, but neither does it derive any Cartesian product. It simply creates an output table that includes all rows from table A with NULLs in the matching columns of table B and vice versa.

The natural and specified joins can be further divided into the following categories:

- INNER JOIN. This is basically any natural or specified join that is not an OUTER JOIN, that is to say, a join that excludes unmatched rows. Joins with predicates are either INNER or OUTER, with INNER being the default.

- OUTER JOIN. An OUTER JOIN is a join that includes unmatched rows from either or both of the joined tables. For a join of two tables, A and B, there are three possible varieties of OUTER JOIN:

  - LEFT OUTER JOIN. This includes all rows from table A, matched or not, with the values from the matched rows of table B, if any.

  - RIGHT OUTER JOIN. This includes all rows from table B, matched or not, with the values from the matched rows of table A, if any.

  - FULL OUTER JOIN. This includes all rows from both tables, merged where matches are found and filled out with NULLs where they are not.

For all of the above types, the word "JOIN", usually accompanied by modifiers that depend on the type, replaces the commas that otherwise separate table names in FROM clauses. You will see what we mean when we deal specifically with all of these types of joins in the following subsections.

CROSS JOINs

A CROSS JOIN is a Cartesian product that performs no selection based on comparing values from the joined tables. All combinations of rows are used. The effect is the same as you would get by performing a join and including no join predicate at all. The syntax for a CROSS JOIN is:

```
table A CROSS JOIN table B
```

Here is an example of a CROSS JOIN:

```
SELECT Salespeople.snum, Customers.city
    FROM Salespeople CROSS JOIN Customers;
```

The output of this query would be too long to list here. It would consist of every snum value in the Salespeople table matched with every city value in the Customers table, regardless of which salespeople were assigned to which customers. Since we did not specify UNIQUE, the repeated city values would be combined independently.

How useful is this syntax? Not very, since it has the same effect as omitting the join predicate in the first place. In other words, it is the same as simply saying:

```
SELECT Salespeople.snum, Customers.city
    FROM Salespeople, Customers;
```

The CROSS JOIN syntax is mostly for clarity, emphasizing that this unusual effect is what you want, which can enhance the readability of your code. Otherwise, someone else reading the code might believe this is simply an error.

NATURAL JOINs

As we mentioned, a natural join as defined by the standard is an equijoin automatically done over all like-named columns in the two tables. This will translate to natural joins in the logical sense only if the database designer has followed a convention where all foreign keys have the same names as their parents, and no other pairs of columns have like names. In our sample tables, we fulfill the first criterion but not the second. All of our foreign keys—snum in the Customers table, and both snum and cnum in the Orders table—have the same names as the parent keys that they reference. There is also a city column in both the Salespeople and Customers tables, however, which is not a foreign or parent key in either table. The likeness of the names reflects the likeness of the content, but it has no relationship to the database structure. Having parent and foreign keys share names is generally a useful practice and has the added benefit that it will make the NATURAL JOIN operators in SQL92 map to actual natural joins, rather than some other arbitrary set of joins suggested by the column names. On the other hand, coming up with two different words for "city" in our sample tables would likely have been awkward. We will shortly show you a workaround for this problem.

This brings up another point about the standard. What if we were to do a natural join of the Salespeople and Customers tables? The two tables have both snum and city columns with names in common, although, as stated, only the first would be a natural join in the logical sense. In the standard, a natural join over these two tables would be a join over a row combination that made *both* pairs of like-named columns equal.

Enough discussion in the abstract. Here is an example of a NATURAL JOIN, SQL92 style:

```
SELECT a.snum, a.sname, b.cnum, b.amt
    FROM Salespeople a NATURAL JOIN Orders b;
```

This is equivalent to the following:

```
SELECT a.snum, a.sname, b.cnum, b.amt
    FROM Salespeople a, Orders b
    WHERE a.snum = b.snum;
```

The output for either query would be as follows:

a.sunum	a.sname	b.cnum	b.amt
1007	Rifkin	2008	18.69
1001	Peel	2001	767.19
1004	Motika	2007	1900.10
1002	Serres	2003	5160.45
1007	Rifkin	2008	1098.16
1003	Axelrod	2002	1713.23
1002	Serres	2004	75.75
1001	Peel	2006	4723.00
1002	Serres	2004	1309.95
1001	Peel	2006	9891.88

Since the only columns in the Salespeople and Orders tables with the same names were the snum columns in each, this worked fine. However, a similar join executed over Salespeople and Customers does not work so well:

```
SELECT a.snum, a.sname, b.cnum, b.cname
    FROM Salespeople a NATURAL JOIN Customers b;
```

This would generate the following:

a.snum	a.sname	b.cnum	b.cname
1001	Peel	2001	Hoffman
1001	Peel	2006	Clemens
1002	Serres	2003	Liu

The equivalent hand-rolled join would be as follows:

```
SELECT a.snum, a.sname, b.cnum, b.cname
    FROM Salespeople a, Customers b
    WHERE a.snum = b.snum
        AND a.city = b.city;
```

Because the city columns had the same name, they were "unnaturally" included in the natural join. How do you get around this? Probably the easiest way is to use the USING form of a specified join, as explained in the next section.

Specified Joins (ON and USING)

Specified joins are joins you directly specify by creating a predicate that states how the join is to be done (the ON form) or by listing a set of columns that are to be equijoined (the USING form).

The ON form is substantially identical to the old-school joins in the WHERE clause with which we started this chapter. The ON clause provides two main advantages:

- Because you can nest joins in the FROM clause and because you can combine predicates in the ON and WHERE clauses, you can get more sophisticated effects than you could easily achieve with the WHERE clause by itself.

- If you adopt the convention of placing your join predicates in ON clauses and save the WHERE clauses for filtering predicates, it will be immediately obvious which is which. This will make your code less confusing to read.

Here is one of the previous examples from this chapter converted to the ON syntax. The original version was:

```
SELECT Customers.cname, Salespeople.sname,
    Salespeople.city
    FROM Salespeople, Customers
    WHERE Salespeople.city IN ('London', 'Barcelona')
        AND Salespeople.city = Customers.city;
```

The ON version will remove the join predicate to the FROM clause while leaving the filtering predicate in the WHERE clause:

```
SELECT Customers.cname, Salespeople.sname,
    Salespeople.city
    FROM Salespeople, Customers
            ON Salespeople.city = Customers.city
    WHERE Salespeople.city IN ('London', 'Barcelona');
```

Since this is, in fact, an equijoin of two like-named columns, the USING form could also be used:

```
SELECT Customers.cname, Salespeople.sname,
     Salespeople.city
     FROM Salespeople, Customers
              USING (city)
     WHERE Salespeople.city IN ('London', 'Barcelona');
```

This is equivalent to the previous example. To generalize, the USING form takes a comma-separated list of column names, where each name matches one column in each table joined, performs equijoins over all the pairs of like-named columns, and combines the results using AND. In other words, it is just like a NATURAL JOIN, except that it uses only the like-named columns that you choose, rather than all like-named columns. The Orders and Customers tables have two like-named columns, so let's use this form on them:

```
SELECT a.cnum, a.snum, onum, amt
     FROM Customers a, Orders b
          USING (cnum, snum);
```

Here is the output.

a.cnum	a.snum	onum	amt
2008	1007	3001	18.69
2001	1001	3003	767.19
2007	1004	3002	1900.10
2003	1002	3005	5160.45
2008	1007	3006	1098.16
2002	1003	3009	1713.23
2004	1002	3007	75.75
2006	1001	3008	4723.00
2004	1002	3010	1309.95
2006	1001	3011	9891.88

Notice the following:

- This is not entirely a natural join in the logical sense because the snum column in Orders references Salespeople not Customers.

- The fact that the cnum component is, in fact, a foreign key/parent key join doesn't matter. The join is based only on the names.

- Most importantly, both the cnum and snum for a given row of the Customers table must match a row of the Orders table for the resulting merged row to be selected for output. For this reason, orders credited to salespeople other than those assigned do not show up in the results of the query. Although the cnums will match, the snums will not.

In the natural join subsection, we pointed out that you could use the USING form of a specified join to deal with the situation where you have like-named columns that you do not want to use in the structure of your join. A natural join of the Salespeople and Customers tables would be an example, as the city columns should be excluded from the predicate of a logical natural join. If you haven't guessed it yet, here is the syntax to do this:

```
SELECT *
    FROM Salespeople, Customers
        USING (snum);
```

UNION JOINs

Before we get into the subcategories of natural and specified joins, we should cover UNION JOINs. UNION JOINs are a bit different from other joins we have seen in that they are not based on Cartesian products, nor do they use predicates, though you could add predicates to them in the WHERE clause, just as with any other query. Rather, a UNION JOIN makes no attempt to correlate the data from the two tables joined. A UNION JOIN of two tables, A and B, outputs all column values from table A, placing NULLs in all columns taken from table B for those rows. Then it outputs all columns from B with NULLs for all columns taken from table A in those rows. For example, here is a UNION JOIN of the Salespeople and Customers tables:

```
SELECT a.snum, sname, b.cnum, b.cname
    FROM Salespeople a UNION JOIN Customers b;
```

The output of this would be as follows:

a.snum	sname	cnum	cname
1001	Peel	NULL	NULL
1002	Serres	NULL	NULL
1004	Motika	NULL	NULL
1007	Rifkin	NULL	NULL
1003	Axelrod	NULL	NULL
NULL	NULL	2001	Hoffman
NULL	NULL	2002	Giovanni
NULL	NULL	2003	Liu
NULL	NULL	2004	Grass
NULL	NULL	2006	Clemens
NULL	NULL	2008	Cisneros
NULL	NULL	2007	Pereira

To make this slightly more useful, let's output all salespeople and customers in London:

```
SELECT a.snum, sname, b.cnum, b.cname
    FROM Salespeople a UNION JOIN Customers b
    WHERE a.city = 'London'
        OR b.city = 'London';
```

In a Full conformance SQL92 implementation, you could simplify this as follows:

```
SELECT a.snum, sname, b.cnum, b.cname
    FROM Salespeople a UNION JOIN Customers b
    WHERE 'London' IN (a.city, b.city);
```

The rest of the join operators in this section are subsets of natural or of specified joins. Each of them must specify one and only one of the following:

- NATURAL, indicating a NATURAL JOIN, as explained earlier
- ON, indicating a specified join of the ON type
- USING, indicating a specified join of the USING type

The subcategories are the INNER and various kinds of OUTER JOINs and are, therefore, all based on what happens to the unmatched rows. They work just the same for NATURAL or for specified joins.

INNER JOINs

For this and the next couple of sections, let's call the first table named in the FROM clause *table A,* and the second, *table B.*

An INNER JOIN is a join that includes no unmatched rows from either table. In other words, it is any join other than an OUTER JOIN. The syntax is as follows:

```
table A [NATURAL] [INNER] JOIN table B
        [{ON predicate} | {USING column list}];
```

INNER is the default and therefore a noiseword (also called "syntactic sugar" by some programmers). If you don't specify a subtype, INNER is what you get. It doesn't matter whether you include the noisewords, but they can clarify your intention to those who later read your code. As we mentioned, you use one and only one of NATURAL, ON, or USING. Here is an example:

```
SELECT onum, odate, amt, o.snum, sname
    FROM Salespeople s NATURAL INNER JOIN Orders o;
```

You also could have phrased it this way:

```
SELECT onum, odate, amt, o.snum, sname
    FROM Salespeople s NATURAL JOIN Orders o;
```

But you cannot use this version:

```
SELECT onum, odate, amt, o.snum, sname
    FROM Salespeople s INNER JOIN Orders o;
```

Since snum is the only column that has the same name in the Salespeople and Orders tables, the tables are joined over snum. Therefore, the example is equivalent to the following:

```
SELECT Customers.cname, Salespeople.sname
    FROM Customers, Salespeople
    WHERE Salespeople.snum = Customers.snum;
```

This is the natural join we used earlier in this chapter. Here is the same join phrased with USING:

```
SELECT onum, odate, amt, o.snum, sname
    FROM Salespeople s JOIN Orders o
    USING (snum);
```

LEFT OUTER JOINs

For this and the next couple of sections, let's call the first table named in the FROM clause *table A* and the second, *table B*. A LEFT OUTER JOIN includes all rows from table A, matched or not, plus the matching values from B if applicable. For the rows from table A where no matches are found, NULLs will be installed in the columns derived from column B. As usual with joins, if there are multiple rows from table B that match table A, there will be a separate row in the results of the query for each such match. The syntax is as follows:

```
table_A [NATURAL] LEFT [OUTER] JOIN table_B
    [{ON predicate} | {USING column_list}];
```

Like INNER previously, OUTER is a noiseword. An OUTER JOIN must specify LEFT, RIGHT, or FULL, and, since these terms apply only to OUTER JOINs, the word "OUTER" is superfluous. Again, though, it helps bring your intention across to those who read your code.

Suppose you wanted to see all the salespeople, coupled with their orders for a particular date. An ordinary join would leave out the salespeople who had no orders on that particular date. Here is a LEFT OUTER JOIN to achieve this effect:

```
SELECT sname, onum
    FROM Salespeople NATURAL LEFT OUTER JOIN Orders
    WHERE odate = '10/03/2000'
    ORDER BY 1;
```

The output from this query would be as follows:

snum	onum
1001	3003
1002	3005
1003	NULL
1004	3002
1007	3001
1007	3006

Although it might seem convenient in the previous example to move the selection predicate—WHERE odate = '10/03/2000'—into an ON clause, if you did that, you could not make it a natural join, as the two are mutually exclusive. Of course, you could express the entire join in an ON clause, as follows:

```
SELECT sname, onum
    FROM Salespeople s LEFT JOIN Orders o
        ON odate = '10/03/2000'
            AND s.snum = o.snum
    ORDER BY 1;
```

This is, however, not much different from putting it in the WHERE clause.

RIGHT OUTER JOINs

Predictably, RIGHT OUTER is the reverse of LEFT OUTER. In other words, all the rows from table B are presented in conjunction with any matches from A or else in conjunction with NULLs. The syntax is as follows:

```
table A [NATURAL] RIGHT [OUTER] JOIN table B
        [{ON predicate} | {USING column list}];
```

You may recall that in the discussion of OUTER JOINs, we added a new salesperson to the Salespeople table and discussed using an OUTER JOIN to deal with the fact that this salesperson had no customers as yet. Normally, you would solve this with a NATURAL JOIN, but that would also include the city columns that have the same names in the Salespeople and Customers tables, which we don't want (because what we want is a natural join in the logical sense). Therefore, we can use the USING form of a specified join to get exactly what we want. Here is the query for a RIGHT OUTER JOIN:

```
SELECT cnum, Salespeople.snum
    FROM Customers RIGHT OUTER JOIN Salespeople
        USING (snum);
```

The output from this query would be as follows.

cnum	snum
2001	1001
2002	1003
2003	1002
2004	1002
2006	1001

Continued on next page

cnum	snum
2008	1007
2007	1004
NULL	1020

A couple of things are worth noting about this query:

- The only reason we need to use a join in this case is because we need to reference the Salespeople table to find those salespeople, like Wang, who have no customers assigned. If we were only interested in the salespeople who did have customers, we could get that information entirely from the Customers table, and we should do so, since joins are usually slower to perform and use more resources than single-table queries.

- It matters that we used Salespeople.snum and not Customers.snum as the output column in the SELECT clause. In INNER JOINs, it often does not matter which of the two matched columns you choose to output, but it does in OUTER JOINs. The snum value 1020 is not present in the Customers table, so that value would not have been output if we had specified Customers.snum. If both of the output columns were taken from the Customers table, where Wang is not represented, both would have been NULL when his row was selected. If this were an INNER JOIN it would not have mattered because we would be selecting only rows where `Salespeople.snum = Customers.snum`. With an OUTER JOIN, we are effectively selecting rows where the parent key matches the foreign key *or* where no match exists. However, we must output the column values from the side where we want all rows to be included.

Note that the above query is the exact reverse of a LEFT OUTER JOIN. In other words, we could have phrased the above query thusly:

```
SELECT cnum, Salespeople.snum
    FROM Salespeople LEFT OUTER JOIN Customers
        USING (snum);
```

It does not matter that the left and right ordering of the output columns in the SELECT clause does not reflect the order in which the tables are referenced in the FROM clause.

FULL OUTER JOINs

As you may have guessed, FULL OUTER is a combination of LEFT and RIGHT OUTER. All rows from both tables are shown, merged where matches are found, or with NULLs filling in the columns from the other table. Here is the syntax:

```
table A [NATURAL] FULL [OUTER] JOIN table B
    [{ON predicate} | {USING column list}];
```

Suppose we were to add a new customer, who did not yet have a salesperson assigned, to the Customers table the output would appear as follows:

cnum	cname	city	rating	snum
2000	Christy	Dangkok	200	NULL

The NULL snum value cannot match anything in the primary key, first of all because primary keys cannot contain NULLs and secondly because NULLs do not match anything, even other NULLs (for most purposes). This is fine. In fact, it is the intention: the NULL indicates that there is no matching salesperson. Now, if we were to repeat the previous query, we would have both a customer and a salesperson who came out unmatched. We are assuming that Wang, from earlier in the chapter, is still present in the Salespeople table.

Here is the query you would use to view all customers, salespeople, and the matches between them, if any:

```
SELECT cnum, Salespeople.snum
    FROM Customers FULL OUTER JOIN Salespeople
        USING (snum);
```

The output from this query would be as follows.

cnum	snum
2001	1001
2002	1003
2003	1002

Continued on next page

cnum	snum
2004	1002
2006	1001
2008	1007
2007	1004
2009	NULL
NULL	1020

This FULL OUTER JOIN is, of course, also a natural join in the logical sense. Notice that a natural FULL OUTER JOIN makes sense only if at least one of the following conditions is TRUE:

- The foreign key permits NULLs, as in this case. Here, the NULLs in the output column are not, strictly speaking, the same as the NULLs in the column itself but are the result of no match being found. This fact probably is significant only if your DBMS supports multiple kinds of NULLs. (At least one product, called FirstSQL, supports this, but it is not a common feature, nor is it part of standard SQL. However, Ted Codd, the father of relational databases, believes that different kinds of NULLs are a good idea. If you come across discussions of four-valued or higher logic in the database literature, this is what they are talking about. In this system, different kinds of NULLs distinguish values that are not present for different reasons: inapplicable, unknown, etc.)

- You are dealing with tables that were created without the proper constraints and therefore may not be in a state of referential integrity. This problem occurs frequently with data ported from older versions of database programs or from sources other than relational databases. In this case, the FULL OUTER JOIN will point out the rows lacking integrity for you. They will be the ones with NULLs inserted on the primary-key side. NULLS on the foreign-key side are not necessarily a problem.

- The proper constraints are in place, but they have been deferred, as is permitted by the standard. In that case, this query could check for the temporary integrity violations. You might want to check these and fix them before you terminate the transaction. For more on transactions and deferrable constraints, see Chapter 17 and "SET TRANSACTION" in Chapter 28.

If none of these conditions are the case, every value in the foreign key should have a match, and the output column based on the foreign key should contain no NULLs. It is, of course, arbitrary whether the foreign-key column is the left or the right, since left and right are simply a function of the order in which the tables are named in the FROM clause.

Summary

You are no longer restricted to looking at one table at a time. Moreover, you can make elaborate comparisons between any of the fields of any number of tables and use the results to decide what information you want to see. We've introduced you to some possible uses for these abilities. You are now familiar with the terms *range variables*, *correlation variables*, and *aliases* (this terminology varies from product to product and writer to writer, so we decided to acquaint you with all three terms). You also understand a bit more about how queries actually work.

The next step after combining multiple tables or multiple copies of a single table in a query is combining multiple queries so that one query can produce output that controls what another query does. We'll introduce this feature in the next chapter.

Putting SQL to Work

1. Write a query that lists each order number followed by the name of the customer who made the order.

2. Write a query that produces all customers serviced by salespeople with a commission above 12 percent. Output the customer's name, the salesperson's name, and the salesperson's rate of commission.

3. Write a query that calculates the amount of the salesperson's commission on each order by a customer with a rating above 100.

4. Write a query that produces all pairs of salespeople who are living in the same city. Exclude combinations of salespeople with themselves as well as duplicate rows with the order reversed.

5. Write a query that produces the names and cities of all customers with the same rating as Hoffman. Write the query using Hoffman's cnum rather than his rating, so that it would still be usable if his rating changed.

6. Revise the following query so that employees who have no managers, such as Atali in our example, will be included in the output:

   ```
   SELECT under.empno, under.name, over.name
        FROM Employees under, Employees over
        WHERE under.manager = over.empno;
   ```

7. Why is the final predicate—a.cnum < b.cnum—included in this query?

   ```
   SELECT sname, Salespeople.snum, a.cname,
        b.cname
        FROM Customers a, Customers b, Salespeople
        WHERE a.snum = b.snum
        AND Salespeople.snum = a.snum
        AND a.cnum < b.cnum;
   ```

CHAPTER

ELEVEN

11

Placing Queries Inside One Another

- How Do Subqueries Work?

- Subqueries and Joins

- Correlated Subqueries

At the end of Chapter 10, we said queries could control other queries. In this chapter, you will learn to do this (for the most part) by placing a query inside the predicate of another query and using the inner query's output in the outer query's predicate. You will find out what kinds of operators can use subqueries and explore how subqueries work with features of SQL such as DISTINCT, aggregate functions, and output expressions. You will learn how to use subqueries with the HAVING clause and receive some pointers on the correct way to use subqueries.

How Do Subqueries Work?

SQL provides you the ability to nest queries within one another. Typically, the inner query generates values that are tested in the predicate of the outer query, determining when it will be TRUE. For instance, suppose we knew the name but not the snum of salesperson Motika, and we wanted to extract all of her orders from the Orders table. Here is one way we could do it (the output is shown in Figure 11.1):

```
SELECT *
    FROM Orders
    WHERE snum =
    (SELECT snum
    FROM Salespeople
    WHERE sname = 'Motika');
```

In order to evaluate the outer (main) query, SQL first had to evaluate the query within the WHERE clause. It did this in the same way it would have had this query been its sole task: it searched through the Salespeople table for all rows where the sname was equal to Motika and then extracted the snum values of those rows.

The only row found, of course, was the one with the snum equal to 1004. Rather than simply outputting this value, however, SQL put it in the predicate of the main query in place of the subquery itself, so that the predicate read

```
WHERE snum = 1004
```

SQL then performed the main query as usual with the above results. Naturally, the subquery must select one and only one column, and the datatype of this column must be comparable to that of the value to which it is being compared in the predicate (to find out which datatypes are comparable, see "Datatypes" in the reference). Often, as above, the selected column and this value will have the same name (in this case, snum), but such is not always the case.

FIGURE 11.1:

Using the subquery

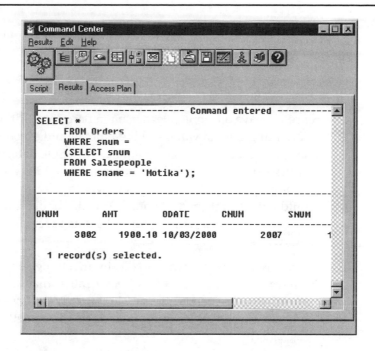

The Values That Subqueries Can Produce

It is rather convenient that our subquery in the previous example returned one and only one value. Had it selected all snums WHERE city = 'London' instead of WHERE sname = 'Motika', it would have produced several values. This would have made the equation in the predicate of the main query impossible to evaluate, and the statement would have produced an error.

When using subqueries in predicates based on relational operators (equations or inequalities), you must be sure to use a subquery that will produce one and only one row of output. If the subquery produces no values at all, the statement will not fail, but neither will the main query produce any output. Subqueries that produce no output cause the predicate to be considered neither TRUE nor FALSE, but UNKNOWN. However, the UNKNOWN predicate has the same effect as FALSE in this case: the main query selects no rows (refer to Chapter 8 for more information on the UNKNOWN predicate).

It is *not* a good idea to do something like this:

```
SELECT *
    FROM Orders
    WHERE snum =
    (SELECT snum
    FROM Salespeople
    WHERE city = 'Barcelona');
```

Since we have only one salesperson in Barcelona, Rifkin, the subquery would select a single snum value and therefore would execute without error. But this is only true because of the current data. Most SQL databases can have multiple simultaneous users, and if another user had added a new salesperson in Barcelona to the table, the subquery would select two values and your statement would fail. The integrity of your SQL code should not be a function of the data, unless you use constraints to force the data to remain within the parameters you specify.

You should also note that predicates involving subqueries normally use the form *scalar expression operator subquery*, rather than *subquery operator scalar expression* or *subquery operator subquery*. In the early versions of the SQL standard and in many commercial products, you could not do something like the following:

```
SELECT *
    FROM Orders
    WHERE (SELECT snum
    FROM Customers
    WHERE cnum = 2001)
    = snum;
```

If your DBMS rejects this query, it may simply mean that you must put the subquery second. The older standard and some products also prevent you from having both of the values in the comparison produced by subqueries. This restriction would prohibit a query like this:

```
SELECT *
    FROM Orders
    WHERE (SELECT snum
    FROM Customers
    WHERE cnum = 2001)
    = (SELECT snum
```

```
    FROM Customers
    WHERE cnum = 2003);
```

Occasionally, subqueries like this can be useful, however, so many products will accept them. They are part of SQL92, but not at the Entry level of conformance where most products currently sit.

Using Aggregate Functions in Subqueries

One type of function that automatically can produce a single value for any number of rows, of course, is the aggregate function. Any query using a single aggregate function without a GROUP BY clause will select a single value for use in the main predicate. For example, you might want to see all orders that are greater than the average for October 4:

```
SELECT *
    FROM Orders
    WHERE amt >
    (SELECT AVG(amt)
    FROM Orders
    WHERE odate = '10/04/2000');
```

The average amount for October 4 is 894.49 (1713.23 + 75.75 divided by 2). The query selected rows with amount columns greater than this value.

Keep in mind that grouped aggregate functions—that is, aggregate functions defined in terms of a GROUP BY clause—can produce multiple values. They are, therefore, not allowed in subqueries of this nature. Even if you use GROUP BY and HAVING in such a way that the subquery outputs only a single group, the statement is still rejected on principle in Entry-level SQL92.

You should use a single aggregate function with a WHERE clause that will eliminate the undesired groups. For example, you cannot use the following query in a subquery to find the average commission of salespeople in London:

```
SELECT AVG(comm)
    FROM Salespeople
    GROUP BY city
    HAVING city = 'London';
```

This is not the best way to form the query anyway. The version you want is

```
SELECT AVG(comm)
    FROM Salespeople
    WHERE city = 'London';
```

Using IN with Subqueries That Produce Multiple Rows

You can use subqueries that produce any number of rows if you use the special operator IN. (The operators BETWEEN, LIKE, and IS NULL cannot be used with subqueries in Entry-level SQL92. Implementations vary on this point, however, and they are supported for Intermediate or better conformance.) As you may recall, IN defines a set of values, one of which must match the other term of the predicate's equation in order for the predicate to be TRUE. When you use IN with a subquery, SQL simply builds this set from the subquery's output. We can, therefore, use IN to perform subqueries that would not work with relational operators and find all orders attributed to salespeople in London (the output is shown in Figure 11.2):

```
SELECT *
    FROM Orders
    WHERE snum IN
    (SELECT snum
    FROM Salespeople
    WHERE city = 'London');
```

FIGURE 11.2:

Using IN with a subquery

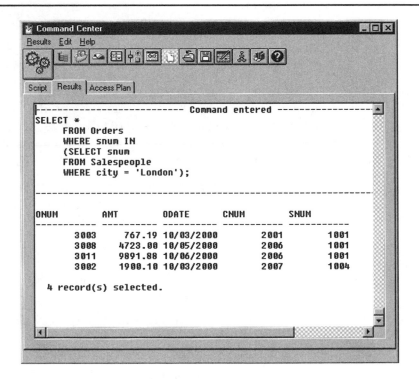

Of course you could use IN even when you are assured that the subquery will produce a single value. In any situation where you can use the relational operator equals (=), you can also use IN. Unlike relational operators, IN will not cause the statement to fail if the subquery selects more than one value. This can be an advantage or a disadvantage. You do not directly see the output from subqueries. Therefore, if you believe that a subquery is going to produce only one value and it produces several, you may not be able to tell the difference from the main query's output. For instance, consider this statement:

```
SELECT onum, amt, odate
    FROM Orders
    WHERE snum =
    (SELECT DISTINCT snum
    FROM Orders
    WHERE cnum = 2001);
```

This query selects all orders, for any customer, assigned to the salesperson who takes the orders for customer 2001. The output for this query is shown in Figure 11.3.

FIGURE 11.3:

All orders for the salesperson of a particular customer using equals

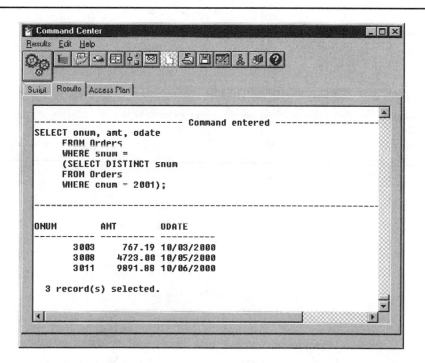

Here is an alternate version using IN, with the output shown in Figure 11.4:

```
SELECT onum, amt, odate
      FROM Orders
      WHERE snum IN
      (SELECT snum
      FROM Orders
      WHERE cnum = 2001);
```

FIGURE 11.4:

All orders for the salespeople of a particular customer using IN

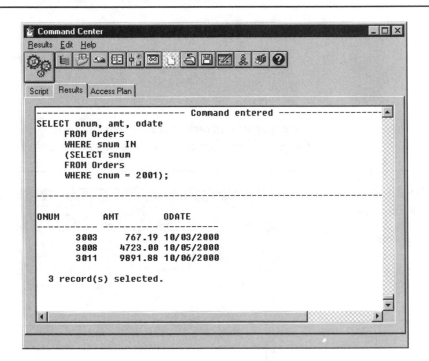

The first version assumes that all of the orders for customer 2001 were credited to her normal salesperson, which happens to be the case for all customers in our data. What happens if such is not the case? The version using IN would give you all orders for all salespeople who were credited with at least one sale for this customer. If your assumption was that these orders would all be for the same salesperson, there would be no obvious way of seeing the mistake, and reports generated or decisions made on the basis of this query would compound the error. The version using equals, on the other hand, would simply fail. This, at least, lets you know there is a problem. You could then troubleshoot by executing the subquery by itself and seeing the values that it produces.

Generally speaking, if you know the subquery should, for logical reasons, produce only one value, you should use equals. IN is appropriate if the query can legitimately produce one or more values, regardless of whether you expect it to. Suppose I want to know the commissions of all salespeople servicing customers in London:

```
SELECT comm
    FROM Salespeople
    WHERE snum IN
    (SELECT snum
    FROM Customers
    WHERE city = 'London');
```

The output for this query, shown in Figure 11.5, is the commission of Peel (snum = 1001), who has both of the London customers. This is a function only of the current data, however. There is no apparent reason why some of the London customers could not be assigned to someone else. Therefore, IN is the most logical form to use for the query.

FIGURE 11.5:

Using IN with a single-value subquery

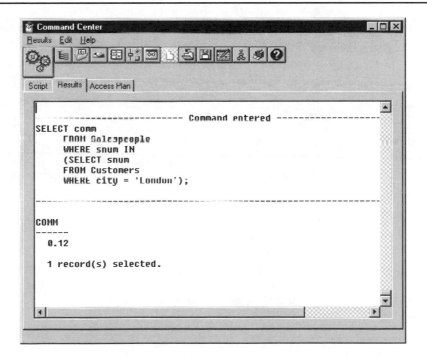

Omitting Table Prefixes from Subqueries

By the way, a table prefix for city is not necessary in the previous example, despite the fact that a city column exists in both the Salespeople and Customer tables. The DBMS always looks first for columns in the table(s) indicated in the FROM clause of the current (sub)query. If it does not find a column with the given name there, the DBMS checks the query containing the subquery, then the query containing that query, and so on, until it either finds a valid reference or reaches the outermost query and produces an error. In the above example, "city" in the WHERE clause was meant to refer to Customers.city. Since the Customers table is named in the FROM clause of the current query, the DBMS's assumption was correct. You can override this assumption with explicit table or alias prefixes, which we will discuss further when we talk about correlated subqueries. If there is any chance of confusion, of course, it is best to use the prefixes.

Subqueries Take Single Columns

A common thread of all the subqueries discussed in this chapter is that they select a single column. This restriction is mandatory, as the select output is being compared to a single value at a time, rather than an entire row at a time. An implication of this rule is that you cannot use SELECT * in a subquery, save in the somewhat unusual case of single-column tables. In the next chapter, we will introduce an exception to this rule, subqueries used with the EXISTS operator.

Using Expressions in Subqueries

You can use an expression based on a column, rather than the column itself, in the SELECT clause of a subquery, using either relational operators or IN. For example, the following query uses the relational operator = (the output is shown in Figure 11.6):

```
SELECT *
    FROM Customers
    WHERE cnum =
    (SELECT snum + 1000
    FROM Salespeople
    WHERE sname = 'Serres');
```

This statement finds all customers whose cnum is 1000 more than the snum of Serres. We are assuming that the sname column has no duplicate values (you can enforce this by using a UNIQUE constraint, discussed in Chapter 4); otherwise the subquery might produce multiple values and the main query fail. Unless the snum and cnum columns have meaning beyond their simple function as primary keys, which is usually not a good idea, a query such as the above is probably not terribly useful, but it does illustrate the point.

FIGURE 11.6:

Using a subquery with an expression

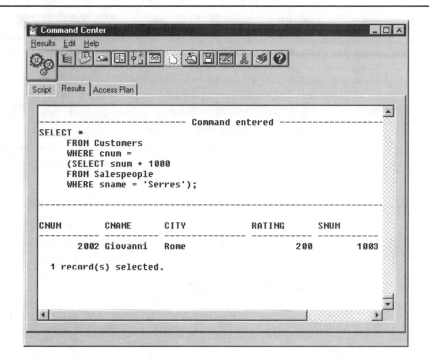

```
----------------------- Command entered ------------------
SELECT *
    FROM Customers
    WHERE cnum =
    (SELECT snum + 1000
    FROM Salespeople
    WHERE sname = 'Serres');

----------------------------------------------------------

CNUM      CNAME     CITY            RATING      SNUM
--------- --------- --------------- ----------- -----------
     2002 Giovanni  Rome                    200        1003

   1 record(s) selected.
```

Subqueries and Joins

If you think a moment about the first query example in the preceding section on IN, you might discover that you also could have phrased it as a join, like this:

```
SELECT onum, amt, odate, cnum, Orders.snum
    FROM Orders, Salespeople
    WHERE Orders.snum = Salespeople.snum
    AND Salespeople.City = 'London';
```

Which version is better? This question gets a little complicated. In principle, the subquery version would execute more efficiently. In the join version, the DBMS would have to go through each possible combination of rows from the two tables and test it against the compound predicate. It is simpler and more efficient to extract from the Salespeople table the snum values where the `city = 'London'`, and then to search for these values in the Orders table, which is what the subquery version does. The inner query gives us the snums 1001 and 1004. The outer query then gives us the rows from the Orders table where those snums are found.

However, whether or not the subquery version would be faster in practice depends on the *implementation*—on how the DBMS program you are using is designed. Your program contains an optimizer that attempts to find the most efficient way to execute your queries. A good optimizer would convert the join version to a subquery anyway, but there is often no easy way for you to determine whether this is being done. It's better to write your queries with efficiency in mind than to rely entirely on the optimizer. We shall cover optimization of queries in Part V of this book.

Although many queries can be phrased as either subqueries or joins, there are some that must be subqueries or must be joins.

Subqueries in HAVING

You can also use subqueries within the HAVING clause. These subqueries can use their own aggregate functions. The following query is an example (its output is shown in Figure 11.7):

```
SELECT rating, COUNT (DISTINCT cnum)
    FROM Customers
    GROUP by rating
    HAVING rating >
    (SELECT AVG(rating)
    FROM Customers
    WHERE city = 'San Jose');
```

FIGURE 11.7:

Finding customers with a rating above San Jose's average

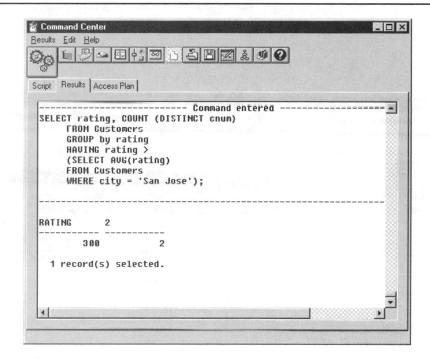

This statement counts the customers with ratings above San Jose's average. Had there been ratings other than 300 that qualified, each distinct rating would have been output with a count of the number of customers who had that rating.

Correlated Subqueries

When you use subqueries in SQL, you can refer in the inner query to the table in the FROM clause of the outer query, forming a *correlated subquery*. When you do this, the subquery is executed repeatedly, once for each row of the main query's table. Correlated subqueries are among the most subtle concepts in SQL because of the complexity involved in evaluating them. Once you have mastered them, however, you will find that they are quite powerful, precisely because they can perform complicated functions with such compact directions.

For example, here is one way of finding all customers with orders on October 3 (the output is shown in Figure 11.8):

```
SELECT *
     FROM Customers outer
     WHERE '10/03/2000' IN
     (SELECT odate
     FROM Orders inner
     WHERE outer.cnum = inner.cnum);
```

FIGURE 11.8:

Using a correlated subquery

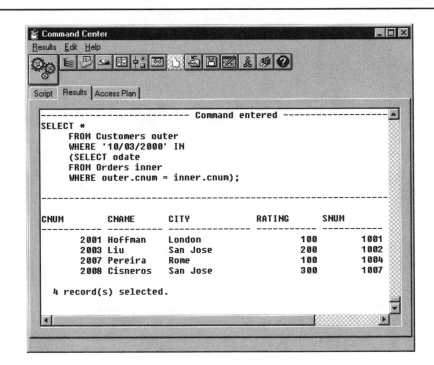

How the Correlated Subquery Works

In the above example, "inner" and "outer" are, of course, aliases, like those discussed in Chapter 10. In some implementations, "inner" and "outer" may be reserved words and therefore prohibited for use as aliases. We chose these names for the sake of clarity, as they refer to values from the inner and outer queries, respectively. Because the value in the cnum column of the outer query varies, the inner query must be executed separately for each row of the outer query. The row of the outer query for which the inner query is being executed at any given time is called the current *candidate row*. Therefore, the procedure to evaluate a correlated subquery is this:

1. Select a row from the table named in the outer query. This will be the current candidate row. If the outer query contains a join, each combination of rows from the tables joined constitutes a candidate row. (If that concept seems slightly confusing, don't worry. We explain it in more detail later in this chapter.)

2. Store the values from this candidate row in the alias named in the FROM clause of the outer query.

3. Perform the subquery. Wherever the alias given for the outer query is found (in this case, outer), use the value for the current candidate row. The use of a value from the outer query's candidate row in a subquery is called an *outer reference*.

4. Evaluate the predicate of the outer query on the basis of the results of the subquery performed in step 3. This will determine whether the candidate row is selected for output.

5. Repeat the procedure for the next candidate row of the outer query and so on until all the candidate rows have been tested.

In the above example, the DBMS implements the following procedure:

1. It selects the row of Hoffman from the Customers table.

2. It stores this row as the current candidate row under the alias outer.

3. It then performs the subquery. The subquery goes through the entire Orders table to find rows where the cnum column is the same as outer.cnum, which currently is 2001, the cnum of Hoffman's row. It then extracts the odate column from each row of the Orders table for which this is TRUE and builds a set of the resulting odate values.

4. Having formed a set of all odate values where the cnum is 2001, it tests the predicate of the main query to see if October 3 is in this set. If it is (and it is), it selects Hoffman's row for output from the main query.

5. It repeats the entire procedure using Giovanni's row as the candidate row and keeps repeating until it has tested every row of the Customers table.

As you can see, the calculations that SQL performs with these simple instructions are fairly complex. Of course, you could also have solved the same problem with a join, such as the following (the output for this query is shown in Figure 11.09):

```
SELECT first.cnum, first.cname
    FROM Customers first, Orders second
    WHERE first.cnum = second.cnum
    AND second.odate = '10/03/2000';
```

FIGURE 11.09:

Using a join in place of a correlated subquery

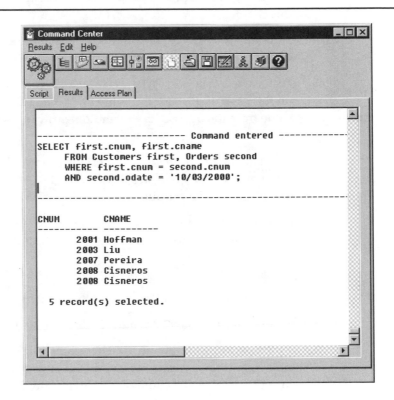

Notice that here Cisneros was chosen twice, once for each order she had on the given date. We could have eliminated this duplication by using SELECT DISTINCT instead of simply SELECT, of course. Doing so is, however, not necessary with the subquery version. The IN operator, as used with the subquery version, makes no distinction between values that are selected by the subquery once and values that are selected repeatedly. Therefore, DISTINCT is not needed.

Suppose we wanted to see the names and numbers of all salespeople who had more than one customer. The following query would accomplish this for us (the output is shown in Figure 11.10):

```
SELECT snum, sname
     FROM Salespeople main
     WHERE 1 <
     (SELECT COUNT(*)
     FROM Customers
     WHERE snum = main.snum);
```

FIGURE 11.10:

Finding salespeople with multiple customers

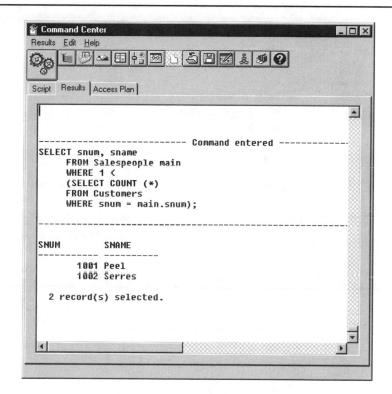

Notice that the FROM clause of the subquery in this example makes no use of an alias. In the absence of a table-name or alias prefix, SQL will initially assume that any column is drawn from the table named in the FROM clause of the current query. If there is no column of the given name (in this case, snum) in that table, SQL will then check the outer queries. To override this assumption, table-name prefixes are usually necessary with correlated subqueries. Aliases are also frequently called for to enable you to reference the same table in an inner and an outer query without ambiguity.

Using Correlated Subqueries to Find Anomalies

Sometimes it is useful to run queries that are solely designed to find anomalies in the data. It is always possible for faulty information to be entered into your database, and, once entered, it can be difficult to spot. You may also want to do certain kinds of pattern recognition. In the previous chapter, under "More Complex Uses of Joins", we showed you how to use a join to find orders not credited to the salesperson generally assigned to a particular customer. Here is a way to do it using a correlated subquery:

```
SELECT *
    FROM Orders main
    WHERE NOT snum =
    (SELECT snum
    FROM Customers
    WHERE cnum = main.cnum);
```

Notice that in this version we get only the information about the order itself, not about the salesperson who normally would have been credited with the sale. This is because the latter information is present in the table accessed in the subquery, and the output of the subquery cannot be used in the output of the main query.

Correlating a Table with Itself

You can also use correlated subqueries based on the same table as the main query, enabling you to extract certain complex forms of derived information. For example, we can find all orders with above-average amounts for their customers (the output is shown in Figure 11.11):

```
SELECT *
    FROM Orders outer
    WHERE amt >
    (SELECT AVG(amt)
    FROM Orders inner
    WHERE inner.cnum = outer.cnum);
```

FIGURE 11.11:

Correlating a table
with itself

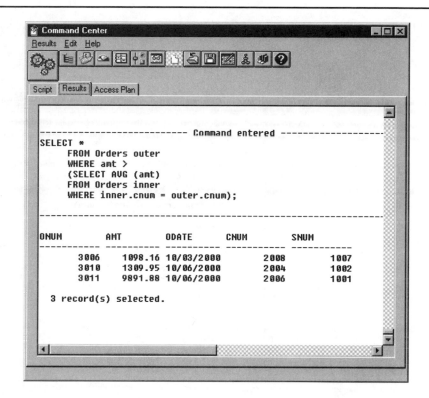

Of course, in our small sample table, with most customers having only one order, the majority of values are the same as the average and therefore not selected. Notice that this is a subquery that cannot be translated into a join, because a join cannot compare simple and aggregate data in this way. More realistically, we may be interested only in the orders that exceed the customer's average by at least 50 percent (the output is shown in Figure 11.12):

```
SELECT *
    FROM Orders outer
    WHERE amt >=
    (SELECT (AVG(amt) * 1.5)
    FROM Orders inner
    WHERE inner.cnum = outer.cnum);
```

FIGURE 11.12:

Selecting orders >= 150 percent of average

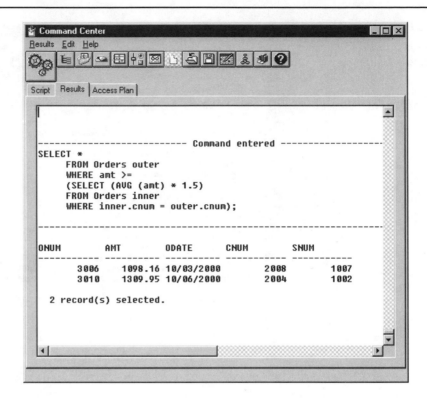

Correlated Subqueries in HAVING

Just as the HAVING clause can take subqueries, it can take correlated subqueries. When you use a correlated subquery in a HAVING clause, you must restrict the outer references to items that could be directly used in the HAVING clause itself. You will recall that the predicate in the HAVING clause is applied to each row that results after the grouping is done. Therefore, HAVING clauses can use only aggregate functions from the SELECT clause or columns used for grouping. These also are the only outer references you can make in correlated subqueries in HAVING. Because the predicate of the HAVING clause is evaluated for each group from the outer query, not for each row, the subquery is executed once for each output group from the outer query, not for each row.

Suppose you want the sums of the amounts from the Orders table, grouped by date, eliminating all those dates where the SUM was not at least 2000.00 above the MAX amount:

```
SELECT odate, SUM(amt)
    FROM Orders a
    GROUP BY odate
    HAVING SUM(amt) >
    (SELECT 2000.00 + MAX(amt)
    FROM Orders b
    WHERE a.odate = b.odate);
```

The subquery calculates the MAX value for all rows with the same date as the current aggregate group of the main query. The subquery must use a WHERE clause, as shown above. The subquery itself must not use a GROUP BY or HAVING clause.

Correlated Subqueries and Joins

As you may have surmised, correlated subqueries are closely related to joins—both involve checking each row of one table against every row of another (or an alias of the same) table. You will find that many operations that can be performed with one of these will also work with the other.

Some differences in application exist between the two, however, such as the aforementioned occasional necessity for using DISTINCT with a join where it is not needed with a subquery. Each can also do some things that the other cannot. Subqueries, for example, can employ aggregate functions in the predicate, making possible operations such as our previous example in which we extracted orders that were above the average for their customers. Joins, on the other hand, can produce rows from both of the tables being compared, whereas the output of subqueries is used only in the predicates of outer queries. As a rule of thumb, the form of query that seems most intuitive will probably be the best to use, but it is good to be cognizant of both techniques for those situations where one or the other will not work.

Summary

Now you are using queries in a hierarchical manner. You have seen how using the results of one query to control another extends the ease with which you can perform many functions. You now understand how to use subqueries with relational operators as well as with the special operator IN, in either the WHERE or HAVING clause of the outer query.

You can also congratulate yourself on mastering what many consider the most abstruse concept in SQL—the correlated subquery. You have seen how the correlated subquery relates to the join, as well as how to use it with aggregate functions and in the HAVING clause. All in all, you have now covered all types of subqueries pretty thoroughly.

The next step is the introduction of some SQL special operators. These take subqueries as arguments, as IN does, but unlike IN, they can be used *only* with subqueries.

Putting SQL to Work

1. Write a query that uses a subquery to obtain all orders for the customer named Cisneros. Assume you do not know his customer number (cnum).

2. Write a query that produces the names and ratings of all customers who have any orders that are above the average for all orders.

3. Write a query that selects the total amount in orders for each salesperson for whom this total is greater than the amount of the largest order in the table.

4. Write a SELECT statement using a correlated subquery that selects the names and numbers of all customers with ratings equal to the maximum for their city.

5. Write two queries that select all salespeople (by name and number) who have customers in their cities whom they do not service, one using a join and one a correlated subquery. Which solution is more elegant? (Hint: one way to do this is to find all customers not serviced by a given salesperson and see if any of them are in his or her city.)

CHAPTER
TWELVE

12

Using Subquery Operators

- How Does EXISTS Work?

- Using EXISTS with Correlated Subqueries

- The Special Operator ANY or SOME

- The Special Operator ALL

- How ANY, ALL, and EXISTS Deal with NULLs, Empty Result Sets, and UNKNOWNs

Now that you are well acquainted with subqueries, we can talk about some special operators that always take subqueries as arguments. The EXISTS operator is used to base a predicate on whether or not a subquery produces output. In this chapter, you will learn how to use this operator with conventional and (more usefully) correlated subqueries. We will also discuss special considerations that come into play when you use this operator as regards aggregates, NULLs, and Booleans. In addition, you will extend your general proficiency with subqueries by examining more complex applications of them than we have been seeing up to now.

You will also learn about the operators ANY, ALL, and SOME (these are actually just two operators, as ANY and SOME are synonyms). ANY, ALL, and SOME are similar to EXISTS in that they take subqueries as arguments. They differ from EXISTS, however, in that they are used in conjunction with relational operators. In this respect, they are similar to the IN operator when it is used with subqueries; they take all the values produced by the subquery and treat them as a unit. However, unlike IN, they can be used only with subqueries, not with enumerated sets.

How Does EXISTS Work?

EXISTS is an operator that produces a TRUE or FALSE value, in other words, a Boolean expression. This means it can stand alone in a predicate or be combined with other Boolean expressions using the Boolean operators AND, OR, and NOT. It takes a subquery as an argument and evaluates to TRUE if it produces any output or FALSE if it does not.

Notice that this makes it different from other predicate operators in SQL. Most SQL operators compare values and produce UNKNOWNs if those values are NULL. EXISTS simply checks whether a query produces output and therefore cannot be UNKNOWN. This situation creates some special issues that we will deal with later in this chapter. The only other operator we have seen that cannot be UNKNOWN is IS NULL, which is specifically designed to deal with NULLs.

For example, we can decide to extract some data from the Customers table if and only if one or more of the customers in the Customers table are located in San Jose (the output for this query is shown in Figure 12.1):

```
SELECT cnum, cname, city
    FROM Customers
```

```
WHERE EXISTS
(SELECT *
FROM Customers
WHERE city = 'San Jose');
```

FIGURE 12.1:

Using the EXISTS operator

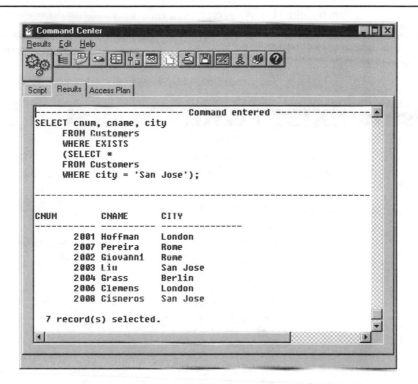

The inner query selected all data for all customers in San Jose. The EXISTS operator in the outer predicate noted that the subquery produced some output and therefore, since the EXISTS expression was the entire outer predicate, made the predicate TRUE. The subquery (not being correlated) was performed only once for the entire outer query and therefore had a single value for all cases. Since EXISTS, when used in this manner, makes the predicate TRUE or FALSE for all rows at once, it is not terribly useful for extracting specific information. For this reason, EXISTS is almost always used with correlated subqueries.

Selecting Columns with EXISTS

In the above example, EXISTS could have just as easily selected a single column, instead of selecting all columns by using the asterisk. This differs from the subqueries we have seen before that can select only a single column, as noted in Chapter 11. However, it generally makes little difference which column EXISTS selects, or if selects all columns, because it simply notes whether or not there is output from the subquery and does not use the values produced at all.

Using EXISTS with Correlated Subqueries

With a correlated subquery, the EXISTS clause is evaluated separately for each row of the table referenced in the outer query, as are other predicate operators used with correlated subqueries. This enables you to use EXISTS as a practical predicate, one that generates different answers for each row of the table referenced in the outer query. Therefore, information from the inner query is, in a sense, preserved, if not directly output, when you use EXISTS in this manner. For example, we can find salespeople who have multiple customers as in the query below, the output of which is shown in Figure 12.2.

```
SELECT DISTINCT snum
    FROM Customers outer
    WHERE EXISTS
    (SELECT *
    FROM Customers inner
    WHERE inner.snum = outer.snum
    AND inner.cnum <> outer.cnum);
```

For each candidate row of the outer query (representing a customer currently being examined), the inner query found rows of the Customers table that matched the snum value (had the same salesperson), but not the cnum value (matched a different customer). If the inner query finds any such rows, it implies that there are at least two different customers serviced by the current salesperson (that is, the salesperson of the customer in the current candidate row of the outer query)—the customer currently matched in the outer query and the different customer currently selected by the subquery. The EXISTS predicate is therefore TRUE for the current row, and the salesperson number (snum) column of the table in the outer query is output. Notice that it does not matter how many customers the salesperson has. EXISTS cares only whether the subquery produces output and makes no distinction as to whether it produces one row or one hundred. We had a good reason to specify DISTINCT in the main query, however. If we had not done so, each of these salespeople would have been selected once for each customer that she or he is assigned. Examine the logic of the query and see if you can tell why this is so.

FIGURE 12.2:

Combining EXISTS
with a join

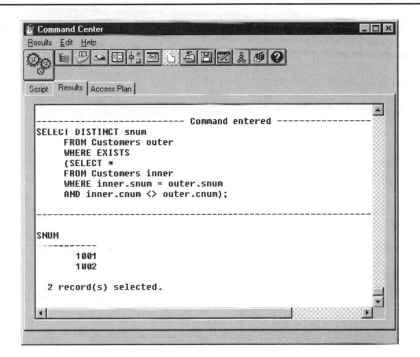

Combining EXISTS with Joins

It might be useful for us to output more information about these salespeople than their numbers, however. We can do this by joining the Customers table to the Salespeople table (the output for the query is shown in Figure 12.3):

```
SELECT DISTINCT first.snum, sname, first.city
     FROM Salespeople first, Customers second
     WHERE EXISTS
     (SELECT *
     FROM Customers third
     WHERE second.snum = third.snum
     AND second.cnum <> third.cnum)
     AND first.snum = second.snum;
```

FIGURE 12.3:

Combining EXISTS with a join

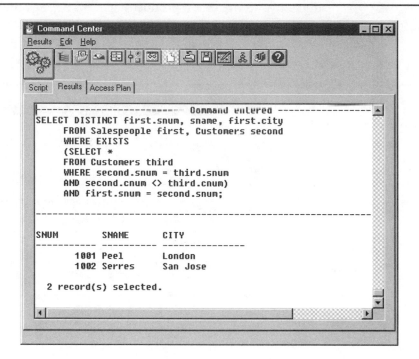

The inner query here is the same as the previous example, save for the fact that we changed the aliases. The outer query is a join of the Salespeople and Customers tables, similar to ones we have seen before. The new clause of the main predicate (AND `first.snum = second.snum`) is, of course, evaluated at the same level as the EXISTS clause. It is the functional predicate of the join itself, matching the two tables from the outer query in terms of the snum column that they have in common. This is, therefore, a natural join. Because of the Boolean operator AND, both of the main predicate's conditions must be TRUE in order for the predicate to be TRUE. Therefore, the results of the subquery matter only in those cases where the second part of the query is TRUE and the join is in effect. Combining joins and subqueries in this way can be a quite powerful way of working with data.

Using NOT EXISTS

The previous example makes it clear that you can combine EXISTS with Boolean operators. Naturally, the one that is easiest to use and probably most commonly used with EXISTS is NOT. One way that we could find all salespeople with only one customer would be to reverse our previous example (the output for this query is shown in Figure 12.4):

```
SELECT DISTINCT snum
     FROM Customers outer
     WHERE NOT EXISTS
     (SELECT *
     FROM Customers inner
     WHERE inner.snum = outer.snum
     AND inner.cnum <> outer.cnum);
```

FIGURE 12.4:

Using EXISTS with NOT

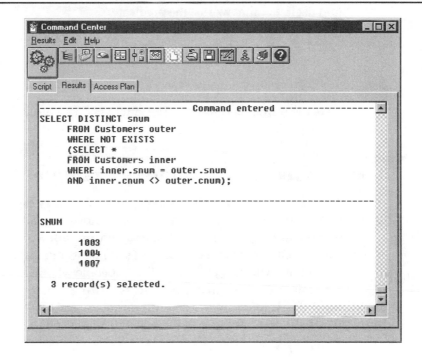

EXISTS and Aggregates

In a strict interpretation of the SQL standard, one thing that EXISTS cannot do is take an aggregate function in its subquery. This makes sense. If an aggregate function finds any rows to operate on, then EXISTS is TRUE, and it does not matter what the value of the function is; if the function finds no rows, then EXISTS is FALSE. Attempting to use aggregates with EXISTS in this way probably indicates that the problem has not been thought out properly, although some products may accept the syntax.

Of course, a subquery to an EXISTS predicate may also use one or more subqueries of its own. These may be of any of the various types we have seen (or that we will see). These subqueries, and any others within them, are allowed to use aggregates, unless there is some other reason why they cannot. The next section offers an example of this situation.

In either case, you could have gotten the same result more easily by selecting the column on which you used the aggregate function, instead of using the function itself. In other words, the predicate

```
EXISTS (SELECT COUNT(DISTINCT sname) FROM Salespeople)
```

would be equivalent to

```
EXISTS (SELECT sname FROM salespeople)
```

were the former permissible. The latter version would also probably execute more quickly.

A More Advanced Subquery Example

The possible applications of subqueries can get very involved. You can nest two or more of them in a single query, even inside one another. While it can take a bit of thought to figure out how these statements will work, you can do things this way in SQL that would take several statements in most other languages. Here is a query that extracts the rows of all salespeople who have customers with more than one current order. It is not necessarily the simplest solution to this problem, but rather is intended to demonstrate advanced SQL logic. Deriving this information means interrelating all three of our sample tables:

```
SELECT *
    FROM Salespeople first
    WHERE EXISTS
    (SELECT *
    FROM Customers second
    WHERE first.snum = second.snum
    AND 1 <
    (SELECT COUNT(*)
    FROM Orders
    WHERE Orders.cnum = second.cnum));
```

The output for this query is shown in Figure 12.5.

We could view the evaluation of the above query like this:

- Take each row of the Salespeople table as a candidate row (outer query) and perform the subqueries.

- For each candidate row from the outer query (Salespeople table), the middle query finds the matching rows from the Customers table, using a natural join. Each customer who satisfies the join becomes a candidate row for the innermost query.

- Whenever we find a customer in the middle query who is matched to the salesperson in the outer query, however, we must look at the innermost query to determine if our middle query predicate will be TRUE.

- The innermost query counts the number of orders of the current customer (current in the middle query). If this number is greater than 1, the predicate of the middle query is TRUE, and rows are selected. This makes the EXISTS predicate of the outer query TRUE for the current salesperson's row, meaning that at least one of the current salesperson's customers has more than one order.

This query, even though it may seem like a convoluted way to extract information, is doing a lot of work. It is correlating three different tables to give you information that would be difficult to derive more directly were the tables larger than they are here, as they likely would be in the real world (although this is not the only, or necessarily the best, way to do it in SQL). Perhaps you would have to see this information on a regular basis—if, for instance, you had an end-of-the-week bonus for salespeople who produced multiple orders from a single customer. In this case, it would be worth deriving the statement and keeping it to use again and again as the data changes (a good way to do this is with a view, which we will discuss in Chapter 15).

The Special Operator ANY or SOME

Let us begin by examining the operator ANY or SOME. SOME and ANY are interchangeable—wherever we use the term ANY, SOME would work just the same. The difference in terminology reflects an effort to allow people to use the term that they find more intuitive and to accommodate differences between products. This is somewhat problematic; as we shall see, intuitive interpretations of these operators can sometimes be misleading.

Here is a new way to find salespeople with customers located in their cities (the output for this query is shown in Figure 12.6):

```
SELECT *
    FROM Salespeople
    WHERE city = ANY
    (SELECT city
    FROM Customers);
```

FIGURE 12.6:

Using the ANY operator

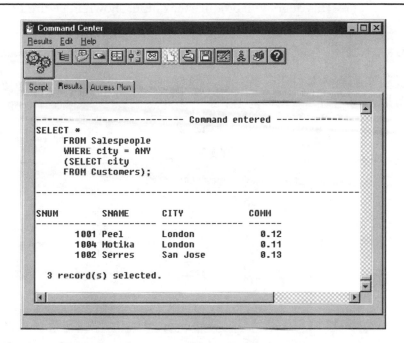

The ANY operator takes all values produced by the subquery, in this case all city values in the Customers table, and evaluates to TRUE if ANY of them equal the city value of the current row of the outer query. Of course, this means that the subquery must select values whose datatype is comparable to what they are being compared to in the main predicate, just as IN and relational operators must (to find out which datatypes are comparable, see "Datatypes" in the reference). This is in contrast to EXISTS, which simply determines whether or not a subquery produces results and does not actually use the results, so that the datatypes of the subquery output columns do not matter.

Using IN or EXISTS Instead of ANY

We could also have used the IN operator to construct the previous query:

```
SELECT *
    FROM Salespeople
    WHERE city IN
    (SELECT city
    FROM Customers);
```

This query will produce the output shown in Figure 12.7.

Using IN as an
alternative to ANY

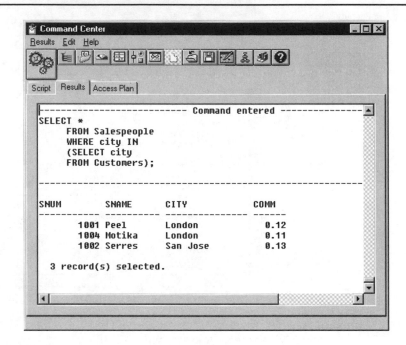

However, the ANY operator can use other relational operators besides = and thereby make comparisons that are beyond the capabilities of IN. For example, we could find all salespeople for whom there are customers who follow them in alphabetical order (the output is shown in Figure 12.8):

```
SELECT *
    FROM Salespeople
    WHERE sname < ANY
    (SELECT cname
    FROM Customers);
```

FIGURE 12.8:

Using ANY with an
inequality

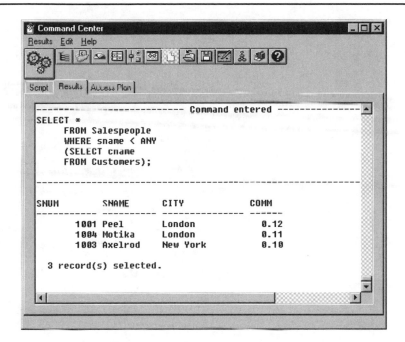

The query selected all rows save for those of Serres and Rifkin, because there
are no customers whose names follow these in alphabetical order. Notice that this
is basically equivalent to the following EXISTS query, whose output is shown in
Figure 12.9:

```
SELECT *
    FROM Salespeople outer
    WHERE EXISTS
    (SELECT *
    FROM Customers inner
    WHERE outer.sname < inner.cname);
```

FIGURE 12.9:

Using EXISTS as an alternative to ANY

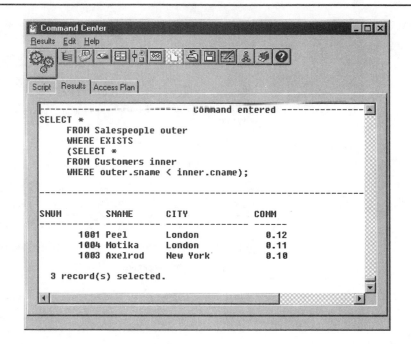

Any query that can be formulated with ANY (or, as we shall see, ALL) could also be formulated with EXISTS, although the reverse is not true. Strictly speaking, the EXISTS versions are not quite identical to the ANY or ALL versions because of a difference in logic (two-valued vs. three-valued), which we will discuss later in this chapter. Nonetheless, technically speaking, you could do without ANY and ALL if you became very adroit with the use of EXISTS (and IS NULL). Many users, however, find ANY and ALL easier to use than EXISTS, which requires correlated subqueries. In addition, depending on the implementation, ANY and ALL can, at least in theory, be more efficient than EXISTS. You can execute an ANY or ALL subquery once and use its output to determine the predicate for every row of the main query. EXISTS, on the other hand, takes a correlated subquery, which requires the DBMS to re-execute the entire subquery for each row of the main query. EXISTS is therefore a less efficient formulation of the query. SQL attempts to find the most efficient way to execute any statement, so it will likely try to convert a less efficient formulation of a query to a more efficient one, but you can't always count on it finding the most efficient formulation.

One reason for offering the EXISTS formulation as an alternative to ANY and ALL is that ANY and ALL can be somewhat counterintuitive, given the way we use these terms in English (as you shall soon see). By being aware of different ways to formulate a given query, you can work around procedures that you happen to find difficult or awkward.

How ANY Can Be Confusing

As we implied above, ANY is not entirely intuitive. If we construct a query to select customers who have a greater rating than ANY customer in Rome, we would get output that might be a little different from what we expected (as shown in Figure 12.10):

```
SELECT *
    FROM Customers
    WHERE rating > ANY
    (SELECT rating
    FROM Customers
    WHERE city = 'Rome');
```

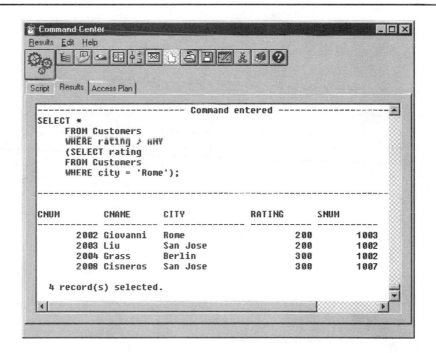

In English, we would normally be inclined to interpret a rating as being "greater than *any* (where the city equals Rome)" by saying that the rating value must be higher than the rating value in *every* case where the city value equals Rome. This is not, however, the way ANY is conceived in SQL. ANY evaluates to TRUE if the subquery finds *any* one or more value(s) that make the condition TRUE.

If we were evaluating ANY the way we normally would in English, only the customers with a rating of 300 would beat Giovanni, who is in Rome and has a rating of 200. However, the ANY subquery also found Periera in Rome with a rating of 100. Because all the customers with a rating of 200 were higher than that, they were selected, even though there was another Rome customer (Giovanni) whose rating they did not beat (the fact that one of the customers selected is also in Rome is irrelevant). Since the subquery did produce at least one value that would make the predicate TRUE for these rows, the rows were selected.

To give another example, suppose we were to select all orders that had amounts that were greater than at least one of the orders from October 6:

```
SELECT *
    FROM Orders
    WHERE amt > ANY
    (SELECT amt
    FROM Orders
    WHERE odate = '10/06/2000');
```

The output for this query is shown in Figure 12.11.

Even though the highest amount in the table (9891.88) is on October 6, the preceding rows have higher amounts than the other row for October 6, which had an amount of 1309.95. Had the relational operator been >= instead of simply >, this row would also have been selected, because it is equal to itself.

Selecting amounts greater
than ANY from October 6

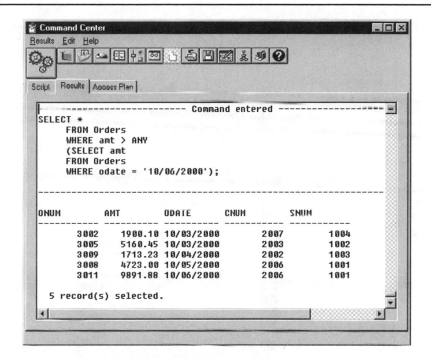

Naturally, you can use ANY with other SQL techniques, such as joins. This query will find all orders with amounts smaller than any amount for a customer in San Jose (the output is shown in Figure 12.12):

```
SELECT *
    FROM Orders
    WHERE amt < ANY
    (SELECT amt
    FROM Orders a, Customers b
    WHERE a.cnum = b.cnum
    AND b.city = 'San Jose');
```

FIGURE 12.12:

Using ANY with a join

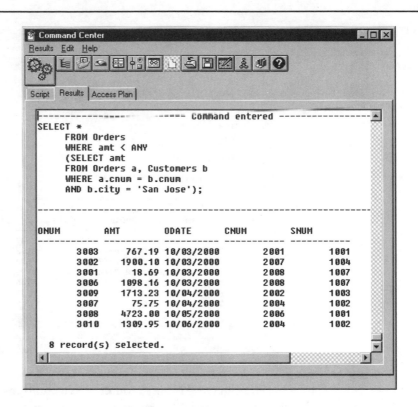

Even though the smallest order in the table was for a customer in San Jose, so was the second-largest; therefore, almost all the rows were selected. An easy thing to remember is that < ANY means less than the largest value selected and > ANY means greater than the smallest value selected. In fact, we could have also phrased the above statement like this (the output is shown in Figure 12.13):

```
SELECT *
    FROM Orders
WHERE amt <
    (SELECT MAX(amt)
    FROM Orders a, Customers b
    WHERE a.cnum = b.cnum
    AND b.city = 'San Jose');
```

FIGURE 12.13:

Using an aggregate
function in place of ANY

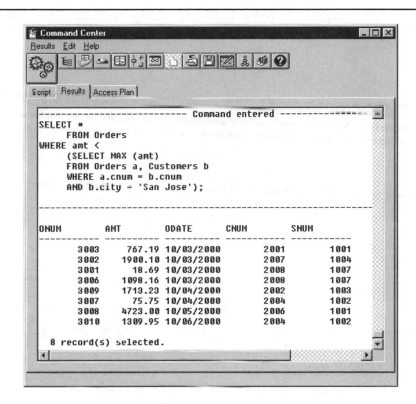

The Special Operator ALL

With ALL, the predicate is TRUE if *every* value selected by the subquery satisfies the condition in the predicate of the outer query. If we wanted to revise our previous example to output only those customers whose ratings are, in fact, higher than every customer in Rome, we would enter the following to produce the output shown in Figure 12.14:

```
SELECT *
    FROM Customers
    WHERE rating > ALL
    (SELECT rating
    FROM Customers
    WHERE city = 'Rome');
```

FIGURE 12.14:

Using the ALL operator

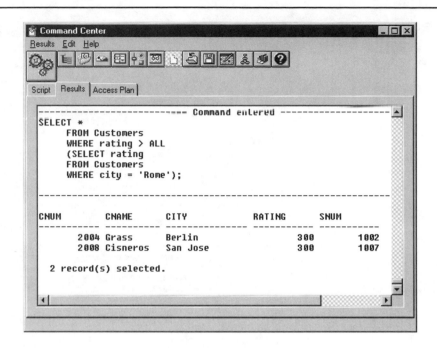

This statement examined the rating values of all customers in Rome. It then found those customers with a higher rating than every one of the Rome customers. The highest rating in Rome is Giovanni, with a value of 200. Therefore, only those customers with a value higher than 200 were selected.

Just as with ANY, we can use EXISTS to produce an alternative formulation of the same query (the output is shown in Figure 12.15):

```
SELECT *
    FROM Customers outer
    WHERE NOT EXISTS
    (SELECT *
    FROM Customers inner
    WHERE outer.rating <= inner.rating
    AND inner.city = 'Rome');
```

Using EXISTS as an
alternative to ALL

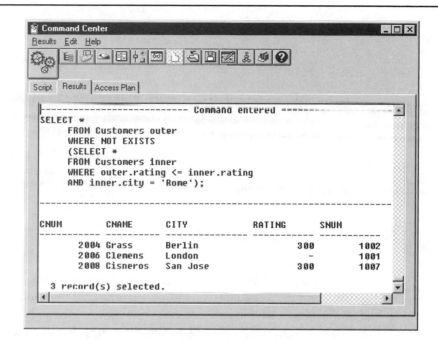

Equalities and Inequalities with ALL

ALL is used primarily with inequalities rather than equalities because a value can
be "equal to all" of the results of a subquery only if all of those results are, in fact,
identical. Examine the following query:

```
SELECT *
    FROM Customers
    WHERE rating = ALL
        (SELECT rating
         FROM Customers
         WHERE city = 'San Jose');
```

This statement would be legal, but we would, with the current data, get no output. The only way this query would produce output is if all rating values in San
Jose happened to be identical. In this case, it would be similar to saying

```
SELECT *
    FROM Customers
    WHERE rating =
```

```
(SELECT DISTINCT rating
 FROM Customers
 WHERE city = 'San Jose');
```

The main difference is that this last statement would fail if the subquery produced multiple values, whereas the ALL version would simply give no output. In general, it is not a good idea to use queries that would work only in special cases like this. Because your data will constantly be changing, it is not a good practice to make assumptions about its content. If you do have a reason for such assumptions, however, it is usually better to have queries that will fail if your assumptions do not hold. This way, you will know that something is amiss and can take appropriate action.

Nonequalities with ALL

You can use ALL effectively with nonequalities, that is to say with the <> operator. To say in SQL that a value does not equal all the results of a subquery, however, is different from saying it in English. Obviously, if the subquery returns multiple distinct values, as is usually the case, no single value can be equal to all of them in the usual sense. In SQL, <> ALL means the same thing that "is not equal to any" means in common English. In other words, the predicate is TRUE if the value is not found among the results of the subquery. Therefore, our previous example put in the negative looks like this (the output is shown in Figure 12.16):

```
SELECT *
    FROM Customers
    WHERE rating <> ALL
    (SELECT rating
    FROM Customers
    WHERE city = 'San Jose');
```

The above subquery selected all ratings where the city was San Jose. This produced a set of two values: 200 (for Liu) and 300 (for Cisneros). The main query then selected all rows whose rating matched neither of these—that is, all rows with a rating of 100.

FIGURE 12.16:

Using ALL with <>

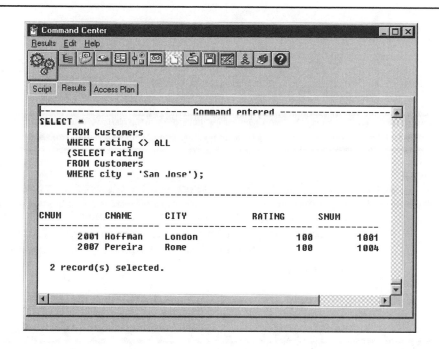

Notice that Clemens was not selected, even though his NULL rating is not the same as that of either Liu or Cisneros. This, of course, is because ALL, like ANY and IN but unlike EXISTS, utilizes three-valued logic. For Clemens' row, the expression being evaluated is

```
(NULL = 200) OR (NULL = 300)
```

This reduces to

```
UNKNOWN OR UNKNOWN
```

which, of course, is UNKNOWN, so Clemens' row is not included.

You could have formulated the same query using NOT IN:

```
SELECT *
    FROM Customers
    WHERE rating NOT IN
    (SELECT rating
    FROM Customers
    WHERE city = 'San Jose');
```

You could also have used ANY:

```
SELECT *
    FROM Customers
    WHERE NOT rating = ANY
    (SELECT rating
    FROM Customers
    WHERE city = 'San Jose');
```

The output would be the same for all three statements.

Keeping ANY, ALL, and EXISTS Straight

In SQL, saying a value is greater (or less) than ANY of a set of values is the same as saying it is greater (or less) than any single one of those values. Conversely, saying a value does not equal ALL of a set of values means that there is no value in the set to which it is equal.

How ANY, ALL, and EXISTS Deal with NULLs, Empty Result Sets, and UNKNOWNs

As we mentioned, there are some differences between EXISTS and the other operators introduced in this chapter with regard to how NULLs are handled. ANY and ALL also differ from each other in how they react if the subquery produces no values to use in a comparison. These differences can give your queries unexpected results if you do not account for them.

When the Subquery Comes Back Empty

One significant difference between ALL and ANY is the way they deal with the situation in which the subquery returns no values. You have to watch out for this, as there is nothing intuitive about it. Basically, whenever a legal subquery fails to produce output, the rules are as follows:

- ALL is automatically TRUE.

- ANY is automatically FALSE.

This means that the following query

```
SELECT *
      FROM Customers
      WHERE rating > ANY
      (SELECT rating
      FROM Customers
      WHERE city = 'Boston');
```

would produce no output, whereas this query

```
SELECT *
      FROM Customers
      WHERE rating > ALL
      (SELECT rating
      FROM Customers
      WHERE city = 'Boston');
```

would produce the entire Customers table. Since there are no customers in Boston, of course, neither of these comparisons is very meaningful.

ANY and ALL vs. EXISTS with NULLs

NULL values are also a bit of a problem with operators like these. When SQL compares two values in a predicate, one of which is NULL, the result is UNKNOWN. The UNKNOWN predicate, like FALSE, causes a row to not be selected, but this will work out differently for some otherwise-identical queries, depending on whether they use ALL or ANY as opposed to EXISTS. Consider our previous examples:

```
SELECT *
      FROM Customers
      WHERE rating > ANY
      (SELECT rating
      FROM Customers
      WHERE city = 'Rome');
```

and

```
SELECT *
      FROM Customers outer
      WHERE NOT EXISTS
      (SELECT *
      FROM Customers inner
```

```
WHERE outer.rating > inner.rating
AND inner.city = 'Rome');
```

These two queries will behave just the same, except for Clemens' row, which has a NULL rating. In the ANY version, when Clemens' rating is selected by the main query, the NULL value makes the predicate UNKNOWN, and Clemens' row is not selected for output. However, when the NOT EXISTS version selects this row in the main query, the NULL value is used in the predicate of the subquery, making it UNKNOWN in every case. This means the subquery will produce no values, and EXISTS will be FALSE. This, naturally, makes NOT EXISTS TRUE. Therefore, Clemens' row is selected for output. This discrepancy stems from the fact that, unlike other types of predicates, the value of EXISTS is always TRUE or FALSE—never UNKNOWN.

This situation constitutes an argument for using the ANY formulation. We do not ordinarily think of a NULL value as being higher than a valid value. Moreover, the result would have been the same if we had been checking for a lower value. NULLs can make NOT EXISTS predicates TRUE when they have no logical reason to be. This is part of a somewhat famous problem in SQL called the EXISTS problem.

Using COUNT in Place of EXISTS

We have pointed out that ANY and ALL formulations can all be (imprecisely) rendered with EXISTS, while the reverse is not true. Although such is the case, it is also true that you can circumvent EXISTS and NOT EXISTS subqueries by executing the same subqueries with COUNT(*) in the subquery's SELECT clause. If more than zero rows of output are counted, it is the equivalent of EXISTS; otherwise it is the same as NOT EXISTS. Let's look at an example (the output is shown in Figure 12.17):

```
SELECT *
    FROM Customers outer
    WHERE NOT EXISTS
    (SELECT *
    FROM Customers inner
    WHERE outer.rating <= inner.rating
    AND inner.city = 'Rome');
```

Using EXISTS with a
correlated subquery

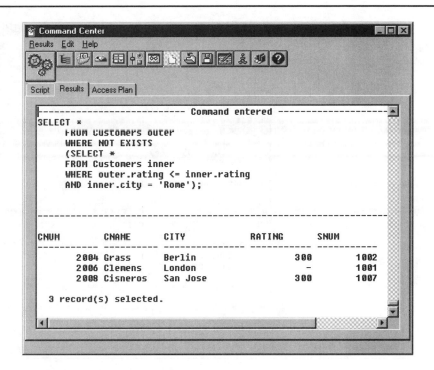

You could also render this query as:

```
SELECT *
     FROM Customers outer
     WHERE 1 >
     (SELECT COUNT(*)
     FROM Customers inner
     WHERE outer.rating <= inner.rating
     AND inner.city = 'Rome');
```

The output to this query is shown in Figure 12.18.

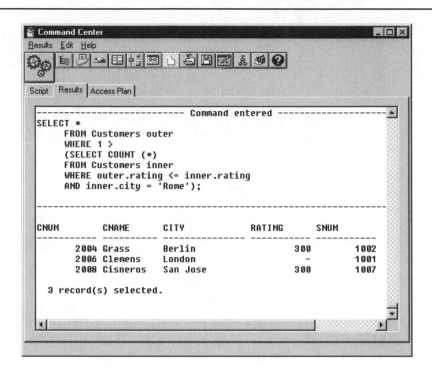

So which version is better? In general, you might as well use EXISTS rather than COUNT for this sort of thing. Although the optimizer may be able to execute the COUNT version just as efficiently as EXISTS, in principle the EXISTS version is more efficient because the subquery need not be completed. As soon as the subquery outputs a row, the DBMS knows that EXISTS is TRUE and need not finish executing the subquery for that row of the outer query. It is helpful to start thinking about alternative ways of formulating SQL statements and how they are likely to be executed. Often, the DBMS has an EXPLAIN PLAN or similar feature that directly shows you how a particular query will be executed and possibly lets you fine-tune its plan.

You are now beginning to see clearly how many ways there are of doing things in SQL. If it all seems a bit confusing at this stage, you needn't worry. You will learn to use those techniques that best suit your needs and are most intuitive for you. At this point, we want to expose you to many different possibilities, so that you will be able to find your own best approach.

Summary

Well, you have covered a lot of ground in this chapter. Subqueries are not a simple topic, so we have spent some time discussing their variations and ambiguities. The mastery you now have of them is not superficial. You know several techniques for solving a given problem, so you can choose the one that best suits your purposes and effectively work around any limitations of the particular product you are using.

EXISTS, although it seems simple, can be one of SQL's more abstruse operators. It is, however, quite flexible and powerful. In this chapter, you have seen and mastered the many possibilities that EXISTS creates for you. In the process, you have considerably extended your comprehension of advanced subquery logic. You have also seen a number of ambiguities of ANY, ALL, and SOME.

You now understand how different formulations of the same query will handle errors and NULL values. The next chapter will show you how to combine the output from any number of queries into a single body by merging the output of multiple queries.

Putting SQL to Work

1. Write a query that uses the EXISTS operator to extract all salespeople who have customers with a rating of 300.

2. How could you have solved the above problem with a join?

3. Write a query using the EXISTS operator that selects all salespeople with customers located in their cities who are not assigned to them.

4. Write a query that extracts from the Customers table every customer assigned to a salesperson who currently has at least one other customer (besides the customer being selected) with orders in the Orders table. (Hint: this is similar in structure to our three-level subquery example.)

5. Write a query that selects all customers whose ratings are equal to or greater than ANY (in the SQL sense) of Serres' ratings.

6. What would be the output of the above statement?

7. Write a query using ANY or ALL that will find all salespeople who have no customers located in their city.

8. Write a query that selects all orders for amounts greater than any (in the usual sense) for the customers in London.

9. Write the above query using MAX.

CHAPTER

THIRTEEN

13

Merging Multiple Queries

- Uniting Multiple Queries as One

- Using UNION with ORDER BY

- Other Ways of Combining Multiple Queries

In the preceding few chapters, we discussed the various ways to place queries inside one another. There is another way of combining multiple queries—that is, by merging their output. In this chapter, you will learn about the clauses in SQL that control how multiple queries are merged. These clauses include UNION, INTERSECT, EXCEPT, and CORRESPONDING.

Uniting Multiple Queries As One

You can put multiple queries together and combine their output using the UNION clause. The UNION clause merges the output of two or more SQL queries into a single set of rows and columns. To output all salespeople and customers located in London as a single body, for example, you could enter

```
SELECT snum, sname
     FROM Salespeople
     WHERE city = 'London'
     UNION
SELECT cnum, cname
     FROM Customers
     WHERE city = 'London';
```

to get the output shown in Figure 13.1.

As you can see, the columns selected by the two statements are output as though they were one. The column headings are omitted because the columns produced by a UNION are not directly extracted from a single table—there are at least two tables. Therefore, the names of the table columns from which the output columns are taken can vary (between the two queries). Because of this ambiguity, the simplest solution is to treat all of the output columns of UNIONs as unnamed, which is what most products—and the standard—do.

Also notice that only the final query ends with a semicolon. The absence of the semicolon is what makes SQL cognizant that another query is coming.

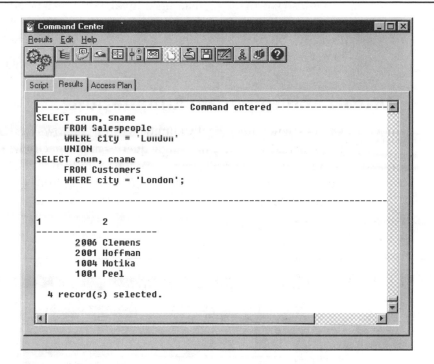

FIGURE 13.1:

Forming a UNION of
two queries

When Can You Make a UNION between Queries?

In order for two (or more) queries to undergo a UNION, their output columns should be *UNION-compatible*. This means, first of all, that all queries in the UNION should select the same number of columns. It also implies that the output columns to be merged should be of comparable datatypes. For example, you would not merge a text column with a set of graphics. In actuality, products vary considerably in how strictly they enforce this rule. Generally, they will attempt to do a datatype conversion automatically if such makes sense. It is better, however, to use a CAST expression to convert the datatypes yourself, if they are not closely related, so that you have control over how the conversion is done.

The basic concept is that two types are UNION-compatible if there is a meaningful way to convert data between them. The official datatype conversions of the SQL92 standard are outlined in the reference under "Datatypes". In older versions of the standard, fixed-length text strings had to be of the same maximum length, and some products may still reflect this restriction.

It is also worth noting that, since any datatype can be NULL, the keyword NULL used in a SELECT clause is UNION-compatible with any datatype. We will see how to use the NULL keyword in UNION in the section "Using UNION to Implement Outer Joins," later in this chapter.

UNION and Duplicate Elimination

UNION will automatically eliminate duplicate rows from the output. This is an idiosyncrasy of SQL, since single queries must specify DISTINCT to eliminate duplicates. For example, this query, whose output is shown in Figure 13.2, has a duplicate combination of values (1001 with London) because we did not tell SQL to eliminate duplicates:

```
SELECT snum, city
    FROM Customers;
```

FIGURE 13.2:

A single query with duplicated output

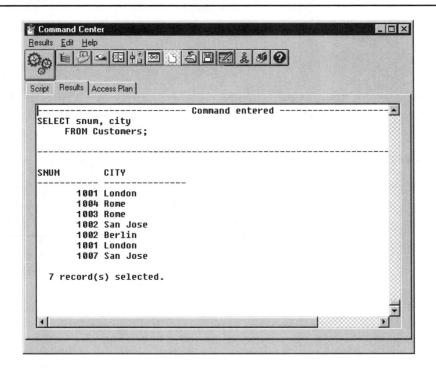

However, if we use UNION to combine this query with a similar one on the Salespeople table, the same redundant combination is eliminated. Figure 13.3 shows the output of the following query:

```
SELECT snum, city
    FROM Customers
    UNION
SELECT snum, city
    FROM Salespeople;
```

FIGURE 13.3:

A UNION eliminates
duplicate output.

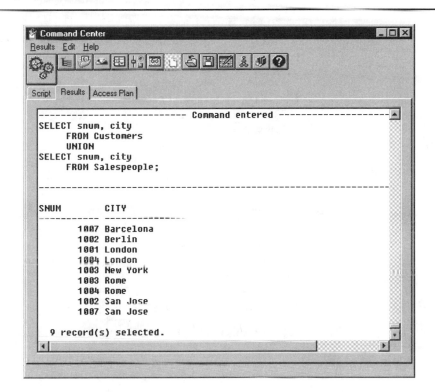

```
-------------------------- Command entered --------------------
SELECT snum, city
    FROM Customers
    UNION
SELECT snum, city
    FROM Salespeople;


SNUM        CITY
----------  --------------
      1007  Barcelona
      1002  Berlin
      1001  London
      1004  London
      1003  New York
      1003  Rome
      1004  Rome
      1002  San Jose
      1007  San Jose

   9 record(s) selected.
```

You can get around eliminating duplicate output by specifying UNION ALL in place of UNION, like this:

```
SELECT snum, city
    FROM Customers
    UNION ALL
SELECT snum, city
    FROM Salespeople;
```

Using Strings and Expressions with Union

In Chapter 9 you saw how to use constants and expressions among the output columns of a query. You can also insert constants and expressions in the SELECT clauses used with UNION. The constants and expressions you use, however, must meet the standards of UNION-compatibility we have outlined. This feature is useful, for example, to provide comments indicating which query produced a given row. You can also use it to merge output columns with expressions, provided they are UNION-compatible.

Suppose you must make a report of which salespeople produced the largest and smallest orders on specific dates. You could unite the two queries, inserting text to distinguish the two cases:

```
SELECT a.snum, sname, onum, 'Highest on', odate
    FROM Salespeople a, Orders b
    WHERE a.snum = b.snum
    AND b.amt =
    (SELECT MAX(amt)
    FROM Orders c
    WHERE c.odate = b.odate)
    UNION
SELECT a.snum, sname, onum, 'Lowest  on', odate
    FROM Salespeople a, Orders b
    WHERE a.snum = b.snum
    AND b.amt =
    (SELECT MIN(amt)
    FROM Orders c
    WHERE c.odate = b.odate);
```

The output from this command is shown in Figure 13.4.

We had to add an extra space to the 'Lowest on' string to make it match 'Highest on' for length. Most implementations do not require you to do so, but since it was part of the SQL89 standard, it may be possible to find one that does. Having the words aligned can also make the output look nicer. Note also that Peel is selected for having both the highest and lowest (in fact, the *only*) order for October 5. Because the inserted strings of the two queries are different (Lowest on as opposed to Highest on), the rows are not eliminated as duplicates.

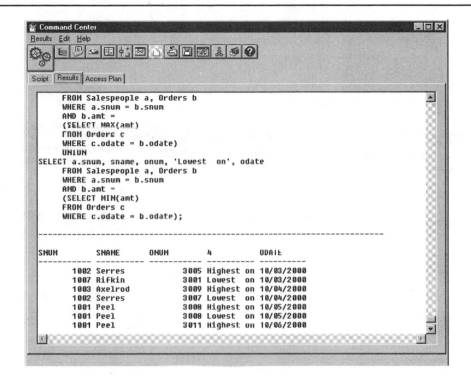

```
FROM Salespeople a, Orders b
WHERE a.snum = b.snum
AND b.amt =
(SELECT MAX(amt)
FROM Orders c
WHERE c.odate = b.odate)
UNION
SELECT a.snum, sname, onum, 'Lowest  on', odate
FROM Salespeople a, Orders b
WHERE a.snum = b.snum
AND b.amt =
(SELECT MIN(amt)
FROM Orders c
WHERE c.odate = b.odate);


---------------------------------------------------------------

SNUM       SNAME       ONUM        4          ODATE
---------- ----------  ----------- ---------- ----------
      1002 Serres           3005 Highest on 10/03/2000
      1007 Rifkin           3001 Lowest  on 10/03/2000
      1003 Axelrod          3009 Highest on 10/04/2000
      1002 Serres           3007 Lowest  on 10/04/2000
      1001 Peel             3008 Highest on 10/05/2000
      1001 Peel             3008 Lowest  on 10/05/2000
      1001 Peel             3011 Highest on 10/06/2000
```

Using UNION with ORDER BY

Up until now, we have not assumed that the data from the multiple queries
would be output in any particular order. We have simply shown the output first
from one query and then from the other. Of course, you could not rely on the output coming in this order automatically. We just did it that way to make the examples easier to follow. You can, however, use the ORDER BY clause to order the
output from a UNION, just as you do the output from individual queries. Let's
revise our last example to order the names by order number. This will make situations such as Peel's in the previous example more obvious, as you can see from
the output shown in Figure 13.5.

```
SELECT a.snum, sname, onum, 'Highest on', odate
    FROM Salespeople a, Orders b
    WHERE a.snum = b.snum
    AND b.amt =
    (SELECT MAX(amt)
    FROM Orders c
    WHERE c.odate = b.odate)
UNION
    SELECT a.snum, sname, onum, 'Lowest  on', odate
    FROM Salespeople a, Orders b
    WHERE a.snum = b.snum
    AND b.amt =
    (SELECT MIN(amt)
    FROM Orders c
    WHERE c.odate = b.odate)
ORDER BY 3;
```

FIGURE 13.5:

Forming a UNION using ORDER BY

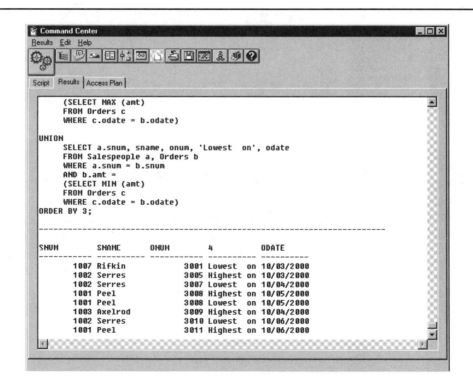

Since ASCENDING is the default for ORDER BY, we did not have to specify it in this example. We can order our output by several columns within one another and specify ASC or DESC independently for each, just as we do for single queries. Notice that the number 3 in the ORDER BY clause indicates which column in the SELECT clause to order. Because the columns of a UNION have no names, you must refer to them by number. This number indicates their placement among the other output columns.

Using UNION to Implement Outer Joins and Similar Operations

You may recall that we introduced in Chapter 10 the concept of the *outer join*. An outer join is a join of two or more tables that includes rows from one or more of the tables where no match was found (Chapter 10 explains outer joins more thoroughly and gives examples of their use). If you are using a product that does not support outer join operators directly, or maintaining code written for such a product, you may have to deal with the situation of outer joins rolled by hand using the UNION operator.

The basic problem is that, in the absence of outer join operators, SQL predicates have no way of dealing simultaneously with row combinations that satisfy predicates and those that do not, given that the latter must have NULLs inserted in the unmatched columns. You deal with this situation by having one query for the matches and another for the unmatched cases, and then merging the two with a UNION.

When we introduced outer joins, we assumed the following row was added to the Salespeople table (see Table 13.1).

TABLE 13.1: A Row Added to the Salespeople Table

Snum	Sname	City	Comm
1020	Wang	Bangkok	.11

There are no orders for this salesperson in the Orders table. If we wanted to see our salespeople listed with their current orders, Wang would not show up in the list. One way you could deal with this deficiency is to make a UNION of two queries, as follows:

- One query would find all orders for salespeople who had any.

- One query would find all salespeople who had no orders and output them with a NULL in the onum column.

Here is an example:

```
SELECT s.snum, sname, onum
     FROM Salespeople s, Orders o
     WHERE s.snum = o.snum

UNION

SELECT snum, sname, NULL
     FROM Salespeople s
     WHERE NOT EXISTS
          (SELECT *
               FROM Orders o
               WHERE s.snum = o.snum)
ORDER BY 1;
```

While support of NULL as a keyword like this is common, some products do not provide it and the standard does not require it in this context. You can work around this by using the NULLIF clause introduced in Chapter 9 and feeding it two equal constants, which will make it always NULL. Here is an example; the output of this query is shown in Figure 13.6:

```
SELECT s.snum, sname, onum
     FROM Salespeople s, Orders o
     WHERE s.snum = o.snum

UNION

SELECT snum, sname, NULLIF(1,1)
     FROM Salespeople s
     WHERE NOT EXISTS
```

```
            (SELECT *
                FROM Orders o
                WHERE s.snum = o.snum)
    ORDER BY 1;
```

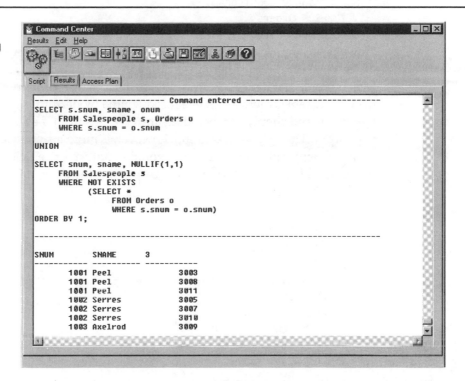

NULLIF(1,1) is always NULL, of course, since 1 always equals 1. This is a good workaround whenever you need to insert a NULL if your product does not recognize NULL as a keyword.

One advantage of doing outer joins this way is that it is considerably more flexible than outer join operators, as it can implement things that are not, strictly speaking, outer joins but present similar problems. For example, in the first of the two queries in the above example, the only reason we had to include the Salespeople table in the join was so we could get the name as well as the snum of the appropriate salesperson.

Suppose we just wanted the snums and the total number of orders for each. We could easily do this using COUNT on the Orders table without reference to the Salespeople table, as follows:

```
SELECT snum, COUNT(onum)
    FROM Orders
    GROUP BY snum;
```

However, Wang would still be excluded. This statement is not technically an outer join, because our query does not require a join to the Salespeople table, or at least it would not if we didn't want to include Wang, who is not represented in the Orders table. You could solve this dilemma by performing an outer join of the two tables and simply not including any columns from the Salespeople table in the output. The following solution, however, is more intuitive and in principle more efficient (although whether it would execute more efficiently, in fact, depends on how the DBMS chooses to optimize the query). The output of this query is shown in Figure 13.7:

```
SELECT snum, COUNT(onum)
    FROM Orders
    GROUP BY snum
UNION
SELECT snum, 0
    FROM Salespeople
    WHERE NOT snum IN
            (SELECT snum
                FROM Orders)
ORDER BY 1;
```

Although each DBMS optimizes these sorts of operations in its own way, probably this version would be faster than the hand-rolled outer join we showed earlier, though not necessarily as fast as an outer join realized with an outer join operator, as shown in Chapter 10.

You can also insert text strings into a UNION to identify the query that produced a given row. Using this technique in outer joins and similar constructs enables you to use predicates to classify, rather than exclude, output.

FIGURE 13.7:

A complete listing of salespeople with orders without
an outer join

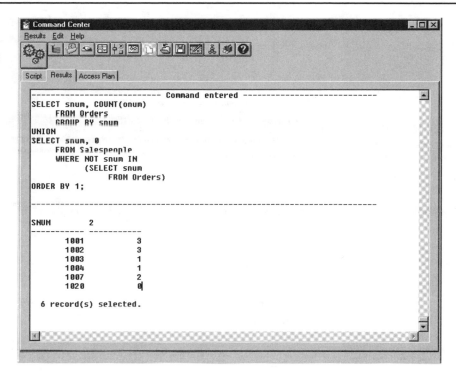

We have previously used in this book the example of finding salespeople with
customers located in their cities. Instead of selecting only these rows, however,
perhaps you want your output to list all of the salespeople and indicate those
who do not have customers in their cities as well as those who do. The following
query, whose output is shown in Figure 13.8, will accomplish this:

```
SELECT Salespeople.snum, sname, cname, comm
    FROM Salespeople, Customers
    WHERE Salespeople.city = Customers.city
UNION
SELECT snum, sname, 'NO MATCH', comm
    FROM Salespeople
    WHERE NOT city IN
        (SELECT city
            FROM Customers)
 ORDER BY 2 DESC;\
```

The second query selects whichever rows the first omits.

FIGURE 13.8:

An outer join with
embedded flags

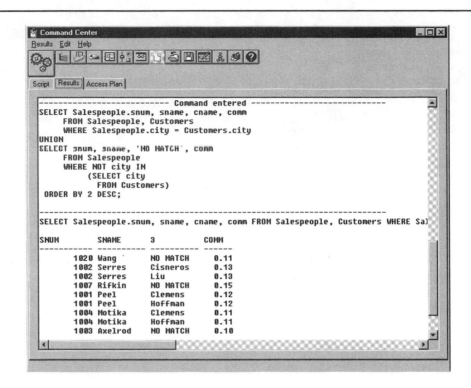

You can also add a comment or expression to your query as an extra output column of the SELECT clause. If you do this, you will have to add some compatible
comment or expression, at the same point in the SELECT clause, to every query in
the UNION operation. UNION compatibility prevents you from adding an extra
field to one of the queries and not the other.

Suppose you wanted a list of salespeople that indicated who had more than
two customers assigned and who did not. Here is one solution; the output is
shown in Figure 13.9:

```
SELECT snum, sname, '   More than one customer assigned'
    FROM Salespeople s
    WHERE 1 <
    (SELECT COUNT(*)
        FROM Customers
        WHERE snum = s.snum)
UNION
SELECT snum, sname, 'No More than one customer assigned'
```

```
FROM Salespeople s
WHERE 1 >=
(SELECT COUNT(*)
    FROM Customers
    WHERE snum = s.snum);
```

FIGURE 13.9:

A UNION that uses a com-
ment to characterize query
results

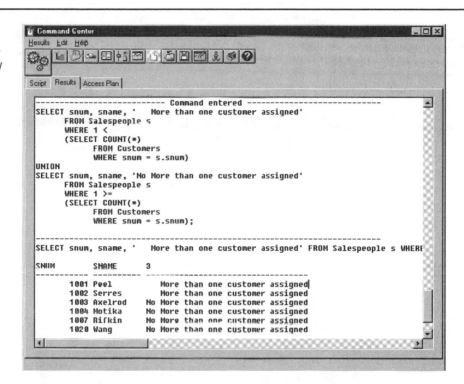

If you were using this query in an application, you could parse the output for
the string you included as a flag and use it to control the flow of the application.

Up until now, the outer joins we have seen implemented with UNION have
been left, rather than full, outer joins (refer to Chapter 10 for a definition of these
terms). Let's do a full outer join of the Salespeople and Customers table over city.
It will include:

- All salespeople who have at least one customer located in the same city

- All customers who have at least one salesperson located in the same city

- All salespeople with no such customers

- All customers with no such salesperson

Here is the query. Notice the use of parentheses, which we will explain shortly. The output is shown in Figure 13.10:

```
(SELECT snum, city, 'SALESPERSON -  MATCHED'
     FROM Salespeople
     WHERE city IN
          (SELECT city
          FROM Customers)
     UNION
  SELECT snum, city, 'SALESPERSON - NO MATCH'
     FROM Salespeople
     WHERE NOT city IN
          (SELECT city
          FROM Customers))
UNION
(SELECT cnum, city, 'CUSTOMER     - MATCHED'
     FROM Customers
     WHERE city IN
          (SELECT city
            FROM Salespeople)
UNION
  SELECT cnum, city, 'CUSTOMER     - NO MATCH'
     FROM Customers
     WHERE NOT city IN
          (SELECT city
            FROM Salespeople))
ORDER BY 2 DESC;
```

The abbreviated outer join that we started with is probably more useful than this last one. This example does, however, bring up another point. Whenever you perform a union on more than two queries, you can use parentheses to determine the order of evaluation. In other words, instead of simply saying

```
query X UNION query Y UNION query Z;
```

you can specify either

```
(query X UNION query Y) UNION query Z;
```

or

```
query X UNION (query Y UNION query Z);
```

FIGURE 13.10:

A complete outer join

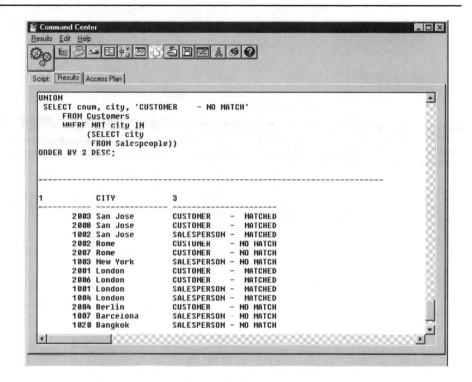

The reason this is useful is that you can combine UNION and UNION ALL to eliminate some duplicates without eliminating others. The statement

  (*query X* UNION ALL *query Y*) UNION *query Z*;

will not necessarily generate the same results as

  query X UNION ALL (*query Y* UNION *query Z*);

if there are duplicate rows to eliminate.

Other Ways of Combining Multiple Queries

Now that we have covered the use of UNION, the other multiple query operators will be fairly simple, because almost all of the principles are the same as for UNIONs. For example, if you have more than two queries to merge, you can use parentheses to force an order of evaluation, the same as with UNION. Also as with UNION, duplicates are eliminated by default, although the use of ALL with these operators can be a little more complex than with UNION.

The difference between these operators and UNION is in the logical operation that decides which rows of the individual queries to include in the output. The general concept is that all of the operators deal with the rows output by the individual queries as a set and decide which members of this set to include in the final output. These operators also have an argument called CORRESPONDING, which is a part of Full SQL92 conformance that is not yet widely implemented. We will not go into CORRESPONDING here, but if you want to know about it, look in the reference under "SELECT".

Note that SQL92 does not actually require these operators with the specified behavior at less than full conformance. Nonetheless, because they are so useful, they are broadly supported (the operator EXCEPT is sometimes found under the synonym of MINUS). However, vendors who choose to implement these operators without claiming Full conformance do not have to give them the specified behavior, and they may not, especially with regard to the ALL argument.

Using INTERSECT

The INTERSECT operator finds the intersection of the rows output by the two or more queries. This is a set-theoretical way of saying it finds those rows in common among the sets output by the individual queries. Suppose we wanted to find which salespeople had more than $1,500.00 total in current orders with less than two customers assigned. Here is one approach. The output is shown in Figure 13.11:

```
SELECT snum
    FROM Orders a
    WHERE 1500.00 <
    (SELECT SUM(amt)
        FROM Orders b
        WHERE b.snum = a.snum)
INTERSECT
SELECT snum
    FROM Salespeople c
    WHERE 2 >
        (SELECT COUNT(*)
        FROM Customers d
        WHERE d.snum = c.snum);
```

FIGURE 13.11:

Merging queries using
INTERSECT

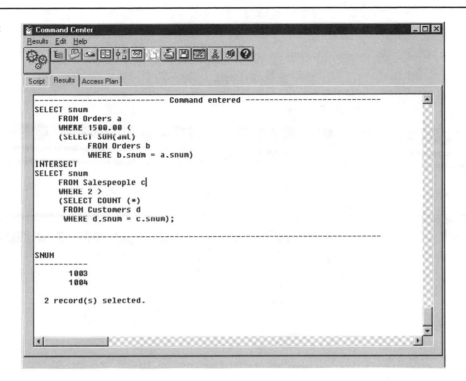

Using EXCEPT or MINUS

EXCEPT is the name of this operator as specified in the SQL standard. MINUS is a common synonym, but its behavior may vary in details. The idea is that EXCEPT takes two queries, A and B, and includes in the output only the rows from A that were not also produced by B. Likewise, it excludes rows produced by B but not by A, so the effect is that no rows output by query B are in the final output in any case.

Let's contrast EXCEPT with INTERSECT by repeating the previous example but with the different operator. This example finds all salespeople with more than $1,500.00 in orders and one or zero assigned customers (the latter is theoretically possible, remember, since we have designed the database so that salespeople could get credit for sales from non-assigned customers). The output is shown in Figure 13.12:

```
SELECT snum
```

```
         FROM Orders a
         WHERE 1500.00 <
                 (SELECT SUM(amt)
                 FROM Orders b
                 WHERE b.snum = a.snum)
EXCEPT
SELECT snum
         FROM Salespeople c
         WHERE 2 >
                 (SELECT COUNT (*)
                 FROM Customers d
                 WHERE d.snum = c.snum);
```

FIGURE 13.12:

Merging queries using
EXCEPT

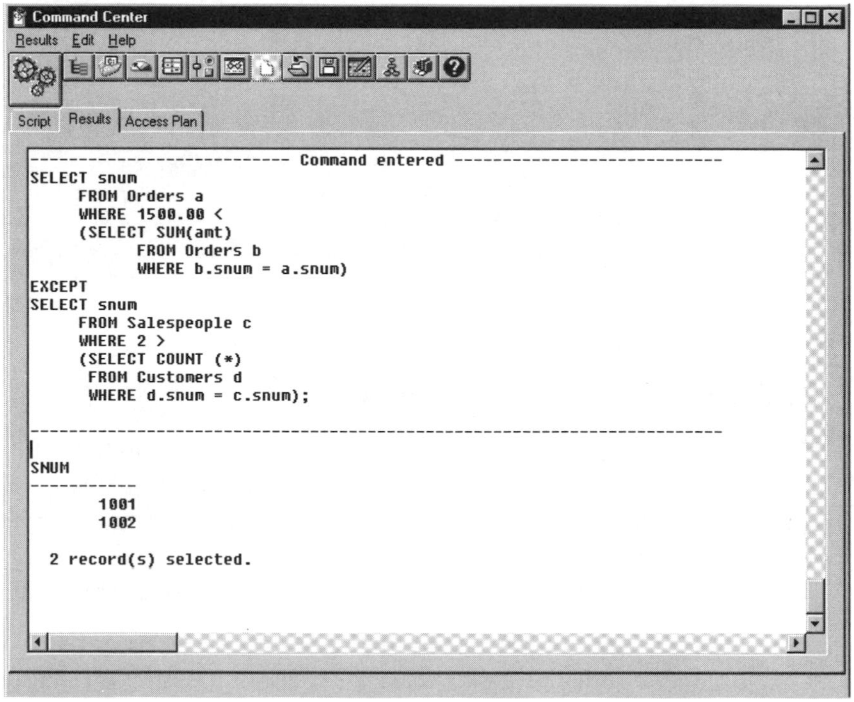

Notice that, unlike the other operators introduced in this chapter, EXCEPT is respective of the order in which the queries are stated. For example, if we were to reverse the previous example, like this, the output, as shown in Figure 13.13, would be quite different:

```
SELECT snum
    FROM Salespeople c
    WHERE 2 >
        (SELECT COUNT (*)
        FROM Customers d
        WHERE d.snum = c.snum)
EXCEPT
SELECT snum
    FROM Orders a
    WHERE 1500.00 <
        (SELECT SUM(amt)
        FROM Orders b
        WHERE b.snum = a.snum);
```

FIGURE 13.13:

EXCEPT with the query order reversed

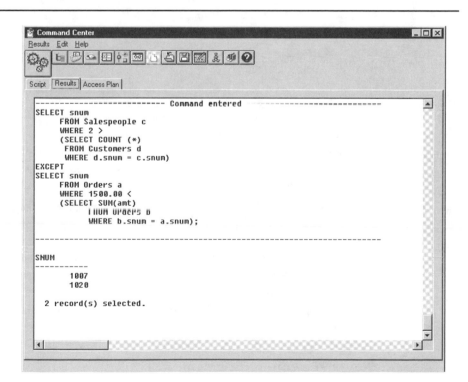

Using ALL with INTERSECT and EXCEPT

The ISO standard specifies some rather sophisticated behavior for these two operators when they are used with an ALL argument. Since, however, these operators are required only for Full SQL92 conformance, which no one is claiming as of this writing (2000), vendors are free not to implement this behavior, and many have not. If the product you are using does not implement ALL as described here, it is probably used as a noiseword and has no effect. If, however, your vendor has implemented this functionality, it is likely to throw you off if you have not accounted for it. For that reason, we explain the behavior specified by the standard here.

Now, since both of these operators eliminate duplicates by default, it does not matter, in the absence of ALL, how many times query A or query B produces a given row. When ALL is introduced, it does matter. The basic idea is that ALL causes the merging (for INTERSECT) or elimination (for EXCEPT) to happen on a per-occurrence basis, rather than once-for-all. To clarify this behavior, let's look again at a previous example:

```
SELECT snum
    FROM Orders a
    WHERE 1500.00 <
        (SELECT SUM(amt)
        FROM Orders b
        WHERE b.snum = a.snum)
EXCEPT
SELECT snum
    FROM Salespeople c
    WHERE 2 >
        (SELECT COUNT (*)
        FROM Customers d
        WHERE d.snum = c.snum);
```

The first query (*query A*) will generally produce the same snum multiple times, once for each order that a given salesperson has in the table. The second query (*query B*) will produce each snum only once, because snum is the primary key of the Salespeople table and therefore cannot be present more than once. In this form, it does not matter how many times a given snum comes up in *query A*; if it comes up at all in *query B*, it is eliminated. If, however, we phrased the query like this

```
SELECT snum
    FROM Orders a
    WHERE 1500.00 <
```

```
(SELECT SUM(amt)
        FROM Orders b
        WHERE b.snum = a.snum)
EXCEPT ALL
SELECT snum
    FROM Salespeople c
    WHERE 2 >
        (SELECT COUNT (*)
        FROM Customers d
        WHERE d.snum = c.snum);
```

it would matter. For each occurrence of an snum value in *query A*, one occurrence of the value would be eliminated from the output. This mean that if *query A* output five duplicate rows and *query B* output the same row twice, the row would show up three times in the output (five occurrences minus two occurrences).

If we specified INTERSECT ALL, each occurrence of an intersection would be counted separately. Though this sounds complicated, all it means in practice is that the smaller number of occurrences of a duplicate row, whether it be in *query A* or *query B*, will be output. If query A output five duplicate rows, and *query B* output the same row twice, the row would show up twice in the output. If *query A* output the row twice and *query B* output it five times, it would still show up twice in the output.

The easiest way to tell how your DBMS behaves is to run the EXCEPT ALL example above and see if the output differs from the same example with EXCEPT.

Summary

Now you know how to use the UNION, INTERSECT, and EXCEPT (MINUS) clauses, which enable you to combine any number of queries into a single body of output. If you have a number of similar tables—tables containing similar information but owned by different users and covering different specifics, perhaps—a UNION can provide an easy way to blend and order the output. Likewise, UNIONs are a good way to deal with outer joins and related problems; they give you a new way to use conditions—not to exclude output, but to label it or to treat the parts of it that meet the condition differently from those that do not.

Now that you have a mastery of queries, we will show you how to treat queries themselves as data objects when we introduce the concept of the view in the next part of this book.

Putting SQL to Work

1. Create a union of two queries that shows the names, cities, and ratings of all customers. Those with a rating of 200 or greater will also have the words "High Rating", while the others will have the words "Low Rating". NULL ratings count as low.

2. Write a statement that produces the name and number of each salesperson and each customer with more than one current order. Put the results in alphabetical order.

3. Form a UNION of three queries. Have the first SELECT the snums of all salespeople in San Jose; the second, the cnums of all customers in San Jose; and the third, the onums of all orders on October 3. Retain duplicates between the last two queries but eliminate any redundancies between either of them and the first. (Note: In the sample tables as given, there would be no such redundancies because the snums, cnums, and onums all fall in different ranges (which is a good idea, by the way). Nonetheless, this UNION is useful as an intellectual exercise.)

4. Write a merged query that finds all salespeople who live in London and have at least one customer in London. Output the salespeople's snums and names.

5. Write a merged query that finds all salespeople with at least one order above $1,000.00 that is not from a customer in their own city. Output the snum and the cnum. Salespeople who have such orders from more than one such customer will appear more than once.

PART IV

More That You Can Do with Data

CHAPTER

FOURTEEN

14

Introducing: Views

■ What Are Views?

■ Using the CREATE VIEW Statement

A view is a data object that contains no data of its own. It is a kind of table whose contents are taken from other tables through the execution of a query. When the view is accessed, the query is executed and its output becomes the content of the view for the duration of that statement. In this chapter, you will learn what views are, how to create them, and a bit about their limitations and restrictions. We will elaborate on the use of views based on advanced query features, such as joins and subqueries, as well as some special considerations that come into play with queries made against views.

What Are Views?

The kinds of tables that you have been dealing with up until now are called *permanent base tables*. These are tables that contain data persistently stored in the database. A view is another kind of table. *Views* are tables whose contents are taken or derived from other tables. In fact, they are also known as *virtual tables*, or even *viewed tables*. You can reference a view within a SELECT, INSERT, or other statement just as though it were a base table, but views contain no data of their own. Views are like windows through which you view information (as is, or in a derived form, as you will see) that is actually stored in base tables. A view is a query that is executed whenever the view is the subject of a statement. The output of the query becomes the content of the view at that moment.

Using the CREATE VIEW Statement

You define views with the CREATE VIEW statement. This consists of the words CREATE VIEW, the name of the view to be created, the word AS, and then a query, as in the following example:

```
CREATE VIEW Londonstaff
    AS SELECT snum, sname, city, comm
    FROM Salespeople
    WHERE city = 'London';
```

This statement, like other SQL statements that create objects, generates no output as such, but merely generates an acknowledgement that a new database object has been created. You now own a view called Londonstaff. Its content is the same information stored in the Salespeople table but restricted to salespeople in London. You can use this view just like any other table. It can be queried, updated, inserted into, deleted from, and joined with other tables and views.

Note that we listed all the columns in the SELECT clause. The reason for this is that this view will still act the same if another column is added to Salespeople. If we had used SELECT *, the view would grow a column whenever the underlying table did, which can be a problem if this view is accessed in applications that rely on its having a stable structure. On the other hand, if a column is dropped from the Salespeople table, this version of the view becomes invalid. That can either mean that the view is automatically dropped or that the column cannot be dropped from the table. For details on this, see "ALTER TABLE" in the reference. In any case, adding columns is both more common and more commonly supported than dropping them, so it is more often useful to list all columns in view definitions, but it is a judgment call you will have to make depending on the situation.

Let's query this view (the output is shown in Figure 14.1):

```
SELECT *
    FROM Londonstaff;
```

FIGURE 14.1:

The Londonstaff view

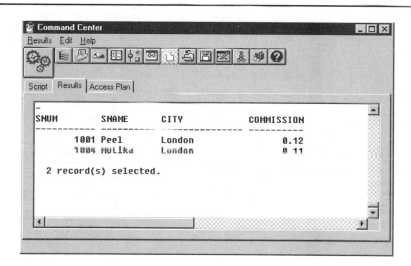

When you told SQL to SELECT all rows from the view, it executed the query contained in the definition of Londonstaff. The output of that query became the content of the view. It then executed a SELECT * against this view.

You may remember that, in Chapter 6, you had a table called Londonstaff, into which you inserted this same content. (Of course, we are assuming that table is no longer extant. If it were, you would have to pick another name for your view. Views are treated as tables and therefore cannot have the same name as tables in the same schema.) The advantage of using a view, instead of a base table, is that the view will be updated automatically whenever the underlying table changes. The contents of the view are not fixed but are reevaluated each time you reference the view in a SQL statement. If you added another London-based salesperson to the Salespeople table tomorrow, she would automatically appear in the Londonstaff view.

You can create a view based on any table, even another view. The query in the view is called the *underlying query*, and the tables it references are called the *underlying tables*. Since views can contain other views, the underlying tables can include tables that are not referenced directly in the view, but rather are more deeply nested within the definitions of other views. All views, however, eventually reference a set of one or more base tables, which are called the *leaf underlying tables* of the view.

Views greatly extend the control you have over your data. They are an excellent way to give people access to some but not all of the information in a table. If you wanted your salespeople to be able to look at the Salespeople table, but not to see each others' commissions, you could create a view for their use (shown in Figure 14.2) with the following statement:

```
CREATE VIEW Salesown
     AS SELECT snum, sname, city
     FROM Salespeople;
```

In other words, this view is the same as the Salespeople table, except that the comm column was not named in the query and is therefore not included in the view.

It is true that the query inside the view is executed when the view is referenced and then not again while that same SQL statement is executing. The content of the view is constant throughout execution of a SQL statement, even though the content of the underlying base table can change. Consider the following merged query on Londonstaff:

```
SELECT *
     FROM Londonstaff
     WHERE comm > .12
EXCEPT
SELECT *
     FROM Londonstaff
     WHERE name LIKE 'G%';
```

FIGURE 14.2:

The Salesown view

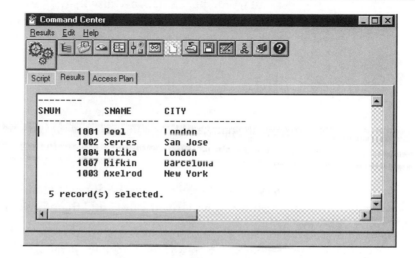

This query should select all salespeople in London with commissions above .12 unless they have names that begin with 'G'. What if a new such salesperson were added to the Salespeople table between when the first and second queries were executed? It doesn't matter. Once you reference Londonstaff in a statement, the query contained in its definition is executed, and its content does not change until SQL reaches the semicolon. If this is a problem, you can lock the Salespeople table. We will address this issue more thoroughly when we talk about concurrency in Chapter 17.

Updating Views

You can now modify the content of the Salesown view using data manipulation statements, but the modifications do not affect the view itself. They will be passed along to the underlying table:

```
UPDATE Salesown
    SET city = 'Palo Alto'
    WHERE snum = 1004;
```

The effect of this statement is identical to performing the same statement on the Salespeople table. However, suppose a salesperson tried to UPDATE his commission:

```
UPDATE Salesown
    SET comm = .20
    WHERE snum = 1004;
```

This statement would be rejected, because there is no comm column in the Salesown view. It is important to note that some views cannot be updated. We will explore the issue of updating views thoroughly in Chapter 15.

Naming Columns

In our examples so far, we have taken the names of the columns of our views directly from the names of the columns in the underlying table. This is the easiest course. However, sometimes you need to provide new names for your columns, for example:

- When some of the columns in the SELECT clause of the underlying query are expressions or derived values and therefore unnamed

- When the query in the view accesses multiple underlying tables, and two or more columns in those tables have the same name

The names that will become the names of the columns are given in parentheses after the name of the view being created. It does not matter if they match the column names of the table being queried; they are matched to the output columns of the query based on the order specified. Their datatypes and sizes are derived from the columns of the underlying query that are "piped" into them. In this scheme, if you rename any of the columns, you must rename all of them.

A more recent variation, supported in most products, is to use the AS argument in the SELECT clause of the underlying query. This is a little more convenient. The AS argument enables you to rename output columns. Here is the Londonstaff view with more complete names than the underlying Salespeople table:

```
CREATE VIEW Londonstaff
     AS SELECT snum AS Salesperson_Number, sname AS Last_Name,
         city, comm AS Commission
     FROM Salespeople
     WHERE city = 'London';
```

Notice that in this version, we didn't rename the city column, because we didn't feel like it. In fact, since the city will always be London, does it make sense to leave this column out? It may, but there are issues involved with updating through this view that may require the city column to be present. We will get to these in the next chapter.

Grouped Views

Grouped views are views that contain a GROUP BY clause or that are based on other grouped views. Grouped views can be an excellent way to process derived information continuously. Suppose each day you have to keep track of the number of customers ordering, the number of salespeople taking orders, the number of orders, the average amount ordered, and the total amount ordered. Rather than repeatedly constructing a complex query, you can simply create the following view:

```
CREATE VIEW Totalforday(Date, Custcount, Salescount, Ordercount,
        Averageamt, Totalorders)
AS SELECT odate, COUNT(DISTINCT cnum),
    COUNT(DISTINCT snum), COUNT(onum),
    AVG(amt), SUM(amt)
    FROM Orders
    GROUP BY odate;
```

Note that we name the columns because most of the underlying output columns are aggregate functions and therefore unnamed. Now you can see all this information with a simple query:

```
SELECT *
    FROM Totalforday;
```

Of course, what's really useful about this view is that you can now ask the same sorts of complicated questions about the aggregate values as you would about simple values. In many cases, you could do this anyway with the underlying query, but it is often easier to do it in two stages, with a view and then a query on that view. If you want to see all days with at least two orders, totaling above $1,000.00, it just became really easy. The output is shown in Figure 14.3

```
SELECT *
    FROM Totalforday
    WHERE Ordercount >= 2 and Totalorders >= 1000.00;
```

As you have seen, SQL queries can get quite complex, so views provide you with an extremely flexible and powerful tool to determine just how your data will be used. They can also make your life easier by reformatting data in useful ways and eliminating repetitive work.

FIGURE 14.3:

A query on a grouped view

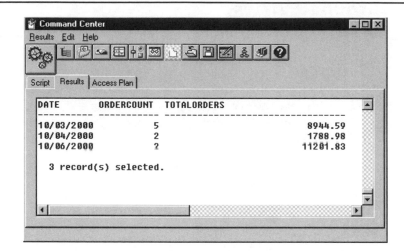

Views and Joins

Views need not be drawn from a single base table. Because almost any valid SQL query can be used in a view, views can distill information from any number of base tables or from other views. We can, for example, define a view that shows, for each order, the salesperson and the customer by name:

```
CREATE VIEW Nameorders
     AS SELECT onum, amt, a.snum, sname, cname
     FROM Orders a, Customers b, Salespeople c
     WHERE a.cnum = b.cnum
     AND a.snum = c.snum;
```

Now you can SELECT all orders by the customer's or by the salesperson's name, or you can see this information for any order. For example, to see all of salesperson Rifkin's orders, you would enter the following query (the output is shown in Figure 14.4):

```
SELECT *
     FROM Nameorders
     WHERE snum = 1007;
```

FIGURE 14.4:

Rifkin's orders as seen in
Nameorders

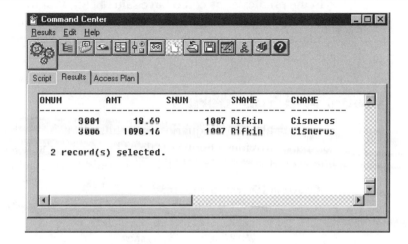

You can also join views with other tables, either base tables or views, so that
you can see all of Axelrod's orders and her commission on each one:

```
SELECT a.sname, cname, amt * comm AS Due_Axelrod
    FROM Nameorders a, Salespeople b
    WHERE a.snum = 1003
    AND b.snum = a.snum;
```

The output for this query is shown in Figure 14.5.

FIGURE 14.5:

A join of a view and a
base table

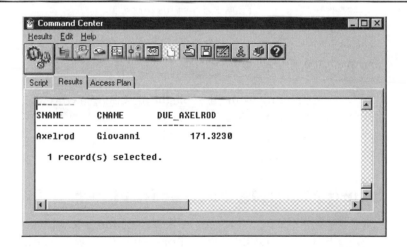

In the predicate, we could have said WHERE a.snum = 1003 AND b.snum = 1003, but the predicate we used is more general. We need only change the snum to make it apply to anyone else. Besides, snum is the primary key of Salespeople and therefore should definitely be unique.

Views and Subqueries

Views can also use subqueries, including correlated subqueries. Perhaps your company provides a bonus for the salesperson who has the customer with the highest order on any given date. You could track that information with this view:

```
CREATE VIEW Elitesalesforce
    AS SELECT b.odate, a.snum, a.sname,
        FROM Salespeople a, Orders b
        WHERE a.snum = b.snum
        AND b.amt =
            (SELECT MAX(amt)
            FROM Orders c
            WHERE c.odate = b.odate);
```

If, on the other hand, the bonus will go only to salespeople when they have had the highest order at least ten times, you might track them in another view based on the first:

```
CREATE VIEW Bonus
    AS SELECT DISTINCT snum, sname
        FROM Elitesalesforce a
        WHERE 10 <=
            (SELECT COUNT(*)
            FROM Elitesalesforce b
            WHERE a.snum = b.snum);
```

Extracting from this table the salespeople who will receive bonuses is simply a matter of entering the following:

```
SELECT *
    FROM Bonus;
```

Using Multiple Queries in Views

As of SQL92, views can be based on multiple queries combined with the UNION, EXCEPT, and INTERSECT operators that we introduced in the previous chapter.

This is highly useful, as it means you can treat material from several tables as though it were from one table. You cannot, however, update such views (more on this in the next chapter). Here is an example showing all salespeople and customers in London:

```
CREATE VIEW Londonpeople
    AS SELECT snum, sname, 'salesperson'
        FROM Salespeople
        WHERE city = 'London'
    UNION
        SELECT cnum, cname, '    customer'
        FROM Customers
        WHERE city = 'London';
```

As with some examples in the previous chapter, we included strings to label which query produced a given row, so that we wouldn't confuse salespeople with customers. We also front-padded the shorter string with blanks, so that the two printed strings would make a nice right-justified column.

What Views Cannot Do

Many types of views (including several of our examples in this chapter) are read-only. This means that you can query them, but you cannot subject them to update statements. (We will explore this topic in the next chapter.)

Also, you cannot use ORDER BY in the definition of a view. The output of the query forms the content of the view, which, like a base table, is by definition unordered. At least this is the position taken by the standard and most purists of database theory. Many products do, in fact, permit ORDER BY in views.

Note that this does not imply the reverse. Queries on views may use ORDER BY. It is important to not confuse the queries *within* the views (the underlying queries) with the queries *on* the views (the queries wherein the views are referenced). Let's return briefly to our first example:

```
CREATE VIEW Londonstaff
    AS SELECT snum, sname, city, comm
        FROM Salespeople
        WHERE city = 'London';
SELECT *
    FROM Londonstaff;
```

The query *within* the view—the underlying query—is:

```
SELECT snum, sname, city, comm
    FROM Salespeople
    WHERE city = 'London';
```

The query *on* the view is:

```
SELECT *
    FROM Londonstaff;
```

Dropping Views

The syntax to eliminate a view from the database is similar to that for removing base tables:

```
DROP VIEW viewname;
```

There is no need, however, to first delete all the contents as there is with base tables, because a view has no contents per se, save for the duration of a particular statement. The underlying table(s) from which the view is drawn are not affected when it is dropped. Remember, you must own the view in order to drop it.

Summary

Now that you can use views, your ability to track and process the content of your database easily is greatly enhanced. Almost anything you can create spontaneously with a query, you can define permanently as a view. Queries on these views are, in effect, queries on queries. We have explored the use of views for both convenience and security, as well as many of the capabilities of views for formatting and deriving values from the ever-changing content of your database. There is one major issue regarding views, updatability, that we chose to defer until Chapter 15. As we indicated, you can update views as you would base tables, with the changes applied to the table(s) from which the view is derived, but such is not possible in all cases.

Putting SQL to Work

1. Create a view that shows all of the customers who have the highest ratings.

2. Create a view that shows the number of salespeople in each city.

3. Create a view that shows the average and total orders for each salesperson after his or her name. Assume all names are unique.

4. Create a view that shows each salesperson with multiple customers.

CHAPTER
FIFTEEN

15

Changing Values through Views

- Updating Views

- Checking the Values Placed in Views

In this chapter, we'll talk about the update statements—INSERT, UPDATE, and DELETE—as they are applied to views. As we mentioned in the previous chapter, using update statements on views is an indirect way of using them on the leaf underlying tables referenced by the queries of the views. However, not all views can be updated. We will discuss the rules for determining whether or not a view is updatable and explore their implications. In addition, we will teach you how to use the WITH CHECK OPTION clause, which controls the specific values that can enter a table through a view.

Updating Views

What happens when you update a view? The simple answer is that the changes are transferred to the base tables that underlie the view. Of course, views can be based on other views, but eventually some set of one or more base tables, the leaf underlying tables, is reached, and this is where the data is actually changed. There are some ambiguities here, however. A view consists of the results of a query, and when you update a view, you are updating a set of query results. But the update does not affect the query or its results per se; it affects the values in the table(s) on which the query was made and thereby changes the output of the query, which is not necessarily a simple matter. The following statement will create the view shown in Figure 15.1:

```
CREATE VIEW Citymatch(custcity, salescity)
    AS SELECT DISTINCT a.city, b.city
    FROM Customers a, Salespeople b
    WHERE a.snum = b.snum;
```

This view shows all matches of customers with salespeople such that there is at least one customer in custcity served by a salesperson in salescity.

For example, one row of this table—London London—indicates that at least one customer in London is served by a salesperson in London. This row could have been produced by the match of Hoffman with her salesperson Peel, both in London. The same value, however, could be produced by matching Clemens, also in London, with his salesperson, who also happens to be Peel. Since we specifically selected distinct city combinations, only one compound row with these values was produced. But which match of underlying table values does it represent?

FIGURE 15.1:

The Citymatch view

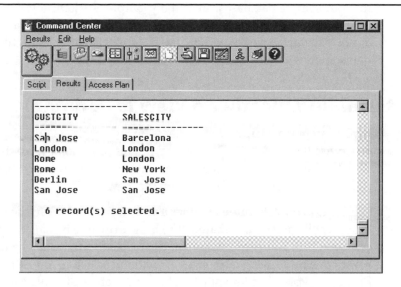

Even if you hadn't selected city combinations using DISTINCT, you would still be in the same boat, because you would then have two rows in the view with identical values, that is, with both columns equal to London. These two rows of the view would be indistinguishable from one another, so you still would not be able to tell which row of the view came from which input values of the underlying tables. (Keep in mind that queries that omit the ORDER BY clause produce output in an arbitrary order. This rule applies as well to queries used within views, which cannot use ORDER BY, in a strict interpretation of the standard. Therefore, you cannot use the order of the two rows to distinguish them.) This means that you would again be faced with output rows that could not be definitely linked to specific rows of the tables queried.

What if you tried to delete the row London London from the view? Would it mean deleting Hoffman, Clemens, or both from the Customers table? Should the DBMS also delete Peel from the Salespeople table? Such questions are impossible to answer definitively, so deletions are not permitted on views of this nature. The view Citymatch is an example of a *read-only view*, one that can be queried but not changed.

Of course, you might think that you could solve this problem by including the snum and cnum columns in the view, so that you could tell in fact which match is represented. This is true, and in this case is the best solution, but keep in mind that our sample database is artificially simple. Realistically, situations like this do arise, although you can limit them by designing your schemas with a high degree of normalization (we cover database design in Chapter 19 of this book). The fact is that some very useful views simply are not updatable.

Determining Whether a View Is Updatable

If you can perform update statements on a view, the view is said to be *updatable;* otherwise it is read-only. Consistent with this terminology, we shall use the expression "updating a view" to mean executing any of the three DML update statements (INSERT, UPDATE, and DELETE) on the view.

How do you determine whether a view is updatable? In database theory, this topic is still somewhat debated. The basic principle is that an updatable view is one on which an update statement can be performed, altering one and only one row of one underlying table at a time without affecting any other rows of any table. Putting this principle into practice, however, can be difficult. Moreover, some views that are updatable in theory are not updatable in fact, at least not in ISO standard SQL. The criteria that determine whether a view is updatable are based on the content of the underlying query. The rules the query must satisfy are as follows:

- It must be drawn on one and only one underlying table.

- It must have no aggregate functions.

- It must not specify DISTINCT.

- It must not use GROUP BY or HAVING.

- It may be defined on another view, but that view must also be updatable.

- It must not use constants, strings, or value expressions (for example, comm * 100) among the selected output columns.

- For INSERT, it must include any columns of the underlying table that have the NOT NULL constraint, unless another default value has been specified.

- In older versions of the SQL standard, it could not use subqueries. Some products still may enforce this, but most do not.

- It should include the primary key of the underlying table. This is not technically a requirement, but you would be well advised to stick to it.

Updatable vs. Read-Only Views

One implication of these restrictions is that updatable views are, in effect, like windows on the underlying tables. They show some, but not necessarily all, of a table's contents. They can be restricted to certain rows (by the use of predicates) or to specifically named columns (with exceptions), but they present the values directly and do not derive information from them, such as by using aggregate functions and expressions. They also do not compare table rows to one another (as in joins and subqueries and as with DISTINCT).

The differences between updatable and read-only views are not merely incidental. The purposes for which you use them are frequently different. Updatable views are generally used just like base tables. In fact, users may not even be aware of whether the object they are querying is a base table or a view and may have no reason to care. These views are an excellent security mechanism for concealing parts of a table that are confidential or are superfluous to a given user's needs. (In Chapter 16, we will show you how to allow users to access a view, but not the underlying table.)

Read-only views, on the other hand, allow you to derive and reformat data extensively. They give you a library of complex queries that you can execute and re-execute, keeping your derived information strictly up to the minute. In addition, having the results of these queries in tables that you can then use in queries themselves (for example, in joins) has advantages over simply executing the queries. Read-only views can also have security applications. For instance, you may want some users to see aggregate data, such as the average salesperson's commission, without being able to see individual commission values.

Determining Which Views Are Updatable

Let's look at some examples of updatable and read-only views:

```
CREATE VIEW Dateorders(odate, ocount)
    AS SELECT odate, COUNT(*)
    FROM Orders
    GROUP BY odate;
```

This view is read-only because of the presence of an aggregate function and GROUP BY.

```
CREATE VIEW Londoncust
    AS SELECT *
    FROM Customers
    WHERE city = 'London';
```

The preceding view is updatable.

```
CREATE VIEW SJsales(name, number, percentage)
    AS SELECT sname, snum, comm * 100
    FROM Salespeople
    WHERE city = 'San Jose';
```

The preceding view is read-only because of the expression comm * 100. Some DBMSs would allow deletions on this view or updates on the snum and sname columns.

```
CREATE VIEW Salesonthird
    AS SELECT snum, sname, city, comm
    FROM Salespeople
    WHERE snum IN
        (SELECT snum
        FROM Orders
        WHERE odate = '10/03/2000');
```

As of SQL92, this view is updatable. In the older SQL standards, this view would have been read-only because of the subquery.

```
CREATE VIEW Someorders
    AS SELECT snum, onum, cnum
    FROM Orders
    WHERE odate IN ('10/03/2000', '10/05/2000');
```

This view is updatable.

```
CREATE VIEW SanJosePeople
    AS SELECT snum, sname, 'salesperson'
        FROM Salespeople
        WHERE city = 'San Jose'
    UNION
        SELECT cnum, cname, '  customer'
        FROM Customers
        WHERE city = 'San Jose';
```

This view is not updatable because of the UNION clause. Since it is a UNION, rather than a UNION ALL, this is only logical: UNION eliminates duplicates by default and therefore should be treated like DISTINCT. If it were UNION ALL, the SQL92 standard still would not allow an update, although some products may permit it as an extension.

Checking the Values Placed in Views

Another issue involving updates of views is that you can enter values that get "swallowed" in the underlying table. Consider this view:

```
CREATE VIEW Highratings
    AS SELECT cnum, rating
    FROM Customers
    WHERE rating = 300;
```

This view is updatable. It simply restricts your access to the table to certain rows and columns. Suppose, then, you INSERT the following row:

```
INSERT INTO Highratings
    VALUES (2018, 200);
```

The INSERT statement on this view is legal. The row would be INSERTed, through the Highratings view, into the Customers table. Once it was there, however, it would disappear from the view, because its rating value is not 300. The fact of such disappearance is usually a problem. The 200 value might have been a simple typo, but now the row is in the Customers table where you cannot even see it through the view. A user may not be aware that he has entered a row he cannot see, and he would be unable to DELETE it using the view in any case.

You can ensure against modifications of this sort by including WITH CHECK OPTION in the definition of the view. Had we used WITH CHECK OPTION in the definition of the Highratings view, like this

```
CREATE VIEW Highratings
    AS SELECT cnum, rating
    FROM Customers
    WHERE rating = 300
    WITH CHECK OPTION;
```

the DBMS would have rejected the above insertion.

WITH CHECK OPTION is a kind of all-or-nothing affair. You put it in the definition of the view, not in an update statement, so either all update statements against the view will be checked or none will. Usually, you do want to employ the CHECK OPTION, so having it in the definition of the view may be a convenience. Generally, you should use this option for updatable views unless you have a specific reason for allowing a view to put into a table values it will not itself contain. For read-only views, of course, CHECK OPTION is meaningless.

Predicates and Excluded Columns

A related problem that you should be aware of involves inserting rows into a view with a predicate based on one or more excluded columns. For instance, it might seem sensible to define Londonstaff like this:

```
CREATE VIEW Londonstaff
     AS SELECT snum, sname, comm
     FROM Salespeople
     WHERE city = 'London';
```

After all, why include the city value when all the city values will be the same, and the name of the view tells us which city this view is for? But picture what happens whenever we try to insert a row. Since we cannot specify a city value, the DBMS would enter a default value, probably NULL, in the city column. (It would use NULL unless we explicitly defined another default. See Chapter 4 for details.) Since the city column would then not equal London, the inserted row would be excluded from the view. The same would be true for any row that you tried to insert into Londonstaff. They would all be entered through the Londonstaff view into the Salespeople table and then be excluded from the view itself (unless the explicitly defined default in the Salespeople table were London, a special case). A user would be unable to enter rows into this view, yet, perhaps unknowingly, could enter rows into the underlying table. Even if we add WITH CHECK OPTION to the definition of the view

```
CREATE VIEW Londonstaff
     AS SELECT snum, sname, comm
     FROM Salespeople
     WHERE city = 'London'
     WITH CHECK OPTION;
```

we would not necessarily solve the problem. The result would be a view that we could UPDATE or DELETE from, but not INSERT into. In some cases, this may be fine; perhaps there is no reason for users with access to this view to be able to add rows. But you should definitely determine that this is the case before you create such a view.

Even though they may not always provide useful information, it is usually a good idea to include in your view all columns referenced in its predicate. If you do not want these columns in your output, you can always omit them from a query *on* the view, as opposed to the query *within* the view. In other words, you could define the Londonstaff view like this:

```
CREATE VIEW Londonstaff
    AS SELECT *
    FROM Salespeople
    WHERE city = 'London'
    WITH CHECK OPTION;
```

This statement would fill the view with identical city values that you could simply omit from the output with a query along these lines:

```
SELECT snum, sname, comm
    FROM Londonstaff;
```

For that matter, there is nothing wrong with putting another view on top of Londonstaff that is intended only for viewing, not for updating, even though it is updatable in principle:

```
CREATE VIEW Londonstafflookie
    AS SELECT snum, sname, comm
    FROM Londonstaff;
```

Note that in this case it makes no sense to add the CHECK OPTION. The underlying query of this view has no predicate. Nonetheless, the idea would be to use Londonstafflookie for reports where you wanted the output to look nice and not be cluttered with Londons. You would use Londonstaff itself for updates to the salespeople in London. Of course, you would still have to update other salespeople through direct access to the Salespeople table itself or through some other set of views.

Checking Views That Are Based on Other Views

A thorny area regarding the CHECK OPTION is whether its restrictions should *cascade up.* That is to say, should a CHECK OPTION clause apply only to predicate of the view in which it was directly contained or also to the predicates of other views contained in that view? For instance, consider the following view:

```
CREATE VIEW Highratings
    AS SELECT cnum, cname, city, rating, snum
    FROM Customers
    WHERE rating = 300;
```

Suppose we create another view based on this one, as follows:

```
CREATE VIEW Myhighratings
    AS SELECT *
    FROM Highratings
    WHERE snum = 1001
    WITH CHECK OPTION;
```

Could we then UPDATE to a rating other than 300, like this?

```
UPDATE Myhighratings
    SET rating = 200
    WHERE cnum = 2001;
```

After all, this does not violate the predicate in the Myhighratings view. The restriction on low ratings is farther down in the Highratings view it references. This is an area that earlier SQL standards did not address. SQL92 does address it, but its solution does not come into play until the Intermediate level of conformance is reached. The sensible default behavior, of course, would be to reject updates of this sort, and that is what most products do. You might double-check, though, just to be sure, by creating the above views as a simple test and attempting the updates.

What SQL92 specifies is that CHECK OPTION can be either CASCADED or LOCAL. CASCADED means that the predicates of all underlying views are checked and updates are rejected if any are violated. LOCAL means that only the predicate within the current view is checked. Implementers need not support LOCAL until they reach Full SQL92 conformance. Even then, the default behavior is CASCADED, which is what you usually will want. Support for CASCADED is required for Intermediate conformance. Products claiming only Entry SQL92 conformance are on their own, but probably support the behavior of CASCADED. The syntax for these variations is simply

```
WITH CASCADED CHECK OPTION
WITH LOCAL CHECK OPTION
```

Even if your product supports this syntax, you could omit CASCADED or LOCAL, and it will default to CASCADED.

Summary

You have now mastered views pretty thoroughly. In addition to having a check-list of rules to determine if a given view is updatable in SQL, you know the basic concept on which the rules are based—updates to views are permissible only if SQL can unambiguously determine which values of the underlying table to change. This means that the update statement, when performed, must require neither changes to multiple rows of the leaf underlying table at once nor comparisons between multiple rows of either the base table or the query output. Since joins involve comparing rows, they are prohibited. You also understand the differences between some of the ways that updatable and read-only views are used.

You have learned to think of updatable views as windows, showing the data of a single table, but optionally omitting or rearranging its columns as well as selecting only certain rows according to a predicate criterion.

Read-only views, on the other hand, can contain most valid SQL queries; they can therefore be a way of keeping queries you need to execute frequently in a permanent form. In addition, having a query whose output is treated as a data object enables you to have the clarity and convenience of making queries on the output of queries.

You now can prevent update statements on a view from producing rows in the underlying table that are not present in the view itself by using the WITH CHECK OPTION clause in the view definition.

In stand-alone queries, you can usually use in a predicate one or more columns that are not present among the selected output without causing a problem. If you use these queries in updatable views, however, they are problematic because they produce views that cannot have rows inserted into them (although, in the absence of WITH CHECK OPTION, the rows may end up in the underlying table). You have seen the implications of, and some approaches to, this problem.

We have mentioned that views have security applications. You can allow users to access views without allowing them to directly access the tables on which the views are based. However, before we can thoroughly discuss this aspect of views, we must cover general questions of user access to data objects, which we will do in the next chapter.

Putting SQL to Work

1. Which of these views are updatable?

```
#1 CREATE VIEW Dailyorders
      AS SELECT DISTINCT cnum, snum, onum, odate
      FROM Orders;
```

```
#2 CREATE VIEW Custotals
      AS SELECT cname, SUM(amt)
      FROM Orders, Customers
      WHERE Orders.chum = customer.cnum
      GROUP BY cname;
```

```
#3 CREATE VIEW Thirdorders
      AS SELECT *
      FROM Dailyorders
      WHERE odate = '10/03/2000';
```

```
#4 CREATE VIEW Thirdorders
      AS SELECT *
      FROM Dailyorders
      WHERE odate = '10/03/2000';
```

2. Create a view of the Salespeople table called Commissions. This view will include only the snum and comm columns. Through this view, someone could enter or change commissions, but only to values between .10 and .20. In fact, only values in the range will be visible in the view.

3. Assume you are using a system that supports LOCAL CHECK OPTION. Create two views, one referencing the other. The first shows all orders for October 3. The second, based on the first, excludes orders for below $1,000.00. The second view has CHECK OPTION, but you can use it to place orders for dates other than October 3, and they will be accepted.

4. With the view you created for question #3, could you enter an October 3 order for $900.00?

CHAPTER
SIXTEEN

16

Determining Who
Can Do What

- Users and Privileges

- Object Privileges

- Taking Privileges Away

- Using Views to Filter Table Privileges

- Privileges on Other Kinds of Objects

- Other Kinds of Privileges

In this chapter, you will learn about privileges. As we mentioned in Chapter 2, SQL is used mostly in environments that require it to recognize and differentiate between the various users of the system. Generally speaking, those in charge of administering the database create the other users and give them privileges. Users who create tables, on the other hand, have control over those tables. *Privileges* are what determine whether a particular user can perform a given operation. The types of privileges correspond to several types of operations. Two SQL statements—GRANT and REVOKE—give and take away privileges. We'll explore how to use these statements in this chapter.

Users and Privileges

In Chapter 1, we quickly went over some basic concepts about users and privileges in a SQL environment. It is time to examine these concepts in a little more detail. Let's reiterate and elaborate on what we said there:

- The formal name for a database user is an Authorization Identifier (Authorization ID).

- Conceptually, database users are similar to Operating System (OS) users. A database user has a name that is associated with certain a set of privileges, a set of objects, and a set of database sessions.

- There is not, however, necessarily any one-to-one correspondence between database and OS users or between either of these and flesh-and-blood people.

- In fact, all the objects under the control of a particular user are said to be in that user's schema. Generally, these objects should be related. Therefore, database users often reflect the identity of the data, rather than the identity of the person using the data. A database user is the owner of a particular set of related database objects. It is not unusual for all applications using the data to connect as this user, regardless of who is executing the application. This is particularly the case with applications such as database-driven Web sites, where you may not even know who is executing the application and you certainly don't want to create a unique database user for each apparently unique Web visitor.

- Database users are identified through a logon procedure, generally involving a username and password. An application can and often does do this invisibly to the end user.

- Once he logs on, a user initiates a *session* (also called a *connection*) with the DBMS. This session continues until terminated. Within the session, the user issues a sequence of statements. Statements from simultaneous sessions of the same or different users form independent sequences.

- Users have a set of privileges that indicate what they may and may not do.

- Just as an OS user typically has ownership of some set of files and directories and may have access to others as well, a database user typically has ownership of one schema and may have access to others as well. A database user can own one or several schemata. Often, an application that must access a schema does so as the same user regardless of which operating system user is executing the application. This simplifies matters considerably.

- Database applications can sometimes execute under privileges associated with the application itself, rather than the user executing it.

Because database user issues have dependencies upon the general software architecture of the database, there are more platform and especially vendor dependencies in this area than in most areas of SQL. In fact, the SQL standard did not even address most of these matters prior to the SQL92 standard, and its approach there is mostly optional prior to Full conformance, which no one currently claims. Luckily, most systems provide high-level database administration tools that make this whole job easier. They do so, however, each in its own sweet way, gleefully frustrating aspiring generalizers.

Suffice it to say for now that any database statement is effectively executed by an Authorization ID. Generally, this will be that of the database user who created the database session, but it may also be one set by an application. For a more thorough explanation of Authorization IDs, see "CONNECT" and "SET CONNECTION"in Chapter 28, as well as "Authorization IDs" in Chapter 29.

Types of Privileges

Database privileges fall into two general categories: *system privileges* and *object privileges*. System privileges control general access to the database and involve such things as the right to connect, the right to create tables and other objects, and the right to administer the database. Object privileges are specific to a particular database object—a particular table or view, for example.

Object privileges are more standardized than system privileges because they are generally independent of system architecture and because they were standardized, at least to a degree, early in the development of the language. However, most vendors support object privileges beyond the standard ones. Generally speaking, the syntax for handling object and system privileges is similar but not identical. The same syntax may also have slightly different meaning for system than for object privileges.

System privileges are basically non-standard. We can give you some idea how they work, but you'll have to refer to your DBMS's own documentation for the gory details. System privileges are not always all grouped together under that name. Sometimes they go by names such as *database authorities* or *admin privileges*. Any privilege that is not specific to a database object is a system privilege in the sense that we use that term here.

Object Privileges

The following basic concepts underlie object privileges:

- Authorization IDs create and own objects.

- The owner of an object grants and revokes the privileges on the object.

- An object privilege consists logically of two components: an object to which the privilege applies and an operation that the privilege allows.

Here are the standard operations that apply to privileges on tables and views:

ALTER   A user with this privilege can perform the ALTER TABLE statement on the table. This privilege does not apply to views. Though not officially part of the ISO standard, this privilege is widely supported. What the standard actually specifies is that ALTER TABLE statements can be issued only by the owner of the schema that contains the table affected.

SELECT	A user with this privilege can perform queries on the table.
INSERT	A user with this privilege can perform the INSERT statement on the table.
UPDATE	A user with this privilege can perform the UPDATE statement on the table. You may limit this privilege to specified columns of the table.
DELETE	A user with this privilege can perform the DELETE statement on the table.
REFERENCES	A user with this privilege can define a foreign key that uses one or more columns of the table as a parent key. You may limit this privilege to specified columns. This privilege does not apply to views.
INDEX	A user with this privilege can create an index on the table. We discuss indexes more fully in Chapter 23. Though not officially part of the ISO standard, this privilege is widely supported. Indexes are widely supported but are not part of the standard. For more on indexes, see Chapter 23.
DROP	A user with this privilege can drop the table. Though not officially part of the ISO standard, this privilege is widely supported. What the standard actually specifies is that DROP TABLE statements can be issued only by the owner of the schema that contains the table affected.

The owner of the table or view automatically has all these privileges and can give them to others using the GRANT statement described in the next section.

Granting Object Privileges

Let us say that Diane owns the Customers table and wants to let Adrian perform queries on it. Diane would enter the following statement:

```
GRANT SELECT ON Customers TO Adrian;
```

Now Adrian can perform queries on the Customers table. Without other privileges, he can only SELECT; he cannot perform any of the actions that affect the values in Customers (including using Customers as the parent table of a foreign key, which restricts the changes that can be made to the values in the Customers table).

When the DBMS receives a GRANT statement, it checks the privileges of the user issuing it to determine if the GRANT is permissible. Adrian himself could not issue this statement. Nor could Adrian grant SELECT to another user: Diane still owns the table (we will show you shortly how Diane could enable Adrian to grant SELECT).

The syntax is the same for granting the other privileges. If Adrian owned the Salespeople table, he could allow Diane to enter rows into it by entering

```
GRANT INSERT ON Salespeople TO Diane;
```

Now Diane could put new salespeople into the table.

You need not restrict yourself to granting a single privilege to a single user per GRANT statement. Lists of privileges or users, separated by commas, are perfectly acceptable. Stephen could grant SELECT and INSERT on the Orders table either to Adrian

```
GRANT SELECT, INSERT ON Orders TO Adrian;
```

or to both Adrian and Diane

```
GRANT SELECT, INSERT ON Orders TO Adrian, Diane;
```

When you list privileges and users in this manner, all of the privileges in the list are granted to all of the users. In a strict interpretation of the ISO standard, you cannot grant privileges on multiple tables in a single statement, but most implementations relax this rule somewhat by allowing you to name several tables, separated by commas, so that all listed users get all listed privileges on all listed tables.

Restricting Table Privileges to Certain Columns

All object privileges use the same syntax except for UPDATE, INDEX, and REFERENCES, which can optionally specify columns. You can grant an UPDATE privilege like the other privileges:

```
GRANT UPDATE ON Salespeople TO Diane;
```

This statement would allow Diane to alter the values in any or all of the columns of the Salespeople table. However, if Adrian wanted to restrict Diane to changing commissions, he could instead enter

```
GRANT UPDATE(comm) ON Salespeople TO Diane;
```

In other words, he simply names the column to which the UPDATE privilege is to apply in parentheses after the privilege name. You can name multiple columns of the table in any order, separated by commas:

```
GRANT UPDATE(city, comm) ON Salespeople TO Diane;
```

The REFERENCES privilege follows this same pattern. When you grant the REFERENCES privilege to another user, he can create foreign keys that reference columns of your table as parent keys. Like UPDATE, the REFERENCES privilege can take a list of one or more columns to which the privilege will be limited. For example, Diane can grant Stephen the right to use the Customers table as a parent-key table with this statement:

```
GRANT REFERENCES(cname, cnum)
     ON Customers TO Stephen;
```

This statement gives Stephen the right to use either or both the cnum and cname columns as parent keys to any foreign keys in his tables. Stephen has control over how this will be done. What he should do, of course, is use cnum, since that is the primary key of the table. But in principle, he could define (cname, cnum) or, for that matter, (cnum, cname) as a two-column parent key, matched by a two-column foreign key in one of his own tables. Or he could create separate foreign keys to reference the columns individually, provided, in either case, that Diane has appropriately constrained the parent key(s) with either a UNIQUE or PRIMARY KEY constraint. There is no restriction on the number of foreign keys he could base on these parent keys, and the parent keys of various foreign keys may overlap.

As with the UPDATE privilege, you can omit the column list and thereby allow all of your columns to be usable as parent keys. Adrian could grant Diane the right to use all of the columns as parent keys with the following statement:

```
GRANT REFERENCES ON Salespeople TO Diane;
```

Naturally, the privilege will be usable only on columns that have the constraints required for parent keys.

INDEX is the privilege to create an index. An index is a database object that exists primarily to enhance performance. However, some indexes can function as

UNIQUE constraints and therefore limit possible column values. For this reason, their use is subject to privilege. The syntax for the INDEX privilege is the same as for REFERENCES, although indexes are not part of standard SQL, so the syntax may vary slightly. For more on indexes, see Chapter 23.

Using the ALL and PUBLIC Arguments

SQL supports arguments to the GRANT statement that have special meaning: ALL PRIVILEGES (or simply ALL) and PUBLIC. You can use ALL in place of the privilege names in the GRANT statement to give the grantee all of the privileges on the table. For example, Diane could give Stephen the entire set of privileges on the Customers table with this statement:

```
GRANT ALL PRIVILEGES ON Customers TO Stephen;
```

(The UPDATE, INDEX, and REFERENCES privileges naturally apply to all columns when granted as part of ALL PRIVILEGES.) The following is an alternate way of saying the same thing:

```
GRANT ALL ON Customers TO Stephen;
```

PUBLIC is a similar sort of catchall argument, but for users rather than privileges. When you grant privileges to the public, all users receive them automatically. Most often, you will apply this argument to the SELECT privilege on certain base tables or views that you want to have available for anyone's perusal. To allow any user to look at the Orders table, for instance, you could enter the following:

```
GRANT SELECT ON Orders TO PUBLIC;
```

Of course, you can grant any or all privileges to the public, but this is generally not advisable. All privileges except SELECT and INDEX allow the user to change (or, in the case of REFERENCES, constrain) the content of the table. Allowing all users to change the content of your tables is inviting problems. Even if you have a small company, and it is appropriate for all of your current users to be able to perform update statements on a given table, it still may be better to grant the privileges to each user individually, rather than to the public. PUBLIC is not restricted to current users. Any new user added to your system will automatically receive all privileges assigned to PUBLIC, so if you want to restrict access to the table at all, now or possibly in the future, it is best to grant privileges other than SELECT to individual users.

Another possibility on some systems is to GRANT privileges to a group. A *group* is simply a database object whose content is a list of users or possibly a list of other groups. This group is not unlike the groups that exist in many operating systems. Groups of this sort are not officially part of the ISO standard, but you may encounter them in practice, and they will make your life easier if you have many users.

Granting with the GRANT OPTION

Sometimes, the creator of a table wants other users to be able to grant privileges on that table. This is particularly true in systems where one or a few people may create most or all of the base tables in the database and then delegate responsibility for them to those who will actually be working with them. SQL allows this situation through the use of the WITH GRANT OPTION clause.

If Diane wanted Adrian to have the right to grant the SELECT privilege on the Customers table to other users, she would give him the SELECT privilege and use the WITH GRANT OPTION clause:

```
GRANT SELECT ON Customers TO Adrian
    WITH GRANT OPTION;
```

Adrian would then have the right to give the SELECT privilege to third parties; he could issue the statement

```
GRANT SELECT ON Diane.Customers TO Stephen;
```

or even

```
GRANT SELECT ON Diane.Customers TO Stephen
    WITH GRANT OPTION;
```

NOTE   Notice that when a user other than the schema owner references the table name, it is preceded by the schema name. This rule applies not only to GRANT but to all SQL statements.

A user with the GRANT OPTION on a particular privilege for a given table can, in turn, grant that privilege on that table, with or without the GRANT OPTION, to any other user. Doing so does not change the ownership of the table; creators own their tables. (And the tables must be prefixed by the Authorization ID of the owner, as above, when other users refer to them). Nevertheless, a user with the

GRANT OPTION on all privileges for a given table wields a great deal of power over that table.

Taking Privileges Away

So now you've given away your privileges like business cards to everyone you meet. People keep reading and revising your data, so that your database is a mess. Now you need to learn how to take privileges away.

The statement is called REVOKE. The syntax of REVOKE is patterned after GRANT, but with the reverse meaning. So, to take away Adrian's INSERT privilege on Orders, you could enter:

```
REVOKE INSERT ON Orders FROM Adrian;
```

Lists of privileges and users are acceptable just as for GRANT, so you could also enter the following statement:

```
REVOKE INSERT, DELETE ON Customers
    FROM Adrian, Stephen;
```

Cascading Revokes

Some questions arise with REVOKE that do not arise with GRANT, however. Who has the right to revoke a privilege? When a user with GRANT OPTION on a privilege loses it, do users to whom he or she has granted the privilege lose it as well?

The general principles are these:

- You can revoke only a privilege you have granted.

- When you revoke a privilege that you have granted with the GRANT OPTION, all users who received the privilege as a consequence of that GRANT OPTION lose it as well.

- Certain objects can depend on certain privileges for their existence. For example, since a view contains a query, you can create a view of a table only if you have the SELECT privilege on that table. If you create such a view and then lose your SELECT privilege, what happens to the view? SQL92 lets you specify CASCADE or RESTRICT when you revoke a privilege. If you specify CASCADE, dependent objects such as the view are automatically dropped. If you specify RESTRICT, the REVOKE statement itself is rejected wherever it would mandate such an action. CASCADE is the default.

- You can also REVOKE the GRANT OPTION on a privilege without revoking the privilege itself. When you do so, you can still specify CASCADE or RESTRICT, as above, to the same effect. For more information, refer to the detailed discussion under "REVOKE" in Chapter 28.

So here is the syntax to the REVOKE statement as we have just described it:

```
REVOKE [ GRANT OPTION FOR ]
{ ALL [PRIVILEGES] } | { privilege .,..}
ON object
FROM PUBLIC | { grantee .,..}
  CASCADE | RESTRICT ;
```

Note that many implementations would permit you to list several objects, although such is not part of the standard. In fact, products declaring only Entry-level SQL92 conformity need not support REVOKE at all. All implementations do, of course, but not strictly as the standard describes. In any case, here are some examples:

```
REVOKE ALL ON Salespeople FROM Linda RESTRICT;
```

This statement eliminates all privileges Linda has on the Salespeople table from her and from everyone to whom she has granted them (if she has the GRANT OPTION). Note that ALL automatically means "all that apply". In other words, it is not necessary for Linda to actually have all privileges for her to have all privileges revoked. Whichever privileges she does, in fact, have will be canceled and the rest ignored. If this REVOKE would cause the automatic destruction of any objects, however—for example, if Linda or one of her grantees has created a view of the Salespeople table—the statement would be rejected with an error. Here is another example:

```
REVOKE GRANT OPTION FOR SELECT, INSERT ON Salespeople FROM George;
```

George retains the SELECT and INSERT privileges on Salespeople but loses the GRANT OPTION for these privileges. Nonetheless, individuals who have received these privileges as a consequence of this GRANT OPTION do not automatically lose them.

Another issue to deal with in revoking privileges is that the same privilege may come from more than one source. For example, suppose Jim has a table called

Leads and gives all privileges on it with the GRANT OPTION to Mary. Jim then gives the SELECT privilege on the table to Tom, while Mary gives him both the SELECT and INSERT privileges. If Jim now revokes SELECT from Tom, does he still retain the privilege? Yes, he does, because he has it from Mary. Since he has a double GRANT of the privilege, only a double REVOKE can remove it.

Using Views to Filter Table Privileges

You can make the effects of privileges more precise by using views. Whenever you grant a privilege on a base table to a user, it automatically applies to all rows and, with the possible exceptions of UPDATE, INDEX, and REFERENCES, all columns of the table. By creating a view that references the base table and then granting privileges on the view rather than the table, you can limit these privileges in any way expressible in the query that the view contains. This greatly refines the basic capabilities of the GRANT statement.

You can, and often should, grant access to a view without providing access to the underlying table. The reverse, however, is not true, at least in SQL92. Privileges granted on a leaf-underlying table of a view apply automatically to the view itself. Note that for views that are not updatable, this means that a user could have automatic access to some columns of the view and not others by having access to one of the leaf-underlying tables and not others (updatable views have only one leaf-underlying table). This situation, however, implies a somewhat stricter reading of the standard than you are actually likely to encounter.

Who Can Create Views?

In order to create a view, you must have the SELECT privilege on all the tables that you reference in that view. If the view is updatable, any INSERT, UPDATE, and DELETE privileges that you have on the underlying table will automatically apply as well to the view. If you lack update privileges on the underlying tables, you will not have them on the views you create, even if the views themselves are updatable. Since foreign keys as such are not used in views, the REFERENCES privilege is never needed to create views. These are the privileges defined by the ISO. Nonstandard system privileges may also be involved. In the following sections, we will assume that the creators of the views we discuss own or have the relevant privileges on all base tables used.

Limiting the SELECT Privilege to Certain Columns

Suppose you wanted to give user Claire the ability to see only the snum and sname columns of the Salespeople table. You could do this by putting these columns in a view

```
CREATE VIEW Clairesview
     AS SELECT snum, sname
     FROM Salespeople;
```

and granting Claire the SELECT privilege on the view but not on the Salespeople table itself:

```
GRANT SELECT ON Clairesview to Claire;
```

You can create column-specific privileges like this using the other privileges as well. However, for the INSERT statement, this will mean the insertion of default values, and for the DELETE statement, the column limitations will not be meaningful. You can, of course, make the UPDATE and REFERENCES privileges column-specific without resorting to a view.

Limiting Privileges to Certain Rows

An even more useful way to filter privileges with views is to use the view to make a privilege apply only to certain rows. You do this, naturally, by using a predicate in the view that determines which rows are included. To grant the user Adrian the UPDATE privilege on all Customers located in London, you could first create this view:

```
CREATE VIEW Londoncust
     AS SELECT *
     FROM Customers
     WHERE city = 'London'
     WITH CHECK OPTION;
```

You could then grant the UPDATE privilege on it to Adrian:

```
GRANT UPDATE ON Londoncust TO Adrian;
```

This method differs from a column-specific UPDATE privilege in that all of the columns of the Customers table are included, but the rows in cities other than London are omitted. The WITH CHECK OPTION clause prevents Adrian from changing the city field to any value besides London.

Granting Access Only to Derived Data

Another possibility is to offer users access to derived data, rather than actual table values. Aggregate functions can often be handy if used this way. You can create a view that gives the counts, averages, and totals for the orders on each order date:

```
CREATE VIEW Datetotals
     AS SELECT odate, COUNT(*), SUM(amt), AVG(amt)
     FROM Orders
     GROUP BY odate;
```

Now you give user Diane SELECT on the Datetotals view:

```
GRANT SELECT ON Datetotals TO Diane;
```

Using Privileges to Refine Constraints

Privileges can interact with constraints in interesting ways. By granting privileges on some tables and not on others, you can effectively create constraints that are more easily modifiable. Suppose you wanted to constrain the city column of the Salespeople table to cities where your company has an office. This would be an easy way to reject some common errors, such as typos, and to force the same city value to be entered always in the same way. Forcing the same string value always to be entered in exactly the same way—e.g., without abbreviations or leading blanks—is helpful because it means that the same value will always be equal to itself in SQL queries, which it logically should and which will make things like GROUP BY work. However, your company may add or close an office from time to time, so it is worthwhile to be able to change the list of valid cities.

There are a few approaches to this problem, but perhaps the most common is to have a separate table of valid values that the Salespeople table will reference. Only a few users will have access to the valid values table, so it will not be easily filled with invalid values. Here is an example:

```
CREATE TABLE Offices
     (city    CHAR(10) NOT NULL PRIMARY KEY);
CREATE TABLE Salespeople
     (snum    INTEGER NOT NULL PRIMARY KEY,
      sname   CHAR(10) NOT NULL,
      city    CHAR(10) REFERENCES Offices,
      comm    DECIMAL);
GRANT ALL ON Salespeople TO PUBLIC;
```

```
GRANT ALL ON Offices TO Jeff;
INSERT INTO Offices
        VALUES ('London', 'San Jose', 'Barcelona', 'New York');
```

Now, only you (as the table creator) and Jeff can add new offices, but anyone can add new salespeople to an existing office. Valid value tables such as this are one of the relatively few common situations where it may be appropriate to have a table that consists solely of a primary key.

Another approach to the same problem is the use of views WITH CHECK OPTION as an alternative to constraints. This entails placing the restrictions you intend for the data in the predicate of the view and granting most users access to the view but not the table. This has the following advantages over constraints placed directly in tables:

- You can have different constraints for different users. For example, you could have entries in an expenses table restricted by the signing authority of the user. With some systems, you could also do this with a constraint in the table that references CURRENT_USER, coupled with a valid values table. If so, this is a purer and less problematic solution than using a view. For more on CURRENT_USER, see "User Value Functions" under "Value Expressions" in Chapter 29.

- It is easier to change than the constraint. Creating a new view is no problem, but DBMSs vary in the degree to which you can modify or drop existing constraints.

On the other hand, this approach has the following disadvantages:

- A constraint effected using views is one to which you can make exceptions. This is sometimes necessary for real-world reasons, but you should avoid it if at all possible. A constraint enables you to make certain assertions about your data that exceptions undermine.

- What you are creating is not, properly speaking, a constraint, and you therefore are in a theoretically ambiguous area when you take this approach.

Privileges on Other Kinds of Objects

So far, we have been concerned only with privileges on base tables and on views. There are, however, other kinds of objects whose access requires privileges, but which we have not yet covered in this book. These include created temporary tables, domains, and collations. For more information on these objects, see "CREATE TABLE", "CREATE DOMAIN", and "CREATE COLLATION" in Chapter 28, as well as "Collations" in Chapter 29. Created temporary tables are base tables that are used for temporary storage. The privileges you can grant on them are the same as for other kinds of base tables. For the other kinds of objects in the list, only one privilege applies: USAGE. The USAGE privilege enables you to reference an object to create another object. For example, you may create a table that utilizes a domain if you have the USAGE privilege on the domain. If that privilege is to be later revoked, you may specify CASCADE or RESTRICT with the effects outlined earlier.

Other Kinds of Privileges

You may have been wondering who has the right to create tables in the first place. While the ISO has not addressed this area of privilege as such, we cannot ignore it. All of the standard privileges emanate from this privilege; it is the creators of tables who grant the table privileges. Likewise, it is the creators of other objects who grant the USAGE privilege on them. Moreover, permitting all of your users to create base tables in a system of any size invites redundancy and inefficiency, to say the least. Associated with this are other concerns: Who has the right to alter, drop, or constrain tables? Should the right to create base tables be distinguished from that to create views or to create permanent tables from temporary? Should there be *superusers*—users who are generally in charge of maintaining the database and therefore have a great many or all privileges without their being individually granted?

Since the ISO doesn't address these concerns, and SQL is used in a variety of environments, there is no DBMS-agnostic answer to these questions. What we present here is an indication of the most common approach to these issues.

Privileges that are not defined in terms of specific data objects are usually called *system privileges*, or *database authorities*. At the most basic level, these will likely include the right to create data objects, probably (and desirably) distinguishing between base tables (usually created by a few users) and views (commonly created by many or all users). A system privilege to create views should supplement, rather than replace, the object privileges that the standard requires of view creators (explained earlier in the present chapter). In addition, in a system of any size, some kind of superuser—a user who automatically has many or all privileges—will generally exist, and the superuser status may be conferred with a privilege or group of privileges. The superuser will generally be identified with a special name such as SYS, System, or DBA (for Database Administrator).

Summary

Privileges have enabled you to see SQL from a new angle, that of SQL actions performed by specific users in a specific database system. The GRANT statement itself is simple enough: with it you grant one or more privileges on an object to one or more users. If you grant a privilege WITH GRANT OPTION to a user, that user can grant the privilege to others in turn. You now understand the previously hinted-at uses of privileges on views—to refine privileges on the base tables or as an alternative to constraints—and some of the advantages and disadvantages of this approach. In the next chapter, we will continue to discuss broader issues in SQL, such as saving or reversing changes, and understanding what happens when different users attempt to access the same object at once.

Putting SQL to Work

1. Give Janet the right to change the ratings of the customers.

2. Give Stephen the right to give other users the right to query the Orders table.

3. Take the INSERT privilege on Salespeople away from Claire and all users to whom she has granted it.

4. Grant Jerry the right to INSERT or UPDATE the Customers table while keeping his possible rating values in the range of 100 to 500.

5. Allow Janet to query the Customers table, but restrict her access to those customers whose rating is the lowest.

CHAPTER

SEVENTEEN

Transactions and Concurrency

- When Does a Change Become Permanent?

- How SQL Deals with Multiple Users at Once

This chapter discusses two related aspects of the SQL language: transactions and concurrency. *Transactions* are groups of SQL statements that are effectively executed as single units. *Concurrency* refers to mechanisms that the DBMS uses to keep operations on the same data by simultaneous users from interfering with one another.

When Does a Change Become Permanent?

It is easy in visualizing a database environment to picture hordes of users entering and changing data constantly, assuming that, if the system is well designed, it will function without glitches. In the real world, however, mistakes due to human or computer error happen all the time, and one of the things that good computer programmers have learned is to give people ways of undoing their actions.

A SQL statement that affects the content or structure of the database—an update statement or a DROP TABLE statement, for instance—is not necessarily irreversible. You can determine after the fact whether a given group of one or more statements will effect permanent changes to the database or be disregarded. For this purpose, statements are treated in groups called transactions. A *transaction* is a sequence of SQL statements that succeed or fail as a unit.

You begin a transaction whenever you initiate a session with SQL. All statements you enter will be part of this same transaction until you complete it by entering either a COMMIT WORK or a ROLLBACK WORK statement. COMMIT will make all of the changes affected by the transaction permanent, and ROLLBACK will reverse them. A new transaction begins after each COMMIT or ROLLBACK statement. The syntax to make all of your changes permanent since logging on, or since the last COMMIT or ROLLBACK statement, is

```
COMMIT WORK;
```

The syntax to reverse them is

```
ROLLBACK WORK;
```

In many implementations, you set a parameter called something like AUTOCOMMIT, which will automatically commit all actions that execute normally. Actions that produce errors are automatically rolled back in any case. If your system offers this feature, you may choose to have all of your actions committed with a statement like this:

```
SET AUTOCOMMIT ON;
```

You could return to regular transaction processing with this statement:

```
SET AUTOCOMMIT OFF;
```

It is also possible for the system to automatically set AUTOCOMMIT on when you log in.

If a user session terminates abnormally—if the system crashes or the user reboots, for example—the current transaction will automatically be rolled back. This is one reason why, if you are doing your transaction processing by hand, you should divide your statements into many different transactions. A single transaction should not contain a lot of unrelated statements; in fact, it can frequently consist of a single statement. Transactions that include an entire group of unrelated changes leave you no choice but to save or reject the whole group, when you probably want to reverse only one specific change. A good rule of thumb is to have your transactions consist of single or of closely related statements.

Let's look at an example. Suppose you want to remove salesperson Motika from the database. Before you DELETE her from the Salespeople table, you first should do something with her orders and her customers. One logical solution would be to set the snum on her orders to NULL, so that no salesperson receives a commission on those orders, while giving her customers to Peel. Then you could remove her from the Salespeople table:

```
UPDATE Orders
     SET snum = NULL
     WHERE snum = 1004;
UPDATE Customers
     SET snum = 1001
     WHERE snum = 1004;
DELETE FROM Salespeople
     WHERE snum = 1004;
```

If you had a problem deleting Motika (perhaps there is another foreign key referencing her that you did not know about or account for), you might want to reverse all of the changes you made until the problem could be identified and resolved. Therefore, this would be a good group of statements to treat as a single transaction. You could precede the group with a COMMIT and terminate it with a COMMIT or a ROLLBACK.

How SQL Deals with Multiple Users at Once

SQL is generally used in multi-user environments—environments where more than one user can perform actions on the database at the same time. This creates a potential for clashes between the various actions performed. For example, suppose you perform the following statement on the Salespeople table:

```
UPDATE Salespeople
    SET comm = comm * 2
    WHERE sname LIKE 'R%';
```

While this statement is executing, Diane enters the following query:

```
SELECT city, AVG(comm)
    FROM Salespeople
    GROUP BY city;
```

Will the averages Diane gets reflect the changes you make to the table? It may be unimportant whether they do or not, but it is often important that they reflect either all or none of the changed commission values. Any intermediate result is purely the accidental and unpredictable result of the order in which the values were physically altered. The output of queries is not supposed to depend on physical details, and neither should it be accidental and unpredictable.

Consider another point. Suppose you find a mistake and roll back your update after Diane gets her output. Now Diane has a series of averages based on changes that were cancelled, but she has no way of knowing her information is inaccurate.

Types of Concurrency Problems

The handling of simultaneous transactions is called *concurrency*, and a number of possible problems can arise in it. Here are some examples:

- Updates can be made without regard to one another. For instance, a salesperson could query an inventory table, find ten pieces of a merchandise item in stock, and order six of them for a customer. Before this change is made, another salesperson queries the table and orders seven of this same item for one of his customers.

- Changes to the database can be rolled back after their effect has already been felt, as when you cancelled your mistake after Diane got her output.

- One action can be affected by the partial result of another action, as when Diane took averages while you were performing an update. Although this is not always a problem, in many cases functions such as aggregates should reflect the state of the database at a point of relative stability. Someone auditing the books, for example, should be able to go back and determine that Diane's averages existed at some point and could have remained the same had no further updates been made after that point. Such is not the case if an update is in progress while the function is being evaluated.

- A deadlock can occur when two users attempt to perform actions that interfere with one another. For example, two users try to change a foreign-key value and its parent-key value at the same time.

Let's describe these situations a little more graphically, using some standard terminology that you may encounter elsewhere in the database literature, for example, in your system documentation. The standard terms for concurrency problems are these:

- Lost update

- Dirty read

- Non-repeatable read

- Phantom insert

We explain each of these terms in Tables 17.1 through 17.4 below.

TABLE 17.1: The Lost Update

Transaction #1	State of Database	Transaction #2
SELECT comm FROM Salespeople WHERE snum = 1001;	comm = .12	SELECT comm
UPDATE Salespeople SET comm = .10 WHERE snum = 1001; COMMIT WORK;	comm = .10	
	comm = .14	UPDATE Salespeople SET comm = .14 WHERE snum = 1001; COMMIT WORK;

At the end of this sequence, the comm is .14. The update to .10 has had no effect. Is this a problem? Not necessarily. Setting the comm to .14 the following week would have had the same override effect. However, changes to data are often based on an understanding of what the previous value was. The user performing transaction #2 was mistaken: she thought the current commission was .12 and it was .10. If her intention were, in fact, to increment the comm by .02, she has failed to do this accurately. Of course, if she had expressed that increment directly, by using a SET comm = comm + .02 clause in the UPDATE statement, she would have avoided this error. However, this is not always easy to do with more complex derivations.

TABLE 17.2: The Dirty (Uncommitted) Read

Transaction #1	State of Database	Transaction #2
SELECT comm FROM Salespeople WHERE snum = 1001;	comm = .12	
UPDATE Salespeople SET comm = .10 WHERE snum = 1001;	comm = .10	
		SELECT comm FROM Salespeople WHERE snum = 1001;
ROLLBACK WORK;	comm = .12	

The query in transaction #2 retrieved a value that has disappeared from the database. Since transaction #1 was rolled back, it is as though the comm value had never been .10, yet that is the value transaction #2 has seen.

TABLE 17.3: The Non-repeatable Read

Transaction #1	State of Database	Transaction #2
	comm = .12	SELECT comm FROM Salespeople WHERE snum = 1001;
UPDATE Salespeople SET comm = .10 WHERE snum = 1001;	comm = .10	
	comm = .10	SELECT comm FROM Salespeople WHERE snum = 1001;

The query in transaction #2 has gotten two different answers to the same question within the same transaction. This is correct: the data has in fact changed. However, it is sometimes necessary for a transaction to be able to ensure that the data it is working on remains constant until it has completed. This is especially true for applications that read the data, perform some operations on it, and then store new values that are in some way derived from or affected by the old. In such a case, this situation would be a problem.

TABLE 17.4:   The Phantom Insert

Transaction #1	State of Database	Transaction #2
		SELECT AVG(comm) FROM Salespeople;
INSERT INTO Salespeople VALUES(1020, 'Tran', 'Bangkok', .15);	Tran's row is added	
		SELECT AVG(comm) FROM Salespeople;

Since the INSERT in transaction #1 occurs in the midst of transaction #2, its value will cause a difference between the same query executed twice. In a sense, this is a special case of an unrepeatable read. The difference is that when the intervening statement is INSERT rather than UPDATE or DELETE, the new row cannot be one that was produced by the previous query but now has different values. It is a new "phantom" row that did not previously exist. In practical terms, the distinction between phantom inserts and other kinds of non-repeatable reads is that phantom inserts are somewhat more limited in their effects. If a query selects a single row, for example, by primary key value, you know that the content of that row will not change because of a phantom insert, whereas other forms of non-repeatable reads may have effects. There therefore exists a class of queries for which phantom inserts are not a problem but other kinds of non-repeatable reads are.

How to Deal with Concurrency Problems

Now that you've seen the kinds of problems that can occur, what do you *do* about them? We could envision any number of nightmare scenarios if simultaneous transactions were uncontrolled. Luckily, SQL provides *concurrency controls* to address precisely these issues. In the original SQL standard, the ISO specified simply that all simultaneous statements shall be executed in such a way that the effect is the same as if no statement were issued until the previous one was completed (including COMMIT or ROLLBACK where appropriate). This rule is, of course, ideal from a data-integrity standpoint, but for practical reasons businesses often need to make their data more accessible than that. This sort of strict standard means that only one transaction will be able to change data at a time (though more than one may be able to read it). If you are running an application that requires a lot of simultaneous updates to the databases, for example, an e-commerce Web site, then you may have to compromise on strict integrity to make your data properly accessible and your performance acceptable.

The mechanisms SQL uses to control concurrent operations are called *locks*. Locks restrict certain operations on the database while other operations or transactions are active. Locks fall into the following two general categories:

- Pessimistic locks are locks that prevent some kinds of data access by simultaneous transactions.

- Optimistic locks keep track of when clashes occur and roll back transactions as necessary. Strictly speaking, these are not locks at all, but the term *optimistic locking* has become standard for this approach.

As the name implies, optimistic locking is more appropriate if you expect clashes to be rare. With optimistic locking, operations can proceed more smoothly in general, because access to the data is unrestricted. Whenever a clash does occur, however, work must be undone, so if clashes are frequent, it will be difficult to get transactions to commit.

Using Pessimistic Locking

In *pessimistic locking*, some types of simultaneous data access are prevented. The first operation that might cause a clash gets a lock on some or all of the data it is using. Subsequent clashing operations are either rolled back or queued up to be re-entered, often using a configurable parameter with a name such as NOWAIT.

Isolation Levels

SQL92 and later deal with locking by defining isolation levels that address whether various sorts of clashes are tolerated. Table 17.5 shows the various isolation levels and the operations they permit.

TABLE 17.5:   Isolation Levels and Permitted Operations

Isolation Level	Lost Update	Dirty Read	Non-Repeatable	Phantom
READ UNCOMMITTED	NO	YES	YES	YES
READ COMMITTED	NO	NO	YES	YES
REPEATABLE READ	NO	NO	NO	YES
SERIALIZABLE	NO	NO	NO	NO

SERIALIZABLE is the default and the highest level of control. It is the same as what had been specified in earlier standards and is the way in principle that relational databases are supposed to work. In SERIALIZABLE mode, each transaction is an island, affecting the operation of no other concurrent transactions. As we mentioned previously, this situation is ideal from a data-integrity standpoint but less than ideal from a performance standpoint.

REPEATABLE READ allows phantom inserts but no other non-repeatable reads. This isolation level is useful for transactions that do not use the kinds of queries that can be affected by phantom inserts. For any given query, simply ask yourself whether the addition of new rows to the table could possibly affect the answer. If not, then REPEATABLE READ may be preferable to SERIALIZABLE, as it will permit INSERTs.

READ COMMITTED allows the same query executed multiple times to return different results but only as the result of concurrent transactions that have been committed.

READ UNCOMMITTED allows the same query executed multiple times to return different results, regardless of whether the concurrent transactions have been committed.

Share and Exclusive Locks

In general, all of the isolation levels are enforced with two logical kinds of locks: share locks and exclusive locks. *Share locks* (or *S-locks*) can be placed by more than one user at a time. This situation enables any number of users to access the data but not to change it. For example, you can use share locks to enforce read repeatability. *Exclusive locks* (or *X-locks*) allow no one but the owner of the lock to access the data. Exclusive locks are used for statements that change the content or structure of the table. You can use them to prevent lost updates. Moreover, you can place both kinds of locks on the data simultaneously.

READ ONLY and READ WRITE Transactions

You may have noticed that all of the isolation levels prevent lost updates. This means a query within a transaction effectively prohibits concurrent transactions from updating or deleting *any of the specific data it selected* until the transactions completes (commits or rolls back). This is generally what you want if you may be updating that data. However, if you know that no such update will occur, you have the alternative of declaring the transaction READ ONLY. The opposite of this is a READ WRITE transaction, which can perform both queries and update operations. A READ ONLY transaction places no locks on the data, but likewise can contain no updates to it. READ UNCOMMITTED transactions are READ ONLY by default; other transactions are READ WRITE by default. The general default for transactions, then, is READ WRITE SERIALIZABLE.

When we cover embedded SQL, you will see that cursors, objects within applications that hold the results of queries, can also be declared READ ONLY for similar reasons to transactions.

Setting Transaction Parameters

So, now that you understand the kinds of locking problems that exist and the solutions that the standard provides, how do you apply these solutions? In the older standards, the solutions were all implementation-dependent, and you can still find implementation-dependent approaches. However, SQL92 did specify a SET TRANSACTION statement that is similar to what most vendors do and is the likely point towards which they will converge. SET TRANSACTION is not required for Entry-level SQL92 compatibility.

Here is an example of a SET TRANSACTION statement. We've provided a more complete description of this statement under SET TRANSACTION in the reference.

```
SET TRANSACTION
    ISOLATION LEVEL REPEATABLE READ,
    READ WRITE;
```

This statement overrides the default setting for the subsequent transaction, but it does leave open the question of how the default is determined. As we stated, the fundamental default is SERIALIZABLE READ WRITE, but it is possible on some systems for a DBA, or possibly even a common user, to define a different default. This default may be specific to a given schema or even a different area of physical storage.

The SQL92 standard does not provide for optimistic locking. Therefore, if your DBMS supports optimistic locking, it will use some sort of non-standard syntax to do so, although such syntax may be incorporated into the SET TRANSACTION statement. See your system documentation for details.

Granularity of Locks (Locking Levels)

When we say that a lock exists on a piece of data, do we mean the entire row, the entire table, just a specific column value, or something else entirely? We are referring to the *granularity* of the lock, also called the *locking level*. The explanation is a little complicated because we can often define the granularity of the lock either in logical or physical terms. That is to say, we can define it either in terms of the logical database objects with which you are now familiar, such as tables and rows, or in terms of objects that are used to define how the data is physically organized on disk (or whatever medium holds it). In the latter case, we are rather heavily in the realm of the platform-specific. Not only the DBMS itself, but also in some cases the operating system and computer architecture on which it resides can affect the locking level. If you encounter locking schemes defined in terms of objects such as dbspaces, tablespaces, or pages, you are in the realm of storage parameters. It is useful to understand these levels so that you will have some idea of how the locking is working, although you will probably not need to engage with this material deeply unless you are a DBA.

Let's look at the most common possibilities:

- Table-level locking means the entire table is locked. Such locks are quickly applied and removed but, of course, maximize the inaccessibility of the data.

- Tablespace or dbspace-level locking refers to locking of a physical storage area on the disk that may hold part of a table or may hold several tables. At the least, these should have been laid out so as to minimize lock conflicts.

- Row-level locking applies to a particular row of a table. It is currently the most common type.

- Page-level locking also refers to a storage parameter. A *page* is a unit of data storage of a particular, often configurable, size, for example, 1K. A DBMS can very efficiently transverse a database formatted into such pages, but the pages will not necessarily have a one-to-one correspondence with any unit of the logical data. Simply locking the page is very efficient performance-wise and may be advisable if the DBA has designed the page setup with this in mind. Otherwise, page-level locking could be a headache.

- Item-level locking means the lock applies only to a single value, a single column of a single row. Although ideal from a concurrency standpoint, this type tends to be slow in practice, so it is not commonly implemented as of this writing. SQL99 provides for large, complex units of data (so-called LOBs), so for these, item-level locking may come to make sense.

Using Optimistic Locking

Although "optimistic locking" is the industry buzzword, "optimistic concurrency control" would probably be as accurate as it is clumsy, which is very. As we mentioned, optimistic locking does not prevent any operations, but it cancels operations that have created clashes. Since this is a common, but not a standard, feature of SQL, the specifics of what your DBMS supports may vary. Nonetheless, in principle, you should be able to apply the isolation levels from the previous section here as well to control which clashes mandate rollbacks. Your DBMS defines the syntax.

The mechanism optimistic locking uses is the *timestamp*. Whenever a transaction touches a piece of data, the DBMS makes a record of the event in the database along with the exact time it occurred. Whenever a transaction reads a piece of data, the DBMS records that too, and it records when every transaction terminates (commits or rolls back). As each change rolls in, the DBMS uses the timestamps to attempt to verify that it is serializable with what preceded it. Failing that, it tries to verify that the transaction has generated none of the kinds of clashes that would violate the specified isolation level. If the transaction does create such a violation, the DBMS rolls it back. Note that the use of the term "timestamp", though common in the industry, differs from that of the SQL92 standard. For an explantion of how this term is used in the standard, look under "Datatypes" in the reference.

Let's look at another table. Table 17.6 is a variation on our lost-update example and could indeed result in a lost update. The optimistic locking scheme allows all operations, but when transaction #2 attempts to update, it notices that there has been an update to the data since that transaction read it. Hence, transaction #2 is rolled back. Yes, transaction #2 does say "COMMIT WORK", but that was our idea, not the database's. The DBMS will reject the COMMIT WORK statement with an error message.

TABLE 17.6:   Variation on the Lost-Update Example

Transaction #1	Timestamp	Transaction #2
SELECT comm FROM Salespeople WHERE snum = 1001;	T = 12:01:44	
	T = 12:14:27	SELECT comm FROM Salespeople WHERE snum = 1001;
UPDATE Salespeople SET comm = .10; COMMIT WORK;	T = 12:53:22	
	T = 12:56:33	UPDATE Salespeople SET comm = .14; COMMIT WORK;

So which way is better? How optimistic are you? Specifically, how often do you expect clashes to occur? If clashes occur frequently, optimistic locking will result in many transactions failing. Otherwise, it may make everything run more quickly. Among the questions you should ask yourself in making the decision are these:

- What is the expected ratio of queries to update operations? If users are frequently reading but infrequently changing the data, clashes will be rare, since concurrency is never a problem unless the data changes. An example of this would be many of the tables in a Human Resources database. Such items as employee salary, vacation time, and dependents may be frequently read, but they do not change often. This database would be a candidate for optimistic locking.

- How long and complicated are my transactions going to be? The longer and more complicated each transaction is, the more painful it will be to roll back. If you have put a client through a whole series of Web pages to provide information and then have to roll back the transaction, that's not good. Of course, this problem is partly a matter of how you design your Web application and the capabilities of your Web server and middleware, all of which are beyond the scope of this book. Nonetheless, you should keep this sort of consideration in mind in choosing your concurrency scheme.

Summary

The key things you have learned about in this chapter are:

- Transaction processing, or how to group changes to the database, and save or disregard them as a unit

- Concurrency control, or how SQL keeps simultaneous statements and transactions from interfering with one another

COMMIT and ROLLBACK are the statements used to take all changes to the database since either the previous COMMIT or ROLLBACK or the beginning of the session as well as to save or disregard them as a group.

Concurrency controls determine to what extent simultaneous statements will affect one another. These are adjustable because of the trade-off between database performance and isolation of the effects of statements.

Putting SQL to Work

1. Which concurrency problem does the following table illustrate?

Transaction #1	Transaction #2
SELECT AVG(rating) FROM Customers;	
	UPDATE Customers SET rating = 500 WHERE cnum > 2002; COMMIT WORK;
SELECT AVG(rating) FROM Customers;	

2. Which concurrency problem does the following table illustrate?

Transaction #1	Transaction #2
SELECT AVG(rating) FROM Customers;	
	INSERT INTO Customers VALUES(2020, 'Harbin', 'Dublin', 300, 1002); COMMIT WORK;
SELECT AVG(rating) FROM Customers;	

3. If there is a power failure, what should happen to all changes contained in the current uncommitted transaction?

4. If you cannot look at a row because a lock is in place, what kind of lock is it?

5. Which lock granularity places the least restriction on data access?

How a SQL Database Is Kept in Order

- The System Catalog

- The Standard Information Schema

In this chapter, you will learn how a typical SQL database keeps itself organized. Not surprisingly, it does so with a relational database created and maintained by the DBMS itself. This method is in keeping with the relational philosophy that all data should be represented as tables. You can access these tables yourself for information about privileges, tables, indexes, and so on. This chapter will show you some typical contents of such a database. After you are familiar with the material in this chapter, you can refer to Appendix D for more detailed information on the standard version of this database.

The System Catalog

In order to operate as a SQL database, your DBMS must keep track of a lot of different things: tables, views, privileges, users, and so on. Such information is called *metadata*—data about data. Clearly the most logical, efficient, sensible, and consistent way to keep track of metadata in a relational environment is to store this information in tables. Doing so enables the computer to arrange and manipulate the information it needs, using the same procedures as it does to arrange and manipulate the data it stores for your needs. In fact, storing the metadata in tables directly controlled by the DBMS is one of Ted Codd's principles that are used to distinguish fully relational from semi-relational and non-relational systems. So there. This set of tables is most commonly referred to as a *system catalog*, or simply the *system tables*.

The SQL standard did not address the issue of system catalogs prior to the publication of the SQL92 standard. Therefore, vendors took their own approaches. When the ISO decided to include the system catalog in the standard then, it realized that vendors had proprietary solutions that they could not simply abandon. Nonetheless, with increasing demand for applications that can transparently access multiple DBMS products, the differences in the catalogs and the consequent differences in the queries that would be used on them became more and more problematic. The system catalog introduced by SQL92 is covered in detail in Appendix D.

The tables of the system catalog are like other SQL tables: rows and columns of data. For example, one table of the catalog contains information about the tables in the database, with one row for each database table; another contains information about the various columns of the tables, with one row per column, and so on. The catalog tables are considered to be created and owned by the DBMS itself, identified by a special name such as SYSTEM. The DBMS creates these tables and updates them automatically as the system is used; you cannot directly subject catalog tables to update commands. If you were to do so, it would greatly confuse the system and make it dysfunctional.

However, users can query the catalog, which is how you find out which objects exist in the database and what their attributes are. In the SQL standard, all users have full access to the catalog, though some products have a more restrictive approach than this.

The Standard Information Schema

SQL92 defines the following two sets of system tables. Each set constitutes a special, system-defined, schema.

- The DEFINITION_SCHEMA consists of a set of base tables that could function very well as the catalog for a SQL92-compliant database. The only problem with the DEFINITION_SCHEMA is that it's mythical. No one expects this schema to be implemented as such. The purpose of the DEFINITION_SCHEMA is to make the semantics of the INFORMATION_SCHEMA unambiguous. The INFORMATION_SCHEMA must behave as though it were implemented over this set of tables, regardless of which set it actually uses.

- The INFORMATION_SCHEMA consists of a series of views that are defined on the tables of the DEFINITION_SCHEMA. Indeed, the main purpose of the DEFINITION_SCHEMA is to make the views of the INFORMATION_SCHEMA intelligible. It is planned (and hoped) that DBMS products will be able to implement these views over their proprietary system catalog, however it is structured, so that there will be a common interface for the system tables of various products. Therefore, the INFORMATION_SCHEMA is the one that actually matters. Various products currently tend to support parts but not the entirety of this schema.

So what you do, then, is query the views of the INFORMATION_SCHEMA just as you would other tables. You cannot, however, perform any operations on these tables other than SELECT. Since the integrity of the database itself relies on the INFORMATION_SCHEMA, the DBMS automatically updates it to reflect the current state of things. You cannot do so. To see a list of the tables, for example, enter the following:

```
SELECT *
    FROM INFORMATION_SCHEMA.TABLES;
```

You would see a table like this:

CATALOG_NAME	SCHEMA_NAME	TABLE_NAME	TABLE_TYPE
MYDATABASE	SAMPLE	SALESPEOPLE	BASE TABLE
MYDATABASE	SAMPLE	CUSTOMERS	BASE TABLE
MYDATABASE	SAMPLE	LONDONSALES	VIEW
MYDATABASE	SAMPLE	ORDERS	BASE TABLE

Regarding the first column of this table: the use of the term *catalog* to refer to a collection of schemata is a feature of SQL92 that is not universally supported. Some DBMS products support such collections under other names, while others do not support them at all. Nonetheless, the standard INFORMATION_SCHEMA was designed with this concept in mind. Therefore, each "catalog" in a database will have a distinct INFORMATION_SCHEMA that describes its contents. For that matter, the standard specifies an even higher level of the ownership hierarchy called *clusters*. It is important to note that some DBMS products use this term with an entirely different meaning, which is explained in Chapter 23 of this book.

Notice also that this table includes views. These are also a kind of table. Please note that this query won't actually enable you to see all tables in the catalog. You will be able to see only those tables on which you have at least some privileges. This restriction is a security feature, as it is not always desirable to expose your entire database structure to all users, and all users automatically have access to the INFORMATION_SCHEMA. The DEFINITION_SCHEMA is inaccessible in any case, even if it were directly implemented.

Commercial products may take a somewhat different approach. Many DBMS products actually have one set of views for you to use to see your own objects and another to see all objects or, perhaps, all objects to which you have some access. These products are likely to retain this feature even as the SQL92 INFORMATION_ SCHEMA gets implemented. It will be a superset of the standard functionality.

Table 18.1 shows the tables of the INFORMATION_SCHEMA. Many of these refer to objects, such as domains and assertions, that are part of the SQL92 standard but are not yet widely implemented. Because you may not actually encounter them, we have not covered features such as these in detail, but we include them in the reference section of the book.

TABLE 18.1: Tables of the INFORMATION_SCHEMA

TABLE	INFORMATION REGARDING
SCHEMATA	Schemata (plural of schema). This refers to all schemata in the current catalog, if catalogs are supported (under any name), or simply all schemata in the database otherwise.
TABLES	Tables.
COLUMNS	Columns of the tables.
VIEWS	Views.
VIEW_TABLE_USAGE	Tables referenced by the views.
VIEW_COLUMN_USAGE	Columns selected by the views.
TABLE_CONSTRAINTS	Constraints on tables.
REFERENTIAL_CONSTRAINTS	REFERENCES and FOREIGN KEY constraints.
CHECK_CONSTRAINTS	CHECK constraints.
KEY_COLUMN_USAGE	Columns used in keys.
ASSERTIONS	Constraints that live independently of tables. A SQL92 feature that lacks wide support. See CREATE ASSERTION in the reference.
CONSTRAINT_TABLE_USAGE	Tables used by constraints.
CONSTRAINT_COLUMN_USAGE	Columns used by constraints.
TABLE_PRIVILEGES	Privileges that exist on tables.
COLUMN_PRIVILEGES	Privileges that exist on specific columns of tables (i.e., REFERENCES and UPDATE).
USAGE_PRIVILEGES	Privileges on objects other than tables. See GRANT in the reference.
DOMAINS	Domains. A SQL92 feature that lacks wide support. See CREATE DOMAIN in the reference.
DOMAIN_CONSTRAINTS	Constraints contained in domains.
DOMAIN_COLUMN_USAGE	Columns that utilize domains.
CHARACTER_SETS	Character sets used in the database.
COLLATIONS	Collating sequences for character sets. See Collations in the reference.
TRANSLATIONS	Translations. See CREATE TRANSLATION in the reference.
SQL_LANGUAGES	Supported languages and APIs (the latter applies only to SQL99, but the table is specified in SQL92).

Logical relationships exist among these tables that would naturally be implemented with primary and foreign keys. For example, each column in the COLUMNS table should identify the table in which the column resides. This will be a column of the TABLES table—logically, a foreign-key-to-parent-key relationship, right? Strictly speaking, it is not such a relationship because these are views, not base tables. Those relationships do exist, but they are among the tables of the DEFINITION_SCHEMA rather than the INFORMATION_SCHEMA. Nonetheless, since you cannot access the DEFINITION_SCHEMA directly, you may as well think of these as relationships among the tables of the INFORMATION_SCHEMA.

Summary

To summarize, SQL systems use a set of tables called the system catalog to structure the database. These tables can be queried but not updated. The SQL92 standard specifies a group of views on such tables that are collectively called the INFORMATION_SCHEMA. As of this writing, no one has fully implemented this schema, both because of the difficulties in accommodating such a set of views over a set of tables that were not designed with them in mind and because not all of the features of SQL92 have been implemented. Now that you understand the catalog, you have completed your orientation to SQL as used in interactive situations. In the next chapter of this book, we will teach you how to design a database.

Putting SQL to Work

1. What is metadata?

2. Which SQL statements can you execute on the system catalog?

3. According to SQL92, when you query the INFORMATION_SCHEMA, can you see all objects in the catalog?

PART V

Advanced Topics

CHAPTER

NINETEEN

Designing a Database

- Modeling a Real-World Situation

- Employing the Entity-Relationship (ER) Model

- Normalizing a Database

19

In this chapter, we'll show you how to design a database schema, informally referred to as "designing a database". We have saved this information for now because not all users will need to design databases, so this may not be of interest to everyone. Nonetheless, if you will be designing database schemata, this chapter offers a systematic approach to doing so. Even if you will not be designing a database yourself, it will deepen your understanding of the principles involved and will make it easier to understand the design of databases you may encounter.

This chapter will start off considerably more abstractly than the others up until now. Database design is, in principle, independent of SQL, since you could implement a good design with another language if you choose. Therefore, in talking about design, we will not get into SQL syntax specifically until it comes to implementation. We will, however, be introducing a number of new concepts.

Though it is mostly beyond the scope of this book, we will touch on some practical aspects of designing a database in a business situation—how to go about getting the information you require.

The approach we will take is to use the Entity-Relationship (ER) model. This is an industry-standard technique, and there are, in fact, numerous database design tools based on it, some of which are bundled with standard relational DBMS products.

Modeling a Real-World Situation

Database design is an iterative process. By this we mean that you are not likely to get it all right the first try. You will come up with a tentative design and check it against the requirements you are trying to meet. When you find where it fails, you will revise it. Therefore, you should plan your project with this in mind. Rather than gathering and analyzing all information and then producing a perfect schema, you are more likely to reach the desired result over a number of passes. So get through the first pass as soon as you can, but don't expect it to be perfect. Many of the potential problems will not become clear until you actually get to the nuts and bolts of the design.

The design process generally begins with a series of interviews with people involved in the business (or other) situation you are trying to support with a database. You need to get at what is essential in the structure of the data and the rules concerning how it is interrelated and which kinds of operations may be performed upon it. These are called the *business rules*. A little later we will introduce you to entities and relationships. You will be looking for entities and the relationships between them to build a model of the data.

Many database books will tell you to keep the needs of the application you are supporting central to your design. While this is true, you are also ahead of the game if your database design is robust enough to support other applications that are not currently planned. While you obviously must make sure that your design supports all the functionality required by the application or applications that are currently envisaged, there is no reason to assume the same database will not later find other uses. Suppose you design a database to support e-commerce on the Web. Over time, that database may come to contain a lot of information about the buying habits of your customers. You could take advantage of this information with a data-mining application, which would examine the data for patterns of interest.

The requirements of a data-mining application are quite different from those of online transaction processing (OLTP). Nonetheless, it would be ideal to be able to use the same database for both, rather than having to export the data, restructure it extensively, and then restore it into a new database structure. If the database has been well and flexibly designed in the first place, you should be able to do this *to a degree*. Realistically, you would not be likely to do data-mining on your live online transaction database. You would copy its content in some stable state (called a *snapshot*) and data-mine the copy. One thing to keep in mind, if you see any data-mining in the future of a database you design, is that it is very helpful to make it a historical database that keeps track of past as well as current information.

Therefore, you should try to make your database a model of those aspects of the world your clients need to manage, if possible going a bit beyond what they may see as the use of the database right now.

When you get to your interviews, keep in mind the following:

- You must pick the brains of both end users and management. End users have the most detailed information about the data and their jobs, and management determines what the priorities are for the database to achieve as well as when you get paid.

- Often, it is best to interview people in groups so you can get a brainstorming effect and use your time more effectively.

- Ask open-ended questions. In speaking freely, the users will give you more information than you would think to ask for specifically.

- Early on, it's best to do in-person interviews with a white board handy. In later stages, when you really are just trying to pin down specifics, e-mail is a good medium. It's fast and you get everything in writing.

- Basically, you ask people to describe their jobs, how they go about them, what information they need, and what information they produce. Try to examine the logical nature of the information itself.

- You're also trying to determine the business rules. You must make sure your schema reflects the actual rules rather than some excessively neat version of them that fits nicely into a data model. We tried to illustrate this point in the sample tables by having salespeople sometimes making sales to customers who are not assigned to them. You need to be able to handle this sort of situation as elegantly as possible.

Employing the Entity-Relationship (ER) Model

The approach to database design we take here is based on the Entity-Relationship (ER) model, which was developed in the 1970s by Dr. Peter Chen. Strictly speaking, what we employ is the Enhanced Entity-Relationship (EER) model, which supplements what that paper originally outlined with other concepts that have proven useful. The industry most commonly uses the term "ER model" regardless of whether the EER extensions are being used, so that's what we'll do here as well.

The ER model is a general data model, as is the relational model that underlies SQL. It provides another way of thinking about and organizing data. The view it provides is more intuitive in terms of how people actually think about the world. This is what makes it so useful for design, which must go from some conception of the world to some model of it that computer programs can use. However, because of its rigorous mathematical foundation and for other reasons, the relational model is generally used for implementation. Therefore, the ER model is used to derive an abstract model of the data that is then implemented with a set of tables that conform to relational principles. However, the ER model itself exists at a higher level of abstraction than tables do and could be implemented differently. For example, some object-oriented databases are based on direct implementation of the ER model.

Luckily, there is a relatively straightforward way to translate from the ER to the relational model, although it does not necessarily produce a one-to-one correspondence between either entities or relationships and tables. We will first explain the ER model in the abstract and show you the conventional means for diagramming it, and then we'll show you how to convert from it to tables.

The Elements of the ER Model

The relational model has one fundamental concept used to model data: the table. The ER model has a few more concepts than that. We describe its most important concepts in the following sections.

Entities

The first basic concept is the *entity*. These correspond fairly closely to how we intuitively think of an entity. They are the items that have a definable existence in the world—Persons, Jobs, Salaries. They are logical categories of items rather than specific items. Therefore, "Person" would be an entity and "Joan" would be an instance of that entity. In this limited respect, entities are somewhat like classes in the object-oriented world, but this comparison should not be taken too far. Entities do not have methods, for example.

Entities can be further characterized as strong or weak. A strong entity is well defined without reference to any other entity in the model, whereas a weak one requires reference to something else in order for its individual instances to be meaningful or to be identifiable. For example, Persons could be a strong entity and Addresses a weak one, if Addresses are significant only in relation to Persons.

Relationships

Entities have *relationships* to one another. A person may have a position, for example. These relationships can have characteristics that are independent of the characteristics of the entities themselves.

Relationships have a couple of important features. One of these is the *degree* of the relationship. This refers to the number of entities that participate in the relationship. The options are:

One   These are called *unary, circular, reflexive,* or *recursive* relationships and occur now and again. They are made possible by the fact that the same entity can participate in a relationship in more than one *role*. For example, most employees have managers who are themselves employees. You can express this as the circular relationship IS_MANAGED_BY between the Employees entity and itself. An employee participates in the relationship in the role of manager, the role of managee, or both. This use of the term "role" here is distinct from its use in SQL99, which relates to privileges. For more information, see the glossary.

Two   These are called *binary* relationships and are by far the most common type.

Three or more   These are called *n-ary* (*ternary* for three-way) relationships and occur now and again.

Another important characteristic of relationships is their *connectivity* (sometimes called *maximum cardinality* or simply *cardinality*), which refers to the mapping of instances of entity A to entity B (for binary relationships; this concept is easily extended to cover n-ary relationships). There are three possibilities:

One-to-one (written 1:1)   For each A, there is no more than one B. This, for example, might be the relationship between noses and mouths, since each face has one of each. In ER models, these relationships often denote subclasses. For example, there is a 1:1 relationship between Dodges and Automobiles because each Dodge is an automobile, though the reverse is not true. Dodges are a subclass of automobiles. You would normally use a subclass if there were considerable information you wanted to track for the subclass item that did not apply to the parent class.

One-to-many (written 1:n)   For each A, there are zero or more Bs, but for each B, there is only one A. Persons and Telephone Numbers could be an example. Each person may have any number of telephone numbers, but each telephone number is possessed by a single person (we could stipulate, although it may not be so in the real world). This is the most common kind of ER relationship.

Many-to-many (written m:n)   For each A, there are zero or more Bs, and for each B, there are zero or more As. Students and Classes could be an example. Students take several classes, and each class has a number of students.

Attributes

These can apply to either entities or relationships. An attribute is a trackable characteristic of the entity or relationship. An attribute can be *single-valued*, meaning it has one value per instance of the entity—for example, the age attribute of a person—or *multi-valued*, meaning it can have several such values—for example, the phone number attribute of a person.

You may have noticed an ambiguity here, in that we earlier used Addresses as an entity with a 1:n relationship to Persons. Are phone numbers so different from addresses in this regard? Most multi-valued attributes could also be modeled as weak entities with 1:n relationships, and both approaches produce the same results when mapped to tables, as we will show below. The major conceptual difference is that an entity, even a weak one, can participate in other relationships, whereas an attribute belongs to only one entity. In practical terms, this distinction is usually unimportant. In fact, an alternative school of thought on the ER model redefines multi-valued attributes as weak entities and m:n relationships as entities, so as to make the mapping to relational tables clearer (you will see how it does this when we cover mapping later in this chapter). This definition does not affect the mapping itself, and it makes the ER model less intuitive as a model of the world, though perhaps more intuitive as a template for a relational structure.

Creating a Simple ER Model

Let's look at a simple example of how we could break a situation down into the above elements. Suppose we are designing a database to model a simplified university enrollment situation. Here are the relevant business rules:

- Classes have one teacher and any number of students.

- Students take one or more classes.

- Teachers teach one or more classes.

- Each student receives one grade in each class.

- For each class, we must track the name, number of units, and the set of zero or more prerequisites.

- For each student, we must track the name and grade level.

- For each teacher, we must track the name and position (Lecturer, Professor, and so on).

What would be the entities, relationships, and attributes in this scenario? The main entities are clearly Classes, Teachers, and Students. Based on the above rules, we can derive the following relationships:

- There is a 1:n relationship, teaches, between Teachers and Classes.

- There is an m:n relationship, enrolled in, between Students and Classes.

- There is a circular relationship, is a prerequisite of, between the Classes entity and itself.

Let's look at this one a minute, because it is a little more complicated. What is the cardinality of this relationship? Since we stated that a given class has zero or more prerequisites, it cannot be 1:1. Is it 1:n or m:n? The pivotal question is whether a given class can be a prerequisite to more than one other class. Our initial description of the situation doesn't say. This situation is something you will commonly encounter in database design: the initial set of questions you got answered was insufficient and brings up more questions. No problem. This is perfectly normal, as we'll get into later in this chapter. In any case, it is normally true that a university class can function as a prerequisite to any of several other classes, so we assume that a class can both have several prerequisites and be a prerequisite to several other classes. This makes it an m:n relationship.

It is worth mentioning that the circular relationship above refers only to the *direct* prerequisites for the class. If class A is a prerequisite to class B and B is a prerequisite to C, then A is, in effect, a prerequisite to C, but it should not be listed as such directly. We can derive this information from the other two prerequisite relationships (A is a prerequisite to B and B is a prerequisite to C). Values that are derivable from other information in the database should be so derived rather than being directly stored. Why? Consider the following:

- If a prerequisite for a class changes, that change has to cascade through all the classes that follow for who knows how many levels. This would be a pain, and there could be more than one path through which a class can be such a prerequisite; in which case, should it remain a prerequisite? Representing the entire path at each point makes it difficult to disentangle the path later.

- Students are frequently granted exemptions from prerequisites, based on examination or other criteria. Students should not have to keep being granted the same exemption as they progress through a sequence of courses. Though this point is specific to school situations, it illustrates how business rules (such as qualification by exam) can affect database design in ways that are not obvious at first glance.

The above illustrates two general principles:

- Data derivable from other data should not, in general, be directly stored in the database. It should be derived as needed, so that it is current up to the second and so that modifications to the database have simpler ramifications. In the infamous real world, exceptions are sometimes made to this rule, primarily for the sake of performance. Such exceptions have a cost in elegance and maintainability, however, that should be included in the calculations.

- Circular relationships should list only first-order relationships. This is a corollary of the above, because all of the other relationships can be derived from the first-order ones. In other words, if we know all the direct prerequisites for all classes, we can determine all the indirect ones.

While we could derive a more complex list of entities and relationships than this, these are the basics. The attributes, then, are those items of information we must track. As a check on yourself, it is good to simply list all the attributes that seem relevant and then match them to entities and relationships, rather than asking what are the attributes of each entity and relationship. The reason is that listing attributes and trying to find places for them may help you discover entities or relationships you did not think of at first. If you need to track a piece of information, you must have an entity or a relationship in which it fits. In a realistic situation, there would probably be more attributes than those implied above, but we keep our examples simple for clarity's sake. The attributes of interest are:

- Student and teacher names
- Class name
- Class number of units
- Student grade in class
- Teacher position
- Student grade level

Now you should try to match these attributes to the entities and relationships. Each attribute *should* describe only one such. Is this the case the way the attributes are listed above? Not quite, because we have already decided that Students and Teachers are separate entities. Given this fact, the name attribute of each should be considered distinct. Therefore, the list could be refined as:

- Student name
- Teacher name
- Class name
- Class number of units
- Student grade in class
- Teacher position
- Student grade level

If an attribute seems like it naturally belongs in more than one place, it may be, as above, that you are thinking of two conceptually similar but distinct attributes as the same. To which entities and relationships do these attributes belong? Most of them obviously link to one of the primary entities as identified by the name we have given the attribute. There is one exception: student grade in class. This attribute involves two entities: Students and Classes. As you may have guessed, this is an attribute of the enrolled in relationship.

The alternative version of the ER model would redefine Enrollments as an entity with 1:n relationships to both Classes and Students. Grades would then be an attribute of this entity. As you will see, both terminologies map to the same set of database tables.

As you might suppose, keeping track of a list of items like this would quickly get cumbersome if the database were realistically complex. That is why there is a standard technique to represent ER data models in ER diagrams. We introduce these diagrams in the next section.

Diagramming Entity-Relationship Models

Entity-Relationship diagrams are a convenient visual representation of the ER model frequently used in database design and other tools. There are actually a number of variations on how these diagrams are presented. We use the following conventions, which we believe to be the most common and clear:

- Entities are shown in rectangles.

- Strong entities have rectangles with sharp corners, and weak entities have rectangles with rounded corners.

- Relationships are shown in diamonds.

- Lines connect the relationships to the participating entities.

- Attributes are shown in ovals and connected to the relevant entity or relationship by a line.

- Single-valued attributes are in a single oval, and multi-valued ones have a double oval.

- Two lines crossing a relationship line indicate a subclass relationship and make the diamond unnecessary. An arrowhead points from the superclass to the subclass.

- The connectivity of the relationships is shown on the connecting lines.

Applying these techniques, then, the University database from the previous section would appear as shown in Figure 19.1

One thing you might notice from the illustration is that showing all the attributes would seriously hinder the readability of the diagram were the number of attributes as great as it probably would be in a realistic situation. For this reason, it is often convenient to make the diagrams without showing all or any of the attributes and just keep a list of the attributes attached to each entity and relationship as an addendum independent of the diagram. In the course of designing the database, you will make many diagrams anyway, so they may not all need to include all the attributes. Many software tools employing ER diagrams enable you to show or hide attributes.

A word about layout: there are, of course, many ways you could lay these items out on the page, but laying them out intelligently will help keep your diagrams readable as they (inevitably) become more complex. You can place the entities anywhere. Therefore, use the relationships to decide where to put the entities, keeping the paths between relationships and their entities as direct as you can manage. For example, since we know both Teachers and Students have relationships to Classes but not to each other, we put Classes in the middle. Of course, if you are using a software tool, it may handle layout for you.

FIGURE 19.1:

ER diagram of the
University database

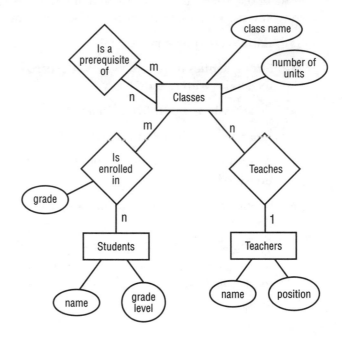

There are some features of the model that are not illustrated by the above. One is the concept of *subclasses*. A subclass is a subset of the instances of an entity. The subclass exists because there is material relevant to it that does not apply to other members of the superclass, which is the original entity. Nonetheless, each instance of the subclass is also an instance of the superclass. This way of thinking may also sound familiar if you are used to object-oriented programming, though, again, you should not take this analogy too far.

In the ER model, one or both of the following will be true of any subclass:

- It has attributes that do not apply to the rest of the superclass.

- It participates in relationships that the rest of the superclass does not.

Let's add a special category of student to our model—the teaching assistant. Regarding this group, the following rules apply:

- Each teaching assistant is a student.

- Teaching assistants are not considered faculty.

- Each teaching assistant has one faculty supervisor. Any number of teaching assistants can have the same supervisor.

- Teaching assistants are assigned to classes. Each can be assigned to any number of classes and any number can be assigned to the same class.

We now have a new entity, Teaching Assistant, that is a subclass of Student. We have also introduced several new relationships into the model.

- There is a 1:n relationship, supervises, between Teachers and Teaching Assistants.

- There is an m:n relationship, assigned to, between Teaching Assistants and Classes.

- There is a subclass relationship, a special kind of 1:1 relationship, between Teaching Assistants and Students. This relationship is of a standard type for subclasses known as IS_A. Some diagramming conventions will use a diamond surrounding IS_A to represent this relationship, instead of the convention we have chosen.

Figure 19.2 shows a revised version of our ER diagram.

FIGURE 19.2:

ER diagram with a subclass

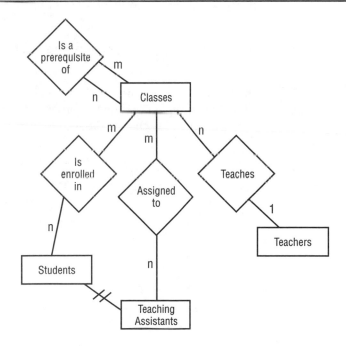

Two other things we have not seen in the example so far are multi-valued attributes and weak entities. As we mentioned, these are closely related. You can often treat a multi-valued attribute as a weak entity, although it may not reflect your intuitive idea of an entity. Weak entities cannot always be sensibly treated as multi-valued attributes, however. For one thing, a multi-valued attribute should be an attribute of only one entity or relationship and participate in no other relationships, whereas a weak entity can participate in relationships with many other entities.

Consider the addition of a phone number to the Teachers entity. Since faculty members are likely to have several such numbers, this would be a multi-valued attribute of Teachers. You could add a similar phone number attribute to the Students entity. You could treat these as weak entities, but it would complexify the diagram to no advantage.

You may have noticed that we have, as yet, made no mention of primary and foreign keys. These are, of course, concepts from the relational, not the ER, world. It is often best in your table design to have special columns for your primary and foreign keys that serve no other purpose. Among the reasons for this are the following:

- You don't have to rely on another source for valid and unique values. If you use social security numbers as primary keys, for example, you must deal with the situation of people who don't have these numbers, such as non-U.S. citizens.

- It is easier to see what the primary and foreign keys are, making the design more transparent.

- Database queries will execute more quickly against short numbers than against, for example, long text or binary strings. Many other possible unique identifiers, such as digitized fingerprints, are simply too inefficient in practice.

- You can effectively ignore the keys in figuring out the attributes of interest in your ER model. None of those attributes will be primary or foreign keys. Rather, the primary and foreign keys will be material you add later, during the conversion process, to enforce the relational structure you want.

Deriving Database Tables from the ER Model

A straightforward algorithm exists for generating a database schema from an ER diagram. This algorithm is what enables some database design tools to generate such schemata automatically. In this case, the tool should generate SQL code that you can modify as needed. Even if you are using such a tool, it is good to understand the process, as you likely will need to tweak its results to meet your needs completely.

The basic algorithm is as follows. Each entity will become a table. A primary key will be created for this table. Each single-valued attribute of the entity will become a column of the table. If the entity is weak, it will also contain a foreign key linking it to the strong entity on which it depends. Other than for primary keys, there are no general rules as to whether columns can contain NULLs. It is a judgement call based on whether that value is required. The concept of NULLs is not relevant to the ER model as such.

For example, here is the first pass at creating a table for the Students entity:

```
CREATE TABLE Students
(studnum       INTEGER NOT NULL PRIMARY KEY,
 name          CHAR(30) NOT NULL,
 gradelevel    CHAR(5) NOT NULL);
```

Now what about name? Is it really a single-valued attribute? The student probably has (at least) a first and a last name. It is single-valued, actually, but it is not *atomic*. It can be meaningfully subdivided into smaller pieces. This violates one of the basic principles of the relational model. Let's therefore break it up into first, middle initial, and last, thusly:

```
CREATE TABLE Students
(studnum       INTEGER NOT NULL PRIMARY KEY,
 firstname     CHAR(15) NOT NULL,
 midinit       CHAR(1),
 lastname      CHAR(15) NOT NULL,
 gradelevel    CHAR(5) NOT NULL);
```

Now the next stage in deriving a set of tables from the ER diagram is to convert each multi-valued attribute into a table with a foreign key referencing the entity table. For example, here is a table we could use to implement Student_Phonenum:

```
CREATE TABLE Student_Phonenum
(studnum       INTEGER NOT NULL REFERENCES Students,
 phonenumber   INTEGER NOT NULL
 PRIMARY KEY   (studnum, phonenumber));
```

A side point: Is it better to store phone numbers as INTEGERs or as CHAR strings? If you store them as INTEGERs, they will take up considerably less storage space, but you will not be able to use dashes, spaces, or parentheses as they are usually used in phone numbers. If the database is likely to be accessed only through applications, this may not be important. You can usually prettify the numbers in the application, so it is better to use INTEGERs in the database. On the other hand, if you don't want to bother with doing this, or if the database will be accessed interactively, it may be better to go for the CHAR strings. In any case, you should pick one approach and be consistent for a given project.

Having a composite primary key consisting of the multi-valued attribute combined with the foreign key is kind of a default approach. It works, but sometimes it would be too inefficient in practice. If the multi-valued attribute were digital pictures, for example, you would not want those huge binaries to be part of your primary key. It would take far too long for the DBMS to search for a particular value. Therefore, you can always just create a primary key for the table, like this:

```
CREATE TABLE Student_Phonenum
(phoneseq     INTEGER NOT NULL PRIMARY KEY,
 studnum      INTEGER NOT NULL REFERENCES Students,
 phonenumber  INTEGER NOT NULL);
```

The phoneseq column will just be some number generated by the system to function as a primary key. You have to make a decision to weigh the proliferation of meaningless numbers against the inefficiency of composite primary keys. The phone number by itself cannot be a primary key because it is possible for students to share a phone (indeed, it is common, given roommate situations).

A 1:1 subclass relationship is implemented by creating a second table for the subclass and having the primary key of the subclass table also be a foreign key to the superclass table. This ensures that for each row in the subclass, there is one and only one matching row in the superclass, the idea being that an instance of the subclass is also an instance of the superclass—for example, each instance of Teaching Assistant is also an instance of Student, since each teaching assistant is a student. With that in mind, let's take a swipe at the teaching assistants. Since this table will reference Teachers, let's show that table first:

```
CREATE TABLE Teachers
(teachnum     INTEGER NOT NULL PRIMARY KEY,
 fname        CHAR(10) NOT NULL,
 midint       CHAR(1),
 lname        CHAR(10) NOT NULL,
 position     CHAR(15) NOT NULL);
```

And then show the Teaching_Assistants table itself:

```
CREATE TABLE Teaching_Assistants
(studnum    INTEGER NOT NULL PRIMARY KEY REFERENCES Students,
 advisor    INTEGER NOT NULL REFERENCES Teachers);
```

Notice that what this effectively has done is add a column called advisor to certain students but not to the rest. This column is not NULL for the others; it simply does not exist. We use this column to implement a relationship that does not exist for the other students.

You can create superclasses as well as subclasses. The procedure for doing this is the same as for creating subclassing, but you simply start with the more specific class. For example, we have phone numbers of both teachers and students. If we wanted to keep all our phone numbers in one table, we would have a problem, because we would have to have a foreign key referencing Students and another referencing Teachers, when they are logically the same key (the foreign key fills the same function in both cases, so this would be poor, illogical design). The solution is to create a superclass of Teachers and Students called Persons. This superclass should contain only what is common to Teachers and Students. Teachers and Students will then have to be revised, so as to be subclasses of Persons. We leave this problem for you as a featured exercise at the end of this chapter.

You implement a 1:n relationship by adding a foreign key to the entity on the n side referencing the entity on the 1 side. We did this in the preceding example of the advisor relationship of the Teaching_Assistants table. Any attributes of the relationship become columns in the table on the n side.

For an m:n relationship, you should create a table independent of each of the entities participating in the relationship. The reason is that either entity can participate in the relationship multiple times. Therefore, neither can function as a primary key; it is the combination of the two that should be unique. Suppose you tried to implement the class enrollments relationship from within the Students table. Since a student can enroll in multiple classes, you would have multiple entries for each student, which is unacceptable in the Students table. The reverse would occur if you tried to put references to the students in the Classes table.

Instead, you must create a new table. First, let's show the definition of the Classes table, since we haven't done that yet:

```
CREATE TABLE Classes
(classnum        INTEGER NOT NULL PRIMARY KEY,
 class_name      CHAR(15) NOT NULL,
 teacher         INTEGER NOT NULL REFERENCES Teachers,
 number_of_units INTEGER);
```

Given that definition, we could implement the Is_Enrolled_In relationship with the following table:

```
CREATE TABLE Enrollments
(classnum       INTEGER NOT NULL REFERENCES Classes,
 studnum        INTEGER NOT NULL REFERENCES Students,
 grade          CHAR(2)
 PRIMARY KEY    (classnum, studnum));
```

Notice that we did not call the table "Is_Enrolled_In". Names like that tend to make ER diagrams clearer but sound awkward for tables. There is no reason you have to keep the names the same in translating from one model to the other, provided, of course, that you do not get confused as to where you are.

Another matter is the circular relationship. Since the circular relationship we have chosen is an m:n relationship, it too must be implemented with a stand-alone table. For 1:n or 1:1 circular relationships, it is possible to define a foreign key within a table that references the same table, but it is problematic, as we will explain shortly. Here is the table to implement prerequisites:

```
CREATE TABLE Prerequisites
(thisclass      INTEGER NOT NULL REFERENCES Classes,
 prereqclass    INTEGER NOT NULL REFERENCES Classes
 PRIMARY KEY    (thisclass, prereqclass));
```

This is rather a neat solution because it doesn't get us into the awkward chicken-and-egg problem that circular relationships can. It does mean you have to enter the classes in the Classes table before you define their prerequisite relationships (otherwise the references would be invalid), but this is probably not a major problem. To see a list of classes and their prerequisites, you would enter the following query:

```
SELECT thisclass, class_name, prereqclass
    FROM Classes, Prerequisites
    WHERE classnum = thisclass
    ORDER BY 1;
```

This, of course, is a straightforward, natural join. Since it is not an outer join, classes without prerequisites are not included. For information on OUTER JOINS, see Chaper 10 and "SELECT" in Chapter 28.

For an example of the chicken-and-egg problem, consider if each class had no more than one prerequisite and you tried to implement it in one table. You could do this as follows:

```
CREATE TABLE Classes
(classnum        INTEGER NOT NULL PRIMARY KEY,
 class_name      CHAR(15) NOT NULL,
 number_of_units INTEGER,
 prereqclass     INTEGER REFERENCES Classes);
```

This solution will work. You just have to INSERT any class before you use it as a prerequisite. But suppose every class had to have a prerequisite. In this case, the prereqclass column should be NOT NULL. But then, how would you INSERT the first row? Whatever the first row references, even itself, it won't be in the table yet.

Such situations do arise. That is one of the reasons why deferrable constraints are a feature of SQL92. With a deferrable constraint, you can allow the constraint to remain violated until the end of the transaction, enabling you to get around such problems. Unfortunately, this feature is not universally supported. For more on deferrable constraints, see "SET CONSTRAINS MODE" in Chapter 28 and "Constraints" in Chapter 29.

Normalizing a Database

A somewhat more formal approach to database design also sees a lot of use. Unlike the ER model, which is fundamentally independent of the relational data model, this approach is an intrinsic part of the body of theory developed by E. F. Codd, the father of relational database theory, also in the 1970s. This approach is called *normalization*.

Earlier, we mentioned that it was helpful to look at all the attributes you need to track independently of the entities and relationships into which you see them fitting. Normalization provides a systematic approach to this. You start out with "attribute soup" (formally speaking, an unstructured body of attributes that comprises an entire intended database schema is called a *universal relation*) and derive the tables into which you want to divide the attributes.

In practical terms, the ER model is more intuitive than normalization. However, normalization is more rigorously defined in terms of the relational model and can prevent certain kinds of anomalies that arise from poor design. Therefore, the ordinary approach is to use the ER model and then to look at the results in terms of normalization. Normalization, then, is generally used for checking and fine-tuning an ER model.

To illustrate the kinds of anomalies normalization is intended to counteract, suppose we had a table showing students with their class enrollments using the following design (all columns are NOT NULL, and (studnum, classnum) is the PRIMARY KEY):

studnum	classnum	teachnum	gradelevel
1899	477	2888	2
1899	376	3999	2
2991	410	2888	3
1777	477	2888	3

Here are some of the problems that could arise when we tried to modify the data:

- Suppose we tried to add a new course and teacher. We could not do so until we had at least one student to enroll in the class. Of course, few students would be likely to volunteer until the class is offered. This is called an *insertion anomaly*.

- Suppose I decide to delete classnum 410? Since this is the only class in which studnum 2991 is enrolled, the number and gradelevel for that student are deleted as well. We have lost more information than we intended to remove. This is called a *deletion anomaly*.

- Suppose I decide to change the teacher of coursenum 477 to 2185. I have to make this change in two places, which introduces the possibility of an inconsistency: I could accidently make the change in one place and not the other. This is called an *update anomaly*.

These are the sorts of anomalies that normalization is designed to address.

Normalization proceeds by degrees. It is not a matter of the database being either normalized or not normalized. The question is: how normalized is it? The answer is expressed as a normal form. A *normal form* is a well-defined standard measure of the degree of normalization a schema possesses. There are six standard normal forms: five of them are simply numbered 1 through 5, and the last is somewhat anomalously called Boyce-Codd Normal Form (BCNF). For the numbered forms, the higher numbers indicate higher degrees of normalization. BCNF doesn't exactly fit in the sequence, but it is above 3, since a database must be in at least third normal form to be in BCNF (but it need not be in BCNF to be in fourth normal form). Happily, there are no abnormal forms, or at least no formal definitions of such. We will stop at BCNF, since that is as far as you commonly need to go. For all the desirability of normalization, it is possible to over-normalize. The more you normalize, the more tables you tend to have, which makes your schema more complex and possibly less efficient in performance.

Since you are by now familiar with the University database example, we will use it again to derive examples of normalization. The attribute soup is as follows:

- Student number
- Student name
- Teacher number
- Teacher name
- Student phone number
- Teacher phone number
- Class number
- Class name
- Class number of units
- Class prerequisites
- Student grade in class
- Teacher position
- Student grade level
- Teaching Assistant Faculty Supervisor

Let's look at the normal forms.

First Normal Form

The first normal form (1NF) is the same as the requirement of a relational database that all data values be atomic. That is to say, if a database is in 1NF, each row of each table will contain no more than one value for each column (it may, of course, contain zero values for a particular column, i.e., it could be NULL). By now, you realize that our classic example of a multi-valued attribute is phone number. If you design a table like this

studnum	name	phonenumbers
3555	Doberman	(477) 378-4673 (477) 839-2839 (523) 482-0012

you are not in the first normal form! As you have seen, the phone numbers should go into a separate table because there are many of them per student.

But what about names? Aren't there also many of those per student? If you wanted to treat the individual portions of a student's name independently, which you generally would, you would indeed also break down name into first, middle initial, last, etc., as we did earlier. First normal form dictates that neither the names nor the numbers get crunched into the space of a single value, but it does not tell us the difference between a value that can usefully be broken up within a table and one that should go into a second table.

Functional Dependencies

Before we get deeper into these questions, we need to explain the concept of functional dependencies. The idea of *functional dependency* is those things I need to know to be able to determine something else. For example, consider the addresses of students. Addresses in our model depend on nothing more than who the student is. If I know which student I mean, I can determine the address (if the attribute we use to identify students is studnum, it would be more precise to say that address has a dependency on studnum, but we're sticking to a conceptual level for now). We say that address has a functional dependency on student. The formal way to express such a dependency is as follows (we use the symbol -> to represent the phrase "is dependent on"):

student -> address

On the other hand, consider students and grades. In order to know which grades a student has earned, I need to know something else besides who the student is. I need to know which classes he is taking. More precisely, to determine a particular grade of a student, I need to know both to which student and to which class I am referring. If someone asks me what grade John got, how could I answer without knowing the class? Therefore, grade has a functional dependency on the combination of student and class, which is written like this:

student, class -> grade

Now, as we go mucking about in the attribute soup, we may notice that certain combinations of attributes can determine entities. For example, if I postulate that all students have unique names, then all I need to know to identify a particular student is her name. On the other hand, if I choose not to make this suspect assumption (keep in mind that the principles you build into your database must *always* be valid; it is not enough that they be valid for the initial or the likely data), I might need more information. Perhaps it seems sufficiently unlikely that two identically named students would live together that I could dare to say that the combination of name and address can determine student. Will Garvin Talisman at 300 Boondale Rd., Richmond, always be one and only one particular student? Pretty likely, but you can't be sure. It could be a father and son combination. Hence, your data integrity rules should not count on this. If you have a logical entity with no logical defining attributes, create such an attribute as a key.

For example, suppose I went swimming in the attributes and came up with a table structured like this:

> **Enrollments**
> studnum   classnum   grade   address

What's wrong with this picture? Well, the address attribute is overdetermined. Address depends only on student, but grade depends on student and class. The practical consequence is that this table will have to store the student's address repeatedly, once for each class in which he is enrolled, and it will have to keep those entries consistent! Not good. Such redundancy wastes space and invites inconsistency. Written formally, here is the problem:

> studnum, class -> grade
>
> studnum > address

The difference in functional dependencies tells us that we are dealing with two different entities (or with an entity and a relationship). These should be in two different tables.

Second Normal Form

Now we're ready to introduce the second normal form (2NF). The second normal form occurs when situations like the above do not. However, let's nail this down a little tighter. In 2NF, you're starting to pinpoint the entities. Any entity will have some set of attributes that determines it, possibly including ID numbers and things you create to make sure that this is the case. You want to get down to the smallest set of attributes possible. This attribute set, then, is the logical key for that entity. You are in second normal form when all the other attributes besides the key depend on nothing but the logical key. If there is no logical key, create one.

So, to modify the previous example, here are two tables in second normal form:

Enrollments

<u>studnum</u>   <u>classnum</u>   <u>grade</u>

Students

<u>studnum</u>   <u>address</u>

These tables do not take care of all the information we need to track, but they do track some information correctly. It is, of course, no problem that the key of one entity (studnum) is a subset of the key of the other one (studnum, classnum). This is likely to end up as a parent key/foreign key relationship.

If the logical key of the table is but a single column, the table is in 2NF.

The formal name for this breaking apart of tables in accordance with functional dependencies is *decomposition*. The above is an example of *lossless decomposition*, because all of the information (including correlations between pieces of information) that was expressed prior to decomposition is preserved once it occurs.

Third Normal Form

Given that any table with a single-column key is in 2NF, and single-column numeric keys are frequently useful anyway, you might think that a good way to kludge the problem of 2NF is simply to create such keys for every table. Doing so, however, would just bring you up against the basic problem that third normal form (3NF) is designed to address: functional dependencies on non-key attributes. For example, suppose we create an enrollment number attribute to force our previous table into 2NF without decomposition:

Enrollments

<u>enum</u>   <u>studnum</u>   <u>classnum</u>   <u>grade</u>   <u>address</u>

This hasn't really solved the problem, has it? Address still depends only on studnum, but now instead of being only part of the key, studnum is not in the key at all. The requirement of 3NF is that every attribute in the table must meet either of these criteria:

- Be part of the key.

- Depend on the value of the key, only on the value of the key, and on the value of the entire key (i.e., 3NF includes 2NF).

A slightly more formal way to put this is that no attribute may have a *transitive* dependence on the key. In this case, studnum does indeed have a dependence on enum, which is the key. Address depends on studnum. Therefore, address has a transitive dependence on enum. But this isn't good enough. Since studnum is not a key, it cannot be assumed to be unique (and generally won't be, in this case). Therefore, an attribute that depends on it would vary directly with it. This is unnecessary redundancy. We should note which address goes with which studnum once and for all. Therefore, to put this table into 3NF, we would essentially do the same thing we did before—separate address into another table:

Enrollments

enum   studnum   classnum   grade

Students

studnum   address

Although this is similar to the solution we used before, the change of key implies some conceptual changes as well. The key of the Enrollments table is no longer the combination of studnum and classnum but is rather the single number enum (enrollment number). Do all the attributes of the Enrollments table depend on enum? Yes, they do because, given a particular enrollment, we can determine the specific student, class, and grade that applies. Notice that what is relevant to the attribute in determining its dependencies is not simply what it is, but what it is intended to express. For example, Classes and Students are both entities independent of Enrollments and do not depend on Enrollments simply to exist. But it is not their simple existence that this table expresses. This table maps them to Enrollments. This mapping has a dependency on Enrollments; therefore, studnum and classnum have a functional dependency on Enrollments in this table. Their *function*, if not their existence, depends on Enrollments.

Now, obviously, both the students and the classes listed in this table should exist. The studnum and classnum attributes in this table have *existence dependencies* on Students and Classes wherever the existence of those entities is established and tracked. Their *functional dependencies*, however, for the functions that they are fulfilling here, are on Enrollments. Given that they do not have existence dependencies on Enrollments, they should not be represented solely in this table. Every entity with an independent existence requires its own table, which this one will reference.

3NF is normally as far as you need go. If you use the ER model correctly, you will generally be there automatically, so the recommended course is to go ahead and use ER and then check your results in terms of the normal forms. Now let's take the attribute soup, identify the functional dependencies, and build a 3NF schema. For quick reference, here are the attributes:

- Student name
- Teacher name
- Student phone number
- Teacher phone number
- Class name
- Class number of units
- Class prerequisites
- Student grade in class
- Teacher position
- Student grade level
- Teaching Assistant Faculty Supervisor

Now, you derive the functional dependencies. If some of them aren't clear, you probably need to get some more information about the business rules. Here's a likely list:

studnum -> student name

studnum -> student phone number

studnum -> student grade level

classnum -> class name

classnum -> class number of units

classnum -> class prerequisite

studnum, classnum -> student grade in class

Now, if we look at the tables we created when we used the ER approach, these should, if we did things well, be in the third normal form, in which case all attributes would have functional dependencies on the keys and only the keys. Let's see if that holds for the following:

```
CREATE TABLE Students
(studnum        INTEGER NOT NULL PRIMARY KEY,
 firstname      CHAR(15) NOT NULL,
 midinit        CHAR(1),
 lastname       CHAR(15) NOT NULL,
 gradelevel     CHAR(5) NOT NULL);
```

The dependencies should be:

> studnum -> firstname
>
> studnum -> midinit
>
> studnum -> lastname
>
> studnum -> grade_level

Yes, these dependencies are all correct and there are no others, so the table is in 3NF. Notice that the dependencies are one way. The firstname attribute depends on studnum because, given studnum, I can figure out the firstname value. However, the reverse is not true: a first name is not enough to tell me which student I mean. Also note that the grade level does not depend on the name attributes, as we are assuming those attributes may not be unique. That is why we need the studnum attribute.

Here's another one:

```
CREATE TABLE Enrollments
(classnum       INTEGER NOT NULL REFERENCES Classes,
 studnum        INTEGER NOT NULL REFERENCES Students,
 grade          CHAR(2)
 PRIMARY KEY    (classnum, studnum));
```

The dependency should be:

> classnum, studnum -> grade

This is correct and is the only one. If we created an enum, of course, we would have three dependencies, but the table would still be in 3NF.

Finally, here's an example with a circular relationship:

```
CREATE TABLE Classes
(classnum        INTEGER NOT NULL PRIMARY KEY,
 class_name      CHAR(15) NOT NULL,
 number_of_units INTEGER,
 prereqclass     INTEGER REFERENCES Classes);
```

The dependencies should be:

classnum -> class_name

classnum -> number_of_units

classnum -> prereqclass

Given a class, can we determine the prerequisites? Yes, so this is also in 3NF.

Boyce-Codd Normal Form

Boyce-Codd Normal Form (BCNF) is rather a refinement of 3NF that deals with the situation that arises when you have multiple possible keys with overlapping components. Suppose we added class and student names as well as numbers to the Enrollments table. Assume that these names are unique, so that they could, in principle, function as keys themselves. Here is what the resulting Enrollments table would look like:

Enrollments

studnum	lastname	firstname	classnum	classname	grade

The combination of first and last student names and the class name are the new attributes. The key for this table could be any combination of a student and a class identifier, like this:

studnum   classnum

studnum   classname

lastname   firstname   classnum

lastname   firstname   classname

However, note the unnecessary redundancy here. Each time a student is enrolled in a class, both her number and name are given. This is redundant and prone to consistency errors. Though either the numbers or the names *could* function as unique identifiers, only one of them *needs* to. The presence of both necessitates the recording of the correlation of a particular name and number, and this correlation does not depend on enrollment but is a characteristic of the student or class itself. Therefore, BCNF would have us separate out the superfluous keys. The names, in all probability, would go into the tables that describe the Student and Class entities, and the numbers would be left to express the enrollments.

Summary

This chapter gave a quick yet reasonably thorough introduction to database design using the Entity-Relationship model. We taught you the meaning of entities, relationships, and attributes and the standard means for diagramming them. We also showed you how to translate this abstract schema into a set of SQL CREATE TABLE statements that could be used to implement it. Finally, we showed you some things about normalization that you could use to verify the soundness of your design. We also included some practical information about how to proceed with database design in terms of what actually happens in the so-called real world.

Putting SQL to Work

1. You have phone numbers of both teachers and students. You want to keep the phone numbers in one table, which means you must create a superclass of Teachers and Students called Persons. This superclass should contain only what the subclasses have in common. Having defined the superclass, you should redefine Teachers and Students as subclasses of Persons. Write the CREATE TABLE statements for Persons, Teachers, Students, and Phone_Numbers.

2. If the database already contains data when you make the change described in # 1, what is the possible conflict?

3. Create an ER diagram showing the University database with the Persons superclass added.

4. You have an entity called Employees. Most employees have managers, who are themselves employees. For each employee, you have a primary key called empno and a name (only one name). Write the CREATE TABLE statement and express the relationship.

Working with International Character Sets

- Working with International Text

- Using Character Sets

- Using Collations

- Using Translations

Although it originated in the United States, SQL is a global standard. For this reason, it is a good idea for database products using SQL to go beyond the English language and the character set used to represent it. This chapter covers special SQL functionality intended for dealing with the various character sets that may be used in textual data. This area is sometimes called National Language Support (NLS).

Working with International Text

Every SQL database product supports at least one set of characters—the set used to express the language itself, including the default representation of the text and other data. This set of characters is called SQL_TEXT. (Usually, the SQL statements are in English characters, since the language is based on English. However, it can be translated into other character sets, provided that these have an unambiguous mapping to the English characters.) Given that databases are now used globally, it is important that SQL acknowledge more than one character set. Therefore, SQL has evolved to deal with the problem of supporting various national languages.

The SQL92 standard provided a uniform approach to this problem that is likely to eventually find wide support among implementers, though it has not as of this writing (2000). Currently, database products handle this matter in a proprietary manner or not at all. Nonetheless, we cover here the approach outlined in the standard, on the assumption that it is the likely point of eventual convergence.

The standard approach uses two sets of text datatypes—conventional text datatypes and national language text datatypes. The difference lies in the default character set used by each. For conventional text datatypes, the default character set is almost invariably one that can support the English language. The national character datatypes take the characters of another language. The idea is that conventional text defaults to a generally used character set, such as English, freeing the national character types to default to a character set usable by the local language, whatever that is. Also, the "plain vanilla" text datatypes preserve backward compatibility because they behave just as they did before NLS datatypes were introduced.

Table 20.1 shows the conventional and national language (NLS) text datatypes.

TABLE 20.1: Conventional and National Language (NLS) Text Datatypes

Conventional Text Datatype (All names in a given cell are equivalent)	NLS Text Datatype (All names in a given cell are equivalent)
CHAR(*length*) or CHARACTER(*length*)	NCHAR(*length*) or NCHARACTER(*length*)
CHARACTER VARYING(*maxlength*) or CHAR VARYING(*maxlength*) or VARCHAR(*maxlength*)	NATIONAL CHARACTER VARYING(*maxlength*) or NATIONAL CHAR VARYING(*maxlength*) or NCHAR VARYING(*maxlength*)

All versions of CHAR are fixed-length and all versions of VARCHAR are variable-length.

When you use NLS types as literals, you must precede them by an N, as shown here:

```
N 'this is a national language literal'
```

Although representing character sets other than the default may seem a straightforward task, a number of issues arise from it. The first is that there is not necessarily a one-to-one mapping of character sets to languages. Multiple languages can sometimes use the same character set, and the same language can sometimes be represented with different characters. This is not too much of a problem for the handling of text data, simply because SQL is indifferent to the semantics of the data. It doesn't care what the symbols mean, so it doesn't matter which human language is being expressed. Nonetheless, you should remember the difference, since the natural inclination is to think of character sets as languages, which is not strictly correct.

In addition, you should be aware that the characters of a human language are a set of symbols for human convenience and are independent of the binary computer numbers that represent them internally. These characters also have multiple mappings; for example, common English characters can follow either an ASCII, EBCDIC, or Latin-1 encoding. These encodings give you the same English characters but with different binary equivalents. Finally, we would like to be able to map one set of characters to another, so that we can perform automatic conversions.

SQL deals with these issues by treating languages in terms of a number of distinct objects. Among these are:

- Character repertoire, which refers to the set of characters to be represented, what we normally would think of as the character set. Though SQL implementations can support which ever character repertoires they like, these repertoires should follow some national or international standard.

- Encoding, which refers to the binary codes that represent the characters internally.

- Form-of-use, which refers to the storage allocation per character of the encoding. In other words, is each character 7 bits, 8 bits, 2 bytes, a variable number of bytes, or some other possibility?

- Collation, which refers to a specification that governs how the character repertoire is to be sorted. The collation controls how comparisons such as less than (<) and greater than (>) are evaluated and generally should map to alphabetical ordering, if that concept applies to the language at hand, or to some other meaningful sorting scheme if possible.

- Character set, which refers to a specific combination of a character repertoire, a form-of-use, an encoding, and a default collation. The same repertoire with a different form-of-use, encoding, or default collation constitutes a distinct character set, although this may differ from how we would think of it informally. As you may have guessed from the term "default", collations can be overridden without changing the character set definition.

- Translation, which refers to a mapping from one character set to another. Given such a mapping, the DBMS can perform conversions automatically.

With all these distinct objects in place, you can have applications that store data in one character set but present it to users in another whenever appropriate.

Using Character Sets

Any DBMS will have at least one character set defined. It may ship with more sets defined, and it may provide some way for you to update it with other character sets, though this is beyond the scope of standard SQL. Using the character sets given to you, however, you may create more sets, which become objects in a schema like tables and views. The basic operation is to take an existing character set and change its default collation, retaining the character repertoire. Collations are also schema objects, and we will show you how to create them shortly. Specifying an alternative form-of-use or encoding for a character repertoire is also useful, of course, but falls into the realm of the implementation-defined (see Appendix I).

Here is a statement to create a new character set from an existing one called Ordinary_text, located in Jim's schema:

```
CREATE CHARACTER SET new_text AS
    GET Jim.Ordinary_text
    COLLATE new_collation;
```

We now have a new character set called new_text that is the same as Ordinary_text except that:

- It is in our schema, not Jim's.

- It uses a collation called new_collation.

In order to execute this statement, we must have the USAGE privilege on Jim.Ordinary_text. Note that, since the new character set is in a different schema than the old, we could have retained the same name and called it Ordinary_text, had we so wished.

You can use this COLLATE clause in several other statements, as we show later in this chapter.

What if you want to change the form-of-use or encoding of a character set? Basically, a change of this type falls into the implementation-defined area. If you want to get rid of this character set, of course, the statement is simply

```
DROP CHARACTER SET new_text;
```

Using Collations

Given that the main action with user-defined character sets is with collations, we will next get into how to use these. Keep in mind that there is a bit more to collations then alphabetical ordering. All the characters in the set, including punctuation marks, numerals, etc., must have a place in the collation. In the common sense of collating sequences, only alphabetic and numeric sequences are generally considered meaningful, and even these are not meaningful in relation to one another.

Nonetheless, the collation must define where all the symbols in the repertoire fall. Such a definition is useful, actually, since you can define the more obscure characters in your set as having a collation that might correspond to special meanings you wish to give them. You could then process these characters in SQL statements using inequalities and similar operations. Since collations can be changed and overridden, you could employ such a specialized use in a particular application without having it be of global significance.

How a collation is defined is something the implementation decides. There are various logical possibilities, among the most important of which are the following:

- The collation can follow the encoding. The characters in the repertoire are, like everything else in a digital computer, represented by binary numbers. Binary numbers are sortable. Therefore, the characters can be sorted according to the binary numbers that represent them. This definition is the default on many systems. It will result in different collations for English characters, depending on whether they employed the ASCII, EBCDIC, or Latin-1 encoding.

- The collation can be enumerated. The characters in the repertoire will be stored in some sequence, and this sequence can be defined as the collation. Since you can place the same characters in many different sequences, you can have multiple enumerated collations for the same character set.

- The collation can be derived from another collation. In principle, any number of such derivations are possible, and you are therefore on your own if you want to use an obscure derivation. What the standard supports is simple reversal, where you can define a collation as the exact reverse of some other collation. The collation can be standard. Basically, this means that it is directly specified in some national or international standard that applies and is used as a basis for the character repertoire. How this will be presented to the DBMS is up to the implementer.

- The collation can be derived in some other way defined by the implementation.

Of these techniques, the only one that is part of standard SQL is to create a variation on an existing collation that came with the DBMS or was added to it later in an implementation-defined manner. The statement to create a collation this way is as follows:

```
CREATE COLLATION collation name
FOR character set
FROM {collation name
```

```
  | { DESC (collation name)}
  | DEFAULT
  | { EXTERNAL ('external collation name')}
  | { TRANSLATION translation name
    [ THEN COLLATION collation name ] }};
  [ NO PAD | PAD SPACE ]
```

Let's look at the elements of the statement in detail:

- CREATE COLLATION *collation name* FOR *character set* gives the name of the new collation and specifies a character set to which it will apply as a default. Collations do not exist in the abstract; they are associated with a particular character repertoire as part of a particular character set. Hence, the FOR *character set* clause is required.

- FROM gives the source of the new collation. The candidates are as follows:

  - *collation name* simply copies another collation over to the new one. It implies that the character repertoires of the two sets are the same (otherwise, it would be unclear how to apply the other collation), although the form-of-use and the encoding may be different.

  - DESC(*collation name*) reverses the collation given in parentheses and makes the result the new collation. This is a derived collation. Again, the character repertoires of the two sets must be identical.

  - DEFAULT specifies that the collation is enumerated and follows the order of the characters in the repertoire as originally presented in the repertoire definition.

  - EXTERNAL ('*external collation name*') specifies that the collation will follow that of an *external collation*. An external collation is an implementation-defined entity, so this is basically a way to support implementation-defined collation techniques. Alternate enumerated collations could also be defined this way.

  - TRANSLATION *translation name* specifies that a translation (explained later in this chapter) is to be applied to the character set, which will result in a different character set. The resulting collation will be that of the second character set but will be applicable only to the first character set. Effectively, this means collating the first character set as though it were the second. This phrase can be optionally followed by THEN COLLATION *collation name*, in which case the preceding procedure is followed and then the specified collation is applied. The specified collation must, of course, be defined for the target character set of the translation, although the resulting collation of the statement will, as before, apply to the source character set of the translation.

- PAD SPACE | NO PAD is the PAD attribute and specifies how strings of unequal length are to be sorted. It is a modification to the specification provided in the FROM clause. There are two possibilities:

    - PAD SPACE means the shorter string is padded with spaces. A space will be some character in the repertoire that functions as a blank character. Its place in the sort will be a function of the collation, however the latter is specified. This is the default.

    - NO PAD means the shorter string is not padded. For sorting purposes, this is the same as padding it with a character that precedes all other characters in the collating sequence.

Coercibility

Any two character sets with the same repertoire may be directly compared. However, two such character sets may not have the same collation applied to those characters. How, then, is it determined which collation is used to evaluate the comparison? The answer standard SQL provides to this question is *coercibility*.

Coercibility is a set of rules that determine which collation is used when such comparisons are made. Each character set will have a coercibility attribute that specifies one of the following:

- A coercibility attribute of *explicit* means that a COLLATE clause has directly specified the collation in the statement at hand. For example, a COLLATE clause (a technique for directly applying a collation explained elsewhere in this chapter) in the ORDER BY list in a query will determine the collating sequence used to sort the output rows (if such sorting is performed; see "SELECT" in Chapter 28). This is an explicit collation and overrides any other.

- A coercibility attribute of *implicit* means that the collation is implied. The results of CONVERT and TRANSLATE expressions, as well as column references, are implicit.

- A coercibility attribute of *coercible* means that the collation can be overridden by an explicit or an implicit collation on the same character set. In general, value specifications, the results of CAST expressions, and columns following a collating sequence are coercible by default.

- An attribute of *no collating sequence* means that the character set cannot be meaningfully sorted. No value expression with this coercibility attribute may be referenced in the query expression contained in a view (see "CREATE VIEW" in the reference) or used with comparison predicates (see "Predicates" in Chapter 29). Actually, every character set defined in the database has a collating sequence—by default the order in which the characters are specified in the repertoire. Characters without a collating sequence can arise, however, as the result of certain operations.

Collations and coercibility are covered in more detail in Chapter 29 under "Collations".

Where Character Sets and Collations Are Specified

Once you specify character sets and collations, you can override them in one of several ways. A character set, for example, can be:

- A default for a schema, which will be set with a DEFAULT CHARACTER SET clause of a CREATE SCHEMA statement.

- A current value for a session, which will be set with a SET NAMES statement.

The value for the current session overrides that of the current schema. This means you can have an application access a schema whose data is in one character set and show that data in another character set, provided a translation between the two is available.

Specifying Collations as Attributes of Objects

A collation can be:

- The default collation of the default character set of the schema.

- An attribute of a domain (see "CREATE DOMAIN" in Chapter 28).

- An attribute of a column (see "CREATE TABLE" in Chapter 28).

- Directly specified in a SQL statement using a COLLATE clause (explained below).

Each of these cases overrides its predecessors in the list.

Specifying Collations Directly

You can directly specify a collation to be applied to the result of an operation using the COLLATE clause. This clause can turn up in the following places:

- In string value functions. These are functions that output text strings. For more information, see "String Value Functions" in Chapter 29.

- Appended to the output columns of a SELECT statement.

- In the GROUP BY clause of the SELECT statement. For more on GROUP BY, see Chapter 8 and "SELECT" in Chapter 28.

- In the ORDER BY clause of the SELECT statement. For more on ORDER BY, see Chapter 9 and "SELECT" in Chapter 28.

- Appended to the column definition in a CREATE or ALTER TABLE statement. In this case, the COLLATE clause will follow all datatype, domain, constraint, and default value clauses and precede the comma that separates column definitions. For more information, see Chapters 3-5 and the following items in Chapter 28: "CREATE TABLE", "ALTER TABLE", and "CREATE DOMAIN"; see "Constraints" in Chapter 29.

- In the definition of domains. Domains are an advanced SQL92 feature that is not yet widely implemented. For more on domains, see "CREATE DOMAIN" in Chapter 28.

The syntax of the COLLATE clause is simply:

```
COLLATE collation name;
```

Here is an example of a COLLATE clause used in a CREATE TABLE statement:

```
CREATE TABLE Customers
     (cnum INTEGER   NOT NULL PRIMARY KEY,
      cname CHAR(10) NOT NULL
                     COLLATE new_collation,
      city CHAR(10),
      snum INTEGER
      FOREIGN KEY (snum) REFERENCES Salespeople(snum));
```

The collation called new_collation is now an attribute of the cname column. As such, it can be overridden by another COLLATE clause specified in a SELECT statement on that column. To wit:

```
SELECT cnum, cname COLLATE old_collation, comm
    FROM Customers
    WHERE cname > 'G';
```

This imposes the old_collation on the cname column, overriding the definition in the table itself for the purposes of this statement. Therefore, the predicate will select values that follow 'G' by the logic of old_collation. Were the COLLATE clause not present in the SELECT statement, the new_collation specified in the CREATE TABLE statement itself would have been used.

Using Translations

A *translation* is a fixed, unambiguous mapping of characters from one character repertoire to another. This, of course, has nothing to do with mapping the content of human languages, which is well beyond the capabilities and purpose of SQL. Translations simply mechanically substitute certain characters for others. Your DBMS may come with some set of predefined translations and may provide you with some implementation-defined way to augment the set. Creating translations as the standard sees it is a matter of applying existing translations to new character sets, which, of course, must have the same character repertoires (though not necessarily the same form-of-use or encoding) as those for which the translation was initially specified. In SQL99, you can invoke external routines from SQL, which enables you to truly define your own translation by specifying some code in a language such as C/C++, Perl, or Java that would actually perform the operation. To see how the syntax actually works, look at "CREATE TRANSLATION" and "DROP TRANSLATION" in Chapter 28. For more on external routines, see Chapter 25.

Summary

This chapter provided an overview of national language support as specified by the SQL standard. Such an approach defines character sets, collations, and translations as built into an implementation and also as user-created portions of schemata. You have seen that character sets consist of repertoires, forms-of-use, encodings, and default collations and that both character sets and collations can be specified independently in several circumstances.

Putting SQL to Work

1. Create a collation that sorts the character set Alpha in the order of the binary numbers that represent it internally (i.e., the encoding). Make sure that the string `'get'` will always sort before the string `'get1'`.

2. Now create an alternate collation based on Alpha that sorts in reverse binary order.

CHAPTER

TWENTY-ONE

21

Using SQL with Other Languages (Embedded SQL)

- How Do You Create Applications in SQL?

- What Is Involved in Embedding SQL?

- Using Host-Language Variables with SQL

- Using SQLCODE and SQLSTATE

- Updating Cursors

- Indicator Variables

In this chapter you will learn how SQL is used to enhance programs written in other languages. Although the nonprocedural character of SQL gives it many strengths, as you have seen, it also produces a great many limitations. The most important of these is that you cannot use plain SQL to develop applications because it lacks flow-control and similar functionality that programs require. To overcome these limitations, you can embed SQL in programs written in a procedural language. The result is a hybrid application where the two languages are combined. For our examples, we have chosen Pascal in the belief that this language is the easiest for the uninitiated to interpret and because Pascal is one of the languages included in the ISO standard.

How Do You Create Applications in SQL?

SQL is designed strictly for database access. It has no flow-control and other structures that would enable you to create complex applications (this changes in SQL99, described in Chapters 24 through 26 of this book). Therefore, to use SQL as a programming language, you must extend its capabilities. Let's look at the fundamental ways in which you can do this:

- You can embed hard-coded SQL statements in a program primarily written in another language. This is Embedded SQL.

- You can write programs that derive SQL statements at runtime. This is Dynamic SQL.

- You can write to an API (application programming interface) designed for this purpose. The program that utilizes the API can have SQL code that is either static or dynamic, though dynamic is more common. The API will be either specific to a given DBMS or a cross-platform standard, such as ODBC, JDBC, SQL/CLI (part of SQL99), or IDAPI. The API comprises a set of hooks into a program. For proprietary APIs, that program is the DBMS itself. For cross-platform APIs, it is a code unit sometimes called a *cartridge* that acts as a universal interface to various DBMS products. The calls are standard actions, some of which take the text of SQL statements as parameters. The cartridge converts the API calls into calls that are appropriate for the DBMS in question, passes the SQL statements to that DBMS, and returns the results to the calling program. The more important cross-platform APIs are shown here:

- The SQL99 standard includes SQL/CLI (SQL Call Level Interface), which is a C-language API.

- The general industry standard as of this writing is ODBC (Open Database Connectivity). This is a C-language API based on the same earlier standard as SQL/CLI. ODBC is thus a variation on and extension of SQL/CLI.

- JDBC (Java Database Connectivity) is patterned after ODBC but is designed to be called from Java rather than C. This is an industry, though not an ISO, standard.

- You can extend SQL with procedural constructs to make it computationally complete. This extended version of SQL will actually be executed by the DBMS itself, rather than some external application. There are several such extended versions (sometimes, though not so much recently, called *4GLs*, i.e., fourth-generation languages) on the market, but all are proprietary, and the differences between products are substantial. SQL99 provides a standard way of extending SQL in this manner, called SQL/PSM, but until (and unless) this standard is implemented, this matter will have to be considered implementation-dependent. We discuss SQL/PSM in Chapter 24.

- You can have bodies of SQL code called *modules* that are callable by programs written in other languages. The approach is called the *module language*. The module language has the same effect as Embedded SQL, since Embedded SQL causes the generation of such modules. An advantage of modules as such over direct Embedded SQL is that multiple applications can access the same module, increasing code reusability. On the other hand, programmers may find it more awkward to switch between the modules and the host programs when coding. In this chapter, we will frequently refer to code modules in a generic sense. We are not speaking of the SQL module language per se, unless so stated or clear from context.

What Is Involved in Embedding SQL?

In order to embed SQL in another language, you must be using a software package that provides support for Embedded SQL in that language as well as, naturally, support for the language itself. Obviously, you have to be familiar with the language you are using. Mainly, you will be using SQL statements to operate on database tables, passing output to and taking input from the program in which it is embedded, commonly referred to as the *host program*.

Why Embed SQL?

Although we have spent some time illustrating what SQL can do, if you are an experienced programmer, you have probably noticed that it is not, in itself, very useful for writing programs. The most immediately apparent limitation is that, while SQL can accomplish a lot with a single statement, interactive SQL basically does things one statement at a time. The `if...then`, `for...do`, and `while... repeat` kinds of logical constructs used to structure most computer programs are absent, so you cannot base a decision about whether, how, or how long to perform an action on the result of another action. In addition, interactive SQL cannot do much with values besides entering them into tables, locating or deriving them with queries, and outputting them directly to some device. To put it a shade more formally, SQL is not computationally complete.

The more traditional languages are, however, strong precisely where SQL is weak. They are designed so that a programmer can begin a process and, based on the results, decide to do one thing or another or to repeat an action until some condition is met, creating logical paths and loops. Values are stored in variables that can be used and changed by any number of statements. This design enables you to prompt users for input or to read it from a file and format the output in elaborate ways (converting numeric data to diagrams, for example).

The purpose of Embedded SQL is to combine these strengths, allowing you to create complex procedural programs that address the database itself through SQL—letting you set aside the complexities of operating on tables in a procedural language that is not oriented to this kind of data structure, while maintaining the strengths of a procedural language.

How Do You Embed SQL?

You place SQL statements in the source code of the host program preceded by the phrase EXEC SQL (think *EXECute SQL*). These include some statements that are special to the embedded form of SQL, which will be introduced in this chapter. The language of the host program, which is called the *host language*, also dictates some variations. The ISO currently supports the following host languages:

- Ada
- C
- COBOL
- FORTRAN
- Java (As SQLJ, an adjunct to SQL99. SQLJ is not yet formally supported by the ISO, though it is by ANSI, the United States equivalent. For more on SQLJ, see Chapter 26.)
- MUMPS, which has more recently been renamed M
- Pascal
- PL/I

How Embedded SQL Actually Works

When you embed SQL statements in your code that is written in another language, you must *precompile* the program before you compile it. A program called a *precompiler* (or a *preprocessor*) will go through the text of your program and convert SQL statements into a form usable by the host language. The precompiler you use will be specific to your host language. The whole procedure consists of the following steps. Usually, you can give the precompiler a single command to perform all of these steps automatically, but it is worth distinguishing them here, because sometimes you must deal with them by hand. The following actions are either performed automatically by the precompiler or by you:

- The source code of the Embedded SQL statements is removed from the program and replaced with subroutine calls in the host language. While the DBMS understands these calls, they are not intended for general use. They are a private interface for use by Embedded SQL applications.

- A file containing the Embedded SQL statements is generated. This is usually called an *access module* or a *database request module* (DBRM).

- Then the ordinary host-language compiler must be run on the host-language program. If this is not done automatically by the precompiler, you will do it in the manner that you would ordinarily compile a program written in that language. Since the Embedded SQL calls have now become external procedure calls, the program can be compiled into object code just as it normally would.

- A program called the *linker* links the private DBMS calls in the host language to a DBMS library that provides their content.

- A program generally called BIND evaluates the contents of the access module. It performs as much of the processing of the SQL statement as it can now, so that the statement can be quickly executed whenever the program is run. Specifically, BIND:

  - Parses each SQL statement if the precompiler has not already done so. This means that it examines the syntax of the statement and builds an appropriate model of its meaning.

  - Validates each SQL statement. This involves ensuring that the statements are valid; BIND also checks privileges to the extent possible beforehand.

  - Derives an *access plan* (sometimes called an *execution plan*) for the statement, which is an approach to executing it. The DBMS can execute a SQL statement in several ways. For example, a join of several tables must decide in which order to look for matches. The decision that it makes could affect performance, so BIND will invoke the optimizer, which attempts to figure out the best way to look for matches (the optimizer does not always succeed in its mission). Having figured out how it wants to execute each statement, the optimizer combines all these approaches into one big access plan, which is associated with the application at hand. Sometimes, you can defer this process until execution time, in which case all access plans are derived when the application is begun, rather than when BIND is run. The advantage to this is that the optimizer can take advantage of information about the state of the database at execution time. This is particularly useful if you are using a cost-based optimizer (see Chapter 23).

- The results of the process thus far are an access plan accompanied by some peripheral information, such as the results of the validation. One of two things happens to these results. Either they are stored directly in the database or they are stored in an external code module called an *executable image*. If they are stored in the database, most products will require you to redo the preprocessing, linking, and so on, each time the DBMS is restarted. (An invocation of a DBMS from startup to shutdown is called an *instance*.) An executable image is arguably a better approach, because it can be reused from instance to instance. In fact, it can be used against any copy of the database that has the appropriate metadata. Either or both of these approaches may be available, depending on your product.

Now when you run the compiled host program, the external procedure calls are interpreted in terms of the library and passed to the DBMS. The DBMS executes them in accordance with the access plan it has stored for this application (or has gotten from the executable image) and passes output and status messages back to the calling program. Two important results of this process are:

- The details of the procedure calls, access plans, and so on are transparent to the application developer. He can continue to deal with things at virtually as high a level as he does for Interactive SQL.

- The execution of SQL statements is much more efficient than for Interactive SQL, however, because so much of the processing is pushed ahead to compile time and therefore does not slow things down at runtime.

Privileges of an Embedded SQL Application

Applications that use Embedded SQL, like any other SQL operation, operate under a set of privileges determining what they can and cannot do. In Interactive SQL, the Authorization ID of the database user determines the privileges. For Embedded SQL, there are two possibilities:

Invoker's rights   This is the same as for Interactive SQL. The relevant privileges are those of the database user executing the application.

Definer's rights   This approach is not universally supported but is arguably superior. Under this plan, the application is always executed under the Authorization ID that created it. Why is this better? For a user to run an application under Invoker's rights, she must have all the privileges required by any operation in that application. However, she will also have these privileges when she executes Interactive or Dynamic SQL. In Embedded SQL, she is restricted to the hard-coded statements in the application, so, even though she may have a great many privileges, she can do little with them. With Invoker's rights, these privileges are hers, to have and to hold, and to turn as loose as she would like. Definer's rights are more secure, especially if there is some way to restrict access to the application itself, which there generally is, often through the operating system.

Using Host-Language Variables with SQL

The basic way in which the SQL and host-language portions of your programs will communicate with each other is through the values in variables. Of course, different languages recognize different datatypes for variables. The ISO defines SQL equivalents for the host languages it recognizes (see Appendix E). The equivalents for any other language an implementer may happen to support are *implementation-defined* (see glossary). More complex host-language datatypes, such as matrices, may not have SQL equivalents, although the extensions to SQL provided in SQL99 make it more compatible with structured data and obscure types. (See Chapter 24 for a discussion of structured data.)

You can use variables from the host program in Embedded SQL statements wherever you would use value expressions. (SQL, when used in this chapter, will refer to Embedded SQL, unless otherwise indicated.) The current value of the variable will be the value used in the command. Host variables must:

- Be declared in a SQL DECLARE SECTION (discussed shortly).

- Be of a compatible datatype for their function in the SQL statement (for example, a numeric type if they are to be inserted into a numeric field). The specific mappings of host-language to SQL datatypes are given in Appendix E.

- Be assigned a value at the time they are used in the SQL statement, unless the SQL statement itself will assign a value.

- Be preceded by a colon (:) when referred to in the SQL statement.

Since host variables are distinguished from SQL column names by a colon, you can use variables with the same names as your columns, if desired.

Suppose you have four variables in your program, called id_num, salesperson, loc, and comm. These variables contain values that you want to insert into the Salespeople table. You could embed the following SQL statement in your program:

```
EXEC SQL INSERT INTO Salespeople
     VALUES (:id_num, :salesperson, :loc, :comm)
```

The current values of these variables would be put into the table. As you can see, the comm variable has the same name as the column its value is being inserted into; the rest of the variables do not. You will also notice that we've omitted the semicolon at the end of the statement. That is because the proper termination for an Embedded SQL statement varies with the language. Basically, it is the conventional statement terminator for that language. The specific terminators used by the standard languages are given in Appendix E. For example, for C, Pascal, and PL/I, the statement terminator is the semicolon; for COBOL, it is the word END-EXEC; and for FORTRAN, no termination mark is used. We will use the semicolon for the sake of consistency with Interactive SQL and with Pascal. Pascal terminates both Embedded SQL statements and its own commands with a semicolon.

The way to make a statement such as the above powerful is to enclose it in a loop and iterate it repeatedly with different values in the variables, such as in the following example:

```
while not end-of-file (input) do
     begin
     readln (id_num, salesperson, loc, comm);
     EXEC SQL INSERT INTO Salespeople
     VALUES (:id_num, :salesperson, :loc, :comm);
     end;
```

This Pascal program fragment defines a loop that will read values from a file, store them in the four named variables, store the values of those variables in the Salespeople table, and then read the next four values, repeating the process until the entire input file has been read. It assumes that each set of values is terminated with a carriage return (for those unfamiliar with Pascal, the readln procedure reads input into a series of variables and moves to the next line of the input). This gives you an easy way to transfer data from text files into a relational database.

Naturally, you can first process the data in whatever ways are possible in your host language, such as excluding any commission under .12:

```
while not end-of-file (input) do
     begin
     readln (id_num, salesperson, loc, comm);
     if comm >= .12 then
     EXEC SQL INSERT INTO Salespeople
     VALUES (:id num, :salesperson, :loc, :comm);
     end;
```

Only rows that meet the comm >= .12 condition are INSERTed. This shows how you can use both loops and conditions as normal in the host language.

Declaring Variables

You must declare all variables that are to be referenced in SQL statements before using them. To do this, you place the variables in a SQL DECLARE SECTION, using the ordinary host-language syntax. You may have any number of these sections in a program, and they may be located anywhere in code before the variable is used, subject to restrictions defined by the host language. Such restrictions boil down to the fact that these are variable declarations for the *host* language and therefore must be located in a section of the program where that language permits such declarations. The DECLARE SECTIONs will begin and end with the Embedded SQL statements BEGIN DECLARE SECTION and END DECLARE SECTION, preceded, as usual for Embedded SQL, with EXEC SQL. To declare the variables used in the previous example, you could enter the following:

```
EXEC SQL BEGIN DECLARE SECTION;
Var
     id-num: integer;
     Salesperson: packed array (1..10) of char;
     loc: packed array (1..10) of char;
     comm: real;
EXEC SQL END DECLARE SECTION;
```

For those unfamiliar with Pascal, Var is a heading that precedes a series of variable declarations, and packed (or unpacked) arrays are variables holding a series of values distinguished by parenthesized numbers (for example, the third character of loc would be loc(3)). The use of a semicolon after each variable definition is a Pascal, not a SQL, requirement.

Notice that there is nothing other than the BEGIN and END DECLARE SECTION statements that distinguish these variables as SQL-declared variables. The Pascal declarations themselves are the same as they would be even if we were using no Embedded SQL in this program. Also, declaring variables in the SQL DECLARE SECTION does not obligate you to actually use them in SQL statements. Hence, the DECLARE SECTION is a subset of the ordinary variable declaration section for the language and may contain a mix of SQL and ordinary host-language variables. If you keep all your variables destined for use in SQL statements separate from the rest, however, the precompiler knows it only needs to examine and allocate resources for those variables. This is something of an optimization, although, with modern machines, it is probably not significant unless you have a huge number of variables. Therefore, it may simply be easier to turn the entire variable declaration section of the host language into a SQL DECLARE SECTION and not worry about which variable is used where.

Retrieving Values into Variables

In addition to putting the values of variables into tables using SQL statements, you can use SQL to obtain values for those variables. One way to do this is with a variation of the SELECT statement that contains an INTO clause. Let's reverse our previous example and put Peel's row from the Salespeople table into our host-language variables:

```
EXEC SQL SELECT snum, sname, city, comm
    INTO :id_num, :salesperson, :loc, :comm
    FROM Salespeople
    WHERE snum = 1001;
```

The values selected are placed in the variables named in the INTO clause in the order named. Naturally, the variables named in the INTO clause must be of the proper datatypes to receive these values, and there must be a variable for each column selected.

Except for the presence of the INTO clause, this query is like any other. The INTO clause adds a considerable restriction to the query, however. It must retrieve no more than one row. If it retrieves multiple rows, they cannot all be inserted into the same variables at the same time. The statement will fail. For this reason, you should use SELECT INTO only under the following conditions:

- When you use the predicate to test for a value that you know will be unique, as in this example. The values that you know will be unique are those that have a constraint forcing uniqueness or a unique index. The constraints forcing uniqueness are PRIMARY KEY and UNIQUE. If a UNIQUE column permits NULLs, you should not use the predicate to test specifically for NULLs with the IS NULL operator. The UNIQUE and PRIMARY KEY constraints are discussed in Chapter 4 and under "Constraints" in the reference. unique indexes are discussed in Chapter 23.

- When you use one or more aggregate functions and do not use GROUP BY. Aggregate functions and GROUP BY are discussed in Chapter 8 in the reference.

- When you use SELECT DISTINCT on a foreign key with a predicate referencing a single value of the parent key, as in the following example. Note that in this case, you are SELECTing only the foreign key value itself, not the entire row:

```
EXEC SQL SELECT DISTINCT snum
        INTO :salesnum
        FROM Customers
        WHERE snum =
              (SELECT snum
              FROM Salespeople
              WHERE sname = 'Motika');
```

Assuming that Salespeople.sname and Salespeople.snum have the UNIQUE and PRIMARY KEY constraints, respectively, of that table and that Customers.snum is a foreign key referencing Salespeople.snum, you can rely on this query to produce a single row. If sname does not have a constraint or index forcing uniqueness, then this query is unreliable. If sname is not unique the query will fail.

Other cases exist where you will know that a query should produce a single row of output, but these are relatively obscure and, in many cases, rely on your data having an integrity that cannot be enforced with constraints. It is not good to rely on such integrity. You are creating a program that is likely to be used for some time, and it is best to play it safe with regard to potential failures. At any rate, there is no need to grope for queries that produce single rows, as SELECT INTO is only a convenience. As you will see, you can deal with queries that produce multiple rows of output by using a cursor.

Using Cursors

One of SQL's strengths is its ability to operate on all rows of a table that meet certain criteria as a unit without foreknowledge of how many such rows there may be. If ten rows satisfy a predicate, a query will output ten rows. If ten million rows qualify, it will produce ten million rows. This does make things difficult, however, when you try to interface to other languages. How can you assign the output of a query to variables when you don't know how much output there will be? The solution is to use what is called a cursor.

A *cursor* is an object that is associated with a query. When the query is executed, the cursor stores its output for processing by the host program, one row at a time. Like host variables, cursors must be declared before they are used. You do so with the DECLARE CURSOR statement, as follows:

```
EXEC SQL DECLARE CURSOR Londonsales FOR
     SELECT snum, sname, city, comm
     FROM Salespeople
     WHERE city = 'London';
```

The query is not executed immediately; this is only a definition. Cursors are somewhat similar to views in that the cursor contains a query and the content of the cursor is whatever the output of the query is at the time the cursor is opened (explained shortly). Unlike base tables or views, however, the rows of a cursor are ordered: there are first, second...last rows of a cursor. This order can either be explicitly controlled with an ORDER BY clause in the query, be arbitrary, or follow an implementation-defined default ordering scheme.

When you reach the point in your program where you are ready to execute the query, you open the cursor with the following statement:

```
EXEC SQL OPEN CURSOR Londonsales;
```

The values in the cursor will be those present when you execute this statement, not the previous DECLARE statement or any subsequent FETCH statements.

Next, you use the FETCH statement to extract the output from this query, one row at a time:

```
EXEC SQL FETCH Londonsales
     INTO :id_num, :salesperson, :loc, :comm;
```

This statement will put the values from the first row selected into the variables. Another FETCH statement will produce the next set of values.

As a side point, suppose we had defined the Londonsales cursor initially like this:

```
EXEC SQL DECLARE CURSOR Londonsales FOR
     SELECT *
     FROM Salespeople
     WHERE city = 'London';
```

Given the current structure of the Salespeople table, this would be the exact equivalent of what we had before. If, however, the structure of the Salespeople table were to change—for example, if another user were to add a new column to the Salespeople table—FETCHes on the Londonsales cursor would fail, because the table would have more output columns than the FETCH has variables. The application would begin to produce runtime errors, which we will show you how to handle later in this chapter. Which approach is better? In practical terms, an application that is being used for actual work generally should continue to run without modification when such changes occur. This fact would argue for enumerating the columns, as we did originally, so that your code will not fail because of such changes. On the other hand, if you let your code fail, you can be sure that such changes will be spotted and that you can make any necessary changes to your application. In general, it is better to go for the more robust approach, which is enumerating the columns, but whichever approach you choose should reflect a conscious decision.

Let's return, then, to the discussion of how to use FETCH. The idea is to put the FETCH statement inside a loop, so that you FETCH a row, do whatever you want with the values from that row, and loop back to FETCH the next set of values into the same variables. For example, perhaps you want to write the output, one row at a time, prompting the user to see if she wants to advance to the next row:

```
Look_at_more:= True;
     EXEC SQL OPEN CURSOR Londonsales;
     while Look_at_more do
     begin
     EXEC SQL FETCH Londonsales
     INTO :id_num, :Salesperson, :loc, :comm;
     writeln (id_num, Salesperson, loc, comm);
     writeln ('Do you want to see more data? (Y/N)');
     readln (response);
     if response = 'N' then Look_at_more:= False
     end;
     EXEC SQL CLOSE CURSOR Londonsales;
```

In Pascal, := means "is assigned the value of", whereas = by itself still has the usual meaning. The writeln procedure writes its output and then starts a new line. The single quotes around character values in the second writeln and in the if...then statement are a Pascal convention that happens to duplicate SQL.

The effect of this fragment is to set a Boolean variable called Look_at_more to TRUE, open the cursor, and enter the loop (since this is Pascal rather than SQL, this is a conventional two-valued Boolean value that cannot be UNKNOWN). Within the loop, a row is FETCHed from the cursor and output to the screen. Then the user is prompted to see if she wants to look at the next row. Unless she responds with N for No, the loop is repeated, and the next row of values is FETCHed. Although you must declare Look_at_more and response as Boolean and char, respectively, in a Pascal variable declaration section, you need not include them in a SQL DECLARE SECTION, because they are not used in the SQL statements.

As you can see, the colons before the variable names are not used for the non-SQL statements. Also notice the CLOSE CURSOR statement corresponding to the OPEN CURSOR statement. This statement, as you may have guessed, empties the cursor of values, so that the query will have to be re-executed, with an OPEN CURSOR statement, before more values can be FETCHed. It is not necessary for all rows selected by the query to have been FETCHed in order to CLOSE the cursor, although this is the usual procedure. Once the cursor is CLOSEd, SQL does not keep track of which rows were FETCHed. If you OPEN the cursor again, the query is re-executed at that point, and you start over from scratch.

This example does not provide any automatic exit from the loop when all the rows have been FETCHed. When FETCH has no more rows to retrieve, it simply places the same the values in the variables of the INTO clause. Therefore, once the data is exhausted, these variables will be repeatedly output with the same values as long as the user fails to terminate the loop with an entry of N. In order to terminate the loop automatically, we need to know the status of the SQL FETCH statement. We also have a more general need for such status, so we can handle errors and such things. The next section shows how to determine the status.

Using SQLCODE and SQLSTATE

It would be nice to know when the data was exhausted, so we could tell the user this and exit the loop automatically. It is even more important that we know if a SQL statement has produced an error. SQL addresses this problem by having host variables whose special function is to return status messages every time a SQL statement is executed. There are two such host variables:

- SQLCODE (called SQLCOD in FORTRAN) is the old way, from SQL86. It is a numeric field indicating whether the previous statement was successful. Although various possible number values for SQLCODE describe various specific errors, there is no standardization, so all of the hundreds of codes are entirely different for each DBMS. This feature is *deprecated*, which is to say, grudgingly supported. Tons of application code exist referencing it, but SQLSTATE is clearly better, so the ISO is doing what it can to promote it.

- SQLSTATE (called SQLSTA in FORTRAN) was introduced in SQL92 with the idea of providing some standardization and richer description. It is a five-character string variable limited to uppercase characters and digits and defined as follows:

  - The first two characters are the *class*, which provides general information about the status. Some classes are specified in the standard and others are implementation-defined.

  - The next three characters are the *subclass*, which elaborates on or narrows the description implied by the class. Subclasses are optional and, like classes, can be either standard or implementation-defined. Standard classes can take either standard or implementation-defined subclasses. Subclasses of implementation-defined classes are, of course, implementation-defined by definition.

  - Classes and subclasses beginning with the numbers 1-4 or the letters A-H are standard; others are implementation-defined. The standard SQLSTATE classes and subclasses are explained in Appendix C.

These are both host-language variables, which, like other host-language variables to be used by SQL, should be defined in a SQL DECLARE SECTION. SQLCODE is of the host-language type that corresponds to SQL INTEGER, and SQLSTATE is of the type that corresponds to SQL CHAR(5). (Appendix E shows which datatypes these are for various languages.) They differ from other variables in that the DBMS will set their values automatically after the execution of each SQL statement. You do not have to pass them in as parameters. You check their values to handle the situations they indicate. Remember that as soon as you execute a new SQL statement, the information from its predecessor is lost: you must copy this information into another variable if you wish to preserve it. If you fail to define either of these variables, SQLCODE is created by default.

For either of these host-language variables, there are three general possibilities: successful completion with no errors or warnings, successful completion with a warning, and error. SQLCODE recognizes only one warning condition, which is called NOT FOUND or NO DATA. This condition means that the statement executed correctly but did not have the ordinary effect; it is defined for various statements as follows:

- For SELECT, no rows were selected by the query.

- For FETCH, the last row had already been FETCHed, or no rows were selected by the query in the cursor.

- For INSERT, no rows were inserted. (This implies that a query was used to generate values for the INSERT and that it failed to retrieve any rows. An INSERT that failed for another reason would produce an error, not the NOT FOUND warning.)

- For UPDATE and DELETE, no rows satisfied the predicate, and therefore no change was made to the data.

In any of these cases, SQLCODE will be set to 100.

The second possibility is that the statement executed normally, without any of the above conditions being true. In this case, SQLCODE will be set to 0.

The third possibility is that the statement generated an error. If this happens, any changes made to the database by the current transaction may be rolled back. It depends on whether your implementation considers the error recoverable. Your implementation will decide, and should document, which errors produce automatic rollbacks. Regardless of whether an automatic rollback is performed, SQLCODE will be set to some implementation-defined negative number. The purpose of this number is to identify the problem as precisely as possible. Generally, your system will provide a subprogram to execute, which will have information about the meaning of the negative numbers your implementer has defined.

So what is different with SQLSTATE? In general terms, the answer is as follows:

- Class '00000' means successful completion with no warning messages, the same as SQLCODE 0. The five zeros mean that both the class and the subclass are zero. In fact, if the class is '00', the subclass must be '000'.

- Class '01' means a warning condition other than NOT FOUND. This class can take any of a variety of subclasses, so that the actual SQLSTATE value will be '01002' or '01000'. You can check for all such values by using numeric ranges. Even though SQLSTATE is a string, rather than numeric, variable, it sorts in numeric order, so that expressions like SQLSTATE > '01001' are meaningful and correct. Class '01' has no exact SQLCODE equivalent.

- Class '02' means NOT FOUND and is the equivalent of SQLCODE = 100. This class can also take any of a variety of subclasses.

- Any class above '02' indicates an error. There are both standard and implementation-defined subclasses for the errors.

If you have an error that produces an automatic rollback, the SQLSTATE class will be '40', and the subclass will be implementation-defined.

SQLCODE is supported primarily for compatibility with old code. If you are creating new code, we recommend that you use SQLSTATE. For a complete description of the standard SQLSTATE codes, see Appendix C.

Using SQLSTATE to Control Loops

Now you can refine our previous example to exit the loop automatically if the cursor is empty, all rows have been FETCHed, or an error is produced. You can do this using either SQLSTATE or SQLCODE. Keep in mind that SQLSTATE is a string datatype and therefore must be delimited by single quotes and that SQLSTATE has both classes and subclasses in the same string and must be dealt with accordingly.

```
Look_at_more:= True;
EXEC SQL OPEN CURSOR Londonsales;
EXEC SQL FETCH Londonsales
      INTO :id_num, :Salesperson, :loc, :comm;
while Look_at_more
   and SQLSTATE = '00000' do
      begin
```

```
            writeln (id_num, Salesperson, loc, comm);
            writeln ('Do you want to see more data? (Y/N)');
            readln (response);
            if response = 'N' then Look_at_more:= False;
            EXEC SQL FETCH Londonsales
                    INTO :id_num, :Salesperson, :loc, :comm;
        end;
    EXEC SQL CLOSE CURSOR Londonsales;
```

Using GOTO and WHENEVER

The above method is fine for exiting when all rows have been FETCHed, but if you produce an error, you need to do something about it. The following modification of the previous example goes to an error-handling routine if an error arises. If a warning arises, the loop exits, but the error-handling routine is not called. Here is the code:

```
Look_at_more:= True;
EXEC SQL OPEN CURSOR Londonsales;
If SQLSTATE >= '02000' then goto error_handler;
EXEC SQL FETCH Londonsales
    INTO :id_num, :Salesperson, :loc, :comm;
    If SQLSTATE >= '02000' then goto error_handler;
while Look_at_more
    and SQLSTATE = '00000' do
    begin
    writeln (id_num, Salesperson, loc, comm);
    writeln ('Do you want to see more data? (Y/N)');
    readln (response);
    if response = 'N' then Look_at_more:= False;
    EXEC SQL FETCH Londonsales
            INTO :id_num, :Salesperson, :loc, :comm;
    If SQLSTATE >= '02000' then goto error_handler;
    end;
EXEC SQL CLOSE CURSOR Londonsales;
```

Notice that the actual error handling is done in Pascal, not SQL in this case. Doing this in the host language is an option. SQL also supports GOTO for the purpose of error handling but only in the context of the WHENEVER statement. The WHENEVER statement allows you to define GOTOs globally, so that the program will execute a GOTO statement automatically if a certain condition occurs. Here are a couple of examples:

```
EXEC SQL WHENEVER SQLERROR GOTO Error_handler;
EXEC SQL WHENEVER NOT FOUND CONTINUE;
EXEC SQL WHENEVER SQLWARNING CONTINUE;
EXEC SQL WHENEVER SQLSTATE >= '03000' GOTO Error_handler;
```

SQLERROR, SQLWARNING, and NOT FOUND have built-in meanings. SQLSTATE >= '03000', of course, is a hand-coded condition and indicates an error class. The built-in values are as follows:

- SQLERROR means an error as opposed to a warning. In other words, it means that SQLSTATE >= '03000' or SQLCODE < 0.

- NOT FOUND is another way of saying a SQLSTATE class of '02' or SQLCODE = 100.

- SQLWARNING means a SQLSTATE class of '01' or '02' or a SQLCODE value of 100.

Error_handler is a name for a place in the program that execution will jump to if an error occurs (GOTO can be either one or two words in SQL). It is defined in whatever manner is appropriate for the host language, such as a label in Pascal or a section name or paragraph name in COBOL (hereafter we shall use the term *label*). Error_handler may identify a generic error-handling routine that has been bundled with the product, or it may indicate a routine you wrote yourself.

CONTINUE means not to do anything special for this SQLSTATE class or SQL-CODE value. This is also the default if you do not use a WHENEVER statement specifying that SQLSTATE class or SQLCODE value. However, having this inactivity defined as an action gives you the ability to switch back and forth between taking and not taking action at various points in your program.

For example, if your program includes a series of INSERT statements using queries that really should produce values, you might want to print a special message or do something to indicate that the queries are coming back empty and no values are being inserted. In this case, you could enter the following:

```
EXEC SQL WHENEVER NOT FOUND GOTO No_rows;
```

No_rows is a label on some code containing an appropriate action. On the other hand, if you are doing a FETCH later in the program, you may want to enter the following at that point

```
EXEC SQL WHENEVER NOT FOUND CONTINUE;
```

because performing a FETCH repeatedly until all rows are retrieved is the normal procedure and does not require or want special handling.

Updating Cursors

You can also use cursors to select a group of rows from a table that can then be UPDATEd or DELETEd one by one. This usage enables you to use the host language to do some specialized operations on your data that may not be doable in SQL.

You do this by using a query to select the appropriate rows, storing these in a cursor, and performing the DELETE using each current row of the cursor in turn. First, you would declare the cursor, like this:

```
EXEC SQL DECLARE Belowavg CURSOR FOR
     SELECT *
     FROM Customers
     WHERE rating <
          (SELECT AVG (rating)
          FROM Customers);
```

Then, you could create a loop to DELETE all the customers selected by the cursor In a more realistic example, you might do some processing of the values retrieved in the host language to determine whether a given row should be DELETEd.

```
EXEC SQL WHENEVER SQLERROR GOTO Error_handler;
EXEC SQL OPEN CURSOR Belowavg;
while SQLSTATE = '0000' do
     begin
     EXEC SQL FETCH Belowavg INTO :a, :b, :c, :d, :e;
     EXEC SQL DELETE FROM Customers
          WHERE CURRENT OF Belowavg;
     end;
EXEC SQL CLOSE CURSOR Belowavg;
```

The WHERE CURRENT OF clause means that the DELETE applies to the row currently retrieved by the cursor. This is called a *positioned DELETE*, and an UPDATE statement using the same technique is called a *positioned UPDATE*. A positioned DELETE requires that the cursor and the DELETE statement both reference the same table and, therefore, that the query in the cursor is not a join. The cursor must also be updatable. To be updatable, a cursor must satisfy the same criteria as a view (see Chapter 15). In addition, the cursor must not use ORDER BY or UNION. Notice in the above example that we still had to FETCH the rows from the cursor into a set of variables, even though we did not use these variables. The syntax of the FETCH statement requires us to do so.

UPDATE works in the same way. You can increase the commission of all salespeople who have customers with a rating of 300 in the following way. First you declare the cursor:

```
EXEC SQL DECLARE CURSOR High_Cust AS
    SELECT *
    FROM Salespeople
    WHERE snum IN
        (SELECT snum
        FROM Customers
        WHERE rating = 300);
```

Then you perform the updates in a loop:

```
EXEC SQL OPEN CURSOR High_cust;
while SQLSTATE = '00000' do
    begin
    EXEC SQL FETCH High_cust
        INTO :id_num, :salesperson, :loc, :comm;
    EXEC SQL UPDATE Salespeople
        SET comm = comm + .01
        WHERE CURRENT OF High_cust;
    end;
EXEC SQL CLOSE CURSOR High_cust;
```

For intermediate conformance to SQL92, a DBMS should permit a cursor to be declared as updatable or as read-only. Although most DBMSs claim only entry-level conformance, this feature is fairly widely supported. The rules are as follows:

- A cursor can be declared FOR UPDATE only if it is updatable according to the principles described above. A FOR UPDATE cursor imposes the same kind of locks on all the data it retrieves as an UPDATE statement would, given the isolation level currently specified.

- In some implementations, and in SQL92 Full conformance, a FOR UPDATE cursor can take a list of columns. UPDATEs will be restricted to those items.

- Any cursor can be declared READ ONLY. A READ ONLY cursor imposes the same kind of locks on all the data it retrieves as a SELECT statement would, given the isolation level currently specified (see Chapter 17).

- A cursor that is updatable in principle can be declared READ ONLY, but the reverse is not true.

- READ ONLY cursors impose less-restrictive locking than updatable ones, enabling more concurrent transactions to access the same data. This is why it can be advantageous to declare an updatable cursor READ ONLY if, in fact, you have no intention of using it for an UPDATE.

To declare High_cust a FOR UPDATE cursor, you would enter this statement:

```
EXEC SQL DECLARE CURSOR High_cust AS
    SELECT *
    FROM Salespeople
    WHERE snum IN
    (SELECT snum
        FROM Customers
        WHERE rating = 300)
    FOR UPDATE OF comm;
```

Indicator Variables

NULLs are special markers defined by SQL. They produce UNKNOWN Boolean values in comparisons. In other languages, UNKNOWN Boolean values are, well, unknown. Therefore, you cannot get proper SQL NULL behavior by directly placing a NULL in a host variable. Whenever you attempt to do this, the value of the host variable into which you attempted to insert the NULL is implementation-defined.

SQLSTATE is set to an error code ('22002' to be exact) or else SQLCODE will be set to a negative number. In either case, an error condition will be raised. You will normally want to avoid this. Frequently, you may select NULLs along with valid values without it being a reason to generate an error in your program. Furthermore, whatever happens to the flow of your program, the values in the host variables will be incorrect because they will not be SQL NULLs. Indicator variables provide an alternative method of dealing with this situation.

Indicator variables are declared in the SQL DECLARE SECTION, like other variables. They will be of the host-language type that corresponds to a SQL EXACT NUMERIC type, as shown in Appendix E. Whenever you perform an operation that might place a NULL in a host-language variable, you should use an indicator variable as a safeguard. You place the indicator in the SQL statement directly after the host-language variable you want to protect, without an intervening blank or comma, although you may optionally insert the noiseword INDICATOR.

An indicator variable in a statement is initially assigned a value of 0. If a NULL is produced, however, the indicator variable is set to a negative number. You may then test the indicator to see if a NULL value was found. Let's assume that we have declared, in the SQL DECLARE SECTION, two Pascal variables of the integer type, i_a and i_b. (There is nothing in the DECLARE SECTION itself that would mark these as indicator variables. They become indicator variables when used as such.) Here is one possibility:

```
EXEC SQL OPEN CURSOR High_cust;
while SQLSTATE = '00000' do
    begin
    EXEC SQL FETCH High_cust
        INTO :id_num, :salesperson,
        :loc:i_a, :commINDICATOR:i_b;
    If i_a >= 0 and i_b >= 0 then
    {This tests the indicator values. If neither
     indicator is negative, no NULLs were produced.}
    EXEC SQL UPDATE Salespeople
        SET comm = comm + .01
        WHERE CURRENT OF High_cust;
    Else
    {one or both NULL}
    begin
    If i_a < 0 then
        {This tests for the first NULL.}
        writeln ('salesperson ', id_num, ' has no city');
        If i_b < 0 then
        {This tests for the second NULL.}
        writeln ('salesperson ', id_num, ' has no
        commission');
    end;
```

```
        {else}
        end; {while}
EXEC SQL CLOSE CURSOR High_cust;
```

As you can see, we chose to include the noiseword INDICATOR in one case and exclude it in the other for the sake of illustration; the effect is the same in either case. Each row is FETCHed, but the UPDATE is performed only if no NULLs were found. If NULLs were found, the else part of the program is executed, which will print a warning message identifying where each NULL was found.

Using Indicator Variables to Emulate SQL NULLs

Another possibility is to treat the indicator variable associated with each host-language variable in a special way so as to emulate the behavior of SQL NULLs. Whenever you use one of these values in your program, for example in an if...then construct, you can check the associated indicator variable first to see if the value is actually a NULL. If so, you treat the variable differently. For example, if a NULL value were retrieved from the city field for the host variable city, which is associated with the indicator variable i_city, you could set city equal to a series of blanks. This would only be necessary if you wanted to print it; its value should make no difference to your program logic. Of course, you use i_city so that it is automatically set to a negative value when a NULL occurs.

To see the necessity for this, suppose you had the following if...then construct in your program:

```
if city = 'London' then
      comm:= comm + .01
else comm:= comm - .01;
```

Any value entered into the city variable either will be equal to 'London' or it will not. Therefore, the commission will be either incremented or decremented in every case. However, the equivalent statements in SQL operate differently:

```
EXEC SQL UPDATE Salespeople
      SET comm = comm + .01
      WHERE city = 'London';
```

and

```
EXEC SQL UPDATE Salespeople
      SET comm = comm - .01;
      WHERE city <> 'London';
```

(Of course, the Pascal version operates only on single values, whereas the SQL version operates on entire tables.) If the city value in the SQL version were NULL, both of the predicates would be UNKNOWN, and the comm value would therefore not be changed in either case. You could use the indicator variable to make the behavior of your host language consistent with this by defining a condition that excludes the NULLs:

```
If i_city >= 0 then
    begin
    If city = 'London' then
    comm:= comm + .01
    else comm:= comm - .01;
    end;
    {begin and end are needed only for clarity in this case.}
```

In a more complex program, you may want to set a Boolean variable to TRUE whenever city is NULL. Then you could simply test this variable whenever appropriate.

Other Uses of Indicator Variables

You can also use indicator variables to assign NULL values. Simply append them to a host-variable name in an UPDATE or INSERT statement in the same way you would in a SELECT statement. If the indicator variable has a negative value, a NULL will be placed in the column. For example, the following statement will place NULLs in the city and comm columns of the Salesperson table whenever the indicator i_a or i_b is negative; otherwise it will place the values of the host variables there:

```
EXEC SQL INSERT INTO Salespeople
    VALUES (:id num, :salesperson, :loc:i_a, :comm:i_b);
```

Indicator variables are also used to indicate string truncation, which occurs if you insert a SQL character value into a host variable that is not large enough to contain all of the characters. This situation is especially a problem with datatypes such as VARCHAR and LONG and with SQL99 elements such as LOBs. In this case, the variable will be filled with the beginning characters of the string, and the trailing characters will be lost. If an indicator variable is used, it will be set to a positive number indicating the length of the string before truncation, thereby letting you know how much text (or whatever) was lost. You will test for this case by seeing if the indicator is > 0 rather than < 0.

Summary

SQL statements are embedded in procedural languages in order to combine the strengths of the two approaches. Some extensions to SQL are necessary to make this work. Embedded SQL statements are translated by a program called a precompiler to a form usable by the compiler of the host language, basically as procedure calls to subprograms that the precompiler creates, called access modules or database request modules. The ISO supports Embedded SQL in these languages: Pascal, FORTRAN, COBOL, C, MUMPS, PL/I, and, as of the SQLJ standard that is an adjunct to SQL99, Java.

In an attempt to describe Embedded SQL in a nutshell, we'll review the most important points in this chapter:

- All Embedded SQL statements begin with the words EXEC SQL and end in a manner that is dependent upon the host language used.

- All host variables to be used in SQL statements must be declared in a SQL DECLARE SECTION before they are used.

- All host variables must be preceded by a colon when they are used in a SQL statement. They are not preceded by a colon when used in the host language.

- Queries can store their output directly in host variables using the INTO clause if and only if they select a single row.

- Cursors can be used to store the output of a query and access it one row at a time. Cursors are declared (which defines the query they shall contain), opened (which executes this query), and closed (which removes the query's output from the cursor). While a cursor is open, the FETCH statement is used to advance it to each row of the query's output in turn.

- Cursors are updatable or read-only. To be updatable, a cursor must satisfy all of the criteria that a view must satisfy; in addition, it must not use ORDER BY or UNION. A cursor that is not updatable is read-only.

- If a cursor is updatable, it can be used to control which rows are affected by embedded UPDATE and DELETE statements through the WHERE CURRENT OF clause. The DELETE or UPDATE must be against the same table that the cursor accesses in its query.

- Every program that uses Embedded SQL will have a host-language variable that is either the string variable SQLSTATE or the exact numeric SQLCODE.

SQLSTATE is recommended, because it is semantically richer and has some standard error information. Nonetheless, SQLCODE is the default if neither is declared. The value of this variable is set automatically after the execution of every SQL statement.

- If a SQL statement executed normally but it did not produce output or the normally expected change to the database, SQLSTATE will equal a string of five characters beginning with '02' or SQLCODE will equal 100. If the statement produced an error, SQLSTATE or SQLCODE will have a value that describes the error. Otherwise, SQLSTATE will equal '00000' or SQLCODE will equal 0.

- The WHENEVER clause can be used to define an action to be taken as soon as a warning or an error occurs. The action can be either to go to some target point in the program (GOTO <label>) or to do nothing (CONTINUE). Naturally, doing nothing is the default.

- Exact numeric variables can also be used as indicator variables. Indicator variables follow another variable name in a SQL statement, without any intervening characters except for the (optional) word INDICATOR.

- Normally, the value of an indicator variable is 0. If a SQL statement attempts to place a NULL into a host variable that uses an indicator, the indicator will be set to a negative number. You can use this fact to prevent errors and to flag SQL NULLs for special treatment in the host program.

- Indicator variables can be used to insert NULLs in SQL INSERT or UPDATE statements. They can also take positive numbers to indicate string truncation.

Putting SQL to Work

NOTE   The answers for these exercises are written in pseudocode, which is an English-language description of the logic that the program should follow. We did this to help the readers who may not be familiar with Pascal (or any other language that could be used). It also keeps the focus on the concepts involved, rather than on the particulars of one or another language. For the sake of consistency with the examples, however, the style of the pseudocode will be very similar to Pascal. We will omit from the programs everything that is extraneous to the matters at hand (such as program initialization, definitions of input/output, and connections to a database). Naturally, there is more than one way to do these exercises, and ours is not necessarily the best way.

1. Company policy has changed and customers can no longer place orders with salespeople other than those to whom they are assigned. You need to write an application that changes the existing content of the database to reflect the new rules. Design a simple program that selects all snum and cnum combinations from both the Orders and Customers tables and checks to see that the combinations in the former are the same as in the latter. If a combination in the Orders table differs from that in the Customers table, the snum value for the Orders table is changed to match. You may assume that a cursor with a subquery is updatable and that the basic integrity of the database, other than the error you are checking for, is sound (primary keys are unique, all cnums in the Orders table are correct, and so on). Include a DECLARE SECTION, and be sure to also declare any cursors used.

2. Suppose your program does not allow cursors or views employing subqueries to be updateable. How would you have to modify the above program?

3. Design a program that prompts the user to change the city values of the salespeople, automatically increasing commissions by .01 for salespeople transferred to Barcelona and decreasing them by .01 for salespeople transferred to San Jose. In addition, salespeople currently in London will lose .02 off their commission regardless of whether their city is changed, while salespeople not currently in London will have theirs increased by .02. The changes in commission based on whether a salesperson is in London will be applied independently of those based on where they are being transferred. Either the city or comm field can contain NULLs, and you should treat them as they would be treated in SQL. Warning: this is a slightly more convoluted program.

CHAPTER

TWENTY-TWO

22

Using Dynamic SQL in Applications

- How Does Dynamic SQL Work?

- Generating Dynamic Statements

- Executing Statements Immediately

- Preparing Statements Once and Executing Them Repeatedly

- Using Dynamic Cursors

In this chapter, we explain how to write applications that generate SQL on the fly. As with Embedded SQL, you can write applications with any number of languages, and, in fact, the language you use is somewhat less significant than it is for Embedded SQL. The most common way to use Dynamic SQL nowadays is to write to an API, such as ODBC, that provides an abstraction layer over any number of DBMSs. The SQL99 standard, discussed in the next part of this book, provides a standard for such an API, called SQL/CLI. SQL/CLI is already compatible with ODBC. For the most part, the industry uses either ODBC or an API specific to a particular DBMS (most DBMS products have such an API). The latter option lets you use functionality specific to that DBMS but at the cost of code portability. Hence, you must decide whether that specific functionality is important to you.

Note that this chapter assumes you have a basic understanding of Chapter 21. Even if you do not plan to use Embedded SQL and therefore skipped that chapter, it would be useful to skim it, as we make references to it here.

How Does Dynamic SQL Work?

The most basic difference between Dynamic and Embedded SQL is that the former does not deal in hard-coded SQL statements but rather relies on program logic to assemble appropriate SQL statements conditionally. These statements may be passed through a call-level interface, which is to say an API, either SQL/CLI, ODBC, IDAPI, or one that is specific to the DBMS at hand. The interface will have various other calls besides those that specifically send SQL statements, which will be concerned with tracking context, initializing resources, and such things. These calls depend entirely on the API you are using and are beyond the scope of the discussion in this chapter. However, in using Dynamic SQL, you have to be aware of some extensions beyond conventional SQL, and these are our present topic.

Specifically, we are covering Dynamic SQL as specified in SQL92. Since this aspect of SQL92 is not required by products claiming less than Intermediate conformance (that is to say, by products claiming Entry conformance or not claiming conformance), not all products may support the functionality quite as it is given here. Nonetheless, support for Dynamic SQL is, in fact, quite widespread and generally conforms to the principles outlined in this chapter, though, as always, you should check your system documentation for variations.

Generating Dynamic Statements

In Dynamic SQL, you assemble SQL statements as strings in your host program logic the same way as you would assemble any other strings in that language. For example, an online shopping application might track a list of items that a user selects as he traverses the site (the ubiquitous "shopping cart"). When it comes time to check out, the application submits this list in an UPDATE statement to the database, which will register the sale, decrement inventory, and so on. The application is written in a language like Perl or Java, generating dynamic HTML pages and using Dynamic SQL for database access. Admittedly, you could also do this much using Embedded SQL, but Dynamic SQL will give you more flexibility.

The capabilities that Dynamic SQL provides above and beyond those of Embedded SQL include the following:

- Since the full text of the SQL statement is generated at runtime, keywords and object names can be dynamically determined. You do not have to decide at coding time which SQL statement will be used, which tables will be referenced, and so on, as you do in Embedded SQL.

- The number of parameters passed to the statement from the host program also can be determined on the fly.

For example, for a shopping-cart application, you will generally have no idea how many items a user is going to order. Therefore, you may not know at coding time how many variables to put in the SQL statement. Dynamic SQL provides an elegant solution to this problem by letting you assemble the entire SQL statement in program logic rather than including it in program code.

You can do this in two basic ways:

- You can send a statement to the DBMS for immediate execution.

- You can prepare a statement in advance of execution, with the idea that the statement may be executed repeatedly. Doing so enables the statement to be validated and optimized prior to execution. It is also required for the execution of queries.

We cover each of these possibilities in the following sections.

Executing Statements Immediately

To simply pass a dynamic statement to the DBMS and execute it, you use the EXECUTE IMMEDIATE statement. For example, suppose you create a character string variable in the host language—Java, C, Pascal, or whatnot (consistent with the Embedded SQL chapter, we use Pascal)—called My_statement, with the following value:

```
My_statement := 'INSERT INTO Orders VALUES
    (3014, 382.22, '10/20/2000', 2001, 1001)';
```

Realistically, the value would probably be derived by concatenating various dynamic elements. Single quotes enclose the entire SQL statement. This usage has nothing to do with SQL per se, but is a Pascal convention for delimiting strings that happens to be similar to the SQL convention. Likewise, the semicolon is in this case the Pascal, rather than the SQL, statement terminator. You do not include the statement terminator in the prepared statement. (In many of our examples in this chapter, we include extra whitespace in the Pascal character arrays that are used for strings. In a real situation, this may not be optimal, but our priority here is readability.)

To execute this statement, you could enter:

```
EXEC SQL EXECUTE IMMEDIATE :My_statement;
```

The EXEC SQL, of course, indicates that this is a SQL rather than a host-language statement, just as in Embedded SQL. As you might expect, the statement is executed immediately. A SQLSTATE or SQLCODE value is set, just as it would be in Embedded SQL, to provide a space for error, warning, or successful completion messages. If this statement were in a loop, you could now change the value of My_statement and repeat the same EXECUTE IMMEDIATE statement to perform a new operation. If this new operation, however, differed from the old only in the values referenced in the statement, i.e., not in SQL keywords or object names, you would be better off using PREPARE and EXECUTE with dynamic parameters as described in the next section of this chapter.

EXECUTE IMMEDIATE is quick without being too dirty, but it does have limitations. Among these are the following:

- It is quick to code but not necessarily quick to execute. Since the DBMS has no idea what kind of SQL statement may be coming, it cannot do any parsing, validation, or optimization ahead of time—all of these will occur at execution time. If you will be executing the same statement more than once, it would be better to use PREPARE and EXECUTE, described in the next section, than EXECUTE IMMEDIATE.

- The SQL statement cannot be a query because EXECUTE IMMEDIATE provides no mechanism to store the results of a query.

- The SQL statement cannot contain dynamic parameters (explained in the next section). Since the entire statement is dynamically constructed, this is not such a problem.

Preparing Statements Once and Executing Them Repeatedly

Another approach is to treat a SQL statement as a temporary object, created by the application, that is executed repeatedly. This approach has the following advantages over EXECUTE IMMEDIATE:

- Queries are possible.

- Performance is much improved. All the parsing, validating, and so on can be done before the statement is executed, and execution itself can therefore proceed more rapidly.

- You can create multiple variations on the same statement by using dynamic parameters.

To achieve these results, you use two statements: PREPARE and EXECUTE.

PREPARE creates an object containing the SQL statement to be executed. When the PREPARE statement is issued, the SQL statement is passed to the DBMS, where it is examined, interpreted, validated, on so on. It is then stored until an EXECUTE (not EXECUTE IMMEDIATE) statement is issued, at which time all that needs to be done is the actual operation. Only single-row queries can be processed this simply. Multiple-row queries are still prepared but are used in cursors rather than being directly executed. We'll explain this procedure later in this chapter.

Here is an example of a PREPARE statement. We assume that the string variable My_statement has the same value as above:

```
EXEC SQL PREPARE :This_SQL_statement
    FROM :My_statement;
```

Again, SQLSTATE or SQLCODE will be set to indicate success or failure. The DBMS will examine the statement contained in My_statement, parsing it, validating it, and so on. If the statement is acceptable, the DBMS will build an execution plan for it and wait for an EXECUTE statement telling it to implement that plan. Effectively, the statement is stored as an object under the name This_SQL_statement, which will be used to execute it later.

Specifying the Scope of Prepared Statements

Another important attribute of the PREPARE statement is its scope. The scope of the PREPARE statement follows the word PREPARE and refers to where EXECUTE statements that reference the object the statement creates can occur. There are two possibilities:

- LOCAL indicates that the statement can be executed only from within the current program, technically the current compilation unit (see the glossary). This is the default.

- GLOBAL indicates that the statement can be executed from anywhere within the DBMS session. Suppose you have a CGI (or similar Web-server protocol) program that accesses a DBMS using Dynamic SQL. A common procedure in such a situation is to keep several database connections available and allocate them to the CGI programs as needed. This saves the performance cost of constantly spawning new DBMS connections, which is considerable. All the processes that access one of these connections will be in the same SQL session unless you do something to specifically reset the session (such as issuing a SET SESSION AUTHORIZATION statement; see the reference).

Here is the previous example revised to provide a global scope:

```
EXEC SQL PREPARE GLOBAL :This_SQL_statement
    FROM :My_statement;
```

The scope specification (GLOBAL or LOCAL) of a prepared statement is considered part of its name. Therefore, you can have identically named prepared statements, one LOCAL and one GLOBAL. You will be able to specify which you want in the EXECUTE statements that utilize this prepared statement.

Normally, a prepared statement remains in existence so long as it is in scope. If you know that you are finished with it, however, and wish to free up the resources it is using, you can *deallocate* the statement. The statement to do this is DEALLOCATE PREPARE, an example of which follows:

```
EXEC SQL DEALLOCATE PREPARE :This_SQL_statement;
```

Using Dynamic Parameters

Finally, we must address the issue of dynamic parameters. The idea of dynamic parameters is that you often want to repeat the same basic statement several times (making PREPARE a more sensible route than EXECUTE IMMEDIATE) but without the statement being quite identical each time. Specifically, you want to be able to put new value expressions in the statement, but you need not change any of the SQL keywords or object names (which would make it a different statement).

Note that these are the same elements you can specify with host-language variables in Embedded SQL. However, since the prepared statement itself is dynamically generated, dynamic parameters give you two levels of variation. You can dynamically decide on a general statement and have several variations on it, depending on the value of the dynamic parameters. Changing value expressions in a statement does not affect how it is parsed, validated, and so on, so it makes sense to PREPARE such a statement once and EXECUTE it repeatedly, filling in the dynamic elements at execute time. Dynamic parameters enable you to do all this, which will become clearer with examples.

Suppose our application decides on the basis of user actions which SQL statement it is to execute. Having chosen a SQL statement, however, the application may still have to execute it several times with different values. This situation could happen with INSERTs, when you cannot know even at PREPARE time how many rows will need to be INSERTed. In this case, you cannot generate a single INSERT statement for all of the rows because you do not know how many values to put in the VALUES clause. The solution is to generate a single-row INSERT and execute it repeatedly with different values. In that case, you will use dynamic parameters for the values.

Let's modify our previous example with some dynamic parameters. Dynamic parameters are represented with simple question marks (?).

```
My_statement := 'INSERT INTO Orders VALUES
    (?, ?, ?, ?, ?)';
EXEC SQL PREPARE GLOBAL :This_SQL_statement
    FROM :My_statement;
```

The idea, is that the EXECUTE statements that invoke This_SQL_statement will provide values to replace those question marks. How in the world, you may wonder, will the DBMS know which value to place in which parameter when all are indicated in the same way? How can it tell one question mark from another? As we will see when we discuss EXECUTE, the answer is simply that it matches parameters to values based on the order in which the latter are provided in the EXECUTE statement or in the SQL descriptor area.

Executing Prepared Statements

The statement to execute a prepared statement is simply called EXECUTE. Here is the syntax of the EXECUTE statement:

```
EXECUTE [ GLOBAL | LOCAL ] prepared statement
[ INTO  { variable.,.. }
    | { SQL DESCRIPTOR [GLOBAL | LOCAL ] descriptor name } ]
[ USING { variable.,.. }
      |  { SQL DESCRIPTOR  [ GLOBAL | LOCAL ] descriptor name } ] ;
```

Now this syntax, obviously, is getting a little more complex. The basic concept is that the EXECUTE statement can use either of two ways to get input parameter values and either of two ways to store output parameter values. Beyond this idea, the relevant concepts are as follows:

- The input parameters are specified in the USING clause and are values that the EXECUTE statement matches to dynamic parameters. If the prepared statement contains no dynamic parameters, EXECUTE statements on it should have no USING clause; otherwise, they must have one.

- The INTO clause stores the output of a single-row query and can be used only with single-row queries—that is to say, with SELECT statements that themselves contain an INTO clause. Multiple-row queries are dealt with by using cursors, as explained later in this chapter. Statements other than queries do not output data and so have no need for places to store it.

First, let's explain the terminology. We use the term *input parameters* for values taken from the host language and placed in the SQL statement. Likewise, we use *output parameters* for values output by the SQL statement and available to the host language. This is standard terminology in most languages for values passed to and from subprograms, although, strictly speaking, it applies in SQL only if the module language (see the glossary) is employed. Nonetheless, these terms are useful for us to speak generically about input and output values regardless of which of the two approaches explained below is used to pass them.

We can summarize the parameter requirements as follows: if the prepared statement contains dynamic parameters, EXECUTE must specify USING, and if the prepared statement is a single-row query, it must specify INTO. Hence, it could specify either, both, or neither of these clauses.

For either USING or INTO, two approaches are possible:

- Employ a list of host-language variables or value expressions separated by commas. In this approach, the host variables are preceded by colons, just as when they are referenced in Embedded SQL statements. For USING, you could use constants, including literals, as well as variables. For INTO, of course, you must use variables, since the EXECUTE operation will assign values to them. In either case, the number of items in the list must match the number of dynamic parameters (for USING) or SELECT output columns (for INTO) in the prepared statement.

- Use a descriptor area. This area is allocated for holding information about Dynamic SQL statements. We describe it later in this chapter.

You can mix and match these approaches if you like, using a descriptor area for output and host variables for input or vice versa. In either case, the datatypes of the parameters must be convertible to the values being placed in them, according to the specifications outlined in the reference under "CAST Expressions".

Here is an EXECUTE statement that invokes our previously prepared statement, filling appropriate values into the dynamic parameters:

```
EXEC SQL EXECUTE :This_SQL_statement
     USING :onum, :amt, :odate, :cnum, :snum;
```

The statement that the DBMS executes is as follows:

```
INSERT INTO Orders VALUES
     (:onum, :amt, :odate, :cnum, :snum);
```

Notice that our host-language variables have the same names as the columns for which their values are destined. This is entirely unnecessary, of course—you can use whichever names you like, subject to the restrictions of the host language—but it is helpful, since the parameters themselves are simple question marks and therefore easily confused. With dynamic parameters, it is seldom obvious which value goes with which parameter, so you can improve the readability of your code by adopting conventions like this that make it as obvious as possible.

Also note that, as with Embedded SQL, host-language variables are preceded by colons in SQL statements. They will not be so preceded in the host language itself, of course; the colons merely serve to alert the SQL statement interpreter that these are host variables, rather than SQL value expressions per se.

Now let's look at an example of an EXECUTE statement using INTO. We assume the statement also uses dynamic parameters. Most prepared statements use dynamic parameters, since the statement would otherwise be identical from iteration to iteration. While there is nothing wrong with a precisely repeated statement, it is less often useful than a varying one. First, here is the Pascal statement that sets the string value and the PREPARE statement that creates an object containing the query:

```
My_statement := 'SELECT snum, sname, city, comm
                    INTO ?, ?, ?, ?
                    FROM Salespeople
                    WHERE snum = ?';
EXEC SQL PREPARE LOCAL :This_SQL_statement
    FROM :My_statement;
```

Notice that we have used the same name for the prepared statement as previously but with a different scope. This makes it, in effect, another statement. Also notice that we used dynamic parameters both for targets for the retrieved values and, as before, for input parameters.

Here is the EXECUTE statement to iterate this statement:

```
EXEC SQL EXECUTE LOCAL :This_SQL_statement
    INTO :targetsnum, :sname,
         :cityINDICATOR:citynull, :commINDICATOR:commnull
    USING :predicatesnum;
```

The statement that the DBMS executes is as follows:

```
SELECT snum, sname, city, comm
    INTO :targetsnum, :sname, :city, :comm
    FROM Salespeople
    WHERE snum = :predicatesnum;
```

Note the following:

- We had to distinguish between targetsnum and predicatesnum. We could not simply use a combination in/out parameter, as we can in some languages.

- We used indicator variables for columns that might contain NULLs. These work the same as indicator variables in Embedded SQL, which are explained in Chapter 21. Had we failed to do this and had a NULL retrieved, it would have produced a runtime error. We can also include indicator variables in the USING clause to generate NULLs—for example, to deliberately INSERT a NULL into the database.

- We specified LOCAL in the EXECUTE statement for clarity. Since LOCAL is the default, we did not, strictly speaking, have to do so. Had we intended to EXECUTE the GLOBAL version, the specification would have been mandatory.

- The datatypes for the host-language variables must be compatible with the corresponding SQL values. If they are not, the DBMS may attempt to make an automatic conversion, as specified in the reference under "CAST Expressions". Failing that, the statement will be rejected.

Using Descriptor Areas

As we mentioned in the preceding section, descriptor areas, sometimes simply called *descriptors*, are an alternative Dynamic SQL technique that enables you to specify input and output parameters for prepared SQL statements. Descriptor areas give you more knowledge about and greater control of the parameters that will be passed to and from the prepared statement. The basic idea is that the DBMS creates a temporary object that stores information about the parameters used in a particular prepared statement. Another prepared statement will use a different descriptor area.

You may recall from our discussion of EXECUTE that you specify input parameters in the USING clause and output in the INTO clause, either, both, or neither of which can use a descriptor area. An implication of this is that you specify descriptor areas independently for input and for output. In fact, a given descriptor area will always be used for one or the other, not for both. Therefore, each prepared statement can have up to two descriptor areas matching it. Likewise, two versions of a prepared statement, one LOCAL and one GLOBAL, take two descriptor areas each, since they are considered two different statements. Although each descriptor area generally is used for only one statement, you could in principle reuse the same descriptor for different statements, provided that their parameters had the same descriptions.

In addition to descriptor areas being an option for EXECUTE IMMEDIATE, you can use them with dynamic cursors, as we will show later in this chapter, or simply to get more information about the output parameters of your SQL statement for use in your program logic.

Each descriptor area is structured hierarchically and contains a number of items, one for each parameter in the statement. Each of those items contains a number of fields providing information about the parameter described by the item. Which of these fields are actually used for a given item will vary depending on its datatype. If a given field is not used for an item, it may still be present, but it will have some implementation-defined value identifying it as junk.

Table 22.1 shows the fields of each item. We also show this table in the reference under "Descriptor Areas", where we provide a more complete description of the fields. We include the table here so you can better picture what a descriptor area is. Keep in mind that the descriptor area will have one entire set of these fields for each item, i.e., each parameter, in the prepared statement.

TABLE 22.1: The Descriptor Area Fields

Name of Field	Function
TYPE	Datatype.
LENGTH	Specified length (if fixed) or maximum length (if varying) in units relevant to datatype, e.g., characters (of whatever byte size) for character datatypes.
OCTET_LENGTH	Specified length or maximum length in octets (bytes).
RETURNED_LENGTH	Actual length of value in units relevant to datatype.
RETURNED_OCTET_LENGTH	Actual length in octets (bytes).
PRECISION	See reference under "Datatypes".
SCALE	See reference under "Datatypes".
DATETIME_INTERVAL_CODE	See reference under "Descriptor Areas".
DATETIME_INTERVAL_PRECISION	See reference under "Descriptor Areas".
NULLABLE	Denotes whether the item can be NULL.
INDICATOR	Denotes an actual NULL—the same function as an INDICATOR variable.

Continued on next page

TABLE 22.1 CONTINUED: The Descriptor Area Fields

Name of Field	Function
DATA	Contains the actual value of the parameter. Matches datatype and description specified by the values in the following fields: TYPE, LENGTH, PRECISION, SCALE, DATETIME_INTERVAL_CODE, DATETIME_INTERVAL_PRECISION, CHARACTER_SET_CATALOG, CHARACTER_SET_SCHEMA, and CHARACTER_SET_NAME.
NAME	The name of the parameter, if any.
UNNAMED	Denotes whether the parameter has a name.
COLLATION_CATALOG	The catalog that contains the collation.
COLLATION_SCHEMA	The schema that contains the collation.
COLLATION_NAME	The name of the collation.
CHARACTER_SET_CATALOG	The catalog that contains the character set.
CHARACTER_SET_SCHEMA	The schema that contains the character set.
CHARACTER_SET_NAME	The name of the character set.

For this discussion, we are interested in only a few of these fields:

- TYPE is numeric code indicating the SQL datatype of the parameter. The valid values are shown in a table in the reference under "Descriptor Areas". The values for the datatypes used in the sample tables are 1 for CHAR, 3 for DECIMAL, 4 for INTEGER, and 9 for DATETIME. Implementation-defined datatypes take negative numbers.

- NULLABLE indicates whether the field can contain a NULL. Although the official datatype is INTEGER, it is effectively a binary field, as its possible values are zero and one. One means that NULLs may be present, and zero means no NULLs.

- INDICATOR functions the same as an indicator variable does when you use that approach. Its value is relevant only if the field is NULLABLE. If this field is a negative number, the value is NULL and the content of the DATA field is irrelevant. If NULLABLE = 1, you should check this field. Otherwise, its value is implementation-defined and irrelevant.

- NAME is the name of the SQL column. There may be no such name. For example, an output column of a query that is a value expression, rather than a simple column reference (see Chapter 9), may be unnamed. In this case, the UNNAMED field is set to 1, and the value of NAME is junk (i.e., it doesn't matter). For input parameters, UNNAMED is always 1, and the value of NAME is implementation-defined and irrelevant.

- DATA is the value of the parameter. It will be of the datatype indicated in TYPE.

OK, so now that you know what descriptor areas are, how do you use them? As we mentioned previously, you employ descriptor areas in EXECUTE statements in place of lists of host-language variables or value expressions. Nevertheless, how do you create them and fill them with values?

The basic procedure is this:

- You create the descriptor area with the ALLOCATE DESCRIPTOR statement.

- You set the values of the descriptor area either automatically, with the DESCRIBE statement, or manually, with the SET DESCRIPTOR statement. You may also initially set them with DESCRIBE and modify them with SET DESCRIPTOR.

- You can, if you like, retrieve the values in the descriptor area with the GET DESCRIPTOR statement. If the descriptor contains output parameters, you will use this statement to retrieve their values. The GET DESCRIPTOR statement can also provide information about the input or output parameters of the statement that may be useful to your program logic.

- You reference the descriptor in an EXECUTE statement or one of the other kinds of statements that we will cover later in this chapter.

- You annihilate the descriptor with a DEALLOCATE DESCRIPTOR statement. If you do not, it will remain in existence as long as it is in scope.

Creating a Descriptor

Depending on what exactly you're up to, all steps in the above list except the first are optional. Let's look at ALLOCATE DESCRIPTOR:

```
EXEC SQL ALLOCATE DESCRIPTOR This_SQL_descriptor
    WITH MAX 7;
```

This statement creates a descriptor area called This_SQL_descriptor, containing seven items. This descriptor will work for any statement with up to seven input or seven output parameters. Fewer are fine. As the syntax implies, the number is intended as a maximum, since you may not know ahead of time how many parameters your prepared statements will have. You can omit the WITH MAX clause, in which case some implementation-defined default will apply. The WITH MAX clause tells the DBMS how much space to set aside for the descriptor. Notice that nothing specifies to which statement this descriptor area applies. That comes later.

Using DESCRIBE to Initialize a Descriptor

As we mentioned, you can fill in the values in two ways. Let's start with DESCRIBE, since it is the easier of the two and is usually where you start. DESCRIBE has the DBMS examine the prepared statement and figure out for itself what the values in the descriptor area should be. For the most part, this method works fine. Parameters based on SQL columns take the datatype and nullability characteristics of the column, for example. Here is the syntax to do this for a descriptor area intended to contain output parameters:

```
EXEC SQL DESCRIBE OUTPUT :This_SQL_statement
    USING SQL DESCRIPTOR This_SQL_descriptor;
```

This statement will use the descriptor area This_SQL_descriptor to store information about the output parameters of This_SQL_statement. Like prepared statements, descriptors can have either a GLOBAL or a LOCAL scope, with LOCAL as the default. Since we did not specify, it is the local versions of This_SQL_statement and This_SQL_descriptor that we are using. The scope for the descriptor should match that of the statement it describes (this rule is not actually enforced, but it is a good idea to follow it).

Likewise, OUTPUT is the default. We could have omitted this noiseword without changing the meaning.

What the statement does is fill This_SQL_descriptor with information about the output columns of This_SQL_statement. For each such column, it creates an item in the descriptor and sets the values for TYPE, NULLABLE, NAME, UNNAMED, and various other fields. Many fields are or are not relevant, depending on the value of TYPE. The statement does not set DATA or INDICATOR, as these are determined by the actual value of the column and are therefore not determined until the statement is EXECUTED.

Here is an example of how to use DESCRIBE for input parameters:

```
EXEC SQL ALLOCATE DESCRIPTOR Another_SQL_descriptor
    WITH MAX 7;
EXEC SQL DESCRIBE INPUT :This_SQL_statement
    USING SQL DESCRIPTOR Another_SQL_descriptor;
```

Since OUTPUT is the default, the word INPUT, following DESCRIBE, is required. This statement fills the descriptor area with information about the dynamic input parameters. If there are no such parameters, you will get an error, of course. The statement decided on the datatype by looking at context in the statement, particularly at the datatypes of values to which the dynamic parameter is compared. Note that, since all dynamic parameters are simple question marks, they are all unnamed. Hence, the value of UNNAMED is always 1, and the value of NAME is undefined for input parameters.

Using SET DESCRIPTOR to Initialize a Descriptor

You can also manually set the content of descriptors areas using the SET DESCRIPTOR statement. Usually, you want to do the initial setup of the descriptors with DESCRIBE and then modify it if necessary with SET DESCRIPTOR. It's just easier and less error-prone than manually setting the fields. Basically, two situations call for SET DESCRIPTOR:

- You need an input descriptor, which implies that you are going to use it in the USING clause of an EXECUTE statement. This means it must have either a value in the DATA field or a negative number in the INDICATOR field (denoting a NULL value). Since DESCRIBE does not set these fields, you have to do it by hand.

- You need to modify some of the values that DESCRIBE has generated. For example, the datatypes it determines for output parameters may not be supported in your host language or may simply not be what you want. In this case, you can manually change the value of the TYPE field for that parameter. When you do this, you automatically clear out any existing values of the DATA and INDICATOR fields, so you should make all changes of this nature first and then set those fields. Changing the TYPE field usually mandates other changes, since which fields of an item need to have values depends on the datatype.

Here is a SET DESCRIPTOR statement that places a value in one item in a descriptor area:

```
EXEC SQL SET DESCRIPTOR Another_SQL_descriptor
     VALUE 1
     DATA = 1001;
```

This statement places the value 1001 in the DATA field of the first item in the Another_SQL_descriptor descriptor area. We don't have to fill in the other fields or specify that this is an input descriptor area because we assume the DESCRIBE statement from the previous section did this for us. Since that statement contains only one dynamic parameter, this is the only parameter value we need to set. Had there been more than one dynamic parameter, we would use a separate SET DESCRIPTOR statement for each.

Here is a SET DESCRIPTOR statement that sets the dynamic parameter NULL:

```
EXEC SQL SET DESCRIPTOR Another_SQL_descriptor
     VALUE 1
     INDICATOR = -5;
```

Now the DATA field value for this item is irrelevant. The choice of -5 is arbitrary. All the standard specifies is that negative values denote NULLs. An implementation could distinguish between different negative numbers to provide additional functionality, but this is uncommon. The most common NULL indicator value is -1 because it is simply the most obvious.

If we wanted to change the datatype of the dynamic parameter to CHAR, we could do it as follows:

```
EXEC SQL SET DESCRIPTOR Another_SQL_descriptor
     VALUE 1
     TYPE = 1;
```

As we mentioned, 1 is the code for datatype CHAR. Of course, this statement just trashed the DATA and/or INDICATOR values we put in previously, so if we actually wanted to do this, we should have done it first. The DBMS will automatically perform any datatype conversions necessary to make the new datatype compatible with any other values to which it is compared, following the rules listed under "CAST Expressions" in the reference. If such a conversion is not possible, the SET DESCRIPTOR statement produces an error.

If you want to use SET DESCRIPTOR as an alternative to DESCRIBE, it gets a little more complicated. First, you must specify the number of items that will be in the descriptor. How will you know? Well, if you are assembling the statements using program logic, just count them as you put them in. If you are having the user enter the statements, or are getting them from another application through some sort of interface between programs (like CORBA), you will have to parse the string variable where you have the statement stored and count the parameters, deciding which are input and which are output parameters on the basis of their placement in the statement. In either case, once you have derived the count, you initialize the descriptor as follows:

```
EXEC SQL SET DESCRIPTOR This_SQL_descriptor
    COUNT = 4;
```

For this example, of course, we went back to the descriptor we used for the output parameters, of which there were four in our example. Although you must use a separate SET DESCRIPTOR statement for each of these four items, you can set all of the fields for a given item in one statement, thusly:

```
EXEC SQL SET DESCRIPTOR This_SQL_descriptor
    VALUE 1
    TYPE = 4,
    NULLABLE = 0;
```

You would repeat this statement, with the appropriate changes, for each of the other three items in the descriptor. This item, of course, matches the output column snum, which is an INTEGER. As we mentioned, INTEGER is TYPE 4, and the NULLABLE = 0 indicates that the column cannot contain NULLs (because the table column for which it is derived contains the NOT NULL constraint). Since INTEGER is a fairly simple datatype, you have to set only these two fields. For some other datatypes, you would have to fill in more fields from Table 22.1.

Retrieving Values from Descriptors

You can also directly retrieve the values in the descriptor area, which is helpful for having them control your program logic. You would normally do this, of course, if you used a descriptor area for the prepared statement output. At the end of such an EXECUTE statement, the output is in the descriptor area and has to be made visible to your program logic. You can also do this anytime you have a programmatic use for the information that the descriptor area provides. The statement to achieve this is GET DESCRIPTOR:

```
EXEC SQL GET DESCRIPTOR Another_SQL_descriptor
      VALUE 1
      :type = TYPE, :nullsok = NULLABLE, :content = DATA;
```

This statement goes to the first item in Another_SQL_descriptor and extracts the TYPE and NULLABLE fields, storing their values in the host-language variables type and nullsok. As you can see, the variable names can match the descriptor fields or not, at your convenience. You can extract however many fields from a given item you wish by separating the assignments with commas as above. To extract fields from another item in the descriptor, however, you must use another GET DESCRIPTOR statement.

You can also use GET DESCRIPTOR to find out how many items are in the descriptor, i.e., how many input or output parameters are in the statement associated with the descriptor. The statement used to do this is as follows:

```
EXEC SQL GET DESCRIPTOR Another_SQL_descriptor
      :numofitems = COUNT;
```

Freeing Up Descriptor Resources

Another statement that operates directly on descriptors is DEALLOCATE DESCRIPTOR. You use this to free up the resources used by descriptor areas that are no longer needed. The statement is simply

```
EXEC SQL DEALLOCATE DESCRIPTOR Another_SQL_descriptor;
```

This statement does not merely empty Another_SQL_descriptor of content. It destroys the descriptor itself, so that it is thereafter undefined.

Using Dynamic Cursors

As with Embedded SQL, Dynamic SQL uses cursors to deal with the sets of data that emerge when you execute queries. For Dynamic SQL, there are two varieties of cursors:

- Declared cursors, which are the same sort of creature we encountered in our discussion of Embedded SQL, though they now can have dynamic elements.

- Allocated cursors, which are even more dynamic than declared cursors in that their names as well as their content can be determined at runtime. This makes it easier for you to not have to know at coding time how many cursors you will need.

The two statements you use to create these two kinds of cursors are DECLARE CURSOR and ALLOCATE CURSOR, respectively. DECLARE CURSOR is, of course, the same statement used in Embedded SQL, but instead of using a hard-coded query, it uses a prepared statement of the type seen earlier in this chapter. Here is an example:

```
My_new_statement :=
    'SELECT snum, sname, city, comm
        FROM Salespeople
        WHERE city = ?';
EXEC SQL PREPARE :Next_SQL_statement
    FROM :My_new_statement;
EXEC SQL DECLARE citycursor
    CURSOR FOR Next_SQL_statement;
```

Of course, the dynamic parameter here behaves just as the previous input parameters we have seen.

The other way to create a cursor is with the ALLOCATE CURSOR statement. This statement works just the same as the dynamic version of DECLARE CURSOR, save that you use a host variable for the cursor name, as follows:

```
EXEC SQL ALLOCATE :somename
    CURSOR FOR :My_new_statement;
```

The advantage of this method is that you can keep changing the value of :somename in a simple and predictable way, such as incrementing a number suffix, to keep generating as many unique names as you need for all the cursors you use. Allocated cursors are sometimes called *extended dynamic cursors*.

Regardless of which technique you use to create the cursor, the rest of the procedure for using it will look familiar from the Embedded SQL chapter. Essentially, you OPEN the cursor, you FETCH the rows from it one by one, and then you CLOSE it. OPEN differs from the embedded version only if dynamic input parameters are involved. In this case, you must use a USING clause just as you would use for an EXECUTE statement. To wit:

```
EXEC SQL OPEN citycursor
    USING :somecity;
```

This statement puts the value of :somecity in the place of the dynamic parameter, executes the query, and fills the cursor with the query's output. Alternatively, the value for the parameter could have come from a descriptor area, just as for EXECUTE. The syntax would be:

```
EXEC SQL OPEN citycursor
    USING The_next_SQL_descriptor;
```

For details on the use either of descriptors or of host variable lists in the USING clause, see the sections on "Executing Prepared Statements" and "Using Descriptor Areas", earlier in this chapter.

FETCH is similar to the embedded version, except that it can optionally include dynamic parameters and that you can optionally store the output in a descriptor area instead of host variables. Here is an example using host variables, which is the same technique that Embedded SQL uses:

```
EXEC SQL FETCH citycursor
    INTO :snum, :sname, :city, :comm;
```

And here is a version using a descriptor area:

```
EXEC SQL ALLOCATE DESCRIPTOR The_next_output_descriptor
    WITH MAX 4;
EXEC SQL FETCH citycursor
    INTO The_next_output_descriptor;
```

You would now use the GET DESCRIPTOR statement, described earlier in this chapter, to retrieve the values from The_next_output_descriptor.

Finally, you would use CLOSE to empty the cursor of content, as follows:

```
EXEC SQL CLOSE citycursor;
```

This statement does not destroy the cursor. Declared cursors stay around as long as they are in scope. You can, however, destroy allocated cursors by deallocating the prepared statements on which they are based. For example, the following statement

```
EXEC SQL DEALLOCATE PREPARE :Next_SQL_statement;
```

would destroy any allocated cursors based on Next_SQL_statement. It would not destroy a declared cursor, but, for either an allocated or a declared cursor, it would automatically deallocate as well any other prepared statements that referenced the cursor (which would be positioned UPDATEs and DELETEs, discussed shortly).

Updating and Deleting through Dynamic Cursors

In addition to all the above methods, you can use either declared or allocated cursors to perform positioned UPDATE and DELETE statements. These statements are much like the embedded variety shown in the last chapter but with the usual dynamic elements. You PREPARE and EXECUTE them just as other dynamic statements. Before you PREPARE them, the cursor they are to reference must be DECLAREd or ALLOCATEd, and before you EXECUTE them, the cursor must be OPEN. Here is an example:

```
My_new_statement :=
    'SELECT snum, sname, city, comm
        FROM Salespeople
        WHERE city = ?';
My_positioned_deletion :=
    'DELETE FROM Salespeople
        WHERE CURRENT OF citycursor';
EXEC SQL PREPARE :Next_SQL_statement
    FROM :My_new_statement;
EXEC SQL DECLARE citycursor
    CURSOR FOR :Next_SQL_statement;
EXEC SQL PREPARE :First_delete
    FROM :My_positioned_deletion;
EXEC SQL OPEN citycursor
    USING The_next_SQL_descriptor;
EXEC SQL FETCH citycursor
    INTO Another_SQL_descriptor;
EXEC SQL EXECUTE :First_delete;
```

Note the following:

- The above code fragment defines a cursor and a statement, FETCHes the first row of the cursor into a descriptor area, and then DELETEs that first row from the table itself. This code fragment would probably be placed in a loop to do a repeated FETCH and DELETE operation. Such loops would work the same as they do in Embedded SQL; see the previous chapter for examples.

- The assignment of My_positioned_deletion could precede the declaration of the cursor it references because it is simply the assignment of a string to a variable in the host language. It is not visible to SQL until it is used in a statement beginning with EXEC SQL, which in this case will be PREPARE.

- Likewise, the PREPARE of the positioned deletion could precede the opening, but not the declaration, of the cursor on which it was based.

- We chose to use PREPARE and EXECUTE partly to show where these operations could be placed in the sequence. In this example, it may have made more sense to simply use EXECUTE IMMEDIATE. If this part of this code fragment were contained in a loop, however, it might make sense to PREPARE once and EXECUTE repeatedly for performance reasons.

Positioned UPDATEs work on exactly the same principles. We will leave the use of a positioned UPDATE as an exercise for the end of this chapter.

You may have noticed that for both positioned UPDATEs and DELETEs, the table references are somewhat superfluous because the only table they can refer to is the one in the cursor. Why, then, do you need to identify the table in the statement itself? For Embedded SQL, this syntax requirement would seem unnecessary but harmless. For Dynamic SQL, it is a bit of a pain, since you may not know in advance which tables you are going to reference, and you could probably just use the same positioned DELETEs for many tables more easily if you didn't have to reference the table name in the statement itself. An aspect of the SQL92 standard, preparable dynamic positioned DELETE (or UPDATE) statements, is designed to address this issue. In these statements, you can leave the FROM clause out of DELETE and the table name out of UPDATE. This, however, is a feature of Full SQL92 conformance, which is not widely supported. For more information on this approach, see INSERT and UPDATE in the reference.

Summary

In this chapter, we've shown you how to generate SQL dynamically in applications. Here are the key points we have covered:

- In Dynamic SQL, you generate SQL statements as text strings in the host language. You will pass these strings, possibly with parameter substitutions, directly to the DBMS to be executed.

- You can use the EXECUTE IMMEDIATE statement to define (prepare) and execute such a statement in one step.

- Alternatively, you can PREPARE the statement in one step and EXECUTE it in another, enabling you to pose queries and to use dynamic parameters represented by question marks. These are assigned values when the statement is executed.

- You can deal with the input and output parameters of dynamic statements either directly through host-language variables or through descriptor areas, which are dynamically created structures that store information about the parameters of a SQL statement.

- You use cursors to deal with queries that return multiple rows of output. These can be declared, which means named at coding time, or allocated, which means named at runtime.

Putting SQL to Work

1. Prepare and execute a query that retrieves the total dollar value of orders for one given customer. Output the customer's number and the total. The customer's number should be a dynamic parameter, and the statement should be executed using host-language variables.

NOTE   For all answers in this chapter, your details of code and host language may vary.

---

2. In the preceding example, what would happen if predicatecnum were given an invalid value, i.e., a value not present in the Customers table? How should you deal with it?

3. Now revise the first answer to use descriptor areas. Allocate both descriptors and set up the input descriptor by hand using the SET DESCRIPTOR statement. Also, retrieve the output values from the descriptor area into host-language variables.

4. Declare a cursor that finds all customers with ratings above a number that will be provided at runtime through a dynamic parameter. Each of these customers has the option to change her city value. The results of their decisions are placed in host variables. You need not worry much about the host logic and variable declarations, etc., only the SQL parts.

CHAPTER

TWENTY-THREE

Optimizing SQL

- Using Indexes

- Rephrasing Queries

23

This chapter covers how to make your SQL operations more efficient, primarily in terms of execution speed. Optimizing SQL is a huge and highly important topic, and for the most part it has to be addressed in a platform-specific manner. We offer some general rules of thumb and give you an idea of the sorts of things you'll need to look for in your system documentation. Chances are good that your system documentation has the information, and chances are decent that the information it has is correct. Without some background, however, it can be difficult to locate the answers you seek in the foot (or more)-long documentation set.

An invaluable aid in SQL optimization is the *access plan*. The precise format name and use of this varies from product to product, but the general concept is that the DBMS provides you with an analysis of how it thinks the query should be executed. In most products, you can make changes to this plan when you know a better way to do it. To find out about this feature, look in your system documentation under "access plan", "explain plan", or "directives". You should use the access plan to evaluate the impact of the techniques from this chapter that you employ, so you can see which ones work well with your system.

The most important ways to improve system performance are:

- Use indexes. These are database objects whose primary purpose is to improve the performance of queries. We will cover indexes in this chapter.

- Phrase your SQL with performance in mind. Unfortunately, the specifics vary greatly from product to product. In this chapter, we introduce the general principles involved and suggest some variations that generally tend to improve performance.

- Adjust the physical parameters of the DBMS. By *physical parameters*, we mean such things as how the data storage space is divided and how large a cache is allocated for statements (if your product supports the caching of statements, which some do). This area is completely product-specific, so we will not be covering it in this chapter. Nonetheless, we mention it because it could be worth looking up in your product documentation.

- Minimize the isolation level of locks or use optimistic locking. We covered this topic in Chapter 17.

Using Indexes

The primary non-platform-specific means to improve the performance of SQL operations is with indexes (although "indices" would be a formally more correct plural for "index", "indexes" is more widely used in the industry, so we will use it as well). A SQL index is akin to the index of a book in that it is an ordered list of the contents. In a way, it is more like a concordance, which is a book index that lists every reference to every word (generally excluding trivial ones) in the book. A SQL index lists all the values in a group of one or more columns, sorted in an order that is meaningful for the datatype (such as numeric order for numbers or following the collation for text strings). Associated with each value is a pointer to the row in the table where the value occurs.

Indexes as such are not a part of any of the ISO SQL standards. The standards tend to be "above" performance issues. Therefore, the syntax to create indexes and their functionality does vary from product to product. There are, however, some common features that we can touch on here.

Generally speaking, indexes operate transparently. They are chiefly used in queries, and the DBMS decides when a query is executed which, if any, indexes are to be used. However, you create the indexes, so you determine the possibilities. Also, you often can use execution hints, called *directives*, to tell the optimizer to do things differently, including to use or not use specific indexes, if you have good reason to believe doing so would give a good result. Some products will use only one index per query, so it can be helpful to specify that it use the best one if you know which one that is.

There are several ways to categorize indexes, but the most fundamental is as *unique* and *non-unique*. A unique index has only one entry for each value; a non-unique index may have any number of entries. In effect, then, a unique index is like a UNIQUE constraint: it prohibits duplicate values in the column or group of columns. In fact, unique indexes were frequently used for this purpose in the early days of SQL before constraints like UNIQUE and PRIMARY KEY were widely supported. Even now, such constraints are often implemented with indexes "under the covers". These days, though, indexes are primarily a performance optimization. Nonetheless, unique indexes are still valid because they improve performance even more than non-unique ones do. If you can use a unique index, you should do so. You can use unique indexes wherever duplicates are prevented from being entered into the table anyway, which is to say wherever a UNIQUE or PRIMARY KEY constraint is already in effect on the same group of columns.

You create an index as an object in a schema like you would other objects. Here is an example:

```
CREATE INDEX Orderdate ON Orders(odate);
```

You are now the proud owner of an index called Orderdate on the odate column of the Orders table. Since you did not specify, this would be a non-unique index, which is the default. Since the odate column already contains duplicate values, you can create only a non-unique index on it. Even if it didn't, you would not want to use a unique index as that would prevent you from adding duplicates in the future. You don't ordinarily view the content of indexes directly, but just so it is perfectly clear what is happening here, let's look at an example of what you have just created:

odate	RID
10/03/2000	000010
10/03/2000	000100
10/03/2000	000030
10/03/2000	000040
10/03/2000	000060
10/04/2000	000070
10/04/2000	000050
10/05/2000	000080
10/06/2000	000090
10/06/2000	000100

RID (Row Identifier) is a unique identifier for each row of the table. (The exact name of this varies from product to product. ROWID is a common variation). RID functions as a pointer to a specific row of the table that contains the value in question. The specific meaning of the number will depend on the implementation, but it either will be an address of the row or it will be a reference that can be converted to such an address. It is distinct from the primary key because it is not part of the content of the table and it is automatically a single numeric field, regardless of whether the table has a primary key or what the primary key is. Notice that the index is sorted by the indexed value, not by the RID.

Some products allow you to directly reference the RID in the predicate of a query. From the standpoint of relational theory, this is cheating a little, because it is making the implementation visible and specifying an operation that is not based on the content of the table (the RID is not part of the content). Nonetheless, if your DBMS supports this method, it is the fastest way to find a specific row. Because it can go directly to the address in the RID, it doesn't even have to access the index, which makes it even faster than searching for the primary key. In order to use the RID, you must first query it from the database, and many database systems will reuse the RID values as rows are deleted.

Many products automatically create unique indexes for columns that use a PRIMARY KEY or a UNIQUE constraint. It is an easy way to implement the constraint, and PRIMARY KEY columns are very frequently referenced in predicates, so the performance benefits should be considerable. Some products will even create indexes for foreign keys, as this will make natural joins using that foreign key much faster. Nonetheless, it is good to explicitly create indexes for these purposes if you can afford the storage space. This "under the covers" behavior could change with the next release of your product, adversely affecting the performance of your code. Since this is an implementation matter, the change may not even be documented.

Given these RID values, queries that reference the odate column in a predicate can execute much more quickly. Note that it is predicate references that matter. It does not matter whether odate is among the selected output columns. The question is whether the DBMS is going to use this value to decide which rows are output. Doing a search on the index is much faster than searching the table because the index is sorted and it uses much less storage. How much faster would this make a query? The following query would be an order of magnitude quicker with the Orderdate index:

```
SELECT *
    FROM Orders
    WHERE odate = '10/04/2000';
```

Once the index exists, the optimizer will use it if it seems helpful. Therefore, you don't have to change anything in the query itself to use the index.

Here is an example of how to create a UNIQUE index:

```
CREATE UNIQUE INDEX onlyonename
    ON Salespeople(sname);
```

There are more complex possibilities for creating indexes, but they vary from product to product. Refer to your system SQL documentation under "CREATE INDEX".

If you decide that an index is no longer useful, you can drop it using the DROP INDEX statement, like this:

```
DROP INDEX Orderdate;
```

An ALTER INDEX statement is uncommon because it is usually easier and better simply to drop the old index and create a new one.

NOTE   Since CREATE INDEX and indexes are not part of standard SQL, you will not find them listed in the reference section of this book.

When to Use Indexes

Are there any disadvantages to using indexes? Certainly. The costs of an index include the following:

- Every time the content of an indexed column is updated or deleted and every time a new row is added, the index must be updated. This does slow down update operations. However, indexes generally do not slow down updates nearly as much as they accelerate queries.

- The index itself takes up storage space in addition to what the table does. The index need not be stored with the table, however, other than being in the same schema.

- If you are going to retrieve the bulk of the rows in the table, accessing the index is literally a waste of time. It will slow down execution (somewhat).

These, then, are the trade-offs you must then consider: is the index worth the space it will take, and will you get enough use and benefit of it with queries to justify slowing down updates somewhat? To bring the matter into greater focus, here are some questions you could ask yourself:

- How frequently will the table be queried and how frequently updated?

- How likely are the common queries and updates to be particularly slow?

- How often will the column(s) you are considering indexing be used in predicates, especially the predicates of queries?

- How often will the column(s) you are considering indexing be used in *join* predicates? Joins tend to run slower and to benefit more from indexes than other queries.

- Which are you more short of: (execution) time or (storage) space? An index sacrifices some of the latter for the former. Usually, the answer is that time is more precious than space, especially since indexes speed queries radically while using up space modestly.

- Are there situations that call for special kinds of indexes, such as bitmap indexes and clusters? We will cover these kinds of indexes and where they are appropriate later in this chapter.

A good way to decide on your constellation of indexes, then, is to examine your application code and see what it requires. If you will be using Interactive or Dynamic SQL, of course, you will have to make the best suppositions you can. It is useful, however, that you can CREATE and DROP indexes as you go, so you can gradually tune up the performance the way you want it.

Types of Indexes

Beyond the unique and non-unique dichotomy, there are numerous categories of indexes. Here we cover some of the major types, so you will understand them if the product you are using supports them. You will specify which of these types you desire your index to be in the CREATE INDEX statement, using syntax that also varies somewhat from product to product.

Here are some of the major types of indexes:

- B+ trees.

- Join indexes and clusters.

- Bitmap indexes.

- R-trees. This is another variation on the idea of the tree. Here, each value is associated with boundary values. R-trees are primarily used in geographical (e.g., GPS), engineering, and virtual reality databases and are beyond the business focus of this book.

B+ Tree Indexes

If you are an advanced programmer, B+ trees will be familiar creatures; otherwise, probably not. Basically, a *tree* in programming is a hierarchical structure that can be quickly traversed to find specific items. A *B+ tree is* a tree designed to optimize binary searches. A *binary search* is a search of a group of sorted values that keeps dividing the set of values still to be searched in half with each comparison it makes. So a binary search for a specific value first finds the value in the middle of the range and asks if its target is greater or less than that number. Depending on the answer, it will search the greater-than subtree or the less-than subtree. It will then test against the midpoint of the subtree, ask the same question, and move to the appropriate subtree in the next level down. The number of values being searched is cut in half with each comparison.

For more on B+ trees, see any standard book on data structures. These indexes are broadly useful, since most predicates that test against a value can be accelerated by binary searches. For many products, B+ trees are the default index type if you do not specify another.

B+ tree indexes can be unique or non-unique. They are even more effective if unique.

Join Indexes and Clusters

Join indexes and clusters are two variations on the same idea. Join indexes themselves are sometimes called *cluster indexes*.

The idea of a *cluster* is to save time matching the values of tables that are frequently joined, by actually storing the joined values as one. In other words, when two tables comprise a cluster, they are stored in the same physical disk location with the frequently joined columns—usually a foreign key and the parent key it references—merged into a single object. Effectively, the tables are converted to a sort of meta-table that is no longer in the first normal form, but it doesn't matter because the clusters, like indexes, are invisible to the users. This will speed joins on these columns greatly but may also adversely affect updates more strongly than indexes do. The fact that some primary key values may match many foreign keys and others match none means that the stored combined rows from the two tables can vary greatly in size. Although beyond the scope of this discussion, it is worth at least pointing out that this variation may require you to be a little careful about how you manage the physical parameters of the cluster, specifically the page size and how the page is specified to grow. Again, consult your system documentation for details.

Note that this meaning of *cluster* is completely different from the one used in SQL92 and later standards.

A join index is basically the same idea, except that there is a common index of the foreign and parent keys, rather than a merging of the tables. Each entry in this index shows a foreign key value, the matching parent key value, the foreign key

RID, and the parent key RID. The index is sorted by parent key. This differs from clusters in that the tables themselves are stored conventionally; it is just the index that is different. Parent key values that do not happen to have foreign keys referencing them at the moment generally are excluded from join indexes, which can mean they are not helpful for outer joins or for restriction predicates testing the parent key.

Join indexes cannot be unique per se, because uniqueness is a quality of a group of columns in a single table, so it doesn't apply. Since join indexes are commonly applied to parent and foreign keys, the parent key will generally have a PRIMARY KEY or a UNIQUE constraint.

Bitmap Indexes

Bitmap indexes are exotic creatures to the relational world, though they are rather an old programming trick. They can not only speed the retrieval of data but, depending on how they are implemented, they can save on storage. However, they can be used only in special situations. Specifically, they are sensible only with very low-cardinality columns.

What is a low-cardinality column? It is a column that has only a small number of possible values: gender, yes or no, marital status, office location (if your company has only a few), etc. The bitmap index creates a binary encoding for this value set by counting the number of distinct values and setting aside that many bits for its structure. Each possible value is represented by a single bit. Each row, then, has this binary number with one and only one bit set to 1: the bit that corresponds to the value in that row. The other bits are set to 0. The advantage of this is twofold:

- The DBMS can use binary operations to find and compare values. Since all other computer operations have to be converted to binary, straight binary math executes very efficiently.

- Instead of storing the actual value, the DBMS can store the index and convert from the bitmap to the value when the value is referenced. The bit length of the index is likely to be considerably less than the value itself. For example, gender stored as CHAR in an ASCII system would take at least seven bits (or eight if your system likes even binary numbers). Stored as a bitmap, it would take two. In principle, it is expressible in one bit, but bitmaps are more concerned with performance than minimizing storage, so this is not the route that was taken. Five office locations can be encoded in five bits, rather than, say, a 10-character (80-bit) string.

An area where bitmaps are really strong is when two or more columns with such indexes are joined. The DBMS can deal with this as one big binary AND operation. The result is very efficient.

Hence, bitmap indexes come in handy when you are correlating a lot of low-cardinality data items. This might be the case if you are performing a demographic analysis of your customer base. Many demographic categories are reduced to low-cardinality value sets to simplify analysis. For example, age as such is probably too high a cardinality for a bitmap index *unless* you group the possible values into a small set of ranges (e.g., under 20, 20-39, 40-59, 60 and over; the cardinality of this value set is 4) and manipulate the data in terms of the ranges.

Although there is no formal reason why bitmap indexes could not be unique, such an arrangement would obviously be of little use. It would mean the column could have no more values than there are bits in the index, making both the column and the index worthless.

Rephrasing Queries

In theory, it makes no difference how you phrase a SQL statement. Even though there are many ways to phrase most queries, the optimizer in the DBMS is supposed to convert all of them to the most efficient formulation and execute that. In fact, however, this is not what happens, but it is close enough to make the whole exercise of rephrasing queries highly ambiguous. Whatever you write, what actually gets executed will probably be neither exactly what you wrote nor the absolutely best formulation. Therefore, we can offer no hard and fast rules about how optimally to write SQL statements. There are general principles, however, that usually will improve performance. Figuring out which tricks apply to your system will involve trial and error.

That said, it is well worth taking the time to understand your optimizer and learning how to manipulate it directly. You should have some way of seeing the access plans it comes up with. For example, in the DB2 interface we used for screen shots in this book, all you have to do is click a folder tab to move to a graphical representation of the access plan.

There are two general flavors of optimizer: *rule-based* and *cost-based*. Your implementation may supply only one of these, or it may allow you to choose which you like. A rule-based optimizer applies a series of rules to determine how to proceed, looking at what indexes are available, whether UNIQUE constraints may limit the possible matches, and so on. Rule-based optimizers do not, however, have any information about the content, as opposed to the structure, of the tables. They do not know how many rows or how many distinct values, etc. there are. This is where cost-based optimizers come in. They keep statistical information about the content of the database, enabling them to more intelligently optimize the queries. They are rather like racing cars; they go like mad but make frequent pit stops. To use a cost-based optimizer, you usually have to do more work than you would for a rule-based, such as telling it to perform the analysis to derive its statistics, not once but regularly, so that its statistics will be up to date.

In any case, even the cost-based optimizer uses rules to determine how to proceed, and, if you are using a rule-based system, you can use your own general statistic knowledge of the data to perform cost-based optimizations. Here are some rules of thumb to make your queries run faster. Again, there are no guarantees with these, but they are likely to work and, in any case, illustrate the kinds of parameters that will affect performance.

1. Be careful about using value expressions or datatype conversions on indexed values used in predicates. For example, suppose our previous index on odate is intact and we do the following:

    ```
    SELECT *
        FROM Orders
        WHERE CAST odate AS char LIKE ('10%');
    ```

    The optimizer will not use the index on odate because the odate value as such is not tested in the predicate; it is converted to another datatype so that it can be tested with a LIKE predicate (for more on CAST, see "CAST Expressions" in the reference). You could get around this for this example by using a BETWEEN predicate, which, unlike LIKE, can operate directly on dates.

    Note that some datatype conversions, including the above, can be done automatically. Therefore, a CAST expression complete with its performance penalties may be taking place even if not expressed. Depending on their level of conformance, some products will accept the following formulation (though many will not):

    ```
    SELECT *
        FROM Orders
        WHERE odate LIKE ('10%');
    ```

    Even though there is no directly stated CAST expression, the effect is the same.

2.   The same applies to <> (does not equal). Most products will ignore indexes on columns that are compared in this way, on the assumption that they will probably be not equal to most values. In fact, for similar reasons, negative predicates (predicates that use NOT) tend to be slower than positive.

3.   ANY is your friend, provided you remember to handle NULLs and empty subqueries correctly (see Chapter 12). EXISTS can either be a friend or not, with the same proviso about NULLs and empties. The advantage of either of these is that they can stop execution of the subquery as soon as a single match is found. ANY is better than EXISTS, however, as the latter requires a correlated subquery, which will be slower unless the optimizer figures out how to convert it to another form, which it can sometimes do.

The performance advantage does not apply to ANY if it is used with NOT or <>. In fact, ALL could be optimal for use with NOT for the same reason that ANY is without it: a single non-match constitutes an answer, so subquery execution can be halted once a non-match occurs. While most optimizers may not be clever enough to realize this, it is worth a try. As Chapter 12 shows, there are many ways to interconvert between ALL, ANY, EXISTS, and other subquery forms. For example, 0 < COUNT used with a subquery is equivalent to EXISTS, save in performance. Most likely, the optimizer will be clever enough to halt the subquery once EXISTS finds a match, but not COUNT. Ergo, EXISTS is better for performance.

4.   Place the predicates that are likely to eliminate the most rows from the output first in the WHERE clause. Often, this means placing join predicates before restriction predicates, since most joins use only a small fraction of the Cartesian product. However, if the restriction predicate is searching for a single value, it may be best to put it first.

5.   LEFT and RIGHT OUTER joins are interconvertible, but LEFT joins may be faster. For more on OUTER joins, see Chapter 10 and the reference under "SELECT".

6.   In a join, place the table with fewer rows first in the FROM clause.

7.   With an indexed column referenced in a predicate, you may do a bit better by combining equalities and inequalities. For example, you could use column_value >= 8, rather than column_value > 7. The reason this would work is that the index scan required for the latter version would first find 7 and then look for the next higher value. The >= 8 version goes right

to 8. This assumes we are dealing with INTEGERs, not DECIMALs, of course.

8. If you want more than 20 percent of the rows of a table, you probably are better off without using an index anyway. Of course, if the index is there, the optimizer may decide to use it automatically, but this is something you may be able to override directly or by using a value expression as above. Meaningless value expressions that serve to disable indexes would be things like *number_value* + 0.

9. NULLs are not values and, therefore, generally not indexed. Depending on your implementation, you might not be able to use an index to speed up a check of whether a value IS NULL or IS NOT NULL.

10. If you are referencing a multi-column index, you need not reference in the query every column, but you must start with the first one and continue through in the order they were indexed. Index usage stops at the first skipped column.

11. Avoid using LIKE with expressions that begin with a wildcard, especially with the any-length-string wildcard (%). This makes any indexes on the column useless and means the entire value must be checked against the rest of the match string.

12. Often a UNION of two queries will do better than a single query, primarily because the individual queries will be simpler and therefore are more likely to be optimized correctly. Also, depending on what kind of DBMS you have, the two UNIONed queries could possibly be executed in parallel. Here is an example:

```
SELECT *
     FROM Salespeople
     WHERE city = 'London'
          OR sname LIKE 'P__1';
```

is likely to be slower than

```
SELECT *
     FROM Salespeople
     WHERE city = 'London'
UNION
SELECT *
     FROM Salespeople
     WHERE sname LIKE 'P__1';
```

Summary

In this chapter, we have given you general guidelines to the use of indexes and to improving query performance through artful phraseology. There are several kinds of unique and non-unique indexes, which improve performance in various ways and have various limitations. We have also shown you how to rephrase queries so as to help the optimizer execute them efficiently.

Putting SQL to Work

1. I have several tables containing statistical information that I want to correlate. The items I will be comparing include age group, gender, marital status, and own/rent home. What kind of index should I put on these columns?

2. On which sorts of columns can I place unique indexes?

3. How could you rephrase the following query to make it possibly more efficient?

```
SELECT *
     FROM Customers
     WHERE cnum > 2002
          OR city = 'London';
```

4. How could you rephrase the following query to make it possibly more efficient?

```
SELECT onum, o.cnum, cname, odate, amt
     FROM Orders o, Customers c
     WHERE NOT amt < 1000.00
          AND o.cnum = c.cnum;
```

5. How could you rephrase the following query to make it possibly more efficient?

```
SELECT *
     FROM Orders
     WHERE amt > ALL
          (SELECT amt
                FROM Orders
```

```
                    WHERE NOT odate > '10/03/2000')
        AND snum IN
            (SELECT s.snum
                    FROM Customers c, Salespeople s
                    WHERE c.city LIKE 'London'
                    AND s.snum = c.snum);
```

The meaning of this query is to find all orders for amounts that exceeds the all amounts on or preceding October 3 from customers assigned to salespeople who have customers in London. Since you happen to know that there are no orders in the table before October 3, you could use this information in your optimization. This last point is the kind of thing you would be able to do that your optimizer may not. It certainly could not if it were rule-based, and it may not even think to keep that particular statistic if it were cost-based.

PART VI

SQL99

SQL99: An Overview

- The Structure of the Standard and the Levels of Conformance

- New Types of Data

- Extensions to SQL Statements

- Programmatic Extensions to SQL

- A Quick Overview of Object Oriented Concepts

- Integrating Objects into the Relational World

SQL99, formerly known as SQL3 (just as SQL92 was formerly known as SQL2), is a new standard, which was approved by the ISO and by ANSI in 1999. This standard greatly extends SQL beyond its previous capabilities. In this chapter, we will show you how the whole standard works and how the various pieces fit together. We will also explain some of its more important features in detail.

First, we will discuss the standard itself and explain the various parts and conformance levels. Then, we will provide an overview of the new functionality, starting with the new datatypes and continuing with the extensions to common SQL statements. Next, we will give an overview of the programmatic extensions to SQL that are part of SQL99. Finally, we will discuss the integration of relational and object-oriented approaches to data, which is one of the most important features of the new standard and the approach that SQL99 takes to this problem. This approach is based on user-defined structured datatypes, which include methods as well as data, and on tables that can function as object classes.

The Structure of the Standard and the Levels of Conformance

The SQL92 standard was structured into three levels of conformance—Entry, Intermediate, and Full—so that implementers could conform to it gradually. As it turns out, most implementers have gotten stuck at Entry level because they are primarily interested in focusing on proprietary features. Hence, SQL99 takes a different approach. It uses a Core functionality that is a prerequisite for any sort of conformance. This is a superset of Entry SQL92, so implementations can go directly from Entry SQL92 to Core SQL99. Beyond that functionality are several types of enhanced conformance. Implementations that support Core can also support any, all, or none of the enhanced levels. Core conformance also requires that the DBMS support either Embedded SQL or directly coded modules.

The standard itself consists of several documents, which correspond to logical subdivisions of the standard. The main purpose of this arrangement is to offer some hope of taming this beast. These document divisions do not correspond directly to the conformance levels, which are specified below. Rather, some of these modules were completed and published independently before the standard itself, but they have since been incorporated into the standard. The versions of these modules in the standard supersede previously published versions. Let's take a brief look at the parts of the standard:

SQL Framework   Provides the logical concepts that underlie the other parts of the standard.

SQL Foundation   Builds on the material in Framework and specifies, for the more fundamental parts of the standard, the actual nuts and bolts of the language, rather than just the conceptual apparatus. Both Framework and Foundation are utilized by the other parts, though neither corresponds directly to Core SQL. Core SQL is rather a subset of Foundation and, as such, is directly based on the material in Framework.

SQL/CLI (Call-Level Interface)   Specifies a standard API (Application Programming Interface) through which SQL operations can be called. This interface is adapted from the old SQL Access Group standard that also forms the basis for the ODBC (Open Database Connectivity) standard, which is currently widely used in the industry. Because of their common pedigree, SQL/CLI and ODBC are already mostly the same, and, if you know ODBC, you should be able to write to a SQL/CLI interface with only minor modification. The general consensus is that SQL/CLI and ODBC should and will converge rather than diverge as time goes on.

SQL/PSM (Persistent Stored Modules)   Refers to procedural extensions to SQL that make it computationally complete and therefore suitable for the development of full applications. More commonly, these extensions will be used to create more sophisticated standard operations that can be invoked by any application that can access the database. For example, SQL/PSM can be used to support *triggers*, which are modules of code automatically executed in response to specified changes in the data. Some proprietary products already do this, such as Oracle's PL/SQL.

SQL/Bindings   Specifies how SQL is to be bound to various host languages, excluding Java, which is dealt with separately. This section is relevant to Embedded and Dynamic SQL. Although neither of those are new features of the language, various new features, such as multimedia and user-defined datatypes, require extensions to the interface between SQL and the host languages.

SQL/MM (Multimedia)   This extends SQL to deal intelligently with large, complex, and sometimes streaming items of data, such as video, audio, and spatial data (for use in Global Positioning Systems or Virtual Reality applications).

SQL/OLB (Object Language Bindings)   Part 0 (as they call it) of the SQLJ specification for embedding SQL in Java. We cover this topic in Chapter 26 of this book. Strictly speaking, this is a distinct standard based on Entry-level SQL92 and developed parallel to SQL99.

These documents, however, generally do not correspond to the levels of SQL99 conformance that are defined. Those levels are defined in terms of "packages" of related SQL functionality that an implementation must support to claim a particular variety of enhanced conformance. The standard also allows itself extensibility by explicitly stating that other groupings of SQL99 features may emerge. We show the types of enhanced conformance that are defined in the SQL99 standard itself in Table 24.1.

TABLE 24.1:   SQL99 Conformance Levels

Conformance Level	Basic Functionality
Core	This level is explained in detail in Chapter 25.
Enhanced Datetime Facilities	This level indicates full support for DATETIME datatypes, including the INTERVAL datatype and TIME ZONE specification. Most of this level was also part of Full SQL92 conformance and is covered under "Datatypes" in the reference.
Enhanced Integrity Management	This level indicates support for advanced referential integrity features, including: • Assertions (See "CREATE ASSERTION" in the reference.) • Referential triggered actions (See Chapter 5 and "CREATE TABLE" in the reference.) • Triggers (Explained in this chapter.) • Subqueries in CHECK constraints (See "CREATE TABLE" in the reference.)
Active Database	This level indicates support for triggers (explained later in this chapter).
OLAP Facilities	This level indicates support for the use of advanced query and table features, including: • Full Outer Joins (See Chapter 10 and "SELECT" in the reference.) • Row and Table Value Constructors (See "Row and Table Value Constructors" in the reference.) • INTERSECT operator (See Chapter 13 and "SELECT" in the reference.)

Continued on next page

TABLE 24.1 CONTINUED: SQL99 Conformance Levels

Conformance Level	Basic Functionality
PSM (Persistent Stored Modules)	This level refers to extensions to SQL to make it computationally complete by providing control-flow and such things. In this case, there is a one-to-one correspondence between the section of the standard and the enhancement conformance level, so that the mapping of SQL parts to conformance levels is neither orthogonal nor consistently non-orthogonal. An implementation has PSM-enhanced conformance if it supports Core SQL and everything in the SQL/PSM document. Among the elements of this document are: • Stored procedures and functions, including variables and flow-control statements (Explained in this chapter.) • Overloading of procedures and functions (Explained in this chapter.) • Additions to the standard INFORMATION_SCHEMA to cover the new functionality
CLI (Call-Level Interface)	This level indicates support for SQL/CLI.
Basic Object Support	This level indicates support for the first level of object relational integration, which includes: • Overloading of SQL invoked external routines (Invocation of external routines from SQL is part of Core.) • User-defined datatypes (UDTs) • Reference datatypes • Typed tables • Arrays, including arrays of reference types and of UDTs Most of these items are explained in this chapter.
Enhanced Object Support	This is the second level of object relational support. It includes all of Basic Object Support with additions such as: • Writing your own constructors • Multiple inheritance, which means that a UDT can have more than one superclass

New Types of Data

As you have seen in this book, SQL has a variety of datatypes that it traditionally supports, including:

- Fixed-length and varying-length CHARACTER strings

- INTEGER, DECIMAL, and FLOATing point numbers

- DATEs and TIMEs

- BINARY data

SQL99 adds several new creatures to the mix. These include:

LOBs (Large Objects)   These are actually special cases of datatypes that SQL had already supported, but the pre-SQL99 versions were of comparatively modest size. New datatypes were needed to deal with items of data that could be much larger than what SQL supported previously. LOBs come in two delicious flavors:

- BLOBs (Binary Large Objects): These are large items of data that, being binary, can be anything but are intended primarily for multimedia data, such as audio, video, and graphics.

- CLOBs (Character Large Objects): These are similar to BLOBs but specifically represent large bodies of text. CLOBs are intended for use in such things as text databases.

Reference   More commonly known in programming as *handles*, these are variables that give the location of a value rather than expressing it directly. This location is not necessarily anything as literal as a memory address. These locations have to be meaningful across networks. Hence, they are some kind of reference that the DBMS can interpret and extract the value of as required. The idea is twofold: to enable coded references to items unknown at coding time, which is one of the traditional uses of pointers in programming, and to enable references to large values as an alternative to direct representation of them, so that they need not be shipped over the network or loaded into memory until and unless needed.

Boolean   Boolean datatypes are now supported. These differ from single-bit BINARY data because they are SQL Booleans: they can be UNKNOWN, as well as TRUE or FALSE. For more on UNKNOWNs and three-valued logic in SQL, see Chapter 7.

Rows   A row can now be treated as a datatype.

Tables   A table can be a datatype. This is primarily done to make tables more like classes, so that the relational model can better support the object-oriented paradigm. Such tables are called *typed tables* and are based on user-defined datatypes (UDTs). We cover both UDTs and typed tables later in this chapter.

Arrays (a.k.a. collections)   An array is an ordered list of elements, where each element is of the same basic type, such as a DATE or an INTEGER. They are standard in many programming languages but are new to standard SQL primarily because, again, they violate the first normal form. Arrays will largely be used for technical or geographical databases.

UDTs (User-defined datatypes)   Users can now define their own datatypes by subclassing the given types or by creating new structured types that behave like objects in the OO world. Along with defining the type, the user can specify functions that can be applied to the type or methods that are included in it. These functions and methods can be used in SQL statements and the values they return referenced in predicates. We cover this subject later in this chapter.

Extensions to SQL Statements

Several familiar SQL statements have been extended in SQL99. In some cases, these statements duplicate advanced features of SQL92 that generally have not been implemented, and in other cases they do not. Among the most important of these new features are:

The use of queries as named objects in SELECT statements

The ability to pattern tables after other tables (the LIKE clause of CREATE TABLE)

The ability to subclass and superclass tables

Recursive queries   *Recursion* is a basic programming concept and is such a favorite conceptual toy of nerds that it has been applied even to acronyms

(GNU's Not Unix, WINE Is Not an Emulator). Essentially, a recursive operation is one defined in terms of itself. Such an operation proceeds by invoking variations on itself until some, generally trivial, case is found that can be solved without invoking a variation. Once this case is solved, all the variations based upon it also can be solved. If you don't understand recursion, refer to any general programming textbook. Recursive queries are, logically enough, queries that invoke variations on themselves. They are used chiefly for expounding circular relationships of the sort explained in Chapters 5 and 19.

Regular expressions in predicates   Regular expressions are another standard programming trick that is new to SQL. A regular expression is a concise way to specify complex string operations for searches and other comparisons. Conceptually, they are similar to the wildcards used in LIKE, but much more complex. SQL supports them with a new predicate called SIMILAR. To find out about regular expressions, search the Web or Linux/Unix documentation for "grep".

The DISTINCT FROM predicate   This, of course, is distinct from DISTINCT as used in the SELECT clause of queries. DISTINCT FROM, the predicate, is equivalent to <>, save that it applies to entire rows rather than single values.

Programmatic Extensions to SQL

SQL99 extends SQL with programmatic capabilities. Most of these extensions are part of SQL/PSM, but some of them are included in Core SQL or in SQL/OLB. Various portions of this functionality are required for the Core, PSM, and Basic Object Support conformance levels. The basic problems that the programmatic extensions are designed to address are as follows:

To make SQL computationally complete   This is a fancy way of saying that SQL will be usable as a stand-alone application language. It will no longer need to be combined with another language, as with Embedded and Dynamic SQL, to create a complete program. This functionality is part of SQL/PSM, and some of it is also used for Basic Object Support. The extensions to achieve this fall into the following categories:

- Flow control: This creates a flow of conditional execution from one SQL statement to another. In other words, this is IF statements, loops, and such things.

- Procedures and functions: Sequences of SQL statements created with flow control can be named and called. Such sequences can include variables that are meaningful only from within them, i.e., they have a local scope.

To enable SQL to function as a data repository for object-oriented (OO) languages, particularly Java   The main problem here is that OO languages combine data (instance variables) with the operations upon it (methods) in objects. These objects are the basic structural foundation of OO languages, just as tables are the basic structural foundation of SQL. Hence, a fully functional *data* repository for an OO language is also a *method* repository, which means it includes executable code. This is a completely different paradigm than SQL was designed to support. This is perhaps the most important part of the standard, so we will cover it later in this chapter and, insofar as it regards Java, in Chapter 26 of this book.

To make SQL extensible   Extensibility is supported by enabling SQL to invoke programs written in other languages, such as Java or C. The term for this is *SQL-invoked external routines*, and the statements that implement it are CALL and RETURN. This is one of the more advanced parts of Core SQL, which we cover in Chapter 25.

To enable SQL to deal with UDTs intelligently   We cover UDTs later in this chapter.

To allow you to create database triggers   *Triggers* are pieces of code stored in the database that are automatically executed whenever specified operations or changes to the data occur. These triggers are called *database triggers* to distinguish them from *application triggers*, which generally have the same function but reside within applications. Database triggers are generally better than application triggers for several reasons, most fundamentally because the specified operation will be performed regardless of which application, or which interactive user, effects the change to the database. Many implementers already support database triggers as a proprietary feature, and application triggers are an older approach that has for the most part been supplanted by database triggers. The referential triggered actions discussed in Chapter 5 of this book can be considered a special kind of database trigger, though they do not use the SQL99 trigger syntax. Triggers are part of SQL Foundation.

Persistent Stored Modules (SQL/PSM)

SQL/PSM is both a section of the SQL99 standard and an enhanced conformance level of that standard. Not unlike Oracle's PL/SQL, it is a programmatic extension of the SQL language that makes it computationally complete and therefore usable for creating applications. You need not use it for complete applications, however. It is fine, and in fact intended, that you use it for procedures and functions that encapsulate a series of SQL statements, including flow-control and variables that are meaningful within the procedure or function. It also interacts well with some features of Basic Object Support. If you are familiar with traditional procedural programming languages, SQL/PSM will actually make SQL into a more familiar creature than it perhaps has been. However, SQL/PSM is simpler and more elegant than SQL combined with procedural languages because it is designed around such SQL peculiarities as three-valued logic (see Chapter 7 and "Predicates" in the reference) and because it uses SQL datatypes directly.

One area of Core SQL99 that complements SQL/PSM particularly well is the invocation of external routines. This refers to the ability to invoke subprograms written in another language from a SQL database. The same SQL statements, CALL and RETURN, are used for invoking SQL routines as are used for external routines.

Since SQL/PSM introduces sequentiality into SQL, we need to introduce a new concept, that of the *SQL statement sequence*. This concept simply refers to a set of SQL statements executed sequentially, rather like a program fragment. Now that SQL is procedural, such sequences become basic units of work.

Let's take a look at the basic features of SQL/PSM:

SQL/PSM includes several flow-control statements of types familiar from other languages. The formal names for these are SQL-control statements, and they are of the following types:

CASE   This statement conditionally executes one of several SQL sequences, depending on whether two values are equal or one is a WHEN clause. It is conceptually similar to, but actually distinct from, the CASE expression from SQL92, which can be used as a value expression (see "CASE Expressions" in the reference).

IF   The old standby; it executes a sequence if a predicate is TRUE. It includes ELSEIF and ELSE.

WHILE   Another favorite; it tests a predicate and repeats a sequence over and over until that predicate is FALSE or UNKNOWN.

REPEAT   A variation on WHILE; it executes the sequence, then tests the predicate. Exits when the predicate is TRUE (not FALSE and not UNKNOWN). REPEAT ensures that the sequence is executed at least once, which WHILE does not do.

LOOP   Repeats a statement sequence until explicitly told to exit or until an error occurs.

FOR   A SQL-oriented variant on the old workhorse; it executes a statement for each row of a table.

As we mentioned, SQL/PSM introduces procedures and functions into SQL. These are like procedures and functions in other languages. They are subprograms that take input and possibly output parameters. Functions additionally return a value directly and so are used in the place of value expressions in SQL statements (see "Value Expressions" in the reference). Methods, which are part of Basic Object Support, are not required for PSM conformance but, if supported, are implemented as a special kind of function. The statements you use to create these things are CREATE PROCEDURE and CREATE FUNCTION (and, possibly, CREATE METHOD). There are also corresponding ALTER and DROP statements for these objects.

Another new feature is error handlers. Previously, SQL supported status parameters, but the actual error handling had to be done in another language. Now, you can have SQL itself react to detected errors.

Finally, there are variables. These stay in scope for the duration of the procedure, method, or function within which they are contained or for the entire "module". (The meaning of this term if modules are not directly supported, which they usually aren't, is implementation-defined. However, it probably means the entire application for Embedded or Dynamic SQL or the entire session for Interactive SQL.) Variables are created with the DECLARE statement and given values with the SET statement. They can be of any standard SQL datatype or, if UDTs are supported, can be UDTs, including structured UDTs. We provide example of UDT variables later in this chapter.

A Quick Overview of Object-Oriented Concepts

If you do not have a background in object-oriented (OO) programming, some of the terms and concepts used to explain this portion of SQL99 are likely to be confusing to you. Therefore, we are going to digress a moment to introduce a few basic OO concepts. If you know this material already, please feel free to skip ahead to the next subsection.

In the OO world, both data and operations upon it are combined and modeled as *objects*. You can do everything that can be done with an object by executing a method on the object. Data can reside in an object, and, if you want to retrieve or change some data that resides in the object, you execute a method on the object. The most important difference between these methods and the functions and procedures used in more traditional programming languages is that the methods are executed *by* the object itself in whatever manner the object sees fit. A procedure is executed by a program; the program finds in memory or storage the data on which it is supposed to operate, and it performs its operation. A method is more like a message sent to the object, which will itself do the executing. This is called *encapsulation*.

Each object, then, consists fundamentally of two things: the methods that it executes and the data that it holds (the latter are called *instance variables*). Objects fall into classes, and each object of a given class will have the same set of methods and the same instance variables, though not necessarily the same values in those variables. To create an object of a given class, you execute a special kind of method on the class called a *constructor*. This creates a new object of the given class. This process is called *instantiation*, and the new object is an *instance* of the class. Now the term *instance variable* may make more sense. An instance variable is a variable that can have different values for each instance of the class; it varies with the instance. The methods remain the same for all instances of a given class.

Any of the methods in an object can invoke other methods on other objects, which is how the control flow of the program is created. A method is invoked on some object and begins a cascade. Of course, the execution of methods is itself conditional, so that OO programs are computationally complete.

A class can be *subclassed*. This means that a new class, called the *subclass*, is created with the old class, called the *superclass*, as a starting point. All of the methods and instance variables of the old class are initially passed to the new. The new class can do either or both of two things:

- It can supplement the instance variables and methods it inherited with new ones.

- It can *override* the methods it inherited. This means that it defines a new method with the same name as, but a different implementation than, one of the methods it inherited. Since instance variables can be accessed only through methods, this technique can also be used to effectively change which instance variables the subclass has.

This brings us to another key concept of the OO world: polymorphism. *Polymorphism* refers to the fact that the same method executed on different objects, or with different parameters or context, need not do the same thing, though it is good programming practice for there to be some conceptual similarity among the various versions of the method (otherwise, it would be more logical to use different methods). For example, in the material world, the verb "to open" has a different meaning for doors than for jars, though the two meanings are not unrelated. In the OO world, "open" would be a method that is executed differently for door objects than for jar objects. Although polymorphism often reflects a method that has been inherited from a superclass and overridden, it need not. Any two objects can use methods with like names and different implementations, but the similarity of names should reflect a conceptual similarity, just as variable names, though in principle arbitrary, should have intelligible meaning where practicable.

Last, we come to the concept of an *interface*, which comes from the Java language. An interface is basically a way of dealing with the fact that there is, in principle, no easy way of telling which methods an object implements. An interface is a group of methods. Any object that supports that interface will have implementations of those methods. The declarations of the object classes indicate which interfaces they support. Unfortunately, they do not, in Java, have to support the entire interface. A single method will do. So, this is hardly a foolproof way to know that a given object supports a given method.

This overview was quick and dirty, but we hope it was sufficient for you to understand what follows. For more information, see a good book on object-oriented programming or a decent text on an OO language like Java or Smalltalk.

Integrating Objects into the Relational World

This section covers the Basic Object Support enhanced conformance level—not to be confused with the Enhanced Object Support enhanced conformance level, though I bet it will be. (The multiple meanings of "enhanced" in the standard will do little to enhance clarity.) Although support for SQL/PSM is not required for implementations that want to support Basic Object, certain SQL/PSM features are also features of Basic Object: basically procedures, functions, and variables.

One of the least enviable tasks of SQL99 was the integration of two different views of the world: the relational one and the object-oriented one. These two horses not only pull in different directions, but they are attached to different carts. Specifically, a key concept of the object-oriented world is *encapsulation*. Everything is an object, but each object is a "black box"—the contents of the object are invisible from outside. Likewise, data and the operations performed on it are both stuffed in that same black box.

Relational systems, on the other hand, do not marry data to the operations upon it and keep both the data and the operations visible, subject to security constraints. All data is stored in tables, and the same operations—the set of valid SQL statements—can be performed on all of it, provided the proper privileges are in place. Even though SQL does divide its data into "objects" called tables, these are hardly black boxes. Not only are the contents of the tables made visible by operations that have nothing to do with the tables per se, but the contents can be mixed from different tables in a completely ad-hoc fashion through the use of joins, subqueries, UNIONs, and similar operations.

One of the strengths of the object-oriented approach is flexibility: each object is its own little world with its own little rules. The relational model, however, makes a virtue of universality: all data is combinatorial fodder for the same relatively simple set of operations.

The fact of the matter is, though, that the relational data model has come to dominate the database field, while the object-oriented approach is becoming more and more important in programming, particularly in C++ and Java. Awkward or not, there are simply too many practical advantages to be gained by gluing an object head onto the relational body. Furthermore, the fact that the two approaches have contrary virtues does mean that a coherent combination of them can be very powerful. It could combine the diversity of the object approach with SQL's ability to efficiently pose general questions about the data regardless of which "object" holds it, which is hard to do in a purely object-oriented system. This, then, is one of the most onerous and valuable tasks to which the SQL99 committee set itself.

The approach that emerged has the following features:

- Users can define their own datatypes (UDTs). These datatypes can behave as objects in the OO sense. A UDT contains data fields (which would be called *instance variables* in the OO world) and methods. Certain basic methods are created automatically.

- A table can also be defined as a datatype. In fact, you do so by basing tables on UDTs. The main purpose of this is so that tables can be subclassed and hence behave more like objects.

- Methods are implemented as a special kind of function that is associated with an object.

- SQL procedures and functions can be *overloaded*. This means that there can be more than one version of the same routine, having the same name but different parameters.

- References and arrays, as described earlier, are part of Basic Object Functionality. This includes arrays of UDTs or of references and references to arrays or UDTs.

You create UDTs with the CREATE TYPE statement. UDTs fall into the following two categories:

Distinct UDTs   These are extensions of datatypes somewhat similar to SQL92 domains (see "CREATE DOMAIN" in the reference). A distinct UDT is based on a standard datatype. It cannot be a subclass or a superclass, and it cannot be instantiated. It does, however, have automatically generated constructor, mutator, and observer methods, all of which we explain later in this section.

Structured UDTs   These are similar to and are intended to emulate classes in the OO world.

UDTs work as follows:

- A UDT has one or more attributes. If it has more than one, it is a structured datatype; otherwise it is distinct. Strictly speaking, the term "attributes" does not apply to distinct types, but it is simpler for this discussion to speak as though it does. In any case, it is a somewhat unfortunate choice of term, because "attribute" is a more formal name for "column" in relational database theory, and the attributes of UDTs do not map to it precisely, save when UDTs are used as typed tables (explained below).

- Distinct types are considerably simpler than structured ones and do not serve quite the same purpose. They function as refinements of datatypes but do not support most of the functionality of objects. Most of the rest of this discussion applies to structured UDTs, which are more complex and interesting. A distinct UDT has these characteristics:

  - It is based on some standard datatype.

  - It can neither be a subclass nor be subclassed (it is always FINAL).

  - It cannot be instantiated.

- For structured UDTs, attributes correspond to instance variables.

- For structured UDTs, a declaration of whether the UDT is instantiable is included in the definition. If it is not, it cannot be directly instantiated. In that case, you must create subclasses of the UDT and instantiate those. This is a common OO feature known as an *abstract superclass*. The idea is that the abstract superclass provides a general definition for a category of objects, all of which will require more elaboration. Again, distinct UDTs are not instantiable by definition.

- An object contains a group of methods. If the datatype is instantiable, one constructor method is created automatically and named for the datatype. Other method types are mutator and observer. One of each of these is created automatically for each attribute. The observer is used to read the attribute value, and the mutator is used to change it. You can also explicitly place methods in classes, which can be implemented with SQL-invoked external routines (part of Core) or with SQL procedures and functions.

- Optionally, it is used as a superclass. This is a type from which the UDT is subclassed. This feature, of course, is provided to support inheritance. A UDT with no superclass is a *maximal superclass*; one with no subclasses is a *leaf class*. A UDT that cannot have subclasses is *final*; other ones are *not final*. The differences between a leaf class and a final class are twofold: a leaf class may just happen not to have subclasses at the moment, whereas a final class cannot have subclasses, and a leaf class does have a superclass, since it is part of a class hierarchy. A final class may simply be a class that is not involved in an inheritance hierarchy, and, in fact, all distinct types fall into this category. Multiple inheritance, which would complexify this simple tree structure, is a feature of Enhanced (rather than Basic) Object Support. Syntactically, subclasses are defined with an UNDER clause and require a new privilege that exists on UDTs, which is also called UNDER. A subclass inherits the attributes and methods of the superclass, which it may supplement and/or override.

- A distinct UDT can be used in a column. A structured UDT can be used in a column *or* be used as a table, with each attribute of the UDT becoming a column of the table. Tables generated from UDTs in this manner are called *typed tables* and have some special features that they inherit from the UDTs. For example, such tables can be subclassed. We explain this concept in greater detail later in this chapter.

NOTE   For the sake of those of you who are familiar with object-oriented programming, we have adopted the standard terms "subclass" and "superclass" for UDTs. However, the SQL99 standard actually uses "subtype" and "supertype".

Creating Your Own Datatypes

A UDT is a database object and therefore resides in a schema like a table, collation, or view. To create a UDT, you use the CREATE TYPE statement; to destroy one, you use DROP TYPE. There is also an ALTER TYPE statement. Here is an example of CREATE TYPE:

```
CREATE TYPE persons AS
    fname           VARCHAR(20),
    lname           VARCHAR(20),
    address         VARCHAR(20),
    picture         BINARY
    NOT INSTANTIABLE
    NOT FINAL;
```

Since it has several attributes, this is a structured UDT. The reason we did not make this type final is that we intend to use it as a superclass; the reason we did not make it instantiable is that we intend to use it as an *abstract* superclass. Recall (or refer back to) the University database we used to explain design in Chapter 19. We ended up creating Persons as a superclass of Students and Teachers, because some aspects of those two entities are common to both, and because both are logically subclasses of Persons. However, any person entered into that schema should not simply be a person; they should fall into a more specific role such as student or teacher. Persons is a class that should be instantiated only through its subclasses. Hence, it is logical to make Persons an abstract superclass with Students and Teachers as subclasses.

Here, then, is how you would create a Students subclass of Persons:

```
CREATE TYPE Students UNDER Persons AS
     gradelevel    INTEGER
     INSTANTIABLE
     NOT FINAL;
```

Now, we have an instantiable class. Note that we did not have to list the fname, lname, etc. again, because they are inherited from the superclass. If these were modified in the superclass, the changes would automatically be reflected here as well.

To instantiate this class, then, we would use the constructor method that is automatically created for us. Here is an example:

```
DECLARE stud1 student;
SET stud1 = student();
```

This statement makes use of the partial procedural feature set that is a part of Basic Object Support (BOS), specifically the use of variables, which, under BOS, can be of UDT datatypes. The DECLARE statement creates a variable to hold our new instance. The constructor for the UDT student is student(). Therefore, the SET statement creates a new student object and stores it in the stud1 variable. We could set the values in this object by using built-in mutator methods named for the attributes they affect. To wit:

```
SET stud1 = student.fname('Gerry');
SET stud1 = student.lname('Dustbin');
```

We are setting further components of the stud1 object. The mutators are student.fname() and student.lname(). Notice that we are not setting a value in anything called "student", although the syntax may give that appearance. The values are not part of the class "student", but of the instance, in this case, stud1. The term "student" is simply telling in which UDT the fname and lname mutators are located, just as schema names can prefix table names to indicate the schema in which the table resides. Mutator methods are very simple: they take a value expression and store it in the appropriate attribute. Keep in mind that stud1 is currently working storage. To put this information into the database, we would have to use an INSERT statement, like this:

```
INSERT INTO Studentlist
    VALUES(stud1.fname, stud1.lname);
```

Of course, we haven't seen that Studentlist table before. Did we just CREATE it as we normally would? We could do so, of course, but we could also base the table directly on the student UDT. We show how to do this in the next section.

Before we get into that, however, we should show you how to retrieve values from attributes. Just as a UDT automatically has a mutator to set the value of each attribute, it automatically has an observer method to retrieve that value. Like the mutator, the observer automatically takes the name of the attribute on which it works. How does the DBMS tell the difference between a mutator and an observer based on a given attribute? By looking at how the method is used, the DBMS can determine whether a value is being set or retrieved. Here is an example:

```
SELECT stud1.fname(), stud1.lname()
    FROM Studentlist;
```

The methods here are obviously observers simply because they fall in the SELECT clause of a query. The parentheses are part of the syntax requirements for methods.

Using UDTs As Tables (Typed Tables)

One of the interesting peculiarities of structured UDTs is that they can function either as column values or as entire tables. In the former case, they violate the first normal form, which will make them many enemies among relational purists. In any case, mapping UDTs to tables is a bit more logical, especially considering how both tables and classes can map to entities in the ER model (see Chapter 19), which is how we have been approaching it. When you make a table of a UDT, the following things happen:

- Each attribute becomes a column. This is logical because "attribute" is a more formal term for "column" in relational theory and because the two concepts are related. An attribute of a table or of a UDT is an atomic value that it stores. Nonetheless, UDT attributes are still peculiar from a relational viewpoint.

- Each row of the table corresponds to an instance of the UDT. Hence, the table is essentially the class, and the rows are the objects. This maps neatly to the ER model, where the entities represent logical classes that are instantiated (see Chapter 19).

- The object aspects of the UDT are retained, even though they do not fit into conventional SQL tables. That is to say:

  - The automatically defined constructor, mutator, and observer methods of the UDT become associated with the table and can still be executed upon it.

  - Any methods you specified directly as part of the UDT are also retained. Such methods are created as schema objects, just as procedures and functions are (in fact, in SQL99 methods are regarded as a special kind of function, though this is not necessarily the case in OO programming generally), but they are associated with UDTs.

The syntax to CREATE a typed table is rather simple:

```
CREATE TABLE Studentlist
    OF students;
```

This statement CREATEs the Studentlist table as described. You can also CREATE typed tables as subclasses of other typed tables. When you do so, each row of the subclass is also a row of the superclass, which is consistent with how subclasses work in the ER model (again, see Chapter 19).

Summary

In this chapter, we have quickly gone over the big picture of SQL99 and offered more detailed coverage of a couple of its more important features, particularly Persistent Stored Modules (PSM) and user-defined datatypes (UDTs). These two items extend SQL into the two prevailing programming paradigms in the world today: procedural and object-oriented, respectively. We have given you some idea of the conceptual and practical difficulties inherent in this, especially in the case of the object-oriented (OO) material. We have also provided a quick and dirty introduction to OO concepts, in case this material was new to you.

Putting SQL to Work

1. Create a Teachers UDT as a subclass of Persons. This subclass will have the following features:

    - It will include a salary column of type DECIMAL.

    - It will include a rank column of type VARCHAR.

    - It will be instantiable.

    - It will not be possible to further subclass this UDT.

2. Now, create a table called current_teachers, based on the Teachers UDT. Note: tables can take the same name as the UDTs on which they are based or other UDTs for that matter. We are just adapting another convention for clarity.

3. Now, create a teacher and place her in the current_teachers table. The teacher will be named Molly Bramm, with a salary of $58,000.00 and a rank of Associate Professor. Rather than simply lobbing values into the table, you will do this:

    - Instantiate the Teachers class using a constructor.

    - Place the proper values into the attributes using mutators.

    - Store the result as a row in the current_teachers table.

CHAPTER
TWENTY-FIVE

25

Core SQL99

■ What Is Core?

Core SQL99 is that portion of the SQL99 standard that is intended to act as a basis for the rest of it. Implementations claiming any sort of SQL99 conformance must support Core SQL99 and may optionally support one of the enhanced conformance levels outlined in the previous chapter. For the sake of brevity, in this chapter we will generally refer to Core SQL99 simply as "Core". This chapter will show you how to use Core, which will apply to any SQL99 system.

What Is Core?

For the most part, Core consists of modest extensions to Entry SQL92, many of which were part of the more advanced portions of SQL92 anyway. However, it does move SQL into some new areas for supporting the enhanced levels as well. The major new areas of functionality in Core are as follows:

LOBs (Large Objects)   These are very large data items, either binary or text string.

External SQL-invoked routines   These are procedures or functions in other languages that can be directly called from SQL, greatly extending the functionality of the DBMS.

Distinct datatypes   These are the simpler of the two types of user-defined datatypes (UDTs). They are atomic and are basically specializations of existing datatypes.

We'll expand each of these areas in the following sections.

LOBs

As we explained in the previous chapter, LOBs come in two flavors: binary (Binary Large Objects, or BLOBs) and character text string (Character Large Objects, or CLOBs). Both of these types address how to deal with data items that are too large to practically manipulate in the same way as the data items with which databases traditionally work. In both cases, the solution is to treat such obese data items as values in columns like you would other SQL data items but to implement them differently.

BLOBs and CLOBs are quite similar in how they work, but the intended uses are different. BLOBs are intended chiefly for what has come to be called *multimedia*—graphics, audio, video, and the like. They are also useful in many scientific and engineering applications. CLOBs are basically intended for dealing with large bodies of text, such as Web pages, rather than the simple text values for which relational databases were designed.

Never use a LOB as a primary key because it would be far too inefficient. Create some short number instead.

Locators

One of the key differences between LOBs and other datatypes is the use of objects called *locators* that access LOBs by reference. This means that whenever you pass a LOB through a parameter or variable of Embedded SQL, Dynamic SQL, the module language, or a SQL-invoked routine (explained later in this chapter), you can use a four-byte integer to retrieve the LOB later, when and where you actually need to use it, rather than retrieving the value directly whenever referenced. Locators are handy for the following reasons:

- Not all languages can handle LOBs stored directly in variables.

- Most often, the DBMS is on a different machine than the application that accesses it. Sending LOBs across the network can bog down everyone using the network, so it is not something to do until and unless it is necessary.

- Even if they are on the same machine, the DBMS generally has one area of allocated working memory, the application another, and the output (say a page dynamically generated and sent through a Web server) possibly a third. This could lead to the same gargantuan LOB being replicated in memory more than once.

Locators deal with these problems by passing to the host language references to the LOBs, rather than passing the LOBs themselves. A locator is a variable in the host language that the DBMS knows to treat differently than other variables. Specifically, it stores a four-byte integer in the variable that acts as a unique identifier for the LOB the locator represents. Hence, a locator is a sort of pointer, but with some rather nifty features that make it easier to use than pointers in most languages. Locators have the following features:

- Locators operate transparently. You need not perform some special operation to go from the pointer to the value it indicates. The application determines based on the context whether it needs the actual value or merely a reference to it and behaves accordingly.

- Locators are typed to match the datatypes to which they point. There are BLOB locators, CLOB locators, and NCLOB (national language support CLOB) locators, as well as UDT and array locators, for products that support those advanced SQL99 features (not part of Core).

- Locators are declared in host programs like other variables but are followed by the keywords AS LOCATOR. They are of the datatype that corresponds to SQL INTEGER or EXACT NUMERIC (see Appendix E or, for Java, Chapter 26).

- Locators are valid until the end of the transaction. These are *non-holdable* locators. SQL99 also specifies *holdable* locators that can remain valid throughout a session, but these are not part of Core.

- Locators are not valid across sessions, so there is no point in storing them.

Here is an example of a locator declaration. This declaration, of course, goes in the code of the host language, in this case Pascal:

```
var
EXEC SQL BEGIN SQL DECLARE SECTION;
picture_handle: integer AS LOCATOR;
EXEC SQL END SQL DECLARE SECTION;
```

Now that picture_handle exists, you can use it to represent a LOB. Let's suppose we have added a snapshot column to the Salespeople table that contains a digitized photograph of each employee. We could do the following:

```
EXEC SQL SELECT snapshot
    INTO :picture_handle
    FROM Salespeople
    WHERE snum = 1003;
```

The locator picture_handle now contains a number that will be used to retrieve the actual value of the snapshot for salesperson 1003 when the time comes. How precisely this is achieved is an implementation-defined matter. When picture_handle has such a value, it is considered *valid*. When it does not, it is *invalid*. All locators automatically become invalid at the end of the current transaction.

NOTE
There are three functions in SQL/CLI that are designed for use with locators: `SQLGetLength()`, `SQLGetPosition()`, and `SQLGetSubString()`. Since SQL/CLI is not part of Core, we will not discuss it in this chapter. We will mention, however, that these three functions, unlike the bulk of SQL/CLI, are not included in ODBC because the latter is not designed with locators in mind.

Using BLOBs

As we mentioned, BLOBs are simply binary data items that can be quite large and can be referenced by locators. BLOBs can be anything, but they will probably be used primarily for large, complex items of data such as graphics, video, and audio—in other words, those datatypes commonly called *multimedia* in the software world. In the SQL99 standard, BLOBs are formally called Binary Large Objects or Binary Strings. Binary Strings are distinct from BIT Strings. The latter term refers to the datatype BIT. BIT Strings are not required to be extraordinarily large as BLOBS are, and there is nothing unconventional in how they are handled. They are part of SQL92 and are appropriate for smaller binary data items.

Whenever you need to refer to a BLOB or other binary data, you do it in hexadecimal (hex) notation. As you may know, hex is a base 16 number system that is used as a more concise way to express binary numbers. There are 16 possible values for each digit, which is the same number of values that four bits can express. Therefore, each hex digit represents four bits. The 16 digits are the numbers 0-9 and the letters a-f. Further information on hex is beyond the scope of this book; see any standard programming text if you need more information. You write hex numbers in SQL as shown here:

```
X 'aa9073f9c79bbe900'
```

This is a hex literal. The uppercase X is necessary to denote that what follows is hex rather than conventional text characters, which, of course, are also enclosed in single quotes. You can also break hex literals across lines, like this:

```
X 'aa9073f9c79bbe900'
  '89e9a6cc45d7d990dca257a'
```

The DBMS automatically concatenates both of these lines into a single hex number. The separate lines are independently bracketed in single quotes, but only the first takes an X argument. The separator between the two parts of the number has to be a newline, rather than just a body of white space, even though, for most other purposes, newlines are simply equivalent to any other white space.

Here is the text to add a snapshot column to the Salespeople table:

```
ALTER TABLE
     ADD COLUMN snapshot BLOB(500K);
```

or

```
ALTER TABLE
     ADD COLUMN snapshot BINARY LARGE OBJECT(500K);
```

This is much the same as adding any other type of column: BLOB (or BINARY LARGE OBJECT) is the datatype and 500K is the length. Although strictly speaking an implementation matter, the length will probably be the maximum rather than the allocated length. If a given snapshot is only 200K, the value won't be padded to 500K. Length functions differently in the VARCHAR datatype than in the CHAR datatype, for example. Length can either be in bytes (the default), kilobytes (expressed as K), megabytes (expressed as M), or gigabytes (expressed as G). (Contrary to the popular misconception, K, M, and G do not correspond to a thousand, a million, and a billion bytes, respectively, because these are not round numbers in the binary world. Rather, they indicate 1,024, 1,048,576, and 1,073,741,824 bytes, respectively, because these numbers are even powers of two.) If the length is omitted, some implementation-defined default will apply.

The operations you can perform on BLOBs are somewhat restricted. Many of the operations you would use for other datatypes are simply not meaningful. For example, BLOBs are not sortable. It makes no sense to say that one BLOB is less than another. Therefore, the only comparison operators you can apply to BLOBs are = and <>. To be =, two BLOBs must be the exact same length; if one is zero-padded and the other is not, the two are not equal. This is because a large set of zeros could well be meaningful in a BLOB—in most raster (pixel map) graphics formats, it would indicate a field of black—so it cannot be assumed to be padding. Keep this in mind if you write any code that manipulates BLOB data directly.

BLOBs can use the concatenation and substring operators that have been available for strings since SQL92. We describe these operators in the reference under "String Value Functions". You can also use a function called LENGTH to determine the size of a BLOB. You will do this frequently while working with a BLOB as a locator so that you know how much data you will be dealing with before you actually retrieve it.

These additional principles apply to BLOBs:

- They cannot be produced by CASE expressions. This functionality is supported at the Extended LOB Support level but not at Core. For more information on this topic, see "CASE Expressions" in the reference.

- They can use most of the functionality of character strings; for example, most string value functions apply, as does the LIKE predicate. Not all of this is required for Core, however.

- They cannot be cast to or from other datatypes with CAST expressions (See "CAST Expressions" in the reference).

- If any of a group of concatenated BLOBs is NULL, the resulting BLOB is NULL.

Using CLOBs and NCLOBs

There are actually two kinds of CLOBs: CLOBs and NCLOBs. The latter are national language support (NLS) CLOBs. The difference between CLOBs and NCLOBs is precisely the same as that between the CHAR and NCHAR datatypes. We described this difference in Chapter 20.

CLOBs are intended primarily for large bodies of text. Picture an online library. What would a data item for such a library be? A page? A book? Clearly not a word. A body of text is something you need to treat as a whole while also being able to independently treat its parts if desired. Even a Boolean search of the sort that Web search engines provide would be complicated and extremely inefficient to implement with LIKE. Hence, large bodies of text form a new category of single items—those that also have components that need to be independently treated. CLOBs also may have uses beyond these relatively obvious ones. For example, VRML (Virtual Reality Modeling Language) is ASCII-based, and VRML components could be treated as CLOBs. Likewise, many potential scientific and technical applications use forms of data that can be expressed as CLOBs. Because it is difficult to generalize about what CLOBs may be used for or how they will be structured, there is little direct functionality in Core for directly manipulating the internals of CLOBs. That will have to be left to the implementation, the application, the user, or to the external routines described elsewhere in this chapter.

For the most part, the rules concerning CLOBs are the same as those for BLOBs, described in the previous section. The main differences are as follows:

- Unlike BLOBs, CLOBs are sortable. You can compare them in terms of inequalities, such as < or >=. In fact, like other text datatypes, CLOBs have collations and can have translations. For more information on these items, see Chapter 20 and "Collations" in the reference.

- Datatypes other than BLOBs can be cast as CLOBs, although CLOBs cannot be cast as other datatypes. Other datatypes can be cast neither to nor from BLOBs. For more on datatype casting, see "CAST Expressions" in the reference.

- CLOBs are a special kind of text datatype, and therefore the special attributes and functions associated with text datatypes are available. For example, CLOBs have character sets and collations and can have translations. You can use string value functions on them.

Let's suppose we wanted to keep our salespeople's resumes in the Salespeople table. Here some variations on the statement to add the resume column:

```
ALTER TABLE Salespeople ADD COLUMN resume CLOB(20K);
ALTER TABLE Salespeople ADD COLUMN resume NCLOB(20K);
ALTER TABLE Salespeople
    ADD COLUMN resume CHARACTER LARGE OBJECT(20K);
ALTER TABLE Salespeople
    ADD COLUMN resume NATIONAL CHARACTER LARGE OBJECT(20K);
```

The national character versions, of course, will have a different character set.

External SQL-Invoked Routines

Another of the important Core SQL extensions is the ability to invoke from SQL routines written in other languages, such as C, Java, Perl, and so on. Core SQL provides a way for you to do this by specifying routines as SQL objects that are essentially wrappers for routines written in another language. The wrapper provides an interface from SQL to the other language, so that the routine can operate as part of SQL despite the fact that it is not written that way. The specification provided in the standard for this is necessarily somewhat incomplete because platform- and language-specific issues inevitably come into play. Since the DBMS cannot itself execute these external routines, it must pass execution elsewhere to do so. Also, these routines will not be stored as data in the DBMS, so there must be some way to specify where they are, such as in a shared (or dynamic linked) library. These are implementation-defined matters.

Nonetheless, Core SQL is relatively sophisticated in the support it does provide. In part, this is because the syntax for creating and invoking external routines is the same as that for SQL procedures and functions. However, the latter are not part of Core but are instead part of the Persistent Stored Modules (PSM) enhanced conformance level. Other than the actual content of the procedure or function, the syntax for creating and executing SQL and external routines is mostly the same.

External routines can be functions, procedures, or methods. Methods are considered a special case of functions and are only relevant if the DBMS supports abstract UDTs, which are not part of Core (for more on abstract UDTs, see Chapter 24). The difference between functions and procedures is the standard one in programming: functions return a value and are therefore used as value expressions, whereas procedures simply do something and are therefore used as statements. Procedures can also return one or more values through output parameters but not directly as functions do. Methods are functions whose return value is an object (a structured UDT).

External routines are objects in a schema, just like tables and views. The actual code will generally reside elsewhere (strictly speaking, this is an implementation matter), but the wrapper will be a database object. There are a number of corollaries to this fact:

- You can create, alter, and drop SQL-invoked routines, using the CREATE, ALTER, and DROP PROCEDURE or FUNCTION statements, respectively, and the DROP ROUTINE statement, which drops either a procedure or a function.

- The use of a routine is controlled by an EXECUTE privilege on the routine. You automatically have the EXECUTE privilege on any routines you create and can GRANT it to and REVOKE it from others at will.

- Routines can be created as part of a CREATE SCHEMA statement but only if they are to be part of the schema being created (for more on CREATE SCHEMA, see the reference under "CREATE SCHEMA").

- A function can take only input parameters. A procedure can take input (IN), output (OUT), or combination (INOUT) parameters. Therefore, a function can produce only one value, the return value, while a procedure can produce as many as you like, one for each output or INOUT parameter. Actually, one of the input parameters to the function can be an INOUT parameter, in which case its final value will be the return value of the function. This enables you to have the effect of functions for routines written in languages that do not support them directly.

- The return values for functions and the parameter values for functions and procedures are SQL datatypes. Conversion to the host-language datatypes is handled just as it is for Embedded SQL (see Appendix E).

- The standard gotchas from Embedded SQL apply. Specifically, this means you can either use or not use indicator variables to indicate NULLs or string truncation. This is a parameter to the CREATE statement, as we shall see.

- If you are using LOBs, you can have the routine return locators.

- The host languages you can use are implemented-defined. The standard supports all of those supported for Embedded SQL. Java, as specified in SQLJ, will be a common extension, as perhaps will be Perl.

- You can use Embedded SQL statements in the external routine, but that complicates matters a lot because you then have to connect to a database from the external routine, which will be independent of the database connection from which you are calling the routine. Doing so is asking for trouble and usually will not achieve anything you could not achieve another way.

So now let's look at some examples of all this in action. First, here is the syntax of the CREATE PROCEDURE and CREATE FUNCTION statements as these are implemented in Core SQL. We omit portions of the syntax relevant only to non-Core features or to external routines that contain SQL:

```
{CREATE PROCEDURE} | {CREATE FUNCTION} routine_name
    ([parameter_declaration.,..])
    [RETURNS datatype [CAST FROM datatype [AS LOCATOR]]
    LANGUAGE language_specification
    [PARAMETER STYLE {SQL | GENERAL}]
    [DETERMINISTIC | NOT DETERMINISTIC]
    [{RETURN NULL ON NULL INPUT} | {CALL ON NULL INPUT}]
    EXTERNAL [NAME external_routine_name]
    [PARAMETER STYLE {SQL | GENERAL}];

parameter_declaration ::=
    [ IN | OUT | INOUT ]
    [ SQL_parameter_name ]
    datatype [AS LOCATOR]
```

The following sections explain the components of the above statements.

Routine Name

The *routine_name* is a SQL identifier. Since Core does not require support for over-loading (having multiple routines with the same name), it may have to be unique for all routines within the schema. Otherwise, the semantics of overloading will be implementation-defined (for Core, though not for more advanced levels of conformance).

Parameter List

Next comes a comma-separated list of parameters. As the syntax diagram above shows, the list must be present, but it may be empty, which is expressed as an empty pair of parentheses.

Each parameter has a mode, either IN, OUT, or INOUT. The mode indicates whether parameter is to pass a value to the routine (IN), receive a value from it (OUT), or both (INOUT). The mode applies only to procedures; the mode of all parameters to functions is IN. For procedures, it is optional for each parameter, and the default for any parameters not specified is IN. We mentioned earlier that a function could take an INOUT parameter. This is true, but you do not declare the INOUT parameter as such. Rather, you set one (and only one) of the parameters in the function in the body and that value becomes the INOUT parameter and the RETURN value of the function. Naturally, the datatype of that parameter must either be the same as the datatype the function returns, as specified by the RETURNS clause, or be CAST to that datatype in the RETURNS clause.

The *SQL_parameter_name* is an optional name that you can use to refer to the parameter within the routine. The reason the name is optional is that parameters are matched to references in the routine on the basis of the order in which they occur. The first parameter in the list gets assigned to the first target available, the second to the second, and so on. The name is merely a convenience to help you keep the parameters straight.

Finally, you specify the datatype of the parameter. This will map to the datatype of the host-language routine according to the rules for Embedded SQL, which are given in Appendix E; for Java, it will map according to the rules for Embedded SQLJ, which are given in Chapter 26. If you wish the parameter to be a locator, of course, you can specify AS LOCATOR.

Returns

The RETURNS clause applies only to functions. It specifies the datatype the function returns, which may be CAST from another datatype. The CAST follows the principles given under "CAST Expressions" in the reference. You generally use it to convert from a SQL datatype that the host language can support to one it cannot. Again, you can include an AS LOCATOR clause to have the function return a locator.

Language

The LANGUAGE clause simply specifies the host language. The Core SQL supported languages are the same as those supported for Embedded SQL (Appendix E). The SQL/PSM enhanced level adds SQL itself as a supported language. Java is a common addition and, if supported, is almost bound to follow the principles of Embedded SQLJ given in Chapter 26. There can be but one language clause and one language. The host language may be able to call subroutines in still other languages (as Java can, for example), but that is of no concern to SQL. It pays attention to only the language it calls directly. By the way, the language the standard supports is called C. If you are using C++, you will still refer to it as C in the LANGUAGE clause, unless your implementation extends the standard by recognizing C++ as such.

In theory, this clause is optional. However, the default is SQL, which is not part of Core. So, for Core SQL, this clause is mandatory.

Parameter Style

If the PARAMETER STYLE is SQL, then you can append indicators to the variables that match the parameters in the host-language routine, and the DBMS will set and use them appropriately (see Chapter 21). Your DBMS may also have the routine set the current value of SQLSTATE, so as to provide you with status information. If the PARAMETER STYLE is GENERAL, you're just passing values around. In this case, you have to be careful of NULLs, of course, although the ON NULL INPUT clause (described below) gives you an alternative way to deal with these.

You can specify the PARAMETER STYLE here or as part of the EXTERNAL clause. It does not matter which you choose, but it must be one or the other, not both.

Deterministic or Non-deterministic

The notion of DETERMINISTIC and NON-DETERMINISTIC routines is based on that of deterministic and possibly non-deterministic queries (see "SELECT" in the reference). The general idea is that a deterministic query or routine is guaranteed to always provide the same answer given the same inputs and the same current data, whereas a non-deterministic one has no such guarantee. Most queries are deterministic (again, the exceptions are outlined under "SELECT" in the reference). How *determinism* will be determined when applied to external routines is implementation-defined, but the general principle is that a routine that will always give the same output provided it has the same input parameters is deterministic and other routines are non-deterministic. You're a bit on your own here: the DBMS has no way of verifying whether the option you choose is, in fact, correct, since this could depend on host-language logic. The default is non-deterministic because that is the safest bet. If you rely on the routine being deterministic when it is not, you could get programming or data-consistency errors, whereas the reverse is likely to be only an inconvenience.

On NULL Input

The question is what to do when one of the input parameters is NULL. The host language cannot necessarily handle SQL NULLs. In fact, it surely cannot, unless you have used indicator variables in the routine and specified the SQL PARAMETER STYLE (see above). Therefore, the best way to deal with NULLs—at least for functions, which must return a value—is to have the function itself return NULL. This is what RETURN NULL ON NULL INPUT does. The response is immediate, since the function is not actually even called. CALL ON NULL INPUT, the default, calls the function as normal and hopes for the best.

External

The EXTERNAL clause specifies that we are dealing with an external, not a SQL, routine. Since only external routines are part of Core, this is a requirement as far as we are concerned in this chapter. The rest of the statement is part of the EXTERNAL clause and therefore also applies only to external routines. The NAME, as indicated, is optional. The binding of the external routine to its SQL wrapper is implementation-defined, so it may or may not rely upon you supplying a name here, and that name may or may not involve some entire path.

Parameter Style

This clause has the same meaning as the previous PARAMETER STYLE above. You may specify it here or there, but not in both places.

Now that we've shown you the pieces, let's see some examples:

```
CREATE PROCEDURE Calculate_payment
      (IN total_balance DEC, IN months_to_pay INT, OUT payment DEC)
      LANGUAGE C
      PARAMETER STYLE SQL
      CALL ON NULL INPUT
      EXTERNAL NAME paycalc;
```

This creates a SQL wrapper called Calculate_payment for a C procedure called paycalc. How the program or library containing paycalc is bound to the DBMS is an implementation-defined matter. This procedure takes the input parameters total_balance and months_to_pay and stores the result of its calculations in the output parameter payment. The CALL ON NULL INPUT goes logically with the SQL PARAMETER STYLE; we can go ahead and call the procedure because we have a way of handling the NULLs. While no relationship is necessary between the PARAMETER STYLE and the ON NULL INPUT clause, when you have to use a GENERAL PARAMETER STYLE you often use RETURN NULL ON NULL INPUT. A GENERAL PARAMETER STYLE might be mandatory if you were invoking a procedure from a library that you were not free to modify.

So how do you invoke this thing? With a CALL statement. Luckily, the CALL statement is considerably simpler than CREATE PROCEDURE. Here is an example:

```
exec sql CALL Calculate_payment(:total_amount,
      :number_of_months, :monthly_payment);
```

Distinct User-Defined Datatypes (UDTs)

As we explained in Chapter 24, user-defined datatypes (UDTs) fall into two categories: distinct and structured. Since only the former are part of Core, we discuss only the former here, though we summarized the latter in Chapter 24.

Distinct UDTs are distinctly less sexy than the structured type. Simply put, a *distinct UDT* is a renamed conventional datatype that restricts possible comparisons. A data item of a given distinct UDT (hereafter, *distinct type*) can be compared only to other items of the same distinct type, not to anything else that happens to be of the same original datatype.

To see the logic of this, let's think a bit about domains. Domains are part of Intermediate SQL92 and are also part of SQL99, though not of Core. Nonetheless, distinct types and domains complement each other. However, the idea of a domain in database theory, as strongly advocated by Ted Codd, the father of relational database, is somewhat different from that found in the standard. In theory, a *domain* denotes a set of values within which, and only within which, direct comparisons make sense. For example, it makes no sense to compare social security numbers and telephone numbers, even though both are numbers and could be of the same datatype: they are in different domains.

A *domain* in the standard, however, is something slightly different. It is a conventional datatype combined with one or more of the following:

- One or more constraints

- A default value

- A collation

All of the above are optional for any given domain, though it would be senseless to have a domain that did not include at least one of them (for more information on domains, see "CREATE DOMAIN" in the reference). Thus, you could create a marital_status domain based on the CHAR datatype. This domain could be restricted to the values 'S', 'M', and 'D', with a default of 'S' and no collation (which would mean the collation of the underlying datatype applies by default). You probably would not do this for only one marital status column, of course, but you would if you had a huge number of such columns in various tables and wanted to standardize the possible values and the default across all of them. What you do is use the domain in place of the datatype in all CREATE TABLE statements that have such columns. Then you do not need to code the constraint and the default separately and can be assured that they will be the same for all marital_status columns. This is very practical, but it does not restrict comparisons as Codd's domains would. Values in the domain marital_status could still be compared in queries to any other text string, such as names, even though the comparison would make no sense. Domains as the SQL standards have defined them do not provide the particular type of integrity protection that Codd sought.

Therefore, the standards committee came up with distinct types, which pretty much do what Codd wanted for domains. Social security numbers (SSNs) could be one distinct type and telephone numbers another. Both could be based on the INTEGER datatype, but attempts to compare SSNs to phone numbers would produce an error. That's the idea. Such a comparison indicates that you are doing something wrong, so the error helps you find the mistake. However, distinct types do not do what SQL92 domains do, which is to standardize constraints and so on. So, if you have an implementation that supports both Core and domains, you can combine them by creating a distinct type and then creating domains based upon the distinct type. You do not *have* to do this, however. Domains and distinct types exist independently of one another, so you can use either, both, or neither, as suits you.

Now that you understand the rationale, here is an example of how to create a distinct type:

```
CREATE TYPE phone_number AS INTEGER(10) FINAL;
CREATE TYPE ssn AS INTEGER(9) FINAL;
CREATE TABLE Student
  (studnum     INTEGER(10) NOT NULL PRIMARY KEY,
   phone_num   phone_number,
   ssn_num     ssn);
```

That's it! The distinct type definition doesn't change the meaning or possible values of the datatype at all; it just restricts comparisons. Since these are both based on INTEGERs, they would have to be strict numbers—no dashes or parentheses. The FINAL argument is a required part of the CREATE TYPE syntax, though it is really more meaningful for structured types. It means the datatype being created cannot be subclassed further, which is always true for distinct types, since they are not subclassed in the first place. While you could consider a distinct type to be a subclass of the base datatype in some logical sense, it is not a subclass according to how that term is used in standard SQL. It is also true, however, that you cannot base distinct types on other distinct types, forming a hierarchy. In this sense, you could say that every distinct type is indeed FINAL.

If you do decide you want to compare a distinct type to some other type, you can always cast it as another datatype in the SQL statement wherein you want to make the comparison. These casts follow the rules laid down in the reference under "CAST Expressions". The valid casts of the distinct type are the same as those of the datatype on which it is based.

A distinct type is an object in a schema, just like a table, or, for that matter, a domain. Although you cannot alter it (what would you change?), you can drop it thusly:

```
DROP TYPE phone_number;
```

Also, like other schema objects, a distinct type is preceded by the schema name if referenced from outside the schema. A USAGE privilege is associated with each distinct type, and anyone who wishes to CREATE a TABLE with a column of that type must have the privilege. The creator of the type, of course, automatically has the USAGE privilege with the GRANT OPTION. For more on privileges, see "GRANT" in the reference.

Summary

You have now seen how the most important parts of Core SQL99 work. Core enables you to deal with multimedia data transparently without most of the difficulty that usually comes from trying to move such unwieldy data items around. It lets you create your own datatypes, which are subtypes of the regular datatypes and which preserve operational integrity by prohibiting certain kinds of illogical comparisons.

Core also lets you invoke host-language routines from within SQL. This capacity somewhat changes the function of the database. Now it becomes not only a repository of data, but also an effective repository of code related to that data, from which it can, to a degree, dynamically construct applications. This capacity is furthered in the PSM and Object Support enhanced conformance levels, which, between them, turn the DBMS into an engine, in effect, for dynamically deriving and executing entire applications in response to changes in the data.

Putting SQL to Work

1. We've decided to begin storing Web pages for our customers. Each customer will have one page, stored as a CLOB. The Web pages themselves will be a distinct type. Create the type and then alter the Customers table so that it contains a column for the pages.

2. Let's elaborate further. Each customer Web page may have any number of graphics. Since these are a multi-valued attribute of the Customers table, they will be stored in a separate table (see Chapter 19 for a refresher on this topic). Create a distinct type for pictures and a new Webpics table to hold the graphics.

Combining SQL and Java—SQLJ and JDBC

- Integrating SQL and Java

- What Is Java?

- What Do SQL and Java Offer One Another?

- General Issues

- Using JDBC

- Using Embedded SQLJ

- Persistent Stored SQLJ—Using Java Methods inside the Database

- SQLJ UDTs—Using Java Classes As SQL User-Defined Types

In this chapter, you will learn how SQL can be combined with Java. This appears to be perhaps the strongest trend in application development and is being driven primarily by two standards: JDBC and SQLJ. These two standards are designed to be interoperable. JDBC is a similar architecture to the ODBC standard whereas SQLJ relates more closely to Embedded SQL.

The purpose of this chapter is to introduce these two emerging standards for application development. In previous chapters we explained the framework for using SQL within other languages but spent little time discussing the different constructs within the languages themselves. In order to fully explain the implementations of JDBC and SQLJ, we need to break this pattern and spend some time providing a background for Java. Those of you who are well versed in this language can fast-forward to the more technical explanations related to SQL. For those of you with limited knowledge of the Java language, we will spend some time explaining the fundamentals so that you might glean more from the technical explanations later in the chapter.

WARNING   This chapter is not meant to provide the reader with a full understanding of the Java language but merely to better explain the topic.

Integrating SQL and Java

As we have seen, there are several ways that SQL can be combined with other languages. All of them apply to Java. There is also progress, in the more advanced portions of SQLJ, in making Java an integral part of the DBMS itself. Hence, Java and SQL appear likely to merge to a greater extent than SQL has been merged with any other language. For this reason, SQL and Java merit a separate, rather long, chapter in this book.

The ways in which Java and SQL come together include the following:

JDBC   This is an API, patterned after ODBC, that enables Java objects to call SQL databases. Effectively, it is Java support for Dynamic SQL.

SQLJ   This breaks into various parts, which are described below. Suffice it to say, SQLJ provides Java support for Embedded SQL and for the integration of Java objects into the DBMS. The first of these has been standard

SQL functionality for other languages since SQL86; the second is a new idea specific to Java/SQL integration, though it has some things in common with the SQL99 external routines and UDTs discussed in the previous two chapters.

Although SQL has been widely integrated into other programming languages and tools, one programming paradigm in which SQL was missing was object-oriented languages such as C++, Eiffel, and Smalltalk. This omission was widely recognized and often discussed during the development of SQL99, but no one took the time and effort to write the specifications for embedding SQL in object-oriented languages—until Java.

Java sprung onto the application development scene in the early 1990s as a programming language with a variety of special features, including:

- An orientation toward working over networks such as the Internet

- The ability to have portable executable code, which is supported through the use of virtual machines

- The ability for applications to be dynamically built from independently compiled code pieces

The Status of JDBC and SQLJ

Early on, the Java developers/specifiers at Sun Microsystems recognized a need for accessing persistent data in a SQL database. To accomplish this, they created a specification for an API called JDBC (Java Database Connectivity).

JDBC is a dynamic interface patterned after ODBC (Open Database Connectivity), which is compatible with SQL/CLI. The difference between the two interfaces is that JDBC is designed to be invoked from Java rather than from C/C++. While JDBC is very useful, not every application needs the power and flexibility of a dynamic interface. For some applications, Static SQL embedded in the Java source code is sufficient.

SQLJ is a new standard for enabling Java to interact with SQL and to be incorporated into the functionality of SQL-based DBMSs. Unlike JDBC, which was drafted by Sun Microsystems, SQLJ is produced by an industry consortium. Hence, SQLJ is an official, though not a complete, standard while JDBC is complete but still unofficial in that it is not the product of a recognized standards body. The SQLJ consortium is closely coordinating its work with ANSI, the U.S.-specific equivalent of the

ISO, and includes many members of the ANSI SQL standards committee. Hence, it is expected that SQLJ standards are likely to be incorporated into both the ANSI and ISO SQL standards (which are themselves coordinated) or at least remain compatible with them.

NOTE

Officially, the SQLJ group is not a consortium, since the term "consortium" implies some legal stuff that isn't there. One term that has been used is the "SQLJ non-consortium." Since we are more interested in the technology than the legal terms, we will stick with the slightly inaccurate but descriptive name "SQLJ consortium".

The JDBC standard is also continuing to progress and is being coordinated with SQLJ, in the hope that the two will remain fully compatible. As of now, you can intermix Dynamic SQL using JDBC with Static SQL using Embedded SQLJ (defined below) to your heart's content.

SQLJ consists of the following parts. Note that the following terms are our own (Gruber's), though we have proposed them to the standards committee. There are, as yet, no concise standard terms, though naturally the published standards have (abstruse and rather epic) names. These names along with those of all documents referenced in this chapter are provided in the References section at the end of this chapter.

> **Embedded SQLJ**   This part of the standard is for embedding SQL in Java source code, similar to Embedded SQL used with other languages (see Chapter 21) and is referred to as SQL/OLB (Object Language Bindings). Since it was completed in 1998, Embedded SQLJ is not an enhanced level of SQL99 conformance and does not require Core SQL99 conformance, but only Entry-level SQL92 conformance. This was done so that this portion of SQLJ could be standardized and implemented more quickly than is usual for SQL and similar standards. Formally speaking, SQLJ is actually based on both SQL92 and the PSM portion of SQL99, which was published before the main SQL99 standard. As it turns out, the only part of PSM that Embedded SQLJ relies on is the CALL statement. The CALL statement has also made it into Core SQL99 and was explained in the previous chapter. The SQLJ consortium refers to Embedded SQLJ as SQLJ Part 0.

> **Persistent Stored SQLJ (PSSJ)**   This part of the standard is for storing and executing Java bytecode in a database. It is therefore conceptually somewhat similar to the PSM features of SQL99 (see Chapter 24), with the

important difference that the language being stored is Java or, more likely, a combination of Java and SQL, rather than an extended version of SQL itself. As this book is written, the SQLJ consortium has finished its work and the standards bureaucracy is crossing the last *t* and dotting the last *i*. The SQLJ consortium refers to Persistent Stored SQLJ as SQLJ Part 1.

SQLJ UDTs   This part of the standard is for treating Java objects like SQL99 structured UDTs (see Chapter 24), so that Java becomes a truly integral part of the DBMS. As we speak, work on this is still in progress. SQL UDTs themselves are, of course, part of the Object Support levels of SQL99, rather than of Core, so they are also not implemented as of this writing. For these reasons, we will not cover SQLJ UDTs in detail in this chapter. SQL99 UDTs, however, are covered in Chapter 24. The SQLJ consortium refers to SQLJ UDTs as SQLJ Part 2.

By processing Embedded SQLJ only as an ANSI standard and not as an ISO standard, the SQLJ consortium was able to complete a standard much quicker than possible with the ISO process (two years, minimum) and to get a standard in place based on Entry-level SQL92. The ISO SQL standards committees are currently processing Embedded SQLJ as an ISO standard, but this version will be completed after SQL99 and so will be based on SQL99, not SQL92.

In fact, the Embedded SQLJ standard is based on Java and JDBC, neither of which are yet official standards. Until recently, it would not have been possible to create an ANSI standard based on a non-standard, proprietary specification such as Java, and it is not yet clear whether the same is possible under ISO requirements. Hence, there is some red tape involved in making SQLJ an official ISO standard. This issue will be resolved, but slowly. In any case, ODBC and JDBC are both pretty much accepted industry standards, despite their lack of canonization by the official committee, so this will not necessarily stop the advance of SQLJ. The embedded level of SQLJ has already been commercially implemented as of this writing (not the case for any level of SQL99).

Embedded SQLJ is based on JDBC V1.20, as specified in *JDBC: A Java SQL API, Version 1.20*. This document is available on the Web at http://java.sun.com/. Since the source URLs for Web documents frequently change, we have not included a complete path.

What Is Java?

Java is a programming language designed to facilitate lots of coffee-related puns.

The details of Java are beyond the scope of this book but it is useful to understand several characteristics of the Java language, some of which are attributes of object-oriented languages in general:

Classes and methods Datatypes and the operations on the datatypes

Java Virtual Machine A runtime environment that executes a special form of Java binary code

JAR files Java archives

Other object-oriented (OO) attributes, such as encapsulation, inheritance, and polymorphism, are covered in Chapter 24.

Java is an object-oriented programming language and therefore conforms to the principles of OO languages outlined in Chapter 24, in the section "A Quick Overview of Object-Oriented Concepts". The explanation below outlines how these concepts apply specifically to Java.

Classes and Methods

A Java class is a potentially complex object that consists of a definition of variables and constants, called *instance variables*, and routines that operate on those variables, called *methods*. The components of a class can be either public or private. Public components can be accessed outside of the class, while private components can be accessed only within the class.

Methods in Java fill the same role as do functions and procedures in other languages and are sometimes informally referred to by those terms. A function is a subprogram that returns a value expression to the location in code where it is referenced. A procedure is a subprogram that does not. Java adopts from C the convention of defining procedures as functions whose return value is void. A Java method declaration includes the datatype of the return value. If this type is the keyword "void", then the method has no return value (i.e., it is a *procedure*). For more on procedures and functions, see Chapters 24 and 25.

In Java, to invoke an instance of a method, the method must be qualified by the instance of the class. In the following example, `prepareStatement()` is a method (function) of the class instance myConn. (In a later example, we will see the declaration of myConn.)

The first line of the example declares UpdateOrders to be an instance of type PreparedStatement and sets the instance to the result of the function prepareStatement().

The second line invokes the method setBigDecimal() to associate the variable surcharge with the first placeholder in the SQL statement stored in UpdateOrders.

The third line invokes the procedure executeUpdate.

The fourth line invokes the destructor close. This releases the statement's database and JDBC resources.

```
PreparedStatement updateOrders = myConn.prepareStatement
                    ("UPDATE ORDERS SET AMT = AMT + ? ");
updateOrders.setBigDecimal(1,surchargeLocalVar);
updateOrders.executeUpdate( );
updateOrders.close( )
```

Java Virtual Machines

Java applications can run in the context of a Java Virtual Machine. A Java *Virtual Machine* (VM) is a runtime environment that executes a special form of Java binary code called *bytecode* and converts this into appropriate calls for the local operating system. Hence, the same bytecode is binary-compatible across any platform that has a Java VM. This is superb from a portability standpoint but less than optimal for performance because of the intervening VM layer. For some platforms, you can get programs that compile Java to native code from either source or bytecode, improving performance but sacrificing binary portability. As a compromise, you can use a Just-in-Time (JIT) compiler, which converts bytecode to native code just before execution, which to some degree limits compile-time optimization. You can also create multiple versions of the program, going native where possible and providing bytecode where not. Bytecode is almost always preferable for applets, since you don't know which OS the user will have (and JIT uses bytecode). On the server, it may be better to go native for performance.

JAR Files

A JAR file is a Java archive. One or more Java classes can be packaged in a JAR file, which can then be distributed and downloaded as needed. As part of the packaging, a JAR file can contain a unique binary signature to verify that the JAR file really contains what it claims to contain. JAR files are the mechanism Persistent Stored SQLJ employs to store and use Java routines in a SQL database.

What Do SQL and Java Offer One Another?

Java and SQL make a highly logical combination, since each has functionality the other lacks. Specifically, SQL adds to Java all of the standard database virtues, including logical data independence, concurrency control, and heightened security control. Also, Java applications that use SQL automatically have access to all the data contained in SQL databases, which is considerable. In other words, SQL is combined with Java for primarily the same reasons it is combined with other languages. Therefore, when Java and SQL are combined, it is done basically the same way as when SQL is combined with other languages: SQL is used for database operations, and Java is used for program logic and non-data functionality. However, Java has some special features in this regard because it is an object-oriented rather than a procedural language. As with other languages, Java can be statically coded, as in Embedded SQL (see Chapter 21), or dynamically generated, as in Dynamic SQL (see Chapter 22). The former is Embedded SQLJ and the latter JDBC.

Java is currently seeing considerable use for Internet and Intranet applications. For these applications, Java can be employed in either or both of two forms:

- Applets, which are small Java programs that are dynamically loaded into a Web browser or other client and executed there

- Server-side applications (sometimes called *servlets*), which are Java programs that are executed within a Web server

Either of these forms may use SQL to access a DBMS, but server-side applications do so more commonly and more extensively. This is primarily because server-side applications perform more complex work with data and because extra complexities are involved in accessing a database from an applet. Applets are most frequently used to enhance a Web page interface. For example, the general pattern of a typical Java e-commerce site would be that it uses a server-side application to execute program logic and dynamically derive Web pages that it then sends to the browser. These Web pages may also include applets to enhance the experience or functionality that the Web page provides.

From the standpoint of a SQL database, a Java application using JDBC or Embedded SQLJ is just the same as any other application. From the SQL database standpoint, there is not necessarily any real difference between a COBOL application with Embedded SQL and a Java application with Embedded SQLJ. There are, however, some special considerations of Java, and of Web-based applications, when used in this way:

- Java is generally used in architectures with at least three tiers: browser, Web server, and DBMS. There may be any number of additional middleware layers between the Web server and the DBMS. From the standpoint of the DBMS, the access is coming from the layer that immediately calls it, not from the browser. Even for applets, calls to the DBMS are likely to be made to a cartridge or module, which then passes them to the DBMS. (The Embedded SQLJ standard does not specify this level of detail, so the details may vary among vendors and also depend on how you write your application.)

- Authentication and security are extremely important. The end user is not necessarily an employee working on a terminal in a facility owned by the enterprise. He could be anyone on the Internet. Authentication and security are important even for Intranet applications, since Intranets are typically connected to the Internet. Therefore, you should keep in mind the security vulnerabilities introduced by the situation. Of course, part of the solution to this problem lies in firewalls and in operating system security.

- For Internet users, performance is even more critical than usual. While an employee may suffer through performance issues, a customer on the Internet probably won't. If two companies offer a similar product at similar prices, the one with the best information and the fastest interface is likely to get the most business. This situation is, of course, made more difficult by the fact that performance on the Internet depends largely on the client connection and on the level of Internet traffic itself, so it is not entirely in your hands. Nonetheless, you must be careful to make conservative assumptions about the conditions that will actually hold and code to those. An application that will be accessed by people with 28.8 modems should be user-tested with such access, from outside the firewall, at times when the Internet is congested.

- Concurrent access is more complicated. How many concurrent users will your application have? On the Internet, concurrent access is no longer limited by the number of devices physically connected to the computer; it is limited by the number of simultaneous ports the Web server will support and the bandwidth of the network connection.

In short, a Java-based SQL database application is just another database application, only more so.

SQL databases get even more interesting when you start storing and using Java routines in the database and mixing Java datatypes and classes with SQL datatypes and UDTs (user-defined types). We will address these issues and possibilities in later sections.

Embedded SQLJ is designed so that it can work as a translator that takes the SQLJ source code and translates it into the appropriate JDBC calls. Though it need not be so implemented, it probably will be by most implementers, as this enables them to mix Embedded SQLJ and JDBC to their heart's content.

Given that Embedded SQLJ can be implemented as a translator to JDBC, what are the advantages of using Embedded SQLJ over JDBC? Let's look at a few:

Simpler source code   Writing directly to an API requires a large number of calls that are encapsulated in the relatively high-level statements that SQLJ employs. Some projects have found a 10:1 reduction in source code complexity, which, of course, speeds development and eases debugging.

Metadata validation at compile time   You will find your programming errors earlier. A consequence of this is that the metadata must be in place at compile time. That is to say, all tables and other database objects referenced in the Embedded SQLJ program have to be created before the program is precompiled.

Strongly typed cursors (iterators)   *By position* iterators are matched to the datatypes of the iterators (explained later in this chapter, but essentially SQLJ's version of a cursor) and the SELECT statement at compile time. If the datatypes are not compatible, the Embedded SQLJ precompiler throws an exception (i.e., generates an error). *By name* iterators take this process a step further and match on both name and datatype.

Offline pre-compilation   This aids performance because compilation does not have to occur at execution time.

Definer's rights   Some DBMSs may allow your Embedded SQLJ program to use definer's rights. That is, the Authorization ID used for checking access rights is the programmer's and not the end user's. Since the concept of definer's rights is very loosely defined in SQL92, not all DBMSs support it. We explained Definer's and Invoker's rights in Chapter 21.

You should use Embedded SQLJ where you can (for simplicity and performance) and JDBC where you must (for runtime flexibility). Since JDBC is independent of the database, Embedded SQLJ is also independent of the database. That is, a compiled Embedded SQLJ program can attach to any SQL database implemented with any SQL DBMS as long as there are appropriate JDBC drivers and the databases have all of the tables and columns used by the program. This is a significant change from SQL embedded in procedural languages where you must compile a program against a specific DBMS or even a specific SQL database.

General Issues

A number of issues are common to both the JDBC and Embedded SQLJ interfaces. The following sections discuss these topics.

SQL in an Object-Oriented World

One of the critical points in understanding how Embedded SQLJ and JDBC interact with Java is that both are based on SQL92, not SQL99. Therefore, neither takes advantage of the SQL99 OO capabilities.

There is no special syntax in Embedded SQLJ or JDBC for creating tables as or mapping them to Java classes. The programmer must create any mappings.

While SQL99 supports complex user-defined datatypes and other object-oriented concepts, SQL database concepts and implementations do not completely map to object-oriented programming languages, and OO programming languages do not completely map to SQL database concepts.

For more details about object-oriented concepts, see the section "A Quick Overview of Object-Oriented Concepts" in Chapter 24.

Datatype Matching

As with the other languages with which SQL interacts (see Appendix E), Java developers face the issue of how to map SQL datatypes to the datatypes used in the other language. With Java, there is an additional issue: Which methods are used to set and retrieve values of that datatype? The reason Java works this way, of course, is that it is an object-oriented language, and therefore all of the items on which it operates are objects. You perform operations on objects using methods.

All Java type specifications are case sensitive. Types prefixed with java.math are defined in the Java math package. Types prefixed with java.sql are defined in the JDBC package. Table 26.1 illustrates mapping from SQL types to Java types. Table 26.2 shows mapping from Java types to SQL types.

TABLE 26.1:   Mapping from SQL Types to Java Types

SQL Type	Java Type
CHAR	java.lang.String
VARCHAR	java.lang.String
LONGVARCHAR	java.lang.String
NUMERIC	java.math.BigDecimal
DECIMAL	java.math.BigDecimal
BIT	boolean
TINYINT	byte
SMALLINT	short
INTEGER	int
BIGINT	long
REAL	float
FLOAT	double
DOUBLE	double
BINARY	byte[]
VARBINARY	byte[]

Continued on next page

TABLE 26.1 CONTINUED: Mapping from SQL Types to Java Types

SQL Type	Java Type
LONGVARBINARY	byte[]
DATE	java.sql.Date
TIME	java.sql.Time
TIMESTAMP	java.sql.Timestamp

TABLE 26.2: Mapping from Java Types to SQL Types

Java Type	SQL Type
java.lang.String	VARCHAR or LONGVARCHAR
java.math.BigDecimal	NUMERIC
boolean	BIT
byte	TINYINT
short	SMALLINT
int	INTEGER
long	BIGINT
float	REAL
double	DOUBLE
byte[]	VARBINARY or LONGVARBINARY
java.sql.Date	DATE
java.sql.Time	TIME
java.sql.Timestamp	TIMESTAMP

The Java type boolean is mapped to a SQL BIT datatype. However, a SQL92 BIT datatype is a BIT string, not a single bit as implied by "boolean". There is no direct support in JDBC for SQL92 BIT and BIT VARYING strings of length greater than one.

SQL also defines ASCII, Binary, and Unicode stream classes that are derived from `java.io.InputStream`. These enapsulate streaming data. The details of using these classes are beyond the scope of this book.

Java and JDBC offer no direct support for the SQL92 INTERVAL datatype.

LONGVARCHAR is a SQL99 datatype that got slipped into JDBC.

The following datatypes listed above are not actually standard SQL datatypes. They will be mapped to standard datatypes as determined by the SQL implementation.

- BIGINT

- TINYINT

- VARBINARY

- LONGVARBINARY

NULL Values

The Java scalar types boolean, byte, short, int, long, float, and double do not support SQL NULL values. However, additional types that *do* support NULL values are available in the java.lang package. Table 26.3 shows mapping from SQL types to Java types with NULLs. Note that these datatypes all begin with a capital letter, distinguishing them from the types that do not support NULLs.

TABLE 26.3:   Mapping from SQL Types to Java Types with NULLs

SQL Type	Java Type with NULL
BIT	java.lang.Boolean
TINYINT	java.lang.Byte
SMALLINT	java.lang.Short
INTEGER	java.lang.Integer
BIGINT	java.lang.Long
REAL	java.lang.Float
FLOAT	java.lang.Double

Continued on next page

TABLE 26.3 CONTINUED: Mapping from SQL Types to Java Types with NULLs

SQL Type	Java Type with NULL
DOUBLE	java.lang.Double
BINARY	java.lang.Byte[]
VARBINARY	java.lang.Byte[]
LONGVARBINARY	java.lang.Byte[]

Java is case-sensitive, and your program's ability to support SQL NULLs can therefore hinge on a single letter. For example, if you place a SQL NULL in a variable defined as type "float" (lowercase f), it will generate an error, while one placed in a "Float" variable will work. All Java datatypes that are composite or that support variable sizes support NULLs, although the primitive fixed-length types do not. You can use the Java NULL to represent the SQL NULL and so avoid the need for NULL indicator variables, discussed in Chapter 21. Of course, if you want, you can use NULL indicator variables with host variables that are simple datatypes. Java is not based on three-valued logic, however. Therefore, to get the full effect of NULLs in SQL, you should detect or create them and structure your logic accordingly. There are methods for working with NULLs that will be mentioned in the next section.

Exception-Handling

The Java language allows you to build very complete exception-trapping and exception-handling into your programs using its `try-catch` syntax. JDBC adds specific support for SQL with the classes `java.sql.SQLException` (a subclass of `java.lang.Exception`), `java.sql.SQLWarning` (a subclass of `java.sql`
`.SQLException`), and `java.sql.DataTruncation` (a subclass of `java.sql`
`.SQLWarning`). These classes add support for both catching and interpreting SQL exceptions and for creating and throwing SQL exceptions. These classes map directly to SQLCODE and SQLSTATE values as follows:

- java.sql.DataTruncation corresponds to a SQLSTATE of '01004'.

- java.sql.SQLWarning corresponds to a SQLSTATE of '02', with any subclass, or to a SQLCODE of 100.

- java.sql.SQLException corresponds to any other non-zero SQLSTATE or SQLCODE.

For more information on these conditions, or on SQLSTATE and SQLCODE, see Chapter 21 and Appendix C.

The following code fragment shows some of the capabilities of Java exception handling:

```
import java.sql.SQLException;
try
{
  //Embedded SQLJ or JDBC statement
  //that generates an exception
} catch (SQLException currExc)
    { // Handle a SQL Exception
      System.err.println( "Exception at location:") ;
      System.err.println(currExc);
      string currSQLState = currExc.getSQLState();
      // could now do something specific based
      // on the SQLstate
    }
```

This example wraps a `try-catch` around a SQL statement that might throw a SQL exception. The exception is assigned to `currExc` in the `catch` statement. As with any other programming language, the appropriate response to a SQL exception in a JDBC or Embedded SQL program depends on what your program needs to do.

Using JDBC

JDBC is a form of Dynamic SQL that provides a uniform API to various DBMSs. It does this through the use of a code module called a *driver* or *cartridge* that receives calls from the executing Java object, translates them into calls to a particular DBMS, and then communicates with the DBMS on behalf of the program that invoked it. This approach is based on that of ODBC, and, in fact, you can get drivers called *jdbc:odbc bridges*, which enable JDBC drivers to call ODBC drivers that then call the DBMS in turn. Although this gives you a way to support DBMSs for which there may not be a JDBC driver available, adding two intervening layers in two different languages is asking for trouble. Don't do it unless you have to.

JDBC comes in the form of a package, which is a formal group of Java classes. Depending on which version of Java Software Development Kit (SDK) you have, this package will have one or the other of the following names:

- package.java.sql
- package.javax.sql

For our purposes, the differences between the two do not matter, and we will assume you are using the former.

Under JDBC, database interaction is encapsulated in methods. Hence, you do not directly code DECLARE CURSOR or EXECUTE IMMEDIATE statements, as you saw in Chapter 22. Rather you invoke Java methods that act as wrappers for these statements. By *wrappers* is meant that you deal with the methods, and the methods generate the Dynamic SQL for you. JDBC has special methods for getting metadata information, although you could also use SQL queries against the INFORMATION_SCHEMA for some of this information, as was shown in Chapter 18. Of course, such SQL statements would still be encapsulated in methods.

Like all other methods in Java, those that encapsulate database operations are contained in classes. Here are the main classes JDBC uses for database operations. Most of these JDBC classes implement interfaces with the same names as the class, so you may encounter these names used for interfaces elsewhere in the literature:

DriverManager   Objects of this class select and interact with JDBC drivers.

Connection   Objects of this class encapsulate database connections (sessions).

Statement   Objects of this class each encapsulate a single SQL statement at a time. They can be reused for multiple statements one after another, however. These are statements prepared and executed in one step.

PreparedStatement   Objects of this class each encapsulate a prepared statement.

ResultSet   Objects of this class store the results of queries. That is to say, they encapsulate cursors, one object per cursor.

DatabaseMetaData   Objects of this class store information about the DBMS, its capabilities, and the objects it contains.

ResultSetMetaData   Objects of this class describe `ResultSets` in detail. We won't be covering this particular class in this discussion, but we mention it so that you can look it up more easily if you need this information.

The following relationships hold among these objects (though somewhat analogous, these relationships are not derived from the ER model like those in Chapter 19):

- There is a 1:n relationship between `DriverManagers` and `Connections`. That is to say, several `Connections` may use the same driver, but each `Connection` will use only one driver, which will, in turn, be under the control of one `DriverManager`.

- There is a 1:n relationship between `Connections` and `Statements` or `PreparedStatements`. That is to say, several `Statements` may take place in the same `Connection`, but each `Statement` takes place in the context of one and only one `Connection`.

- There is a 1:n relationship between `Statements` or `PreparedStatements` (for the rest of this discussion, lowercase statement objects will be a generic term covering both variations) and `ResultSets`. That is to say, each statement object can have several `ResultSets` (if the statement is not a query, it can produce none) because the statement object can be iterated multiple times (for distinct statements with `Statement` or for the same statement for `PreparedStatement`). A given `ResultSet` contains the output of one statement object.

These relationships become important because they determine the context relationships among the objects. A `Connection` has to exist in the context of a driver, and therefore of a `DriverManager` object. For that reason, it is a method in `DriverManager` that is used to create a database connection for a `Connection` object. The `Connection` object, like all Java objects, does have a constructor that is invoked when you create an instance of the class. However, this constructor merely allocates the object; it does not create the actual connection. To do this, you use the `getConnection()` method of the `DriverManager` class, as you will see shortly.

Likewise, statement objects exist in the context of `Connections` and are given values by methods in `Connections`. `ResultSets` exist in the context of statement objects and are given values by methods in those classes. Later, in the Embedded SQLJ section, we will elaborate further on the concept of context.

Making and Managing Database Connections

The basic procedure to make a database connection is as follows:

- Load the JDBC driver. Although setting up and configuring your system with JDBC is beyond the scope of this discussion, loading the appropriate JDBC driver is something you do from within your Java code using the forname() method.

- Create a Connection object

- Use DriverManager.getConnection() to create a database connection associated with the Connection object.

The following code fragment illustrates these steps. Note the comments in the code for explanation:

```
Connection myConn = null;
// This line creates an instance of the Connection class
   // called "myConn". It is initialized to an empty value,
   // which is distinct from a SQL NULL.
   try {
        Class.forName("jdbc.driver1");
        //This method loads the driver called "jdbc.driver1"
        // The quotation marks are not part of the name.
        myConn = DriverManager.getConnection
                        ("jdbc:default:connection",
                         "Ashley",
                         "LeFanu");
        // This is the method that actually creates the
        // connection. Note that it is a method in the DriverManager,
        // not the Connection, class. It connects to the database
        // identified by jdbc:default:connection (this is
        // called a db-url}. Ashley and LeFanu are
        // the username and password respectively.
        // The Connection object myConn is now associated
        // with a specific database connection.

        catch (Exception currException)
           {
            System.err.println("JDBC connection error:") ;
            System.err.println(currException);
            System.exit(1);
           }
```

Driver Classes

In the previous example, `jdbc.driver1` is the name of a class that is a valid JDBC driver. This name is specific to a particular JDBC driver implementation. Examples are:

- `sun.jdbc.odbc.JdbcOdbcDriver`

- `oracle.jdbc.driver.OracleDriver`

According to the JDBC 1.2 specification, a JDBC driver should register itself with the JDBC driver manager when its class is loaded. However, some drivers may require the programmer to register the driver after it is loaded. The previous example could be expanded to register the driver using the `DriverManager .registerDriver()` method, as shown here:

```
Connection myConn = null;
try {
    Class.forName("jdbc.driver1");
    DriverManager.registerDriver
                    ((Driver)myDrvrClss.newInstance()
                     );

    myConn = DriverManager.getConnection(...)
    ...
}
```

You will need to read the documentation for the drivers you are using to find out whether they register themselves or you need to register them.

Database Universal Resource Locator

A *db-url* string has the form `jdbc:jdbc-vendor:vendor-specific-info`. Some examples are:

- `jdbc:default:connection`

- `jdbc:my_subprotocol:my_subname`

- `jdbc:odbc:odbc-data-source`

The vendor-specific-information is, well, vendor specific. You will need to read the documentation for your DBMS or JDBC driver vendor to locate the information you must include.

getConnection()

There are three forms of `DriverManager.getConnection()`:

- `DriverManager.getConnection(String)`

- `DriverManager.getConnection(String, Properties)`

- `DriverManager.getConnection(String, String, String)`

The first string in each form is always the *db-url*. The first form uses only the *db-url*. In the second form, Properties is a list of tag-value pairs. This list will probably include a username and password. A vendor would require this form when additional information is needed. The third form is the one used above where the second and third parameters are the username and password.

Building Statements

From within a database connection, you issue statements. Therefore you use a method in the `Connection` class to create values for the objects that encapsulate SQL statements. The most important of these objects are `Statement` and `PreparedStatement` (there are other classes for more specialized operations, some of which we will introduce shortly). The `Statement` class wraps EXECUTE IMMEDIATE, whereas the `PreparedStatement` class wraps EXECUTE (PREPARE itself is wrapped by `Connection.prepareStatement()`). `PreparedStatements` can take dynamic parameters (which are usually called *placeholders* in the Java world) and be executed multiple times with differing values for these. For more on this, see Chapter 22. The methods used to create statement objects are as follows.

To create a one-time statement:

```
Connection.createStatement();
```

To create a prepared statement:

```
Connection.prepareStatement("SELECT * FROM Salespeople");
```

These methods return objects of types `Statement` and `PreparedStatement`, respectively. Note that in the case of the prepared statements, you give the query string when the object is initialized. This is the equivalent of Dynamic SQL PREPARE. For `Statements`, you give the statement later at execute time, which will be the equivalent of Dynamic SQL EXECUTE IMMEDIATE (though you need not include the EXECUTE IMMEDIATE syntax, only the content of the dynamic statement). The statement objects use the following methods.

executeQuery() This executes a query. For `Statement` objects, the text of the query or a string variable containing the same is passed as an input parameter (if it is the text, it will be double-quoted). Also, for `Statement` objects, the query can return but a single row (in other words, it must be usable in a SELECT ...INTO form, as shown in Chapter 21). For `Prepared-Statement` objects, `executeQuery()` takes no parameters. There are other methods used to set the dynamic parameter values. In either case, the results of the query will be stored in a cursor wrapped in a `ResultSet`. Since this method returns a `ResultSet` object, there should be a `ResultSet` declared to receive it.

executeUpdate() This executes a DML update statement in the generic sense—that is to say, either an INSERT, an UPDATE, or a DELETE. It follows the same rules as `executeQuery()`, save that it does not produce a `ResultSet` object, but merely a count of the number of rows affected by the operation.

close() This is used only by the `Statement` class and frees the resources (allocated memory and so on) used by the statement. The `Connection` and `ResultSet` classes have similar `close()` methods that also free up resources.

For `PreparedStatements`, you use a group of methods beginning with "set" to set the dynamic parameter values. Some examples are `setDate()`and `setInt()`. The other datatypes have corresponding methods. There is also a `setNull()` method you can use to set an input parameter of any datatype to a SQL NULL. Here is a code fragment that creates a PreparedStatement:

```
PreparedStatement updateOrders = myConn.prepareStatement
                    ("UPDATE ORDERS
                            SET amt = amt + ? ");
// Creates a PreparedStatement object
updateOrders.setBigDecimal(1,surchargeLocalVar);
// Assigns a value to the dynamic parameter
int updatedCount = updateOrders.executeUpdate( );
// Executes the statement. updatedCount is a variable that holds
// the number of rows updated (the return value of
// executeUpdate().)
PreparedStatement insertOrders = myConn.prepareStatement
("INSERT INTO ORDERS(onum, amt, odate, cnum, snum)
        VALUES(?,?,?,?,?)" };
```

```
// Creates another PreparedStatement object
insertOrders.setInt(1, onumLocalVar);
insertOrders.setBigDecimal(2, amtLocalVar);
insertOrders.setDate(3, odateLocalVar);
insertOrders.setInt(4, cnumLocalVar);
insertOrders.setInt(5, snumLocalVar);
// Sets several dynamic parameters.
insertOrders.executeUpdate( );
// Executes the statement
```

In the previous examples, the statement is prepared and then executed only once. However, once a statement is prepared, it could be executed many times. For example, the insertOrders statement could be prepared once, then the input of data accepted from a form and the insert into the database performed in a loop. When the statement is executed, the contents of the variables are evaluated and used to fill in the dynamic parameters.

If the statement is syntactically invalid, the prepareStatement() method will throw a SQLException.

Results Sets

A SQL query processed by the executeQuery() method creates a cursor that returns rows into a JDBC ResultSet. Initially, the ResultSet is positioned before the first row in the cursor. The next() method is used to fetch the next record in the cursor. Therefore, the next() method wraps the SQL FETCH statement. Each column in the cursor can be accessed using getXXX() methods where XXX is the datatype of the column. Each of the getXXX() methods has two forms. One accepts the column name as the parameter, while the other accepts the column index—its relative position in the SELECT statement. The column index form is likely to be faster and is unambiguous. The column name form is more immune to change, but if a ResultSet contains two columns with the same name, only the first matching column is returned. It is possible for a ResultSet to have more than one like-named column because it is based on the SELECT columns of the query, rather than the columns of any particular table. You can retrieve SQL NULLs using the getNull() method. Let's look at this example:

```
int snum = 0;
String sname = null;
String city  = null;
float  commission = 0.0;
```

```
// The above are program variables that will hold values
// from the query output. Note that they can but need not
// be the same as the column names on which they are based.
PreparedStatement GetSalesPeople = myConn.prepareStatement
      ("SELECT snum, sname, city, comm
            FROM Salespeople" };
// Creates a PreparedStatement holding the indicated query.
ResultsSet SalesPeople = GetSalesPeople.executeQuery();
// Creates a ResultSet holding the output of the query.
SalesPeople.next();
// Performs a FETCH on the ResultSet cursor, i.e., advances it
// one row.
While (SalesPeople.getWarnings() == null )
    // While neither error nor no data.
    {
    snum = SalesPeople.getInt(1);
    sname = SalesPeople.getString(2);
    // The above two retrieve column values by index.
    city = SalesPeople.getString("city");
    commission = SalesPeople.getFloat("comm");
    // The above two retrieve column values by name.
    System.out.println (sname + " has an SNUM of " + snum);
    // Print a string involving snum and sname.
    SalesPeople.next();
    // FETCH cursor.
    }
SalesPeople.close();
// This closes and deallocates the cursor, freeing the resources
// used.
```

Managing JDBC Transactions

By default, a JDBC connection is created in autocommit mode. That is, a transaction is implicitly started each time a statement is executed. If the statement is successful, the transaction is committed. If the statement fails, the transaction is rolled back.

While this may be desirable behavior in some instances, in others it is useful to have the JDBC program explicitly control the transaction characteristics. JDBC includes a number of methods that allow you to find out the current transaction characteristics and change them. Look at the methods in this code fragment:

```
if (myConn.getAutoCommit())
// The getAutoCommit() method returns true if autocommit is set on.
then
    {myConn.setAutoCommit(false);
// Disable autocommit. Now autocommit is definitely false.
    }
boolean everythingOK = true;
// We'll pretend that there is some code here
// that uses exception handling to set
// everythingOK to false if there is a problem
if (everythingOK)
then
    {myConn.commit();
    }
else
    {myConn.rollback();
    }
// The above manually commits on no error and rolls back on error.
// Whether there was an error was determined by whatever you did
// with everythingOK, rather than automatically. Therefore, you get
// to define which conditions mandate a rollback.
```

The method isReadOnly() enables you to find out if a connection is read only, and setReadOnly() lets you change that characteristic. The method getTransactionIsolation() enables you to find out the current isolation level while setTransactionIsolation() enables you to change the isolation levels. Invoking setReadOnly() and setTransactionIsolation() while a transaction is active will throw a SQLException. For more on transactions, see Chapter 17 and "SET TRANSACTION" in Chapter 28.

Cleanup

The following example uses the close() method to clean up the resources used by the insertOrders statement and myConn connection.

```
myConn.close(); // Close the connection
```

Closing the Connection automatically closes all Statement, PreparedStatement, ResultSet, and other objects associated with it. This is important to remember, because, if you close the Connection, references to the ResultSet also become invalid. You can close ResultSets and Statements, but not PreparedStatements, without closing the Connection. It is generally a good idea to clean up after yourself to free up resources.

DatabaseMetaData

The JDBC DatabaseMetaData interface is a set of methods for finding out information about a database. Using these methods allows you to create a program that first queries the SQL database to find out what syntax it supports and what tables are available, then create SQL statements to query and update that data.

The `Connection.getMetaData()` method returns a `DatabaseMetaData` object:

```
DatabaseMetaData myConnMetaData = myConn.getMetaData();
```

You can get information about the JDBC driver associated with your connection as shown here:

```
String drvrNam = myConnMetaData.getDriverName();
String drvrVer = myConnMetaData.getDriverVersion();
```

You can get information about the SQL product to which you are connected like this:

```
String dbProdName =
        myConnMetaData.getDatabaseProductName();
String dbProdVersion =
        myConnMetaData.getDatabaseProductVersion();

boolean entrySQL92 =
        myConnMetaData.supportsANSI92EntryLevelSQL();
boolean intermediateSQL92 =
        myConnMetaData.supportsANSI92IntermediateLevelSQL();
boolean fullSQL92 =
        myConnMetaData.supportsANSI92FullLevelSQL();
```

All JDBC drivers are supposed to return a true for the method `supportsANSI92EntryLevelSQL()`.

You can get information about the SQL database to which you are connected in this manner:

```
String currDBURL = myConnMetaData.getURL();

ResultSet myTables = myConnMetaData.getTables
                (catalogNameString
                ,schemaPatternString
```

```
                ,tableNamePatternString
                ,tableTypesList[]
                );

ResultSet myColumns = myConnMetaData.getColumns
                (catalogNameString
                ,schemaPatternString
                ,tableNamePatternString
                ,columnNamePatternString
                );
```

The `tableTypesList` argument is an array of strings that contain values such as TABLE, VIEW, SYSTEM TABLE, GLOBAL TEMPORARY, and LOCAL TEMPORARY. These values are the types of objects that the DBMS recognizes.

Using Embedded SQLJ

In many respects, Embedded SQLJ is just SQL embedded in another programming language, as described in Chapter 21. As with other languages, Static SQL statements are intermingled with the ordinary code of the language. A program called a precompiler converts these embedded statements to Java calls to an API that can be executed against a database. In the case of SQLJ, it is most commonly converted to JDBC calls, although it could also be converted to another API. If another API is used, however, the behavior must emulate JDBC in several respects, such as the handling of connection context. This feature enables you to intermix SQLJ and JDBC seamlessly. As with other embedded forms of SQL, syntax checking and optimization occur at precompile time, rather than runtime. The advantages and disadvantages of SQLJ as opposed to JDBC are pretty much the same as Embedded vs. Dynamic SQL generally, save that Embedded SQLJ also has a considerably simpler syntax than JDBC.

As with other forms of Embedded SQL, Embedded SQLJ is implemented primarily as a feature by DBMS vendors. Such vendors will supply the precompiler that examines Java source (not byte) code and converts the flagged SQL statements. As of this writing, vendors supporting Embedded SQLJ include IBM, Oracle, Informix, Sybase, and Compaq. Installing and configuring tools for these vendors is a platform-specific matter and therefore beyond the scope of this discussion. The package of classes that support SQLJ is usually called `sqlj.runtime`.

In most languages, the text that flags Embedded SQL code is the keywords EXEC SQL; in Embedded SQLJ, it is the string `#sql`. The statement terminator is the semicolon. The SQLJ class libraries you reference in your code are in the package `sqlj.runtime`, and classes you create that use SQLJ end in the extension `.sqlj`.

Connecting to Databases and Managing Database Connection Context

Applications that access a DBMS over a network generally need to be concerned with one or more kinds of *context*. The reason is that all traffic between the two entities—the application and the DBMS—is realized as a series of network calls, and each entity may be communicating with several others. The DBMS could be communicating with different Web servers, for example, and each Web server with different DBMSs. However, both the DBMS session and the application generally have *state* (a DBMS session always does), which means that certain things must be consistent. If a variable is set when an application initiates a session, it should still be set when the application contacts that session again, unless something has specifically been done to change it. This is called *maintaining state*. Since potentially numerous entities can simultaneously use the DBMS, and these entities in some cases can also be in contact with other DBMSs, there must be a way to consistently correlate the state of the DBMS with the state of the application—and possibly with other kinds of state as well. This is called *context*, and it is generally maintained by passing identifiers between the application and the DBMS. Each of these identifies a particular context and is called a *context handle*. Sometimes, context must be handled simultaneously at multiple levels, e.g., the DBMS session context, the network context, and the SQL transaction context.

In the case of SQLJ, there are the following kinds of context handles:

ConnectionContext   This tracks the SQL database connection. The convention is a little different here, as `ConnectionContext` is the name of the interface, but you create and name the class that implements it yourself, as you will see. The class you create effectively wraps a JDBC `Connection` object (discussed earlier in this chapter) and any number of `ExecutionContext` objects (below). A given SQL statement can either specify a connection context or use the default.

ExecutionContext   This is for tracking information relevant to the execution of a particular SQL statement. Each `ExecutionContext` tracks information for one statement. If a new statement is issued using this context, the information for the previous statement is lost. You can retain this information by having multiple ExecutionContexts in the Connection-Context. You should do this for statements that are intended to be executed concurrently.

The creation of a SQLJ connection context takes place in two stages. First, you use the keyword "context" to create a new context class. This is called a *generated context class*, and it automatically inherits a body of appropriate methods and variables. Then you instantiate this generated class using arguments that also create the JDBC Connection object that will underlie it. Here is an example that creates a SQLJ connection context and then performs two database operations, one using the new context and one using the default:

```
#sql context MyDBContext;
// This creates a generated context class called MyDBContext.
MyDBContext myContext = new MyDBContext
    ("jdbc:default:connection", "Ashley", "LeFanu")
// This instantiates the MyDBContext class as the object
// myContext. It also creates the JDBC Connection object
// that will underlie the SQLJ context object. Note that
// the parameters you pass in are the same as for the
// getConnection() JDBC method, as shown in the previous
// section of this chapter.
#sql [myContext] { UPDATE ORDERS
                    SET amt = amt + :surchargeLocalVar};
// This statement takes place on the created
// connection context.
#sql { INSERT INTO ORDERS(onum, amt, odate, cnum, snum)
          VALUES(:onumLocalVar,:amtLocalVar,
                 :odateLocalVar,:cnumLocalVar,
                 :snumLocalVar) };
// This statement takes place on the default connection
// context.
```

If myContext is the current default context, these two SQL statements operate on the same database connection. If not, they operate on different database connections and possibly on different DBMSs entirely.

Clearly, you need a mechanism to both set the default context and find the current default context. You accomplish this using the setDefaultContext() and getDefaultContext() methods. Since the default context object is a static variable, Embedded SQLJ programs that are multi-threaded or reentrant should use an explicit connection context.

In a SQL statement, the database context is a variable that is evaluated at runtime. Therefore, it is possible to use the same SQL statement against different connection contexts, as shown here:

```
#sql context CurrDBContext;
if {some condition}
// We assume there is a test here to control program flow.
then
    {CurrDBContext = myContext;}
else
    {CurrDBContext = yourContext;}
// The following statement is executed against whichever
// context was set by the preceding test.
#sql [currDBContext] {UPDATE ORDERS
                        SET amt = amt + :surchargeLocalVar };
```

An Embedded SQLJ connection context object is similar to but slightly different than a JDBC Connection object. The primary difference is the default transaction characteristics. We'll discuss transaction characteristics in more detail in a later section.

An Embedded SQLJ connection context object can be constructed from a JDBC Connection object. In the following example, myConn is a JDBC Connection object:

```
#sql context MyDBContext;
MyDBContext myContext = new MyDBContext(myConn);
```

A JDBC Connection object can be created from an Embedded SQLJ connection context object using the getConnection() method, which is one of the methods that your generated context class will automatically have. In the following example, myContext is an Embedded SQLJ connection context object:

```
Connection sharedConn = null;
sharedConn = myContext.getConnection();
```

This sharing of connections enables you to seamlessly mix SQLJ and JDBC operations.

Execution Context

The execution context methods defined in the class sqlj.runtime.Execution-Context allow the developer to control some characteristics of the execution environment and to get information about the execution of the most recent SQL statement. The Execution Context is implemented with the class sqlj.runtime

`.ExecutionContext`. You can specify the execution context for a statement following the connection context, as you will see.

There are a number of statement parameters that you can either set or retrieve using methods in the `ExecutionContext` class. The set versions, which, of course set the values, are listed below. To retrieve these values, substitute `get` for `set` in the method name.

setMaxRows()   The maximum number of rows that a ResultSetIterator can contain. If the query produces more rows than this, the remainder are discarded and no exception(error) is thrown. Iterators, which are explained later in this chapter, are SQLJ objects that wrap JDBC ResultSet objects. For a ResultSetIterator of unlimited size, set this option to 0.

setMaxFieldSize()   The maximum number of bytes returned from a column of datatype BINARY, VARBINARY, LONGVARBINARY, CHAR, VARCHAR, or LONGVARCHAR. Truncated bytes are not returned and no exception is thrown. The `setMaxFieldSize()` method deals strictly in bytes and is not affected by the number of bytes in either the Java or SQL characters.

setQueryTimeout()   The maximum number of seconds a query will process. Zero, the default, is unlimited. If the timeout is exceeded, a SQLException is thrown.

The following information can be returned from the last SQL statement execution:

getUpdateCount()   Returns the number of rows affected by the last INSERT, UPDATE, or DELETE statement.

- 0 is returned if the last SQL statement was not a DML (Data Manipulation Language) statement.

- QUERY_COUNT is returned if the last statement created an iterator or a result set.

- EXCEPTION_COUNT is returned if the last statement produced an exception.

getWarnings()   Returns the first SQL warning returned by the last SQL statement. Additional warnings are chained to the first warning.

Let's look at an example that uses both connection and execution contexts:

```
ExecutionContext execContext = new ExecutionContext();
```

```
// Creates an execution context. We assume the connection
// context is an in the previous examples.
execContext.setQueryTimeout(1);
// Wait for only 1 second for query results. Otherwise, cancel.
#sql [myContext, execContext]
// This specifies both the connection and the execution
// context, in that order.
        { UPDATE ORDERS
                SET amt = amt + :surchargeLocalVar };
System.out.println
("Updated " + execContext.getUpdateCount() + " rows");
```

Note that the characteristics set for and the information returned from an execution context apply *only* to SQL statements that use that execution context. In this example

```
#sql [myContext, execContext1]
        { UPDATE ORDERS
                SET amt = amt + :surchargeLocalVar };
System.out.println
("Updated " + execContext2.getUpdateCount() + " rows");
```

the `println()` information is from some previous SQL statement, not the immediately preceding UPDATE statement.

Selecting Data

Selecting a single row in an Embedded SQLJ program looks exactly like selecting a single row in any other language with Embedded SQL. For more details on doing this, see Chapter 21.

A SQL statement that returns multiple rows is handled differently in Embedded SQLJ programs than in the other Embedded SQL languages. With SQL embedded in a procedural language, you would use a cursor to loop through multiple rows returned by a SELECT statement. SQLJ uses a similar but not identical construct, called an *iterator*. You can use two different forms of iterators: bind by position and bind by name.

Bind by Position Iterators

In the following example, a *bind by position* iterator class is generated with a list of Java datatypes. The generated class, ByPos in this example, is used to declare an instance, positer, that is then associated with a SQL SELECT statement.

```
#sql iterator ByPos (int, String, String, BigDecimal)
{
    ByPos positer;
    // declare a by position iterator object
    int sNum = 0;
    String sName = null;
    String City = null;
    BigDecimal commission = 0.0;
// In this example, the variable names can but do not have
// to match the column names whose values they will hold.
// Since the matching is case-insensitive, all but commission
// do happen to match, though.

    // populate it
    #sql positer = { SELECT snum, sname, city, comm
                        FROM Salespeople };
    #sql { FETCH :positer INTO :sNum,:sName,:City,:commission };
    while ( !positer.endFetch() )
        {
         System.out.println
                (sName + " has an SNUM of " + sNum);
         System.out.println
                ('City: ' + positer.City);
         System.out.println
                ('Commission: ' + positer.commission);

         #sql { FETCH :positer INTO :sNum
                            ,:sName
                            ,:City
                            ,:commission };
        }
    positer.close();
    // done with iterator so clean up
}
```

The SELECT statement effectively populates the iterator. Each FETCH returns the next row into the Java variables. The predicate method endFetch() is set to true after the last row is fetched. This is not so different from how FETCH works with cursors, as we discussed in Chapter 21.

In this example, the data could be retrieved from the SQL database when the SELECT statement is executed, or each row could be retrieved when the FETCH is executed. The exact timing depends on the SQL database and may even depend on the strategy chosen by the query optimizer.

The iterator generates accessor methods for each of the columns with a name of getColN(), where N is the specific column number.

Bind by Name

A *bind by name* iterator class includes pairs of datatypes and names. Columns in the SELECT statement are bound to variables in the iterator by name, not by position, and the names are case insensitive. That is, the names specified in the generated iterator class ByName have to match the names when an instance of the iterator (namiter) is associated with a SELECT statement, but the case and the order of the names do not. Let's look at an example:

```
#sql iterator ByName (int sNum,
                      String sName,
                      String City,
                      BigDecimal Comm);
// Although these names have to match the table columns
// whose values they will hold. The matching is not
// case-sensitive, unlike most things in Java.
// Therefore, the above versions work.
{
    ByName namiter = null;
    // declare a by name iterator object
    #sql namiter = { SELECT snum, sname, city, comm
                        FROM Salespeople };
    String s;
    int i;
    // advances to next row
    while ( namiter.next() )
    {
        i = namiter.SNum();
        // set variable to sNum
        s = namiter.SName();
        // set variable to sName
```

```
        System.out.println (s + " has an SNUM of " + i);
        System.out.println('City: ' + namiter.City());
        System.out.println('Commission: ' + namiter.Comm());
    }
    namiter.close();
    // done with iterator so clean up
}
```

The iterator method next() advances the iterator by one row. If a record is found, the predicate method returns a true. (We use lower-case to distinguish Java true and false from SQL's TRUE and FALSE. Java's logic is not three-valued, although JDBC does provide methods for dealing with SQL NULLs.) If the end of the iterator is reached, the predicate method returns a false.

The iterator generates accessor methods for each of the columns, in this example, sNum(), sName(), City(), and Comm(). These names are case sensitive.

Updating Data

You can update data using either a searched UPDATE or a positioned UPDATE.

A searched UPDATE is based on a SQL predicate. This is the form of UPDATE we have generally used in this book. The following example modifies the rows of the Salespeople table based on the current value of the Java variable sNum:

```
#sql [myContext]
        { UPDATE Salespeople
            SET comm = comm + .01
            WHERE snum = :sNum];
```

A positioned UPDATE is based on which row is currently in the iterator. This is similar to the use of positioned UPDATEs through cursors, which is explained in Chapter 21 and in the reference under "UPDATE". Here's an example:

```
#sql [myContext]
        { UPDATE SALESPEOPLE
            SET comm = comm + .01
            WHERE CURRENT OF :namiter};
```

For positioned UPDATEs, a by-position iterator works exactly the same as a by-name iterator.

Managing SQLJ Transactions

When you create an Embedded SQLJ connection context, the fourth parameter controls whether or not autocommit is enabled:

```
#sql context MyDBContext;
MyDBContext myContext = new MyDBContext
                          ("db-url"
                          ,"username"
                          ,"password"
                          ,true        // enable autocommit
                          );
```

This code enables autocommit. In SQLJ, unlike JDBC, the default for autocommit is false. You can change the autocommit characteristic by mapping a JDBC Connection to an Embedded SQLJ connection context, then using the JDBC setAuto-Commit() method.

With the exception of the autocommit characteristic, you control Embedded SQLJ transactions the same way as you control transactions in any other language with Embedded SQL, save that the keyword "WORK" is optional, as shown here:

```
#sql [myContext] commit;
```

```
#sql [myContext] rollback;
```

If you specify a connection context, the commit and rollback statements apply only to that context. If you do not specify a context, the commit and rollback apply to the current default connection context.

Cleanup

With Embedded SQLJ, you have less control over cleanup than with JDBC. You can close an iterator and you can close a database connection. Iterators should be closed as soon as you are finished with them. Database connections should be closed when you are finished with everything you need to do to a particular SQL session.

The following example closes the database connection context myContext along with any underlying JDBC Connection:

```
myContext.close(CLOSE_CONNECTION);
```

You could keep the underlying JDBC Connection active by invoking `close()` with the value KEEP_CONNECTION. CLOSE_CONNECTION and KEEP_CONNECTION are predefined static variables.

Persistent Stored SQLJ—Using Java Methods inside the Database

SQL/PSM-1996, which later evolved into the PSM portion of SQL99, introduced the concepts of creating, storing, and invoking routines (functions and procedures) within a SQL database. It also introduced the ability to define SQL interfaces for external routines. The latter feature found its way into Core SQL99. In PSM96, stored routines must be written in SQL, while external routines can be written in any language. Persistent Stored SQLJ simply expands these abilities to allow the stored routines to be written in Java, using expansions to the PSM96 syntax for defining external routines. This is what became the Core SQL external routine syntax explained in the previous chapter. In other words, Java code is invoked like external routines, but is, in fact, stored in the database. These Java routines can be Java without any sort of database access, Java with JDBC, or Java with embedded SQLJ. The routines are invoked from SQL statements that could be SQL embedded in a program written in Java or some other language. The additional points you must learn to use Persistent Stored SQLJ are really quite small.

To insert a Java class into your database, the class must be contained in a Java JAR file. The mechanism you use to create a Java JAR file depends on the Java development tool you are using and so is beyond the scope of this book. The basic sequence you will use is:

- Install a JAR file with the `sqlj.install_jar` procedure.

- Create a SQL name for each Java method in the JAR that you want to access using CREATE PROCEDURE or CREATE FUNCTION. You do not need to create SQL names for methods that you do not want to use.

- GRANT and REVOKE usage privileges either on the individual methods in the JAR or to the entire JAR.

- You may need to use `sqlj.alter_java_path` to specify a path for name resolution of support classes within Java classes.

Once you have a JAR installed in your database, you may need to update it using the procedure `sqlj.replace_jar` or to get rid of it using the procedure `sqlj.remove_jar`.

The examples in the following sections use the `MyClass` class, as shown below:

```java
public class MyClass
{
    //A method that returns a string. "Public" means it is
    // visible from outside of this object.
    public static String Continent(String city)
                throws SQLException
    {
        if (city.equals("London") ||
            city.equals("Barcelona") ||
            city.equals("Rome"} ||
            city.equals("Berlin"))
            return "Europe";
          else if
            (city.equals "San Jose" ||
             city.equals "New York"
            )
            return "North America";
        else
            return "Unknown"; }
// end of continent

    // Update all orders
    public static void updateOrders
            (java.math.BigDecimal surchargeLocalVar)
                throws SQLException
    {
        // database context is current database
        #sql { UPDATE ORDERS
                SET amt = amt + :surchargeLocalVar)
                        };
    // end of update_orders
}
// end of class MyClass
```

For the purposes of further discussion, we assume that this class has been compiled and placed in the JAR file `h:/sqlj/ClassExample.jar`.

Installing a JAR File

The `sqlj.install_jar` procedure takes three parameters:

- A URL pointing to a JAR file.

- The JAR name that will be used inside the SQL database.

- An integer. If the integer is non-zero and there are install actions in a deployment descriptor in the JAR file, the install actions are executed at the end of the `install_jar` procedure.

The following example installs the JAR with a local filename of `h:/sqlj/ClassExample_jar` as `ClassExample_jar` within a SQL database:

```
sql.install_jar('file:h:/sqlj/ClassExample.jar'
                ,'ClassExample_jar'
                ,0);
```

Note that while it is entirely possible to give a JAR a completely different name within a SQL database than the outside filename, it will lead to confusion and maintenance problems later. As always, consistent naming is extremely important.

Once a JAR file is installed, you must create SQL procedure and function specifications for the methods you wish to access. You can access a Java method only if it is *visible*. A Java method is *visible* in SQL only if it is public, static, and mappable. A method is *mappable* if the Java datatypes of the parameters (and the return type for functions) can be mapped to SQL datatypes. Methods that are not visible cannot be accessed from SQL, but they can be accessed from visible methods.

The following is an example of the code you would execute from SQL to create SQL FUNCTION and PROCEDURE wrappers for the Java methods `Continent()` and `UpdateOrders()`. This code conforms to the principles of Core SQL99, as outlined in Chapter 25. Since the FUNCTION you are creating is a database object, you do not have to do this from within Java, although you may. You can use interactive SQL or any other SQL interface. Since this code is not necessarily entered from within Java, we have omitted the specific Embedded SQLJ syntax, such as the `#sql` string:

```
CREATE FUNCTION continent(city VARCHAR(30))
```

```
        RETURNS VARCHAR(30)
        NO SQL
        EXTERNAL NAME 'ClassExample_jar:myClass.Continent'
        LANGUAGE JAVA
        PARAMETER STYLE JAVA;
GRANT EXECUTE ON FUNCTION continent TO PUBLIC;


CREATE PROCEDURE update_orders(surcharge DECIMAL)
    MODIFIES SQL DATA
    EXTERNAL NAME 'ClassExample_jar:myClass.UpdateOrders'
    LANGUAGE JAVA
    PARAMETER STYLE JAVA;
GRANT EXECUTE ON PROCEDURE update_orders TO PUBLIC;
```

The characteristics NO SQL, CONTAINS SQL, and MODIFIES SQL DATA are hints that the DBMS can use. These have the same meanings as for external routines, as described in the previous chapter. The default is CONTAINS SQL. The Persistent Stored SQLJ standard says that a CONTAINS SQL method "can invoke SQL operations, but cannot read or modify SQL data, i.e., the method cannot perform SQL OPEN, CLOSE, FETCH, SELECT, INSERT, UPDATE, or DELETE operations." That is, with a CONTAINS SQL method you can do such things as control transactions and call procedures, but you cannot change data in the database.

You probably have noticed that defining the SQL FUNCTIONS and PROCEDURES could get very tedious for a JAR file with numerous methods. This script could be included in the JAR file using an `afterInstall()` method (see your Java documentation for details). This is a Java script that, in this case, chiefly executes SQL. It does not require Embedded SQL syntax because Java simply passes the script content to the database. It may require some configuration, however.

```
SQLActions[ ] = {
"BEGIN INSTALL
  -- include CREATE and GRANT statements here
CREATE FUNCTION continent(city VARCHAR(30))
    RETURNS VARCHAR(30)
    NO SQL
    EXTERNAL NAME 'ClassExample_jar:myClass.Continent'
    LANGUAGE JAVA
    PARAMETER STYLE JAVA;
GRANT EXECUTE ON FUNCTION continent TO PUBLIC;

CREATE PROCEDURE update_orders(surcharge DECIMAL)
```

```
      MODIFIES SQL DATA
      EXTERNAL NAME 'ClassExample_jar:myClass.UpdateOrders'
      LANGUAGE JAVA
      PARAMETER STYLE JAVA;
GRANT EXECUTE ON PROCEDURE update_orders TO PUBLIC;

END INSTALL ",
"BEGIN REMOVE
      -- include any REVOKE and DROP statements here
END REMOVE "
}
```

Note that you use `thisjar` instead of the SQL JAR name. When this script is executed by `sql.install_jar`, the SQL JAR name will replace `thisjar` with the actual name of the JAR file.

If this JAR file has a name of `classexample_deploy.sql`, you could build a JAR file that contains the following:

- The text file `classexample_deploy.sql`

- The class file for `MyClass`

- A manifest file (look this up in your Java documentation) with the following manifest entry:

```
Name: classexample_deploy.sql
SQLJDeploymentDescriptor: TRUE
```

This manifest entry identifies `classexample_deploy.sql` as a deployment descriptor in the JAR. With this script in place, you can call `sqlj install_jar` with a non-zero as the third parameter:

```
--
--  Get the city and continent for customers.
--
SELECT city, continent(city)
  FROM Customers;
--
-- Add a 10.00 surcharge to all orders
--
CALL update_orders(10.00);
```

After the JAR is installed, the SQL commands between the BEGIN INSTALL and END INSTALL are executed.

You can also add statements to revoke access and drop the procedure and function definitions before the JAR is deleted by a call to `sqlj.remove_jar`.

What Does Java Look Like in the Database?

Once you have installed a JAR file in the database and defined the appropriate procedures and functions, you can access it the same way you access any other stored procedure or function. For example:

```
-
- GET the city and continent for customers.
-
SELECT city, continent(city)
  from customers;
-
- ADD a 10.00 surcharge to all orders
-
CALL update_orders(10.00);
```

The Persistent Stored SQLJ standard does not define the details of exactly how Java routines are executed within your SQL database—this is left to each DBMS vendor.

Given the volume and diversity of Java classes that are now available, Persistent Stored SQLJ allows you to quickly add very powerful, pretested capabilities to the database.

SQLJ UDTs—Using Java Classes As SQL User-Defined Types

The goal of SQLJ UDTs is to allow Java classes to be used within a SQL database as the base for defining SQL99 UDTs. This is an expansion of Persistent Stored SQLJ and so takes advantage of `sql.install_jar` and `sql.remove_jar`. Additional syntax allows you to create a UDT from a class in a JAR installed in your SQL database. Not only can you store and manipulate these UDTs in your SQL database, but you can also pass them to a Java program without change.

SQLJ UDTs require at the very least the SQL99 package Basic Object Support and may require some features from Enhanced Object Support. Since the SQLJ UDT specification is still a work in progress, it is not completely clear how all of the pieces fit together.

Summary

There are two ways to integrate Java and SQL: JDBC and SQLJ.

JDBC, defined by Sun, is a uniform API for accessing various DBMSs. It is based on ODBC and uses Dynamic SQL. In JDBC, there are various standard objects that encapsulate the Embedded SQL statements.

SQLJ falls into three parts: Embedded SQLJ, Persistent Stored SQLJ, and SQLJ UDTs.

Embedded SQLJ is basically embedded SQL applied to Java, but it is based on JDBC so that the two can be seamlessly intermingled. Embedded SQLJ provides an easier syntax and improves performance by moving some operations from runtime to compile time, as do other forms of embedded SQL. Embedded SQLJ also provides facilities for handling context, so that state can be maintained between the DBMS and application. As of this writing (2000), there are several implementations of SQLJ on the market. These are mostly implementations of Embedded SQLJ.

Persistent Stored SQLJ is a technique for storing Java bytecode in a database and executing it from within SQL. For execution, it utilizes the external routine functionality, which is part of Core SQL99 (see Chapter 25). Hence, the bytecode can be stored and invoked, but the DBMS understands little of its content or structure. Implementations of this are emerging as we speak.

SQLJ UDTs are a way to achieve a true hybrid of the object-oriented and relational database approaches by treating Java objects as SQL99 structured UDTs (see Chapter 24). Structured UDTs are executable objects treated as datatypes or as table types by the DBMS. As of this writing, SQLJ UDTs are still in the future.

References

ANSI X3.135-1992 (R1998), Information Systems - Database Languages SQL, and ISO/IEC 9075:1992, Information technology - Database Languages SQL

ANSI/ISO/IEC 9075-4-1996, Information technology - Database Languages SQL - Part 4: Persistent Stored Modules (SQL/PSM)

ANSI X3.135.10-1998, Information systems - Database Languages SQL - Part 10: Object Language Bindings (SQL/OLB)

ANSI 331.1-1999 Database Languages - SQLJ - Part 1: SQL Routines using the Java(TM) Programming Language

The Java Language Specification, James Gosling, Bill Joy, and Guy Steele, Addison-Wesley, 1996

JDBC: A Java SQL API, Version 1.20, Graham Hamilton and Rick Cattell, JavaSoft, 10 January 1997

Putting SQL to Work

1. Prepare and execute a JDBC statement to insert a new Salesperson record for Faloon, who lives in Pittsburgh, gets a 10% commission, and has a Salesperson number of 1042. Use the connection myConn and clean up after you are finished.

2. Rewrite your answer to question 1 as an Embedded SQLJ statement against the connection context myContext.

PART VII

Syntax and Command Reference

CHAPTER

TWENTY-SEVEN

27

Introduction to the Syntax and Command Reference

- Notable Features of Standard SQL

- Contents Grouped by Subject

The following is a complete reference to the SQL92 standard, which is the version implemented commercially as of this publication (2000). It also includes some coverage of common variations on the standard. The reference has the following structure.

- Chapter 27: Introduction. This is the part you're reading now.
- Chapter 28: Statement Reference. This is an alphabetical reference on every SQL statement in the standard.
- Chapter 29: Common Elements. This is an alphabetical reference on elements that are common to many of the SQL statements in Chapter 28.

The rest of this introduction provides a listing of contents grouped by subject and an overview of the notable features of the standard. The contents listing is at the end of this Chapter.

Notable Features of Standard SQL

This section provides a brief overview of some of the more specialized features of the SQL92 standard that may have only been touched on in the rest of this book. It is introductory to the reference that follows it.

Users, Schemas, and Sessions

Here is an overview of the SQL environment as defined in the standard. This aspect is little changed by SQL99.

First, there is the organization of the data itself. Data is contained in tables, tables are group into schemata, and schemata are grouped into catalogs. The catalogs can be further grouped into *clusters*.

NOTE Some database products have been using these terms slightly differently than defined in the standard, and your system documentation may reflect this.

From the viewpoint of a particular SQL session, a cluster is the world. It contains all of the tables that session can access, and all interrelated tables must be in the same cluster. The standard does, however, give implementations the option of using cross-cluster catalogs.

Clarifying the context of SQL requires identifying who or what issues SQL statements. In the standard, an entity that produces SQL statements is technically called a *SQL agent*. A SQL agent is associated with an Authorization ID, which is an identifier that has a group of privileges permitting certain actions. For the most part, this reference will simplify by just using the term "Authorization ID". The Authorization ID could be a user directly executing SQL, or it could be an application. It is the Authorization ID that establishes a connection to a DBMS. Once the connection is made, a session is begun. Optionally, implementations may allow SQL agents to switch to some other connection and session possibly as a different Authorization ID. (Hence, SQL Agent and Authorization ID are not strictly synonymous, but only the latter concept is relevant to the execution of SQL itself, generally speaking. Almost all of how connection switching is actually done is still implementation-defined.) At any one time, there will be a current session that is active and perhaps some others that are dormant. The Authorization ID under which the statements are run is that of the user or, if the module language is being used, that of the module.

Schema Definition Statements

A *schema* is a named set of database objects that are under the control of a single Authorization ID and can be treated as a whole for certain purposes. Previously, the SQL standard defined procedures for creating and dropping tables and other objects, but it simply equated schemata with Authorization IDs. To accommodate users who may want to create more than one schema, the new standard includes statements for creating and dropping schemata as well as tables and other objects. It also allows schemata to be grouped into catalogs and these into clusters.

> **NOTE**   See Also: CREATE SCHEMA, DROP SCHEMA, and SET SCHEMA in Chapter 28.

Temporary Tables

We have in this book kept the discussion of base tables primarily confined to permanent base tables. These are base tables that store data whose content remains intact from session to session. Since such data is the whole point of a database, permanent base tables are by far the most important kind. However, you can also create temporary base tables, whose data is not retained from one session to the next. These are primarily useful for intermediate results and other kinds of working storage.

Temporary tables fall into two categories: created and declared.

Created temporary tables are objects with a persistent identity in the database from session to session. Although the data is not held between sessions, the empty tables are there for you when you begin each session, so you do not have to create them afresh each time. Created temporary tables come in two flavors: local and global. The difference between these is the scope. For more on created temporary tables, see CREATE TABLE, which is the statement used to create them, in Chapter 28.

Declared temporary tables are objects that exist only in applications (or modules) and do not have a persistent identity in the database. You include the code to create these in applications. Once the application exits, the DBMS never heard of the declared temporary table. For the sake of completeness, these tables are usually called declared local temporary tables, though there is no global variety. For more on declared temporary tables, see DECLARE LOCAL TEMPORARY TABLE, which is the statement used to create them, in Chapter 28.

NOTE   See Also: CREATE TABLE, DECLARE LOCAL TEMPORARY TABLE, and DROP TABLE in Chapter 28.

Read-Only, Scrollable, Insensitive, and Dynamic Cursors

A *cursor* is an object used to store the output of a query for processing in an application. In SQL89, a cursor that was updatable in principle—that is, one that didn't violate any of a series of rules that prohibited update statements—was updatable in fact. In SQL92, you have the option of declaring it read-only. Besides enhancing security, read-only cursors can improve performance by reducing the need to lock the data.

Sensitivity has to do with the reflection in the cursor of external changes to the data. Since a cursor translates SQL's set-at-a-time operation into the item-at-a-time operation of conventional languages, it spreads what would otherwise be a simultaneous occurrence over time. In other words, a cursor can be opened and then read (FETCHed) gradually. This creates the possibility that the cursor's data could be changed while it still is being read. What happens if another statement changes some data yet to be read in an opened cursor? In the early standards, the answer was "God only knows." Possibly, this is not the ideal answer. In SQL92, on the other hand, you can declare the cursor to be *insensitive*, in which case the rest of the world will be gleefully ignored by the cursor. Only read-only cursors can be insensitive. Currently, you cannot, in the standard, declare a cursor sensitive, meaning that external changes to the data will be reflected in the cursor. (You still have the option of leaving the cursor indeterminate. What happens when you do this is implementation-dependent. It is not unreasonable, however, to hope that the implementation at least will behave consistently in this matter and tell you what to expect in the system documentation.)

You can also *scroll* cursors now. Although the rows of a table are, in principle, unordered, once these rows are placed in a cursor they will have some order, whether arbitrary or imposed. Previously, you had to operate on these rows one at a time, beginning with the first and proceeding straight through to the end. Now you can jump around, go back to where you were, and so on. A cursor that permits this is called a *scroll cursor*; such a cursor must be read-only.

NOTE   See Also: CLOSE, DECLARE CURSOR, FETCH, and OPEN in Chapter 28. For additional information specifically on the use of cursors in Dynamic SQL, see ALLOCATE CURSOR, EXECUTE, EXECUTE IMMEDIATE, and PREPARE.

Client/Server Orientation

Standard SQL is designed around the concepts of client/server or of multi-tiered architectures. It enables you to manage connections, recognizing that a very common database configuration is one in which front-end software on one computer, called the *client*, attempts to extract information from a back-end DBMS located on another computer, called the *server*. Many of the new features regarding standardized connection procedures, locking schemes, and error diagnostics were motivated by the desire to enable clients to communicate with a variety of DBMSs, possibly on a variety of servers, in the same way.

What Is a Client/Server Architecture?

In a client/server architecture, multiple computers are connected over a network. The computers are grouped into clients and servers. Users directly interact with clients to perform most of the front-end user interface functions. Servers perform various intensive tasks in response to requests from clients. A DBMS typically resides on a server and responds to SQL requests from the clients. SQL is well suited to such an arrangement because as a declarative language it is very concise, and the network therefore does not get bogged down passing detailed instructions back and forth between the client and server. Nonetheless, the language is sufficiently precise for the server to perform the required task autonomously without further client input. Particularly for queries, this is an improvement over the older file server approach, where the server may transmit an entire table to the client and leave it to extract the data that it needs.

Client/server architectures do, however, introduce the issue of connections. A client must be connected to a server in order to communicate with it. Since the standard has to be neutral with regard to the particularities—which platforms and networks are being used, for example—much is necessarily left up to the implementation here. But the 92 standard does define what a SQL connection is and provide some ground rules for how one behaves. The standard is tailored to the realities of client-server computing, in which clients may want to interface to multiple servers and servers normally interface to multiple clients.

This is not to say that the standard can be applied only to client/server architectures, however. SQL92, like its predecessors, is a functional specification. Any configuration— stand-alone PC, traditional minicomputer, or mainframe computer—that functions as specified is acceptable.

How Do the Internet and Intranets Fit into This?

The Web and Intranets that utilize the HTTP protocol are sometimes viewed as simple client/server architectures. In this analysis, the Web browser is commonly regarded as a "client" of a Web server, such as Apache or iPlanet. When a DBMS is involved, however, it is usually as another layer behind the Web server. This is called a *three-tiered architecture*. There may, in fact, be any number of additional layers, particularly between the web server and the DBMS. These situations are generally termed *n-tiered architectures*. In these situations, the web server is a server to the browser but a client to the DBMS. Since "client" and "server" refer to functions of a software module rather than its fundamental nature, there is nothing wrong with this approach. Since this is a database-centric book, we will be viewing Web servers and middleware chiefly as clients.

> **NOTE**   See Also: CONNECT, DISCONNECT, and SET CONNECTION in Chapter 28.

Enhanced Transaction Management

As discussed in Chapter 17, a *transaction* is a group of successive SQL statements that succeed or fail as a unit—a failure in the transaction causes the whole sequence to be canceled, or *rolled back*. The DBMS automatically begins a transaction whenever you issue a statement that calls for one and no other transaction is active. Transactions are ended by a COMMIT WORK statement (to save the changes) or a ROLLBACK statement (to disregard them) or by a system crash or disconnect. If a transaction cannot be committed, it will be rolled back; ROLLBACK can never fail.

SQL92 provides features that make transactions considerably more sophisticated. However, these features are part of Intermediate, rather than Entry, SQL92 conformance. These features are useful enough that many of them are, in fact, implemented, but variations abound. Among the special features of transactions in SQL92 are the following:

- Transactions can be specified as read-only. This means that statements within the transaction that attempt to change the content or structure of the database will produce an error. This will tend to improve performance of concurrent operations as it reduces the need to lock the data.

- You can defer constraint checking until the end of the transaction, and you can choose which constraints you wish to defer. Constraints control the data that may be placed in the database. See the discussions under SET CONSTRAINTS MODE in Chapter 28 and Constraints in Chapter 29.

- Transactions can specify the isolation levels of the locks placed on the data. See the discussion under SET TRANSACTION in Chapter 28.

- Transactions can specify the size of the diagnostics area for statements within the transaction. See the discussion in Appendix C.

> **NOTE**
>
> See Also: COMMIT WORK, ROLLBACK, SET CONSTRAINTS MODE, and SET TRANSACTION in Chapter 28.

Application-Owned Privileges (Definer's Rights)

Actions performed on a database are associated with an Authorization ID, a name that's unique within the database. This allows the privileges linked to a particular Authorization ID to determine which actions may be taken by a user. For example, an Authorization ID could have the privilege to retrieve data from a table or to use a translation on a character set. Generally, an Authorization ID is associated directly with a user and defines possible actions whether the user is employing stand-alone SQL or running an application that interfaces to the database. It is often useful with applications to grant privileges to the application itself instead of to the user, so that users can execute the statements in the application without having the same privileges in other contexts. Applications, especially if they use Static SQL, can greatly control what users do with their privileges and thus offer a good deal of security. There is further discussion of this in Chapter 21.

Application-owned privileges are sometimes said to embody *definer's rights*, whereas a module that makes users execute it under their own privileges is enforcing *invoker's rights*. There are other terms as well, since some products have had application-owned privileges for a while as a nonstandard feature.

> **NOTE**
>
> See Also: Chapter 16; Authorization IDs and User Value Functions in Chapter 29; and Appendix F on the CD.

Standardized Connection Procedure

In earlier standards, SQL statements were associated with Authorization IDs, but how a particular Authorization ID was associated with a particular statement was up to the implementation. Authorization IDs had privileges to perform certain statements and, if they created objects such as tables, had control over those objects. They were generally understood to be users, although the standard did not actually say this. And in fact, users, from the standpoint of a DBMS or an operating system, may not have a one-to-one correspondence to each other or to real-world users. In some commercial environments, a single Authorization ID could be shared by several real-world users, or users could have multiple Authorization IDs. This is particularly common with a

DBMS for which a Web server is a client. Also, the way an Authorization ID was identified by the DBMS—the connection procedure—was left up to the implementers.

The SQL92 standard standardizes much of this and makes it explicit that users, directly or through applications, establish connections to the DBMS. Thus, it is possible for a given user to have several concurrent connections, only one of which will be active at a time. Users explicitly switch between connections using the SET CONNECTION statement.

NOTE   See Also: CONNECT, DISCONNECT, and SET CONNECTION in Chapter 28.

Standardized System Tables

A catalog in the standard is a collection of schemata. It contains an INFORMATION_ SCHEMA, which is a set of tables that describes the contents of the schemata—what columns are in the various tables, what views are defined, what privileges are associated with which Authorization IDs, and so on. It is these tables themselves that are called the "catalog" in some commercial products. The standardized INFORMATION_ SCHEMA specified by SQL92 allows both users and applications to use the same SQL statements to get information about any schema under any DBMS that they may be using. The INFORMATION_SCHEMA is laid out in Appendix D and described in Chapter 18.

Standardized Error Codes and Diagnostics

Two standard error variables are supported. In the old approach, information about the result of a SQL operation was transmitted through a numeric variable called SQL-CODE. This variable would be set automatically after the execution of each SQL statement to indicate what happened when the statement was executed. There were three possibilities:

- A value of 0 indicated successful completion.

- A value of 100 indicated that the statement executed properly but had no effect or produced no output. For example, a query that produced no data or an attempt to delete a row that wasn't there would produce a SQLCODE value of 100.

- Any negative number indicated an error.

Of course, the idea was for the specific negative number to indicate the specific error, but the mapping was left up to the implementation, so now they are all different. For the sake of the upward-compatibility of existing products and maintainability of existing applications, SQLCODE is still supported, but it has been deprecated, which means that it is not recommended now and may not be supported in the future.

The new approach is to use another variable called SQLSTATE. This is a five-character text string with standard values for various error classes. It also provides for implementation-defined error conditions. In fact, errors are classified at two levels of detail: class and subclass. Often, an error message will use a standard class and a proprietary subclass, so that the standard tells you the general nature of the error and the subclass gives you more specific information. There are no standard subclasses, but if the class describes the error adequately, the subclass may be omitted (set to '000').

The standard also now provides a diagnostics area with multiple error messages and codes produced by the execution of a single statement. You access this using the GET DIAGNOSTICS statement. For a detailed description of the diagnostics area, see Appendix C.

NOTE   See Also: GET DIAGNOSTICS in Chapter 28 and Appendix B.

Domains

Relational theorists such as E. F. Codd, the father of relational database theory, have long promoted the use of *domains* to account for the fact that data may need to be typed more precisely than can be achieved with a standard set of datatypes. For example, telephone numbers are not the same type of data as social security numbers even though both are numbers. Although they could be of the same datatype, it makes no sense to directly compare them; they are in different domains.

SQL92 supports domains, but they are not quite what Codd had in mind, because they do not restrict possible comparisons. As discussed in Chapter 25, the distinct UDTs of SQL99 are closer to Codd's conception of domains and complement SQL92 domains rather well. A domain in SQL92 is effectively a standard datatype accompanied by some combination of standard refinements. It gives you a convenient way to bundle the refinements. You create these domains as objects in a schema and then declare columns of tables to be of domains rather than datatypes. A domain definition contains a datatype, but it may also contain clauses that specify a default value, one or more constraints (rules that restrict the values allowed in particular columns), and a collation (a sorting order for character sets) to apply to the domain. Domains once defined can still be altered or even dropped.

Domains are a convenient way to reproduce customized packages of constraints, default values, and collating sequences uniformly across a schema. They will be particularly useful to apply the same constraint to several tables, for example, to perform check-digit validation on ID codes. They could also come in handy in large and complex schemata or in schemata that use complex data requiring many constraints, as in some engineering applications.

NOTE   See Also: Chapter 25; ALTER DOMAIN, CREATE DOMAIN, and DROP DOMAIN in Chapter 28; and Constraints and Datatypes in Chapter 29.

Assertions and Deferability of Constraints

Constraints are rules that you establish to restrict the values that can be placed in your columns. In basic SQL, constraints are contained in the definitions of base tables and are of two kinds: column constraints and table constraints. The former are part of a column definition and check their rules whenever a statement attempts to insert or change a value in that column. The latter are part of the table definition and therefore can accommodate rules that involve checking multiple columns of the table. In both kinds, the constraints can be either of certain predefined kinds—NOT NULL, for example, or UNIQUE—or can be CHECK constraints that allow the table creator to create value expressions using the column values. If the expression is FALSE, the constraint is not satisfied, and the statement is rejected.

An extension of this concept is *assertions*—constraints that exist in the schema as independent objects, not in a table. This means that they can refer to multiple tables in their predicates. They can also be used to ensure that a table is never empty, which cannot be done within the table itself. Assertions allow you to design general principles that your data must meet, for example, to design validity checks. Assertions can be created and dropped. You can also put constraints in domains, as discussed under "Domains" elsewhere in this chapter.

SQL92 constraints are named, either explicitly or automatically by the DBMS. This enables them to be deferred (explained shortly) or dropped from tables or domains. You drop constraints using the ALTER TABLE, ALTER DOMAIN, and DROP ASSERTION statements.

You have the option of deferring the checking of constraints (for the rest of this discussion, "constraints" can be taken to mean constraints in tables, constraints in domains, or constraints in assertions, unless otherwise specified) until the end of the transaction. This gets rather sophisticated. Basically, a constraint can be checked at any of the following times:

1. After every statement that affects the table(s) to which it refers

2. At the end of every transaction that contains one or more statements that affect the table(s) to which it refers

3. At any time between 1 and 2 when the user or application decides it should be checked and therefore forces the issue

When you define a constraint, you specify whether it must be checked immediately after each statement or may be deferred until the end of the transaction. If you choose the latter, you can also specify whether it will default to being checked immediately or default to being deferred. Then, during your transaction, you can change this default by setting a *constraints mode*, which explicitly controls whether your deferrable constraints are checked immediately after each statement or deferred until the end of the transaction (your non-deferrable constraints, by definition, must be checked immediately). You can set the constraints mode for all constraints at once or for specified ones. If you set your constraints mode at any time to immediate, the constraints you indicate will be checked immediately. Use this technique when you want the third type of checking listed above. The statement to force or defer the checking of constraints is SET CONSTRAINTS MODE.

There are certain things you can do only if you can defer constraints. For example, you may want to have two tables each with a foreign key referencing the other. Suppose additionally that the foreign keys both have the NOT NULL constraint, so that neither table can have a foreign key value entered until a matching parent key value exists in the other, and neither can accept any rows without having some foreign key values. Whichever table you attempt to insert into first will get an integrity violation, because the parent key in the other table will not yet exist. This is an example of *circularity*. The solution is to defer the checking of the FOREIGN KEY constraint until after you have been able to insert rows into both tables. Circularity is discussed further in Chapters 5 and 19.

Keep in mind, however, that if you get a constraint violation at the end of a transaction, you will lose all of the work accomplished in that transaction. Unless you are very concerned with performance and can save a bit of time by performing all of your checks at once, you probably should check your constraints as soon as possible, rather than putting it off until the end of a long transaction. If you use SET CONSTRAINTS MODE to force checking of constraints before you terminate the transaction, you're better off. If any constraint is currently violated, setting the constraints mode to immediate will fail. This lets you know there is a problem without rolling back the transaction. For more on transactions, see Chapter 17.

NOTE See Also: Chapters 4, 5, 17, 19; CREATE ASSERTION, CREATE TABLE, DROP ASSERTION, and SET TRANSACTION in Chapter 28; and Constraints in Chapter 29.

International Language Support

One of the things that truly qualifies SQL92 as a worldwide standard is its support for customized character sets. No longer is SQL anchored to English. The standard enables implementers and users great flexibility in defining their own character sets. For example, characters need not be one-byte long as English-language letters usually are; they can even vary in length. They do have to be sortable. There must be some defined collation (ordering) sequence so that a statement like *character 1 < character 2* can be evaluated as TRUE or FALSE (provided neither character 1 nor 2 is NULL). Normally, collations should correspond to alphabetical ordering. In any case, collations can be overridden, even for standard character sets. You can also define your own translations from one character set to another. The character sets, collations, and translations are all defined as objects in the schema, and users must have the USAGE privilege on them to use them.

> **NOTE** See Also: Chapter 20; CREATE CHARACTER SET, CREATE COLLATION, CREATE TRANSLATION, DROP CHARACTER SET, DROP COLLATION, and DROP TRANSLATION in Chapter 28; and CAST Expressions, Collations, and Datatypes in Chapter 29.

Date, Time, and Interval Datatypes

Dates and times have special features that make it difficult to handle them properly as simply character strings or numbers. Hence, they have their own datatypes. There is also an interval datatype for doing math with date and time values. These types work as follows:

- A date value consists of a year, a month, and a day.

- A time value consists of hours, minutes, seconds, and decimal fractions of a second.

- A timestamp is a combination of date and time.

With time and timestamp, you also have the option of specifying decimal fractions of seconds. Timestamp, in fact, defaults to four decimal places, e.g., 11:09:48.5839. Time itself defaults to no decimal. Either time or timestamp can also have a time zone indication that shows how far the indicated time is offset from Universal Coordinated Time (UCT).

The standard also supports two types of intervals: year-month and day-time. Intervals are used to represent the differences between various days and times; they enable you to perform date and time arithmetic. For example, if you subtract the time 2:00 from the time 5:30, you get the interval 3:30, for three hours and thirty minutes. Likewise, you could take the date value of July 2003, add an interval month value of three, and get the date value of October 2003. Note that, although intervals are either year-month or day-time, not all of the components of the year or time have to be expressed. Interval arithmetic will work with what you give it. The reason for the two types is that we cannot say in general how many days are in a month. It depends on the month. This means we would not know, when incrementing the day values in a theoretical month-day interval, when we could switch and increment the month value. It is undetermined.

> **NOTE**   See Also: Datatypes in Chapter 29.

Binary Datatypes

SQL92 support binary data. This is different from the BLOBs (Binary Large Objects) of SQL99 in that SQL92 provides no special features, such as SQL99 locators, for managing binary data. In SQL92, binary data is treated simply as string data. For more on SQL99 BLOBs, see Chapter 25. For more on SQL92 binary datatypes, see Datatypes in Chapter 29.

There are two types of binary data in SQL 92: fixed-length and varying-length. Although you will frequently need to use varying-length data, using the fixed-length type improves performance and reduces storage space. One place where you may be able to use fixed-length is with digitized images. If all of the images are of the same size and resolution (which is likely), and no image compression is used (which is possible), they should all be of the same size.

> **NOTE**   See Also: Chapters 24 and 25 and Datatypes in Chapter 29.

Datatype Conversions

SQL is a strongly typed language. Although all datatypes are, of course, ultimately represented in the DBMS as binary numbers, operations cannot freely mix them or operate on them as binaries or as numbers, as is possible in some computer languages. This has advantages and disadvantages. Often it is useful to convert from one datatype to another, but problems can arise if this process is not controlled. The standard allows you to convert datatypes by using the CAST expression. This enables you to instruct the DBMS to convert an integer to a character string or a character string to binary data. This is especially handy for joins and unions, where all columns being joined or merged have to be of similar datatypes.

> **NOTE**   See Also: CAST Expressions and Datatypes in Chapter 29.

Built-In Value Functions

SQL provides system values in the form of built-in string variables whose values are automatically set by the system to reflect the Authorization IDs being used to identify the current user and the currently applicable privileges. There are three types: SESSION_ USER, CURRENT_USER, and SYSTEM_USER.

CURRENT_USER, also known as USER, refers to the Authorization ID used to determine which actions currently can be performed. This will be the Authorization ID either of the user or of a (possibly emulated) module. The latter would be the case whenever a module that has an Authorization ID of its own is being executed (see "Application-Owned Privileges" elsewhere in this chapter). Otherwise, CURRENT_ USER identifies the user. In any case, the Authorization ID associated with the user will be contained in the variable SESSION_USER. (Note that although SESSION_ USER is set automatically, implementations do have the option of allowing user override with the SET SESSION AUTHORIZATION statement.)

SYSTEM_USER is the current user as identified by the operating system. Most often, this would be the same as SESSION_USER, but how operating system users correspond to Authorization IDs is implementation-defined, so the two may differ. Refer to your system documentation for details on this. There are also built-in functions for DATE and TIME values. These are as follows: CURRENT_DATE, which provides (surprise!) the current date, CURRENT_TIME, which does the same for time, and CURRENT_TIMESTAMP, which is a combination of the other two.

NOTE See Also: SET SESSION AUTHORIZATION in Chapter 28 and Authorization IDs, Privileges, and Value Expressions in Chapter 29.

New Operators for Strings

The standard provides a concatenation operator and several functions that operate on text strings. We can divide these into two categories. First, there are those that operate on strings and produce strings as output: the CONCATENATE operator (written | |), SUBSTRING, UPPER, LOWER, TRIM, TRANSLATE, and CONVERT. Then there are those that operate on strings but produce numeric output: POSITION, CHAR_LENGTH, OCTET_LENGTH, and BIT_LENGTH.

Of the first group, only CONCATENATE is *dyadic*, meaning it operates on two strings at once. It simply appends the second string to the first, so that `'Mary ' || 'Schmary'` becomes `'MarySchmary'`. SUBSTRING takes a string, a starting position within it, and a number of characters to extract and produces a new string, so that `SUBSTRING ('Astarte' FROM 2 FOR 4)` returns `'star'`. UPPER and LOWER convert a string to all upper or all lowercase, respectively; either of these operations is called a *fold*. TRIM is used to remove leading or trailing blanks from strings. You can specify leading, trailing, or both.

TRANSLATE and CONVERT address SQL's use of various and customized character sets. TRANSLATE converts from one character set to another. CONVERT keeps the character set the same but switches to a different definition of how the character set is represented.

POSITION finds the starting position of one string within another, so that POSITION ('star' IN 'Astarte') returns 2. If there is no match for the substring, POSITION returns 0. The other three functions all give you the length of a string, either in the number of characters, the number of octets (8-bit sequences, commonly called bytes), or the number of bits.

NOTE   See Also: Chapter 20; CREATE CHARACTER SET, CREATE COLLATION, and CREATE TRANSLATION in Chapter 28; and Collations and String Value Functions in Chapter 29.

Row and Table Value Constructors

Predicates in SQL compare values in terms of operators like = or in terms of SQL's own operators and return a value of TRUE, FALSE, or (in the presence of NULLs) UNKNOWN, based on the result of the comparison. Previously, SQL predicates could compare single values to single values or could, in some situations, compare single values to a column of values derived from a subquery (a query used to derive values for use within another query). In SQL92, SQL can deal with sets of values that correspond to entire rows or entire tables. This functionality is part of Full SQL92 conformance, which, as of this writing (2000), is claimed by few if any vendors. Nonetheless, the feature is useful enough that some products support it as an extension to their standard conformance level. For example, previously you could have a predicate that said

```
WHERE c1 = 3
```

or one that said

```
WHERE c1 = 3 AND c2 = 5
```

In SQL92, you could express the latter as

```
WHERE (c1, c2) = (3, 5)
```

This functionality is more than just a convenience, however. It enables you to do things you could not do before, such as comparing a row produced by a subquery to an enumerated row of values. You can even use subquery operators such as ANY or ALL (see Chapter 12) with such subqueries.

If an inequality is used instead of =, the expression is evaluated as a sort with the first value having the highest priority and each subsequent value the next highest. In other words,

```
(1, 7, 8) < (2, 0, 1)
```

is TRUE because $1 < 2$ and once a pair of unequal values is found, the rest of the values don't matter.

A table value constructor consists of a set of row value constructors, preceded by the word VALUES and separated by commas. This syntax enables table value constructors to neatly extend the standard syntax for INSERT.

NOTE   See Also: INSERT in Chapter 28 and Predicates and Row and Table Value Constructors in Chapter 29.

Referential Integrity Refinements

In SQL89, foreign keys consisted of one or more columns in a table (*table A*) that referenced one or more columns in another table (*table B*). This meant that, for every row of *table A* where the foreign key was not NULL, there had to be a row in *table B* with the same values in its referenced columns—the parent key. The parent key in *table B* had to have either the UNIQUE or the PRIMARY KEY constraint, so that it would be assured of having unique values.

In SQL92, things have grown more complex. First, matches of a foreign key to its parent can be either partial or full. The distinction comes when you have a composite (multicolumn) foreign key that is partially NULL. A partial match is a match of values that are not NULL in the foreign key; a full match is a match of all values. You specify in the FOREIGN KEY constraint which type of match is enforced.

Also, the standard supports referential triggered actions, known in some existing products as update effects and delete effects. These specify what happens when you change a parent key value that is referenced by one or more foreign key values. You can specify this effect independently for ON UPDATE and for ON DELETE, and for each there are four possibilities:

SET NULL   This sets to NULL all foreign keys that reference a parent key being deleted or changed.

SET DEFAULT   This sets all columns in the referencing foreign keys to the value defined as a default in the default value clause that applies to them. If there is no such value, the default is NULL.

CASCADE   A change in the parent key value automatically produces the same change in the foreign key value(s).

NO ACTION   The foreign key value does not change. If this would produce an integrity violation, the statement is disallowed. Keep in mind, however, that you can defer checking for an integrity violation until the end of the transaction, so there is time to change the foreign key value to a new one that would still be valid. For more information on deferring the check of the integrity constraint, refer to the discussion of "Assertions and Deferability of Constraints" in this chapter.

If none of the four is specified, NO ACTION is the default.

NOTE   See Also: Chapter 5; CREATE TABLE in Chapter 28; and Constraints in Chapter 29.

Conditional Expressions

CASE (conditional) expressions are similar to the case statements found in many programming languages. They are not statements, however, but expressions. Rather than directing actions, they have values and can be used practically anywhere a value expression can. The expressions list one or more predicates and give a value for each. The predicates are tested in the order listed. As soon as one is found that is TRUE, the CASE expression the CASE expression returns the value corresponding to that predicate to the SQL statement in which it is contained. There may be an ELSE clause at the end of the CASE expression that determines the value of the clause if none of the predicates are TRUE. If there is no ELSE clause, ELSE NULL is implied.

Two other new expressions are actually just shorthand for certain types of CASE expressions: NULLIF and COALESCE. NULLIF relates two values. If the two are the same, the condition is TRUE and NULLIF returns the value NULL. Otherwise, NULLIF returns the first of the values. COALESCE lists a series of values. It traverses the list until it finds the first one that is not NULL. It then assumes this value. If no non-NULL value is found, it assumes the NULL value. Both NULLIF and COALESCE can be expressed, albeit less succinctly, with CASE.

NOTE   See Also: Chapter 9 and CASE Expressions in Chapter 29.

Automatic Flagging of Variations on the Standard

This feature is very useful for knowing when you can simply follow the standard and this book and when you have to resort to reading the system documentation. It also helps you to write SQL code that will work the same on all engines. Basically, the flagger is a program that reviews the SQL source code in applications or modules and determines whether each statement conforms to SQL92, is an implementer extension or variation, or is in error. It then flags (marks) the statement appropriately. Of course, if the statement contains syntactic errors, the flagger may not be able to tell whether the intended statement is standard or an implementation extension. The flagger will flag at a certain level of standard conformance: Entry, Intermediate, or Full. Features that conform to a higher level of conformance than specified will be flagged as extensions. In addition to extensions, the flagger will also indicate variations—statements that are acceptable to the standard in syntax but behave somewhat differently in the implementer's version. ISO accepts these if flagged, so that the implementer's existing products can be upwardly compatible.

Modules and Compilation Units

Although this is not actually a new feature of SQL92, it is an aspect of how the SQL standard works that seems to get more complicated as time goes on, so it is worth explaining here. As mentioned in Chapter 21, the standard supports multiple "binding styles": one is the module language where modules of SQL code are called, and the other is Embedded SQL, where SQL code is directly interspersed in the source code of another language. Dynamic SQL is an extension of Embedded SQL in this regard. The standard is actually written in terms of the (infrequently used) module language and then specifies ways for Embedded SQL to emulate its behavior. Hence, things like scope, application-owned privileges, and the like are frequently specified in terms of modules. When Embedded SQL code is pre-compiled, it does indeed generate modules called *compilation units*, but the mapping of these to the module language modules is implementation-defined and not necessarily one-to-one. The upshot is that the meaning of things like scope and application-owned privileges is largely left up to the implementation. The implementation, should, however, have well-defined compilation units that have a well-defined mapping to modules. For details, however, you will have to resort to your system documentation.

Contents Grouped by Subject

This section groups the statements and common elements in the reference according to their logical function, which will make it easier to find the statement you need to perform a specific task. Once you find the desired statement, you can search for it alphabetically in the reference itself.

Defining and Changing Objects

CREATE SCHEMA   Creates a schema.*

DROP SCHEMA   Eliminates a schema.*

CREATE TABLE   Creates a table.

DECLARE LOCAL TEMPORARY TABLE   Creates a temporary table.*

ALTER TABLE   Changes the definition of a table.

DROP TABLE   Eliminates a table.

CREATE DOMAIN   Creates a domain.*

ALTER DOMAIN   Changes the definition of a domain.*

DROP DOMAIN   Eliminates a domain.*

CREATE CHARACTER SET   Defines a custom character set.

DROP CHARACTER SET   Eliminates a character set.

CREATE COLLATION   Specifies a collating sequence.*

DROP COLLATION   Eliminates a collating sequence.*

CREATE TRANSLATION   Defines a translation.

DROP TRANSLATION   Eliminates a translation.

CREATE VIEW   Creates a persistent derived table.*

DROP VIEW   Eliminates a derived table.*

ALLOCATE CURSOR   Dynamically creates a cursor.*

DECLARE CURSOR   Creates a cursor.*

Constraints*   Details on data restrictions.

Datatypes   Details on types of data.

Row and Table Value Constructors   Direct specifications of rows and tables.

Appendix D   INFORMATION_SCHEMA

Manipulating Data

SELECT   Retrieves rows from tables.

INSERT   Puts rows in tables.

UPDATE   Changes data values.

DELETE   Removes rows from tables.

COMMIT WORK   Makes changes permanent.

ROLLBACK   Disregards changes.

OPEN   Readies a cursor* for use.

FETCH   Retrieves rows from cursors.*

CLOSE   Empties a cursor* of data.

Aggregate Functions   Take totals, counts, averages, etc.

CASE Expressions   Specify conditional values.

CAST Expressions   Convert datatypes.

Datetime Value Functions   Reference current date or time.

Numeric Value Functions   Perform arithmetic operations.

Predicates   Define sophisticated tests of data for operations.

Row and Table Value Constructors   Specify rows and tables.

String Value Functions   Operate on character or bit strings.

Subqueries   Queries* used within other statements.

Establishing Security and Data Controls

CREATE ASSERTION   Defines a general rule for data.

DROP ASSERTION   Eliminates a general rule for data.

SET CONSTRAINTS MODE   Controls when constraints* are checked.

SET SESSION AUTHORIZATION   Specifies the current session user.

SET TRANSACTION   Prevents or allows changing of data.

GRANT   Gives users or applications privileges on objects.*

REVOKE   Takes away privileges on objects.*

Constraints   Details on restricting data.

Setting Up the Session Parameters

CONNECT   Starts a SQL session.

DISCONNECT   Ends a SQL session.

SET CONSTRAINTS MODE   Controls when constraints* are checked.

SET NAMES   Sets name defaults.

SET SCHEMA   Specifies the current schema.*

SET SESSION AUTHORIZATION   Specifies the current session user.

SET TIME ZONE   Specifies the current time zone.

SET TRANSACTION   Prevents or allows changing of data.

Static Coded Applications

CLOSE   Empties a cursor* of data.

DECLARE CURSOR   Creates a cursor.*

OPEN   Readies a cursor* for use.

FETCH   Retrieves rows from cursors.*

Appendix E   Mapping SQL to Other Languages.*

Appendix F   Specification of the Module Language*

Dynamic Coded Applications

ALLOCATE CURSOR   Defines a cursor* dynamically.

ALLOCATE DESCRIPTOR   Sets aside descriptor area.*

DEALLOCATE DESCRIPTOR   Destroys descriptor area.*

DESCRIBE   Automatically fills descriptor area.*

SET DESCRIPTOR   Manually fills descriptor area.*

GET DESCRIPTOR   Retrieves information from descriptor area.*

Descriptor Areas   Details on descriptor* contents.

PREPARE   Generates a SQL statement dynamically.

DEALLOCATE PREPARE   Destroys a prepared SQL statement.

EXECUTE   Executes a prepared SQL statement.

EXECUTE IMMEDIATE   Prepares and executes a SQL statement.

DECLARE CURSOR   Creates a cursor.*

OPEN   Readies a cursor* for use.

FETCH   Retrieves rows from cursors.*

Appendix H   Specification of Dynamic SQL*

Troubleshooting

GET DIAGNOSTICS   Retrieves error messages from diagnostics area.*

Appendix E   Embedded SQL   Includes information on status parameters*

Appendix C   Error Codes

NOTE   The asterisk (*) indicates terms that may be found in the Glossary in Appendix I.

CHAPTER

TWENTY-EIGHT

28

SQL Statement Reference

This is an alphabetical reference to the statements recognized by the SQL92 standard. Although SQL99 is published, as of this publication (2000), it is SQL92 that you will find in the marketplace. We cover SQL99 elsewhere in this book, though at a lesser level of detail than this reference provides. Elements common to multiple statements, such as datatypes, predicates, and value expressions, are covered in the next chapter. If you are unsure of the name of the statement you need, see the Contents Grouped by Subject chart at the end of Part VII or the Index. To understand the context in which these statements are used, consult the earlier parts of the book.

Each entry presents the following information: the purpose of the statement, its syntax and usage rules, its requirements for various levels of standard conformance, and cross-references to related subjects. References that appear in UPPERCASE letters are to statement entries in this chapter; those in Mixed Case are to entries for other SQL elements in Chapter 29.

The SQL92 standard is designed so that implementers can bring their products into conformance gradually. The standard defines three levels of conformance, each incorporating its predecessor: Entry, Intermediate, and Full. The entire standard builds on the previous SQL86 and SQL89 standards, so these can be considered prior levels of conformance. Unless otherwise noted, any feature required for some level of conformance is also required for any higher level, so that all Entry features are also required for the Intermediate level, and all SQL86 features are also part of SQL89 and SQL92. SQL99 is an exception; it builds directly on Entry-level SQL92. Keep in mind that conformance to the standard is, in any case, optional. ISO does not enforce or officially certify conformance. The National Institute of Standards and Technology (NIST) used to certify SQL conformance but has abandoned this role. It is not clear at this writing whether anyone else will take it up.

Each entry describes the features of the statement as required for Full ISO SQL92 conformance. Following each description is an outline of the conformance levels, showing what features are not required by products claiming lesser levels of conformance to the 92 standard or claiming conformance to an earlier standard. The conformance levels are shown here:

Intermediate	Not required for Intermediate-level conformance to the ANSI/ISO SQL92 standard.
Entry	Not required for Entry-level conformance to the ANSI/ISO SQL92 standard.
SQL89	Not required for conformance to the 1989 ANSI/ISO SQL standard.
SQL86	Required for conformance to the 1986 ANSI/ISO SQL standard.

| Non | Not required by any ANSI/ISO official standard, but commonly used. |

Except for Non, each of these levels implies conformance to all of its predecessors unless otherwise noted, so that any SQL code that conforms to Entry 92 also conforms to SQL89, and code that conforms to Full 92 also conforms both to Intermediate and Entry.

The syntax diagrams use conventions that mostly follow the BNF (Backus Naur Form) standard, but we have introduced some variations to enhance readability. The conventions we use are as follows:

- The symbol ::= means "is defined as". It is used to further clarify parts of a statement's syntax diagram.

- Keywords appear in all uppercase letters. These reserved words are literals that are actually written as part of the statement.

- Placeholders for specific values, such as *domain name* in the CREATE DOMAIN statement, appear in *italic* type. These placeholders identify the type of value that should be used in a real statement; they are not literals to be written as part of the statement. The Usage discussion explains their possible values and any restrictions on them. This is not a standard BNF convention.

- Optional portions of a statement appear in square brackets ([and]).

- A vertical bar (|) indicates that whatever precedes it may optionally be replaced by whatever follows it.

- Braces ({ and }) indicate that everything within them is to be regarded as a whole for the purpose of evaluating other symbols (e.g., vertical bars or ellipses).

- Ellipses (…) indicate that the preceding portion of the statement may be repeated any number of times.

- Ellipses with an interposed comma (.,..) indicate that the preceding portion may be repeated any number of times, with the individual occurrences separated by commas. The final occurrence should not be followed by a comma.

NOTE Ellipses with an interposed comma, as described above, are not a standard BNF convention; we use them for simplicity and clarity in representing the many SQL statements that use this construct. Without them, the diagrams would be considerably more complex.

- Parentheses (()) used in syntax diagrams are literals. They indicate that parentheses are to be used in forming the statement. They do not specify a way of reading the diagram as braces or square brackets do.

Carriage returns or line feeds in SQL are treated the same as blanks—they simply delimit the elements of statements. In other words, they are white space. Carriage returns and spacing are used in our syntax diagrams for readability only; you need not duplicate them in your SQL code.

It is worth pointing out here the distinction between two terms that will frequently turn up in discussion of the standard: *implementation-dependent* and *implementation-defined*. The two are not quite the same. The former means that the implementation can simply do what it likes; the latter also allows the implementation to do as it sees fit but requires that it commit itself—the implementation's behavior must be both documented and consistent.

NOTE

The terminology we use here is not always the official ISO terminology. The official terminology can get quite labyrinthine, so we have simplified things somewhat. For this reason, we sometimes use different terms than the ISO or even use the same terms somewhat differently. For example, "predicate" in the standard is an expression using =, BETWEEN, EXISTS, or similar operators that can be TRUE, FALSE, or UNKNOWN. A "search condition" is some combination of predicates using AND, OR, NOT, and parentheses and also can be TRUE, FALSE, or UNKNOWN. In this book, we have effectively defined "predicate" recursively to incorporate both of these terms into a single term.

ALLOCATE CURSOR

(Dynamic SQL Only) Associates a Cursor with a Prepared Statement

Syntax

```
ALLOCATE extended cursor name
[INSENSITIVE] [SCROLL]
CURSOR FOR extended statement name;
```

Usage

The ALLOCATE CURSOR statement is used in Dynamic SQL to associate a cursor with a SQL statement previously readied by a PREPARE statement. It differs from the dynamic version of DECLARE CURSOR in that the cursor name is a host-language variable. This means you can use an ALLOCATE CURSOR statement to create an indefinite number of cursors by executing it repeatedly with different values for the name parameter. For examples of ALLOCATE CURSOR in use, see Chapter 22.

The extended statement name is the name of an object previously created with a PREPARE statement, which must be a properly formed SELECT statement, suitable for use in a cursor. ALLOCATE CURSOR must conform to the rules for cursors specified under DECLARE CURSOR. INSENSITIVE means that the content of the cursor will not be changed if the data changes while it is in use. SCROLL enables you to retrieve the rows of the cursor in any order you want, but it may only be used with read-only cursors. Both of these are explained in more detail under DECLARE CURSOR. If applicable, an updatability clause may be appended to the SELECT statement in order to restrict the cursor's updatability and thus limit its lock usage. If so, it is included in the SELECT string given to the PREPARE statement, rather than part of this statement. Again, see DECLARE CURSOR. For an explanation of locking, see Chapter 17.

The extended cursor name is a simple target specification, that is, a host-language variable that cannot have an indicator variable appended. At the time the ALLOCATE CURSOR statement is executed, the variable must have a value, and that value must be different from the names of all existing allocated cursors in the same module or compilation unit.

To destroy (deallocate) the cursor, close it using the CLOSE statement and then simply deallocate the prepared statement on which it is based, using the DEALLOCATE PREPARE statement.

Example

In the following example, the content of the host variable cursorname will be set to the name of the allocated scrollable cursor. We assume that cursorname is of a text string type, although the specific type will depend upon the host language. The current value of cursorname will become the name used to refer to the cursor in other SQL statements. Statement5 is a prepared SELECT statement. It is assumed that the application numbers statements as they are prepared.

```
ALLOCATE :cursorname SCROLL CURSOR

FOR :statement5;
```

Conformance Levels

Intermediate   The implementation is not required to support the ALLOCATE
                   CURSOR statement at this level.

NOTE   See Also: Chapter 22, DECLARE CURSOR and PREPARE in this chapter, and Appendices E and H.

ALLOCATE DESCRIPTOR
(Dynamic SQL Only) Creates a Descriptor Area

Syntax

```
ALLOCATE DESCRIPTOR descriptor name
  [ WITH MAX num occurrences ];
```

Usage

A descriptor area is an area used in Dynamic SQL to store information about the parameters of a dynamically generated SQL statement. There can be one descriptor area for input variables and another for output. Host-language variables provide an alternative to descriptor areas for either or both of these purposes. Descriptor areas are used because the statements in Dynamic SQL are generated spontaneously at runtime, with dynamic parameters represented by simple question marks. The ALLOCATE DESCRIPTOR statement creates a descriptor area with the given name and the number of allocated descriptor items specified by *num occurrences*. The actual descriptor area can have this number of items or fewer. If the WITH MAX clause is not used, some implementation-dependent default greater than zero will apply. For examples of descriptor areas in use, see Chapter 22. For a detailed explanation of the content of descriptor areas, see Descriptor Areas in Chapter 29.

Example

The following statement allocates a 17-item descriptor area called descrip_stat5.

```
ALLOCATE DESCRIPTOR 'descrip_stat5'
  WITH MAX 17;
```

Conformance Levels

Intermediate	The name of the descriptor and the number specified in the WITH MAX clause may be restricted to being literals rather than variables. This is not true for Full conformance.
Entry	There is a discrepancy in the standard in that it does not state that descriptor areas are not required for Entry-level conformance, but it does state that Dynamic SQL generally is not so required. Since descriptors are used only in Dynamic SQL, we assume the intent is that descriptors are not required at this level.
SQL89	Dynamic SQL and descriptors areas were not part of the standard.

NOTE See Also: Chapter 22; DEALLOCATE DESCRIPTOR, DESCRIBE, GET DESCRIPTOR, and SET DESCRIPTOR in this chapter; and Descriptor Areas in Chapter 29.

ALTER DOMAIN

Changes the Definition of a Domain

Syntax

```
ALTER DOMAIN domain name
  { SET DEFAULT default   }
| { DROP DEFAULT  }
| { ADD constraint clause }
| { DROP CONSTRAINT constraint name };
```

Usage

ALTER DOMAIN changes the definition of a domain by adding or dropping a default or constraint. Domains are alternatives to datatypes on which columns can be based. For more on domains, see CREATE DOMAIN. ALTER DOMAIN can be issued only by the owner of the schema that contains the domain. Any changes you specify with it instantly affect all columns based on the domain.

SET DEFAULT defines a default value that will be applied to all columns based on the domain unless overridden by a default defined on the particular column (see CREATE TABLE). The new default applies to rows added to the tables after this statement is issued; default values already present in the data are unaffected. For example, if you change a default city from London to Tokyo, rows in columns based on this domain that previously had London set by default will not have their values changed, but new rows will have Tokyo.

DROP DEFAULT removes the existing default. In the absence of an existing default, it will produce an error.

ADD places a new constraint on the domain. This constraint will use the keyword VALUE wherever it references the column value to be checked. In other words, VALUE replaces a specific column reference, as any number of columns could be based on this domain.

DROP CONSTRAINT eliminates a constraint. If the constraint was not assigned a name when created, it will have some name assigned by the DBMS (for any level of SQL92 conformance). Any such generated name will be listed in the INFORMATION_ SCHEMA. The standard does not allow multiple changes in the same ALTER DOMAIN statement. In other words, you cannot drop a default and add a constraint at the same time.

Example

The following statement restricts the range of values that can be entered into the domain id_nums to those between 0 and 10000 inclusive (the domain, of course, is assumed to have a numeric datatype).

```
ALTER DOMAIN id_nums ADD range_check
CHECK(VALUE BETWEEN 0 AND 10000);
```

This constraint is not deferrable.

Conformance Levels

Intermediate	ALTER DOMAIN is not required at this level.
Entry	No support for domains is required at this level.

> **NOTE**
> See Also: CREATE DOMAIN and DROP DOMAIN in this chapter, Constraints in Chapter 29, and Appendix D.

ALTER TABLE
Changes the Definition of an Existing Base Table

Syntax

```
ALTER TABLE table name
{ ADD [COLUMN] column definition }
| { ALTER [COLUMN] column name alter action}
| { DROP [COLUMN] column name RESTRICT | CASCADE }
| { ADD table constraint definition }
| { DROP CONSTRAINT constraint name
```

```
RESTRICT | CASCADE };
```

```
alter action ::=
{ SET DEFAULT default option } | { DROP DEFAULT }
```

Usage

The table affected cannot be a view or a declared local temporary table. (See CREATE VIEW and DECLARE LOCAL TEMPORARY TABLE, respctively, in this chapter.) The ALTER TABLE statement must be issued by the owner of the schema in which the table is located.

ADD COLUMN places a new column in the table, which will be its new last column. The optional word COLUMN is allowed for clarity; it is not needed and has no effect. The DBMS can distinguish ADD COLUMN from ADD used for table constraints because the latter use begins with a keyword while the former begins with a column name, which cannot be a keyword. The new column is defined just as it would have been in a CREATE TABLE statement. It may include constraints, a default, and a collating sequence.

If the table is not empty at the time the new column is added, the column will be initially set to the default value for every row in the table. This implies that there must be a default value for the added column. The default will be that defined for the column or, if none such, that defined for the domain or, if none such, NULL. If the column has the NOT NULL constraint, and the table is not empty when the column is added, either the column or its domain, if any, must have a default value. Users with privileges on the table will also have them on the new column, unless those privileges are column-specific (see Chapter 16).

ALTER COLUMN is used to create or drop a default value for the column. Again, the word COLUMN is optional. The default value, of course, should match the datatype of the column or of its domain, whichever is applicable. The default may include user value functions. (See Value Expressions in Chapter 29 for more information.)

DROP COLUMN is used to eliminate a column from the table. Any data currently in the column is destroyed. Naturally, there are restrictions. First, the column to be dropped may not be the only one in the table. (If this is what you want to do, use DROP TABLE.)

If you specify RESTRICT, the statement will fail if the column is currently referenced in any views, constraints, or assertions, except for constraints that are contained in the table and reference only the specified column. Sometimes, references to a column can be hidden; for example, a view that includes SELECT * (SELECT all columns) will include the column even without naming it. So may one that uses the NATURAL JOIN operation (see SELECT).

If you specify CASCADE, such referencing objects will be dropped, and all column-specific privileges on the column will be revoked from all users.

> **WARNING** With CASCADE, views referencing the column will not be modified—they will be dropped.

ADD *table constraint definition* will add a new table constraint to the table, and DROP will drop an existing one. If RESTRICT is specified for DROP, the column must not currently be used as the parent key to any foreign key. If CASCADE is specified, any such foreign keys will have their REFERENCES or FOREIGN KEY constraint dropped as well. If the foreign key is also a parent (possible but unusual), any foreign keys that reference it will also lose their constraints.

Example

This statement adds a column called country to the Clients table. The column is a fixed-length text string with a ten-character maximum length and a default value of USA.

```
ALTER TABLE  Clients ADD country CHAR(10) DEFAULT = 'USA';
```

Conformance Levels

Intermediate   ALTER TABLE is required for Intermediate or Full SQL92 conformance. It has been supported by many products for some time but not in a fully standardized fashion.

> **NOTE** See Also: Chapter 3; CREATE TABLE, DROP TABLE, and CREATE DOMAIN in this chapter; and Constraints and Datatypes in Chapter 29.

CLOSE

(Static or Dynamic SQL) Closes a Currently Open Cursor

Syntax

```
CLOSE cursor name;
```

Usage

If the cursor is not currently open, the CLOSE statement will produce an error. It does not matter whether any or all of the rows have been fetched. Once the cursor is closed, its content is lost. If it is reopened, the query contained will be executed again with possibly different results (if the data has been changed in the interim). For more on cursors, see DECLARE CURSOR and Chapter 21.

Conformance Levels

SQL86   CLOSE is required by the original 86 standard.

NOTE

See Also: Chapter 21 and ALLOCATE CURSOR, DEALLOCATE CURSOR, DECLARE CURSOR, FETCH, and OPEN in this chapter.

COMMIT WORK

Makes Current Changes Permanent

Syntax

```
COMMIT [WORK];
```

Usage

The COMMIT WORK statement terminates a transaction (a group of statements executed together) and attempts to make the changes dictated by statements within the transaction permanent. This attempt can fail because, for example, of a system crash or a constraint violation. If the transaction cannot be committed, it will be rolled back (aborted). In the more advanced conformance levels, WORK is an optional word provided for clarity; it has no effect. For examples of transactions and the COMMIT statement, see Chapter 17.

If your system is configured so that transaction management is under the control of the operating system, this statement produces an error.

Before the COMMIT is performed, all constraints that were deferred are checked. After the execution of all statements in the transaction, the database must be in a state that satisfies all constraints. Otherwise, the transaction is rolled back. For more on deferring constraints, see Constraints in Chapter 29.

When the transaction is committed, all open cursors are closed, and any temporary tables whose definitions specify ON COMMIT DELETE ROWS are emptied of data.

Conformance Levels

Intermediate   Deferability of constraints is not required by the standard.

Entry   The keyword WORK is not optional.

NOTE   See Also: Chapter 17; CLOSE, ROLLBACK, and SET TRANSACTION in this chapter; and Constraints in Chapter 29.

CONNECT
Establishes a Connection to the DBMS

Syntax

```
CONNECT TO { SQL environment spec
    [ AS connection name ]
    [ USER user name] }
    | DEFAULT ;
```

Usage

Since some connection procedure is necessary in most SQL environments, most products already have their own approach to this problem. The standard technique indicated here won't be required until Full SQL92 conformance is reached, although many products may try to implement it even if they do not claim such conformance.

If there is already an active connection between the user and the DBMS, the previous connection becomes dormant, and the new one is current.

DEFAULT indicates implementation-defined values for *SQL environment spec*, *connection name*, and *user name*. Likewise, omitting the AS or USER clauses implies that the implementation has some technique for naming the connection and for ascertaining the Authorization ID under which the statement should be run. The Authorization ID may be obtained from the operating system, for example, or it and a password may be prompted for. Other than meeting the basic conventions (outlined in Appendix G), restrictions as to format and possible values of all of these are implementation-defined.

It is also up to the implementation to determine from the *SQL environment spec* which server to connect to, what protocol to use, and so on.

If the CONNECT statement is issued by a SQL module or compilation unit emulation thereof, this module may have its own Authorization ID. If so, it is implementation-defined whether the user name must be that Authorization ID or could instead be the user's own ID. In any other case, the username would be the Authorization ID normally identifying the user. For more on modules, see Appendix F.

If the user already has a connection with the indicated connection name, the statement will produce an error. This includes the DEFAULT. If the statement produces an error, the current connection, if any, will remain the current connection.

Example

The following statement initiates a connection to the environment called Marketing_Dept under the Authorization ID (for SESSION_USER) Carrie:

```
CONNECT TO Marketing_Dept USER Carrie ;
```

Conformance Levels

Full Only required at this level.

Non Some form of connection initiation is supported by all major products, but it may not precisely follow the standard.

> **NOTE** See Also: DISCONNECT and SET CONNECTION in this chapter and Authorization IDs in Chapter 20.

CREATE ASSERTION

Defines an Assertion

Syntax

```
CREATE ASSERTION constraint name
CHECK ( predicate )
[ constraint attributes ];
```

Usage

An assertion is a schema object whose content is a CHECK constraint, which is to say a predicate preceded by the keyword CHECK. The constraint is violated if the predicate is FALSE. The rules, behavior, and syntax of CHECK constraints are described in Chapter 29 under Constraints. An assertion is not part of a table definition but exists independently of any particular table and can refer in its predicate to any tables in the schema. It can be used to ensure that tables are not empty, which cannot be done from within the tables because constraints within tables are checked only when table values are inserted, updated, or deleted. The assertion must conform to the following principles:

- The name must be supplied. With other types of constraints, you have the option of letting the DBMS name the constraint for you (although it is usually not a good idea). For assertions, you do not have this option.

- If the assertion is created as part of a CREATE SCHEMA sequence, and the assertion's name is qualified by a schema name, the latter must be the name of the schema being created.

- The predicate cannot reference a temporary table. Temporary tables are explained under CREATE TABLE.

- The predicate cannot use target specifications (the variables used to output data to the host language in Static SQL) or dynamic parameter specifications (which serve a similar function in Dynamic SQL).

- The predicate may not use datetime value functions or user value functions (CURRENT_USER and so on).

- The assertion is named as a constraint. Therefore, its name must be different from the name of every other constraint in the schema.

- The predicate cannot contain a query that is possibly non-deterministic (possibly non-deterministic queries are defined in this chapter under SELECT).

- For every column specifically referenced in the predicate, the creator of the assertion must have the REFERENCES privilege on that column or the CREATE ASSERTION statement will fail.

- For every table referenced without regard to column names (for example, if an assertion containing the aggregate function COUNT (*) were used on the table to impose a maximum size), you must have the REFERENCES privilege on at least one column of that table.

- The assertion fails if it is FALSE at the time the constraint is checked. A value of UNKNOWN, which can be caused by NULLs, will not cause a failure (see Chapter 7 or Predicates in Chapter 29 for an explanation of NULLs and UNKNOWNs).

- The *constraint attributes* clause allows you to define whether the constraint can be deferred and whether it is deferred by default. If no constraint attributes are included, the constraint will not be deferrable and will be effectively checked after every relevant statement (see Constraints in Chapter 29).

If the text of the constraint is too long to fit in the allocated space in the INFORMATION_ SCHEMA (the set of tables that describe the content of the database), you will get a warning message, but the statement will not fail. The text will be truncated in the INFORMATION_SCHEMA but will still execute as though it were present in full.

Example

The following statement defines an assertion on the Salespeople table that ensures that either the salary or commission columns must have a value (both may have values). The constraint will be deferrable but checked immediately by default.

```
CREATE ASSERTION Check_on_pay
CHECK (Salespeople.salary IS NOT NULL
OR Salespeople.commission IS NOT NULL)
DEFERRABLE INITIALLY IMMEDIATE;
```

Conformance Levels

Intermediate   Support for assertions is not required at this level.

> **NOTE**
> See Also: CREATE SCHEMA, DROP ASSERTION, and SET CONSTRAINTS MODE in this chapter; Constraints, Datetime Value Functions, Predicates, and Value Expressions (for User Value Functions) in Chapter 29; and Appendix G.

CREATE CHARACTER SET

Defines a Character Set

Syntax

```
CREATE CHARACTER SET character set name [ AS ]
GET character set source
[ COLLATE collation name
| COLLATION FROM collation source ];
```

Usage

The CREATE CHARACTER SET statement defines a character set for text strings. As part of its internationalization, SQL92 provides this facility primarily to enable the use of languages other than English. This statement can also be used to change the default collation of a character set by defining a new version of it with a different collation.

Each SQL implementation comes with one or more character sets already defined. These will either follow national or international standards or be defined by the implementer. One of these sets is the SQL TEXT character set that is used to express the SQL language itself. This statement enables you to create new character sets by changing the existing definitions and supplying new names.

A character set consists of a *repertoire*, an *encoding* a *form-of-use*, and a *collation*. A repertoire is a set of characters, an encoding is a way of representing them internally in the database (i.e., as binary numbers), a form-of-use is a data format used by the encoding, and a collation is a way of sorting them. The form-of-use is associated with the repertoire and generally need only be considered separately if you want to change it (see String Value Functions in Chapter 29). This statement combines the repertoire of some existing character set with a collation to define a new character set. A character set is an object in the schema. It has an owner, and other users must be granted the USAGE privilege on it to access it.

A character set follows the ordinary rules for schema objects. That is to say, it must be created by the schema owner, its name must be unique within the schema, and if it is part of a CREATE SCHEMA sequence, it will be part of the schema being created and cannot specify another with a qualified name. The creator of the character set will be able to grant the USAGE privilege on it to others. If the CREATE CHARACTER SET statement is contained in a module or compilation unit, the current Authorization ID, whether that of the user or the module, must be that of the schema owner.

The GET clause identifies the character set that provides the repertoire. To use a character set as the source of your repertoire, you must have the USAGE privilege on that character set. In this case, you would simply be creating a new character set with the same repertoire but a different collation than the old. For example, you might use this to make ASCII and EBCDIC collate the same way, which of course they normally do not. You would own and control access over this new character set.

Lastly, you define the default collation for this character set. If a CREATE CHARACTER SET statement is part of a CREATE SCHEMA sequence, you may use a COLLATE clause to explicitly specify a collation. Otherwise, you must use COLLATION FROM and apply some predefined collation or other collation source as defined under CREATE COLLATION.

Example

The following statement defines a new character set based on the ASCII repertoire but with the reverse collating sequence, so that `'a' > 'b'`.

```
CREATE CHARACTER SET Backwards_ASCII
GET ASCII COLLATION FROM DESC(ASCII);
```

Conformance Levels

Intermediate   At this level, being able to simultaneously define a character set and collation in a CREATE SCHEMA sequence is not required.

Entry   Entry-level conformance does not require support for the CREATE CHARACTER SET statement.

NOTE   See Also: Chapter 20; CREATE SCHEMA and DROP CHARACTER SET in this chapter; Collations in Chapter 29; and Appendix G.

CREATE COLLATION

Defines a Collating Sequence

Syntax

```
CREATE COLLATION collation name
FOR character set specification
FROM collation source
[ NO PAD | PAD SPACE ]


collation source ::=
collation name
| DESC ( collation name )
| DEFAULT
| EXTERNAL ('external collation name')
| { TRANSLATION translation name
 [ THEN COLLATION collation name ] };
```

Usage

Text strings in SQL are normally sortable. This means that they fall in some intrinsic sequence, such as alphabetical order. You can apply relational operators such as less than and greater than to such strings, and the expression will be evaluated in terms of the collating sequence. For example, `'a' < 'b'` means "`'a'` precedes `'b'` in the collating sequence," and `'c' > 'b'` means "`'c'` follows `'b'` in the collating sequence". Strings of more than one character are sorted by comparing the first character of each, then the second, and so on until a difference between the two strings is found. That difference determines the sorting order.

A collation is a named schema object that defines a collating sequence. As with other schema objects, all collations in a schema must have distinct names. If they are part of a CREATE SCHEMA sequence, and a schema name is prefixed to their own, it must be the name of the schema being created.

The Authorization ID issuing the CREATE COLLATION statement must have the USAGE privilege on all collations and translations referenced within it. This Authorization ID will own and have the USAGE privilege on the created collation but will have the GRANT OPTION on this privilege only if it also has the GRANT OPTION on all the contained collations and translations.

If the *collation source* is a collation name, that collation is duplicated. It may be a collation from a different schema, so you can transfer customized collations between schemas this way. You can also define a new version of a collation with a different pad attribute (explained below). Naturally, if the collation is drawn from a schema other than the current default, the name must be preceded by the schema name and a dot.

If the *collation source* specifies DESC (descending) followed by a collation name, the new collation will be the reverse of the old.

If the *collation source* specifies DEFAULT, the collation will be the order in which the characters are represented in the repertoire. This is implementation-defined.

If the *collation source* specifies EXTERNAL, the nature of the collation and any restrictions upon it are implementation-defined.

If the *collation source* specifies TRANSLATION, an already-existing translation will be applied to the character set. The source character set of the translation must be the same as that of the collation being here defined. If the THEN COLLATION clause is used, its character set must match the target of the translation. For more on tranlations, see CREATE TRANSLATION.

Example

The following statement defines a collation based on the Cursive character set. The collation will follow the order in which the characters are represented in the repertoire.

```
CREATE COLLATION Normal_cursive
```

```
FOR Cursive
FROM DEFAULT;
```

Conformance Levels

Intermediate   Support for the CREATE COLLATION statement is not required

NOTE   See Also: Chapter 20; CREATE CHARACTER SET, CREATE SCHEMA, and CREATE TRANSLATION in this chapter; Collations in Chapter 29; and Appendix G.

CREATE DOMAIN

Defines a Domain

Syntax

```
CREATE DOMAIN domain name [ AS ] datatype
[ DEFAULT default value    ]
[ constraint definition... ]
[ COLLATE collation name    ];

constraint definition ::=
[ constraint name definition ]
check constraint
[ [NOT] DEFERRABLE ]
[ {INITIALLY IMMEDIATE}
| {INITIALLY DEFERRED}]
```

Usage

The CREATE DOMAIN statement creates a domain, an object in the schema that serves as an alternative to a datatype in defining columns. A domain specifies a datatype and additionally offers options for defining a default value, a collation, and one or more constraints. Ideally, it denotes a logical category of values.

AS is provided for clarity; it is not necessary and has no effect. You can create a domain without specifying any of the optional clauses. You might do this to group columns into comparisons that make sense. For example, it makes no sense to compare social security numbers and telephone numbers even though both may be the same datatype—they are in different domains. Domains can also be a useful way to standardize complex packages of constraints or an unusual collation. The UDTs in Core SQL99 provide another approach to this that complements domains, as we discuss in Chapter 25.

Only the Authorization ID that owns the schema can create, and thus own, the domain. This Authorization ID must have the REFERENCES privilege on every column referenced in the domain and the USAGE privilege on every domain, character set, translation, or collation so referenced. This Authorization ID will have the USAGE privilege on the domain. If the Authorization ID was granted all of the privileges listed above with GRANT OPTION specified, it will be able to pass along the USAGE privilege on the domain itself.

If the CREATE DOMAIN statement is part of a CREATE SCHEMA sequence, and the domain name is prefixed with a schema name, the domain must be part of the schema being created. Also, if a character string datatype is used with no character set or no collation specified, the schema defaults apply. (Collations can only be specified for character string datatypes.)

The optional arguments follow the same rules as the same arguments used in other contexts. See CREATE TABLE and Constraints and Collations in Chapter 29.

All constraints must be expressed as CHECK constraints. As is ordinarily the case with constraints, the naming and attributes are optional. The attributes determine the deferability of the constraint, as described in Chapter 29 under Constraints. If the attributes are omitted, the constraint cannot be deferred. If the name is omitted, and your system conforms at least to Entry SQL92, the DBMS will assign a name, which you can determine by querying the INFORMATION_SCHEMA (see Appendix D).

Note also that domains cannot be circular. That is, a domain may contain constraints that reference columns; and these columns may be based on domains that have constraints of their own that reference columns in turn. But at no point in this chain should the domain we started with come up again. All domains referenced directly or indirectly in the constraints of a domain are said to be in usage by those constraints. No domain may be in usage by its own constraints.

Example

The following statement creates a domain called id_nums, which is to be filled with positive integers. The default value will be NULL.

```
CREATE DOMAIN id_nums AS integer CHECK(VALUE > 0);
```

Conformance Levels

Intermediate   At this level, the user cannot name the constraints or specify a collation. The constraints are named, but by the DBMS rather than the user.

Entry   Domains are not required at this level.

NOTE   See Also: Chapter 25; ALTER DOMAIN, CREATE TABLE, and DROP DOMAIN in this chapter; and Constraints in Chapter 29.

CREATE SCHEMA

Defines a Schema

Syntax

```
CREATE SCHEMA schema name clause
[ DEFAULT CHARACTER SET character set ]
[ { CREATE DOMAIN statement
| CREATE TABLE statement
| CREATE VIEW statement
| GRANT statement
| CREATE ASSERTION statement
| CREATE CHARACTER SET statement
| CREATE COLLATION statement
| CREATE TRANSLATION statement
  [ character set ] } ]...;

schema name clause ::=
schema name
| AUTHORIZATION authorization ID
| schema name AUTHORIZATION authorization ID
```

Usage

The CREATE SCHEMA statement creates a schema, a named group of related objects. It may contain several other statements to create objects in the schema, such as tables, character sets, and domains, and to grant privileges on them. All of these objects are effectively materialized at the same time. Therefore, some circular references are possible that would not be normally, such as having two tables each with a foreign key referencing the other table as parent. Objects and privileges may also be added later to the schema.

The creator of a schema owns it and largely controls the usage of the objects in it. The right to create schemas is itself implementation-defined. The schema is part of a group of one or more schemas called a *catalog*. Its name must be unique within the catalog.

The schema name clause specifies the name of the schema. This may be a full name, in the form

```
cluster.catalog.schema
```

If the cluster and catalog are not specified, defaults may apply in an implementation-defined manner.

If no AUTHORIZATION clause is used, there are two possibilities:

- If the CREATE SCHEMA statement is part of a module or compilation unit (see Appendix F, and the module has its own Authorization ID, the schema will be under the Authorization ID of the module. This means that use will be controlled by any user executing the module (see Appendix F and Chapter 21).

- Otherwise, the schema will be under the Authorization ID of the SQL session user who creates it. For more on SQL session users, see User Value Functions in Chapter 29.

If no *schema name* is given in the CREATE SCHEMA statement, but just the AUTHORIZATION clause, the Authorization ID is used as the *schema name*. The implicit assumption is that one Authorization ID will create only one schema, at least within the current catalog. This was the approach of the SQL86 standard, and SQL92 supports it, in large part for compatibility.

If both the Authorization ID and the schema name are indicated, the first indicates the owner and the second the schema. In any case, the schema name must be unique within its catalog.

The DEFAULT CHARACTER SET clause determines the character set that will be used for all columns and domains with CHARACTER STRING datatypes if none other is specified. If it is omitted, there will be some implementation-defined default.

If the AUTHORIZATION clause is used and the CREATE SCHEMA statement is part of a module, then the CREATE SCHEMA statement and any other statements that are part of it (for example, CREATE TABLE, CREATE DOMAIN, or any of the statements listed in the syntax diagram above) will operate under the indicated Authorization ID. After the CREATE SCHEMA statement and all of its contained statements have executed, the rest of the statements in the module will revert to the Authorization ID and the schema that were in effect before the CREATE SCHEMA statement.

Example

The following statement creates a schema called Joes_Schema, populated with a single domain and a single table and performing a single GRANT.

```
CREATE SCHEMA Joes_Schema  AUTHORIZATION Joe
DEFAULT CHARACTER SET ASCII
CREATE DOMAIN id_nums AS integer CHECK(VALUE > 0)
CREATE GLOBAL TEMPORARY TABLE Fluctuations
(  item_num    id_nums NOT NULL PRIMARY KEY,
item_name    CHAR(10) NOT NULL,
start_price  DEC(4,2),
max_price    DEC(4,2),
min_price    DEC(4,2),
avg_price    DEC(4,2),
end_price    DEC(4,2)
ON COMMIT PRESERVE ROWS )
GRANT SELECT ON Fluctuations TO Sarah;
```

Conformance Levels

Intermediate   Intermediate-level conformance need not allow assertions, collations, or translations as parts of a CREATE SCHEMA sequence.

Entry   Entry-level conformance does not require support for domains or character sets. It also does not mandate being able to name the schema—your only option may be to omit the name clause so that the schema is named after the Authorization ID of its creator (as specified in SQL89).

NOTE   See Also: CREATE ASSERTION, CREATE CHARACTER SET, CREATE COLLATION, CREATE DOMAIN, CREATE TABLE, CREATE TRANSLATION, CREATE VIEW, DROP SCHEMA, GRANT, and REVOKE in this chapter; Authorization IDs and Collations in Chapter 29; and Appendix G.

CREATE TABLE

Creates a Permanent or Temporary Base Table

Syntax

```
CREATE [ {GLOBAL | LOCAL} TEMPORARY ] TABLE table name
( {column definition
| [table constraint ] }.,..
[ ON COMMIT { DELETE | PRESERVE } ROWS ] );


column definition ::=
column name
  {domain name | datatype[(size)]    }
  [ column constraint...]
  [ default value  ]
  [ collate clause ]
```

Usage

If TEMPORARY is specified, the table is temporary, and either GLOBAL or LOCAL must be specified; otherwise the table is a permanent base table and neither GLOBAL nor LOCAL apply. The disctinction between permanent and temporary base tables will be clarified later in this entry. The ON COMMIT clause can only be used for temporary tables. If the table is temporary, and the ON COMMIT clause is omitted, then ON COMMIT DELETE ROWS is implied.

The table will contain one or more column definitions and zero or more *table constraints*, all separated by commas. The order of the columns in the CREATE TABLE statement determines their order in the table. A column definition must include:

- The name of the column. The column must be named as outlined in Appendix G.
- Either a datatype or a domain that will apply to all column values.

The table creator must have the USAGE privilege on a domain to define a column on it. Some datatypes will accept size arguments indicating, for example, the length of a fixed-length character string or the scale and precision of a decimal number. The meaning and format of these vary with the datatype, but there will be defaults in any case. See Datatypes in Chapter 29 for more information on these arguments. For examples of CREATE TABLE in use, see Chapters 3, 4, and 5.

In addition to the elements shown above, there are a number of optional elements that can be included in column definitions. These elements, discussed below, may be specified in any order.

Default Values and Collations

One such element is a default value for the column. If a default is given for a column specified on a domain that already has its own default, the default of the column overrides that of the domain. If the NOT NULL constraint (described below) is specified for a column, then either a default value must be defined or every INSERT or UPDATE command on the column must leave it with a specified value.

You may also specify a collating sequence for the column, if that column has a character string datatype or is defined on a domain with such a datatype. This sequence overrides the ordinary collating sequence of the character set or of the domain. See Collations in Chapter 29 for more detail on collating sequence.

Column and Table Constraints

You may also place one or more constraints on the table. Constraints following the definition of a column apply to that column; those standing alone as table constraints may reference any one or more columns in the table. Starting with SQL92 (any level), constraints are named, although the names may be generated internally, rather than defined by the table creator. The following description of the types of constraints is an overview; see Chapters 4 and 5 and Constraints in Chapter 29 for more detailed information. The possible constraints are:

NOT NULL	In the standard, this can only be a column constraint. This forbids NULLs from being entered into a column.
UNIQUE	This mandates that every column value, or combination of column values if a table constraint, be unique.
PRIMARY KEY	This has the same effect as UNIQUE, except that none of the columns in a PRIMARY KEY constraint may contain NULLs, while those in a UNIQUE constraint may. (Note that this is not true for Entry-level SQL92 conformance, as noted under the conformance levels. In fact, Entry-compliant implementations may allow NULLs in UNIQUE \as an extension to the standard.) Also, the PRIMARY KEY constraint behaves a bit differently with foreign keys (explained later in this entry). This constraint may be used only once in a given table.

CHECK	This is followed by a predicate, in parentheses, that uses column values in some expression whose value can be TRUE, FALSE, or (in the presence of NULLs) UNKNOWN. The constraint is violated only when the predicate is FALSE. See Predicates in Chapter 29.
FOREIGN KEY | REFERENCES	FOREIGN KEY is the table constraint version; REFERENCES is for column constraints. For a table constraint, the words FOREIGN KEY are followed by a parenthesized list of the column names in this table that will do the referencing. After that, the two versions are the same: the keyword REFERENCES followed by the name of the table containing the parent key and a parenthesized list of the column(s) that are to be referenced. This constraint identifies the columns as a foreign key referencing a parent key in the same or (usually) another table. The parent key must have the PRIMARY KEY or the UNIQUE constraint. If the former, the column name(s) can be omitted from the FOREIGN KEY or REFERENCES constraint. Note that you can specify what happens when a parent key is changed or deleted, and you can specify full or partial matches of foreign to parent keys, which behave differently when NULLs are present. See Constraints in Chapter 29 for details.

You can define constraints so that they are not checked until the end of the current transaction. This is very useful when, for example, you want to update a table that references itself as a parent key. This operation usually creates intermediate states where referential integrity has to be violated. By default, constraints are not deferrable. See SET CONSTRAINTS MODE or Constraints in Chapter 29 for more information.

Temporary Tables

Temporary tables are tables whose data is destroyed at the end of every SQL session, if not earlier. They are used for intermediate results or working storage. There are three kinds: global temporary tables, created local temporary tables, and declared local temporary tables. The first two are created with the CREATE TABLE statement by specifying GLOBAL TEMPORARY or LOCAL TEMPORARY, respectively. Declared local temporary tables are created with the DECLARE LOCAL TEMPORARY TABLE statement. The difference between the first two types, which we will call created temporary tables, and the third, the declared tables, is that the created tables have definitions that are permanent parts of the schema, even though their data is not. Declared tables are created at runtime by a SQL module or a program that uses SQL; outside that module or program, their names and definitions are not stored in the database.

The difference between the global and local tables created by this statement is their visibility. Although neither can be seen by other SQL sessions (and thus by other users), the data in global temporary tables can be accessed by any program or module within the session. Created local tables, on the other hand, cannot share data between modules or compilation units. For further discussion of modules and compilation units, see Appendix F.

To summarize, temporary tables are base tables. The data they contain is their own, not (as with views) an indirect representation of the data in other tables. They typically are created and filled with data by applications or modules. But this data is not saved in the database. It is automatically destroyed at the end of a SQL session, and when the table is to be used again, new data must be inserted into it. Global temporary tables have definitions stored permanently (that is, until dropped like any other table with a DROP TABLE statement) in the schema. Their data can be accessed by any statement within the same SQL session. Created local temporary tables also have definitions that are permanent parts of the database schema, but their data can be accessed only by the SQL module or program that called them. Declared local temporary tables, created with the DECLARE LOCAL TEMPORARY TABLE statement, do not even have definitions that are part of the database schema. Their definitions are part of the code in a module or Embedded SQL program, and they are defined when that code is executed. Table 28.1 summarizes the characteristics of the various types of base tables. Since declared tables are created with a different statement, we will omit them from the remainder of this discussion.

TABLE 28.1:   Characteristics of Base Tables

Table Type	Visibility of Data	Definition	Data Persistence
Permanent	Universal (subject to privileges)	Permanent	Permanent
Global Temporary	Session	Permanent	Session
Created Local	Module or C.U.	Permanent	Session
Declared Local	Module or C.U.	Module or C.U.	Session

The ON COMMIT clause specifies what happens at the end of the transaction. DELETE ROWS will empty the table, while PRESERVE ROWS will retain the data for the next transaction in the session. If the transaction rolls back (is aborted), the table is returned to its state at the end of the previous transaction, with the rows either deleted or preserved. If the aborted transaction was the first in the session, the table is emptied. As we mentioned, DELETE is the default, so be sure to specify PRESERVE if you will ever want to retain the data across transaction boundaries. You can always empty the table, but you cannot preserve the data in a table that specifies ON COMMIT DELETE ROWS.

Ownership and Access Control

Like all database objects, a table resides in a schema and is created by the owner of that schema. If the table name is qualified by a schema name in the CREATE TABLE command, it identifies the containing schema. If the table name is not so qualified, it will be part of the current default schema. (See Appendix G for details.) As with all schema objects, if the table is part of a CREATE SCHEMA sequence, then the schema being created will be the containing schema. In any case, the table name must be unique within its schema.

Tables and other database objects are created and owned by Authorization IDs, which means users in most contexts (the exception is with modules, see Appendix F). The owner of an object controls the privileges others have on it. In a sense, then, all privilege flows from the right to create objects. Who has this right? In SQL89, it was undefined. In SQL92, tables are grouped into schemas and can only be created by the owner of the schema (which can be a module) in which they reside. Who has the right, then, to create a schema? That is still undefined.

There are, of course, very good reasons why it is impractical to standardize this point, but since it must be addressed, implementers have taken their own approaches. One that is used in some major products is to define a privilege called, for example, "resource" that gives the user the right to create objects. This is granted by some user with the DBA privilege—a superuser privilege. Users without the resource privilege will at least have the connect privilege—the right to log on.

Example

The following statement creates a global temporary table whose rows will be preserved between transactions. The primary key is based on the id_nums domain; the other columns are based on standard datatypes.

```
CREATE GLOBAL TEMPORARY TABLE Fluctuations
(  item_num id_nums NOT NULL PRIMARY KEY,
item_name CHAR(10) NOT NULL,
start_price   DEC,
```

```
max_price DEC,

min_price DEC,

avg_price DEC,

end_price DEC

ON COMMIT PRESERVE ROWS );
```

Conformance Levels

Intermediate	Implementations at this level are not required to support temporary tables and collation definitions. Certain special features of foreign keys, namely partial matches and update effects (see Constraints in Chapter 29), do not come into play at this level. Also, at this level you may have to name the columns of a multicolumn FOREIGN KEY constraint in the same order that the parents they match were named in the UNIQUE or PRIMARY KEY constraint that applies to them. Note: If your system has conformed to the new standardized INFORMATION_SCHEMA (and perhaps even if it has not), you can find the order there. In the standard INFORMATION_SCHEMA, you would look in the view KEY_COLUMN_USAGE. At this level you may not be able to name constraints. If that is the case, internal names must be generated.
Entry	If UNIQUE or PRIMARY KEY is specified, NOT NULL should be specified too (this was the old standard's approach, and it remains permissible until the Intermediate level of SQL92 conformance).
SQL89	Naming of constraints, either by the user or the system, is not supported at this level.
SQL86	Use of the FOREIGN KEY and REFERENCES constraints is not supported at this level; they were added to the standard in SQL89.

NOTE

See Also: Chapters 3, 4, and 5; ALTER TABLE, COMMIT WORK, CREATE SCHEMA, CREATE VIEW, DECLARE LOCAL TEMPORARY TABLE, DROP TABLE, and ROLLBACK in this chapter; Constraints and Datatypes in Chapter 29; and Appendix F.

CREATE TRANSLATION

Translates Text Strings from One Character String to Another

Syntax

```
CREATE TRANSLATION translation name
FOR source character set
TO target character set
FROM translation name
| { EXTERNAL ('translation name') }
| IDENTITY ;
```

Usage

The CREATE TRANSLATION statement defines a translation from one character set to another. Once defined, the translation can be applied by using the TRANSLATE statement. A translation is an object in the schema and follows the conventional rules for such objects.

The translations that a given product supports are implementation-defined. This statement effectively allows you to define new translations based on the existing ones.

Example

The following statement imposes an external translation on the ASCII character set. The resulting character set is called Czech. The external translation is called Convert1, and the translation defined here is called Convert2. Effectively, this makes an imported translation part of the schema.

```
CREATE TRANSLATION Convert2 FOR ASCII TO CZECH
FROM EXTERNAL ('Convert1');
```

Conformance Levels

Intermediate   Not required at the Intermediate level or below.

NOTE See Also: Chapter 20; CREATE CHARACTER SET and CREATE COLLATION in this chapter; Collations and Datatypes in Chapter 29; and Appendix G.

CREATE VIEW

Defines a View

Syntax

```
CREATE VIEW table name [(column list)]
(AS SELECT statement
[WITH [CASCADED | LOCAL] CHECK OPTION] );
```

Usage

The CREATE VIEW statement creates a view, also known as a virtual or derived table. A view is an object that is treated as a table but whose definition contains a query, which is to say a valid SELECT statement (see SELECT). Views are referenced in SQL statements just like base tables are. When the view is referenced in a statement, the query is executed and its output becomes the content of the view for the duration of that statement. In some cases, views can be updated, in which case the changes are transferred to the underlying data in the base table(s) referenced by the query. Views are not the same as temporary tables, which do contain their own data, even though it is not preserved between sessions (see CREATE TABLE and DECLARE LOCAL TEMPORARY TABLE).

As with a base table, the rows of a view are by definition unordered. Therefore, ORDER BY may not be specified in the query. Note that the query may access more than one base table and that therefore a view may combine data from several tables.

As is usual with database objects, views are part of a schema and can be created only by the schema owner. If the CREATE VIEW statement is part of a CREATE SCHEMA sequence and the view name is preceded by a schema name, the names must match. The name of the view must be distinct from all other table names—both base tables, including temporary tables, and views—in the same schema. Views can be based on other views, but at some point must refer to some set of base tables.

Let's look at some terminology. The tables or views directly referenced in a query—whether that query stands alone or is part of a view definition—are called the "simply underlying tables" of the query (or the view). These combined with all the tables they reference, and all the subsequently referenced tables—all the way down to and including the base tables that contain the data—are called the "generally underlying tables". The base tables—the ones that do not reference any other tables but actually contain the data—are called the "leaf underlying tables". View definitions cannot be circular. That is, no view can be among its own generally underlying tables.

The view also may not contain a target specification (a host vaiable, possibly accompanied by an indicator viariable) or a dynamic parameter specification. (These are relevant only to Static and Dynamic SQL, respectively. If you want to pass parameters in this fashion, you probably want to use a cursor; see DECLARE CURSOR).

The list of columns is used to provide the columns with names that will be used only in this view. You may use it if you do not want to retain the names that the columns have in the underlying base table(s). You must name the columns whenever the following apply:

- Any two of the columns would otherwise have identical names.

- Any of the columns contain computed values or any values other than column values directly extracted from the underlying tables, unless an AS clause is used in the query to name them.

- There are any joined columns with distinct names in their respective tables, unless an AS clause is used in the query to name them.

If you do name the columns, you naturally cannot use the same column name twice in the same view. If you name the columns, you must name all of them, so the number of columns in the name list has to be the same as that in the SELECT clause of the contained query. You may use SELECT * in the query to select all columns; if you do this, it will be converted internally to a list of all columns. This conversion is for your protection, because it means that if someone were to add a column to an underlying table using the ALTER TABLE statement, it would not change the definition of your view.

Note that the columns in the view may not have a coercibility attribute of No Collating Sequence. This is only relevant for character string datatypes. Coercibility attributes are discussed under Collations in Chapter 29.

Views and Privileges

Privileges exist on views just as on other tables. In order to create a view, you must have the SELECT privilege on every simply underlying table referenced within it, including any underlying views. If you have this privilege with the GRANT OPTION for every such table, then you will also have it with GRANT OPTION on the view. Otherwise, you will own the view but still be unable to grant others to right to query it—it will basically be a view for your personal use. You can grant INSERT, UPDATE, and DELETE privileges on the view as well if you have these privileges on the underlying tables with GRANT OPTION, provided that the view is updatable (as explained below). The REFERENCES privilege works in a similar manner: if you have it on all referenced columns, you have it on the view; and if you have it with GRANT OPTION, then you retain the GRANT OPTION for the privilege on the view.

Inserting, Updating, and Deleting Values in Views

When you perform any of these operations on a view, the changes are transferred to the base table that contains the data. Such operations can be permitted only if the changes that must be made to the underlying table (always singular, as we shall see shortly) are unambiguous. The principle is that an insertion of or change to one row in the view must translate to an insertion of or change to one row in the leaf underlying table. If this is the case, the view is said to be updatable. The specific conditions outlined in the standard for a view to be updatable are these:

- It must be drawn on one and only one simply underlying table; in other words, no joins.

- It must contain one and only one query; in other words, no usage of UNION, EXCEPT, or INTERSECT.

- If the simply underlying table is itself a view, that view also must be updatable.

- The SELECT clause of the contained query may specify only column references, not value expressions or aggregate functions, and no column may be referenced more than once.

- The contained query may not specify GROUP BY or HAVING.

- The contained query may not specify DISTINCT.

- In SQL92, subqueries are permissible, but only if they do not refer to any of the generally underlying tables on which the view is based.

These are fairly stringent restrictions, and some products may relax some of them.

CHECK OPTION

The CHECK OPTION clause can be specified only for updatable views. It verifies that INSERT and UPDATE statements against the view do not populate the generally underlying tables with rows that will be excluded from the view. In other words, if I wanted a view of employees that would show only those working in London, I could put WHERE city = 'London' in the query. If I then inserted a row into the view that had Barcelona in the city column, it would be inserted into the leaf underlying table but would not show up in my view. Usually, such an insertion is a mistake, so you normally should use CHECK OPTION with updatable views. With CHECK OPTION, INSERTs and UPDATEs are allowed only if they produce rows that satisfy the predicate of this view.

The CASCADED | LOCAL option determines whether the predicates of any underlying views are checked as well. You could have several layers of views between this view and the base table data. If an UPDATE or INSERT produces a row that violates the predicates of any of them, that row will not "trickle up" into the view. Should all of the predicates therefore be checked for every INSERT or UPDATE? The CASCADED option says yes, and it is the default. The LOCAL option will check only the predicate contained in this view. This does not override the predicates in the underlying views; if any of them excludes a row, it still will be added to the leaf underlying table without appearing in the present view. This can create subtle problems, as rows may disappear for reasons that are not obvious from examining the topmost view alone. For this reason, it is probably better in most cases to specify CASCADED or leave it as the default.

Note that CHECK OPTION is a sort of constraint. Unlike most types of constraints, however, it cannot be deferred. It will be effectively checked after every INSERT or UPDATE command.

Views and Security

Views are very useful to control what users do with the data. By granting access to views rather than the base tables, you can prevent users from seeing various rows and columns. In certain situations, you can use CHECK OPTION to effectively define constraints that are specific to various users. Place the constraints in the predicate of the view, specify CHECK OPTION, and give the users privileges on the view rather than the base table. Keep in mind that these users also will not see any existing rows that violate the constraint through the view, which may or may not be a problem.

Example

The following statement creates a read-only view called Price_Variations based on the Fluctuations table (see the CREATE TABLE example). Since the view calculates the extent of price variation between the minimum and the maximum, and this is a calculated column, the output columns must be named. WITH CHECK OPTION cannot be specified, as the view is not updatable.

```
CREATE VIEW Price_Variations (item_id, item_name, price_variation)
(AS SELECT item_id, name, max_price - min_price
 FROM Fluctuations
 WHERE start_price > end_price);
```

Conformance Levels

Intermediate	Not required to allow specification of CASCADED or LOCAL for CHECK OPTION. If no specification is supported, it will default to CASCADED.

Entry   Not required to support UNION, EXCEPT, or INTERSECT, even for read-only views. Not required to support subqueries in updatable views.

NOTE   See Also: CREATE TABLE, DROP VIEW, GRANT, and SELECT in this chapter; Predicates in Chapter 29; and Appendix G.

DEALLOCATE DESCRIPTOR

(Dynamic SQL Only) Destroys a Descriptor Area

Syntax

```
DEALLOCATE DESCRIPTOR descriptor name;
```

Usage

The DEALLOCATE DESCRIPTOR statement deallocates, which is to say effectively removes, the named descriptor area, which must have been previously created with an ALLOCATE DESCRIPTOR statement. Descriptor areas are used in Dynamic SQL to provide information about and values for the parameters of dynamically generated SQL statements. For more on descriptor areas, see Chapter 22 and Descriptor Areas in Chapter 29.

Conformance Levels

Intermediate   Implementations at this level are required only to support literals as descriptor names.

Entry   No Dynamic SQL or descriptor support is required.

NOTE   See Also: Chapters 14 and 15; Chapter 22; ALLOCATE DESCRIPTOR, DESCRIBE, GET DESCRIPTOR, and SET DESCRIPTOR in this chapter; and Descriptor Areas in Chapter 29.

DEALLOCATE PREPARE

(Dynamic SQL Only) Destroys a Prepared Statement

Syntax

```
DEALLOCATE PREPARE prepared statement;
```

Usage

Prepared statements are statements generated from text strings at runtime. They are created using the PREPARE statement and destroyed using the DEALLOCATE PRE-PARE statement. If the prepared statement is currently referenced in a cursor, that cursor must be closed when the DEALLOCATE PREPARE statement is issued. The cursor and all prepared statements referencing it will be destroyed as well.

Conformance Levels

Intermediate   Implementations at this level are not required to support this statement.

NOTE   See Also: Chapter 22; ALLOCATE CURSOR, CLOSE, DECLARE CURSOR, OPEN, and PREPARE in this chapter.

DECLARE CURSOR

(Static or Dynamic SQL) Defines a Cursor

Syntax

```
DECLARE cursor name [ INSENSITIVE ] [ SCROLL ] CURSOR
FOR { SELECT statement
[ updatability clause ] }
  |{ prepared statement };

updatability clause::=
FOR { READ ONLY | UPDATE [ OF column list] } ]
```

Usage

The DECLARE CURSOR statement defines a *cursor*, an object used in applications to contain the output of a query and sometimes to perform updates on the tables referenced in the query. It is similar to a view in that its definition is a query and its content is the output of that query when it is opened (see OPEN). It differs from a view in that it does not act as a table, but rather as a way of breaking down the set-at-a-time operation of SQL into item-at-a-time operations for handling by an application. It is a sort of variable that stores the output of the query so that it can be processed by the application one row at a time.

The cursor name chosen must be unique within the module or compilation unit. The cursor can either be hard-coded (Static SQL) or created at runtime from a statement previously readied with a PREPARE statement (Dynamic SQL). In the former case, a SELECT statement and optional updatability clause will be specified. With the latter, a prepared statement containing the SELECT statement—and including the updatability clause if one is desired—will be used.

Ordering the Rows

Unlike those of a base table or view, the rows of an opened cursor have a definite order. If you wish, you may use an ORDER BY clause in the SELECT statement to impose an order. Otherwise, the order is implementation-dependent and possibly arbitrary. Even if your implementation provides a default ordering (which is common), for example by primary key, you should not consider it reliable unless your system documentation says it is. Generally, if the order of the rows is significant, you should use an ORDER BY clause. ORDER BY allows you to sort the rows by any one or more columns of the cursor. You may specify ascending or descending independently for each column used to sort, with ascending as the default. For more detail on ORDER BY, see SELECT.

Sensitivity of Cursors

If you specify INSENSITIVE, the cursor's contents will be fixed once it is opened. Any changes made by other statements to the underlying data while the cursor is open will be ignored by the cursor. Only read-only cursors (explained below) can be defined as INSENSITIVE.

Scroll Cursors

If you specify SCROLL, you will not have to fetch the rows of the cursor in order once it is opened. SCROLL defines the cursor so that you can go back and forth through the rows when you fetch them. SCROLL can be specified only for read-only cursors.

Updating Cursors

A cursor is either updatable or read-only. Some cursors are not updatable by their nature and are therefore read-only even if this is not explicitly specified. If a cursor is updatable in principle, you can make it read-only with an updatability clause, although the reverse is not true. The updatability clause can also restrict the updatability of the cursor to specified columns. This clause can specify FOR UPDATE only if the cursor is updatable in principle. If the cursor is not updatable in principle, READ ONLY may be specified for clarity but will not change the behavior of the cursor. To be updatable in principle, a cursor must satisfy the following conditions:

- It may not specify INSENSITIVE, SCROLL, or ORDER BY.

- It must be drawn on one and only one simply underlying table (see CREATE VIEW). In other words, no joins.

- It must contain one and only one query. In other words, no use of UNION, EXCEPT, or INTERSECT.

- If the simply underlying table is a view, that view must itself be updatable.

- The SELECT clause of the contained query may specify only column references, not derived values or aggregate functions, and no column may be referenced more than once.

- The contained query may not specify GROUP BY or HAVING.

- The contained query may not specify DISTINCT.

A cursor that satisfies the above conditions is updatable in principle and by default permits UPDATE statements on all columns. Therefore, if FOR UPDATE is specified for such a cursor with no column list, it is simply for clarity and has no effect.

If you know that you will do no updating through an updatable cursor, declaring it read-only is a good idea. Data that might be changed must be locked, and this can slow down operations by other users. For the same reason, you may want to specify FOR UPDATE OF with a column list to lock only specific columns in the table. For more information on locking, see Chapter 17.

Dynamic Cursors

Dynamic cursors are cursors created in Dynamic SQL at runtime. In Dynamic SQL you generally do not know, when you are writing the application, the specific content of the cursors the users will need. You may not even know how many cursors will need to be created. Therefore you can define cursors and have the SELECT statement and perhaps even the name filled in at runtime. You implement the latter option with the ALLOCATE CURSOR statement, which allows you to define any number of cursors with the same statement by simply executing the statement repeatedly with different values for the name parameter and query. See ALLOCATE CURSOR for more information on this topic.

With the Dynamic SQL version of DECLARE CURSOR, you define a cursor name in the code but leave the query to be filled in at runtime. In this case, you use a prepared statement in place of the SELECT statement and the updatability clause. The content of this prepared statement will in fact be a SELECT statement, possibly appended by an updatability clause, but the text of this statement will be generated dynamically at runtime by the application. For examples, see Chapter 22.

See PREPARE for information on how to define the query that the cursor will use.

Example

The following statement defines a scrollable, insensitive cursor called London_Clients, which contains the entries for all clients located in London. Because it is scrollable and insensitive, the cursor will automatically be read-only.

```
DECLARE London_Clients INSENSITIVE SCROLL CURSOR
FOR SELECT ID_NUM, NAME
  FROM Clients
  WHERE city = 'London';
```

Conformance Levels

Intermediate   Implementations at this level are not required to support insensitive cursors.

Entry   Implementations at this level are not required to support scroll cursors or updatability clauses (FOR UPDATE without a column list is implicit if the cursor is updatable; otherwise, read-only is implicit). They need not support Dynamic SQL or dynamic cursors at all.

NOTE   See Also: Chapters 21 and 22; Read-Only, Scrollable, Insensitive, and Dynamic Cursors in Chapter 27; and ALLOCATE CURSOR, CLOSE, CREATE VIEW, DEALLOCATE PREPARE, FETCH, OPEN, PREPARE, and SELECT in this chapter.

DECLARE LOCAL TEMPORARY TABLE

Defines a Local Temporary Table

Syntax

```
DECLARE LOCAL TEMPORARY TABLE qualified table name
```

```
(    {column definition
|    [table constraint ] }.,..
[ ON COMMIT { DELETE | PRESERVE } ROWS ] );
```

Usage

Temporary tables, unlike views, contain data of their own, but that data is not preserved between SQL sessions. In the case of declared local temporary tables, which are created with the DECLARE LOCAL TEMPORARY TABLE statement, the table definitions are not preserved either; the tables are defined at runtime (the other two types of temporary tables, which do have persistent definitions, are defined with the CREATE TABLE statement). The DECLARE LOCAL TEMPORARY TABLE statement is contained in some application SQL code, such as a module, or some Embedded SQL code. When that code is executed, the declared table is created. When the module or compilation unit is exited, the definition and content of the declared local temporary table (which we will refer to as "declared tables" for the remainder of this discussion) is destroyed. In other words, a DELETE and a DROP TABLE statement are effectively executed. Not being a persistent part of the database, the definition of the declared table is not recorded in the INFORMATION_SCHEMA.

> **NOTE** In the module language approach, all temporary table declarations must precede all procedures, which will contain the various other SQL statements used in the module.

A declared table does not reside in a schema as other tables do. The "schema" of which it is a part is derived in some implementation-dependent manner from the SQL-session identifier that invoked the module and the name of the module itself. Since you generally cannot know when writing Static SQL code what the SQL-session identifier will be, the standard provides a built-in variable that represents the containing schema. That variable is the word *MODULE*, which is to be prefixed to the declared table's name wherever referenced just as a schema name would be, for example, MODULE.MY_TABLE. This system allows a unique instance of the table to be defined for each session that invokes the containing module. Each such instance will be invisible to other sessions or modules. If Embedded or Dynamic SQL is used rather than the module language, support for declared tables is an implementation extension that should behave in a similar manner to the module approach.

The rules for columns, datatypes, constraints, defaults, and so on in declared tables are the same as for the other kinds of temporary tables described under CREATE TABLE. Likewise, the ON COMMIT clause operates in the same way as it does in CREATE TABLE: if DELETE ROWS (the default) is specified, the table is automatically emptied of values at the close of each transaction, although its definition will survive the transaction so that a second DECLARE TABLE within the same module will not be necessary. If PRESERVE ROWS is specified, the table will be emptied of values at the end of the session or when it is destroyed, whichever comes first. The table will be destroyed (dropped) when the module or compilation unit that contains the DECLARE statement is exited.

All of the conventional table privileges—INSERT, UPDATE, DELETE, SELECT, and REFERENCES—exist on declared tables but are not grantable. Therefore, each user will have these privileges on the versions of the table that she creates.

Example

The following statement creates a temporary table called Daily_Stats, which presumably will contain data to be used for further calculations by the application. The data inserted in the table will persist across transactions.

```
DECLARE LOCAL TEMPORARY TABLE Daily_Stats

(statnum   INTEGER NOT NULL PRIMARY KEY,

average    DECIMAL(4,2),

maximum    DECIMAL(4,2),

minimum    DECIMAL(4,2)

ON COMMIT PRESERVE ROWS  );
```

Conformance Levels

Intermediate   Implementations at this level are not required to support this statement.

> **NOTE**
> See Also: CREATE SCHEMA, CREATE TABLE, DROP TABLE, and GRANT in this chapter; Authorization IDs in Chapter 29; and Appendix F.

DELETE

Removes Rows from Tables

Syntax

```
DELETE FROM table name
[  {  WHERE predicate }
|  {  WHERE CURRENT OF cursor name } ];
```

Usage

The DELETE statement can be coded directly or, in Dynamic SQL, be a prepared statement, which is a statement whose text is generated at runtime (see PREPARE). The DELETE statement removes rows from temporary or permanent base tables, views, or cursors. In the last two cases, the deletions are transferred to the base table from which the view or cursor extracts its data.

The WHERE CURRENT OF form is used for deletions from cursors. The row currently in the cursor is removed. This is called a *positioned deletion*. The WHERE *predicate* form is used for deletions from base tables or views. All rows that satisfy the predicate are removed at once. This is called a *searched deletion*. If the WHERE clause is absent, it is also a searched deletion, but all rows of the table or view are removed (be careful!). The following restrictions apply to both types:

- The Authorization ID performing the deletion must have the DELETE privilege on the table.

- If the deletion is performed on a view or cursor, that view or cursor must be updatable (see CREATE VIEW and DECLARE CURSOR).

- If the current transaction mode is read-only (see SET TRANSACTION), and the table being deleted from is not temporary, then the deletion is disallowed. Note that this logically should include views that are based on temporary tables, although the standard seems ambiguous on this point.

Using Searched Deletions

The predicates used in DELETE statements, like those in SELECT and UPDATE, use one or more expressions—for example, location = 'London'—and test whether they are TRUE, FALSE, or (in the presence of NULLs) UNKNOWN for each row based on the values within that row. Each row for which the predicate is TRUE will be deleted.

NOTE   If a row that satisfies the predicate for a searched deletion has been marked for deletion or update, by this or another transaction, through a cursor that is still open (see OPEN), it will produce the warning "Cursor operation conflict", but the deletion will proceed.

Using Positioned Deletions

Positioned deletions use cursors and therefore only apply to Static or Dynamic, not to Interactive, SQL. You can use a positioned deletion if there is a cursor within the current module or compilation unit that references the table, and this cursor has been opened within the current transaction, has had at least one row FETCHed, and has not yet been CLOSEd (see OPEN and FETCH). The last row FETCHed will be deleted.

Using Prepared DELETE Statements

In Dynamic SQL, you generally do not know in advance the statements that will need to be issued. You may not even know the name of the table from which the values are being deleted when you write the code. For these situations, SQL provides the PREPARE statement, which you use to generate the text of dynamic statements at runtime. When you use PREPARE to generate a positioned deletion, the FROM table name clause of the DELETE statement may be omitted, and whatever table underlies the cursor will be assumed. This frees you from having to know the table name in advance, and the cursors can simply be generated dynamically as needed with the ALLOCATE CURSOR statement (see Chapter 22 and ALLOCATE CURSOR).

Example

The following statement removes from the Clients table everyone whose name begins with *W*:

```
DELETE FROM Clients
    WHERE NAME LIKE 'W%';
```

Conformance Levels

Intermediate	Implementations at this level are not required to support prepared statements.
Entry	Implementations at this level are not required to support Dynamic SQL.

NOTE   See Also: Chapters 2, 6, 21, and 22; ALLOCATE CURSOR, CREATE VIEW, DECLARE CURSOR, OPEN , PREPARE, and SET TRANSACTION in this chapter; and Predicates in Chapter 29.

DESCRIBE

(Dynamic SQL Only) Provides Information about a Prepared Statement

Syntax

```
DESCRIBE [ INPUT | OUTPUT ]
```

```
SQL statement
 USING SQL DESCRIPTOR descriptor name;
```

Usage

The DESCRIBE statement stores information about the input or output parameters of the prepared SQL statement in the named SQL descriptor area, which previously must have been allocated with an ALLOCATE DESCRIPTOR statement. The prepared statement itself must have been created with a PREPARE statement. To access the information that DESCRIBE stores, use the GET DESCRIPTOR statement. If neither INPUT nor OUTPUT is specified, OUTPUT will be used by default.

The basic idea is that a given DESCRIBE statement examines either all input or all output parameters in the Dynamic SQL statement. It uses the context of how these parameters are used in the statement to figure out datatypes, nullability characteristics, and so on of the parameters. It then stores this information about the parameters in the descriptor area. Each item in the descriptor area describes one parameter. The actual value of the parameter is set with a SET DESCRIPTOR statement or automatically. For more information, see SET DESCRIPTOR, Descriptor Areas, in Chapter 29 and Chapter 22.

Describing Output Columns

You specify OUTPUT in order to provide information about the output columns of the statement. If the statement is not SELECT or FETCH, then the descriptor item COUNT is set to zero and the others are not set (this indicates a problem, as other statements will not use output parameters). Otherwise, COUNT is set to the number of output columns. If this number is greater than the number of descriptor items, a warning condition is raised and no other descriptor fields are set. Otherwise, the descriptor item areas are set in the same sequence as they appear in the SELECT list. Each descriptor item area will have values set as follows:

- TYPE is set to a code indicating the datatype. The codes are listed under Descriptor Areas in Chapter 29.

- NULLABLE is set to 1 if the resulting column may contain NULLs or to 0 if it may not.

- NAME is set to the name of the column.

- UNNAMED is set to 1 if the name of the output column is implementation-dependent; otherwise, it is set to 0. (If the name is implementation-dependent, it's because the output column is not a simple replicant of an input column but is part of a value expression, aggregate function, union, or similar operation and has not been named in an AS clause. See SELECT for more information.)

How the other relevant fields are set depends on the datatype of the column. However, the settings of these fields for a particular datatype are the same whether DESCRIBE INPUT or DESCRIBE OUTPUT is specified, so they are explained later in this entry.

Describing Input Parameters

You specify DESCRIBE INPUT to provide information about the dynamic parameter specifications in the prepared statement. COUNT is set to the number of parameter specifications in the statement. If this number is greater than the number of allocated descriptor areas, a warning message is produced and the other descriptor areas are not set. Also, if this number is zero, the other descriptor areas are not set. Otherwise, they are set as follows:

- TYPE is set to the code listed under Descriptor Areas in Chapter 29 that matches the datatype of the column.

- NULLABLE is set to 1. This indicates that the input parameter may be NULL.

- NAME and UNNAMED are set to implementation-dependent values.

Settings That Are the Same for Either Input or Output

Whether you specify INPUT or OUTPUT, the DATA and INDICATOR are not relevant; these and other unused fields are set by DESCRIBE to implementation-dependent values. To set the DATA or INDICATOR fields, use the SET DESCRIPTOR statement. The values that depend on the datatype are described below for various datatypes. For more on the meaning of these paramenters, for example, precision and scale, see Datatypes in Chapter 29.

If the datatype is any CHARACTER STRING type, then:

- LENGTH is set to the length (if fixed) or maximum length (if varying) of the string in characters.

- OCTET_LENGTH is set to the maximum possible length in octets (bytes).

- CHARACTER_SET_CATALOG, CHARACTER_SET_SCHEMA, and CHARACTER_ SET_NAME are set to the catalog, schema, and name of the string's character set.

- COLLATION_CATALOG, COLLATION_SCHEMA, and COLLATION _NAME are set to the catalog, schema, and name of the string's collation.

Note that if the language being interfaced to is C or C++, the LENGTH and OCTET_ LENGTH values will not include the implementation-defined string-termination character.

If the type is a BIT (binary) STRING, LENGTH is set to the length (if fixed) or maximum length (if varying) in bits, and OCTET_LENGTH is set to the maximum possible length in octets (bytes).

If any EXACT NUMERIC type is indicated, PRECISION and SCALE are set to the appropriate precision and scale.

If any APPROXIMATE NUMERIC type is indicated, PRECISION is set to the appropriate figure.

If a DATETIME type is indicated, then:

- LENGTH is set to the length in positions.
- DATETIME_INTERVAL_CODE is set to the code indicated in Descriptor Areas in Chapter 29.
- PRECISION is set to the TIME precision or the TIMESTAMP precision, if either applies, that is, if the datatype is TIME or TIMESTAMP, respectively.

If an INTERVAL type is indicated, then:

- DATETIME_INTERVAL_CODE is set to the code indicated in Descriptor Areas in Chapter 29.
- DATETIME_INTERVAL_PRECISION is set to the INTERVAL's leading field precision.
- PRECISION is set to the fractional seconds precision, if applicable.

Conformance Levels

Intermediate	Implementations at this level are not required to support variables for descriptor names.
Entry	Implementations at this level are not required to support Dynamic SQL at all.

NOTE   See Also: Chapter 22; , ALLOCATE DESCRIPTOR, DEALLOCATE DESCRIPTOR, GET DESCRIPTOR, and SET DESCRIPTOR in this chapter; and Datatypes and Descriptor Areas in Chapter 29.

DISCONNECT

Destroys Connections to the DBMS

Syntax

```
DISCONNECT connection | ALL | CURRENT;
```

Usage

The DISCONNECT statement terminates one or more connections between the current SQL-agent and the DBMS. If ALL is specified, it means all connections for the current user. If a connection is named, that connection is terminated; alternatively, you can specify either ALL connections or the CURRENT connection, by using those keywords. To start a connection, which will initially be the current one, use the SET CONNECTION statement while some connection is still current. If there is no current connection, of course, you use CONNECT to set a new current connection. In most implementations, CURRENT is also the default.

Conformance Levels

Intermediate   Implementations at this level are not required to support DISCONNECT.

NOTE   See Also: Chapter 3 and CONNECT and SET CONNECTION in this chapter.

DROP ASSERTION

Removes an Assertion from the Schema

Syntax

```
DROP ASSERTION constraint name;
```

Usage

The DROP ASSERTION statement is used to remove an assertion from the schema. Assertions are constraints that stand alone as objects, rather than being part of a table or domain definition; they are created with the CREATE ASSERTION statement. You can use assertions to ensure that a table is not empty, which you could not do from a constraint within the table itself. Assertions are also more logical for constraints that enforce business rules that are not a function of a particular table. The Authorization ID dropping the assertion must own the schema in which it resides.

Conformance Levels

Intermediate   Implementations at this level are not required to support DROP ASSERTION. But, of course, most or all DBMSs support some kind of DISCONNECT procedure.

NOTE   See Also: CREATE ASSERTION in this chapter and Authorization IDs and Constraints in Chapter 29.

DROP CHARACTER SET

Destroys the Definition of a Character Set

Syntax

```
DROP CHARACTER SET character set name;
```

Usage

The DROP CHARACTER SET statement destroys a character set, which must have been previously defined with a CREATE CHARACTER SET statement. It must be issued by the owner of the schema that contains the character set, and no constraints, views, collations, or translations may be referencing the character set at the time it is dropped. If there are any, this statement produces an error, and the character set is not dropped. When the character set is destroyed, all Authorization IDs lose their privileges on it.

Conformance Levels

Entry   Implementations at this level are not required to support the DROP CHARACTER SET statement.

NOTE   See Also: Chapter 20; CREATE CHARACTER SET and CREATE SCHEMA in this chapter; and Authorization IDs and Collations in Chapter 29.

DROP COLLATION

Destroys a Collation

Syntax

```
DROP COLLATION collation name;
```

Usage

The DROP COLLATION statement destroys a collation, which must have been previously defined with a CREATE COLLATION statement. It must be issued by the Authorization ID that owns the schema in which the collation resides. Except in a COLLATE FROM clause, no view may reference it in a query; neither may any constraint—whether contained in a table definition, domain, or assertion—reference it in a predicate. If any views or constraints do so reference it, the DROP COLLATION statement is rejected with an error.

If collx is the name of the collation being deleted, other references to collx are dealt with as follows:

- The definitions of all other collations that reference collx are modified by deleting all THEN COLLATION collx or DESC (collx) clauses.

- All character-set definitions that reference collx are modified by deleting all COLLATION FROM collx or DESC (collx) clauses.

- The definitions of all column or domain definitions that reference collx are modified by deleting COLLATE collx clauses.

- All views and constraints that use a COLLATE FROM collx clause have that clause deleted.

Conformance Levels

Intermediate   Implementations at this level are not required to support the DROP COLLATION statement.

NOTE   See Also: Chapter 20; CREATE CHARACTER SET, CREATE COLLATION, and CREATE SCHEMA in this chapter; and Collations and Constraints in Chapter 29.

DROP DOMAIN

Destroys a Domain

Syntax

```
DROP DOMAIN domain name CASCADE | RESTRICT ;
```

Usage

The DROP DOMAIN statement destroys a domain, which must have been previously created with a CREATE DOMAIN statement. It must be issued by the owner of the schema in which the domain resides. If RESTRICT is specified, the domain must not be currently referenced by any tables, views, or constraints. If it is, the statement will get an error. If CASCADE is specified, the effects on all columns based on the domain are as follows:

- The datatype of the domain becomes the datatype of the column.

- If the column has no default value and the domain does, the default of the domain becomes the default of the column. If both the column and the domains have defaults, that of the column overrides that of the domain.

- Each constraint that is part of the domain is passed on to the column, provided that the Authorization ID dropping the domain has the necessary privileges to effect the change to the column. In other words, for each constraint C that is contained in the domain to be dropped, the following statement is effectively attempted under the privileges of the current SQL-session Authorization ID:

  ```
  ALTER TABLE table name ADD C;
  ```

  If the Authorization ID lacks the requisite privileges to execute this statement, the change is not made, but the domain is still dropped.

All users lose their privileges on the domain, and its definition is destroyed.

Conformance Levels

Entry　　　　Implementations at this level are not required to support the DROP DOMAIN statement.

NOTE　　　See Also: Chapter 25; ALTER TABLE, CREATE DOMAIN, and GRANT in this chapter; and Constraints in Chapter 29.

DROP SCHEMA

Destroys a Schema

Syntax

```
DROP SCHEMA schema name CASCADE | RESTRICT ;
```

Usage

The DROP SCHEMA statement drops the named schema. The current Authorization ID must own the schema being dropped. If RESTRICT is specified, the schema must currently be empty of objects—permanent, global temporary, or created local temporary tables, as well as views, domains, assertions, character sets, collations, and translations—or the DROP SCHEMA statement will fail. If CASCADE is specified, any such objects are dropped along with the schema. This syntax form has the same effect as explicitly dropping each object with the appropriate DROP statement and specifying CASCADE where applicable (which would be for DROP TABLE, DROP VIEW, and DROP DOMAIN).

Conformance Levels

Entry   Implementations at this level are not required to support DROP SCHEMA.

NOTE   See Also: CREATE SCHEMA, DROP ASSERTION, DROP CHARACTER SET, DROP COLLATION, DROP DOMAIN, DROP TABLE, DROP TRANSLATION, and DROP VIEW in this chapter.

DROP TABLE

Destroys a Base Table

Syntax

```
DROP TABLE table name CASCADE | RESTRICT ;
```

Usage

The DROP TABLE statement is used to drop the various kinds of tables that can be created with a CREATE TABLE statement: permanent base tables, global temporary tables, and created local temporary tables. Views are dropped with the DROP VIEW statement, and declared local temporary tables are automatically dropped at the end of the session wherein they are declared. The Authorization ID that issues that statement must be the owner of the table or the DROP TABLE statement will produce an error.

If RESTRICT is specified, no views or constraints may currently be referencing the table to be dropped. If CASCADE is specified, such referencing objects will be dropped along with the table. For constraints, this means that the constraint itself will be dropped. If the constraint is contained in a table or domain definition, the containing object will not be dropped.

The definition of the table is destroyed and all users lose their privileges on it.

Conformance Levels

Entry   Implementations at this level are not required to support DROP TABLE.

NOTE   See Also: Chapters 3; CREATE TABLE in this chapter; and Constraints in Chapter 29.

DROP TRANSLATION

Destroys a Translation

Syntax

```
DROP TRANSLATION translation name;
```

Usage

The DROP TRANSLATION statement destroys a translation previously created using a CREATE TRANSLATION statement. The Authorization ID issuing the statement must own the schema in which the translation resides. The translation must not be currently referenced by any views or constraints or the DROP statement will produce an error. If any character sets or collations use a translation collation based on this translation, that collation is removed from their definitions. The translation definition is destroyed, and all users lose their privileges on it.

Conformance Levels

Intermediate   Implementations at this level are not required to support the DROP TRANSLATION statement.

NOTE   See Also: Chapter 20; CREATE TRANSLATION in this chapter; and Collations in Chapter 29.

DROP VIEW

Destroys a View

Syntax

```
DROP VIEW view name   CASCADE | RESTRICT ;
```

Usage

The DROP VIEW statement drops a view, which must previously have been created with a CREATE VIEW statement. The Authorization ID issuing the DROP VIEW statement must own the schema within which the view resides. If RESTRICT is specified, the view may not be referenced by any other views or by any assertions or the DROP statement will produce an error. If CASCADE is specified, such referencing objects are dropped along with the view. The view definition is destroyed, and all users lose their privileges on the view.

Conformance Levels

Entry   Implementations at this level are not required to support the DROP VIEW statement.

NOTE   See Also: Chapters 14 and 15 and CREATE VIEW and CREATE ASSERTION in this chapter.

EXECUTE

(Dynamic SQL Only) Executes a Prepared Statement

Syntax

```
EXECUTE [ GLOBAL | LOCAL ] prepared statement
[ INTO { output parameter.,.. }
   | { SQL DESCRIPTOR [GLOBAL | LOCAL ] descriptor name } ]
[ USING { input parameter.,.. }
     |  { SQL DESCRIPTOR  [ GLOBAL |LOCAL ] descriptor name } ] ;
```

Usage

The EXECUTE statement executes a statement previously generated with the PREPARE statement. It provides values for any dynamic input and output parameters associated with the prepared statement. The USING clause is for input parameters and the INTO clause for output. A given EXECUTE statement will use either or both of these clauses depending on whether the prepared statement contains input parameters, output parameters, or both. Conceivably, the EXECUTE statement could use neither USING nor INTO, if no dynamic parameters are present in the prepared statement. This would be somewhat unusual, however, since such statement are generally better suited for EXECUTE IMMEDIATE. Prepared statements do not contain INOUT parameters (parameters functioning as both an INPUT and an OUTPUT). For more on prepared statements, see PREPARE. For either input or output parameters, you can use a descriptor area or a list of host-language variables (or parameters for the module approach; in this entry, we use the term *variables* for both approaches to simplify the discussion) to provide the values for the dynamic parameters embedded in the prepared statement.

The GLOBAL and LOCAL options refer to the scope of the prepared statement or descriptor area. If the scope is LOCAL, the statement or area is accessible only by statements within the module or compilation unit in which it was created (see Appendix F); otherwise, it is accessible to any statement in the session. If the scope of the statement or descriptor is GLOBAL, it must be specified. LOCAL is the default. Since the scope is technically part of the name, two prepared statements or descriptor areas may have the same names but a different scope and still be distinctly named.

In the USING and INTO clauses, variable are preceded by colons (:) and may be appended by indicators (see Chapter 21). Any SQL descriptor areas used must previously have been allocated with an ALLOCATE DESCRIPTOR statement and not yet deallocated with DEALLOCATE DESCRIPTOR.

The USING clause indicates from where the values for the dynamic input parameters contained in the prepared statement are to be taken. It will indicate either a list of variables that will have been assigned values by the host-language procedure calling the SQL EXECUTE statement or a descriptor area from which the values are to be drawn. If the former, the variables from the host language will be matched to the dynamic parameters (represented in the prepared statement by simple question marks) contained in the prepared statement on an ordinal basis. If the latter, the descriptor items will be matched to the dynamic parameters on an ordinal basis.

The INTO clause indicates where the output from the prepared statement will be stored. If output parameters are used, they will be assigned values by the EXECUTE statement. The host-language variables or descriptor items will be matched to the output columns on an ordinal basis. The decision to use variables or descriptor areas for input or output is actually two independent decisions; the two approaches may be mixed.

Note that either, both, or neither of these clauses (USING and INTO) may be used, but neither may be used more than once in a given EXECUTE. The following rules apply:

- If the prepared statement contains dynamic input parameters, the USING clause must be present.

- If the prepared statement is a SELECT or FETCH statement, the INTO clause must be present. These are the statements that use output parameters.

- If the prepared statement is a SELECT, it must be of the single-row variety. SELECT statements that retrieve multiple rows should be put in dynamic cursors (see DECLARE CURSOR and ALLOCATE CURSOR).

- If the prepared statement references a created or declared local temporary table, this EXECUTE statement must be located in the same module or compilation unit as the corresponding PREPARE statement.

For the USING clause, if any, the following rules also hold:

- If a variable list is used, and its number of variables does not match the number of input variables in the prepared statement, an error is generated and the EXECUTE statement fails.

- If a descriptor area is used, the items within it must have been already set, including, for each item, either the DATA or the INDICATOR field, using a SET DESCRIPTOR statement.

- If a SQL descriptor area is used, the current value of COUNT in that area must equal the number of input parameters used in the prepared statement and must be between zero and the MAX number of items specified when the descriptor was allocated, inclusively.

- If a descriptor area is used, the descriptor items naturally must match the parameters in the prepared statement. (See Descriptor Areas in Chapter 29.)

- If an indicator parameter or the INDICATOR field of a descriptor item is negative, a NULL is placed in the matching input parameter in the prepared statement, and the value of the parameter or of the DATA field of the descriptor item is irrelevant. Otherwise, the value of the parameter or the DATA field of the descriptor area will be placed in the matching parameter.

- If the datatype of a descriptor item or parameter is not the same as the matching dynamic parameter of the prepared statement, an automatic CAST expression will be attempted to convert the parameter or descriptor item to the datatype of the dynamic parameter. The rules for CAST conversions are explained in CAST Expressions in Chapter 29. If the CAST fails, an error is generated, and the EXECUTE statement fails.

- If a descriptor area is used, the values of the NAME and UNNAMED fields of the descriptor items are ignored.

For the INTO clause, the following rules apply:

- The number of listed output parameters, or the count of descriptor area items, as the case may be, must equal the number of output columns in the prepared statement.

- If a descriptor area is used, your implementation may require that you already have set its fields to match the dynamic parameter specifications in this prepared statement. If so, you would do this with the DESCRIBE or the SET DESCRIPTOR statement. These settings will become invalid once the DATA field is set by the EXECUTE statement. Hence, you must reset the descriptor each time you execute the prepared statement. Some implementations may relax this restriction.

- If the datatypes of the parameters or the value of the TYPE fields of the descriptor items do not match the datatypes of the output columns of the prepared statement, an automatic CAST expression will be attempted, conforming to the principles outlined in CAST Expressions in Chapter 29, to convert the value to the appropriate datatype. If the CAST expression fails, an error is generated, and the EXECUTE statement fails.

- If a descriptor area is used, the values in the fields of each of its items must accurately describe the output column value to be inserted into the item's DATA field (provided that the column is not NULL), possibly after the casting specified above.

- If output parameter variables are used, they must be able to hold the value produced by the casting specified above, or an error is produced.

- If the value of an output column is NULL, then either the descriptor item's INDICATOR field or the indicator appended to the variable, as appropriate, is set to -1. If variables are used without appended indicators and NULLs arise, an error is produced. In the presence of a negative indicator, the value of the descriptor item's DATA field, or of the variable, as appropriate, is implementation-dependent.

- If the value of the output column is not NULL, the indicator DATA field or the variable is set to that value, possibly after the casting specified above.

- If a descriptor area is used, and the value of an item after casting is a VARCHAR or BIT VARYING type, RETURNED_LENGTH is set to the length of the value in characters or bits, respectively, and RETURNED_OCTET_LENGTH to the length in octets (bytes).

Example

The following statement executes a prepared statement called stmt6, taking a series of values from a set of three input parameters and storing the results in a SQL descriptor area called Desc_11. The descriptor area has a global scope, but the prepared statement does not.

```
EXECUTE stmt6

USING :name, :city, :occup

INTO GLOBAL Desc_11;
```

Conformance Levels

Intermediate   Implementations at this level are required only to support literals (no variables) for descriptor names.

Entry   Implementations at this level are not required to support Dynamic SQL.

NOTE   See Also: Chapter 22; EXECUTE IMMEDIATE, PREPARE, and SELECT in this chapter; and CAST Expressions and Descriptor Areas in Chapter 29.

EXECUTE IMMEDIATE

(Dynamic SQL Only) Prepares a Statement from a Text String and Executes It

Syntax

```
EXECUTE IMMEDIATE SQL statement variable;
```

Usage

The EXECUTE IMMEDIATE statement prepares a statement for execution from a variable containing a text string that expresses the statement to be executed. It then executes the statement, effectively combining the functionality of the PREPARE and EXECUTE statements, albeit with certain limitations—for example, the statement cannot be prepared once and executed repeatedly as can be done using the separate PREPARE and EXECUTE statements. Also, neither input nor output parameters may be used. This restriction implies that the statement to be executed cannot be SELECT or FETCH.

EXECUTE IMMEDIATE fails if any of the following conditions is TRUE:

- The datatype of the SQL statement variable does not correspond to a CHARACTER STRING type. To see which datatypes in your host language correspond to which SQL types, see Appendix E.

- The content of the SQL statement variable does not equal the text of a valid and legal (for the current Authorization ID) SQL statement.

- The SQL statement variable contains a comment. For information on comments, see Appendix G.

- The SQL statement contains one or more dynamic input parameters.

- The SQL statement is SELECT or FETCH.

- The SQL statement references a cursor that does not exist.

- The SQL statement references a cursor name that can match more than one cursor. This implies that one of the cursors is an extended dynamic (allocated) cursor whose name was generated at runtime.

If none of these conditions hold, the statement is prepared and immediately executed.

Example

The following statement takes a string variable called Delete_7, whose content is the text of a valid SQL statement (presumably DELETE), and executes it.

```
EXECUTE IMMEDIATE :Delete_7;
```

Conformance Levels

Entry   Implementations at this level are not required to support Dynamic SQL.

NOTE   See Also: Chapter 22 and ALLOCATE CURSOR, DECLARE CURSOR, EXECUTE, PREPARE, and SELECT in this chapter.

FETCH

Retrieves a Row from an Open Cursor

Syntax

```
FETCH [ [ orientation ] FROM ]
cursor name INTO target spec .,.. ;


orientation ::=
NEXT | PRIOR | FIRST | LAST |
{ ABSOLUTE | RELATIVE  offset }
```

Usage

The FETCH statement retrieves the values from one row of a cursor into the list of target specs in order, so that the first output column of the cursor goes in the first target spec, the second column in the second target, and so on. The target spec is an output parameter in the module language and a host-language variable in Embedded or Dynamic SQL. The cursor will have been created with a DECLARE CURSOR or an ALLOCATE CURSOR statement and opened with an OPEN CURSOR statement, before any rows are fetched.

Recall that the rows of cursors, unlike those of base tables or views, are by definition ordered, although this order may be arbitrary. At any time, an opened cursor has a position among the rows it contains; it may be before a row, on a row, or after the last row. When first opened, it is positioned before the first row. The FETCH statement repositions the cursor and then copies the values from the row on which it is currently positioned to the target specifications. By repositioning the cursor, the FETCH statement also determines which row of the cursor is the current row and therefore can be used in conjunction with the positioned versions of the DELETE and UPDATE statements to change the contents of the table retrieved by the cursor (assuming it is updatable; see DECLARE CURSOR).

The orientation specifies where the cursor is to be repositioned. NEXT is the default if the orientation is omitted and is, in any case, the only possibility unless SCROLL was specified for the cursor when it was defined (see DECLARE CURSOR). SCROLL may be specified only for read-only cursors. The offset is of an EXACT NUMERIC type with a scale of zero—in effect, an integer. This may be a literal or a host-language variable of an appropriate type—that is to say, a type that maps to SQL INTEGER. The options for orientation are defined as follows.

- If the cursor is currently positioned before the first row, NEXT moves the cursor onto that row. If it is on a row, NEXT moves it onto the next one. If it is after the last row, NEXT produces the no-data condition (explained below).

- If the cursor is currently positioned after the last row, PRIOR moves it onto that row. If it is currently positioned on a row other than the first one, PRIOR moves it onto the previous one. If it is currently positioned on or before the first row, PRIOR produces the no-data condition.

- FIRST moves the cursor onto the first row.

- LAST moves the cursor onto the last row.

- ABSOLUTE *offset* moves the cursor onto that row (i.e., if *offset* = 7, it moves to the seventh row). If *offset* is greater than the number of rows, the no-data condition is produced.

- RELATIVE *offset* moves forward *offset* rows if *offset* is positive or backward *offset* rows if *offset* is negative. If this option moves the cursor before the first or after the last row, the no-data condition is produced.

The no-data condition indicates that there is no row to be FETCHed in the indicated position. In this case, a warning message is produced, and the target specs are not set. Since rows are normally FETCHed until this happens, the no-data condition does not necessarily denote an error. FETCHing from an empty cursor also produces the no-data condition. When the no-data condition arises, the cursor position is defined as follows:

- If the last FETCH specified (or defaulted to) NEXT, specified LAST, or specified ABSOLUTE or RELATIVE using numeric arguments that were too large, the cursor is positioned after the last row.

- Otherwise, the cursor is positioned before the first row.

If an error arises during derivation of any derived columns in the cursor, the position of the cursor remains unchanged. Unless an orientation is specified, FROM is optional. It may be omitted; if included, it has no effect.

Example

The following statement moves the cursor Paris_Sales back three rows and places its output in a series of target specifications. It assumes Paris_Sales is a scrollable cursor.

```
FETCH RELATIVE -3
FROM Paris_Sales
INTO :name, :id_num, :num_of_clients;
```

Conformance Levels

Entry Implementations at this level are not required to support orientations (in which case NEXT is effectively used) or to allow the word FROM. Also, they may require that only EXACT NUMERIC column values can be fetched into EXACT NUMERIC targets, rather than performing an automatic CAST

NOTE   See Also: Chapters 21 and 22 and ALLOCATE CURSOR, CLOSE CURSOR, DECLARE CURSOR, and OPEN in this chapter.

GET DESCRIPTOR

(Dynamic SQL Only) Retrieves Information from a SQL Descriptor Area

Syntax

```
GET DESCRIPTOR descriptor name
{ simple target spec = COUNT }
| { VALUE item number
   {simple target spec = desc field}.,.. };
```

Usage

The GET DESCRIPTOR statement retrieves information from SQL descriptor areas, which store information about input and output parameters for dynamically created SQL statements and can also store values for them. Each descriptor area describes all the input or all the output parameters of one statement. The content and structure of descriptor areas are described in detail in Chapter 29 under Descriptor Areas. By "simple target specifications" is meant host variables (or parameters for the module language) without appended indicator variables. The descriptor areas must first be allocated with the ALLOCATE DESCRIPTOR statement; then the information is stored in them with either the DESCRIBE or the SET DESCRIPTOR statement. The *descriptor name* can be either a literal or a host-language variable.

A descriptor area consists of a list of descriptor items and a COUNT field denoting the size of the list. Each descriptor item corresponds to one parameter or target specification in the statement and contains a number of fields:

- TYPE indicates the datatype. (Depending on the datatype, there may also be a variety of related fields providing descriptive information such as the length.

The irrelevant fields for a given datatype, such as PRECISION for a character string, are ignored.)

- DATA gives the actual content of the parameter or target if it is not NULL.
- INDICATOR will set to a negative value to indicate whether the parameter or target is NULL, in which case the value of DATA is irrelevant.

This statement will retrieve either the COUNT, which is the number of descriptor items in the descriptor area, or specific information about a specific descriptor item. The items are listed in the descriptor area in the order in which they are used in the statement being described, so they can be referred to by this ordinal number (*item number*). The fields of the item that you want to see are referred to by name (*desc field*) as listed under Descriptor Areas in Chapter 29.

Since it is the INDICATOR field of a descriptor item that establishes whether a value is NULL, neither the DATA field nor any of the descriptive fields of the item can contain SQL NULLs. For any given datatype, some of the fields in the item will be inapplicable. These will be set to implementation-dependent defaults but not to SQL NULLs. If you retrieve DATA and its value is NULL, you must retrieve the INDICATOR in the same statement, or you will get an error. Therefore, you should retrieve the INDICATOR whenever the DATA value might be NULL, check the INDICATOR to see if it is NULL, and have the program logic act appropriately. If the INDICATOR is negative, and the descriptor item therefore NULL, the value of DATA is implementation-dependent and does not matter.

You will also get an error if you specify an item number greater than the maximum number of items in the descriptor area, i.e., the number of occurrences defined when the descriptor area was allocated. If your item number is within this range but still greater than the number of descriptor items actually used—the value of COUNT—you will not get an error but merely a no-data condition. For an explanation of NO DATA, see Appendix E.

Example

The following statement retrieves the TYPE, NULLABLE, and NAME fields from the seventh descriptor item (corresponding to the seventh dynamic parameter in the described statement) into a series of target specifications.

```
GET DESCRIPTOR :Desc_7
VALUE 7
  :data_type = TYPE,
  :can_contain_nulls = NULLABLE
  :column_name = NAME;
```

Conformance Levels

Intermediate   Implementations at this level are not required to support the use of anything but literals for descriptor names.

Entry   Implementations at this level are not required to support Dynamic SQL.

NOTE   See Also: Chapter 22; ALLOCATE DESCRIPTOR, DEALLOCATE DESCRIPTOR, DESCRIBE, and SET DESCRIPTOR in this chapter; and Datatypes and Descriptor Areas in Chapter 29.

GET DIAGNOSTICS

Retrieves Diagnostic Information about the Previous SQL Statement

Syntax

```
GET DIAGNOSTICS { statement information item.,..}
| condition information;

statement information item ::=
simple target spec = NUMBER | MORE
| COMMAND_FUNCTION | DYNAMIC_FUNCTION
| ROW_COUNT

condition information ::=
EXCEPTION condition number
condition information item.,...

condition information item ::=
simple target spec = cond info item name

cond info item name ::=
CONDITION_NUMBER
| RETURNED_SQLSTATE
| CLASS_ORIGIN
```

```
|  SUBCLASS_ORIGIN

|  SERVER_NAME

|  CONNECTION_NAME

|  CONSTRAINT_CATALOG

|  CONSTRAINT_SCHEMA

|  CONSTRAINT_NAME

|  CATALOG_NAME

|  SCHEMA_NAME

|  TABLE_NAME

|  COLUMN_NAME

|  CURSOR_NAME

|  MESSAGE_TEXT

|  MESSAGE_LENGTH

|  MESSAGE_OCTET_LENGTH


condition number ::= simple value specification
```

Usage

The GET DIAGNOSTICS statement retrieves information from the DBMS regarding the exception and completion conditions of the immediately preceding SQL statement within the same session. Exception conditions are errors that prevent a statement from being executed; completion conditions are warnings that indicate possible errors but still allow the statement to execute. This information is stored in a diagnostics area and further clarifies the codes provided through SQLCODE or (preferably) SQL-STATE. It is in the form of various fields that are retrieved into simple target specifications—target specifications without indicator variables.

The statement information items provide information about the statement—which statement it was, how many rows were affected (for example, if it was an UPDATE statement), and so on. The condition information provides the SQLSTATE or SQL-CODE value along with supplemental information—for example, if an error was a cursor conflict, you can find out the name of the cursor with which the conflict arose. Also, the diagnostics area can specify several error codes produced by the same statement, whereas SQLSTATE and SQLCODE can only specify one. The diagnostics area is discussed in detail in Appendix C.

Example

The following statement retrieves the error conditions for the previous statement, which we will assume was a prepared statement. It will find out the number of error or warning conditions this statement raised (NUMBER), whether this number exceeded what could be stored in the diagnostics area (MORE), and what the prepared statement itself was (DYNAMIC_FUNCTION). These values are stored in three target specifications.

```
GET DIAGNOSTICS

        :how_many_errors = NUMBER,

        :diagnostics_overflow = MORE,

        :prepared_statement = DYNAMIC_FUNCTION;
```

Conformance Levels

Entry	Implementations at this level are not required to support GET DIAGNOSTICS.
SQL89	Implementations at this level are not required to support SQLSTATE.
Non	Diagnostic areas are widely used but in a nonstandardized way.

NOTE   See Also: Appendix C.

GRANT

Gives Privileges to Users

Syntax

```
GRANT privilege.,.. ON object name
TO { grantee.,.. } | PUBLIC
[ WITH GRANT OPTION ];


privilege  ::=
 { ALL PRIVILEGES }
 | { SELECT
 | DELETE
```

```
| { INSERT [ (column name.,..) ] }
| { UPDATE [ (column name.,..) ] }
| { REFERENCES [ (column name.,..) ] }
| USAGE   }

object name ::=
[ TABLE ] table name
| DOMAIN domain name
| COLLATION collation name
| CHARACTER SET character set name
| TRANSLATION translation name
```

Usage

The GRANT statement gives the grantees—that is, Authorization IDs that represent users or, possibly, modules—the right to perform the specified actions on the named objects. The USAGE privilege applies to all other types of objects besides tables, whereas the other kinds of privileges apply only to tables. Tables here may be permanent base tables, temporary tables, or views. The Authorization ID issuing the GRANT, which we will refer to as the *grantor* for the remainder of this discussion, must have the privilege itself with the GRANT OPTION and may grant it with this option, which allows the grantee to grant the privilege further.

ALL PRIVILEGES confers all the applicable privileges that the grantor is entitled to grant. For global or created local temporary tables, only ALL PRIVILEGES may be specified. Privileges may not be granted on declared local temporary tables. PUBLIC denotes all Authorization IDs, present and future.

SELECT, INSERT, UPDATE, and DELETE allow the grantee to execute the statements of the same names on the object. USAGE confers the ability to use the object to define another object—for example, to use a translation to define a collation. REFERENCES confers the ability to use the table as a parent to a foreign key or to refer to it in a constraint. INSERT, UPDATE, and REFERENCES may be restricted to specified columns of the tables; if the list of columns is omitted, however, they apply by default to all columns, including columns added to the table later. If there are any columns that the grantor has not the right to confer (does not have the GRANT OPTION on), those columns are ignored by the GRANT, but the privilege is GRANTed on the others.

NOTE   There is interest in a column-specific SELECT privilege for a future upgrade of the standard, and provision has been made for this in the current design of the standard INFORMATION_SCHEMA, but the fields of the INFORMATION_SCHEMA provided for this purpose currently have no meaning.

Cascading of Privileges

Privileges can cascade up, meaning that privileges granted on some object can imply grants of privileges on other objects. These situations are covered by the following principles:

- If the grantee owns an updatable view and is being GRANTed privileges on its leaf underlying table (the base table wherein the data finally resides, regardless of any intervening views), these privileges will be GRANTed for the view as well. If specified, the GRANT OPTION also cascades up. There is only one leaf underlying table for an updatable view; see CREATE VIEW.

- If the grantee owns an updatable view that immediately references the table on which privileges are being GRANTed (in other words, if the reference appears in the FROM clause without an intervening view), these privileges also cascade up, including the GRANT OPTION if applicable.

- If the grantee owns a view, updatable or not, that grantee will already have the SELECT privilege on all tables referenced in its definition as well as on the view itself. If the grantee gains the GRANT OPTION on SELECT on all the referenced tables, he also acquires the GRANT OPTION on the SELECT privilege on the view.

- Likewise, the GRANT OPTION cascades up in domains. If a grantee owns a domain and acquires the GRANT OPTION on REFERENCES for all tables referenced in any domain constraints and on USAGE for all domains, character sets, collations, and translations referenced in the domain, that grantee gets the USAGE privilege on the domain with the GRANT OPTION.

- Likewise, if a grantee owns a collation or translation and gets the GRANT OPTION on the character set on which it is based, the GRANT OPTION cascades up to the collation or translation.

- The REFERENCES privilege cascades up in a more complex fashion. If the grantee owns a view and, after this GRANT statement has been executed, will have the REFERENCES privilege on every column referenced in the view, and if the grantor has the REFERENCES privilege on at least one column of each table referenced in that view, then the grantee gets the REFERENCES privilege on the view, with the GRANT OPTION if such was specified for this statement.

In all of the above situations, the grantor of the privilege is _SYSTEM, which denotes an automatic GRANT.

For each privilege that is GRANTed, a privilege descriptor is created. For column-specific privileges, a separate descriptor is generated for each column. The privilege descriptor indicates:

- The grantee that has received the privilege.
- The privilege itself (the action that can be performed).
- The object on which the privilege is GRANTed, which may be one of those listed above or a column.
- The grantor that conferred the privilege. For automatic GRANTs, this is the built-in value _SYSTEM.
- Whether the privilege is grantable (GRANTed with the GRANT OPTION).

Multiple identical privilege descriptors are combined, so that a privilege GRANTed twice by the same grantor need only be revoked (cancelled) once. Likewise, if two privilege descriptors differ only in that one confers the GRANT OPTION and the other does not, they are merged into a single privilege with the GRANT OPTION. If the grantor lacks the ability to GRANT the privileges attempted, a completion condition is raised—a warning that privileges were not GRANTed will appear. Revocation of privileges is also complicated. See REVOKE for details.

Example

The following statement gives the user (or, theoretically, the module) Emil column-specific INSERT and UPDATE privileges with the GRANT OPTION on the Salespeople table:

```
GRANT INSERT(snum, name, city), UPDATE(name)
ON Salespeople
TO Emil
WITH GRANT OPTION;
```

Conformance Levels

Intermediate   Implementations at this level are not required to support privileges on character sets, domains, collations, or translations.

Entry   Implementations at this level are not required to support the optional word TABLE.

NOTE See Also: Chapter 16; CREATE CHARACTER SET, CREATE COLLATION, CREATE DOMAIN, CREATE TABLE, CREATE TRANSLATION, and CREATE VIEW in this chapter; and Authorization IDs and Collations in Chapter 29.

INSERT

Inserts Rows into a Table

Syntax

```
INSERT INTO table name
[ (column_name.,..) ]
{ VALUES(value.,..) }
| query
| {DEFAULT VALUES};
```

Usage

The INSERT statement enters one or more rows into *table name*. The rows are either the output of the query or a table value constructor. A table value constructor consists of the keyword VALUES followed by one or more row value constructors, separated by commas. A row value constructor is a parenthesized, comma-separated lists of values. Hence, the VALUES clause can be followed by one or more parenthesized lists of values, and each such parenthesized list constitutes a row to be INSERTed. For more on row and table value constructors, see Row and Table Value Constructors in Chapter 29. In Entry SQL and older versions of SQL, the VALUES clause can take but a single list of values and INSERT but a single row unless a query were used.

Naturally, these rows must have the same datatypes as the columns being inserted into. The column name list identifies which columns of the table the values are being INSERTed into; all columns not in the list will have their default values INSERTed automatically. If any such columns cannot receive defaults (for example, if they have the NOT NULL constraint but have no other default value specified), the INSERT will fail. If the list is omitted, all columns of the table are the target of the INSERT. The number of columns and the order in which you list them must match the number and order of the output columns of the corresponding query or the number and order of the columns of all row value constructors in the VALUES clause version.

The Authorization ID under which this statement is issued must have the INSERT privilege on all named columns of the target table or on all such columns if the list is omitted. The table may be a view. If so, the view must be updatable (see CREATE VIEW), in which case the new rows are INSERTed into the base table ultimately containing the data from which the view is derived (the leaf underlying table). Keep in mind that the view may specify WITH CHECK OPTION, which restricts the values that can be inserted through it. In fact, there can be any number of intervening views before the base table is reached, and if these specify WITH CASCADED CHECK OPTION, they also can cause INSERTs to be rejected. (Views may be used in this manner as a security mechanism, enabling some users to make changes within tightly controlled parameters without constraining the base table itself.) Also, if the current TRANSAC-TION MODE is read-only, the table must be temporary or the INSERT is rejected.

Example

The following statement puts a row into the table Salespeople, using a single-row table value constructor. Even though table value constructors generally were not part of the pre-92 SQL standards, the particular language construction has been specified since SQL86.

```
INSERT INTO Salespeople (ID_num, lname, fname, city, country)

VALUES ( 1023, 'Blanco', 'Mercedes', 'Barcelona', 'Spain');
```

Conformance Levels

Intermediate   Implementations at this level may exclude references to the target table in the query expression, except where they are column qualifiers.

Entry   Implementations at this level may limit the table value constructor to that of a single row—in effect, to a row value constructor but with the VALUES keyword present. Also, EXACT NUMERIC types may be restricted to matching only other EXACT NUMERIC types (see Datatypes in Chapter 29). Entry-level implementations are also allowed to exclude truncation, so that, for character string datatypes, the length of the target must be at least as great as the length of the value being INSERTed or the INSERT fails.

NOTE   See Also: Chapter 6 and 15; CREATE VIEW, SELECT, and SET TRANSACTION in this chapter; and Authorization IDs, Datatypes, Predicates, and Row and Table Value Constructors in Chapter 29.

OPEN

(Static or Dynamic SQL) Readies a Cursor for Use

Syntax

```
OPEN cursor name [USING values source];
```

```
values source ::=
    parameter list
| {SQL DESCRIPTOR descriptor name}
```

Usage

The OPEN statement opens a cursor that will have been previously defined with a DECLARE CURSOR or (an alternative in Dynamic SQL) an ALLOCATE CURSOR statement. Any parameters or variables (including built-in variables such as CURRENT_USER) are filled in with their current values. The query contained in the cursor is executed and the data retrieved. The data is now ready to be processed one row at a time through the use of the FETCH statement.

If the cursor is INSENSITIVE, changes made to the data by other statements within the same transaction will not affect the content of the cursor while it is open. If it is not INSENSITIVE, whether such changes are visible is implementation-defined. You declare a cursor INSENSITIVE when defining it with the DECLARE CURSOR or the ALLOCATE CURSOR statement. The cursor will remain open until a CLOSE statement is issued or until the end of the transaction, regardless of whether all of its rows are FETCHed.

The USING clause only comes into play in Dynamic SQL and only if the query in the cursor uses dynamic input parameters, which are indicated with question marks (?). The OPEN CURSOR statement does not produce the output of the query; FETCH does that. Therefore, it cannot take output parameters, and all dynamic parameters in the statement must be input parameters. The USING clause specifies, in order, the values to put in the dynamic parameters. You have two options. One is to list a series of conventional variables (or parameters for the module language) passed from the application. You must prefix these with colons, and you may append indicator, if you want to make it possible to insert NULLs into the dynamic parameters (see Chapter 22; Parameters and Variables under Value Expressions in Chapter 29; and Appendix H).

The other option is to take the values from a descriptor area. In this case, the words SQL DESCRIPTOR precede the name of the descriptor area. If a descriptor area is used, its COUNT field must equal the number of dynamic input parameters in the query. Otherwise, the number of variables listed in the USING clause (excluding indicators) must equal that of the dynamic input parameters in the query. In either case, the USING parameters or descriptor items must match or be convertible to, in order, the datatypes of dynamic parameters in the query, based on the criteria for comparability of datatypes described in Chapter 29 under Datatypes.

Conformance Levels

Entry   Implementations at this level are not required to support Dynamic SQL and therefore not required to support dynamic cursors.

NOTE   See Also: ALLOCATE CURSOR, CLOSE, COMMIT WORK, DECLARE CURSOR, FETCH, PREPARE, and ROLLBACK in this chapter and Datatypes in Chapter 29.

PREPARE

(Dynamic SQL Only) Generates a SQL Statement from a Character String

Syntax

```
PREPARE [ GLOBAL | LOCAL ] SQL statement name
FROM character string variable;
```

Usage

In Dynamic SQL, you frequently cannot know beforehand the SQL statements that will be required at runtime. Therefore, the standard enables you to generate statements at runtime by first storing the text of the desired statement in a character string variable and then converting this variable into a SQL statement. Providing a technique for generating proper SQL syntax based on the actions of the user or application is the application's responsibility. Once the character string is generated, however, there are two statements that can effect the conversion. EXECUTE IMMEDIATE converts the character string and executes the statement at once. The PREPARE statement creates a SQL statement from the text that can then be repeatedly executed using EXECUTE or, if the statement is a query, incorporated into a cursor using an ALLOCATE CURSOR or DECLARE CURSOR statement. Prepared statements can use dynamic parameters.

PREPARE neither provides values for input parameters nor retrieves them for output parameters. EXECUTE, OPEN CURSOR, and FETCH do so. This is one of the points of repeated execution of prepared statements: you can repeat the statement with different values for the input parameters each time and get different values for the output as well.

NOTE If a statement has already been prepared with the same name as the one we are attempting to prepare here, it will automatically be replaced, possibly without warning (no warning is required by the standard).

You have the option of specifying a scope of GLOBAL or LOCAL. The scope refers to the visibility of the prepared statement. If GLOBAL is specified, the prepared statement may be accessed by any EXECUTE, DECLARE CURSOR, or ALLOCATE CURSOR statement in the session. Otherwise, it may be accessed only from within the module or compilation unit (see Chapter 21 and Appendix H). If the scope is not specified, LOCAL is the default. Two prepared statements with the same name but with different scopes are considered two distinctly named statements.

The character string stored in the variable must, once leading and trailing blanks are removed, match the text of some valid SQL statement without comments. It may use dynamic parameters, but all of the following criteria must be satisfied:

- No dynamic parameter may be contained in a SELECT clause.

- A dynamic parameter may not be used on both sides of a dyadic operator. That is to say, expressions such as ? = ? or ? > ? are prohibited.

- No dynamic parameter may be used in the following expressions:

    - ? COLLATE *collation* (See Collations in Chapter 29.)

    - EXTRACT (*extract* field FROM ?) (See Datetime Value Functions in Chapter 29.)

- No dynamic parameter specification may be the argument to an aggregate function (see Chapter 8 and Aggregate Functions in Chapter 29).

- No dynamic parameter may be used in a row value constructor that is tested with the IS NULL predicate (see Predicates and Row and Table Value Constructors in Chapter 29).

- No dynamic parameter may be the second element in a row value constructor used with the OVERLAPS operator (see Row and Table Value Constructors and Datetime Value Functions in Chapter 29).

- No dynamic parameter may be the first operand of COALESCE or of the first WHEN condition in a CASE expression, or both operands of a NULLIF expression (see CASE Expressions in Chapter 29).

- No dynamic parameter may be in the same column position for each row of a table value constructor, unless the statement is an INSERT and the constructor is used to generate values for it (see Chapters 5 and 22; INSERT, and Row and Table Value Constructors in Chapter 29).

- If a dynamic parameter is a row value constructor used with an IN predicate, it may not be both the entire constructor and the first element in the list to be matched (see Predicates and Row and Table Value Constructors in Chapter 29).

NOTE
Since ALLOCATE CURSOR generates cursor names at runtime, these are allowed to duplicate the names of the more permanent cursors created with DECLARE CURSOR. The text of the prepared statement may refer to cursors of either type but will produce an error if the reference is ambiguous because of name duplication.

Once the conditions described above have been met, the statement is ready to be executed. Whether a prepared statement continues to be valid past the end of a transaction or needs to be prepared once again is implementation-dependent.

Example

The following statement converts the text string variable SQLstmt5 to the prepared statement Statement5. This statement will be accessible throughout the session. The content of the string variable is also shown. The statement uses a dynamic parameter for the city value that must be matched; this will be assigned a value when the statement is executed using an EXECUTE statement. The leading and trailing blanks will be removed automatically. As you can see, the statement terminator (;) is not part of the prepared statement.

```
SQLstmt5 ::= ' DELETE FROM Salepeople WHERE city = ? '
PREPARE GLOBAL Statement5 FROM :SQLstmt5;
```

Conformance Levels

Intermediate   Implementations at this level are not required to support any of the following as prepared statements: CREATE ASSERTION, DROP ASSERTION, CREATE COLLATION, DROP COLLATION, CREATE TRANSLATION, DROP TRANSLATION, SET SCHEMA, SET CATALOG, SET NAMES, SET CONSTRAINTS MODE, SELECT (used outside of cursors; in other words, a single-row SELECT).

Entry   Implementations at this level are not required to support Dynamic SQL at all.

NOTE
See Also: Chapter 22; ALLOCATE CURSOR, DECLARE CURSOR, EXECUTE and EXECUTE IMMEDIATE in this chapter; and Predicates and Row and Table Value Constructors in Chapter 29.

REVOKE

Removes the Privilege to Perform an Action

Syntax

```
REVOKE [ GRANT OPTION FOR ]
{ ALL PRIVILEGES } | { privilege .,..}
ON object
FROM PUBLIC | { grantee .,..}
 CASCADE | RESTRICT ;
```

Usage

The REVOKE statement removes privileges or the GRANT OPTION on them from Authorization IDs that will have previously received them with the GRANT statement. Authorization IDs generally refer to users but may also mean modules or compilation untis (see Authorization IDs in Chapter 29). The privileges follow the definitions and rules outlined under GRANT. The GRANT OPTION is the ability to grant the privileges received in turn to others. If GRANT OPTION FOR is specified, the grantee loses the ability to grant the named privileges on the named object but retains the privileges themselves for his own use; if GRANT OPTION FOR is not specified, the grantee loses the named privileges. A grantee that loses a privilege automatically loses GRANT OPTION as well, so a separate statement to REVOKE the GRANT OPTION is not necessary. If no column list is given for a column-specific privilege, the REVOKE statement applies to all columns on which the privilege (or GRANT OPTION on the privilege) currently is held and which the issuer of this statement has the authority to REVOKE.

NOTE

Although REVOKE has been part of commercial SQL implementations throughout the history of the language, it is not required for Entry SQL92 and earlier SQL standards. In practice, this means everyone supports it but may not follow precisely what the standard specifies, especially in the area of dependencies, where the standard is highly abstruse.

In any case, the revoker of the privilege will be the same Authorization ID that GRANTed it. To clearly explain CASCADE and REVOKE, we must explain dependencies. Following are the basic principles that govern dependencies. The standard is slightly more complicated than this, but our explanation conforms to what you are likely to actually find in practice.

- GRANT OPTION on a privilege includes subsets of that privilege. That is to say, if you have GRANT OPTION on SELECT for five columns of a table, you can GRANT SELECT on any of those five columns independently; you do not have to GRANT it on all of them.

- A privilege is either dependent or independent.

- An independent privilege is one directly GRANTed by the owner of the object in question or automatically GRANTed by the DBMS. Automatic GRANTs have a grantor of _SYSTEM and include such things as the GRANT of all privileges on an object to its creator. For more on automatic GRANTs, see GRANT.

- If a user (user A) is not the creator of an object but has GRANT OPTION on a privilege (privilege X), she can GRANT the privilege to user B. The privilege user B now has is considered a separate privilege (privilege Y) that is directly dependent on privilege X.

- If user A GRANTed privilege X WITH GRANT OPTION, and user B GRANTs privilege Y to a third user (C, who now has privilege Z), privilege Z is directly dependent on privilege Y and indirectly dependent on privilege X.

- Several people can GRANT the same privilege to any given user. If these GRANTs differ only in their dependencies, that is, on who is GRANTing them, the privileges are merged, and we say that these privileges have multiple dependencies. The multiple dependencies are treated independently unless they are redundant (for example, the same GRANT executed twice by the same grantor to the same grantee would not result in two dependencies. If the grantors were different, it would).

- Privileges with GRANT OPTION are also merged with identical privileges without, but the GRANT OPTION has a separate dependency. Suppose user A GRANTs user B a privilege WITH GRANT OPTION, and user C GRANTs the same privilege without GRANT OPTION. If user A REVOKEs the privilege, user B still has it but without GRANT OPTION.

- Some objects require privileges on other objects. For example, to CREATE a VIEW, you must have the SELECT privilege on all columns of all tables directly referenced in the view. Likewise, to CREATE a DOMAIN using a particular COLLATION, you must have the USAGE privilege on that COLLATION. The objects that can have such dependencies are as follows:

  - Base tables can contain constraints that reference other tables. Such constraints rely on the REFERENCES privilege on those tables. Table constraints can also utilize domains, character sets, collations, and translations, all of which require the USAGE privilege.

  - Views require the SELECT privilege on all columns referenced in them. The query contained in a view can also make direct use of some other kinds of objects, such as domains (for CAST expressions) or collations. These objects require the USAGE privilege.

- Domains can use constraints, with the same consequences as for base tables.

- Assertions use constraints, with the same consequences as for base tables.

- Note that some objects, like character sets, require privileges but do not depend on them.

- The above objects are said to be directly dependent on the privileges used to create them and indirectly dependent on any privileges on which those privileges depend.

- Consider a database full of privileges GRANTed like this. Picture each privilege as an oval having an arrow pointing to each other privilege that directly depends on it. Each independent privilege has a star on top of the oval. Now add rectangles indicating all objects that depend on privileges (other objects are not relevant). There are also arrows pointing to them from the privileges on which they directly depend. This type of picture is called a dependency graph; it may or may not actually be implemented by the DBMS as a data structure, but it is a useful tool for you to use to understand dependencies. (For complex schemata, having an application or tool that actually draws these things can be handy.)

- When a privilege or GRANT OPTION on one is REVOKEd, all privileges directly or indirectly dependent can be REVOKEd as well. All arrows indicating such dependencies are removed from the dependency graph. Arrows to objects that depend on these privileges are also removed.

- At this point, examine the graph and see if there are any privileges, other than independent privileges, or any objects with no arrows pointing to them. If so, these are "abandoned". Also, see if there are any groups of privileges and objects that point to one another but do not include any independent privileges. These also are abandoned. The principle is that *from any dependent privilege or object, you should be able to trace a path back through the arrows to an independent privilege. If you cannot, the privilege or object is abandoned.*

OK, now that you know all this, how do RESTRICT and CASCADE work? If the revocation of a privilege creates abandoned privileges or objects, the following happen:

- If the REVOKE statement specifies RESTRICT, then REVOKE fails and nothing is changed. REVOKE RESTRICT is the safe approach.

- If the REVOKE statement specifies CASCADE, then any or all of the following occur, depending on what dependencies exist. All abandoned privileges are automatically REVOKEd.

  - All abandoned views are dropped.

  - All abandoned constraints residing directly in tables are removed from those tables. This is achieved with an automatically executed ALTER

TABLE statement, which may be how the CASCADE effect will show up in the logs. The tables are otherwise unaffected.

- The same for abandoned constraints residing in domains. In effect, an ALTER DOMAIN statement is issued.
- If an abandoned constraint resides in an assertion, the assertion is dropped.

> **NOTE** It does not matter whether the user performing the REVOKE has the right to perform the above operations. They are automatic. You should keep the security implications of this in mind when GRANTing privileges.

Example

The following statement removes the SELECT privilege on Salespeople from Authorization ID Burns. Any dependent privileges are revoked, and dependent objects are dropped or altered as indicated.

```
REVOKE SELECT ON Salespeople FROM Burns CASCADE;
```

Conformance Levels

Entry   Implementations at this level are not required to support REVOKE.

Non   Most if not all nonconformant products do support REVOKE but it may not behave exactly as described here. The syntax is fairly, but not absolutely, standard.

> **NOTE** See Also: Chapter 16 and GRANT in this chapter.

ROLLBACK

Ends a Transaction, Canceling All Changes

Syntax

```
ROLLBACK [ WORK ];
```

Usage

The ROLLBACK statement terminates the current transaction. A transaction is a group of one or more SQL statements that are effectively executed at the same instant and succeed or fail as a group. With ROLLBACK, they all fail, and their effects are canceled (the successful transaction-termination statement is COMMIT). ROLLBACK can never fail, but it can be overridden, if the SQL transaction is part of some implementation-dependent encompassing transaction. If this happens, you will get an invalid transaction state error. Otherwise, the ROLLBACK will proceed. All open cursors will be closed.

Conformance Levels

Entry   Implementations at this level may require the word WORK rather than having it be optional.

NOTE   See Also: COMMIT WORK and SET TRANSACTION in this chapter.

SELECT

Retrieves Rows from One or More Tables

Syntax

```
SELECT [DISTINCT]
{ { aggregate function | value expression
  [AS column name]},....}
| {qualifier.*}
| *
INTO target spec.,..
FROM { {table name [AS] [correlation name]
[ (column name.,..) ] }
| {subquery
| joined table
| table value constructor
| {TABLE table name} }
```

```
        [AS] correlation name [(column name.,..)]}
  } .,..
  [ WHERE predicate ]
  [ GROUP BY {table name | correlation name}.column name
     [ COLLATE collation name ] ]
  [ HAVING predicate ]
  [ {UNION | INTERSECT | EXCEPT} [ALL]
  [CORRESPONDING [BY (column name.,..)] ]
  select statement | {TABLE table name}
  | table value constructor ]
  [ ORDER BY {{output column [ ASC | DESC ]}.,..}
   | {{positive integer [ ASC | DESC ]}.,..};
```

Usage

The SELECT statement is used to formulate queries—requests for information from the database. The issuer of the statement must have the SELECT privilege on all tables accessed. Queries may be stand-alone statements or used in the definitions of views and cursors. You can also use them as subqueries to produce values that will be used within other statements, including the SELECT statement itself. Sometimes, a subquery will be evaluated separately for each row processed by the outer query. Values from that outer row will be used in the subquery. Queries of this type are called correlated subqueries. For more information, see Chapters 11 and 12 and Subqueries in Chapter 29.

The output of a query is itself a table, and the SELECT clause defines the columns of that table (the output columns). The output columns can either be taken directly from the table(s) on which the query operates, be derived from the values in those tables, or be direct value expressions not using the content of the tables.

The INTO clause is used only in Embedded SQL, Dynamic SQL, or the module language and only for queries that return but a single row. It simplifies operations for these queries by making a cursor (see Chapter 21 and DECLARE CURSOR) unnecessary.

The FROM clause determines the one or more tables from which the data will be taken or derived. These sources may include temporary or permanent base tables, views, or the results of subqueries and other operations that return tables.

The WHERE clause defines the criteria that rows must meet in order to be used for deriving the output. These criteria are defined using predicates, which are described later in this entry and discussed in more detail in Predicates in Chapter 29.

The GROUP BY clause groups the output over identical values in the named columns. If the GROUP BY clause is used, every value expression in the output columns that includes a table column must be included in it, unless the columns are used as arguments to aggregate functions. GROUP BY is used to apply aggregate functions to groups of rows defined by having identical values in specified columns. If no GROUP BY clause is used, either all or none of those output columns in the SELECT clause based on tables must use aggregate functions. If all of them use aggregate functions, all rows satisfying the WHERE clause (if any) or all rows produced by the FROM clause (if there is no WHERE clause) are treated as a single group for deriving the aggregates.

The HAVING clause defines criteria that the groups of rows defined in the GROUP BY clause must satisfy to be output by the query. HAVING is meaningful only with GROUP BY, although some products may not reject the use of HAVING without GROUP BY.

UNION, INTERSECT, and EXCEPT are used to combine the output of multiple queries. They are explained in detail below.

ORDER BY forces the output of the one or more queries to emerge in a particular sequence.

The following list shows the order in which the clauses of the SELECT statement are effectively evaluated:

1. FROM
2. WHERE
3. GROUP BY
4. HAVING
5. SELECT
6. UNION or EXCEPT
7. INTERSECT
8. ORDER BY
9. INTO

The individual clauses are described in greater detail in the following sections, in the order in which they are specified in the syntax.

The SELECT Clause

The SELECT clause appears first but is not the first logical step. The other clauses produce a set of rows, the source rows, from which the output is to be derived. The SELECT clause determines which columns from these rows are output. It may directly output these columns, or it may use them in aggregate functions or value expressions. Value expressions can be NUMERIC, STRING, DATETIME, or INTERVAL; they may include CAST expressions, CASE statements, aggregate functions, and subqueries (for more information, see Aggregate Functions, CASE Expressions, CAST Expressions, and Value Expressions in Chapter 29). If DISTINCT is specified, the rows are compared and, if any duplicate rows are found, only one copy appears in the output. This comparison occurs after all expressions have been evaluated, as the last step before output. The SELECT clause may contain any of the following:

- Aggregate functions, which are functions that extract single values from groups of column values—for example, SUM or COUNT.

- An asterisk (*), which means all of the columns of all tables listed in the FROM clause are output, in the order in which they appear in the FROM clause.

- A value expression, which in a SELECT clause usually is or includes a column name from one of the tables identified in the FROM clause. Either the column's value is directly output or it becomes part of some expression, such as `AMOUNT *` 3. The column name that you can specify with the AS clause is the name of the output column. If the output columns are directly taken from one and only one column referenced in the FROM clause, it will inherit the name of that column by default. You can override this name by using the AS clause, if desired. The names of columns not directly taken from input columns are implementation-dependent. You are not required to name any output columns. It makes no difference whether you include the word noiseword AS—if omitted, it is implied.

- The {*qualifier.**} sequence, which produces all input columns as output columns, except that the common columns of any joined tables are removed. The qualifier is a name or correlation variable denoting a table referenced in the query. In order for the qualifier to have a point, this should be a joined table, probably created in the FROM clause using the join operators we will introduce later in this entry.

An output column from the query can contain NULLs if any of the following are true:

- It includes the name of a column that can contain NULLs.

- It is suffixed with an indicator parameter or an indicator variable. For example, `SELECT :prog-var:prog-var-indicator FROM tablename`.

- It contains a subquery.

- It contains a CASE, COALESCE, or NULLIF argument.

- It contains an aggregate function other than COUNT.

- The query contains an outer join (explained later in this entry).

Otherwise, the output column cannot contain NULLs. It is important to know whether NULLs may be present because, if you are using either Static or Dynamic SQL, you probably will want to use an indicator parameter or variable if NULLs may be encountered. If you don't, they could cause you an error (see Chapter 21).

NOTE In the last case listed above, the output column value would be NULL whenever no rows are selected from which the aggregate can be derived. With COUNT, the value in this situation is 0 rather than NULL.

The INTO Clause

You can use this clause whenever you know that a particular query will produce only one row and when you have a host language into whose variables you can store the output. Situations where you know you will output only one row include when you are searching for a specific primary key value and when you are using aggregate functions with no GROUP BY clause. The *target specs* consists of host-language variables, possibly appended by indicator variables, that can hold the values in the output columns in the SELECT clause. The *target specs* should match the SELECT columns in the order given. For more on the use of INTO, see Chapters 21 and 22.

The FROM Clause

The FROM clause names the source tables for the query. These tables may be any of the following:

- Tables or views named and accessed directly.

- Tables derived on the spot with a subquery.

- Built-in joins (explained later in this entry).

- Table value constructors. This is a way to directly specify a set of values as constituting a table for the duration of this statement. See Row and Table Value Constructors in Chapter 29.

- Explicit tables. These consist simply of the word TABLE followed by the name of a table or view. It is the equivalent of SELECT * FROM *tablename*.

You can follow tables specified with any of the above techniques with correlation names. A correlation name (also called a range variable or an alias) provides an alternative name for the table it follows. These names last only for the duration of the statement. They are an option of convenience for base tables and views but are required for tables produced by subqueries or table value constructors. They can be used to qualify ambiguous column references in the rest of the statement, as can the table names that they replace.

A join, explained later in this entry, is a technique for combining multiple tables into one. You may choose to join a table to itself, which is treated as a join of two identical tables; in this case, you will have to use correlation names to distinguish the two copies. The correlation name will prefix the column name—separated by a period, as usual (see Appendix G). The column name lists here are for renaming columns, just as they are in the SELECT clause. The names used here, however, are not for the output; they are for references to the columns made in the remainder of the statement, particularly in the WHERE clause. They are optional but may be required to clarify column references in some cases.

Joins

If more than one table is named in the FROM clause, they are all implicitly joined. This means that every possible combination of rows (one from each table) will, in effect, be derived, and that this concatenation will be the table on which the rest of the query operates. The concatenated table is called a Cartesian product or a cross join.

Usually, you want to eliminate most of the rows and focus on the data you want, typically in terms of some relationship. To do this, you can use the WHERE clause. As an alternative, you can use built-in join operators to perform the entire join in the FROM clause, treating the result as a derived table for processing by the rest of the query. For that matter, the two techniques can be combined, although this usually produces more confusion than it is worth. The old standard did not support built-in join operators, so if you have already learned to perform your joins by hand, you may find it natural to stick with that method. Otherwise, you are likely to find the built-in joins simpler for any of a group of standard operations. For more detail on joins than is provided here, see Chapter 10.

First, let's look at the built-in join operators that you would use in the FROM clause. The syntax to create a joined table this way is as follows:

```
cross join ::=
table A CROSS JOIN table B


natural join ::=
table A NATURAL
  [join type] JOIN table B


union join ::=
table A UNION JOIN table B


specified join ::=
table A
  [join type] JOIN table B
  {ON predicate}
 | {USING (column name.,..)}


join type ::=
INNER
 | { { LEFT | RIGHT | FULL } [OUTER] }
```

All of that just to replace a table name in the FROM clause! Nonetheless, it can be simpler than doing the same joins by hand, as you will see. The syntax above refers to a join of two tables (it is possible to join any number of tables, but these operations can be broken down into multiple joins of two tables). The result of this join is a table, which can be treated as a source table for the rest of the query. One and only one of the following is to be specified: CROSS, NATURAL, UNION, ON, or USING. The join type arguments (INNER, LEFT, and so on) serve to further qualify joins that use NATURAL, ON, or USING.

You can optionally place the entire join in parentheses. Why would you want to do this? Correlation names can follow either the entire join, to rename the table and possibly columns that result from it, or simply follow the individual tables being joined. Sometimes you must use correlation names for the individual tables to avoid ambiguity. If the join is parenthesized, a correlation name following it, outside the parentheses, applies to the result table of the join. Correlation names following the individual tables specified as part of the join apply to the tables and can be referenced in the join itself. In the absence or parentheses, a correlation name following a join is assumed to apply to the last table in the join, not the result table. The use of correlation names will become clearer in the examples that follow.

The two tables joined actually can be the same table, in which case the join is performed as though two identical tables are being joined. This is called a self-join and can be useful in some situations.

A join over a column is a join in which only those rows from the Cartesian product of *table A* and *table B* where the values in that column are the same are retained; these two columns are merged into one (the join column or common column). Naturally, the datatypes of the joined columns have to be comparable (as defined in Chapter 29 under Datatypes).

The joins fall into the following categories:

- A CROSS join, as defined above, is a straight Cartesian product. A CROSS join is shown in Table 28.2.

- A natural join has a slightly different meaning in the SQL standard than it does in database theory generally. In theory, a natural join is a join of a foreign to its parent key. In the standard, a natural join is a join of two tables over all columns that have the same name, one in each table. You can make the standard joins the same as theoretical ones by making sure that all your foreign keys have the same names as their parents and that all other columns have unique names. Natural joins in either the standard or theoretical sense fall into the following categories, which in the standard are called join types. In all of these, the word OUTER, if used, is optional and has no effect:

  - INNER, which means that only rows where matches are found are included in the output. This type is shown in Table 28.3.

- LEFT [OUTER], which means that all rows from *table A* are included, with matching rows from *table B* where found and NULLs where not found. This type is shown in Table 28.4.

- RIGHT [OUTER], which is the reverse of a LEFT OUTER join. All rows for *table B* are included with NULLs in rows unmatched in *table A*. This type is shown in Table 28.5.

- FULL [OUTER]. This is a combination of LEFT and RIGHT OUTER. All rows from both tables are included, merged where matches are found, and filled out with NULLs where not. This type is shown in Table 28.6.

- A UNION join consists of all columns of both tables, with no matching or Cartesian product derivation. You concatenate all of the columns from *table B* onto *table A*. All the rows from *table A* are output, with NULLs in the columns from *table B*. Then all the rows from *table B* are output, with NULLs in the columns from *table A*. This is a fairly exotic type of join that sees little use. (Note that a UNION join is not the same as the UNION operator used to merge the output of multiple SELECT statements, described later in this entry.) This type is shown in Table 28.7.

- A specified join uses ON or USING. Either of these can use the join types explained under natural joins:

  - USING is just like a natural join, except that you name the columns to be used in the join. The columns still have to have the same names in both tables. If your foreign and parent keys have the same names, but you may have other like-named columns as well (watch for common column names like "city" or "last name"), this is a way to restrict your join to the actual matching columns to directly name the columns to be joined. The standard calls this a named columns join. This type is shown in Table 28.8.

  - ON lets you specify a predicate, and the row combinations that satisfy that predicate are considered matched. This is pretty much the same way you hand-code a join in the main query anyway, but if you want to do all the work in the FROM clause, or if you want to have an easy way to embed joins, ON is your baby. The standard calls this a join condition, though all joins are over (written or implied) predicates (conditions). This type is shown in Table 28.9.

A CROSS Join

A complete CROSS join of these two tables would take 35 rows (seven rows in one table times five in the other). We're just going to show you enough to get the idea. In this and many other of these join examples, we are not including all columns of the joined tables. That would require the table to be too wide to make easily readable. The letters *s* and *c* are simple correlation names for the joined tables (not the result table).

```
Salespeople s CROSS JOIN Customers c
```

TABLE 28.2: A Portion of a CROSS Join

S.snum	Sname	S.city	Cnum	Cname
1001	Peel	London	2001	Hoffman
1001	Peel	London	2002	Giovanni
1001	Peel	London	2003	Liu
1001	Peel	London	2004	Grass
1001	Peel	London	2006	Clemens
1001	Peel	London	2008	Cisneros
1001	Peel	London	2007	Pereira
1002	Serres	San Jose	2001	Hoffman
1002	Serres	San Jose	2002	Giovanni

A NATURAL INNER Join

The NATURAL INNER join retrieves all rows where both the city and snum columns of both tables have the same value. It is based on the fact that they have the same name. Although for an INNER JOIN, it does not strictly matter which table the commonly named columns come from (since the values are the same in both), it does matter for an OUTER JOIN, and the syntax requires you to specify. This mandates the use of correlation names.

```
Salespeople s NATURAL INNER JOIN Customers c
```

Table 28.3 shows a NATURAL join, in the standard, not theoretical, sense, of the Salespeople and Customers tables.

TABLE 28.3: A NATURAL INNER Join

Sname	S.snum	C.city	Cnum	Cname
Peel	1001	London	2001	Hoffman
Serres	1002	San Jose	2003	Liu
Peel	1001	London	2006	Clemens

A LEFT OUTER Join

Here is the previous example as a LEFT OUTER join:

```
Salespeople s NATURAL LEFT OUTER JOIN Customers c
```

TABLE 28.4: A LEFT OUTER Join

Sname	S.snum	C.city	Cnum	Cname
Peel	1001	London	2001	Hoffman
Serres	1002	San Jose	2003	Liu
Peel	1001	London	2006	Clemens
Motika	1004	NULL	NULL	NULL
Rifkin	1007	NULL	NULL	NULL
Axelrod	1003	NULL	NULL	NULL

A RIGHT OUTER Join

Here is the previous example as a RIGHT OUTER JOIN:

```
Salespeople s NATURAL RIGHT OUTER JOIN Customers c
```

TABLE 28.5: A RIGHT OUTER Join

Sname	S.snum	C.city	Cnum	Cname
Peel	1001	London	2001	Hoffman
Serres	1002	San Jose	2003	Liu
Peel	1001	London	2006	Clemens
NULL	NULL	Rome	2002	Giovanni
NULL	NULL	Berlin	2004	Grass
NULL	NULL	San Jose	2008	Cisneros
NULL	NULL	Rome	2007	Pereira

A FULL OUTER Join

Here is the previous example as a FULL (RIGHT and LEFT) OUTER join:

```
Salespeople s NATURAL FULL OUTER JOIN Customers c
```

TABLE 28.6: A FULL OUTER Join

Sname	S.snum	C.city	Cnum	Cname
Peel	1001	London	2001	Hoffman
Serres	1002	San Jose	2003	Liu
Peel	1001	London	2006	Clemens
Motika	1004	NULL	NULL	NULL
Rifkin	1007	NULL	NULL	NULL
Axelrod	1003	NULL	NULL	NULL
NULL	NULL	Rome	2002	Giovanni
NULL	NULL	Berlin	2004	Grass
NULL	NULL	San Jose	2008	Cisneros
NULL	NULL	Rome	2007	Pereira

A UNION Join

Here is a UNION join. Note that it is basically a way to concatenate the two tables, while keeping the result in a tabular structure:

```
Salespeople UNION JOIN Customers
```

TABLE 28.7: A UNION Join

Snum	Sname	City	Cnum	Cname
1001	Peel	London	NULL	NULL
1002	Serres	San Jose	NULL	NULL
1004	Motika	London	NULL	NULL
1007	Rifkin	Barcelona	NULL	NULL

Continued on next page

TABLE 28.7 CONTINUED: A UNION Join

Snum	Sname	City	Cnum	Cname
1003	Axelrod	New York	NULL	NULL
NULL	NULL	NULL	2001	Hoffman
NULL	NULL	NULL	2002	Giovanni
NULL	NULL	NULL	2003	Liu
NULL	NULL	NULL	2004	Grass
NULL	NULL	NULL	2006	Clemens
NULL	NULL	NULL	2008	Cisneros
NULL	NULL	NULL	2007	Pereira

A Specified Join with USING

The following is a natural join in the theoretical sense between the two tables.

```
Salespeople s JOIN Customers c USING snum
```

TABLE 28.8: A Specified Join with USING

Cnum	Cname	C.city	S.snum	Sname
2001	Hoffman	London	1001	Peel
2002	Giovanni	Rome	1003	Axelrod
2003	Liu	San Jose	1002	Serres
2004	Grass	Berlin	1002	Serres
2006	Clemens	London	1001	Peel
2008	Cisneros	San Jose	1007	Rifkin
2007	Pereira	Rome	1004	Motika

A Specified Join with ON

Here's a specified join using ON. Not a commonly useful predicate, but we got bored with simple equalities:

```
ON snum + 1000 = cnum
```

TABLE 28.9: A Specified Join with ON

Snum	Sname	City	Cnum	Cname
1001	Peel	London	2001	Hoffman
1002	Serres	San Jose	2002	Giovanni
1004	Motlka	London	2004	Grass
1007	Rifkin	Barcelona	2007	Pereira
1003	Axelrod	New York	2003	Liu

Note that all of these kinds of joins determine which rows are included in the output. Even joins over specified columns, such as natural and specified USING joins, actually retrieve all the columns of the underlying tables. The determination of which *columns* of these rows to include in the output is an independent matter determined by the SELECT clause.

Subqueries can be used in the FROM clause, but these may not use aggregate functions. WHERE clause subquery predicates are discussed in the next section and under Predicates in Chapter 29.

The WHERE Clause

The WHERE clause contains a *predicate*, which is a set of one or more expressions that can be TRUE, FALSE, or UNKNOWN. NULLs compared to any value, including other NULLs, produce UNKNOWNs. Other values are compared according to collating sequence (for character string types), numerical order (for numeric types), chronological order (for datetime types), or magnitude (for interval types). These comparisons are expressed using the following operators: =, <, <=, >, >=, and <> (does not equal). Operators such as * (multiplication) or || (concatenation) may be applied depending on the datatype (see Datatypes in Chapter 29).

In addition to the standard comparison operators, SQL provides the following special predicate operators. (These are explained in more detail in Chapter 29 under Predicates.) Assume that A, B, and C are all value expressions, which can be or include column names or be direct expressions (possibly using column names or aggregate functions) in the appropriate datatype. They could also be variables (Embedded SQL), parameters (module language), or dynamic parameters (Dynamic SQL). For more information, see Value Expressions in Chapter 29. For example, assuming they are numbers, A could be 1000 (a direct expression, in this case, a literal), B could be snum (a column name), and C could cnum/2 (a value expression incorporating a column name). Following are the predicates.

BETWEEN

```
B BETWEEN A AND C
```

This statement is equal to (A <= B) AND (B <= C). A and C must be specified in ascending order. B BETWEEN C AND A would be interpreted as (C <= B) AND (B <= A), which would be FALSE if (A <= B) AND (B <= C) were TRUE, unless all three values were the same, in which case, both component predicates would be TRUE. If any of the values is NULL, the predicate is UNKNOWN.

IN

```
A IN (C, D .,..)
```

This statement is TRUE if A equals any value in the list. If any of the values is NULL, the predicate is UNKNOWN.

LIKE

```
A LIKE 'string'
```

This statement assumes that A is a character string datatype and searches for the specified substring. Fixed and varying-length wildcards may be used (see Predicates in Chapter 29). If A or the string is NULL, the predicate is UNKNOWN.

IS NULL

```
A IS NULL
```

This statement specifically tests for NULLs. Unlike most other predicates, it can only be TRUE or FALSE—not UNKNOWN. It is TRUE if A contains a NULL, FALSE otherwise.

SOME or ANY

```
A comp op SOME | ANY subquery
```

SOME and ANY have equivalent meanings. The *subquery* produces a set of values. If, for any value V so produced, A *comp op* V is TRUE, then the ANY predicate is TRUE. The comparison operators are the standard ones outlined above (=, <=, etc.)

ALL

```
A comp op ALL subquery
```

ALL is similar to ANY except that all of the values produced by the *subquery* have to make A *comp op* V TRUE.

EXISTS

> EXISTS *subquery*

This statement is TRUE if the *subquery* produces any rows, and FALSE otherwise. It is never UNKNOWN. To be meaningful, it must use a correlated *subquery* (explained later in this entry).

UNIQUE

> UNIQUE *subquery*

If the *subquery* produces no identical rows, UNIQUE is TRUE; otherwise, it is FALSE. For the purposes of this predicate, identical rows are devoid of NULLs; otherwise, they are not identical.

MATCH

> *row value constructor* MATCH *arguments subquery*

MATCH tests for the presence of the constructed row among those of the table produced by the *subquery*. The *arguments* allow you to specify FULL or PARTIAL matches and whether the matched row has to be unique. MATCH is examined in more detail in Chapter 29 under Predicates; also look at Row and Table Value Constructors.

OVERLAPS

> *row value constructor* OVERLAPS *row value constructor*

OVERLAPS is a rather specialized predicate for determining when two date or time periods overlap. It must be used with DATETIME datatypes, possibly in conjunction with INTERVAL datatypes. Again, see Predicates in Chapter 29.

Combining Predicates

These predicates are combined using the conventional Boolean operators AND, OR, and NOT. For TRUE and FALSE values, these predicates have the conventional results; if UNKNOWNs are involved, the results are those outlined in Chapter 29 under Predicates. Parentheses may be used to force an order of evaluation. When all is said and done, the rows selected by the WHERE clause, whether directly extracted from tables or based on Cartesian products, are the ones that go on to be processed by the subsequent clauses. For a given row to be SELECTed, it must make the predicate TRUE.

The GROUP BY Clause

The GROUP BY clause is used to define groups of output rows to which aggregate functions (COUNT, MIN, AVG, and so on) can be applied. If this clause is absent, and aggregate functions are used, the column names in the SELECT clause must all be contained in aggregate functions, and the aggregate functions will be applied to all rows that satisfy the query. Otherwise, each column referenced in the SELECT list outside an aggregate function will be a grouping column and be referenced in this clause. All rows output from the query that have all grouping column values equal will constitute a group (for the purposes of GROUP BY, all NULLs are considered equal). The aggregate function will be applied to each such group. Let's look at a simple example:

```
SELECT snum, AVG(amt), MAX(amt)

FROM Orders

GROUP BY snum;
```

All orders with the same snum value—the same salesperson—constitute a group, and the highest and the average amount for each group are calculated and output. If we wanted these figures calculated independently for each date, we could also make odate a grouping column. Then the aggregates would be calculated for each unique combination of snum and odate. Grouping can be done over joins, in which case table or correlation name prefixes to the column names may be necessary to resolve ambiguities.

If a COLLATE FROM clause is used, it will provide the collation defined for the output column derived from the grouping column. The coercibility attribute of the output column is then explicit. Naturally, the COLLATE CLAUSE can only be applied if the grouping column is a character set datatype. See Collations and Datatypes in Chapter 29.

The HAVING Clause

Just as the WHERE clause defines a predicate to filter rows, the HAVING clause is applied after the grouping performed by GROUP BY to define a similar predicate for filtering groups based on the aggregate values. It is needed to test for aggregate function values, as these are not derived from single rows of the Cartesian product defined by the FROM clause, but from groups of such rows, and therefore cannot be tested in a WHERE clause.

UNION, INTERSECT, EXCEPT, and CORRESPONDING

These statements take entire SELECT statements (queries), minus any ORDER BY clauses, as arguments in this form:

```
query A {UNION | INTERSECT | EXCEPT} [ALL] query B
```

The output columns of each of the queries must be comparable (as defined in Chapter 29 under Datatypes) in the order specified—the first output column of *query A* with the first of *query B*, the second of each, and so on—because these columns will now be merged. If CORRESPONDING, described below, is used, the output columns can be in any order.

UNION includes any row output by either query. If ALL is specified, duplicate output rows are all retained. Otherwise, only one copy of each duplicate is retained.

EXCEPT outputs the rows from *query A*, except for any also produced by *query B*. These are eliminated from the output, and duplicates within the output of *query A* are output only once. If EXCEPT ALL is specified, the number of times a duplicate row appears in the output of *query B* is subtracted from the number of times it appears in *query A*, and it is output that many times—provided, of course, that the number is greater than zero.

If INTERSECT is specified, any rows that appear in the output of both *query A* and *query B* are output once each. Other rows are not output. INTERSECT ALL will have the duplicate rows appear the number of times that they appear in *query A* or the number they appear in *query B*—whichever is smaller.

Note that you may string together any number of queries with the above operators. You may also use parentheses to force an order of evaluation.

CORRESPONDING restricts the operation to columns in the SELECT clauses of the two queries whose names are the same and whose datatypes are comparable. (Of course, you may be able to force this by using the AS clause to assign names or a CAST expression to convert datatypes. See CAST Expressions in Chapter 29.) If a list of columns is supplied with CORRESPONDING, they all must be commonly named and typed columns as just described. The operation is restricted to these columns. If no list is supplied, all such like named and typed columns are used.

In either case, only the like named and typed columns will be output. They will emerge in the order listed or, if no list is used, in the order in which they appear in the first query. With CORRESPONDING, it is not necessary for each SELECT list to have the same number of columns with matching datatypes in the same order—otherwise, it is necessary.

The ORDER BY Clause

Finally, the ORDER BY clause is used to sort the output. The rows are sorted according to the values in the columns listed here; the first column listed gets the highest priority, and the second column determines the order within duplicate values of the first, the third within duplicate values of the second, and so on. You may specify ASC (for ascending, the default) or DESC (for descending) independently for each column. Character sets will be sorted according to their collations. You may also use integers rather than names to indicate columns. The integers refer to the placement of the column among those in the SELECT clause, so that the first column is indicated with a 1, the fifth with a 5, and so on. If any output columns are unnamed, of course, you will have to use a number.

Possibly Nondeterministic Queries

In some cases, it is possible for the same query to produce different output tables on different implementations because of subtle implementation-dependent behaviors. Such queries are called *possibly nondeterministic queries*. A query is possibly nondeterministic if any of the following is true:

- It specifies DISTINCT and the datatype of at least one column of the source row is character string.

- One column of the source rows is of a character string datatype and is used in either the MIN or the MAX aggregate function.

- A character set column is used as a grouping column in GROUP BY or in a UNION.

- A HAVING clause uses a character string column within a MIN or MAX function.

- It uses UNION without specifying ALL.

- It uses INTERSECT or EXCEPT.

Possibly nondeterministic queries cannot be used in constraints (see Constraints in Chapter 29).

Example

The following statement determines the total and average sales for each salesperson on each day of a given week, excluding days where the total was less than $100.00.

```
SELECT snum, SUM(amt), AVG(amt), odate
FROM Orders
WHERE odate BETWEEN '10-01-2000' AND '10-08-2000'
GROUP BY snum, odate
HAVING SUM(amt) > 100.00;
```

Conformance Levels

Intermediate   Implementations at this level are not required to support the use of table value constructors or the use of the TABLE clause (explicit tables). They are not required to support multiple specifications of DISTINCT in the same SELECT list. This would apply to uses of DISTINCT within aggregate functions. They are not required to support a COLLATE clause for GROUP BY, UNION joins, or CROSS joins. Nor are they required to support the use of subqueries to derive tables for the FROM clause.

Entry Implementations at this level are not required to support the built-in join operators. If the FROM clause directly references a view based on aggregate data, and that view uses a GROUP BY clause, you may be restricted from referencing any other tables in the FROM clause, and WHERE, GROUP BY, HAVING, and further aggregates in the SELECT list of the present query may all be prohibited. Predicates may be prohibited from referencing aggregate functions. Qualifiers may be disallowed. EXCEPT, INTERSECT, and CORRESPONDING may all be excluded, and it may not be possible to make UNIONs of joins.

NOTE   See Also: Chapters 7 and 12; ALLOCATE CURSOR, CREATE VIEW, DECLARE CURSOR, and GRANT in this chapter; Aggregate Functions, Collations, Datatypes, Predicates, Row and Table Value Constructors, and Subqueries in Chapter 29; and Appendix G.

SET CATALOG

Determines the Default Catalog

Syntax

```
SET CATALOG catalog name;
```

Usage

SQL schemata are grouped into catalogs, and these into clusters, although implementations have the option of allowing cross-cluster catalogs. This statement defines the default catalog within which the current session operates. Any unqualified schema names used in SQL statements will be implicitly qualified by this catalog name. The default prior to the use of this statement is implementation-defined. Once the leading and trailing blanks, if any, are removed, the catalog name must conform to the proper conventions for such names, which is to say it must be a properly formed SQL identifier (see Appendix G) and conform as well to any implementation-defined restrictions on catalog names.

Conformance Levels

Intermediate   Implementations at this level are not required to support this statement or to support catalogs.

NOTE   See Also: Users, Schemas, and Sessions in Chapter 27 and CREATE SCHEMA and SET SCHEMA in this chapter.

SET CONNECTION

Determines Which Connection Is Active

Syntax

```
SET CONNECTION connection name | DEFAULT ;
```

Usage

The SQL92 standard gives you the ability to have more than one simultaneous connection between a user and a DBMS. The connections are created with the CONNECT statement and destroyed with DISCONNECT. Once you have created several connections using CONNECT, you can use the SET CONNECTION statement to switch between them. The named connection becomes current, and the current one becomes dormant with no other change in its state. The connection name may be a variable (Embedded SQL), parameter (module language), or literal.

Conformance Levels

Intermediate   Implementations at this level are not required to support this statement.

NOTE   See Also: CONNECT and DISCONNECT in this chapter.

SET CONSTRAINTS MODE

Determines When Constraints Are Checked

Syntax

```
SET CONSTRAINTS MODE constraint name.,.. | ALL
[DEFERRED | IMMEDIATE];
```

Usage

Constraints are expressions involving table data, functioning as tests that must be satisfied for the data to be allowed into the database. They can be part of table definitions, domain definitions, or assertion definitions. When created as part of one of these objects, they are specified as DEFERRABLE or NOT DEFERRABLE. If they are NOT DEFERRABLE, they are effectively checked after every statement. Otherwise, checking can be deferred until the end of the transaction. This statement determines when the DEFERRABLE constraints are checked. If ALL is specified, the statement applies to all DEFERRABLE constraints. If not, it applies to the constraints that are named in the list. If IMMEDIATE is specified, all specified constraints are effectively checked now and after every subsequent statement. If DEFERRED is specified, all specified constraints are effectively checked at the end of the transaction. If any DEFERRED constraints are violated when you attempt to set their mode to IMMEDIATE, the SET CONSTRAINTS MODE statement fails.

Example

The following statement will cause all constraints to be checked immediately. If any are violated, the transaction will be rolled back.

```
SET CONSTRAINTS MODE ALL IMMEDIATE;
```

Conformance Levels

Intermediate   Implementations at this level are not required to support this statement.

NOTE   See Also: Chapter 17 and ALTER DOMAIN, ALTER TABLE, COMMIT WORK, CREATE ASSERTION, CREATE DOMAIN, CREATE TABLE, and ROLLBACK in this chapter.

SET DESCRIPTOR

(Dynamic SQL Only) Directly Stores Values in a Descriptor Area

Syntax

```
SET DESCRIPTOR  [GLOBAL | LOCAL] descriptor name
{ COUNT = integer }
| { VALUE item number
{ descrip item = value }.,.. };
```

Usage

This statement stores values in the descriptor area, or simply descriptors, or changes the number of parameters described therein. Descriptors are used in Dynamic SQL to provide and retrieve values for parameters of dynamically generated statements; see Chapter 22 and Descriptor Areas in Chapter 29. A given descriptor describes either all dynamic input or all dynamic output parameters of a given statement. For each such parameter, there is one item consisting of a number of fields.

The descriptor shall have been previously created with an ALLOCATE DESCRIPTOR statement. GLOBAL or LOCAL refers to the scope and, if specified, must agree with the scope of the descriptor as defined in the ALLOCATE DESCRIPTOR statement that created it. If the scope is GLOBAL, it must be specified in this statement. LOCAL is the default and therefore optional. The following descriptor items cannot be changed by this statement but must be set automatically by the system: RETURNED_LENGTH, RETURNED_OCTET_LENGTH, NULLABLE, COLLATION_CATALOG, COLLATION_SCHEMA, COLLATION_NAME, and NAME.

If you set values other than DATA, the value of DATA becomes undefined. Therefore, a given SET DESCRIPTOR statement either sets the DATA field, which contains a value for the parameter, or sets the other fields that describe the parameter. In some situations, when you set certain fields, others are set automatically, as follows:

- If you set TYPE to CHARACTER or CHARACTER VARYING, then CHARACTER_SET_CATALOG, CHARACTER_SET_SCHEMA, and CHARACTER _SET_NAME are all set to the value for the default character set, and LENGTH is set to 1.

- If you set TYPE to BIT or BIT VARYING, then LENGTH is set to 1.

- If you set TYPE to DATETIME, then PRECISION is set to 0.

- If you set TYPE to INTERVAL, then DATETIME_INTERVAL_PRECISION is set to 2.

- If you set TYPE to NUMERIC or DECIMAL, then SCALE is set to 0 and PRECISION to the implementation-defined default value.

- If you set TYPE to FLOAT, then PRECISION is set to the implementation-defined default value. (This reflects the state of the standard as of this writing. The default SCALE of 0 may be subject to change.)

- If you set DATETIME_INTERVAL_CODE and TYPE to DATETIME, and you specify DATE, TIME, or TIME WITH TIME ZONE, then PRECISION is set to 0.

- If you set DATETIME_INTERVAL_CODE and TYPE to DATETIME, and you specify TIMESTAMP or TIMESTAMP WITH TIME ZONE, then PRECISION is set to 6.

- If you set DATETIME_INTERVAL_CODE and TYPE to INTERVAL, then, if you specify DAY TO SECOND, HOUR TO SECOND, MINUTE TO SECOND, or SECOND, PRECISION is set to 6, and if you do not specify one of the above, PRECISION is set to 0.

For all of the above cases, fields not mentioned may be automatically set to implementation-dependent values. In any case, the above are defaults that generally can be overridden by subsequently setting the descriptor field directly with this statement. When a group of descriptor fields are set in a single statement, they are set in the following order: TYPE, DATETIME_INTERVAL_CODE, DATETIME_INTERVAL_PRECISION, PRECISION, SCALE, CHARACTER_SET_CATALOG, CHARACTER_SET_SCHEMA, CHARACTER_SET_NAME, LENGTH, INDICATOR, and DATA. So, for example, the default PRECISION created when you set TYPE can be overridden with a PRECISION specification in the same statement. Note that this effect is independent of the order in which the fields are listed in the SET DESCRIPTOR statement.

Naturally, the datatypes of the values being set must match those of the descriptor item targets, and values being inserted into the DATA field must match the description of that field given by the other items, as least for TYPE, LENGTH, OCTET_LENGTH, PRECISION, and SCALE. Also note that the values of the descriptor area items following a failed SET DESCRIPTOR statement are implementation-dependent; this differs from most statements, which definitely leave the data in its previous state if they fail. Also, there may be implementation-dependent restrictions on changing fields previously set by a DESCRIBE statement. DESCRIBE is an alternative way to set descriptor areas; it automatically derives values by examining a prepared statement.

Example

The following statement sets the TYPE (to the code for CHARACTER) and LENGTH fields of the fourth item (which would describe the fourth dynamic parameter) of the descriptor area called Statement5_Desc. The scope of GLOBAL must be specified, as it is part of the descriptor name.

```
SET DESCRIPTOR GLOBAL :Statement5_Desc VALUE 4
TYPE = 1, LENGTH = 25;
```

Conformance Levels

Intermediate   Implementations at this level may require a descriptor name to be a literal—a simple name. Otherwise, it could be a variable.

Entry   No Dynamic SQL support is required.

> **NOTE**
>
> See Also: ALLOCATE DESCRIPTOR, DESCRIBE, and GET DESCRIPTOR in this chapter and Descriptor Areas in Chapter 29.

SET NAMES

Sets the Default Character Set

Syntax

```
SET NAMES character set name;
```

Usage

The SET NAMES statement defines the default character set used for SQL statements. Trailing and leading blanks are removed, and then the *character set name* must identify a character set suitable for SQL text. The default remains in force for the duration of the session or until a new one is defined. The *character set name* may be a variable or parameter.

Conformance Levels

Intermediate   Implementations at this level are not required to support this statement.

> **NOTE**
>
> See Also: Chapter 20 and CREATE CHARACTER SET and CREATE SCHEMA in this chapter.

SET SCHEMA

(Dynamic and Interactive SQL) Sets the Current Schema

Syntax

```
SET SCHEMA schema name;
```

Usage

The SET SCHEMA statement defines the schema that will be used by default to qualify unqualified object names in interactive or prepared SQL statements. After leading and trailing blanks are removed, the schema name must identify an existing schema to which the current Authorization ID has access. The schema name may be prefixed with a catalog name; if so, both the schema and the catalog are set, and the named schema naturally must reside within the named catalog. Otherwise, some implementation-defined default catalog containing the schema will apply. It may be useful to override this default because schema names need only be unique within their catalogs. You could have a development and a production schema with the same name in different catalogs, for example. The default schema remains in force until a new one is defined or until the end of the session.

Conformance Levels

Intermediate   Implementations at this level are not required to support this
                      statement.

NOTE   See Also: CREATE SCHEMA and SET CATALOG in this chapter.

SET SESSION AUTHORIZATION

Changes the Authorization under Which Statements Are Executed

Syntax

```
SET SESSION AUTHORIZATION Authorization ID;
```

Usage

Once leading and trailing blanks are removed, the Authorization ID named in the statement must be one that the current Authorization ID can access and switch to. The rules for determining which other Authorization IDs, if any, an Authorization ID may switch to are implementation-defined. If the switch is legal, the SQL-session Authorization ID— the value of the built-in variable SESSION_USER—is changed, as are the Authorization IDs controlling access to temporary tables.

Conformance Levels

SQL89   Implementations at this level are not required to support this statement.

NOTE   See Also: Authorization IDs in Chapter 29.

SET TIME ZONE

Defines the Local Time Zone Displacement

Syntax

```
SET TIME ZONE interval value | LOCAL;
```

Usage

Time zones in SQL are used for clock arithmetic and for time stamps. The default time zone for your session is implementation-defined. This statement changes that time zone. The INTERVAL value must be of the INTERVAL HOUR TO MINUTE type and must be between '-12:59' and '+13:00'. The time zone will be incremented or decremented by the indicated amount. Alternatively, LOCAL returns you to the initial default.

Conformance Levels

Entry   Implementations at this level are not required to support this statement.

> **NOTE**   See Also: Datetime Value Functions in Chapter 29.

SET TRANSACTION

Sets the Attributes of the Next Transaction

Syntax

```
SET TRANSACTION { ISOLATION LEVEL
  { READ UNCOMMITTED
  | READ COMMITTED
  | REPEATABLE READ
  | SERIALIZABLE }
  | { READ ONLY | READ WRITE }
  | { DIAGNOSTICS SIZE num of conditions } }.,.. ;
```

Usage

The SET TRANSACTION statement specifies whether a transaction shall be read-only or read/write, what the level of isolation from concurrent transactions will be, and how many conditions to allocate for the diagnostics area for the transaction. It must be specified while no transaction is active, and it will apply to the subsequent transaction. If you specify ISOLATION LEVEL, you will follow it with one of these: READ UNCOMMITTED, READ COMMITTED, REPEATABLE READ, or SERIALIZABLE. You may also specify READ ONLY or READ WRITE or allocate a diagnostics area by specifying DIAGNOSTICS SIZE. You may specify any or all of these, separated by commas.

The ISOLATION LEVELs determine whether and how this transaction will be affected by concurrent transactions—transactions from different SQL sessions that are accessing the same data. There are three phenomena that the isolation levels are designed to address:

- Dirty Read: One transaction modifies a row, and another reads it before the change is committed. If the transaction is rolled back (canceled), the change does not take place, and the second transaction has read a row that never really existed.

- Non-repeatable Read: One transaction reads a row. A second transaction deletes or modifies it and COMMITS before the first one does. Now the first transaction could perform the same read and get different results.

- Phantom: One transaction reads a group of rows that satisfy a predicate. Another INSERTs or UPDATEs rows, so that they too satisfy the predicate. Now the same query performed by the first transaction will get different results.

Table 28.10 shows which isolation levels permit which of these phenomena.

TABLE 28.10: Isolation Levels and Permitted Reads

Isolation Level	Dirty Read	Non-Repeatable	Phantom
READ UNCOMMITTED	Yes	Yes	Yes
READ COMMITTED	No	Yes	Yes
REPEATABLE READ	No	No	Yes
SERIALIZABLE	No	No	No

READ ONLY and READ WRITE simply refer to the updatability of the transaction—whether the transaction is permitted to make changes to the structure or content of the database or merely to extract data. If you know that no writes will be necessary, declaring the transaction READ ONLY may improve the performance of this or of concurrent transactions.

When specifying ISOLATION LEVELs and updatability, you must conform to the following principles:

- If you omit the ISOLATION LEVEL, SERIALIZABLE is implied.

- If READ WRITE is specified, the ISOLATION LEVEL may not be READ UNCOMMITTED.

- If the ISOLATION LEVEL is READ UNCOMMITTED, the transaction is READ ONLY by default; otherwise it is READ WRITE by default.

- The number of conditions must be a positive integer.

The DIAGNOSTICS SIZE clause allocates a number of items within which diagnostics information may be stored. This information can be retrieved with the GET DIAGNOSTICS statement. The content of diagnostics areas and the specific error codes are listed in Appendix C.

Example

The following statement will specify that the subsequent transaction can write as well as read data, that it will have a REPEATABLE READ isolation level, and that room for 14 error messages will be allocated in the diagnostics area.

```
SET TRANSACTION ISOLATION LEVEL REPEATABLE READ,
READ WRITE, DIAGNOSTICS SIZE 14;
```

Conformance Levels

Entry   Implementations at this level are not required to support this statement.

NOTE   See Also: Chapter 17; COMMIT WORK, GET DIAGNOSTICS, and ROLLBACK in this chapter; and Appendix C.

UPDATE

Changes the Values in a Table

Syntax

```
UPDATE table name
SET { column name =
{ value expression
|   NULL
|   DEFAULT }}.,...
[ {WHERE predicate }
| {WHERE CURRENT OF cursor name } ];
```

Usage

This statement changes one or more column values in an existing row of a table. The table may be a temporary or permanent base table or a view. Any number of columns may be set to values, and the whole *column name = value expression* clause is followed by a comma if there is another such to follow. As an alternative to an explicit value, the column may be set to NULL or to the DEFAULT defined for the column (see CRE-ATE TABLE) or the domian (see CREATE DOMAIN). The *value expression* may refer to the current value in the columns. Any such references refer to the values of all of the columns before any of them were updated by this statement. This allows you to do such things as double all column values (if numeric) by specifying

```
column name = column name * 2
```

Value expressions also can use subqueries, CASE expressions, and CAST expressions (see Value Expressions in Chapter 29).

The UPDATE will be applied to all rows that fulfill the WHERE clause or, if the WHERE clause is omitted, to all rows. The WHERE clause is one of two types. The WHERE predicate form is like the WHERE predicate clause in the SELECT statement (see SELECT and Predicates in Chapter 29). It uses an expression that can be TRUE, FALSE, or UNKNOWN for each row of the table to be updated, and the UPDATE is performed wherever it is TRUE. The WHERE CURRENT OF form can be used in Static or Dynamic SQL if an updatable cursor directly (in other words, not through views) referencing the target table is open and positioned on a row (see OPEN, FETCH). The UPDATE is applied to the row on which it is positioned. When using WHERE CURRENT OF in Dynamic SQL, you can omit the table name from the UPDATE clause, and the table in the cursor is implied.

In either case, for the UPDATE to be successful, the following conditions must be met:

- The issuer of the statement must have the UPDATE privilege on each column of the table that is being set (see GRANT).

- If the target table is a view, it must be updatable (see CREATE VIEW).

- If the current transaction state is read-only, the target table must be temporary.

- If the UPDATE is done through a cursor that specifies ORDER BY, it may not set the values of any columns specified in the ORDER BY clause.

- The value expression in the SET clause must not, directly or through views, reference the leaf-underlying table (the base table where the data ultimately resides) of the target table.

- The value expression may not use aggregate functions save in subqueries (see Aggregate Functions and Subqueries in Chapter 29).

- Each column of the target table can be altered only once by a given UPDATE statement.

- If the UPDATE is on a cursor that specified FOR UPDATE, each column being set will have been specified or implied by that FOR UPDATE (see DECLARE CURSOR).

- If the UPDATE is made through a view, it may be constrained by a WITH CHECK OPTION clause (see CREATE VIEW).

Example

The following statement doubles the commission of salespeople in Hong Kong and sets their salary to some default value already defined for the column.

```
UPDATE Salespeople SET comm = comm * 2, salary = DEFAULT
WHERE city = 'Hong Kong';
```

Conformance Levels

Intermediate	Implementations at this level are not required to support UPDATEs on cursors that use ORDER BY. In an UPDATE using the WHERE predicate that is made on a view, neither the predicate nor the value expression in the FROM clause can reference the leaf-underlying table. Also at this level, letting the table name be implied for a Dynamic SQL UPDATE using WHERE CURRENT OF may be disallowed.
Entry	No support for Dynamic SQL is required. Neither is support for specifying DEFAULT in place of a value expression. Also, matches of the value expression to the column in which it is being put are defined fairly tightly, so that for character strings, the value expression may not be longer than the column (no truncation allowed), and exact numeric types cannot be updated to approximate numerics. (That is, there are no automatic conversions; see Datatypes in Chapter 29.)

NOTE See Also: Chapters 6 and 21; CREATE TABLE, CREATE VIEW, DECLARE CURSOR, FETCH, GRANT, OPEN, and SELECT in this chapter; and Aggregate Functions, Datatypes, Predicates, Subqueries, and Value Expressions in Chapter 29.

CHAPTER

TWENTY-NINE

29

Common Elements

This part of the reference contains detailed information about the elements of SQL statements; it supplements what is listed in Chapter 28 under the statements themselves, as material included in this chapter is common to several statements.

Both chapters are extensively cross-referenced. References that appear in UPPER-CASE letters are to statement entries in Chapter 28; those in Mixed Case are to entries for other SQL elements in this chapter.

Aggregate Functions

Calculate a Single Value from a Set of Values

Syntax

```
aggregate function ::=
{ COUNT (*) } |
{{   AVG
|   SUM
|   MAX
|   MIN
|   COUNT }
([DISTINCT | ALL] value expression) }
```

Usage

Aggregate functions, sometimes called set functions, take a group of values in the SELECT or HAVING clause of a query (which can be a subquery) and produce a single value. The group will be either one defined with a GROUP BY clause or all of the values produced by the query. (Queries are requests for information from the database and are implemented in SQL with the SELECT statement, as discussed in Chapters 7 through 12 and under SELECT in Chapter 28. This discussion will assume you understand the basics of queries.)

The COUNT function has two forms. The first listed above, which uses the asterisk (*), counts the number of rows output by the query. It does not count individual column values and pays no attention to whether rows are DISTINCT or whether NULLs are included. The other form of COUNT and all of the other functions automatically disregard NULLs, although they should raise a completion condition (send a warning message) when this happens.

The elimination of NULLs is performed after the value expression is evaluated, so NULLs in the data may be counted if the value expression uses CASE or COALESCE expressions. For that matter, values could be eliminated based on a predicate specified in a NULLIF expression, although they are normally eliminated based on the predicates in the WHERE clause of the containing query.

If DISTINCT is specified for these aggregates, duplicate values will be counted only once in the aggregate figure; otherwise, duplicate values are treated the same as other values, regardless of whether ALL is specified (ALL is the default). Let's examine the role of the functions:

- The second form of COUNT counts all non-NULL column values.

- AVG takes the average (mean) of all the values. This function and SUM (below) may not be applied to CHARACTER STRING, BIT STRING, or DATETIME datatypes, although they may be applied to INTERVAL and, naturally, NUMERIC datatypes.

- SUM totals the values. It may be applied to the same datatypes as AVG.

- MAX returns the largest of the values, based on the rules for comparisons outlined under Predicates. MAX may be applied to any datatype and will follow the rules for comparison specified for comparison predicates under Datatypes.

- MIN is the reverse of MAX. It returns the least of the values.

You should also be aware of a number of rules. Among these rules are the following:

- If the query returns no rows—or no rows in a given group—so that the aggregate function has no data to be applied on, COUNT produces a zero, and the other functions produce NULLs.

- The value expression may not itself contain an aggregate function or a subquery.

The effect of taking an aggregate of an aggregate—for example, the highest average—can often be achieved by defining a view using the innermost aggregate (AVG) and then putting the outermost aggregate (MAX) in the query on (rather than the query within) the view.

- If the aggregate function is used in a subquery, the value expression may contain an outer reference, but if it does, no other column references are allowed in the same expression. (An outer reference is a reference in a subquery to values in a containing query; see Subqueries.) An aggregate using an outer reference also must be contained either directly in a SELECT clause or in a subquery in a HAVING clause (see Chapter 8 and SELECT in Chapter 28). If the latter, it must be contained in a subquery defined in the HAVING clause (not the WHERE), and the table referenced must come from that query at the same level of nesting as that HAVING clause.

- The result of COUNT is an INTEGER. Other aggregates inherit the datatypes of their value expressions, although the precision is implementation-defined in the case of SUM and both the precision and scale are implementation-defined in the case of AVG, with the value expression's precision and scale being the minimum values allowed. For an explanation of precision and scale, see Datatypes.

- If SUM produces a value that is out of range for its datatype, you will get an error.

When contained in the SELECT list of a query that does not use GROUP BY, the aggregate functions are applied to the whole output of the query. If GROUP BY is used, each set of rows that has equal values for the column or group of columns specified in the GROUP BY clause constitutes a group, and the aggregate functions are applied independently to each such group. HAVING filters groups based on aggregate rather than individual values. GROUP BY and HAVING are explained in more detail under SELECT in Chapter 28.

Conformance Levels

Intermediate	Implementations at this level may require the value expression to be a simple column reference if DISTINCT is specified.
Entry	Implementations at this level need not allow ALL to be specified for COUNT and may require that the value expression contain a column reference to the output columns of the SELECT clause (which it normally does, except when using an outer reference). If the value expression uses an outer reference, implementations may require that expression to be a simple column name. No value expression may generally contain an aggregate function (for example, in the view referenced; this may prevent you from using views to take aggregates of aggregates as suggested, although many products don't enforce this restriction).

NOTE See Also: Chapter 8; SELECT in Chapter 28; and Collations, Datatypes, Predicates, Subqueries, and Value Expressions in this chapter.

Authorization IDs

Determine the Privileges under Which Statements Are Issued

Usage

An Authorization Identifier (Authorization ID) is a unique identifier that is associated with a SQL session, a set of owned objects, and a set of privileges on objects. Its format is that of an identifier as outlined in Appendix G. Up to three Authorization IDs may be active at any given moment in a session. You can refer to these in statements by the built-in user value functions SESSION_USER, SYSTEM_USER, and CURRENT_USER.

The SESSION_USER is the Authorization ID named in the USER clause of the CONNECT statement that initiated the session. If the CONNECT statement lacked a USER clause, or if the session was initiated in some implementation-defined manner, then the SESSION_USER is implementation-defined. The SESSION_USER can be changed with the SET SESSION AUTHORIZATION statement; the restrictions on this are implementation-defined.

The CURRENT_USER (also referred to simply as the USER) is the Authorization ID whose privileges determine what can actually be done. By default, it is the same as the SESSION_USER, but there are two exceptions: in CREATE SCHEMA sequences and in the module language. Either a schema definition or a module may specify an Authorization ID, which will become the CURRENT_USER while that CREATE SCHEMA statement or module is being executed.

The SYSTEM_USER is the user as defined by the operating system. It is derived in an implementation-dependent manner and is provided primarily so that there is a way to map DBMS users to operating system users, as there is no requirement that there be consistent name usage or a one-to-one correspondence between the two. Indeed, there frequently is not.

When a CREATE SCHEMA is issued under the privileges of an Authorization ID, that Authorization ID becomes the owner of the schema and the objects within it. Objects include base tables, views, domains, assertions, character sets, collations, and transla-tions. This owner will have the right to create new objects in the schema. As the owners of objects, Authorization IDs may GRANT privileges on them to other users, subject to one restriction (explained below). They may also have privileges on other objects, which will have been explicitly or implicitly GRANTed (through a GRANT to PUBLIC, for example) by the owners of those objects (see Chapter 16 and GRANT in Chapter 28). Whenever a statement is issued on an object, the privileges of the CURRENT_USER are evaluated, and an error is produced if sufficient privileges to perform the operation do not exist.

> **NOTE**
> If you create an object that references other objects—such as a domain referencing a character set or a view referencing a base table—that you do not own, you will be prevented from granting any privileges on your own object that imply grants of privileges on the referenced objects unless you have the GRANT OPTION on the implied privileges (for more detail, see GRANT and the various CREATE statements in Chapter 28).

Conformance Levels

SQL89   Each statement and each schema is associated with an Authorization ID, effectively corresponding to the current user, but how this association is determined is implementation-defined.

Non   A widely used convention is that Authorization IDs may have system-level privileges as well as privileges on objects.

> **NOTE**
> See Also: Chapter 16; CREATE ASSERTION, CREATE CHARACTER SET, CREATE COLLATION, CREATE DOMAIN, CREATE SCHEMA, CREATE TABLE, CREATE TRANSLATION, CREATE VIEW, GRANT, and REVOKE in Chapter 28; Value Expressions in this chapter; and Appendix F.

CASE Expressions

Allow Values to Be Specified Conditionally

Syntax

```
{CASE value expression
{ WHEN value expression
   THEN   { value expression | NULL } }...)


|{CASE
{ WHEN predicate
   THEN   { value expression | NULL } }...}
[ ELSE { value expression | NULL } ]
   END }
| { NULLIF (value expression, value expression) }
| { COALESCE (value expression.,..) }
```

Usage

A CASE expression is used in a SQL statement in place of a value when there is more than one possible value you might want to use depending on conditions. CASE is the most general form; it allows you to define either a predicate or a value expression you attempt to match and then to set the value as desired if the predicate is TRUE or the match occurs. NULLIF and COALESCE both represent situations that could be covered by the CASE form, but they are more elegantly expressed using these forms.

The CASE Form

The CASE form takes one or more WHEN and THEN clauses of either of the two forms and one optional ELSE clause. The WHEN clauses are all tried in sequence. As soon as one succeeds, the matching THEN clause provides the value of the CASE expression. If none of the WHEN clauses succeed, the ELSE clause provides a value. If the ELSE clause is omitted, ELSE NULL is implied. At least one of the THEN clauses or the ELSE clause must specify a result other than NULL (otherwise, since NULL is the default ELSE value, the CASE expression would always produce NULLs and would therefore be senseless). The CASE form is terminated with the keyword END.

All of the WHEN clauses in a given CASE expression must be of the same form—either *value expression* WHEN *value expression* or WHEN *predicate*. In the first form, the WHEN condition is satisfied whenever the value expression in a WHEN clause equals the value expression in the CASE clause. This means, of course, that the datatypes of all the value expressions following WHEN clauses must be comparable to the first value expression. (Datatypes are comparable if they are convertible. See Datatypes in this chapter for the standards on convertibility.) In the second form, the WHEN condition is satisfied whenever the predicate is TRUE. In both forms, the value expression in the THEN clause indicates the value that will be the result of the CASE expression if the matching WHEN condition is satisfied, and the value expression in the ELSE clause indicates the value that will result if none of the WHEN clauses are satisfied. If more than one WHEN condition is satisfied, the first one in the statement is used to determine which THEN clause produces the result.

The datatype of the result of the CASE expression depends on the datatypes of the values contained in the various THEN clauses and the ELSE clause, if any. We will call these the *candidate values*. The candidate values must all be comparable. The following are the criteria that the candidate values must meet and that determine the datatype of the result:

- If any of the candidate values are CHARACTER strings, they must all be CHARACTER strings using the same repertoire. The result will be a CHARACTER string.

- If any of them is a BIT string, they must all be BIT strings, and the result will be, too.

- If they are CHARACTER or BIT strings and any of them are varying-length, the result is a varying-length CHARACTER or BIT string, respectively; otherwise, the result is a fixed-length CHARACTER or BIT string equal in length to the longest of the specified strings (measured in characters or bits as appropriate).

- If they are all EXACT NUMERIC, the result will be EXACT NUMERIC with a scale equal to the largest of their scales and an implementation-defined precision.

- If any of them is APPROXIMATE NUMERIC, they must all be EXACT or APPROXIMATE NUMERIC, and the result will be APPROXIMATE NUMERIC with an implementation-defined precision.

- If any of them is a DATETIME type, they all will be the same DATETIME type, and this will be the type of the result.

- If any of them is an INTERVAL, they all will be INTERVALs. If any specifies YEAR or MONTH, they all will specify only YEAR or MONTH. If any specifies DAY, HOUR, MINUTE, or SECOND (precision), then none of them will specify YEAR and MONTH. Within these parameters, the precision of the result includes all time units from the largest to the smallest specified by any of the THEN clauses.

The NULLIF and COALESCE Forms

The NULLIF form compares the two values given to it. If they are equal according to the principles outlined under comparison predicates (see Predicates), NULL is the result. Otherwise, the result is the first value. If V1 and V2 are the two values, NULLIF (V1, V2) is equivalent to the following CASE expression:

```
CASE WHEN V1=V2 THEN NULL ELSE V1 END
```

COALESCE takes a series of comparable values and returns the first one that is not NULL or returns NULL if there is none such. Again using V1 and V2, COALESCE (V1, V2) is equivalent to:

```
CASE WHEN V1 IS NOT NULL THEN V1 ELSE V2 END
```

COALESCE expressions with more than two values as arguments are equivalent to CASE expressions with more THEN clauses, one for each argument. If V1, V2, and so on to Vn (where n is an arbitrary number) are the arguments, the equivalent CASE expression is:

```
CASE WHEN V1 IS NOT NULL THEN V1
ELSE COALESCE (V2, . . . ,Vn ) END
```

In other words, try each value in sequence. If its value is NULL, perform the COA-LESCE operation with the remaining values until you find a non-NULL value or until there are no values left, in which case COALESCE returns a NULL.

Conformance Levels

Entry   Implementations are not required to support CASE expressions at this level.

NOTE   See Also: Chapter 9 and Datatypes and Predicates in this chapter.

CAST Expressions

Used to Convert from One Datatype to Another

Syntax

```
CAST ( { value expression | NULL }
AS { datatype | domain } )
```

Usage

Use this expression in place of a value expression when the result of that value expression needs to be converted to another datatype or domain. If the CAST is into a domain, the Authorization ID performing the action must have the USAGE privilege on that domain.

We can call the datatype of the value expression we are converting from the source datatype (SD) and the datatype we are converting to—or the datatype of the domain we are converting to, as the case may be—the target datatype (TD). Not all conversions are allowed. Table 29.1 shows which conversions are valid. There are three possibilities: Y (yes) means that the conversion is valid without restriction, N (no) means that the conversion is not valid, and M (maybe) means that the conversion is valid if certain conditions to be outlined are met. The source datatypes are listed vertically along the left edge, while the targets are listed horizontally across the top.

TABLE 29.1: Valid Datatype Conversions

	EN	AN	VC	FC	VB	FB	D	T	TS	YM	DT
EN	Y	Y	Y	Y	N	N	N	N	N	M	M
AN	Y	Y	Y	Y	N	N	N	N	N	N	N
C	Y	Y	M	M	Y	Y	Y	Y	Y	Y	Y
B	N	N	Y	Y	Y	Y	N	N	N	N	N
D	N	N	Y	Y	N	N	Y	N	Y	N	N
T	N	N	Y	Y	N	N	N	Y	Y	N	N
TS	N	N	Y	Y	N	N	Y	Y	Y	N	N
YM	M	N	Y	Y	N	N	N	N	N	Y	N
DT	M	N	Y	Y	N	N	N	N	N	N	Y

Note: The following abbreviations are used: EN = EXACT NUMERIC, AN = APPROXIMATE NUMERIC, C = CHARACTER (Fixed- or Varying-length), FC = Fixed-length CHARACTER, VC = Varying-length CHARACTER, B = BIT STRING (Fixed- or Varying-length), FB = Fixed-length BIT STRING, VB = Varying-length BIT STRING, D = DATE, T = TIME, TS = TIMESTAMP, YM = YEAR-MONTH INTERVAL, DT = DAY-TIME INTERVAL.

The following are the applicable restrictions:

- If SD is INTERVAL and TD is EXACT NUMERIC, then SD is allowed only one DATETIME field.

- If SD is EXACT NUMERIC and TD is INTERVAL, then TD is allowed only one DATETIME field.

- If SD and TD are both CHARACTER STRINGS, they must have the same character repertoires.

- If TD is a CHARACTER STRING, the collating sequence of the result is the default collating sequence for its repertoire, and the result is coercible (See Collations).

If NULL or the result of the value expression is specified, the result of the CAST expression is NULL. This helps you to define empty columns of appropriate datatypes where needed—for example, in queries combined in a UNION expression (see SELECT in Chapter 28) without having to actually define columns or insert data. If NULL is not specified, the target value (TV, the value that will result from the CAST expression) is derived from the source value (SV, the value of the value expression) following the specifications outlined below.

If the target datatype (TD) is EXACT NUMERIC then:

- If the source datatype (SD) is EXACT or APPROXIMATE NUMERIC, and SV can be represented in TV without losing any leading digits, the conversion to a number of equivalent value in the new type is effected; otherwise, an error—numeric value out of range—is produced. Trailing digits can be rounded or truncated, although which of these will be done is implementation-defined.

- If the source datatype (SD) is a CHARACTER STRING, then leading and trailing blanks are removed, and what is left must be the character representation of an optionally signed exact number.

- If the source datatype (SD) is INTERVAL, then the same rules as outlined above for EXACT and APPROXIMATE NUMERICs apply.

If the target datatype (TD) is APPROXIMATE NUMERIC, then the rules are the same as outlined above for EXACT NUMERICs, except that the source datatype may not be an INTERVAL.

If the target datatype (TD) is a CHARACTER STRING, then let its length, if it is fixed-length, or its maximum length, if it is varying-length, be called the target length (TL). The target length is measured in the number of characters. The following stipulations apply:

- If the source datatype is EXACT or APPROXIMATE NUMERIC, the character repertoire of the target must include all of the characters actually used to represent the number. (It need not include all that could be used to express a number of that type, although it normally would. So, for example, if the character repertoire did not include the minus sign, you would have no problem unless a negative number were actually encountered.)

- If the source datatype is EXACT or APPROXIMATE NUMERIC, and the number of characters needed to represent the source value (SV) is shorter than the target length, the SV is padded with blanks; if SV is longer, an error is produced. If the source is APPROXIMATE NUMERIC and its value is zero, the representation will be x '0E0' (zero exponent zero).

NOTE

Some host languages interpret 0E0 as 1. This obviously will garble APPROXIMATE NUMERIC zeros produced by SQL and introduce subtle or dramatic errors. When building applications, you should handle these zeros as a special case, unless you know that your host language adopts the same convention as SQL.

- If the source datatype is fixed or variable-length STRING, and the number of characters in the source value exceeds the target length, truncation occurs and produces a warning, unless the truncation is only of trailing blanks.

- If the source datatype is BIT STRING, things get complicated. Let's call the length of the source value (SV) in bits the source length (SL) and the bit length of the character with the shortest bit length in the form-of-use of the target datatype (TD) the minimum character length (MCL). SL is divided by MCL, and the remainder is the number of zero-valued bits that are appended to the source value (SV). If that remainder (and thus the number of such bits added) is not zero, then a warning—implicit zero-bit padding—is raised. In any case, the BIT STRING is converted according the form-of-use of the target datatype. If the resulting string is of a different length than the target length (TL), then either truncation (if it is too long) or zero-bit padding (if too short) occurs, and an appropriate warning condition is raised.

- If the source datatype is DATETIME or INTERVAL, then it is converted to the shortest character string that can express its value with the appropriate precision. If this character string is longer than the target length, an error is produced; no truncation is allowed in this case. Otherwise, if it is shorter, it is padded with blanks. Again, the character repertoire of the target must be able to express the character string produced from the DATETIME or INTERVAL source.

If the target value (TV) is BIT STRING, then let SL be the length of the source value in bits and TL be the length in bits of either the target value, if the target is fixed-length, or of the maximum target value, if it is varying-length. The source value (SV) is converted to a BIT STRING. If this string is longer than TL, truncation occurs. If it is shorter and the target is fixed-length, it is padded on the right with zero-bits. In either of these cases, an appropriate warning condition is raised.

If the target datatype (TD) is DATE, then:

- If the source datatype is CHARACTER STRING, leading and trailing blanks are removed, and if the remaining string represents a valid DATE value, the conversion is effected. Otherwise, an error is produced.

- If the source datatype is DATE, the conversion is automatic.

- If the source datatype is TIMESTAMP, the target value is set to the YEAR, MONTH, and DAY fields of the source value, adjusted by the time-zone displacement if any.

If the target datatype is TIME, then:

- If the source datatype is CHARACTER STRING, leading and trailing blanks are removed, and if the remaining string represents a valid TIME value, the conversion is effected. If not, an error is produced.

- If the source datatype is TIME, and if the target specifies WITH TIME ZONE, the implied or explicit time-zone displacement of the source is inherited. Otherwise, the target inherits the time-zone displacement of the current SQL session.

- If the source is TIMESTAMP, the target value is set to the HOUR, MINUTE, and SECOND fields of the source value. If the target specifies WITH TIME ZONE, the implied or explicit time-zone displacement of the source is inherited. Otherwise, the target inherits the time-zone displacement of the current SQL session.

If the target datatype is TIMESTAMP, then:

- If the source datatype is CHARACTER STRING, leading and trailing blanks are removed, and if the remaining string represents a valid TIMESTAMP value, the conversion is effected. Otherwise, an error is produced.

- If the source datatype is DATE, the values of its YEAR, MONTH, and DAY fields become the values of the same fields in the target. The HOUR, MINUTE, and SECOND fields of the target are set to zero. If WITH TIME ZONE is specified for the target, the time-zone displacement for the current SQL session is inherited.

- If the source datatype is TIME, the values of its HOUR, MINUTE, and SECOND fields become the values of the same fields in the target. The YEAR, MONTH, and DAY fields of the target are set to those produced by an execution of CURRENT_DATE (see Datetime Value Functions). If WITH TIME ZONE is specified for the target, the explicit or implied time-zone displacement for the source is inherited.

If the target datatype is INTERVAL, then:

- If the source datatype is EXACT NUMERIC, and if the source value can be represented in the target without the loss of leading significant digits, the conversion is effected. Otherwise, an error is produced.

- If the source datatype is CHARACTER STRING, leading and trailing blanks are removed, and, if the result is a valid INTERVAL value, the conversion is effected. Otherwise, an error is produced.

- If the source datatype is INTERVAL, and the precisions of the source and target are the same, the conversion is automatic. If not, the source is converted to a single number expressed in its least significant (smallest) units. If this number cannot be converted to the precision of the target without loss of precision of its most significant field, an error is produced. Otherwise, the conversion is effected.

Finally, if the target datatype is contained in a domain, the target value produced must satisfy any constraints in that domain.

Conformance Levels

Entry   Support for CAST expressions is not required at this level.

NOTE   See Also: Chapter 9; CREATE DOMAIN in Chapter 28; and Datatypes and Datetime Value Functions in this chapter.

Collations

Objects in the Schema That Define Collating Sequences

Usage

Character sets in SQL are normally sortable, which means they can be placed in some order, called a *collating sequence*, and compared in terms of it—for example, 'a' < 'b' means 'a' precedes 'b' in the collating sequence. A *collation* is a schema object that defines a collating sequence used on a character set. In most cases, it is desirable to design the collating sequence to approximate alphabetical order, although this necessarily will be imperfectly realized with many character sets. Each character has a unique place in the collating sequence, and a given letter in upper- and lowercase is two different characters. The default collations for the standard ASCII and EBCDIC character sets place all the characters of one case before all the characters of the other because they collate in terms of the encoding—the numeric values that constitute the internal representation of the characters. For this reason, it may be desirable to define custom collations for these character sets (if your implementation has not done this for you already), as well as for any others that you may use.

Where You Use Collations

You use the CREATE COLLATION statement to define a collation (see Chapter 16 and CREATE COLLATION in Chapter 28). You must have the USAGE privilege on all character sets and translations referenced in that statement. You will now have the USAGE privilege on your collation and possibly will be able to share it with others using the GRANT statement (see GRANT in Chapter 28).

Once created, a collation may be referenced in a number of statements in a COLLATE clause following the value expression to which it is to apply. The syntax of the COLLATE clause is:

```
COLLATE collation name
```

For example, this can be used in a CREATE CHARACTER SET statement to define the default collating sequence for that character set. It also can define a default for a domain that overrides that of the character set or for a column that overrides that of its domain, if any (see CREATE DOMAIN, ALTER DOMAIN, CREATE TABLE, and ALTER TABLE in Chapter 28). Any of these, in turn can be overridden with COLLATE clauses appended to value expressions, which can include column references, aggregate functions, scalar subqueries, CASE expressions, and CAST specifications (see Value Expressions, Subqueries, CASE Expressions, and CAST Expressions), and string value functions, such as SUBSTRING, FOLD, CONVERT, TRANSLATE, and TRIM (see String Value Functions). These value expressions are used in the SELECT and GROUP BY clauses of queries (see SELECT in Chapter 28) and in predicates (see Predicates).

Coercibility

Each collating sequence has a coercibility attribute with one of the following values:

- An *explicit* coercibility attribute means that a COLLATE clause has directly specified the collation in the statement at hand. For example, a COLLATE clause in the GROUP BY list in a query will determine the collating sequence used to sort the output rows, if such sorting is performed (see SELECT in Chapter 28). This is an explicit collation and overrides any other.

- An *implicit* coercibility attribute means that the collation is implied. The results of CONVERT and TRANSLATE expressions, as well as column references, are implicit.

- A *coercible* value for the coercibility attribute means that the collation can be overridden by an explicit or an implicit collation on the same character set. In general, value specifications, the targets (results) of CAST expressions, and columns following a collating sequence are coercible by default.

- An attribute of *no collating sequence* means that the character set cannot be meaningfully sorted. No value expression with this coercibility attribute may be referenced in the query expression contained in a view (see CREATE VIEW in Chapter 28) or used with comparison predicates (see Predicates). Actually, every character set defined in the database has a collating sequence—by default the order of the binary numbers that represent the characters in the encoding. Characters without a collating sequence can arise, however, as the result of certain operations (see Collations).

The following tables show how the collating sequence and coercibility are determined whenever operators are used on character strings or whenever characters strings are compared. A collating sequence labeled "default" indicates the default collating sequence, and X means any collating sequence. Of course, if the coercibility attribute is "no collating sequence", the collating sequence does not exist.

Table 29.2 shows the rules for monadic operators. These are operators that reference only a single string, namely FOLD and TRIM. SUBSTRING is also treated for this purpose as a monadic operator, with the string being examined considered the operand. The leftmost two columns of the table indicate the coercibility and collating sequence for the character string before the operator is applied. For each such combination, the resulting coercibility and collating sequence are shown on the right.

Table 29.3 shows the coercibility and collating sequences that result from using operators that take two strings as arguments and produce a string as a result; these are called *dyadic operators*. In this and Table 29.4, X means any collating sequence of the first operand, Y means any collating sequence of the second operand, and Y<> X means Y does not equal X.

Table 29.4 shows how comparison of character strings with differing collations will be collated.

TABLE 29.2: Collating Sequences and Coercibility Rules for Monadic Operators

Operand		Result	
Coercibility	**Collating Sequence**	**Coercibility**	**Collating Sequence**
Coercible	Default	Coercible	Default
Implicit	X	Implicit	X
Explicit	X	Explicit	X
No Collating Sequence		No Collating Sequence	

TABLE 29.3: Collating Sequences and Coercibility Rules for Dyadic Operators

Operand 1		Operand 2		Result	
Coercibility	**Collating Sequence**	**Coercibility**	**Collating Sequence**	**Coercibility**	**Collating Sequence**
Coercible	Default	Coercible	Default	Coercible	Default
Coercible	Default	Implicit	Y	Implicit	Y
Coercible	Default	No Collating Sequence		No Collating Sequence	
Coercible	Default	Explicit	Y	Explicit	Y
Implicit	X	Coercible	Default	Implicit	X
Implicit	X	Implicit	X	Implicit	X
Implicit	X	Implicit	Y<> X	No Collating Sequence	
Implicit	X	No Collating Sequence		No Collating Sequence	
Implicit	X	Explicit	Y	Explicit	Y
No Collating Sequence		Any, except Explicit	Any	No Collating Sequence	

Continued on next page

TABLE 29.3 CONTINUED: Collating Sequences and Coercibility Rules for Dyadic Operators

Operand 1		Operand 2		Result	
Coercibility	**Collating Sequence**	**Coercibility**	**Collating Sequence**	**Coercibility**	**Collating Sequence**
No Collating Sequence		Explicit	X	Explicit	X
Explicit	X	Coercible	Default	Explicit	X
Explicit	X	Implicit	Y	Explicit	X
Explicit	X	No Collating Sequence		Explicit	X
Explicit	X	Explicit	X	Explicit	X
Explicit	X	Explicit	Y<> X	Not Permitted: Invalid Syntax	

TABLE 29.4: Collating Sequences Used for Comparisons

Comparand 1		Comparand 2		Collating Sequence Used for Comparison
Coercibility	**Collating Sequence**	**Coercibility**	**Collating Sequence**	
Coercible	Default	Coercible	Default	Default
Coercible	Default	Implicit	Y	Y
Coercible	Default	No Collating Sequence		Not Permitted: Invalid Syntax
Coercible	Default	Explicit	Y	Y
Implicit	X	Coercible	Default	X
Implicit	X	Implicit	X	X
Implicit	X	Implicit	Y<> X	Not Permitted: Invalid Syntax

Continued on next page

TABLE 29.4 CONTINUED: Collating Sequences Used for Comparisons

Comparand 1		Comparand 2		Collating Sequence Used for Comparison
Coercibility	**Collating Sequence**	**Coercibility**	**Collating Sequence**	
Implicit	X	No Collating Sequence		Not Permitted: Invalid Syntax
Implicit	X	Explicit	Y	Y
No Collating Sequence		Any except Explicit	Any	Not Permitted: Invalid Syntax
No Collating Sequence		Explicit	X	X
Explicit	X	Coercible	Default	X
Explicit	X	Implicit	Y	X
Explicit	X	No Collating Sequence		X
Explicit	X	Explicit	X	X
Explicit	X	Explicit	Y<>X	Not Permitted: Invalid Syntax

Operations that involve more than two operands, for example CASE expressions with more than two THEN clauses, are treated for the purpose of determining collation as a series of dyadic operations. The first two operands are compared, and the resulting collating sequence and coercibility attribute are used in comparison to the third operand, and so on until all the operands have been included in the comparison.

Conformance Levels

Intermediate   Support for explicit collations is not required at this level.

NOTE See Also: Chapter 20; CREATE CHARACTER SET, CREATE COLLATION, and DROP COLLATION in Chapter 28; and Datatypes, Predicates, and String Value Functions in this chapter.

Constraints

Put Restrictions on the Data That May Be Entered into Tables

Syntax

```
table constraint ::=
[ CONSTRAINT constraint name ]
{ PRIMARY KEY  (column name.,..)}
| { UNIQUE (column name.,..)}
| { FOREIGN KEY  (column name.,..)
REFERENCES table name [(column name.,..)]
[ referential specification ] }
| { CHECK predicate }
[ [NOT] DEFERRABLE ] ]
column constraint ::=
[ CONSTRAINT constraint name ]
{ NOT NULL }
| { PRIMARY KEY }
| { UNIQUE }
| { REFERENCES table name [(column name)]
[ referential specification ] }
| { CHECK predicate }
 [ [ INITIALLY DEFERRED | INITIALLY IMMEDIATE ]
[ [NOT] DEFERRABLE ] ]

referential specification::=
[ MATCH { FULL | PARTIAL } ]
[ ON UPDATE { CASCADE
    | SET NULL
    | SET DEFAULT
    | NO ACTION } ]
[ ON DELETE { CASCADE
    | SET NULL
    | SET DEFAULT
    | NO ACTION } ]
```

Usage

Constraints define conditions that data must meet in order to be entered into the database. They can be included in the definitions of columns, temporary or permanent base tables, domains, or assertions. Although constraints cannot be used in views, views also offer facilities for controlling column values (see CREATE VIEW in Chapter 28). Table constraints apply to one or more columns of one or more tables; they are used in table definitions, domains, and assertions. Column constraints apply to single columns, except for the REFERENCES constraint, which applies to two columns—the referencing column and the referenced column—which are usually in separate tables. Column constraints follow the definition of the constrained column within its table definition (for REFERENCES, this is the table containing the referencing, rather than the referenced, column). There are equivalent table constraints for all column constraints. Domains and assertions use only CHECK constraints.

You may optionally name the constraint; this will allow you to drop or alter it later by referring to its name. If the constraint is not named, an implementation-dependent default name will be generated (this was not true in SQL89).

If the data is in such a state that a deferred constraint is violated, and a statement causes the constraint to be checked, one of two things happens. If the statement that causes the constraint to be checked is COMMIT WORK, the transaction is rolled back. Otherwise, the statement that causes the constraint to be checked will fail. This includes SET CONSTRAINTS MODE itself, so if you want to know whether a constraint has been violated, you can attempt to change the constraint's mode and see if you get an error.

In general, all references in table constraints to columns are to columns in the table where the table constraint resides. (The exceptions are in some CHECK predicates and the REFERENCES list within FOREIGN KEY constraints.) The meanings of the various table constraints are as follows:

- PRIMARY KEY means that the group of one or more named columns is the unique identifier for the table. The combination of values in a PRIMARY KEY is constrained to be distinct for each row; duplicates and NULLs will be rejected. Only one PRIMARY KEY constraint may exist for a given table. Formally speaking, PRIMARY KEY is equivalent to the following CHECK constraint (see Predicates):

    ```
    CHECK(UNIQUE (SELECT key columns FROM table name)

    AND

    (key columns) IS NOT NULL)
    ```

- UNIQUE is like PRIMARY KEY, except that any number of UNIQUE constraints may coexist in the same table. For Entry-level SQL92, columns that take the PRIMARY KEY or the UNIQUE constraint must be declared NOT NULL. The NULL check need not be built into the constraint, as above. However, at Intermediate-level and in SQL99, NOT NULL is implied for PRIMARY KEY and optional for UNIQUE. Here is the CHECK constraint that is the equivalent to UNIQUE:

```
CHECK(UNIQUE (SELECT key columns FROM table name))
```

- FOREIGN KEY names a group of columns in this table that will be a foreign key referencing a group of columns in this or another table. The group of columns in the referenced table must have either the PRIMARY KEY or the UNIQUE constraint. In the former case, the column name list can be omitted from the REFERENCES clause—the table's PRIMARY KEY is the default. The referenced columns must be of the same datatypes as the referencing columns, in the specified order. A table may reference itself, which enables circular relationships. See Chapters 5 and 9. This constraint is discussed in more detail below.

- CHECK defines a predicate that will refer to one or more values from one or more tables, unless it is contained in a domain. If the predicate is FALSE when the constraint is checked, the constraint is violated. This constraint is also discussed in more detail below.

These are the definitions of the column constraints:

- NOT NULL means that the column may not contain the NULL value.

- PRIMARY KEY is the same as the table-constraint version, except that no column list may be used. As a column constraint, it automatically applies only to the column whose definition it follows.

- UNIQUE is the same as the table-constraint version, also with the proviso that a column list need not and cannot be used.

- REFERENCES is the column-constraint version of the FOREIGN KEY constraint. A referencing column list is not used; the column being constrained is the referencing column. A referenced column list, if used, will have only one column. If the referenced column has the PRIMARY KEY constraint, it need not be named.

- CHECK is also the same as the table-constraint version, except that all column references in the predicate must be to the constrained column unless they are contained in subqueries (see Subqueries).

The FOREIGN KEY and REFERENCES Constraints

As noted above, these are two variations on the same constraint, and we will use the term "FOREIGN KEY constraint" to refer to both of them unless otherwise noted.

A FOREIGN KEY constraint requires that all values present in the foreign key be matched by values in the parent key—in other words, that the foreign key have referential integrity. This means that someone using a set of columns as a parent key is placing controls on what can be done with those columns. For this reason, the REFERENCES privilege on those columns is required to define a foreign key on them. In addition, the following rules must be satisfied:

- Each column in the foreign key must reference a column of the same datatype in the parent key. The columns must be specified in the same order in the FOREIGN KEY and in the UNIQUE or PRIMARY KEY constraints, and no column may be specified more than once.

- If the foreign key table is a persistent base table, the parent key table must also be such a table.

- If the foreign key table is a global local temporary table, the parent key table must also be such a table.

- If the foreign key table is a created local temporary table, the parent key table must be either a global or created local temporary table.

- If the foreign key table is a declared local temporary table, the parent key table can be any sort of temporary table.

- If the parent key table specifies ON COMMIT DELETE ROWS, the foreign key table must do so as well.

In addition to the above, there are two issues that must be addressed in ensuring that the values in the foreign key are matched in the parent:

- What is meant by a match?

- What happens when a change to the parent key data is attempted that would affect the match?

The first of these two questions is addressed by the *match type*, determined by the MATCH FULL or PARTIAL clause. The second is addressed by *referential triggered actions*, determined by the ON UPDATE and ON DELETE clauses.

Match Types

A match, of course, basically means that the values in any row of the foreign key are present in some row of the parent. The complexity arises when NULLs are factored in. NULLs in principle represent data items whose values are unknown. Strictly speaking, then, we cannot say whether they match known data items or even each other. There is considerable debate in this area, which we won't go into here. Suffice it to say that NULLs don't match anything—not even other NULLs. Other than that, the standard lets you take one of three approaches:

- If the MATCH clause is omitted, then a partially NULL foreign key is acceptable regardless of whether there are parent key values that match. Otherwise, all of the values in the foreign key must be present in some row of the parent.

- If MATCH FULL is specified, then each row of the foreign key must be entirely NULL, or it must have no NULLs and be entirely matched by some row of the parent key.

- If MATCH PARTIAL is specified, then the foreign key may be partially NULL, and the non-NULL values of each row of the foreign key must match the corresponding values in the parent key. Since parent key values may be identical in those columns where they match the foreign key and differ in others, it is possible for more than one parent key row to match the same foreign key row. Such parent key rows are called *nonunique matching rows*; others are *unique matching rows*. Notice that unique matching rows are unique *in the parent key*; it is possible for more than one foreign key row to reference the same parent key row, and, for each foreign key that matches only one such row, this parent key row will be the unique matching row. A parent key row may be a unique matching row of some group of foreign key values and a nonunique matching row of others, since the matches could be based on different non-NULL columns in the foreign keys. Unique and nonunique matching rows work differently with referential triggered actions, as discussed below (don't worry, we have examples coming).

To illustrate the types of matches, we will use the Client_Phone table shown in Table 29.5. In this table, the combination of ID_NUM and PHONE is the primary key. We will also use another table, shown in Table 29.6, that tracks each phone call made to a client. This table has a foreign key (CLIENT_ID, PHONE) that references Client_Phone (ID_NUM, PHONE). The primary key of the Calls_to_Clients table is CALL_ID.

TABLE 29.5: The Client_Phone Table

ID_NUM	PHONE	TYPE	AVAIL
1809	415 555 8956	home	after 6 P.M.
1809	510 555 6220	work	9-5 MF
1996	212 555 0199	work	app. 10-7
1996	212 555 7878	cell	any
1777	503 555 2279	fax	any
1777	503 555 9188	home	after 7 P.M.

TABLE 29.6:   The Calls_to_Clients Table

CALL_ID	CLIENT_ID	PHONE	MADE_BY
2201	1809	415 555 8956	Terrence
2202	1809	NULL	Liu
2204	NULL	212 555 0199	MacLeish
2207	NULL	NULL	MacLeish
2209	1811	503 555 9188	Liu

Rows of Calls_to_Clients are identified by CALL_ID; those of Client_Phone are identified by the combination of PHONE and ID_NUM. However, we will refer to them simply by their order as shown to make the discussion less awkward. For each of the three types of MATCH specification (FULL, PARTIAL, and neither), the following list identifies the rows of Client_Phone that each row of Calls_to _Clients matches and, for PARTIAL, whether it matches them uniquely (in other words, whether the matching Client_Phone rows are unique matching rows).

- If FULL is specified, call 2201 matches the first row, and call 2207 is an acceptable foreign key value, but it does not match anything (foreign keys can be NULL). The other rows of Calls_to_Clients violate referential integrity and would be rejected.

- If PARTIAL is specified, call 2201 matches the first row, and call 2207 is still an acceptable, unmatched value. In addition, call 2202 matches the first and second rows, and call 2204 uniquely matches the third row. Call 2209 violates referential integrity and would be rejected.

- If neither FULL nor PARTIAL is specified, call 2201 matches the first row. None of the other calls match any row, but since the foreign keys are partially or entirely NULL, they would not be rejected.

As you can see, omitting the MATCH clause produces the most tolerant and possibly the most problematic behavior. It is usually safest and least confusing to specify MATCH FULL by default.

For column constraints, or for foreign keys where all columns have the NOT NULL constraint, MATCH clauses are ignored, and the effect is the same as if none were used.

Referential Triggered Actions

The referential triggered actions specify what happens when a change to a parent key could affect its match with a foreign key. The ON UPDATE and ON DELETE versions allow you to specify this effect separately for UPDATE and for DELETE statements.

(INSERT statements, of course, don't directly affect referential integrity, since the rows generated could not have been previously referenced.) You may specify at most one ON DELETE and one ON UPDATE clause in a given constraint. The options are discussed in the following paragraphs.

CASCADE makes the same change to the foreign key as is made to the parent. If the operation is DELETE, the entire row of the foreign key table is deleted; if UPDATE, the changes made to the parent key table cause the same changes in the corresponding columns of the foreign key table. If MATCH PARTIAL is specified and the triggered action is ON DELETE CASCADE, only the unique matching rows are deleted. If MATCH PARTIAL is specified and the triggered action is ON UPDATE CASCADE, the change is made to all unique matching rows, provided that this change can be cascaded consistently to all matching rows.

If SET NULL is specified with an ON DELETE triggered action, then all foreign key columns in matching rows—or all in unique matching rows if MATCH PARTIAL is specified—are set to a value of NULL. With an ON UPDATE triggered action, then, if no match type was specified, those columns that reference altered values are set to NULL. Otherwise, if MATCH FULL is specified, the entire referencing foreign key is set to NULL. If MATCH PARTIAL is specified, then only the columns that reference altered values are set to NULL and only for unique matching rows.

SET DEFAULT works almost like SET NULL, except that the columns are set to the default value specified in their table definition or in their domain definition (see CREATE TABLE and CREATE DOMAIN in Chapter 28). A second difference from SET NULL is that, when MATCH FULL is specified with an ON UPDATE SET DEFAULT triggered action, the change is made only to those columns whose referenced values have been altered, not to all columns of the foreign key. Note that, since NULLs don't match anything, they don't reference anything, and that therefore a change to a column in the parent key that is NULL in the foreign key will leave the foreign key NULL rather than install its default value.

NO ACTION is the default if you do not specify a triggered action. NO ACTION specifies that no automatic change will be made to the foreign key data in response to changes in the parent key. If such changes would leave the data without referential integrity—in other words, if the FOREIGN KEY constraint would be violated—the changes are not allowed.

We will use Tables 29.5 and 29.6 again to illustrate the operation of referential triggered actions. If the second and third rows of the Client_Phone table are deleted, then:

- If FULL or neither is specified, there are no matching rows, and therefore no changes to the Calls_to_Clients table are made. If a triggered action of NO ACTION is specified, the delete is still allowed because there are no matches.

- If PARTIAL were specified, then, since call 2202 is a nonunique matching row of row 2, it would not be changed by any referential action and, if NO ACTION were specified, would not prevent the deletion of row 2, as it would still have a valid reference to row 1. The deletion of row 3, on the other hand, would be rejected because 2204 is a unique matching row of row 3 (of course, if the deletions of rows 2 and 3 were part of the same statement or transaction, the one rejection would cause both to fail). If SET CASCADE were specified, the deletion of row 3 would cause call 2204 to be deleted also.

- If SET NULL were specified, the CLIENT_ID and PHONE for call 2204 would be set to NULL; for SET DEFAULT, the PHONE column would be set to the default of the column or domain.

Let's say we updated rows 1 and 3 to the following:

ID_NUM	PHONE	TYPE	AVAIL
NULL	415 555 8956	home	after 6 P.M.
1996	212 555 8888	work	app. 10-7

This changes the first ID_NUM and the third PHONE values; the referential triggered actions would be as follows:

- If MATCH FULL is specified, the change to row 3 would have no effect on the Calls_to_Clients table, nor would it be rejected: there are no matching rows. If ON UPDATE CASCADE is specified, the update would be rejected, because the attempt to cascade the change of row 1 to NULL to the foreign key in Calls_to_ Clients would produce a partially NULL foreign key there, which is not permissible for MATCH FULL. Likewise, NO ACTION would fail, because it would leave call 2201 without a valid reference. If SET NULL or SET DEFAULT is specified, the CLIENT_ID and PHONE columns of Calls_to_Clients would both be set to NULL or to default values, respectively.

- If neither FULL nor PARTIAL is specified, the effects are the same as for MATCH FULL with two exceptions:

  - If CASCADE is specified, the update will be permitted, and the CLIENT_ ID column for call 2201 in Calls_to_Clients will be set to NULL.

  - If SET NULL is specified, only the CLIENT_ID will be set to NULL, whereas with MATCH FULL the PHONE column would be set to NULL as well.

- If MATCH PARTIAL is specified, then the effects deriving from the update of row 1 are the same as if neither were specified. For the update of row 3, if NO ACTION is specified, the update would be rejected, as it would leave call 2204 without a valid reference (it would still contain the old phone number, which is not now present in the parent key). If CASCADE, SET NULL, or SET DEFAULT is specified, the PHONE column for 2201 would be set to the new phone number, to NULL, or to a default value, respectively.

The CHECK Constraint

Formally speaking, a CHECK constraint is violated if the following predicate is TRUE:

```
EXISTS ( SELECT * FROM tables WHERE NOT (predicate))
```

where *tables* are the tables referenced in or containing the constraint, and *predicate* is the predicate contained in the constraint (see Predicates). Notice that if the predicate is UNKNOWN, EXISTS will be FALSE and the constraint will be satisfied (see "Three-Valued Logic" in the Predicates entry and Chapters 7 and 12).

If the CHECK constraint is contained in a domain, the keyword VALUE will be used instead of a column reference. Whenever a column based on that domain is updated, the constraint will be checked by substituting the name of that column for the keyword VALUE and checking the value in the row that is under examination by the constraint.

A CHECK constraint must also meet the following criteria:

- If it is contained in a permanent base table or a domain, then the predicate may not reference temporary tables.

- If it is contained in a global temporary table, then the predicate can reference only global temporary tables.

- If it is contained in a created local temporary table, then the predicate can reference only global or created local temporary tables.

- If it is contained in a declared local temporary table, then it may not reference a permanent base table.

- If it is contained in a temporary table definition that specifies ON COMMIT PRESERVE ROWS, then it may not reference a temporary table that specifies ON COMMIT DELETE ROWS.

- It may not reference a datetime value function or a user value function.

- It may not use a query that is possibly nondeterministic (see SELECT in Chapter 28).

- The creator of the CHECK constraint must have the REFERENCES privilege on any columns named in the constraint.

- If a table is referenced in the constraint, but no columns from it are specifically indicated (for example, if SELECT * is used), the creator of the CHECK constraint must have the REFERENCES privilege on at least one column of that table.

- If the text of the predicate is too long for the allocated space in the INFORMATION_ SCHEMA, it is truncated and a warning condition is raised.

When Constraints Are Checked

A constraint is defined when created as either DEFERRABLE or NOT DEFERRABLE. If neither is specified, NOT DEFERRABLE is the default. A constraint that is NOT DEFERRABLE is checked after every statement (INSERT, UPDATE, or DELETE) that may produce values in violation of it. A DEFERRABLE constraint can be checked immediately or at the end of each transaction; that is, its mode may be either IMMEDIATE or DEFERRED (the mode of constraints that are NOT DEFERRABLE is always effectively IMMEDIATE).

Constraints whose mode is IMMEDIATE are checked whenever a statement is issued that may produce values that violate the constraint or one (SET CONSTRAINTS MODE) that directly mandates the immediate checking of the constraint. A constraint's mode at the beginning of a session is determined by whether INITIALLY IMMEDIATE or INITIALLY DEFERRED was specified when it was created. The SET CONSTRAINTS MODE statement can then be used to change the mode of a DEFERRABLE constraint at any time. The two clauses—DEFERRABLE or NOT DEFERRABLE and INITIALLY IMMEDIATE or INITIALLY DEFERRED—may be specified in either order.

Conformance Levels

Intermediate — Implementations at this level are not required to support temporary tables. FOREIGN KEY constraints need not allow the MATCH type to be specified or to support ON UPDATE referential triggered actions. It may be required that the order of the columns as named in the FOREIGN KEY constraint match the order they were named in the PRIMARY KEY or UNIQUE constraint. Intermediate-level implementations do not have to allow subqueries in the predicate of a CHECK constraint, and they may allow that predicate to access tables without the constraint creator having the REFERENCES privilege on them. They might not support ALTER DOMAIN.

Entry — Implementations at this level are not required to support user naming of constraints. If PRIMARY KEY or UNIQUE is specified, NOT NULL must be specified for each column in the constraint (the old approach from SQL89). Entry-level implementations are not required to support referential triggered actions. They are not required to support adding and dropping table constraints or to support domains.

SQL89 — Constraints are not named.

NOTE   See Also: ALTER DOMAIN, ALTER TABLE, CREATE ASSERTION, CREATE DOMAIN, CRE-
ATE TABLE, CREATE VIEW, DELETE, ROLLBACK, SELECT, SET CONSTRAINTS MODE, and
UPDATE in Chapter 28 and Predicates and Subqueries in this chapter.

Datatypes

Definitions and Characteristics of SQL Datatypes

Syntax

```
datatype ::=
{ {CHARACTER[(length)]}
| {CHAR[(length)]}
| {CHARACTER VARYING(length)}
| {CHAR VARYING(length)}
| {VARCHAR(length)}
[CHARACTER SET(repertoire name | form-of-use name )] }
| {NATIONAL CHARACTER[(length)]}
| {NATIONAL CHAR[(length)]}
| {NCHAR[(length)]}
| {NATIONAL CHARACTER VARYING(length)}
| {NATIONAL CHAR VARYING(length)}
| {NCHAR VARYING(length)}
| {BIT[(length)]}
| {BIT VARYING(length)}
| {NUMERIC[ (precision[, scale]) ]}
| {DECIMAL[ (precision[, scale]) ]}
| {DEC[ (precision[, scale]) ]}
| INTEGER
| INT
| SMALLINT
| {FLOAT[(precision)]}
| REAL
```

```
| {DOUBLE PRECISION}
| DATE
| {TIME[(precision) ]
[ WITH TIME ZONE ]}
| {TIMESTAMP[(precision)]
[ WITH TIME ZONE ]}
| {INTERVAL interval qualifier}
```

Usage

Every column of every table in a SQL database must have a datatype. The datatype will be part of either the column definition itself (see CREATE TABLE in Chapter 28) or the definition of the domain on which the column is based (see CREATE DOMAIN in Chapter 28). The SQL standard takes a two-tiered approach to datatypes. Officially, there are seven basic datatypes, but most of these have several variations that go by different names, and it is the names of the variations that you use when you specify a datatype for a column or a domain. For clarity, we will define each variation as a separate datatype and consider the larger groupings categories. The DBMS itself, however, does not necessarily distinguish datatypes within categories. The category plus values for the relevant arguments (*precision*, *length*, and so on) can be sufficient to define the datatype. Therefore, INTEGER in the standard is usually referred to as "EXACT NUMERIC with scale 0", i.e., a decimal number with no didgits following the decimal point, and the datatypes of SQL items (such as descriptor area fields) are officially defined as such. The categories are as follows:

CHARACTER STRING   All datatypes that represent text, whatever the character set used.

NATIONAL CHARACTER   Effectively the same as the CHARACTER STRING types, except that the character set is some implementation-defined set that corresponds to the language that will be in most general use. For our purposes, we will put these types in the same category with CHARACTER STRING for the remainder of this discussion.

BIT STRING   Straight binary data.

EXACT NUMERIC   Numbers that represent exact figures.

APPROXIMATE NUMERIC   Numbers expressed in scientific notation (mantissa and exponent) that represent approximate figures.

DATETIME   Dates, times, or combinations of both.

INTERVAL   The quantity of time between various dates and times.

The specific types for each of the categories are described in later sections of this entry.

Comparability of Datatypes

If values are to be compared, or if columns are to be joined or to be combined using UNION, EXCEPT, or INTERSECT operators (see SELECT in Chapter 28), the values or columns must be of comparable datatypes. All datatypes within categories other than CHARACTER, NATIONAL CHARACTER, DATETIME, or INTERVAL are comparable (the restrictions on DATETIME and INTERVAL comparability are discussed under "DATETIME Types" and "The INTERVAL Type", respectively, later in this entry). CHARACTER and NATIONAL CHARACTER types are comparable, within or between the CHARACTER and NATIONAL categories, if they use the same character repertoire. EXACT NUMERIC and APPROXIMATE NUMERIC are also comparable. If datatypes are not comparable, they can in some cases be converted by using a CAST expression (see CAST Expressions for a table of the valid type conversions).

CHARACTER STRING Types

CHARACTER STRINGs can be fixed- or varying-length. CHARACTER STRINGs are set off in SQL statements with single quotes (apostrophes—not left and right single quotes in the standard, though some products relax this restriction) before and after. Blank spaces between quotes represent blank spaces, and single quotes themselves are represented within a string with a concatenation of two single quotes ('') for each single quote expressed. Double quotes are different characters than pairs of single quotes and do not require this special treatment within strings.

NATIONAL CHARACTER STRING types behave in the same way as CHARACTER STRING types, except that, when specified as literals in SQL statements, NATIONAL CHARACTER types are preceded by an N and a space. The CHARACTER STRING and NATIONAL CHARACTER STRING datatypes are each described below along with any arguments, other than character set specifications, that may be appended to them when they are specified:

- CHARACTER [(*length*)], which can be abbreviated CHAR, is a fixed-length text string. The length is a positive integer specifying the number of characters that the column holds. It is effectively a maximum; values of lesser length will be padded with blanks. Although the *length* argument is technically optional, the default (and the minimum) is 1, so it is usually necessary.

- NATIONAL CHARACTER [(*length*)] is the NATIONAL CHARACTER STRING equivalent of CHARACTER. It can be abbreviated NATIONAL CHAR or NCHAR.

- CHARACTER VARYING (*length*), also known as CHAR VARYING and VARCHAR, is a text string of varying length. Here the *length* argument literally specifies a maximum and is not optional; it can be anything from 1 to the implementation-defined maximum. The length of the data value can be anything from 0 to the value of *length*.

- NATIONAL CHARACTER VARYING, NATIONAL CHAR VARYING, and NCHAR VARYING are all names for the NATIONAL CHARACTER STRING equivalent of VARCHAR.

For all of the types listed above, there will be some implementation-defined maximum for the *length* argument.

If a character set specification is used, it will be of the following form:

```
CHARACTER SET(repertoire name | form-of-use name )
```

In other words, either the repertoire or the form-of-use may be specified and the other will be implied. Which repertoires and forms-of-use are supported and how they are associated is implementation-defined. They may follow national or international standards, or they may themselves be implementation-defined. If the character set specification is omitted, some default will apply.

Every implementation is required to support a character repertoire called SQL_ TEXT. This will contain all the characters necessary to express the SQL language, plus all characters contained in other character sets supported by the implementation.

BIT STRING Types

BIT strings, of course, are binary numbers—sequences of zeros and ones. Long BIT strings containing complex data—for example, digitized images or sound—are often called BLOBS (Binary Large Objects). There are two bit datatypes (that's "two bit" not "two-bit"): BIT and BIT VARYING. Each is followed by a parenthesized positive integer indicating the length in bits. BIT strings are fixed-length. The length may be omitted, but the default is 1, so usually a length will need to be specified. Unlike fixed-length CHARACTER strings, fixed-length BIT strings impose a minimum as well as a maximum length. In other words, any attempt to insert a string shorter than the indicated length will produce an error. BIT VARYING strings are varying-length, and the length, which will be the maximum length, must be specified. There will be some implementation-defined length that cannot be exceeded in any case (some implementations may not enforce this restriction).

BIT strings can be represented in SQL statements in binary or hexadecimal form. Hexadecimal is a base-16 number system where each digit represents four binary digits; it provides a more concise and readable way to express binary values. The characters used to represent hexadecimal (or hex) are the digits 0–9 and the letters A–F. (Either upper- or lowercase letters A–F may be used to the same effect.) If a BIT string literal is represented in a SQL statement in binary form, it will be preceded by the letter B; if it is hex, it will be preceded by the letter X and delimited with single quotes.

BIT strings in the standard can be compared and thus sorted. The details for how this is done are described under Predicates.

EXACT NUMERIC Types

EXACT NUMERIC numbers have a specified or implied precision and scale. The precision is the total number of significant digits used to express the number; the scale is the number of significant digits to the right of the decimal point. Naturally, the scale cannot exceed the precision. Also, the precision may be either binary, meaning that it is expressed as the bit-length of the number, from which the number of digits can be derived, or decimal, in which case it directly indicates the number of digits. The scale is decimal. If the precision is omitted, an implementation-defined default applies; if the scale is omitted, the default is 0, which means that the number is effectively an INTEGER and the decimal point is dropped. The EXACT NUMERIC types are these:

- NUMERIC [(*precision*[, *scale*])]. This may specify neither precision nor scale, specify both precision and scale, or just specify precision and leave scale as the default, which is 0. The precision, whether specified or default, is decimal rather than binary.

- DECIMAL [(*precision*[, *scale*])], also known as DEC. This is very similar to NUMERIC, but with the subtle difference that the implementation may choose a precision greater than that specified. NUMERIC specifies an actual precision; DECIMAL specifies a minimum precision. Of course, in either case the precision could be omitted in favor of the implementation's default.

- INTEGER, also known as INT. The scale is 0, and the precision is an implementation-defined default. Whether this default is decimal or binary is also implementation-defined.

- SMALLINT. This is the same as INTEGER except that the precision may be less than that of INT. Whether the precision actually is less is implementation-defined. INT and SMALLINT precisions will be either both decimal or both binary—whichever the implementation chooses.

APPROXIMATE NUMERIC Types

APPROXIMATE NUMERIC numbers are expressed in scientific notation and have a precision, but no scale as such. The mantissa and the exponent are both signed, and the sign and magnitude of the exponent essentially determine the scale. The precision is binary (see EXACT NUMERIC above) and is that of the mantissa. The number of digits that can be in the exponent (not, properly speaking, a precision) is implementation-defined. The capital letter E (without quotes; this is not a text string) is the exponentiation symbol. The APPROXIMATE NUMERIC types are as follows:

- FLOAT [(*precision*)]. The precision you specify here is a minimum. The implementation is free to exceed it. There is, however, an implementation-defined maximum precision, and the precision you specify here cannot exceed that number. For FLOAT and only FLOAT, the precision is always binary. This means the number you give will be the number of bits rather than a number of digits.

- REAL. For this type, the precision is decimal and implementation-defined.

- DOUBLE PRECISION. Here, too, the precision is decimal and implementation-defined but is greater than that of REAL.

In any case, there will be some implementation-defined maximum precision that applies to all the above types.

DATETIME Types

DATETIME types in SQL consist of multiple fields representing different parts of an expression indicating the date and/or time. These are delimited with separators— minus signs (-) separate the fields of a date, and colons (:) those of a time. Where dates and times are combined, the two are separated with a blank space.

DATETIME values are comparable if they have the same fields. Individual fields of DATETIME values can be accessed with the EXTRACT expression. (See Numeric Value Functions. Although it works on DATETIMEs, EXTRACT produces a numeric result and is so considered a numeric value function.) There are three DATETIME datatypes:

- DATE is a set of three integer fields: YEAR, MONTH, and DAY. Four positions are allocated for years and two each for months and days, in the format *yyyy-mm-dd*. With separators, the total number of positions is 10.

- TIME [(*precision*)] [WITH TIME ZONE] is also a set of three numeric fields: HOUR, MINUTE, and SECOND. With separators, the length is 8 positions. You can optionally use the precision argument to specify fractional seconds up to an implementation-defined maximum number of positions, which will be at least 6. SECOND is therefore a DECIMAL; the other fields are INTEGERs. When fractional seconds are used, the total number of positions in the TIME item increases by the positions of the fractional seconds plus 1 to account for the decimal point. You can also optionally specify a time zone displacement. This indicates an amount to offset the time to account for divergence from UCT (Universal Coordinated Time). The time zone displacement adds two new fields—TIMEZONE_HOUR and TIMEZONE_ MINUTE— to the value of the TIME datatype. The possible values for TIMEZONE_HOUR are integers ranging from -12 to +13. For TIMEZONE_MINUTE, they are 0 to 59. In effect, the sign on the TIMEZONE_HOUR field applies to both. If WITH TIME ZONE is omitted, the default for the session applies. The addition of a time zone increases the length of the column by 6 positions.

- TIMESTAMP [(*precision*)] [WITH TIME ZONE] is a combination of DATE and TIME. Fractional seconds and time zones are options just as with TIME. The length of the TIMEZONE datatype is 19 positions plus whatever is added by fractional seconds or the time zone option.

When values for any of these types are given as literals in a SQL statement, they are surrounded by single quotes and preceded by the name of the type followed by a blank space. For example, a TIMESTAMP value would look like this:

```
TIMESTAMP '2000-07-12 10:38:54'
```

The possible values for DATETIME fields are shown in Table 29.7.

TABLE 29.7: Valid Values for DATETIME Fields

Field Name	Valid Values
YEAR	0001 to 9999
MONTH	01 to 12
DAY	Within the range 1 to 31, but further constrained by the values of the MONTH and YEAR fields, according to the rules for well-formed dates in the Gregorian calendar
HOUR	00 to 23
MINUTE	00 to 59
SECOND	00 to 61.9..., where 9... means repeating 9s for as many digits as are specified by the precision
TIMEZONE_HOUR	00 to 13
TIMEZONE_MINUTE	00 to 59

NOTE   DATETIME datatypes allow dates in the Gregorian format to be stored in the date range 0001-01-01 CE (Common Era, the same as AD in ISO nomenclature) through 9999-12-31 CE. The range for SECOND allows for as many as two "leap seconds". Interval arithmetic that involves leap seconds or discontinuities in calendars will produce implementation-defined results (we hope).

The syntax for assigning a value to the TIME ZONE is to append

```
AT {TIME ZONE interval } | LOCAL
```

to the end of the DATE value. LOCAL indicates that the time zone should be the default for the session. If the entire AT clause is omitted, LOCAL is the default. If TIME ZONE is specified, it will be indicated with a value of type INTERVAL containing the fields HOUR and MINUTE. INTERVALs are described in the following section.

The INTERVAL Type

INTERVALs are datatypes that denote the quantity of time between two DATETIME values. For example, between 12:00 and 12:30 is an interval of 00:30, or a half-hour. DATETIME values can be incremented or decremented by INTERVALs or added or subtracted to produce INTERVALs. The fields of the INTERVAL are numbers as in the DATETIME fields, but the numbers can be signed to indicate a direction in time. When used as literals, INTERVALs are preceded by the word *INTERVAL* and delimited with single quotes. The separators used are the same as for the DATETIME types. The definition of an INTERVAL includes an interval qualifier that indicates which fields of the DATE and TIME fields are to be included in the INTERVAL. The syntax diagram of this element is:

```
interval qualifier ::=
range of fields | single field


range of fields ::=
{ { YEAR | DAY | HOUR | MINUTE }
[(precision)] }
TO { YEAR | MONTH | DAY | HOUR | MINUTE }
| { SECOND [(precision)] }


single field ::=
{ { YEAR | MONTH | DAY | HOUR | MINUTE }
[(precision)] }
| { SECOND [(leading precision[, frac precision])] }
```

In other words, the interval qualifier may specify either a range of fields or a single field. If it specifies a range, the field before TO is called the *start field*, and the field following TO is called the *end field*. The start and end fields may be the same, in which case the effect is the same as if a single field had been specified.

The start field may not be SECOND. If you want seconds as the only field, specify SECOND as a single field. The optional precision argument following the start field is a positive integer indicating the number of positions to place in the leading field. The default is 2. The optional precision argument following the SECOND field represents the fractional precision—the number of digits to the right of the decimal point that will be used to represent the value. The following criteria must be met:

- The start field must be of equal or greater significance than the end field, where the descending order of significance of the fields is YEAR, MONTH, DAY, HOUR, MINUTE, SECOND.

- All fields falling between the start and end fields in the descending order of significance are included. In other words, an interval cannot be DAY, MINUTE without the intervening HOUR.

- If the start field is YEAR, the end field must be MONTH.

- The start field cannot be MONTH.

In effect, these restrictions mean that INTERVALs are either any single DATETIME field, YEAR possibly subdivided into MONTH, or fields less significant than MONTH, possibly subdivided into fields that are less significant still. YEAR and DAY are always either start fields or single fields. INTERVALs with YEAR and/or MONTH fields are called *year-month INTERVALs*; others are called *day-time INTERVALs*. Year-month and day-time INTERVALs are not comparable to each other in the terms discussed at the beginning of this entry. However, other INTERVALs are comparable.

For single-field INTERVALs, you may specify any DATETIME field, again with the optional precision. If the single field is SECOND, the precision can have two parts—the leading precision and the fractional (frac) precision. The former is the number of digits preceding the decimal point, with a default of 2. The latter is the number following the decimal point, with a default of 6.

The length of the INTERVAL is calculated according to the following principles:

- If the interval qualifier is a single field, the INTERVAL is the length of that field. If that field is SECOND, the length is the leading precision plus the fractional precision plus 1 (for the decimal point); otherwise, the length equals the specified or implied precision.

- All fields between the start and end fields have a length of 2, but each adds 3 positions to the length of the INTERVAL because of the necessary separator.

- The length of an INTERVAL that uses a range of values is calculated as follows: add the start field precision, the length of the end field (which is calculated just as though the end field were a single field as described above) plus 1 (for the separator), and the length of the intervening fields plus separators, which is 3 for each intervening field.

Anything that can be expressed in the precision specified or implied is a valid value for the start field or the sole field of an INTERVAL. YEAR and DAY are always start or sole fields. The valid values for the fields when not used as start or sole fields are shown in Table 29.8.

TABLE 29.8: Valid Values for Intervening and End Fields in INTERVAL Items

Field	Valid Value Range
MONTH	-1 to 11
HOUR	-23 to 23
MINUTE	-59 to 59
SECOND	-59.9° to 59.9°, where 9° means repeating 9s for as many digits as are specified by the precision

Operations Involving DATETIMEs and INTERVALs

Arithmetic operators can be used on DATETIMEs and INTERVALs. The result will be a value expression that can be used in SQL statements where value expressions normally are—for example, among the output columns of queries or as values to be placed into a table with an INSERT statement. See Value Expressions and Chapter 10. Table 29.9 defines the operations that are possible.

TABLE 29.9: Valid Operators Involving DATETIMEs and INTERVALs

Operand 1	Operator	Operand 2	Result Type
DATETIME	-	DATETIME	INTERVAL
DATETIME	+ or -	INTERVAL	DATETIME
INTERVAL	+	DATETIME	DATETIME
INTERVAL	+ or -	INTERVAL	INTERVAL
INTERVAL	* or /	NUMERIC	INTERVAL
NUMERIC	*	INTERVAL	INTERVAL

These operations, of course, also obey the natural rules associated with dates and times according to the Gregorian calendar. The meanings are as follows:

- DATETIME - DATETIME = INTERVAL. This compares two DATETIMEs and finds the INTERVAL of time between them. The two DATETIMEs must be comparable (as defined under DATETIME earlier in this entry). If the first DATETIME is chronologically later, the INTERVAL is positive.

- DATETIME (+ or -) INTERVAL = DATETIME. This increments (+) or decrements (-) the DATETIME by the INTERVAL. If the DATETIME has a TIME ZONE component, it is preserved in the resulting DATETIME value.

- INTERVAL + DATETIME = DATETIME. This is equivalent to DATETIME + INTERVAL described above.

- INTERVAL (+ OR -) INTERVAL = INTERVAL. Adds or subtracts the numbers in the various fields of the INTERVALs. Keep in mind that INTERVAL values are signed and that subtracting a negative increases the value of the answer.

- INTERVAL (* or /) NUMERIC = INTERVAL. NUMERIC here means any EXACT or APPROXIMATE NUMERIC type. The various fields of the INTERVAL are multiplied or divided by the NUMERIC figure and values are converted to appropriate units and carried into fields of greater or lesser significance as necessary.

- NUMERIC * INTERVAL = INTERVAL. This is the equivalent of INTERVAL * NUMERIC, described above.

For example, the following expression increments the value of a DATETIME value by a year-month INTERVAL value:

```
DATE '2000-11-28' + INTERVAL '0002-4'
```

This will evaluate to the following DATETIME value:

```
DATE '2003-03-28'
```

In addition to the above operations, time periods can be compared to see whether they overlap. This is done with the OVERLAPS predicate as described in the Predicates entry of this chapter.

Compatibilities with Other Languages

When it needs to pass values to or from an application, SQL will either use variables (in Embedded SQL), parameters (in the module language), or dynamic parameters (in Dynamic SQL). However, the datatypes supported by various languages differ both from each other and from the SQL datatypes. In particular, DATETIME and INTERVAL are supported by none of the languages specified in the standard. Also, SQL values can be NULL, which has no equivalent in most languages because NULLs produce UNKNOWN values in comparisons, whereas even values such as zero or an empty string will produce TRUE or FALSE values in comparisons in conventional languages. Indicator variables are appended to conventional variables to indicate the presence of NULLs and allow the application to respond appropriately. The details of how to pass SQL values through variables or parameters, as well as the exact equivalents for SQL datatypes in the various standard-supported languages, are outlined in Chapter 21 and Appendices E and F.

Conformance Levels

Intermediate   At this level, support for BIT STRINGs is not required, CHARAC-
TER STRINGs need not allow character set specifications, and
DATETIME and INTERVAL datatypes need not support a speci-
fied precision for fractional seconds.

Entry   At this level, support for varying-length character strings, as well
as NATIONAL CHARACTER, DATETIME, and INTERVAL
datatypes is not required, although VARCHAR, DATE, and TIME
are very widely supported, sometimes augmented with TIME-
STAMP and INTERVAL. Also, empty strings may be disallowed,
although most implementations do allow them.

NOTE

See Also: Chapters 1, 3, 9, 20, 24, and 25; CREATE CHARACTER SET and SELECT in
Chapter 28; CAST Expressions, Collations, Datetime Value Functions, and Predicates
in this chapter; and Appendices E and F.

Datetime Value Functions

Functions That Produce Date and Time Values

Usage

Datetime value functions are used in place of value expressions and produce system-
determined values when referenced. There are three kinds, one for each of the DATE-
TIME datatypes:

- CURRENT_DATE. The date according to the system clock. The datatype of this
item is DATE.

- CURRENT_TIME [(*precision*)]. The time according to the system clock. The current session TIME ZONE is automatically included. The precision argument, if
supplied, specifies the decimal fractions of a second to be included in the time.
This follows the principles outlined in the Datatypes entry under "DATETIME
Types". The datatype of this item is TIME WITH TIME ZONE.

- CURRENT_TIMESTAMP [(*precision*)]: A combination of CURRENT_DATE
and CURRENT_TIME. The precision argument has the same meaning as specified under CURRENT_TIME. The datatype of this item is TIMESTAMP WITH
TIME ZONE.

Conformance Levels

Intermediate   Implementations at this level are not required to allow a specification of the fractional seconds for CURRENT_TIME or CURRENT_TIMESTAMP.

Entry   Implementations at this level are not required to support datetime value functions.

NOTE   See Also: Datatypes and Value Expressions in this chapter.

Descriptor Areas

(Dynamic SQL Only) An Effective Way to Deal with Dynamic Parameters

Usage

Dynamically-generated SQL statements can often use dynamic parameters as input or output parameters. There are two ways to set the values for the input parameters or retrieve them from the output parameters. You can use host-language variables (or parameters in the module language), or you can use descriptor areas. This entry is concerned with descriptor areas. For examples of both approaches in practice, see Chapter 22.

A *descriptor area*, sometimes just called a *descriptor*, consists of a series of items, each of which stores information about a single dynamic parameter. Each item has a number of fields. One field can hold a value for the parameter, another indicates whether it is NULL, and the rest provide descriptive information, such as the datatype, length, and so on of the parameter. Which of these fields are relevant depends on the datatype of the parameter.

When you execute a dynamic statement, you can specify that a descriptor area is to be used for all input parameters, all output parameters, or both. In the case of "both", you use a separate descriptor area for input and for output. You specify a descriptor for the input parameters with the USING clause, and you specify one for the output parameters with an INTO clause. These clauses are the same for any of the statements that use them, and either of them can take a list of host-language variables or the name of a descriptor area. The statements that use these clauses are as follows:

- EXECUTE is used to execute statements previously assembled with the PREPARE statement. The prepared statements can include most SQL statements, including queries that are known to produce only one row of output (single-row queries). EXECUTE can use either USING or INTO. INTO would be used only for queries.

- OPEN CURSOR in Dynamic SQL can execute a cursor that was dynamically created with either a DECLARE CURSOR or an ALLOCATE CURSOR statement. Such a cursor may have dynamic input parameters, and these will be given values with a USING clause in the OPEN CURSOR statement.

- FETCH is the statement that actually retrieves the data from open cursors. Therefore, it will use an INTO clause to store the output columns of the query in the cursor. FETCH retrieves the cursor contents one row at a time.

Of course, a given statement can have either, neither, or both kinds of dynamic parameters. The upshot is that a given descriptor area handles either all input or all output parameters for a given statement. A single descriptor does not handle both kinds of parameters, nor would it normally be used for more than one statement, though it could if the parameters for the statements were the same. However, you can execute the same statement repeatedly with different values specified in or entering the descriptor, which is largely the point.

Descriptor areas are created with the ALLOCATE DESCRIPTOR statement. When you create (allocate) a descriptor, you specify the maximum number of items it can hold. The values in the fields can either be manually specified with the SET DESCRIPTOR statement or automatically set with the DESCRIBE statement. However, for input parameters, you must use SET DESCRIPTOR to set the values. DESCRIBE cannot do this. The normal situation would be to:

- Use DESCRIBE to initialize the descriptor.

- Use SET DESCRIPTOR to change any fields you think you need to change.

- For input parameters, use SET DESCRIPTOR again to set the DATA field. You cannot set the DATA field, which actually contains the value for the parameter, at the same time as the other descriptor fields.

You can retrieve the content of the descriptor with the GET DESCRIPTOR statement.

The fields of a descriptor area item are shown in Table 29.10.

TABLE 29.10: The Descriptor Area Fields

Name of Field	Datatype
TYPE	INTEGER
LENGTH	INTEGER
OCTET_LENGTH	INTEGER

Continued on next page

TABLE 29.10 CONTINUED: The Descriptor Area Fields

Name of Field	Datatype
RETURNED_LENGTH	INTEGER
RETURNED_OCTET_LENGTH	INTEGER
PRECISION	INTEGER
SCALE	INTEGER
DATETIME_INTERVAL_CODE	INTEGER
DATETIME_INTERVAL_PRECISION	INTEGER
NULLABLE	INTEGER
INDICATOR	INTEGER
DATA	Matches datatype and description specified by the values in the following fields: TYPE, LENGTH, PRECISION, SCALE, DATETIME_INTERVAL_CODE, DATETIME_INTERVAL_ PRECISION, CHARACTER_SET_CATALOG, CHARACTER_SET_ SCHEMA, and CHARACTER_SET_NAME
NAME	CHARACTER string with character set SQL_TEXT and length not less than 128 characters
UNNAMED	INTEGER
COLLATION_CATALOG	CHARACTER string with character set SQL_TEXT and length not less than 128 characters
COLLATION_SCHEMA	CHARACTER string with character set SQL_TEXT and length not less than 128 characters
COLLATION_NAME	CHARACTER string with character set SQL_TEXT and length not less than 128 characters
CHARACTER_SET_CATALOG	CHARACTER string with character set SQL_TEXT and length not less than 128 characters
CHARACTER_SET_SCHEMA	CHARACTER string with character set SQL_TEXT and length not less than 128 characters
CHARACTER_SET_NAME	CHARACTER string with character set SQL_TEXT and length not less than 128 characters

Most of the fields apply only to particular datatypes and therefore may or may not be relevant depending on the value of the datatype of the parameter, which is specified in the TYPE field. The values in those fields that are not relevant are implementation-dependent. The fields that do not depend on the value of TYPE are described below:

- TYPE itself, naturally, will always be present and indicate the datatype of the parameter following the codes indicated in Table 29.10.

- NULLABLE indicates whether the parameter may contain NULL values. A value of 1 indicates that it may, and a value of 0 indicates that it may not.

- INDICATOR is a descriptor field that indicates whether the parameter actually does contain a NULL. If NULLABLE is 1, you should always check this value (for output parameters) or set it when you want to specify NULLs (for input parameters). If an output parameter is NULL, and the INDICATOR field is not retrieved (with the GET DESCRIPTOR statement, naturally), an error is produced. A negative INDICATOR value means that the parameter is NULL, and the value of DATA is irrelevant; otherwise, the parameter is not NULL, and the value of DATA must be appropriate for its datatype and description as indicated in the other fields. This applies to both input and output parameters, so INDICATOR fields may be set negative to insert NULLs.

- DATA is the content of the parameter. Its value must match the description given by the TYPE and other relevant fields (precision and so on), unless the INDICATOR field shows that it is NULL, in which case its value is implementation-defined and effectively undefined (and irrelevant).

- NAME indicates the name of the parameter.

- UNNAMED specifies whether the name of the parameter is implementation-dependent or imposed. The name is imposed if SQL syntax dictates what the name is—for example, if it is taken directly from a column name or specified with an AS clause (see SELECT in Chapter 28). If the name is implementation-dependent, UNNAMED is set to 1; otherwise, it is set to 0.

The numeric codes for the various datatypes as used in the TYPE field are shown in Table 29.11.

TABLE 29.11: Valid Values for the TYPE Descriptor Field

Datatype	Code
Implementation-defined	< 0
BIT	14
BIT VARYING	15
CHARACTER	1

Continued on next page

TABLE 29.11 CONTINUED: Valid Values for the TYPE Descriptor Field

Datatype	Code
CHARACTER VARYING	12
DATE, TIME, or TIMESTAMP	9
DECIMAL	3
DOUBLE PRECISION	8
FLOAT	6
INTEGER	4
INTERVAL	10
NUMERIC	2
REAL	7
SMALLINT	5

The CODE number indicates the datatype of the parameter specified on the left in the above table. The fields that are relevant for the various datatypes indicated by TYPE are defined below:

- If TYPE indicates NUMERIC, then PRECISION and SCALE are the precision and scale values for the NUMERIC datatype.

- If TYPE indicates DECIMAL, then PRECISION and SCALE are the precision and scale values for the DECIMAL datatype.

- If TYPE indicates FLOAT, then PRECISION is the precision value for the FLOAT datatype.

- If TYPE indicates BIT or BIT VARYING, then LENGTH is the length or maximum length value for the BIT datatype.

- If TYPE indicates CHARACTER or CHARACTER VARYING, then LENGTH is the length or maximum length value for the CHARACTER datatype, CHARACTER_SET_NAME indicates the character set on which it is based, and CHARACTER_SET_CATALOG and CHARACTER_SET_SCHEMA indicate the catalog and schema where that character set resides. Likewise, COLLATION_ NAME, COLLATION_CATALOG, and COLLATION_SCHEMA contain the same information for the collation of the character set.

- If TYPE indicates DATE, TIME, or TIMESTAMP, then DATETIME_INTERVAL_ CODE is a code specified in Table 29.10, and PRECISION is the fractional seconds precision, if any, of the TIME or TIMESTAMP.

- If TYPE indicates INTERVAL, then DATETIME_INTERVAL_CODE is a code specified in Table 29.11, and DATETIME_INTERVAL_PRECISION and PRECISION are the leading field precision and fractional seconds precision, if any, respectively.

All implementation-defined datatypes are negative numbers, and the set of fields that are relevant for such types is also implementation-defined.

For DATETIME and INTERVAL datatypes, the DATETIME_INTERVAL_CODE is used to indicate which fields are present in the DATETIME or INTERVAL. The meaning of the value in the field can vary depending on whether the datatype is DATETIME or INTERVAL. The possible values for DATETIMEs are shown in Table 29.12, while those for INTERVALs are shown in Table 29.13.

TABLE 29.12: Valid Values for DATETIME_INTERVAL_CODE if the Datatype Is DATE

Datetime Datatype	Code
DATE	1
TIME	2
TIME WITH TIME ZONE	4
TIMESTAMP	3
TIMESTAMP WITH TIME ZONE	5

TABLE 29.13: Valid Values for DATETIME_INTERVAL_CODE if the Datatype Is INTERVAL

Interval Fields	Code
DAY	3
DAY TO HOUR	8
DAY TO MINUTE	9
DAY TO SECOND	10
HOUR	4
HOUR TO MINUTE	11
HOUR TO SECOND	12
MINUTE	5

Continued on next page

TABLE 29.13 CONTINUED: Valid Values for DATETIME_INTERVAL_CODE if the Datatype Is INTERVAL

Interval Fields	Code
MINUTE TO SECOND	13
MONTH	2
SECOND	6
YEAR	1
YEAR TO MONTH	7

Conformance Levels

Entry   Support for Dynamic SQL, which is where descriptor areas are used, is not required at this level. In fact, most products support it, but not necessarily conforming to the specifications of the standard.

NOTE   See Also: ALLOCATE DESCRIPTOR, DEALLOCATE DESCRIPTOR, DESCRIBE, GET DESCRIPTOR, and SET DESCRIPTOR in Chapter 28; Predicates (for discussion of three-valued logic and NULLs) and Datatypes in this chapter; and Appendix H.

Numeric Value Functions

Functions That Produce Numeric Values

Syntax

```
numeric value function ::=
{ POSITION (character string IN character string) }
| {EXTRACT ( datetime field
  FROM {datetime value expression | interval value expression} ) }
| {CHAR_LENGTH | CHARACTER_LENGTH (string value expression)}
| {OCTET_LENGTH (string value expression) }
| {BIT_LENGTH (string value expression) }
```

Usage

Numeric value functions operate on nonnumeric datatypes but produce numeric results. They can be used in SQL statements wherever numeric value expressions are used. When a numeric value expression produces a number, it is said to equal that number. The rules are outlined in the following paragraphs.

POSITION

For POSITION, both strings must have the same character repertoire but not necessarily the same character set (see Chapter 20). In other words, their collating sequences and forms-of-use may differ. The result is an INTEGER. If either string is NULL, POSITION is also NULL. If the first string is a subset of the second, POSITION is set to the character position in the second string where the first string begins. All matches after the first are ignored. If the first string is empty, POSITION = 1. If no match is found, POSITION = 0. For example, the following expression finds the starting position of the first occurrence of 'press' in 'Express':

```
POSITION ('press' IN 'Express')
```

The resulting value would, of course, be 3.

EXTRACT

For EXTRACT, if the DATETIME or INTERVAL on which the extract is performed is NULL, EXTRACT is NULL as well. Otherwise, EXTRACT equals the value of the field specified. The fields that can be extracted are YEAR, MONTH, DAY, HOUR, MINUTE, SECOND, TIMEZONE_HOUR, and TIMEZONE_MINUTE. The last two can be extracted only from DATETIME values of type TIME or TIMESTAMP that specify WITH TIME ZONE. If the extracted field is SECOND, the datatype of EXTRACT is EXACT NUMERIC with some implementation-defined precision and scale, such that the fractional seconds can be expressed without truncation. Otherwise, the datatype is INTEGER. For example, the following expression produces an integer corresponding to the month value of the INTERVAL literal:

```
EXTRACT MONTH FROM INTERVAL '2010-05'
```

The resulting value would, of course, be 05.

CHARACTER_LENGTH

CHARACTER_LENGTH may be abbreviated as CHAR_LENGTH. The string literal, string datatype, or other string value expression on which it operates is a CHARACTER or BIT STRING as specified under String Value Functions in this chapter. If the string value function output (hereafter *string*) is NULL, then CHAR_LENGTH is NULL. Otherwise, if the string is a CHARACTER datatype, CHAR_LENGTH returns the number of characters in it, which will be an INTEGER.

> **NOTE**   An empty character string is not NULL; it will produce a CHAR_LENGTH of zero. For BIT STRINGs, CHAR_LENGTH is equivalent to OCTET_LENGTH.

OCTET_LENGTH

OCTET_LENGTH also is NULL if the string is NULL. Otherwise, OCTET_LENGTH is the BIT_LENGTH of the string divided by 8 and rounded up to the nearest INTEGER. Octets are sequences of 8 bits each, and in some obscure circles are called *bytes* (although people have been known to take liberties with the definition of bytes, which is why the standard went for octets).

BIT_LENGTH

BIT_LENGTH, too, returns NULL if the string is NULL. Otherwise, it returns an INTEGER indicating the number of bits used to represent the value, which will be zero for a zero-length (as opposed to NULL) string.

Conformance Levels

Intermediate	Support for POSITION and BIT_LENGTH is not required at this level.
Entry	Support for numeric value functions is not required at this level.

> **NOTE**   See Also: Datatypes, String Value Functions, and Value Expressions in this chapter.

Predicates

Expressions That Can Be TRUE, FALSE, or UNKNOWN

Syntax

```
predicate ::=
[(] [NOT]
```

```
{ comparison predicate

| between predicate

| in predicate

| like predicate

| null predicate

| quantified comparison predicate

| exists predicate

| unique predicate

| match predicate

| overlaps predicate    }

[AND | OR predicate ] [)]

[IS [NOT] truth value]


truth value ::=

TRUE | FALSE | UNKNOWN
```

Usage

Predicates are expressions that apply comparison operators (the *comp op* element shown in the syntax) and/or SQL predicate operators (IN, EXISTS, and so on) to values, to produce a truth value of TRUE, FALSE, or UNKNOWN. Predicates may be either a single such expression or a combination of any number of them using the standard Boolean operators AND, OR, and NOT, as well as the special SQL operator IS, and possibly using parentheses to impose an order of evaluation. Predicates are used in the WHERE and HAVING clauses of SELECT statements and subqueries to determine which rows or aggregate groups are to be selected (see SELECT in Chapter 28 and Subqueries), in constraints to determine whether a constraint is violated (see Constraints), and in the UPDATE and DELETE statements to determine on which rows the change should be made (see the UPDATE and DELETE entries in Chapter 28). The individual types of predicates are explained in separate sections later in this entry.

Many of these predicates use row value constructors, which are parenthesized lists of one or more values. We note here that the parentheses may be omitted if a list contains but a single value. For more information, see Row and Table Value Constructors.

Three-Valued Logic (3VL)

With the exceptions of the EXISTS, IS NULL, UNIQUE, and MATCH predicates, predicates in SQL can be TRUE, FALSE, or UNKNOWN. UNKNOWNs arise when NULLs are compared to any value including other NULLs. Since we don't know what the value is, we can't say what the result of the comparison should be. UNKNOWN truth values can be operated on by the Boolean operators AND, OR, and NOT, as well as by the SQL operator IS, with the results shown in Tables 29.14 through 29.17.

TABLE 29.14:   Truth Values Using NOT in Three-Valued Logic

Expression	Truth Value
NOT TRUE	FALSE
NOT FALSE	TRUE
NOT UNKNOWN	UNKNOWN

TABLE 29.15:   Truth Values Using OR in Three-Valued Logic

OR	TRUE	FALSE	UNKNOWN
TRUE	TRUE	TRUE	TRUE
FALSE	TRUE	FALSE	UNKNOWN
UNKNOWN	TRUE	UNKNOWN	UNKNOWN

TABLE 29.16:   Truth Values Using AND in Three-Valued Logic

AND	TRUE	FALSE	UNKNOWN
TRUE	TRUE	FALSE	UNKNOWN
FALSE	FALSE	FALSE	FALSE
UNKNOWN	UNKNOWN	FALSE	UNKNOWN

TABLE 29.17:   Truth Values Using IS in Three-Valued Logic

IS	TRUE	FALSE	UNKNOWN
TRUE	TRUE	FALSE	FALSE
FALSE	FALSE	TRUE	FALSE
UNKNOWN	FALSE	FALSE	TRUE

In Table 29.14, the expression on the left produces the truth value on the right. The other tables should be read like multiplication tables; the value indicated at the intersection of a column and a row is that produced by applying the operation (OR, AND, or IS) to the values indicated on the left and on top.

The rules of thumb (which cover most but not all combinations, hence the tables) are these:

- TRUE OR anything is TRUE.
- FALSE AND anything is FALSE.
- Any truth value ANDed or ORed with itself produces itself.
- IS is TRUE if the two truth values are the same and FALSE otherwise.

It is important to keep in mind that NULLs can not only be stored in the database, they can be generated by queries or CAST expressions (see CAST Expressions). In particular, outer joins (see Chapter 10 and SELECT in Chapter 28) can insert NULLs into the output of a query, even if none are present in the tables being joined. Outer joins merge the rows of two tables wherever matching values are found in one or more columns. Where no matches are found for a row from one of the tables, that row may be included (depending on the type of outer join) but with NULLs inserted into the columns whose values would have been taken from the other table had there been a match. Although useful, three-valued logic is problematic and controversial. (If you love a good fight, the legitimacy of 3VL is the biggest one in SQL.) The IS operator is provided primarily to give you a way to test for UNKNOWNs and ensure that the results are either TRUE or FALSE, as IS never produces an UNKNOWN.

Among the problems to be careful of in 3VL is its inability to generalize. Consider this predicate:

```
X > 1 OR X < 2
```

Obviously, any integer X will make this predicate TRUE. If X is NULL, however, the predicate will still come out UNKNOWN, as its two components would individually be UNKNOWN, and UNKNOWN AND UNKNOWN is UNKNOWN. This is one of the arguments against 3VL.

When all is said and done, the predicate will finally be either TRUE, FALSE, or UNKNOWN. Rows are selected by SELECT statements or subqueries if their values make the predicate in the WHERE clause TRUE. Likewise, rows are changed by INSERT or UPDATE statements if their values make the predicate in the WHERE clause TRUE. The predicate in the HAVING clause of a SELECT statement applies to values derived from groups of rows (see SELECT in Chapter 28 and Aggregate Functions); groups are selected for output if their values make the predicate TRUE. Constraints, however, are satisfied if the predicate is either TRUE or UNKNOWN; only a truth value of FALSE violates a constraint.

Comparison Predicates

```
comparison predicate ::=
row value constructor comp op row value constructor
```

```
comp op ::=
=
| <
| <=
| >
| >
| <>
```

NOTE   The syntax for a row value constructor is shown under Row and Table Value Constructors.

Comparison predicates compare two sets of one or more values that are in the form of simple value expressions, subqueries, or row value constructors. A row value constructor is a sequence of one or more values. Each row value constructor must have the same number of values and in such an order that the values in corresponding positions are of comparable datatypes (see Datatypes for the precise definition of comparability). Each such pair of values is called a *pair of corresponding values*. For subqueries, the values produced by the subquery are treated as though they were the content of a row value constructor. Likewise, for simple value expressions, although, in this case, the row value constructor would have only one element. For the rest of this discussion, we shall speak mostly in terms of row value constructors, but the substance applies to sets of values specified by any of these techniques, unless otherwise stated or clear from context.

If either or both of a pair of corresponding values is NULL, the result of the comparison of those two values is UNKNOWN. Otherwise, the two values are compared in terms of the comparison operator, which will be one of the following: =, <, <=, >, >=, <>, and the resulting expression is evaluated as TRUE or FALSE. NUMERIC values are compared according to their algebraic values. CHARACTER STRINGs are compared according to their collating sequences, as determined by the rules specified under Collations in Table 29.4. If the strings are of unequal length, then the shorter is padded prior to comparison according to the pad attribute of the applicable collating sequence. If the attribute is PAD SPACE (the default), the shorter string is padded with whatever character in the repertoire is defined as the blank space character. If the attribute is NO PAD, then the shorter string is padded with some implementation-dependent character from outside the character set that collates lower than any character within it. Then the strings are compared.

Two strings are equal if they collate the same. For example, the following two strings are not the same but would be considered equal, provided that they were collated with the PAD SPACE attribute:

```
'Weston'
```

```
'Weston      '
```

In some cases, it is possible for two strings of unequal length or representing different sequences of characters to collate the same. If such strings are referenced in an aggregate function, are subject to exclusion by a DISTINCT argument in a SELECT clause, are used in UNION, INTERSECT, or EXCEPT operations, or are used in a GROUP BY clause to partition aggregate groups (for all of these, see SELECT in Chapter 28), which of these distinguishable but equal values is used is implementation-dependent.

BIT STRINGs are compared bit by bit until the first difference is found or until the end of at least one of the strings is reached. On the first bit difference, the BIT STRING value that equals 1 is the greater. If there is no bit difference and the strings are of unequal length, then the longer string is greater. If there is no bit difference and no difference in length, then the strings are equal.

DATETIMEs are compared according to their placement in chronological time. A later date has a greater value.

INTERVALs are first converted into appropriate units, meaning that all fields are converted into the units of the least significant field of either value, and these values are compared as NUMERICs.

Now that we understand how the individual elements of the row value constructor list are compared, we will examine how the entire lists are compared in terms of the results of the individual comparisons. We can call the first row value constructor RC1 and the second RC2. The rules are these:

- If all of the corresponding values are equal, then RC1 = RC2.

- Otherwise, both lists are traversed until the first difference or NULL is found among the corresponding values. If a difference is found, then those corresponding values are compared, and the truth value using any given comparison operator is the same as it would be using the same comparison operator on those two values. RC1 <> RC2 is TRUE if there are any differences in the corresponding non-NULL values.

- RC1 <> RC2 is FALSE if and only if RC1 = RC2 is TRUE.

- RC1 = RC2 is FALSE if and only if RC1 <> RC2 is TRUE.

- If either RC1 > RC2 or RC1 = RC2 is TRUE, then RC1 >= RC2 is TRUE.

- If either RC1 < RC2 or RC1 = RC2 is TRUE, then RC1 <= RC2 is TRUE.

- RC1 < RC2 is FALSE if and only if RC1 >= RC2 is TRUE.

- RC1 > RC2 is FALSE if and only if RC1 <= RC2 is TRUE.
- RC1 <= RC2 is FALSE if and only if RC1 > RC2 is TRUE.
- RC1 >= RC2 is FALSE if and only if RC1 < RC2 is TRUE.
- In any other case, the truth value of the comparison is UNKNOWN.

Some of the above may seem obvious, but it is useful for reference because of the subtleties of 3VL. For example, if the only difference between the RC1 and RC2 is the presence of NULLs in one or the other, then RC1 = RC2 is not TRUE; nor is it FALSE. It is UNKNOWN, as is RC1 <> RC2. Notice that this effect will be achieved even if both row value constructors have the NULLs only in corresponding values. NULL = NULL is UNKNOWN. For example, assuming a collating sequence that corresponds to alphabetical ordering, the first of the following comparison predicates would be TRUE, the second FALSE, and the third UNKNOWN:

```
('bat', 'raven') >= ('bat', 'cat')
('bat', 'beat')  >= ('cat', NULL)
('bat', NULL)    >= ('bat', 'man')
```

The BETWEEN Predicate

```
between predicate ::=
row value constructor [NOT] BETWEEN
    row value constructor AND row value constructor
```

NOTE   The syntax for a row value constructor is shown under Row and Table Value Constructors.

BETWEEN predicates check to see whether the first row value constructor falls in an ascending range specified by the other two. As with comparison predicates, the row value constructors must all have the same number of values, and the corresponding values must be comparable. We can call the first row value constructor RC1, the second RC2, and the third RC3.

```
RC1 BETWEEN RC2 AND RC3
```

is equivalent to

```
RC1 >= RC2 AND RC1 <= RC3
```

and

```
RC1 NOT BETWEEN RC2 AND RC3
```

is equivalent to

```
NOT (RC1 BETWEEN RC2 AND RC3)
```

(parentheses added for clarity). Notice that if RC1 BETWEEN RC2 AND RC3 is TRUE, this does not mean that RC1 BETWEEN RC3 AND RC2 is also TRUE. The first would be translated as

```
RC1 >= RC2 AND RC1 <= RC3
```

whereas the second would be translated as

```
RC1 >= RC3 AND RC1 <= RC2
```

These statements could both be TRUE only if RC1, RC2, and RC3 were all equal.

Here are some examples. The first of the following BETWEEN predicates would be TRUE, the second FALSE, and the third UNKNOWN.

```
(4, 6) BETWEEN (3, 9)  AND (5, NULL)

(4, 6) BETWEEN (5, 3)  AND (NULL, 9)

(4, 6) BETWEEN (3, 9)  AND (NULL, 5)
```

The IN Predicate

```
in predicate ::=

row value constructor

[NOT] IN table subquery

| (value expression.,..)
```

> **NOTE** The syntax for row value constructors is shown under Row and Table Value Construc-
> tors, and that for table subqueries is shown in Subqueries.

IN predicates determine whether the row value constructor is found in the set of values that either is specified directly or is produced by a table subquery. If the values are specified, it is equivalent to a table value constructor. The table subquery is a SELECT statement that produces zero or more rows of one or more columns each—in other words, a conventional table (see Subqueries in this chapter and SELECT in Chapter 28 for more information). In any case, the row value constructor preceding the word IN (the *match target*) is compared to the output rows of the table subquery or the row value constructors of the table value constructor as the case may be (in either case, call these the *specified rows*). If the match target is equal to at least one of the specified rows according to the rules laid out in the Comparison Predicates section of this entry, then the truth value of the IN predicate is TRUE. If for every specified row (X) the match target <> X, then the truth value is FALSE. If a subquery is used and comes back empty (returns no rows) then the IN predicate is FALSE. If none of the foregoing conditions are met, the truth value is UNKNOWN. This happens when a partially NULL row matches in all of its non-NULL components.

For example, the first of the following IN predicates would be TRUE, the second FALSE, and the third UNKNOWN:

```
(4, 6) IN VALUES (3, 9), (5, NULL), (4, 6)

(4, 6) IN VALUES (3, 9), (5, NULL), (3, 6)

(4, 6) IN VALUES (3, 9), (5, 0), (NULL, 6)
```

Although the above examples are specified with row value constructors, subqueries that produce the same sets of rows would have the same effect.

Note that IN used with a subquery is equivalent to the quantified comparison predicate SOME used with an equals operator and the same subquery.

The LIKE Predicate

```
like predicate ::=

string value expression

[NOT] LIKE string value expression

[ ESCAPE character ]
```

LIKE compares two strings, one of which can contain wildcards, to see if they match. These strings are value expressions of some string datatype and may be generated however value expressions may (see Value Expressions). The first string, the *match value*, is searched for substrings that are specified by the second, the *pattern*. The optional ESCAPE clause allows you to define an escape character as described below. All three expressions must be comparable as defined under Datatypes. Two wildcards may be used in the pattern:

- The underscore (_) stands for any single character in the match value.

- The percent sign (%) stands for any sequence of zero or more characters in the match value.

If you want to search for either of these wildcards as literals, you must use the ESCAPE clause to define an escape character. Whenever this character is used in the pattern, it must precede either the underscore or the percent sign and will indicate that the underscore or percent sign is to be interpreted literally, not as a wildcard.

The truth value of a LIKE predicate conforms to the following principles:

- If either the match value, pattern, or escape character is NULL, the truth value is UNKNOWN.

- If both the match value and the pattern are zero-length strings, the truth value is TRUE.

- Otherwise, if the match value can be subdivided into segments such that each equals (as defined under Comparison Predicates) a string in the pattern or is represented in the pattern by a wildcard, where the segments and wildcards are in the same sequence in the pattern as the matching segments in the match value, then LIKE is TRUE.

- If none of the above conditions hold, LIKE is FALSE.

No padding or truncating of the match value is done. If the pattern does not describe the entire match value, but really just a substring, you must place percent signs at the beginning and/or the end of the pattern to match (account for) the extraneous material in the match value. This implies that two strings that are equal according to the standards outlined under Comparison Predicates in this entry still may not be LIKE one another as defined here. The comparison predicate may pad the shorter string with blanks automatically, whereas LIKE will not match trailing blanks unless a trailing percent sign wildcard is used.

In the following examples, the first LIKE predicate is TRUE, the second FALSE, and the third UNKNOWN.

```
'Sherwood_Forest ' LIKE '%wood|_For%' ESCAPE '|'

'Sherwood_Forest ' LIKE '%wood|_Forest' ESCAPE '|'

'Sherwood_Forest ' LIKE '%wood|_For%' ESCAPE NULL
```

The comparison between the match value and the pattern must follow some collating sequence and coercibility attribute. These are based on the tables in the Collations entry as specified below.

If the escape character is not specified, then the collating sequence used is determined by Table 29.4, taking the match value as comparand 1 and the pattern as comparand 2. Otherwise, let C1 be the coercibility attribute and collating sequence of the match value and C2 be the coercibility attribute and collating sequence of the pattern. Taking C1 as the operand 1 coercibility and C2 as the operand 2 coercibility, calculate the resulting collating sequence and coercibility according to Table 29.3. Call this result C3. Now take C3 as the coercibility attribute and collating sequence of comparand 1 and the escape character—with its coercibility attribute and collating sequence—as comparand 2, and let Table 29.4 determine the collating sequence and coercibility used in the LIKE predicate. Fun, eh?

The NULL Predicate

```
null predicate ::=
row value constructor IS [NOT] NULL
```

NOTE   The syntax for a row value constructor is shown under Row and Table Value Constructors.

NULL predicates are designed specifically to check for the presence of NULL values. For this reason, they are never UNKNOWN—only TRUE or FALSE. If all of the values in the row value constructor are NULL, then IS NULL is TRUE. If they are all

FALSE, then IS NOT NULL is TRUE. Notice that IS NOT NULL will not necessarily have the same value as NOT (IS NULL). This was not true in older SQL standards. There, the NULL predicate took a column reference where it now takes a row value constructor, and therefore *value* IS NOT NULL was the same as NOT (*value* IS NULL). This is no longer the case, unless the row value constructor happens to contain a single value. Table 29.18 shows the truth table for the NULL predicate.

The expression column on the left indicates the number of values in the row value constructor and whether they are NULL, not NULL, all NULL, some NULL, or none NULL. The other columns show the appropriate truth values for variations of the NULL predicate to row value constructor R.

For example, the first and last of the following predicates are TRUE, and the second and third are FALSE:

```
(NULL, NULL) IS NULL

(NULL, 5) IS NULL

(NULL, 5) IS NOT NULL

 NOT ((NULL, 5) IS NULL)
```

TABLE 29.18: Truth Table for the NULL Predicate

EXPRESSION	R IS NULL	R IS NOT NULL	NOT R IS NULL	NOT R IS NOT NULL
1 value: NULL	TRUE	FALSE	FALSE	TRUE
1 value: NOT NULL	FALSE	TRUE	TRUE	FALSE
> 1 value: all NULL	TRUE	FALSE	FALSE	TRUE
> 1 value: some NULL	FALSE	FALSE	TRUE	TRUE
> 1 value: none NULL	FALSE	TRUE	TRUE	FALSE

Quantified Comparison Predicates

```
quantified comparison predicate ::=
row value constructor comp op { ANY | ALL | SOME }
  table subquery
```

NOTE   The syntax for row value constructors is shown under Row and Table Value Constructors, and that for table subqueries is shown in Subqueries.

Quantified comparison predicates are a special type of comparison predicate that, rather than comparing two row value constructors, compares a row value constructor to the set of rows produced by a table subquery. The row value constructor (RC) is compared individually to each row from the subquery, but a single value is produced that describes the results of the entire set of comparisons. Either all of the comparisons were TRUE, some of them were, or none of them were. As in comparison predicates, RC and the subquery output must have the same number of columns, and corresponding values must be comparable. The rules for determining collating sequences and coercibility for character string datatypes are also the same as for comparison predicates. Simple single value expressions may also be used, which are treated like row constructors of only one column. In the earlier standards, only simple value expressions could be used.

The quantifier that precedes the comparison operator is one of three types: ANY, ALL, or SOME. ANY and SOME are synonymous, and we will use SOME to indicate either of them for the remainder of this discussion. The truth value result is determined as follows:

- Whether SOME or ALL is specified, if all of the comparisons between RC and each row produced by the subquery are TRUE, the result is TRUE.

- If the subquery returns zero rows and ALL is specified, the result is TRUE. If the subquery returns zero rows and SOME is specified, the result is FALSE.

- If ALL is specified and any of the comparisons between RC and the subquery rows are FALSE, then the result is FALSE.

- If SOME is specified and there is at least one comparison between RC and the subquery rows that is TRUE, the result is TRUE.

- If SOME is specified and every comparison between RC and the subquery rows is FALSE, the result is FALSE.

- In any case not covered by the preceding, the result is UNKNOWN.

ANY and ALL can be confusing in certain situations. For example, in ordinary English a value is normally considered greater than any of a set of values if it is greater than every member of the set. In SQL, that meaning would be expressed by > ALL. The expression > ANY would be true if RC were greater than at least one member of the set. SOME is probably a less-confusing term in this regard. The thing to remember is that you are looking at a group of comparisons between RC and each row returned by the subquery. Of this group, are ALL of the comparisons TRUE? Are SOME of the comparisons TRUE? Another point of confusion comes when using a zero-row subquery. Comparing a value to ANY (zero-row subquery) will result in a FALSE. Comparing a value to ALL (zero-row subquery) will result in a TRUE.

In the following examples, we show the rows produced by a subquery rather than the subquery itself. This, of course, is not the proper syntax, but it makes the predicate more readable.

Of the following SOME predicates, the first is TRUE, the second FALSE, and the third UNKNOWN:

```
(2100.00, 97) > ANY
(2500.00, 99
 18000.00, NULL
 2000.00, 118)


(2100.00, 97) = SOME
(2500.00, 97
 2100.00, NULL
 2000.00, 118)


(NULL, NULL) = SOME
(2500.00, 99
NULL, NULL
2000.00, NULL)
```

Of the following ALL predicates, again, the first is TRUE, the second FALSE, and the third UNKNOWN:

```
(2100.00, 97) > ALL
(2000.00, 97
1800.00, NULL
2000.00, 118)


(2100.00, 97) <> ALL
(2100.00, 77
2100.00, 97
NULL, 97)


(2100.00, 97) = ALL
(2100.00, 97
2100.00, NULL
2100.00, 97)
```

The EXISTS Predicate

exists predicate ::=

EXISTS *table subquery*

NOTE   The syntax of the table subquery element is shown under Subqueries.

EXISTS is a predicate that takes a subquery as an argument and is TRUE if that subquery produces any rows and FALSE otherwise. Although predicates determine when subqueries produce rows, and most predicates can be TRUE, FALSE, or UNKNOWN, subqueries either produce rows or they do not. If the predicates are UNKNOWN, of course, they do not.

Normally, EXISTS is used with a correlated subquery. This is a subquery that has an outer reference, which is a reference to a value in some containing query. The subquery may have different results depending on this value and must be evaluated differently for each row of the containing query (see Subqueries). Therefore, a correlated subquery produces different answers for the different rows of the containing query, and EXISTS can also have different values for each such row. Otherwise, EXISTS would have the same value for every row of the query, which is not a very useful predicate.

Be careful in the presence of possible NULLs. If the predicate of the subquery is UNKNOWN, no row is produced, and EXISTS is FALSE. That might not be a problem, but if the predicate of the containing query is NOT EXISTS, this FALSE becomes TRUE, whereas UNKNOWN would stay UNKNOWN. This problem has been thoroughly analyzed by Chris Date, a leading relational theorist. A rule of thumb is that if the subquery in an EXISTS predicate tests a value that might be NULL, use the IS NULL predicate to find the NULLs and handle them appropriately. Many but not all EXISTS predicates can also be expressed as quantified predicates.

Since EXISTS uses correlated subqueries, clarity requires that examples use entire queries rather than the EXISTS predicates in isolation. The following example uses the Salespeople table as shown elsewhere in this book. For the sake of simplicity, we have built both the outer query and the subquery on the same table—this is not required by the EXISTS syntax. This query finds all rows with city values that are also present in some other row. This produces a list of salespeople with other salespeople in their cities (alerting us to territory conflicts). It will produce two rows of output for each such match (matching salesperson A to B and then matching B to A), so we specified DISTINCT.

```
SELECT DISTINCT *
FROM Salespeople outerquery
WHERE EXISTS
  (SELECT *
```

```
FROM Salespeople innerquery
WHERE innerquery.city = outerquery.city
    AND innerquery.snum <> outerquery.snum);
```

The innerquery.snum <> outerquery.snum predicate is necessary to prevent every row from being selected in a match with itself.

The UNIQUE Predicate

```
unique predicate ::=
UNIQUE table subquery
```

NOTE   The syntax of the table subquery element is shown under Subqueries.

UNIQUE tests to see whether a subquery has produced any duplicate rows. It is either TRUE or FALSE never UNKNOWN. All of the rows from the subquery are compared as *row value constructor = row value constructor* comparison predicates. If this expression is TRUE for any combination of two subquery rows, UNIQUE is FALSE; otherwise, it is TRUE. This implies that if any NULLs are present in a row, it is automatically UNIQUE.

The following examples show the rows that would be produced by the subquery rather than the subquery itself. This is not the proper syntax, but it enhances readability. The first predicate is TRUE, and the second is FALSE.

```
UNIQUE (3, 7, NULL
        3, 7, NULL
        3, 7, 9)


UNIQUE (3, 7, NULL
        3, 7, 9
        3, 7, 9)
```

The MATCH Predicate

```
match predicate ::=
row value constructor MATCH [UNIQUE]
[PARTIAL | FULL] table subquery
```

NOTE   The syntax for row value constructors is shown under Row and Table Value Constructors, and that for table subqueries is shown in Subqueries.

MATCH checks to see whether the row value constructor matches any of the rows
produced by the subquery. It differs from IN in that it enables you to specify ways of
handling partial matches, which are matches between partially NULL rows. Such
matches are ignored by IN or the equivalent = ANY. The comparability and collating
sequence of the row value constructor (RC) and the rows produced by the subquery
follow the rules outlined earlier in this entry under Comparison Predicates.

MATCH behaves differently depending on whether PARTIAL, FULL, or neither is
specified. "Neither" is its own case; there is no default. If PARTIAL is specified, then:

- If RC is entirely NULL, then MATCH is TRUE.

- Otherwise, if UNIQUE is not specified, and there is at least one row from the
  subquery that contains all the corresponding non-NULL values of RC, then
  MATCH is TRUE.

- Otherwise, if UNIQUE is specified, and there is only one row from the subquery that matches the non-NULL values of RC as described above, then
  MATCH is TRUE.

- Otherwise, MATCH is FALSE.

In the following examples, we show the rows produced by the subquery rather
than the subquery itself. This is not the proper syntax, but it enhances readability. The
first of the following predicates is TRUE, and the second is FALSE:

```
(34, NULL, 99) MATCH UNIQUE PARTIAL
(34, 87, 96
 34, 87, 99
 NULL, 87, 96)


(34, NULL, 99) MATCH UNIQUE PARTIAL
(34, 45, 99
 34, 87, 99
 NULL, 87, 96)
```

FULL essentially follows the same principles, except that if RC is partially NULL, it
won't match anything. Specified more formally, the rules are:

- If RC is entirely NULL, then MATCH is TRUE.

- Otherwise, if RC contains any NULLs, then MATCH is FALSE.

- Otherwise, if UNIQUE is not specified, and there is at least one row from the subquery that equals RC (as defined under Comparison Predicates), then MATCH is TRUE.
- Otherwise, if UNIQUE is specified, and there is only one row from the subquery that equals RC, then MATCH is TRUE.
- Otherwise, MATCH is FALSE.

The first of the following predicates is TRUE, and the second is FALSE:

```
(NULL, NULL, NULL) MATCH UNIQUE FULL

(NULL, 88, 99

34, 88, 99

34, 88, 99)


(34, 88, 99) MATCH UNIQUE FULL

(34, 88, 99

34, 99, 88

34, NULL, 88

34, 88, 99)
```

If neither PARTIAL nor FULL is specified, the rules are as follows:

- If RC is partially or entirely NULL, then MATCH is TRUE.
- Otherwise, if UNIQUE is not specified, and there is at least one row from the subquery that equals RC (as defined under Comparison Predicates), then MATCH is TRUE.
- Otherwise, if UNIQUE is specified, and there is only one row from the subquery that equals RC, MATCH is TRUE.
- Otherwise, MATCH is FALSE.

The first of the following predicates is TRUE, and the second is FALSE:

```
(34, NULL, 99) MATCH

(34, 87, 96

34, 87, 103

NULL, 87, 34)


(34, 88, 99) MATCH UNIQUE

(34, 88, 99

NULL, 88, 99

34, 99, 88

34, 88, 99)
```

> **NOTE**
>
> If you specify neither PARTIAL nor FULL, be careful of NULLs. If there are any NULLs in your row value constructor (RC), they will match anything. You can prevent this by using CASE expressions to convert the NULLs to something else, like zeros or blank strings.

The OVERLAPS Predicate

```
overlaps predicate ::=
row value constructor OVERLAPS row value constructor
```

> **NOTE**
>
> The syntax for a row value constructor is shown under Row and Table Value Constructors.

OVERLAPS is a specialized predicate for determining whether time periods overlap each other. The row value constructors will each have two elements, and the first of each will be DATETIME values with the same group of fields (see Datatypes). The second element of each row value constructor may be either a DATETIME or an INTERVAL datatype, and they do not have to be the same. If the second element is a DATETIME, it must have the same group of fields as the first element. If it is an INTERVAL, the fields in the INTERVAL must be such that it can be added to the DATETIME first element. The two row value constructors specify two periods of time. The first element of each is one boundary date, and the second, if a DATETIME type, is the other boundary date or, if an INTERVAL, is added to the first element to derive the second boundary date. If the INTERVAL is negative, the second boundary date will fall before the first; likewise if the second DATETIME specified chronologically precedes the first. In either case, call the chronologically earlier of the two boundary dates the start date and the later of the two the termination date. The start and termination dates derived from the first row value constructor are S1 and T1; those derived from the second are S2 and T2.

If the first element of either list is NULL, the other boundary date, however derived, becomes the start date, and NULL becomes the termination date. Note that, if the first element of a list is NULL and the second an INTERVAL, the start and termination dates will both be NULL, and the result of OVERLAPS will be UNKNOWN. If the second element is NULL, the first element is the start date and the termination date again is NULL.

Using the values derived from the preceding paragraphs, the following expression (a single predicate) is evaluated:

```
( S1 > S2 AND NOT ( S1 >= T2 AND T1 >= T2 ) )
OR
```

```
( S2 > S1 AND NOT ( S2 >= T1 AND T2 >= T1 ) )

OR

( S1 = S2 AND ( T1 <> T2 OR T1 = T2 ) )
```

Although complex, the effect of this fits with the intuitive sense of overlapping periods of time.

In the first of the following examples, OVERLAPS is TRUE; in the second, it is FALSE; and in the third, it is UNKNOWN:

```
(DATETIME '2001-11', INTERVAL '0004-01')

OVERLAPS (DATETIME '2001-11', DATETIME '2001-02')


(DATETIME '2001-11', INTERVAL '-0004-01')

OVERLAPS (DATETIME '2001-11', DATETIME '2001-02')


(DATETIME NULL, INTERVAL '0004-01')

OVERLAPS (DATETIME '2001-11', DATETIME '2001-02')
```

Conformance Levels

Intermediate   Implementations at this level are not required to support MATCH. Nor are they required to support value expressions other than value specifications (literals, host variables, parameters, or user value functions) in an enumerated list of values for IN.

Entry   Implementations at this level are not required to support UNIQUE or OVERLAPS. They may require that, in LIKE predicates, MATCH values be column references rather than general value expressions and that patterns and escape characters be value specifications. They may refuse to accept row value constructors for IS NULL—only references to single columns.

NOTE   See Also: Chapters 6, 7, and 12; SELECT, UPDATE, DELETE, and CREATE TABLE in Chapter 28; and Aggregate Functions, CAST Expressions, Datatypes, Constraints, and Subqueries in this chapter.

Row and Table Value Constructors

Structures That Define Sets of Values to Be Used in Expressions

Syntax

```
constructor element ::=
{ value expression }
| NULL
| DEFAULT


row value constructor ::=
constructor element
| (constructor element.,..)
|  row subquery


table value constructor ::=
VALUES row value constructor.,..
```

Usage

Row value constructors are groups of one or more value expressions in the specified sequence and are comparable to table rows, to which they can be compared in many predicates (see Predicates). If the row value constructor is a single element, the parentheses can be omitted.

A table value constructor is a group of row value constructors corresponding to a set of rows. Table value constructors are comparable to tables, including those resulting from queries. For example, you can have a query and exclude rows with certain values by using the EXCEPT operator and putting the values you want to exclude in a table value constructor following EXCEPT (see SELECT in Chapter 28).

Row value constructors obey the following principles:

- NULL or DEFAULT can be specified only if the row value constructor (RC) is contained in a query that is producing rows for an INSERT statement. For NULL, however, many implementations may choose to disregard this restriction and support the specification of NULL in contexts other than INSERT as an extension of the standard.

- If a subquery is used, it must be a row subquery (see Subqueries). In other words, an error is produced if the results of the subquery contain more than one row.

- If a subquery is used and produces no rows, the RC is entirely NULL.

The following is an example of a row value constructor:

```
(24, NULL, 'Demetrious')
```

For a table value constructor, all the row value constructors must have the same number of values (including NULLs) and must align vertically (speaking logically, not visually) in columns of comparable values, so that the first, second, third, and so on columns of each match. The following is an example of a table value constructor:

```
VALUES
(24, NULL, 'Demetrious'),
(98, 77, 'Lamark'),
( 0, 444, NULL)
```

Conformance Levels

Intermediate   Implementations at this level may restrict row value constructors to single elements, unless they are contained in table value constructors. Such implementations also may be limited to using the table value constructor as a query expression to produce values to be inserted into a table (see INSERT in Chapter 28), and the table constructors themselves may be restricted to a single row, in the form of a list even if it contains a single element. Effectively, these caveats emulate the structures used in SQL89.

Entry   Implementations at this level may disallow the specification of DEFAULT in row value constructors.

SQL89   Implementations at this level need not support row or table value constructors.

NOTE   See Also: INSERT and SELECT in Chapter 28 and Predicates and Subqueries in this chapter.

String Value Functions

Functions That Operate On and Produce Strings

Syntax

```
string value function ::=
{
```

```
{SUBSTRING (character value expression
  | bit value expression
  FROM start position
  [ FOR string length ] ) }
| { {UPPER | LOWER} (character value expression) }
| { CONVERT (character value expression
    USING form-of-use conversion name)  }
| { TRANSLATE (character value expression
    USING translation name)  }
| {  TRIM ([ [LEADING | TRAILING | BOTH]
    [character value expression]
    FROM character value expression)   }
}
[COLLATE FROM collation name]
[ || {string value expression | string value function} ]
```

Usage

String value functions operate on strings and produce strings. The strings may be of a CHARACTER datatype or, for concatenation (| |) and SUBSTRING, a BIT datatype. The various functions are described in the following paragraphs.

SUBSTRING extracts a substring from the character or bit value expression, starting at the position indicated in the FROM clause and running for the number of positions indicated in the FOR clause or to the end of the value expression, whichever comes first. If the FOR clause is omitted, it runs to the end of the value expression by default. A *position* here is one character or bit in the value expression, as appropriate. If the value expression, starting position, or length is NULL, the result of the function is also NULL. If the starting position exceeds the length of the string or if the string length is zero, the result is a zero-length string. The datatype of the SUBSTRING result is a varying-length character or BIT string with a maximum length equal to the length (if fixed) or maximum length (if varying) of the value expression from which the substring was extracted. If the value expression is a character string, the collating sequence and coercibility of the result are as determined by Table 29.2 (see Collations), with the value expression being the single operand.

UPPER | LOWER converts the string to all uppercase or all lowercase, respectively. Either of these operations can be referred to as a *fold*. The character set of the result is that of the string, and the collating sequence and coercibility follow Table 29.2 (see Collations).

CONVERT changes the string's form-of-use, the specification for the encodings used to represent the character repertoire internally—for example, the number of bits per character. The form-of-use used must be defined for the character repertoire of the string being converted. The result will have the Implicit coercibility attribute, and its collating sequence will be the default for its character repertoire (see Collations).

TRANSLATE changes the character set of the string. This differs from changing the form-of-use in that the character repertoire—the set of characters as represented visually, rather than just internally—may be changed. The translation must have already been defined by the implementation or with a CREATE TRANSLATION statement. It will consist of some one-to-one or many-to-one mapping of character elements from two (not necessarily distinct) repertoires. The result is a varying-length character string with an implementation-defined maximum length and the character repertoire of the target character set of the translation. If the string being translated is NULL, the result of the expression is still NULL.

TRIM removes occurrences of the specified character from the beginning and/or end of the string. By default, it removes blank spaces from both ends of the string. You may specify any single character in the repertoire of the string instead of blank, and you may just TRIM the characters from the beginning (LEADING) or end (TRAILING) of the string. Specifying BOTH is equivalent to the default and so is used only for clarity. The character being removed must have a length of one (no multiple-character sequences), and if either it or the value expression being trimmed is NULL, the result of the function is also NULL. The collating sequence and coercibility of the result follow Table 29.2 (see Collations); the value expression being trimmed is considered that table's monadic operand.

The COLLATE FROM clause, if specified, imposes a different collation on the result of the string value function. The coercibility attribute in this case is Explicit (see Collations).

Concatenate (| |) takes two strings—either of which can be directly expressed as a literal, be taken or derived from a column value, or be the result of one of the other functions—and appends the second to the first. It can append characters to character strings or bits to BIT strings but may not mix the two, nor may it mix character repertoires. The collating sequence and coercibility of the result follow Table 29.3. The two strings being concatenated are the two operands. If either of the strings being concatenated is NULL, the result of the concatenation also is NULL. If both of the strings are fixed-length, the result of the concatenation is fixed-length; otherwise, it is varying-length. If the result of the concatenation is varying-length and exceeds the implementation-defined maximum length for varying-length strings, and it cannot be shortened sufficiently by eliminating trailing blanks (for character strings) or zeros (for BIT strings) to fall within this length, an error is produced. If it is fixed-length and exceeds the implementation-defined maximum, an error is produced without truncation being attempted.

Conformance Levels

| Intermediate | Implementations at this level may disallow the use of a COLLATE FROM clause, the use of BIT strings, and/or the use of UPPER I LOWER, TRANSLATE, or CONVERT. |
| Entry | Implementations at this level may disallow SUBSTRING, TRIM, or concatenate (I I). |

> **NOTE**   See Also: Chapter 20; CREATE CHARACTER SET, CREATE COLLATION, and CREATE TRANSLATION in Chapter 28; and Collations and Value Expressions in this chapter.

Subqueries

Queries Used to Produce Values for Processing within Other Statements

Usage

Queries are SELECT statements, which are statements that extract or derive data from tables and views (see SELECT in Chapter 28). Subqueries are queries that produce data that is not the final output of the statement but will be further processed within the statement. Subqueries can be used in the predicates of other queries or of DELETE or UPDATE statements and may be used as well in the FROM clauses of queries, in row value constructors, or in value expressions. Wherever used, they are enclosed in parentheses. The fact that subqueries can be used in the predicates of queries means that they can also be used within other subqueries to any level of nesting. There are three types of subqueries:

- Subqueries that can produce any number of rows are called *table subqueries*.

- Subqueries that can produce no more than one row, but may contain any number of column values in that row, are called *row subqueries*.

- Subqueries that can produce no more than one value are called *scalar subqueries*.

Since each of these three types is a more restricted case of its predecessor, each may be used wherever its predecessors may; scalar may be used as row subqueries (provided a row with a single value is acceptable in context) and row as table subqueries. Scalar subqueries are used in comparison predicates that are not quantified (in other words, do not use ANY, ALL, or SOME; see Predicates) and, in SQL92, may be used anywhere value expressions may unless explicitly excluded. Row subqueries may be used in row value constructors, and table subqueries are used in FROM clauses (see

SELECT in Chapter 28) and in those predicates other than simple comparison predicates that use subqueries.

The syntax for all three kinds of subqueries is the same. Row subqueries are distinguished from table subqueries by the effect; the predicate of the row subquery, combined possibly with the use of DISTINCT in the SELECT clause, must ensure that no more than one row is returned or else an error will be produced by the statement containing the subquery. In general, a row subquery should test for a primary key or unique value or use aggregate functions without specifying a GROUP BY clause. A scalar subquery is distinguished from a row subquery by only having one output column specified in the SELECT clause. However, it must still satisfy the same criteria for producing but a single row. A subquery with only one output column but multiple rows is still defined as a table subquery.

Often, a subquery contained in a predicate may refer to a value from the table(s) being tested in that containing predicate. This is called an *outer reference* and a subquery that employs it is a *correlated subquery*. An outer reference may have different values for each candidate row being evaluated by the containing predicate; therefore, the subquery must be evaluated independently for each such value. This is normally the case with the EXISTS predicate (see Predicates) and is not uncommon with other types of predicates. The containing predicate may contain the subquery at any level of nesting. It is possible that the name of some column referenced in a subquery may be the same as the name of a column referenced in the containing query or in some outer query in which the containing query is itself a subquery. By default, a column name applies to the matching table with the most local scope—that is to say, the table referenced in the current query or in the first containing query encountered as one moves out in levels of nesting. If the column name can match more than one table with the same scope, in other words, at the same nesting level, the name is ambiguous and must be qualified with a table or correlation name prefix (correlation names are temporary names for tables used for clarifying ambiguities and for convenience; see Chapter 10 and SELECT in Chapter 28). Such prefixes also can be used to override the default interpretation and specify that a column name is to match a table at some level of nesting farther "outside" than would otherwise apply.

Conformance Levels

Entry   At this level, subqueries may prohibit the use of UNION, INTERSECT, and EXCEPT, and subqueries used in comparison predicates may prohibit the use of the GROUP BY or HAVING clauses, either directly in the subquery or in any views referenced by the subquery at any level of nesting.

NOTE   See Also: Chapter 10; CREATE CURSOR, CREATE VIEW, DELETE, INSERT, SELECT, and UPDATE in Chapter 28; and Predicates and Row and Table Value Constructors in this chapter.

Value Expressions
Specify a Value to Be Used in a Statement

Usage

Value expressions are used in SQL statements to produce values of various types for output or for further processing by the statement. Provided they conform to the principles outlined in this entry, they may be any combination of literals (values that represent themselves), column references, aggregate functions, numeric or string value functions, CAST expressions, CASE expressions, user value functions, scalar subqueries, host variables possibly appended with indicator variables (in Embedded SQL), parameters possibly appended with indicator parameters (in the module language), and dynamic parameters (in Dynamic SQL). Complete value expressions may also be used as elements of value expressions, in which case parentheses to force an order of evaluation may be necessary.

Value expressions have datatypes, and all of the datatypes used to construct them (except for indicator parameters or variables, hereafter called *indicators* in this entry) must be comparable, and all operations performed must be suitable for those types (see Datatypes). The various value expressions categorized by datatype are as follows:

- Numeric value expressions are constructed from combinations of values of EXACT NUMERIC and APPROXIMATE NUMERIC datatypes.

- Character value expressions are constructed from combinations of values of CHARACTER and/or NATIONAL CHARACTER datatypes.

- Bit value expressions are constructed from combinations of values of the BIT datatypes.

- Datetime value expressions are constructed from combinations of DATETIME datatypes or from combinations of DATETIME and INTERVAL datatypes.

- Interval value expressions are constructed from combinations of INTERVAL datatypes.

- User value functions such as CURRENT_USER or SESSION_USER (see Authorization IDs) also are value expressions.

The various types of value expressions are described in the following sections.

Numeric Value Expressions

In numeric expressions, the expression is evaluated as a series of numeric values and monadic or dyadic (one-operand or two-operand) operations performed in a specified or implied order. The monadic operands are monadic plus (+) and monadic minus (-). The latter changes the sign of the operand, while the former does nothing but is allowed by the syntax. The dyadic operators are addition (+), subtraction (-), multiplication (*), and division (/). The order of evaluation can be controlled by parentheses. In the absence of these, numeric value functions (such as POSITION; see Numeric Value Functions) are evaluated before operations like multiplication (*) and division (/), and these are performed before addition (+) and subtraction (-). Beyond that, evaluation is left to right. The following principles hold:

- If any of the operands is NULL, the result of the expression also is NULL.

- The result of any dyadic operation with two EXACT NUMERIC operands is EXACT NUMERIC. The result of any dyadic operation with at least one APPROXIMATE NUMERIC operand is APPROXIMATE NUMERIC. In either case, the precision is implementation-defined.

- If the result of an addition or subtraction is EXACT NUMERIC, the scale is that of the larger of the two operands.

- If the result of a multiplication is EXACT NUMERIC, the scale is the sum of the scales of the two operands.

- If the result of a division is EXACT NUMERIC, the scale is implementation-defined.

- If the result of an operation other than division is EXACT NUMERIC, and that result cannot be precisely represented in the precision and scale specified, a range error is produced.

- If the result of a division operation is EXACT NUMERIC, that value may be rounded or truncated, implementation-defined, to fit into the given precision and scale. If leading significant digits must be lost for it to fit, however, an error is produced.

- If the result of an operation is APPROXIMATE NUMERIC, the scale does not apply (see Datatypes).

- If the result of an operation is APPROXIMATE NUMERIC, the exponent must fall within the implementation-defined maximum range or a range error is produced.

Character and Bit Value Expressions

In CHARACTER types, the values expressed may be literal strings set off with single quotes (apostrophes), column values, or string value functions. If they are literals, they optionally may be preceded by an underscore (_) followed without intervening characters by the name of the character set. If this character-set specification is omitted, the default for the session will apply. All the values expressed must be drawn from the same character repertoire (not necessarily the same set). Different character repertoires can be mixed only if there is a defined translation to convert some of them to the repertoire of the others (see CREATE TRANSLATION in Chapter 28).

The other string types are preceded by an uppercase letter that identifies the type. This letter precedes the left quote that begins the string and does not itself go in quotes. The letter is N for NATIONAL CHARACTER types, B for BIT strings represented in binary form, and X for BIT strings represented in hexadecimal form (see Datatypes).

If multiple strings are specified with one or more intervening separators, they will be concatenated.

Datetime Value Expressions

Datetime value expressions consist of values of type DATETIME (see Datatypes), optionally incremented or decremented by values of type INTERVAL. The DATETIME values may be represented by datetime value functions such as CURRENT_DATE (see Datetime Value Functions) or by column references or literals. When a literal is used, it must be preceded by the name of the DATETIME datatype (DATE, TIME, or TIMESTAMP), followed by a separator, and it must be delimited by single quotes ('). If an INTERVAL modifier is given, it may be preceded by a plus (+) or minus (-) sign. Since the interval is itself signed, either of these may result in an increment or decrement of the DATETIME value. Naturally, the INTERVAL and DATETIME values must match according to the rules described under Datatypes. If either the DATETIME or INTERVAL value is NULL, the result of the expression is NULL.

The DATETIME value optionally may append an AT TIME ZONE clause, which may specify either a time zone or the keyword LOCAL. LOCAL indicates the session default and is also the default if the TIME ZONE clause is omitted. The TIME ZONE, if specified, may take a variable or parameter as an argument but without an appended indicator (see Parameters and Variables later in this entry), which means in effect that it cannot be NULL (since NULLs in variables and parameters can exist only with the use of indicators). It may also take a literal but not a column reference.

INTERVAL Value Expressions

An INTERVAL value expression consists of an INTERVAL value possibly modified by the addition or subtraction of another comparable INTERVAL value (all year-month INTERVALS are comparable, as are all day-time INTERVALS; see Datatypes) or by being multiplied or divided by a number. The INTERVAL value may be derived by subtracting two comparable DATETIME values, in which case the pair of DATETIME values must be parenthesized to force the order of evaluation, and an interval qualifier must be appended to indicate the fields that the resulting INTERVAL value should contain. If any of the DATETIME or INTERVAL values is NULL, the result of the expression is also NULL. If the INTERVAL value is a literal (rather than, say, a column reference or a variable), it must be preceded by the keyword INTERVAL and a separator and delimited with single quotes ('). The interval arithmetic to produce the resulting INTERVAL value is performed according to the principles outlined under "The INTERVAL Type" in Datatypes.

User Value Functions

Value expressions may also be user value functions. These are special built-in SQL variables with the following meanings:

- CURRENT_USER (or simply USER) indicates the Authorization ID under whose privileges SQL statements are currently being evaluated.

- SESSION_USER indicates the Authorization ID associated with the current SQL session.

- SYSTEM_USER indicates the user name associated with this session by the operating system.

All three of these can have the same value or they all can be different. They are explained in greater detail under Authorization IDs.

Parameters and Variables

Finally, value expressions may be variables, parameters, or dynamic parameters. All of these are used to pass values back and forth between the DBMS and the application. Variables are used in Embedded SQL, parameters in the module language, and dynamic parameters in Dynamic SQL (see Appendices E, F, and H, respectively). Variables and non-dynamic parameters (for the remainder of this discussion, *parameters* will mean non-dynamic parameters unless otherwise indicated) are prefixed with a colon (:) and generally may have integer variables or parameters called *indicators* appended to them. The indicators are set negative to indicate a NULL value, in which case the value of the variable or parameter is undefined for the purposes of the host language and NULL for the purposes of SQL. A positive indicator value occurs if a CHARACTER or BIT string is too long to fit in the variable or parameter. In this case, the value is truncated, and the indicator is set to the number of characters or bits, as appropriate, that were in the string prior to truncation. If this number is too great to be expressed in the precision of the indicator, an error is produced. In the absence of a NULL or truncated value, the indicator is set to zero.

Dynamic parameters are represented with question marks and may not be appended by indicators. Dynamic parameters can be described by descriptor items in lists created with an ALLOCATE DESCRIPTOR statement (see ALLOCATE DESCRIPTOR in Chapter 28 and Descriptor Areas in this chapter); each item has a number of fields, one of which is INDICATOR. That field can be used in the same way as the appended indicators for variables and parameters. In any case, variables, parameters, and dynamic parameters may be used to pass values in either direction between the DBMS and the application.

Conformance Levels

Intermediate   At this level, implementations are not required to support character set or collation specifications for CHARACTER literals, BIT STRING literals of either variety (binary or hexadecimal), or fractional seconds beyond six digits.

Entry   At this level, implementations are not required to support NATIONAL CHARACTER, DATETIME, or INTERVAL type expressions or to support empty strings or automatic or specified concatenation. CASE and CAST expressions may be excluded, as may scalar subqueries, except when the latter are used in a row value constructor for a comparison predicate (see Predicates, Row and Table Value Constructors).

NOTE

See Also: ALLOCATE DESCRIPTOR, CREATE TRANSLATION, DELETE, INSERT, SELECT, and UPDATE in Chapter 28; Authorization IDs, CASE Expressions, CAST Expressions, Datatypes, Datetime Value Functions, Descriptor Areas, Numeric Value Functions, Predicates, Row and Table Value Constructors, and String Value Functions in this chapter; and Appendices E, F, and H.

APPENDIX

A

Answers

Chapter 1

1. onum

2. Record. Field. The more formal terms are tuple and attribute, respectively, but we did not introduce those in the chapter.

3. Because the rows of a table are by definition in no particular order. Some database systems do allow you to wriggle out of this, however.

Chapter 2

1. INSERT

2. Data Definition Language (DDL)

3. A set of criteria that determine whether a given SQL statement will be executed against a particular row of a table, for example, whether a particular row would be retrieved by a SELECT statement.

4. A statement that retrieves data from the database; a SELECT statement.

Chapter 3

1.
```
CREATE TABLE Customers
    (cnum integer,
    cname char(10),
    city char(10),
    rating integer,
    snum integer);
```

NOTE   This statement could be further refined with constraints we will introduce in the next chapter.

2.
```
ALTER TABLE Customers DROP rating;
```
or
```
ALTER TABLE Customers DROP COLUMN rating;
```

3.   DROP TABLE Customers CASCADE;

Chapter 4

1.   CREATE TABLE Orders
     (onum INTEGER NOT NULL PRIMARY KEY,
     amt DECIMAL,
     odate DATE NOT NULL,
     cnum INTEGER NOT NULL,
     snum INTEGER NOT NULL,
     UNIQUE (snum, cnum));

     or

     CREATE TABLE Orders
     (onum INTEGER NOT NULL UNIQUE,
     amt DECIMAL,
     odate DATE NOT NULL,
     cnum INTEGER NOT NULL,
     snum INTEGER NOT NULL,
     UNIQUE (snum, cnum));

     The first solution is preferable.

2.   CREATE TABLE Salespeople
     (snum INTEGER NOT NULL PRIMARY KEY,
     sname CHAR(15),
     city CHAR(15),
     comm DECIMAL NOT NULL DEFAULT = .10);

3.   CREATE TABLE Orders
     (onum INTEGER NOT NULL PRIMARY KEY,
     amt DECIMAL,
     odate DATE,
     cnum INTEGER NOT NULL,
     snum INTEGER NOT NULL,
     CHECK ((cnum > snum) AND (onum > cnum)));

Chapter 5

1. CREATE TABLE Cityorders
    (onum INTEGER NOT NULL PRIMARY KEY,
    amt DECIMAL,
    cnum INTEGER,
    snum INTEGER,
    city CHAR (15),
    FOREIGN KEY (onum, amt, snum)
    REFERENCES Orders (onum, amt, snum),
    FOREIGN KEY (cnum, city)
    REFERENCES Customers (cnum, city));

2. CREATE TABLE Orders
    (onum INTEGER NOT NULL,
    amt DECIMAL,
    odate DATE,
    cnum INTEGER NOT NULL,
    snum INTEGER,
    prev INTEGER,
    UNIQUE (cnum, onum),
    FOREIGN KEY (cnum, prev) REFERENCES Orders (cnum, onum));

3. CREATE TABLE Items
    (inum   INTEGER NOT NULL PRIMARY KEY,
    iname   CHAR(15) NOT NULL,
    price   DECIMAL(6,2),
    onum   INTEGER NOT NULL REFERENCES Orders);

4. CREATE TABLE Customers
    (cnum INTEGER NOT NULL PRIMARY KEY,
    cname CHAR(10) NOT NULL,
    city CHAR(10),
    rating INTEGER,
    snum INTEGER REFERENCES Salespeople ON UPDATE CASCADE
         ON DELETE SET NULL);

Chapter 6

1. INSERT INTO Salespeople (city, cname, comm, snum)
    VALUES ('San Jose', 'Blanco', NULL, 1100);

2. DELETE FROM Orders WHERE cnum = 2006;

3. UPDATE Customers
    SET rating = rating + 100
    WHERE city = 'Rome';

4. UPDATE Customers
    SET snum = 1004
    WHERE snum = 1002;

Chapter 7

1. SELECT onum, amt, odate
        FROM Orders;

2. SELECT *
        FROM Customers
        WHERE snum = 1001;

3. SELECT city, sname, snum, comm
        FROM Salespeople;

4. SELECT DISTINCT snum
        FROM Orders;

5. SELECT sname, city
        FROM Salespeople
        WHERE city = 'London'
            AND comm > .10;

6. SELECT *
        FROM Customers
        WHERE rating > 100
            OR city = 'Rome';

    or

    SELECT *
        FROM Customers
        WHERE NOT rating <= 100
            OR city = 'Rome';

    or

    SELECT *
        FROM Customers
        WHERE NOT (rating <= 100
            AND city <> 'Rome');

There may be other solutions as well.

7.

onum	amt	odate	cnum	snum
3001	18.69	10/03/2000	2008	1007
3003	767.19	10/03/2000	2001	1001
3005	5160.45	10/03/2000	2003	1002
3009	1713.23	10/04/2000	2002	1003
3007	75.75	10/04/2000	2004	1002
3008	4723.00	10/05/2000	2006	1001
3010	1309.95	10/06/2000	2004	1002
3011	9891.88	10/06/2000	2006	1001

8.

onum	amt	odate	cnum	snum
3001	18.69	10/03/2000	2008	1007
3003	767.19	10/03/2000	2001	1001
3006	1098.16	10/03/2000	2008	1007
3009	1713.23	10/04/2000	2002	1003
3007	75.75	10/04/2000	2004	1002
3008	4723.00	10/05/2000	2006	1001
3010	1309.95	10/06/2000	2004	1002
3011	9891.88	10/06/2000	2006	1001

9.
```
SELECT *
    FROM Salespeople;
```

Chapter 8

1. Any two of the following:

```
SELECT *
    FROM Orders
    WHERE odate IN ('10/03/2000', '10/04/2000');
```
or
```
SELECT *
    FROM Orders
    WHERE odate BETWEEN '10/03/2000' AND '10/04/2000';
```

or

```
SELECT *
    FROM Orders
    WHERE (odate = '10/03/2000') OR (odate = '10/04/2000');
```

or

```
SELECT *
    FROM Orders
    WHERE (odate >= '10/03/2000') AND (odate <= '10/04/2000');
```

The last formulation is poor. Depending on your program, it may run ineffi-ciently because it is deriving a range when all it needs are two values. For the same reason, the IN version may be more efficient than the BETWEEN, although there is a greater likelihood of your DBMS being intelligent enough to make the conversion in this case.

2.  ```
    SELECT *
        FROM Customers
        WHERE cname BETWEEN 'A' AND 'GZ';
    ```

NOTE
For most common collations, BETWEEN 'A' and 'G' would fail to produce names beginning with G, as these would follow the plain letter G in alphabetical order.

3.  ```
    SELECT *
      FROM Customers
      WHERE (cname LIKE 'C%') or (cname LIKE 'c%');
    ```

4.  ```
    SELECT *
        FROM Orders
        WHERE amt <> 0
            AND (amt IS NOT NULL);
    ```
    or
    ```
    SELECT *
        FROM Orders
        WHERE NOT (amt = 0
            OR amt IS NULL);
    ```

5.  ```
    SELECT COUNT(*)
        FROM Orders
        WHERE odate = '10/03/2000';
    ```

6.  ```
    SELECT COUNT(DISTINCT city)
        FROM Customers;
    ```
    ```

7. SELECT cnum, MIN(amt)
       FROM Orders
       GROUP BY cnum;

8. SELECT MIN(cname)
       FROM Customers
       WHERE cname LIKE 'G%';

9. SELECT city, MAX(rating)
       FROM Customers
       GROUP BY city;

10. SELECT odate, COUNT(DISTINCT snum)
       FROM Orders
       GROUP BY odate;

Chapter 9

1. SELECT onum, snum, amt * .12;

2. SELECT 'For the city ', city, ', the highest rating is ',
       MAX(rating)
       FROM Customers
       GROUP BY city;

3. SELECT rating, cname, cnum
       FROM Customers
       ORDER BY rating DESC;

4. SELECT odate, SUM(amt)
       FROM Orders
       GROUP BY odate
       ORDER BY 2 DESC;

5. SELECT cnum, cname,
       CASE city WHEN 'London' THEN 'Brussels' ELSE city END
       FROM Customers;

6. UPDATE Customers
       SET rating = COALESCE(rating, 0) + 100;

Chapter 10

1. SELECT onum, cname
        FROM Orders, Customers
        WHERE Customers.cnum = Orders.cnum;

2. SELECT cname, sname, comm
        FROM Salespeople, Customers
        WHERE Salespeople.snum = Customers.snum
        AND comm > .12;

3. SELECT onum, comm * amt
        FROM Salespeople, Orders, Customers
        WHERE rating > 100
        AND Orders.cnum = Customers.cnum
        AND Orders.snum = Salespeople.snum;

4. SELECT first.sname, second.sname
        FROM Salespeople first, Salespeople second
        WHERE first.city = second.city
        AND first.sname < second.sname;

   You need not use these particular aliases.

5. SELECT a.cname, a.city
        FROM Customers a, Customers b
        WHERE a.rating = b.rating
        AND b.cnum = 2001;

6. SELECT under.empno, under.name, over.name
        FROM Employees under LEFT OUTER JOIN Employees over
        WHERE under.manager = over.empno;

7. If it were not included, each match of customers would appear in the output twice, with the second time in the reverse order of the first. Also, each customer would be selected as matching himself.

Chapter 11

1.  ```
    SELECT *
        FROM Orders
        WHERE cnum =
        (SELECT cnum
        FROM Customers
        WHERE cname = 'Cisneros');
    ```

    or

    ```
    SELECT *
        FROM Orders
        WHERE cnum IN
        (SELECT cnum
        FROM Customers
        WHERE cname = 'Cisneros');
    ```

2.  ```
    SELECT DISTINCT cname, rating
        FROM Customers, Orders
        WHERE amt >
        (SELECT AVG(amt)
        FROM Orders)
        AND Orders.cnum = Customers.cnum;
    ```

3.  ```
    SELECT snum, SUM(amt)
        FROM Orders
        GROUP BY snum
        HAVING SUM(amt) >
        (SELECT MAX(amt)
        FROM Orders);
    ```

4.  ```
    SELECT cnum, cname
        FROM Customers outer
        WHERE rating =
        (SELECT MAX(rating)
        FROM Customers inner
        WHERE inner.city = outer.city);
    ```

5. Correlated subquery solution:

    ```
    SELECT snum, sname
        FROM Salespeople main
        WHERE city IN
        (SELECT city
        FROM Customers inner
        WHERE inner.snum <> main.snum);
    ```

Join solution:

```
SELECT DISTINCT first.snum, sname
    FROM Salespeople first, Customers second
    WHERE first.city = second.city
    AND first.snum <> second.snum;
```

The correlated subquery finds all customers not serviced by a given sales-person and checks to see if any of them are located in his or her city. The join solution is simpler and more intuitive. It finds cases where the city fields match and the snums do not. Therefore a join is a more elegant solution to this problem, given what we have studied up till now. However, there is a more elegant subquery solution that we will encounter later.

Chapter 12

1.
```
SELECT *
    FROM Salespeople first
    WHERE EXISTS
    (SELECT *
    FROM Customers second
    WHERE first.snum = second.snum
    AND rating = 300);
```

2.
```
SELECT a.snum, sname, a.city, comm
    FROM Salespeople a, Customers b
    WHERE a.snum = b.snum
    AND b.rating = 300;
```

3.
```
SELECT *
    FROM Salespeople a
    WHERE EXISTS
    (SELECT *
    FROM Customers b
    WHERE b.city = a.city
    AND a.snum <> b.snum);
```

4.
```
SELECT *
    FROM Customers a
    WHERE EXISTS
    (SELECT *
    FROM Orders b
    WHERE a.snum = b.snum
    AND a.cnum <> b.cnum)
```

5. SELECT *
       FROM Customers
       WHERE rating >= ANY
       (SELECT rating
       FROM Customers
       WHERE snum = 1002);

6.

cnum	cname	City	Rating	snum
2002	Giovanni	Rome	200	1003
2003	Liu	San Jose	200	1002
2004	Grass	Berlin	300	1002
2008	Cisneros	San Jose	300	1007

7. SELECT *
       FROM Salespeople
       WHERE city <> ALL
       (SELECT city
       FROM Customers);

   or

   SELECT *
       FROM Salespeople
       WHERE NOT city = ANY
       (SELECT city
       FROM Customers);

8. SELECT *
       FROM Orders
       WHERE amt > ALL
       (SELECT amt
       FROM Orders a, Customers b
       WHERE a.cnum = b.cnum
       AND b.city = 'London');

9. SELECT *
       FROM Orders
       WHERE amt >
       (SELECT MAX(amt)
       FROM Orders a, Customers b
       WHERE a.cnum = b.cnum
       AND b.city = 'London');

Chapter 13

1.  ```
    SELECT cname, city, rating, 'High Rating'
        FROM Customers
        WHERE rating >= 200
        UNION
    SELECT cname, city, rating, ' Low Rating'
        FROM Customers
        WHERE rating < 200
        OR rating IS NULL;
    ```

    or

    ```
    SELECT cname, city, rating, 'High Rating'
        FROM Customers
        WHERE rating >= 200
        UNION
    SELECT cname, city, rating, ' Low Rating'
        FROM Customers
        WHERE NOT rating >= 200
        OR rating IS NULL;
    ```

2.  ```
    SELECT cnum, cname
        FROM Customers a
        WHERE 1 <
            (SELECT COUNT(*)
            FROM Orders b
            WHERE a.cnum = b.cnum)
         UNION
    SELECT snum, sname
        FROM Salespeople a
        WHERE 1 <
            (SELECT COUNT(*)
            FROM Orders b
            WHERE a.snum = b.snum)
        ORDER BY 2;
    ```

3.  ```
    SELECT snum
        FROM Salespeople
        WHERE city = 'San Jose'
        UNION
    (SELECT cnum
        FROM Customers
        WHERE city = 'San Jose'
        UNION ALL
    ```
    ```

```
SELECT onum
      FROM Orders
      WHERE odate = '10/03/2000');
```

4.   ```
     SELECT snum, sname
           FROM Salespeople
           WHERE city = 'London'
     INTERSECT
     SELECT a.snum, sname
           FROM Customers a, Salespeople b
           WHERE a.snum = b.snum
                 AND a.city = 'London';
     ```

5.   ```
     SELECT snum, cnum
           FROM Orders
           WHERE amt > 1000.00
     EXCEPT
     SELECT a.snum, cnum
           FROM Salespeople a, Customers b
           WHERE a.snum = b.snum
           AND a.city = b.city;
     ```

Chapter 14

1.   ```
     CREATE VIEW Highratings
           AS SELECT cnum, cname, city, rating, snum
                 FROM Customers
                 WHERE rating =
                 (SELECT MAX(rating)
                 FROM Customers);
     ```

2.   ```
     CREATE VIEW Salescount(city, salesperson_count)
           AS SELECT city, COUNT(snum)
                 FROM Salespeople
                 GROUP BY city;
     ```

3.   ```
     CREATE VIEW DailyOrders(sname, average, total)
           AS SELECT sname, AVG(amt), SUM(amt)
                 FROM Salespeople s, Orders o
                 WHERE s.snum = o.snum
                 GROUP BY snum;
     ```

4.   ```
     CREATE VIEW Multicust
           AS SELECT *
     ```

```
FROM Salespeople a
WHERE 1 <
        (SELECT COUNT(*)
        FROM Customers b
        WHERE a.snum = b.snum);
```

Chapter 15

1. #1 is not updatable because it uses DISTINCT. Since onum is a primary key, as a practical matter, no duplicates can be eliminated, but in the ISO standard and in most products, this view would be rejected on the basis of syntax.

   #2 is not updatable because it uses a join, an aggregate function, and GROUP BY.

   #3 is not updatable because it is based on #1, which is not updatable.

   #4 is updatable.

2. ```
   CREATE VIEW Commissions
         AS SELECT snum, comm
                FROM Salespeople
                WHERE comm BETWEEN .10 AND .20
                WITH CHECK OPTION;
   ```

3. ```
   CREATE VIEW Oct3orders
         AS SELECT onum, odate, amt, cnum, snum
                FROM Orders
                WHERE odate ='10/03/2000';
   CREATE VIEW HighOct3orders
         AS SELECT onum, odate, amt, cnum, snum
                FROM Oct3orders
                WHERE amt >= 1000.00
                WITH LOCAL CHECK OPTION;
   ```

4. No.

Chapter 16

1. GRANT UPDATE(rating) ON Salespeople to Janet;

2. GRANT SELECT ON Orders TO Stephen WITH GRANT OPTION;

3. REVOKE INSERT ON Salespeople FROM Claire CASCADE;

4. CREATE VIEW Jerrysview
       AS SELECT cnum, cname, city, rating, snum
           FROM Customers
           WHERE rating BETWEEN 100 AND 500
           WITH CHECK OPTION;
   GRANT INSERT, UPDATE ON Jerrysview TO Jerry;

5. CREATE VIEW Janetsview
       AS SELECT cnum, cname, city, rating, snum
           FROM Customers
           WHERE rating =
               (SELECT MIN(rating)
                FROM Customers)
           WITH CHECK OPTION;
   GRANT SELECT ON Janetsview TO Janet;

Chapter 17

1. A non-repeatable read.

2. A phantom insert.

3. They should be rolled back.

4. An exclusive lock (X-lock).

5. Item-level locking.

Chapter 18

1. Data that describes data.

2. SELECT.

3. No. You can see only those on which you have at least one privilege.

Chapter 19

1.  ```
    CREATE TABLE Persons
            (personnum          INTEGER NOT NULL
                PRIMARY KEY,
            firstname           CHAR(15) NOT NULL,
            midinit             CHAR(2),
            lastname            CHAR(15) NOT NULL);

    CREATE TABLE Teachers
            (teachnum           INTEGER NOT NULL
                PRIMARY KEY
                REFERENCES Persons,
            position            CHAR(10) NOT NULL);

    CREATE TABLE Students
            (studnum            INTEGER NOT NULL
                PRIMARY KEY
                REFERENCES Persons,
            grade_level         CHAR(5) NOT NULL);

    CREATE TABLE Phone_Numbers
            (phonenum           INTEGER NOT NULL,
            personnum           INTEGER NOT NULL
                REFERENCES Persons,
            PRIMARY KEY (phonenum, personnum));
    ```

2. Previously, there was no reason a student and a teacher could not have the same primary key number (studnum or teachnum), since they were entirely distinct entities. Now that they are both subclasses of Persons, such a clash cannot be allowed. It would violate the PRIMARY KEY constraint in the Persons table. This likely means that one or the other will have to have their primary key updated, which is something to avoid if possible. It's always good to check for problems like these beforehand. Here is a query to do it:

    ```
    SELECT studnum
        FROM Students
    INTERSECT
    SELECT teachnum
        FROM Teachers;
    ```
    If this query produces any output, it will be a list of clashes. Otherwise, you're OK.
    ```

3. See the graphic below.

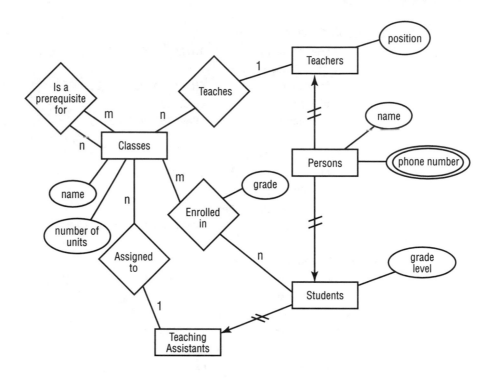

4.
```
CREATE TABLE Employees
    (empno              INTEGER NOT NULL
        PRIMARY KEY,
    name                CHAR(15) NOT NULL,
    manager             INTEGER
        REFERENCES Employees);:
```

Note that, since the manager column allows NULLs, there is no chicken-and-egg problem here. Presumably the CEO has no manager.

Chapter 20

1.
```
CREATE COLLATION new_collation
    FOR Alpha
    DEFAULT
    NO PAD;
```

2. CREATE COLLATION new_collation2
        FOR Alpha
        DESC new_collation
        NO PAD;

Chapter 21

NOTE

The answers for these exercises are written in pseudocode, which is an English-language description of the logic that the program should follow. We did this to help the readers who may not be familiar with Pascal (or any other language that could be used). It also keeps the focus on the concepts involved, rather than on the particulars of one or another language. For the sake of consistency with the examples, however, the style of the pseudocode will be very similar to Pascal. We will omit from the programs everything that is extraneous to the matters at hand (such as program initialization, definitions of input/output, and connections to a database). Naturally, there is more than one way to do these exercises, and ours is not necessarily the best way.

1. EXEC SQL BEGIN DECLARE SECTION;
        SQLSTATE: char(5);
        cnum: integer;
        snum: integer;
        custnum: integer;
        salesnum: integer;
   EXEC SQL END DECLARE SECTION;
   EXEC SQL DECLARE Wrong_Orders AS CURSOR FOR
        SELECT cnum, snum
        FROM Orders a
        WHERE snum <>
             (SELECT snum
             FROM Customers b
             WHERE a.cnum = b.cnum);
   {We are still using SQL to do the main work here.
   The query above locates the rows of the Orders table
   that are not in agreement with the Customers table.}
   EXEC SQL DECLARE Cust_assigns AS CURSOR FOR
        SELECT cnum, snum
        FROM Customers;

```
{This cursor is used to provide the correct snum values.}
begin {main program}
EXEC SQL OPEN CURSOR Wrong_Orders;
while SQLSTATE = '00000' do
{Loop until Wrong_Orders is empty}
      begin
      EXEC SQL FETCH Wrong_Orders INTO
      (:cnum, :snum);
      if SQLSTATE = '00000' then
{If Wrong_Orders is empty, we don't want this loop to do anything.}
      begin
      EXEC SQL OPEN CURSOR Cust_Assigns;
      repeat
      EXEC SQL FETCH Cust_Assigns
      INTO (:custnum, :salesnum);
      until :custnum = :chum;
{The repeat FETCH until... command will go through the
Cust_Assigns cursor until the row that matches the current
cnum of Wrong_Orders is found.}
      EXEC SQL CLOSE CURSOR Cust_assigns;
      {We close the cursor, so that we will start out fresh
      next time through the loop.
      The value we need from this cursor is stored
      in the salesnum variable.}
      EXEC SQL UPDATE Orders
            SET snum = :salesnum
            WHERE CURRENT OF Wrong_Orders;
      end; {If SQLSTATE = '00000'}
      end; {While SQLSTATE...do}
EXEC SQL CLOSE CURSOR Wrong_Orders;
end; {main program}
```

2. Given the program we used, the solution would be to simply include onum, the primary key of the Orders table, in the Wrong_Orders cursor. In the UPDATE statement, you would then use the predicate WHERE onum = :ordernum (assuming a declared integer variable ordernum) instead of a WHERE CURRENT OF Wrong_Orders. The resulting program would look like this (we omitted most comments from the previous version):

```
EXEC SQL BEGIN DECLARE SECTION;
      SQLSTATE: char(5);
```

```
            ordernum: integer;
            cnum: integer;
            snum: integer;
            custnum: integer;
            salesnum: Integer;
    EXEC SQL END DECLARE SECTION;
    EXEC SQL DECLARE Wrong_Orders AS CURSOR FOR
            SELECT onum, cnum, snum
            FROM Orders a
            WHERE snum <>
                    (SELECT snum
                    FROM Customers b
                    WHERE a.cnum = b.cnum);
    EXEC SQL DECLARE Cust_assigns AS CURSOR FOR
            SELECT cnum, snum
            FROM Customers;
    begin {main program}
    EXEC SQL OPEN CURSOR Wrong_Orders;
    while SQLSTATE = '00000' do {Loop until Wrong_Orders is empty.}
            begin
            EXEC SQL FETCH Wrong_Orders
                    INTO (:ordernum, :cnum, :snum);
            if SQLSTATE = '00000' then
            begin
            EXEC SQL OPEN CURSOR Cust_Assigns;
            repeat
            EXEC SQL FETCH Cust_ Assigns
                    INTO (:custnum, :salesnum);
                    until :custnum = :cnum;
            EXEC SQL CLOSE CURSOR Cust_Assigns;
            EXEC SQL UPDATE Orders
            SET snum = :salesnum
            WHERE CURRENT OF Wrong_Orders;
            end; {If SQLSTATE = '00000'}
            end; {While SQLSTATE...do}
    EXEC SQL CLOSE CURSOR Wrong_Orders;
    end; {main program}

3.  EXEC SQL BEGIN DECLARE SECTION;
            SQLCODE: integer;
            {Decided to do an example using SQLCODE.}
            Newcity: array[1.. 12] of char;
```

```
            Commnull: boolean;
            Citynull: boolean;
            Response: char;
EXEC SQL END DECLARE SECTION;
EXEC SQL DECLARE CURSOR Salesperson AS
            SELECT * FROM SALESPEOPLE;
begin {main program}
EXEC SQL OPEN CURSOR Salesperson;
EXEC SQL FETCH Salesperson
            INTO (:snum, :sname, :city:i_cit, .comm:i_com);
{FETCH first row.}
while SQLCODE = 0 do
{While there are rows in Salesperson.}
            begin
            if i_com < 0 then commnull: = true;
            if i_cit < 0 then citynull: = true;
{Set Boolean flags that will indicate NULLs.}
            if citynull then
            begin
            write ('No current city value for salesperson ',
            snum,' Would you like to provide one? (Y/N)');
{Prompt indicates city is NULL.}
            read (response);
{The response will be used later.}
            end {if citynull}
else {not citynull}
            begin
            If not commnull then
{To perform comparison and operations only on nonNULL comm values.}
            begin
            if city = 'London' then comm: = comm - .02
            else comm: = comm + .02;
            end;
{end If not commnull, begin and end
            are for clarity, as there is but one statement.}
            write ('Current city for salesperson ',
            snum, ' is ', city,
            'Do you want to change it? (Y/N)');
{Note: Salespeople not currently assigned a city will not have their
commissions changed on the basis of whether they reside in London.}
            read (response);
```

```
{Response now has a value regardless of whether citynull is true or
false.}
     end; {else not citynull}
     if response = 'Y' then
     begin
     write ('Enter new city value: ');
     read (newcity);
     if not commnull then
{This operation can be performed only on nonNULL values.}
     case newcity of:
     begin
     'Barcelona': comm:= comm + .01,
     'San Jose': comm:= comm - .01
     end; {case and if not commnull}
     EXEC SQL UPDATE Salespeople
     SET city = :newcity, comm = :comm:i_com
     WHERE CURRENT OF Salesperson;
{Indicator variable will put a NULL in comm if appropriate.}
     end; {If response = 'Y', if response <> 'Y', no
     change is made.}
     EXEC SQL FETCH Salesperson
     INTO (:snum, :sname, :city:i_cit,
     :comm:i_com);
{FETCH next row}
     end; {while SQLCODE = 0}
EXEC SQL CLOSE CURSOR Salesperson;
end; {main program}
```

Chapter 22

NOTE   For all answers in this chapter, your details of code and host language may vary.

---

1. Another_query :=
        'SELECT a.cnum, SUM(amt)
                FROM Customers a, Orders b
               WHERE a.cnum = b.cnum
                    and a.cnum = ?';

```
EXEC SQL PREPARE Custtotal FROM :Another_query;
EXEC SQL EXECUTE Custtotal
      USING :predicatecnum
      INTO :targetcnum, :total;
```

2. The query would produce no rows. As a result, a NOT FOUND, also known as NO DATA, condition would arise. This would be reflected in the current value of SQLCODE or SQLSTATE. You should check this value for this situation and write your program code to deal with it appropriately.

3.
```
Another_query :=
    'SELECT a.cnum, SUM(amt)
            FROM Customers a, Orders b
            WHERE a.cnum = b.cnum
                and a.cnum = ?';
EXEC SQL ALLOCATE DESCRIPTOR Custinput
      WITH MAX 5;
{This maximum is arbitrary, of course. We only need one item for
  input and two for output.}
EXEC SQL ALLOCATE DESCRIPTOR Custoutput
      WITH MAX 5;
EXEC SQL SET DESCRIPTOR Custinput
      COUNT = 1;
EXEC SQL SET DESCRIPTOR Custinput
      VALUE 1
      TYPE = 4,
      NULLABLE = 0;
EXEC SQL SET DESCRIPTOR Custinput
      VALUE 1
      DATA = :predicatesnum;
EXEC SQL PREPARE :Custtotal FROM :Another_query;
EXEC SQL EXECUTE :Custtotal
      USING Custinput
      INTO Custoutput;
EXEC SQL GET DESCRIPTOR Custoutput
      VALUE = 1
      DATA = :targetcnum;
EXEC SQL GET DESCRIPTOR Custoutput
      VALUE = 2
      DATA = :total;
```

4. A_query :=
```
    'SELECT cnum, cname, city, rating, snum
        FROM Customers
        WHERE rating > ?';
EXEC SQL PREPARE :rating_query
    FROM :A_query;
EXEC SQL DECLARE rating_search
    CURSOR FOR :rating_query;
EXEC SQL OPEN rating_search
    USING :ratingthreshold;
WHILE SQLCODE >= 0 DO
BEGIN
EXEC SQL FETCH rating_search
    INTO :custnumber, :custname, :custcity,
        :custrating, :custsalesperson;
EXEC SQL UPDATE Customers
    SET city = :newcity
    WHERE CURRENT OF rating_search;
END;
EXEC SQL CLOSE rating_search;
```

Chapter 23

1. Bitmap.

2. Always on columns that have the PRIMARY KEY or the UNIQUE constraint. But you can increase performance by putting them on any combination of columns where a business rule requires uniqueness.

3.
```
SELECT *
    FROM Customers
    WHERE cnum >= 2003
UNION
SELECT *
    FROM Customers
    WHERE city = 'London';
```

4.
```
SELECT onum, o.cnum, cname, odate, amt
    FROM Customers c, Orders o
    WHERE c.cnum = o.cnum
        AND amt >= 1000.00;
```

5.  ```
    SELECT *
        FROM Orders
        WHERE amt >
            (SELECT MAX(amt)
                    FROM Orders
                    WHERE odate = '10/03/2000')
        AND snum IN
            (SELECT snum
                    FROM Customers
                    WHERE city = 'London');
    ```

Some things to note about this answer:

- The aggregate function version of the first subquery (> MAX) would probably do better than > ALL if there is an index on odate and amt.

- For doing a MIN or MAX comparison, there is a reasonable chance that the compiler would refer to the index. For an ALL comparison, this is less likely. If this were a correlated subquery, there would be a strong argument for ALL, however, because the > ALL version can abort the subquery as soon as it finds a value greater than the amt in the main query. The MAX version will have to complete the subquery. However, using MAX, the optimizer will definitely realize that it has to make a comparison to only one value produced by the subquery. With ALL, it may think it has to make separate comparisons for each value produced.

- Since there are no dates before 10/03/2000, NOT > 10/03/2000 is the same as = 10/03/2000 (it is never less than). Equalities do better than inequalities.

- Since we are looking at the salespeople assigned to the customers, rather than those credited with the sale, the join in the second subquery was superfluous.

Chapter 24

1.  ```
    CREATE TYPE Teachers UNDER Persons AS
        salary      DECIMAL,
        rank        VARCHAR
        INSTANTIABLE
        FINAL;
    ```

```
2.   CREATE TABLE current_teachers
         OF teachers;

3.   DECLARE teach1      teachers;
     SET teach1 = teachers();
     SET teach1 = teachers.fname('Molly');
     SET teach1 = teachers.lname('Bramm');
     SET teach1 = teachers.salary(58000.00);
     SET teach1 = teachers.rank('Associate Professor');
     INSERT INTO current_teachers
         VALUES(teachers.fname, teachers.lname,
         teachers.salary, teachers.rank);
```

Chapter 25

```
1.   CREATE TYPE webpage AS CLOB(40k) FINAL;
     ALTER TABLE Customers ADD COLUMN customer_page webpage;

2.   CREATE TYPE webgraphic AS BLOB(1M) FINAL;
     CREATE TABLE Webpics
         (picnum      integer NOT NULL PRIMARY KEY,
          cnum        integer REFERENCES Customers,
          picture     webgraphic);
```

Chapter 26

```
1    String snameLocalVar = "Faloon";
     String cityLocalVar = "Pittsburgh";
     BigDecimal commLocalVar = 0.10;
     Integer snumLocalVar = 1042;

     PreparedStatement insertSalesperson = myConn.prepareStatement
     ("INSERT INTO Salespeople(snum, sname, city,comm)
         VALUES(?,?,?,?,?)" };

     insertSalesperson.setInt(1, snumLocalVar);
     insertSalesperson.setString(2, snameLocalVar);
     insertSalesperson.setString(3, cityLocalVar);
```

```
insertSalesperson.setBigDecimal(4, commLocalVar);

insertSalesperson.executeUpdate();
```

2.  ```
    String snameLocalVar = "Faloon";
    String cityLocalVar = "Pittsburgh";
    BigDecimal commLocalVar = 0.10;
    int snumLocalVar = 1042;

    #sql [myContext] {INSERT INTO Salespeople
                        (snum, sname, city, comm)
                    VALUES
                      (:snumLocalVar, :snameLocalVar,
                       :cityLocalVar, :commLocalVar) };

    #sql [myContext] commit;
    ```
    ```

INDEX

Note to the Reader: Throughout this index **boldfaced** page numbers indicate primary discussions of a topic. *Italicized* page numbers indicate illustrations.

A

ABSOLUTE clause, 642
abstract superclasses, 488, 490
access control, **610**
access modules, 404
access plans, 404–405, 456
active connections, **680**
Active Database conformance level, 476
Ada language, 403
ADD clause
   in ALTER DOMAIN, 589
   in ALTER TABLE, 591 592
ADD COLUMN clause, 591
adding table elements, 40
addition
   of date values, 147
   in expressions, 767
admin privileges, 314
afterInstall() method, 552
aggregate functions, **127**, *128*, **694–696**
   COUNT, **129–131**, *129–130*
   duplicates in, **130–131**
   EXISTS with, **229–230**

expressions in, **131**, *132*
with GROUP BY, **132–136**, *133–137*
with host-language variables, 410
nesting, **137**
ordering with, **155**, *155*
with privileges, 324
in subqueries, **203**, 695
with views, 300
aliases
   in self joins, **172–175**, *173–174*
   in subqueries, 216
ALL argument and operator, **241–243**, 752–753
   for constraints, 681
   with COUNT, 130
   vs. DISTINCT, **97–98**
   with empty results, **246–247**
   equalities and inequalities with, 243 244
   with GRANT, 318
   with INTERSECT and EXCEPT, **276–277**
   with nonequalities, **244–246**, *245*
   with NULLs, **247–248**
   for object privileges, **318–319**
   in optimizing, 466
   with WHERE, 674

C

E

G

I

J

M

P

X

W

Y

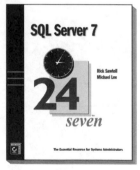
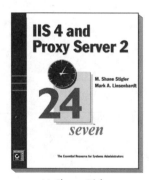

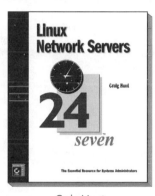
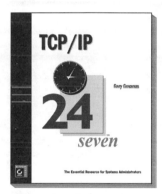

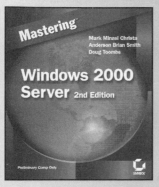

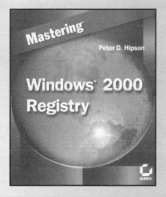
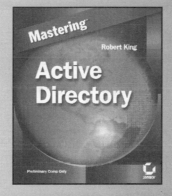

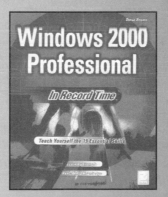

What's on the CD?

This book is accompanied by a CD that contains:

- Sybase's SQL Anywhere Studio 6.0.3 for Linux

- IBM's DB2 Universal Database Version 6.1 for Linux*

- Nine Appendixes

  - Appendix A: Answers

  - Appendix B: Upgrade Path from SQL92 to Core SQL99

  - Appendix C: Error Codes

  - Appendix D: Information Schema

  - Appendix E: Mapping SQL to Other Languages

  - Appendix F: Specification of the Module Language

  - Appendix G: SQL Linguistic Definitions and Conventions

  - Appendix H: Specification of Dynamic SQL

  - Appendix I: Glossary

- Adobe Acrobat Reader 4